AF506889

Please Leave us a Review on Amazon

New
Eclogion

by

Saint Nicodemus of the Holy Mountain

New Eclogion

Translated and edited by
Dean Marais

Published by Based Books
©2025 Dean Marais

Originally published
1803

This edition is a faithful English rendering of the New Eclogion, preserving the theological depth, structure, and tone of the Orthodox patristic tradition for contemporary readers.

Cover Designed by Based Books

Icon on Pg 6. is Public Domain
Source: Ιερά Μονή Οσίου Νικόδημου
https://commons.wikimedia.org/wiki/File:Nikodemos_of_the_Holy_Mountain_Icon.jpg

Other Orthodox Works Published by Based Books

The Lives of the Saints for Orthodox Christians

The New Testament Commentaries of Saint Theophylact of Ohrid

The Complete Discourses of Saint Symeon the New Theolgian

The Sayings of the Desert Fathers: The Patericon of Saint Ignatius Brianchaninov

The Arena - Saint Ignatius Brianchaninov

Unseen Warfare – Saint Theophan the Recluse

History of the Byzantine Empire – Fyodor Uspensky

Philokalia: Volumes 1-5 – Saint Theophan the Recluse

New Eclogion – Saint Nicodemus of the Holy Mountain

Ο Α ΝΙΚΟΔΗΜΟΣ
ο Αγιορείτης
ΠΗΔΑΛΙΟΝ
ΔΕΗΣΙΣ ΓΕΩΡΓΙΒ Κ ΠΑΝΑΓΙΩΤΑΣ
ΤΕΚΤΕΡΙΔΗ
ΙΕΡΑ ΜΟΝΗ ΟΣ. ΝΙΚΟΔΗΜΒ 2006

New Eclogion

by
Saint Nicodemus of the Holy Mountain

Table of Contents

The Life of Saint Nicodemus of the Holy Mountain

Athonite Monk, Theologian, Reviver of Hesychasm, Compiler of the Philokalia, and Interpreter of the Sacred Canons

Feast Day: July 14 (Old Calendar) / July 27 (New Calendar)

Early Life and Education

Nicholas Kallivourtzis was born in 1748 (some sources give 1749) on the Greek island of Naxos in the Aegean Sea, which was at that time under Ottoman rule. His parents, Anthony and Anastasia Kallivourtzis, were devout Orthodox Christians who raised their son in the fear of God. His mother Anastasia later completed her earthly life as a nun, taking the monastic name Agathi, at the Monastery of Saint John Chrysostom on Naxos—a testament to the deep piety of the household in which young Nicholas was formed.

From his earliest years, Nicholas displayed exceptional gifts that would later serve the Church in extraordinary ways. According to his biographer, he was possessed of "great acuteness of mind, accurate perception, intellectual brightness, and vast memory"—qualities that were readily apparent to all who furthered him along in his learning. He avoided bad company and everything that might harm his soul, showing a zeal for all that was good and beneficial. His love for both sacred and secular learning manifested early, and he assisted his parish priest during the Divine Liturgy and other services, already drawn to the mysteries of the faith.

Nicholas received his elementary education on his native island under the tutelage of his parish priest, who instilled in him a deep love for Christ and His Church. He then studied under Archimandrite Chrysanthos, brother of the great missionary and equal-to-the-apostles Saint Cosmas Aitolos, who recognized in the young Nicholas tremendous intellectual potential and introduced him to the riches of sacred and secular letters. From there, Nicholas proceeded to the renowned Evangelical School in Smyrna (modern-day Izmir, Turkey), one of the finest educational institutions in the Greek world of that era.

At Smyrna, Nicholas received a classical education of remarkable breadth. He studied theology, ancient Greek, Latin, French, and Italian, mastering these languages with facility. His teachers noted not only his linguistic abilities but also his philosophical acumen and his capacity for deep theological reflection. However, Turkish persecution of Christians during the Russo-Turkish War of 1768–1774 forced him to abandon his studies and return to Naxos around 1770, cutting short what had promised to be a distinguished academic career.

The Call to Monastic Life

Upon returning to Naxos, the young Nicholas became secretary to Metropolitan Anthimos Vardis, who appreciated his gifts and had great hopes for his future. It was during this period that a series of providential encounters would redirect the course of his life forever.

On Naxos, Nicholas met certain Athonite fathers—the hieromonks Gregory and Niphon, and the virtuous Elder Arsenios of the Peloponnese—monks who had come from Mount Athos and who embodied the hesychastic tradition of inner prayer. These men, described by his biographer as "possessing much virtue and modesty," taught Nicholas about noetic prayer and the Jesus Prayer: "Lord Jesus Christ, Son of God, have mercy on me, a sinner." Their example of ascetic struggle and their teaching on the interior life awakened in Nicholas an ardent desire for the monastic vocation.

He also encountered the holy Metropolitan Macarius of Corinth (now also venerated as a saint), a man "shining with every virtue and holiness," and Elder Sylvester of Caesarea, a hesychast monk devoted to the contemplative life. These were self-exiled Athonites known as Kollyvades—followers of a movement that sought to restore authentic Orthodox practices, particularly the frequent reception of Holy Communion and proper observance of memorial services on Saturdays rather than Sundays, in accordance with patristic tradition.

Through these encounters, Nicholas became convinced that his calling lay not in ecclesiastical administration or worldly scholarship, but in the monastic life on Mount Athos—the Holy Mountain that had been a beacon of Orthodox monasticism for over seven centuries.

Entry into Monastic Life

In 1775, at the age of twenty-six, Nicholas traveled to Mount Athos and received the monastic tonsure at the venerable Monastery of Dionysiou, one of the twenty ruling monasteries on the Holy Mountain. Following monastic custom, his name was changed to Nicodemus, symbolizing his death to the world and rebirth in Christ. His first obedience was to serve as the monastery's secretary, a task that utilized his education and administrative abilities while he learned the ascetic disciplines of cenobitic life.

At Dionysiou, Nicodemus was initiated into the practice of hesychia—the inner stillness that lies at the heart of Orthodox spirituality. He learned the method of prayer involving controlled breathing, inner recollection, and the continual repetition of the Jesus Prayer, descending with the mind into the heart to find there the living presence of Christ. This practice would inform all his future labors and writings.

Nicodemus aligned himself with the Kollyvades fathers, who were at that time engaged in a controversial but spiritually vital movement to revive traditional Orthodox practices and patristic literature. Against the spiritual laxity that had crept into the Church under centuries of Ottoman domination, the Kollyvades advocated for: the frequent reception of the Eucharist as essential for spiritual growth; the observance of memorial services on Saturdays rather than Sundays, to preserve the Lord's Day as a celebration of the Resurrection; rigorous adherence to fasting rules; and the cultivation of hesychastic prayer for all Christians, not merely monks.

The Beginning of Literary Labors

In 1777, two years after his arrival at Dionysiou, a momentous event occurred that would shape the remainder of Nicodemus's life. Metropolitan Macarius of Corinth visited Mount Athos and arrived at the monastery. Recognizing the exceptional abilities of the young monk, Macarius entrusted him with a task of immense importance: the editing and preparation for publication of the *Philokalia*.

Macarius had discovered manuscripts of patristic writings on prayer and the spiritual life scattered among the libraries of Athonite monasteries, particularly at Vatopedi. These texts—spanning authors from the fourth to the fifteenth centuries, including Evagrius Ponticus, Maximus the Confessor, Symeon the New Theologian, and Gregory Palamas—contained the accumulated wisdom of Orthodox spirituality on nepsis (watchfulness), hesychia (stillness), and theosis (deification). Macarius conceived the idea of gathering these writings into a single anthology that could guide both monks and laypeople in the path of inner transformation.

The task of compiling, editing, and annotating this vast collection fell to Nicodemus. While compiling the Philokalia, he included the titles of various passages from both the Old and New Testaments based solely on his own memory, as he possessed what can only be described as a photographic memory. He knew the Holy Scriptures by heart, remembering even the chapter, verse, and page, and could recite long passages from the writings of the Holy Fathers from memory.

Simultaneously, Macarius entrusted Nicodemus with editing the treatise *On Frequent Holy Communion* and the *Evergetinos*, a classic eleventh-century collection of spiritual teachings drawn from the lives and sayings of the Desert Fathers. These three works—the Philokalia, the treatise on Communion, and the Evergetinos—marked the beginning of Nicodemus's lifelong vocation as an editor, compiler, and author of spiritual literature.

The *Philokalia* was published in Venice in 1782 and immediately sparked a spiritual renewal throughout the Orthodox world. Its influence spread from Greece to Russia (through the Slavonic translation by Paisios Velichkovsky), Romania, and eventually to the West, becoming one of the most important spiritual classics of Eastern Christianity.

Years of Asceticism and Scholarly Labor

After completing his initial work at Dionysiou, Nicodemus moved to a cell near the Monastery of Pantocrator, where he placed himself under the spiritual guidance of Elder Arsenios of the Peloponnese, one of the Kollyvades fathers. Under this experienced guide, Nicodemus devoted himself to intense prayer, the study of Holy Scripture, and the works of the Church Fathers, developing the theological and spiritual depth that would characterize all his subsequent writings.

During this period, he spent time with his elder on the isolated island of Skyropoulos near the Holy Mountain. It was here, at the request of his cousin Hierotheos, the newly appointed Bishop of Euripos, that Nicodemus composed his original work *Handbook of Spiritual Counsel* (also known as the *Enchiridion of Counsels* or *On the Preservation of the Five Senses, Imagination, Mind, and Heart*). This treatise displays both deep psychological insight and a keen philosophical mind, addressing the practical dimensions of the spiritual life for both clergy and laity. Published in 1801, it continues to guide Orthodox spirituality to this day.

In 1783, returning to Mount Athos, Nicodemus received the Great Schema—the highest degree of Orthodox monasticism, signifying complete dedication to the ascetic life and continual prayer. For the next six years, he withdrew into strict silence and seclusion, devoting himself entirely to prayer and contemplation. This period of hesychastic withdrawal deepened his spiritual life and prepared him for the immense literary labors that lay ahead.

His solitary life was interrupted when Metropolitan Macarius again visited Athos and entrusted Nicodemus with a new obedience: the editing and publication of the complete works of Saint Symeon the New Theologian, the great eleventh-century mystic and theologian of divine light. He also cared for the publication of the works of Saint Gregory Palamas. Obediently setting aside his beloved hesychastic quiet, Nicodemus returned to literary work—a labor he would continue without ceasing until his death.

Major Works and Contributions

The scope of Saint Nicodemus's literary output is staggering, encompassing nearly every field of Orthodox theology and spirituality. His works transformed the spiritual landscape of the Orthodox world and continue to nourish the faithful to this day.

His most influential work is undoubtedly the *Philokalia* (1782), compiled in collaboration with Saint Macarius of Corinth—an anthology of writings on watchfulness and prayer by thirty-six Church Fathers spanning from the fourth to the fifteenth centuries. This collection sparked a renewal of hesychastic spirituality throughout the Orthodox world. Alongside this, he prepared the *Evergetinos* (1783–1784), four volumes of teachings from the Desert Fathers, and edited the complete works of Saints Symeon the New Theologian and Gregory Palamas, making these crucial patristic texts accessible to a wider audience.

In the field of canon law, Nicodemus produced his monumental *Pedalion* ("The Rudder," 1800), prepared in collaboration with Hieromonk Agapios, containing the canons of the Holy Apostles, the Ecumenical and Local Councils, and the Holy Fathers, together with extensive commentary. This work remains the standard collection of Orthodox canon law. His ascetical writings include *Unseen Warfare*, an Orthodox adaptation of Lorenzo Scupoli's *Spiritual Combat* enriched with teachings on the Jesus Prayer; the *Handbook of Spiritual Counsel* (1801); and *Christian Morality* (1803), which he considered his most edifying book.

Nicodemus made substantial contributions to liturgical studies through works such as the *Heortodromion*, a commentary on the canons sung on feasts of the Lord and the Theotokos, and *The New Ladder*, an interpretation of the Hymns of Degrees from the Octoechos. His hagiographical labors produced the *New Eklogion* (1803) and the posthumously published *New Synaxarion* in three volumes (1819). He also composed original liturgical poetry, including sixty-two canons to the Most Holy Theotokos gathered in the *New Theotokarion* (1796), and his Canon to the Mother of God "Quick to Hear" remains in liturgical use. His *Exomologetarion* ("Manual of Confession," 1794) provided comprehensive guidance for confessors and penitents, while his biblical commentaries included an interpretation of the Seven Catholic Epistles and a modern Greek translation of Saint Theophylact's commentary on the Pauline Epistles.

The Kollyvades Controversy

Saint Nicodemus was a central figure in the Kollyvades movement, which despite its eventual vindication, caused him considerable suffering during his lifetime. The movement took its name from the kollyva—boiled wheat offered in memorial services for the departed. The controversy began when certain Athonite monks, out of practical convenience, began performing memorial services on Sundays rather than Saturdays. The Kollyvades fathers objected, arguing that Sunday, as the day of the Resurrection, was inappropriate for such commemorations, and that this innovation contradicted liturgical tradition.

More significantly, the Kollyvades advocated for frequent Holy Communion—a practice that had fallen into disuse, with many Orthodox Christians communing only once or twice a year. This teaching, expounded in the treatise *On Frequent Holy Communion* prepared by Nicodemus and Macarius, was initially condemned as erroneous by Patriarch Procopius of Smyrna in 1785. The Kollyvades were accused of innovation and even heresy, and some were exiled from Mount Athos.

Nicodemus suffered calumny and opposition for his association with this movement. However, his position was accepted as orthodox by the Synod of Constantinople in 1819—ten years after his death. Today, the Kollyvades fathers are recognized as prophetic voices who called the Church back to its authentic tradition, and several of them, including Saints Macarius of Corinth, Nicodemus, and Athanasios of Paros, have been glorified as saints.

Service to the Athonite Academy

Beyond his scholarly work, Saint Nicodemus contributed to the institutional life of the Holy Mountain. In 1801, when the Athonite Academy (Athoniada School) was passing through a difficult period both financially and spiritually, the Holy Assembly of Athonite Fathers appointed Nicodemus to a three-member committee responsible for the school's management. Along with the former Metropolitan Ambrose of Trikki and the teacher Christophoros Prodromitis, "the boast of Mount Athos" Saint Nicodemus was "more than others a beneficial presence at Athoniada." He contributed to the economic improvement of the school and zealously worked for its progression, allowing it to remain in operation until the brink of the Greek Revolution in 1821.

Character and Personal Qualities

According to the testimony of his contemporaries, Saint Nicodemus was a simple man, without malice, unassuming, and distinguished by his profound concentration. Despite his immense learning and the reverence in which he was held, he remained humble and accessible, devoted entirely to prayer and his labors for the Church.

His intellectual gifts were extraordinary. He was fluent in several languages, including ancient and modern Greek, Latin, French, and Italian, and was well-versed in both Eastern patristic theology and Western spiritual literature. He studied the writings of Western authors on asceticism and contemplative prayer, adapting them within an Orthodox framework when he found them beneficial. This willingness to learn from all sources of spiritual wisdom, while maintaining rigorous Orthodox criteria, demonstrates both his intellectual breadth and his pastoral concern for the salvation of souls.

Saint Nicodemus was a brilliant theoretician of the hesychastic life, writing complex philosophical and theological discourses on the subject of human transformation, the cleansing of the spiritual mind and passions, the enlightenment of man, and man's union with God through theosis. He was not merely an academic theologian but a practitioner of the spiritual life he described, one who had descended into the depths of hesychastic prayer and emerged bearing fruit for the Church.

He also maintained important relationships with other spiritual figures of his time, including the Hieromartyr Gregory V, Patriarch of Constantinople (martyred in 1821), who assisted in publishing some of his works. Saint Gregory sent to Saint Nicodemus the New Martyr Constantine of Hydra so that Nicodemus might catechize and prepare him for martyrdom—and afterward, Nicodemus wrote his life.

Final Years and Blessed Repose

Not long before his repose, Father Nicodemus, worn out by his literary work and ascetical struggles, went to live at the cell of the iconographer Hieromonks Stephen and Neophytos Skourtaios, who were brothers by birth. Finding himself hindered by infirmity and unable to continue his work alone, he entrusted them with assisting in the publication of his remaining manuscripts, many of which would appear only after his death.

On the eve of his departure from this life, Father Nicodemus was able to make his confession, receive Holy Unction, and partake of Holy Communion—the sacraments he had so ardently encouraged all Christians to receive frequently throughout his life.

On the night of his death, Wednesday, July 14, 1809, Father Nicodemus remained in prayer, giving thanks to God and asking for His mercy. He reposed peacefully at the age of sixty (or sixty-one), having spent over thirty years on the Holy Mountain in prayer, asceticism, and tireless labor for the Church.

His first biographer, Father Euthymios, describes the Saint's repose in this manner: "When the sun rose on the earth that day, the intelligible sun of the Church set. The fiery pillar, the guide

16

of the New Israel into piety disappeared; the cloud which refreshed those who were melting in the heat of sin, hid itself."

His many friends and acquaintances mourned, and the words of a certain Christian were typical of the thoughts of many individuals of that time: "Oh, my Fathers, it would have been better for a thousand Christians to have died today, and not Nikodemos."

He was buried near the Skourtaios cell in Karyes, the administrative center of Mount Athos.

Glorification and Veneration

Following his death, veneration of Father Nicodemus emerged among the monastic communities of Mount Athos and on his native island of Naxos. His writings continued to spread throughout the Orthodox world, nourishing countless souls and contributing to spiritual renewal wherever they were read.

On May 31, 1955, Ecumenical Patriarch Athenagoras I officially glorified Nicodemus as a saint, along with his associate Saint Macarius of Corinth and other figures of the Kollyvades movement. This act integrated Nicodemus into the universal calendar of the Orthodox Church, confirming the holiness of his life and the enduring value of his teaching.

Saint Nicodemus is commemorated annually on July 14 (Old Calendar) / July 27 (New Calendar). The precious relic of his holy skull is preserved on Mount Athos and is venerated by pilgrims who seek his intercessions.

Legacy

Saint Nicodemus the Hagiorite is one of the greatest theological and instructive figures of the period of Turkish occupation. His works elevated the morals of monastics and all the faithful by making known the wisdom of the holy fathers, the fragrance of hagiography, and the grace of hymnography. Rightly is he the boast of the Holy Mountain and the glory of the Orthodox Church.

Writings of Saint Nicodemus the Hagiorite have been translated into Turkish, Russian, Romanian, English, and other languages. It is a fact that the writings of Saint Nicodemus circulate and are read in our days by thousands of Christians.

The Philokalia alone has transformed Orthodox spirituality across the world, inspiring countless Christians—both Eastern and Western—to undertake the path of hesychastic prayer. His canonical commentaries remain authoritative. His hagiographical collections preserve the memory of the saints. His hymns are still sung in churches. His manuals on confession and spiritual counsel continue to guide clergy and laity alike.

Saint Nicodemus stands as a model of how learning and holiness, scholarship and prayer, can be united in a single life dedicated entirely to God and the service of His Church. In an era of cultural and spiritual crisis under Ottoman rule, when Western influences threatened to erode

Orthodox identity, he looked to the patristic sources, gathered their wisdom, and made it accessible to his contemporaries—and through them, to all subsequent generations.

Troparion to Saint Nicodemus the Hagiorite, Tone 3

Adorned with the grace of wisdom, O Father, / you appeared as the divine trumpet of the Spirit / and a teacher of virtues, O God-speaking Nicodemus, / for you give saving teachings to all, / showing the radiance of a pure life / with the wealth of your divine words, // with which, like light, you shone upon the world.

Another Troparion to Saint Nicodemus of the Holy Mountain, Tone 1

Let us, O faithful, honor the luminary of Athos and the offshoot of Naxia, and the God-inspired teacher of the whole Church, Nicodemus, who was filled with divine wisdom, for he pours out abundant heavenly teachings to those who cry out: Glory to Christ who glorified you, glory to him who crowned you, glory to him who through you gives us help.

Prayer to Saint Nicodemus of the Holy Mountain

O divinely inspired and universal teacher of truth, excellent praise of the Holy Mountain, brightest star of the Catholic Orthodox Church, all-venerable and holy Father Nicodemus! Grant us enlightenment through your prayers in fulfilling the divine will, direct our steps to the paths of virtuous living, overshadow us with the grace given to you and enlighten our minds to understand your God-wise teachings, so that we may find in them repentance, healing, joy, peace, meekness, tranquility, love, and whatever is good and gracious and salvific, and in the end, eternal life, and pray always to the Lord for us all, sincerely those who love you and call upon your fatherly goodness and help every day and hour. Amen.

Through the prayers of our venerable father Nicodemus of the Holy Mountain, O Lord Jesus Christ our God, have mercy on us and save us. Amen.

Preface to the New Eclogion

Νέον Ἐκλόγιον

Among the manifold labors of our venerable father Nicodemus of the Holy Mountain, whose tireless pen produced works spanning nearly every field of Orthodox theology, his hagiographical writings hold a place of special honor. Saint Nicodemus, whom the Orthodox Church has glorified as theologian, teacher, reviver of hesychasm, canonist, and hagiologist, possessed what his biographer describes as a "special love for hagiography"—a love that found expression in several major works, chief among them the *New Eclogion* (Greek: Νέον Ἐκλόγιον), first published in Venice in the year 1803.

The title *Eclogion* derives from the Greek word ἐκλογή (*eklogê*), meaning "selection" or "anthology"—and indeed, this work represents a careful selection, a gathering of spiritual treasures from the manuscript collections of the Holy Mountain. Saint Nicodemus, who spent over three decades on Mount Athos immersed in prayer, ascetic struggle, and scholarly labor, had access to the rich libraries of the Athonite monasteries, where countless hagiographical texts lay hidden in manuscripts, many of them unpublished and unknown to the wider Church. With the same meticulous care he brought to the compilation of the *Philokalia*, the editing of the *Pedalion*, and the preparation of scores of other works, Saint Nicodemus gathered these neglected lives of the saints and presented them to readers as, in his own words, "a delicate bouquet of spiritual flowers."

His purpose in compiling the *New Eclogion* was not merely historical or literary, but profoundly spiritual. He wished to help believers "free themselves from their passionate attachment to earthly things and experience intelligent spiritual delight, filling their souls with Divine love." This goal reflects the saint's understanding—shared by the entire Orthodox tradition—that hagiography serves a soteriological purpose: the lives of the saints are written not simply to inform, but to transform; not merely to record history, but to lead readers toward salvation.

The saints themselves are icons of Christ. In their lives, we see the commandments of the Gospel embodied in flesh and blood; we encounter men and women who struggled against the passions, who loved God above all things, who persevered through persecution and temptation, and who attained union with the Divine. As Saint Justin Popovich has written, "When we read the Lives of the Saints, we are reading the Life of our Lord Jesus Christ"—for Christ lives in His saints, and their lives are continuations of His life in the world. Thus, the reading of saints' lives is not a secondary devotion but an essential element of Orthodox spiritual formation.

The tradition of hagiography stretches back to the earliest centuries of the Church, when communities began to commemorate their martyrs on the anniversaries of their deaths and to preserve written accounts of their witness. Over time, the genre expanded to include confessors, ascetics, hierarchs, and all who had manifested the grace of God through holy living. Collections such as the Synaxarion, the Menologion, and various Paterika preserved these lives for liturgical reading and personal edification. Saint Nicodemus stands in this venerable tradition, yet he also brought to it the particular gifts of his age and person: a critical eye for manuscripts, a mastery of Greek that allowed him to render ancient texts accessible to contemporary readers, and a pastoral heart that sought always the spiritual benefit of the faithful.

The *New Eclogion* is structured in three parts, reflecting both chronological progression and thematic development. This arrangement takes the reader on a journey through the entire history of Christian holiness, from apostolic times to the relatively recent period of Saint Nicodemus's own day.

The First Part covers the period from the first to the fifth centuries, presenting the lives of saints from the early Christian era: martyrs who shed their blood for Christ, confessors who suffered for the faith, and the first great ascetics who withdrew to the desert to wage spiritual warfare against the passions. Here we encounter such luminaries as the Martyr Photina (the Samaritan Woman who met Christ at the well), the Hieromartyr Polycarp of Smyrna (the apostolic father who was burned alive for refusing to deny Christ), Saint Epiphanius of Cyprus (the great defender of Orthodoxy against heresies), Saint Macrina the sister of Saint Basil the Great (who consecrated herself to virginity and asceticism from childhood), and Saint Paisius the Great (the Egyptian hermit renowned for his miracles and spiritual insight). These lives establish the foundation upon which all subsequent Christian sanctity would be built.

The Second Part is dedicated to the saints of the fifth through twelfth centuries, the era of Byzantine flourishing when monasticism reached its full development and the Church defended the Orthodox faith against successive waves of heresy. This section presents the lives of archbishops, confessors, and venerable ascetics whose struggles took place during the golden age of patristic theology and ecclesiastical organization. Among those included are Saint Cyril of Alexandria (the great champion of Christological orthodoxy), Saint Andrew of Crete (the hymnographer who composed the Great Canon), Saint Paul of Xeropotamou, Saint Euthymius the New, Saint Lazarus of Gallicea, and many others who exemplify the diverse paths to holiness that flourished within the Byzantine Christian world.

The Third Part spans the twelfth through the nineteenth centuries, with particular attention to the Athonite ascetics and saints of the late Byzantine and post-Byzantine eras. Here the reader encounters figures from the Holy Mountain itself, men who lived in the very places where Saint Nicodemus himself labored and prayed, and whose memory remained alive in the monastic communities of his day. Among these are Saint Leontios of Jerusalem, Saint Gregory of Sinai (the great teacher of hesychasm), Saint Maximos the Kavsokalyvite,

Saint Gregory Palamas (the defender of the hesychastic tradition and theologian of the Divine Light), Saint Nectarios the Athonite, and others who demonstrate that the grace of sanctity did not cease with the ancient fathers but continued to flow undiminished through the centuries.

The collection concludes with several edifying narratives that complement and enrich the main theme, offering additional spiritual nourishment for the reader.

This three-part structure serves a profound theological purpose: it demonstrates the continuity of holiness throughout Christian history. The same Holy Spirit who sanctified the martyrs of the first century continued to work in the hesychasts of the fourteenth century and in the new martyrs who suffered under Ottoman rule. The paths to holiness are many—martyrdom, monasticism, episcopal service, the life of the family—but the goal is one: union with God through Christ in the Holy Spirit. By presenting saints from every era and every condition of life, Saint Nicodemus shows that sanctity is possible for all who seek it with sincerity of heart.

Saint Nicodemus also rendered an invaluable linguistic service in preparing this collection. Many of the ancient texts he gathered were written in forms of Greek that had become difficult for ordinary readers to understand. Just as he did with so many of his other works, Saint Nicodemus translated and adapted these texts into accessible and understandable language, ensuring that the spiritual wisdom they contained would not remain locked away from those who most needed it. This pastoral concern—making the treasures of the tradition available to all the faithful, not merely to scholars—characterizes all of Saint Nicodemus's literary work.

It is fitting to recall that the *New Eclogion* appeared as one of several hagiographical works that Saint Nicodemus produced or prepared during his life. In 1799, he and Saint Macarius of Corinth edited the *New Martyrologion*, a collection of lives of the New Martyrs—those who had suffered death rather than convert to Islam under Ottoman rule. This work was intended "to demonstrate that the Orthodox Church continues to produce Saints, particularly Martyrs, who were subjected to the same trials, torments, and death as the ancient Martyrs," thereby strengthening and encouraging the Orthodox faithful to remain true to Christ amid persecution. The *New Synaxarion*, published posthumously in three volumes in 1819, represented another major hagiographical undertaking. Together with the *New Eclogion*, these works constitute a magnificent treasury of sanctity gathered by a saint for the benefit of all who seek to follow Christ.

The spiritual benefit of reading the lives of the saints cannot be overstated. As the fathers have taught, the lives of the saints warm our souls and motivate us to imitate their virtues. Saint Paisios of Athos counseled: "By studying the lives of the saints, our soul is warmed and motivated to imitate them, and to proceed with manly courage in the struggle to acquire the virtues." When we read of the saints' struggles, we realize that we are not alone; that others have faced the same temptations and emerged victorious through the grace of God; that the commandments of Christ, far from being impossible ideals, have been lived out by countless men and women throughout history. Their lives show us what is possible when human freedom cooperates with divine grace.

Moreover, the saints become our companions and intercessors. "If we live with all the saints by attentively reading their lives each day as we walk in the spiritual garden of the Synaxarion," writes Hieromonk Macarius of Simonos Petra, "we shall discover little by little those whom our heart especially goes out to. They will become our close friends... and a great comfort to us along the strait and narrow way that leads to Christ." Thus the reading of hagiography is not merely an intellectual exercise but an encounter with living persons who, having completed their earthly course, now stand before the throne of God and intercede for those who honor their memory.

The Orthodox priest who spoke to a convert and said, "You will never be truly Orthodox without reading the Lives of the Saints," expressed a truth confirmed by the experience of generations. The most pious faithful, the most spiritually advanced Christians, are invariably those who have nourished themselves on the lives of the saints. In an age of distraction and spiritual confusion, when the soul is bombarded with images of vice and worldliness, the lives of the saints offer a saving alternative: images of virtue, models of repentance, examples of faith, hope, and love that can illuminate the darkness and show the way to the Kingdom.

May this *New Eclogion*, gathered with such love and care by our holy father Nicodemus of the Holy Mountain, serve as a "delicate bouquet of spiritual flowers" for all who read it. May the saints whose lives are contained herein intercede for us, inspire us, and guide us along the path of salvation. And may we, through the reading of their lives, be freed from passionate attachment to earthly things and come to experience that intelligent spiritual delight which fills the soul with Divine love—to the glory of the Father, and of the Son, and of the Holy Spirit, now and ever and unto ages of ages. Amen.

Part 1

The Struggles of the Holy Glorious Martyr Photina and Those Who Suffered with Her in the Year 66

This holy martyr Photina (Svetlana) is the same Samaritan woman about whom the Apostle John the Theologian speaks in his Gospel. She conversed with our Lord Jesus Christ at the well of the Patriarch Jacob and believed in the Savior. After His Ascension and after the descent of the Holy Spirit upon the divine apostles on the Day of Pentecost, Photina, together with her two sons and five sisters, was baptized by the disciples of Jesus. Then she began to pass from country to country preaching about the Risen Son of God, thereby converting many idolaters to the true faith and leading them to piety.

In the days of the impious Roman Emperor Nero, a great persecution was raised against Christians. After the martyric death of the chief apostles Peter and Paul, in a vain attempt to destroy the name of Christ throughout the whole world, the persecutors began to seek out His disciples and all those who believed in the One Lord. And the fools did not know that the more they persecuted the Christian faith, the more it was strengthened and spread, for *"the gates of Hades shall not prevail against it"* forever (Matthew 16:18).

At that time, holy Photina, together with her younger son Josias, was in Carthage, one of the African cities, where she boldly preached the Gospel. Her elder son Victor served as a soldier in the Roman army. For the valor and courage he displayed during the war against the Avars, who were raiding Roman lands, Emperor Nero made him a military commander and, not knowing that he was a Christian, sent him to Italy to punish all the Christians there.

Sebastian, the Governor of Italy, tried to persuade Victor to carry out the emperor's command despite his convictions:

"I know, most excellent commander, that you, like your mother and your brother Josias, are a Christian. You are all followers of the Apostle Peter. However, I advise you to carry out the emperor's command and punish the Christians, so as not to endanger your own life."

"I will fulfill the will of the Heavenly and Immortal King Christ, the True God, but as for the command of Emperor Nero to punish Christians, I will not only not carry it out, but I do not even wish to hear of it," Victor answered him.

"As your true friend, I advise you to do what will serve your own benefit," Sebastian again addressed the commander. "If you sit in judgment and seek out Christians, and having found them, punish them, you will please the emperor and inherit their property. I also advise you to warn your mother and brother that they should not boldly preach Christ, teaching the Hellenes to renounce their ancestral faith, lest you yourself be endangered because of them."

"May it never be that I should do all that you tell me: punish Christians, or take anything from them, or advise my mother or brother not to preach that Christ is God. Indeed, I myself am and will be a preacher of Christ, just as they are. Let us see what will happen then," the Christ-loving warrior objected.

"Brother, I am advising you what is for your benefit, but you consider what you must do," the governor again began to counsel Victor.

However, before he could finish his speech, Sebastian was immediately struck blind and, falling to the ground from severe and terrible pain in his eyes, remained speechless. The servants lifted him and placed him on a bed, where he lay silent for three days, and on the fourth day he cried out loudly: "There is one God, the God of the Christians!"

"Why have you so suddenly changed your opinion, Sebastian?" Victor asked, entering his chambers.

"Because Christ is calling me, my sweetest Victor," replied the emperor's legate in Italy.

And immediately, instructed by Victor in the Christian faith, he was baptized, and as soon as he came up from the holy font, he could see again and glorified God. Observing this strange miracle, all the idolaters from Sebastian's household became frightened lest the same thing might happen to them for their unbelief as had happened to their master. They all ran to Victor and, having been catechized in the Christian faith, received Baptism.

A short time passed, and word reached Nero that the military commander and the governor were preaching in Italy the teaching of Peter, Paul, and the other apostles, that they had converted many Hellenes to the Christian faith, and that the commander's mother, Photina, together with her other son Josias, had been sent to Carthage to preach the Crucified One there as well.

Hearing this, the emperor was inflamed with anger and sent soldiers throughout Italy to bring to Rome all those who professed the Christian teaching. Meanwhile, the Lord Himself appeared to many men and women and said: *"Come to Me, all you who labor and are heavy laden, and I will give you rest"* (Matthew 11:28). "Do not be afraid, for I am with you, and Nero will be defeated together with his servants."

Among those who beheld this vision was Victor, to whom Jesus Christ said: "From now on your name shall be Photinus (light), for through you many shall be enlightened and believe in Me. Strengthen Sebastian for martyrdom with your words. Blessed and happy is he who shall struggle to the end." After these words, the Lord ascended to Heaven.

The coming events were also revealed to Photina. Therefore, together with a multitude of Christians, she set out from Carthage to Rome, where she also began to preach Christ with extraordinary boldness. And all the inhabitants of the capital of the Great Empire were troubled, saying: "Who is she who has come here with such a multitude of people?" At this same time, her son Photinus was brought to Rome by soldiers together with Sebastian, the Governor of Italy. All together they appeared before the emperor, who personally interrogated the Christians brought before him.

At first the emperor tried, through conversation, without intimidation or the application of torture, to compel the confessors to renounce their faith:

"Renounce Christ or you shall die an evil death," Nero threatened them in his anger.

"May this never be, O Christ the King, that we should renounce Thee and be separated from Thy faith and love," the martyrs prayed in response. Among them were: Anatolia, Photo, Photis, Parasceva, Kyriake, the sisters of Photina, and Photinus and Josias, her sons. They were all in agreement to die with joy and gladness for love of the Crucified Lord.

Then the tyrant commanded that their hand joints be crushed with iron balls. Seizing the saints, Nero's servants brought them to the place of torture and placed their hands on an anvil. The tortures began. From the third hour of the day until the sixth, the torturers changed three times, yet the martyrs felt no pain whatsoever, nor were their hands even broken. This strange miracle confounded Nero, and he commanded that the martyrs' hands be cut off. Immediately seizing Photina and binding her hands, the servants repeatedly struck at the holy woman's hands with swords, but could do nothing. They were paralyzed and fell to the ground as dead, while the martyr remained unharmed and thanked God, saying: *"The Lord is my helper; I shall look upon my enemies"* (Psalm 117:7).

The emperor began to think how he might overcome these Christians and persuade them not to worship their God. He commanded that the men be cast into prison, while holy Photina, together with her five sisters, be brought to him in the golden hall. He ordered a golden table and seven golden thrones to be set there, and much money, golden ornaments, garments, and golden belts to be brought, supposing that with these enticements he might change their faith. He also commanded his daughter Domnina, together with all her handmaidens, to come into this hall and be with the saints. Should the martyrs renounce Christ, Nero promised not only to give them all that was in this luxurious room, but also to honor them with great glory and honor. The wretch was deluded: for these women, thinking on heavenly things, despised all earthly goods and did not even wish to look upon them.

Such a Christian worldview, incomprehensible to the pagan mind, amazed the emperor's daughter. Noticing this, Photina addressed her with these words:

"Rejoice, bride of my Lord!"

"Rejoice also, my lady, lamp of Christ," Domnina answered her. Hearing that the princess had mentioned the name of Christ, the saint rejoiced greatly and, thanking the Lord, embraced and kissed her. She then instructed the emperor's daughter in the Christian faith and baptized her together with a hundred palace handmaidens. After the celebration of this great Mystery, during which Domnina was given the name Anthusa, the emperor's daughter commanded Stephanida, the chief of her handmaidens, to distribute to the poor all the golden ornaments and money that were in the golden hall.

Learning of this, Nero groaned and commanded that a furnace be immediately heated, and then that holy Photina be thrown into it together with her companions. In this fire the martyrs spent three days and remained alive and unharmed. When the inhabitants of the city of Rome heard of this miracle and saw them, at first they were perplexed as to how such a thing could happen, and then, following the Christians, they glorified God.

Then the tyrant commanded that all the confessors be given deadly poison, prepared by the skilled magician Lampadius. First the poison was given to holy Photina; taking it in her hands, she said: "We should not have taken this poison in our hands and drunk it, because you yourself are unclean. But so that you, O emperor, and this magician may know the power of my Christ, I shall drink it first in the name of the Lord and God our Jesus Christ before the others, and then all who are with me shall drink it." And so it happened to them: the poison caused the martyrs no harm whatsoever.

Seeing this, the sorcerer was amazed and said: "I have another strong poison. But if you drink it and do not die that very hour, I shall believe in your God." When the new potion was brought, the martyrs again drank it and suffered no harm. The magician was astonished and, gathering all his books of magic, threw them into the fire. Following his promise, he believed in Christ, was baptized, and was renamed Theoclitus. Learning of this, the emperor commanded the soldiers to seize the former magician and lead him outside the city wall. There his head was cut off with a sword. Thus the blessed Theoclitus received the crown of martyrdom before all the others.

After this, the lawless Nero commanded that the sinews of these disobedient Christians be cut. The soldiers carried out the order, while the martyrs mocked and derided the powerlessness of the emperor and his gods, counting as nothing the sufferings they were enduring. Then the emperor commanded that lead be melted, mixed, and when it boiled, poured into the mouth of holy Photina, and onto the backs of the other saints. Yet even after this the martyrs continued to glorify the Creator: "We thank Thee, O Christ our God, that with boiling lead Thou hast refreshed our hearts thirsting from this great heat."

This did not stop Nero, and he devised another torture for them. The saints were hung up, their bodies were mercilessly scraped and burned with torches, but the more torment the emperor's servants inflicted upon the Christians, the more they were strengthened by Divine grace and glorified God. Then the pitiful and vain Nero thought to break their unconquerable spirit with another torment: ash mixed with the strongest vinegar was poured into their nostrils. But even these actions were unsuccessful. The saints continued to thank God and said that this hellish mixture was to them *"sweeter than honey and the honeycomb"* (Psalm 18:11).

Such behavior drove the tyrant into a frenzy. He commanded that the confessors be blinded and then imprisoned for three years in a foul-smelling dungeon swarming with venomous serpents.

By their presence and constant prayers, the martyrs sanctified this terrible place: all the venomous creatures inhabiting the dungeon died, the stench was transformed into fragrance, and the darkness into brilliant light. And our Lord Jesus Christ stood in the midst of the saints, saying to them: *"Peace be with you"* (John 20:19). Then, taking holy Photina by the hand, He raised her up and said: *"Rejoice always"* (1 Thessalonians 5:16)... because *"I am with you even to the end of the age"* (Matthew 28:20). At that moment sight returned to the martyrs, and seeing God, they worshipped Him. Blessing the ascetics, Christ said: "Be of good courage and be strengthened," and with these words ascended to Heaven. Something like scales fell from the bodies of the saints, and they were completely healed, becoming as they were before.

After three years, the emperor ordered that one of his servants, who had been imprisoned there, be brought from the dungeon. When the messengers came to the prison, they saw that the martyrs were in good health: the blind Galileans could see again, the dungeon was filled with light and ineffable fragrance, crowds of people were coming there and, believing in the Risen Savior, were receiving Baptism.

After such a report, Nero lost his temper and again summoned the martyrs for interrogation. Asking why they had not obeyed him and continued to preach the name of Christ, he decided to subject the Christians to new punishments for violating his decree. First the saints were crucified upside down and their bodies were scraped for three days in a row until the tendons came apart. Having done this, the beast-like and inhuman servants left the martyrs hanging thus for four days. When this time had passed, they came to see if the confessors were still alive, but before they could even approach them, they were immediately struck blind. At that very moment an Angel of the Lord descended from Heaven, untied the saints, and kissing them, healed all their wounds. Taking pity on the blinded servants, holy Photina prayed to God for them, and they immediately could see again, after which they believed in Christ and received Baptism.

When Nero was informed of yet another miracle that had occurred with the Christians he was torturing, the emperor commanded that the skin be flayed from Photina. During this torture the saint, like the Psalmist, cried out: *"O Lord, Thou hast proved me and known me"* (Psalm 25:2). The flayed skin was thrown into the river, and the saint was thrown into a dry well. Then Sebastian, Photinus, and Josias had their reproductive organs cut off and thrown to dogs; then their skin was also flayed and thrown into the river, and the martyrs themselves were locked in an old bathhouse. The five sisters of holy Photina, brought before the tyrant, had their breasts cut off, and their skin was also flayed. When it came to the turn of holy Photis, she did not want to be held by force, but with great courage flayed her own skin, so that the tyrant marveled at her endurance. But even after this torment, the all-evil tyrant devised another terrible punishment for her: in Nero's garden, the tops of two trees were bent down, the blessed Photis was tied to them, and they were released. The saint was torn in two, and thus she surrendered her soul into the hands of God. Then the vile Nero commanded that the remaining martyrs be beheaded with the sword, while the blessed Photina was to be taken from the well and imprisoned in a dungeon.

Since she remained alone and had not been crowned with the crown of martyrdom together with the others, she was grieved and asked God for this. He appeared to her and, signing her three times with the Precious and Life-giving Cross, healed her of all her wounds. After a few days, singing praises and blessing God, Photina surrendered her honorable soul to the Lord. The Church celebrates her memory on March 20 / April 2.

Thus all came to the Desired God and received His Heavenly Kingdom, which may we also be granted through their prayers. Amen.

The Life, Struggles, and Martyrdom of the Holy Glorious Hieromartyr Polycarp, Bishop of Smyrna, Who Suffered in the Year 143

This glorious hieromartyr of Christ Polycarp came from the city of Ephesus. His parents were very wealthy and pious people: his father was called Pancratius, and his mother Theodora. When Theodora was pregnant with holy Polycarp, it was reported to Marcion, the governor of Ephesus, that they were Christians. The parents were seized and brought before him for interrogation, during which Marcion tried to find out why they did not submit to the imperial command and despised the great gods, worshipping Christ instead.

"O governor, we were taught by the apostles of our Lord to believe in and worship the True God, the Creator of heaven and earth, our Lord Jesus Christ, in whose name we were baptized, whom we confess and preach. But the soulless and senseless idols, which you consider to be gods, we abhor and despise," the parents of Polycarp fearlessly testified.

Hearing this, the governor grew angry and commanded the soldiers to throw them to the ground and beat them severely. Then Pancratius and Theodora were cast into prison, where they remained for a long time, deprived of all human help, suffering from hunger and thirst and enduring other sufferings. In this prison the future hieromartyr was destined to be born.

But the all-good God, who knows all things before they come to pass, foreseeing that the governor would seek the infant to raise him and teach him his own delusion, sent His Angel to the prison. The Angel first healed the infant's parents of the wounds inflicted upon them by the beatings, and then told them that the governor would put them to death. After this, the messenger of God took the infant and carried him to a very wealthy Christian widow, commanding her to baptize him and, without revealing the truth to anyone, to raise him with all diligence. After this the Angel became invisible.

The lawless Marcion searched many days for the infant, but did not find him and grew even more angry, subjecting the saint's parents to cruel tortures. Finally, seeing their steadfastness, he decided to put Pancratius and Theodora to death. The governor commanded the soldiers to lead them far outside the city and behead them, and to leave their bodies to be devoured by wild beasts. But in vain did the wretch labor, for not a single beast approached the honorable remains of the holy martyrs. A little later Christians came to this place and, according to Christian custom, reverently buried them.

The pious Christian widow baptized the child and named him Pancratius, after his father. She raised him as her own child. When the child reached the age suitable for learning, the woman sent him to school, and within a short time he learned all the church services. Having even from childhood the mind of an elder, Pancratius did not play with other children, but associated with wise and virtuous men. As the son of martyrs, he strove, as far as possible, to imitate them in all virtues with all his might, striving to acquire love for all, humility, gentleness, temperance, and chastity. He especially loved mercy, for which reason he was nicknamed Polycarp (Greek for "fruitful," "abundant in fruit"). Listen and marvel.

As we have already said, that God-loving woman who raised him was exceedingly wealthy and had storehouses full of wheat and other grain. Being merciful and very compassionate, the blessed Pancratius secretly gave abundant alms to the poor without his foster mother's knowledge, so that he emptied all the stores. Once his mother came for wheat and, finding the storehouses empty, was astonished, not understanding how this could have happened. However, knowing the good disposition and mercy that her ward showed to the poor, she understood that it was Pancratius who had emptied the granaries. When she returned and looked at him angrily, the youth with a cheerful face tried to persuade her to go to the storehouses once more to see that they were full. But the woman was greatly angered and would not go under any circumstances.

Then the saint went to the storage place alone, prayed to the Most Merciful God, and, O miracle! immediately all the granaries were filled with grain. Calling his mother, he joyfully said to her: "My lady, go to the storehouses to see the power and grace of God." When the woman entered and saw the storehouses full of grain, and even jars filled with oil and wine, she loudly glorified the Generous God and, kissing the blessed Pancratius, said to him: "My beloved child, from now on give to the poor as much as you wish, and henceforth I shall call you not Pancratius, but Polycarp." From that time this name remained with the saint. From that very day the blessed one generously distributed grain to all who were in need, and by God's mercy the storehouses never became empty, because, seeing the saint's good disposition, the Almighty multiplied the supplies.

At that time a severe famine struck the region of Ephesus, and then the most blessed Polycarp showed great mercy and compassion not only to the poor, but also to the rich, because many, although they possessed great wealth, did not know where to buy food and were in danger of dying from hunger. And the saint generously distributed provisions to them. Thus crowds of rich and poor came to him every day, and he sent no one away empty-handed, mercifully receiving all and doing good to each one.

When the saint was twenty-five years old, he heard that John the Theologian was preaching the Gospel in other parts of Asia. Having a strong desire to receive benefit, Polycarp took leave of his mother and went to the Theologian, with whom were Ignatius the God-bearer and the blessed Bucolus. The divine Polycarp followed them and, passing from place to place, from country to country, like the Apostle John, preached the word of Christ. He experienced great deprivations, suffering from hunger, thirst, and nakedness. After some time, the Roman Emperor Domitian learned that the apostle was converting idolaters to the Christian faith. This displeased the ruler, and he exiled the beloved disciple of Christ to the island of Patmos. Before his departure, John the Theologian ordained the blessed Bucolus as Bishop of Smyrna and gave him the holy Polycarp as his companion.

On the way to Smyrna, holy Bucolus ordained the divine Polycarp to the priesthood. And although he did not consent, justifying himself as unworthy of bearing such a high office in the Church, the bishop elevated the young priest to the dignity of orphanotrophus (guardian of orphans). However, the blessed Polycarp was so humble-minded that he did not wish to be distinguished from others, and even in the assembly of priests he did not sit according to his rank, but lower than everyone, as a simple man.

Because of such great humility, the all-good God exalted and glorified Polycarp: foreknowing his death, holy Bucolus gathered all the bishops, clergy, and Christians of the diocese, informed them of his approaching death, and asked the assembly whether they agreed that henceforth Polycarp should be Bishop of Smyrna. All agreed to this proposal with great joy. Thus, against his own will, holy Polycarp was ordained Bishop of Smyrna.

Having accepted the great burden of the episcopate, the blessed one carried out his office with special diligence, constantly teaching his flock the word of the Gospel, and through his deeds becoming an example of every good thing for the entire Christian community of Smyrna. He did not cease visiting his verbal flock day and night: everywhere strengthening the weak, consoling the sorrowful, healing the sick, caring for orphans, showing mercy to the poor, and helping all Christians. He had special, both secret and open, care for the martyrs, strengthening them in the faith of Christ, for at that time the tyrants constantly subjected them to cruel tortures.

The bishop was worthily called Polycarp, because he was filled with every divine fruit, being a wonderful calm harbor and great refuge not only for Christians, but also for numerous pagans, whom he constantly taught without any fear or timidity, converting them to the faith of Christ. Even during his lifetime, the saint performed countless miracles. Once a great and terrible fire broke out in Smyrna. Moreover, the fire raged not only in the city itself and in the houses, but also in the fields outside the city, in the vineyards, where trees and animals burned. This terrible disaster did not abate for seven days. The foolish and deluded idolaters called upon their gods for help. But they labored in vain, because the more they implored the idols, the more God was angered against them, and the fire kept growing stronger. As a result, the Christians came to the saint, asking him to pray to the Lord for the cessation of the fire. The bishop took pity on them and, in accordance with their request, prayed to the Almighty, and then, rebuking the idolaters, because of whose impiety all the evil was happening, he addressed the fire with these words: "In the name of our Lord Jesus Christ, whom I, unworthy as I am, serve and worship, I command you to be completely extinguished this very hour!" And, O strange miracle! that terrible fire at that very moment was completely extinguished and disappeared, and those present cried out in amazement: "Great is the God of the Christians!" And many idolaters believed in Christ and were baptized to the glory of our Creator.

One of the pagans, a nobleman named Petronius, moved by the devil, who always envies every good, began to speak blasphemous words against the Christian faith and holy Polycarp, and immediately suffered an attack of possession. He fell to the ground, began to roll about, foam at the mouth, and convulse. Some Christians took pity on him and asked the bishop to heal Petronius. Imitating the Master Christ, the blessed hierarch took pity on him and granted the nobleman a twofold healing: forbidding the crafty and unclean spirit and driving it out of Petronius, he thereby also enlightened his soul. Through the benefit he received, the rich man came to know the power that the servants of Christ have, and believing, was baptized together with all his household.

Four years passed, and a severe drought struck the region of Smyrna, as a result of which the entire harvest could perish. The people were in sorrow and did not know how to save it. The Christians again came to their bishop Polycarp and asked him to pray to the Lord. And, O Thy wonders, O Christ the King! Such a heavy rain poured down that it watered all the crops. But since the rain did not cease for several days in a row, the Bishop of Smyrna again, by means of prayer, halted its excess.

From these few miracles performed by the saint during his lifetime, one can judge the boldness he had before God. We shall briefly recount the glorious feat of the martyrdom of the hierarch Polycarp.

When Marcus Aurelius ruled in Rome, a great persecution was raised against believing Christians, and many city rulers mercilessly tortured them. So did the governor of Smyrna: finding a Christian, he would subject him to inhuman and deadly torments, and he went so far as to decide to seize holy Polycarp as the head of the local Christian community. Hearing of this, the divine bishop was not troubled in the least and decided to remain in the city. However, the Christians, loving him and not wishing to be deprived of such a worthy archpastor, persuaded the saint by various means to leave the city. He departed from Smyrna and arrived at a certain village, where he spent days and nights in prayer for all Christians and for all the Churches of Christ throughout the world. Praying thus for three days in a row, he dozed off and saw in a dream that his pillow caught fire and burned. Immediately awakening, the saint prophetically said to those with him that for the love of Christ fire must change his life. Meanwhile, the governor's servants continued to seek Bishop Polycarp, and the bishop, impelled by the love of the brethren, moved to another village. And as soon as the hierarch left his first refuge, soldiers came there and, not finding him there, seized two children living in that house. To find out where the blessed Polycarp was, they subjected them to tortures. Unable to endure the torments, one of the children revealed the location of the Bishop of Smyrna.

Taking the child, the soldiers came that same evening to the house where the archpastor was hiding. This time the hierarch did not want to go anywhere, but, trusting in God's will, insisted on his decision and went down fearlessly, with a cheerful and joyful face, to meet the uninvited guests, which greatly surprised the soldiers. While the legionnaires were dining at the saint's request, the bishop prayed, after which they placed him on a donkey and brought him to Smyrna.

When Polycarp was entering the governor's palace, a voice was heard from Heaven: "Be strong, Polycarp, and be of good courage." Many Christians heard these words, but no one saw Him who spoke them. The emperor's viceroy was not certain that the famous Polycarp had been brought to him. However, when the saint convinced him of this, the governor began to persuade him to renounce Christ and blaspheme Him, but the Bishop of Smyrna objected:

"For eighty-six years I have served Him, and He has done me no wrong. How then can I now blaspheme my King, my Savior and Redeemer?"

But the tyrant again began to compel the hierarch to renounce Christ:

"If you do not renounce Christ, I shall throw you to be devoured by wild beasts," the judge threatened the martyr.

"Do not delay, but throw me to the beasts, because I shall not waver in my faith, but rather I shall be very grateful to you if you transfer me an hour earlier from this false and most burdensome world into the true and immortal one," Polycarp insisted.

"Since you," the governor continued to oppose the hierarch, "count the beasts as nothing, then, if you do not repent, I shall burn you with fire."

"Why do you threaten me with temporal fire, which soon goes out? Or do you not know of the unquenchable fire of eternal torment, which is prepared for the impious? Therefore, do not waste time, but do as you wish," the divine bishop replied in a confessional manner.

Speaking these and many other words with great boldness and joy, the martyr amazed the governor, so that he sent a herald in perplexity to proclaim three times that Polycarp was a Christian. Hearing the announcement, the whole crowd of Hellenes and Jews cried out with a loud voice: "This is the father of the Christians, who teaches the people not to worship the gods. We must burn him alive." Immediately they brought wood and brushwood from the workshops and baths. The Jews especially strove to excel in this impious deed, for it is their custom, because of the hatred they bear toward Christ and all Christians, to zealously serve such evil. When the pyre was ready, the Bishop of Smyrna removed his garments and loosened his belt. The soldiers wanted to nail the saint with nails so that he would stand motionless in the fire. But he said to them: "Leave me, for He who gives me strength to endure the fire will strengthen me to remain motionless." They tied his hands behind his back, and Polycarp was offered as a well-pleasing whole burnt offering to God, like a festal ram chosen from a great flock. Before entering the fire, the martyr, raising his eyes to heaven, began to pray: "Lord God Almighty, I thank Thee that Thou hast deemed me worthy from this day and hour to be numbered among Thy martyrs in the resurrection to eternal life, both of soul and body. May I only be offered this day before Thee as an acceptable sacrifice, as Thou, O True God, hast prepared, revealed beforehand, and accomplished. For this I bless Thee for all things, I glorify Thee with Thy Beloved Son and with the Holy Spirit, now and ever and unto the ages of ages. Amen."

After this he entered the fire, and, O miracle! that fire, like a vault, like a sail filled with air, surrounded the body of the martyr. And he stood in the midst of it not as burning flesh, but as gold refined in a goldsmith's furnace, and there was a strong fragrance, as if frankincense or some other precious aromatic substance were burning.

Finally, seeing that the saint's body was not burning, the lawless men commanded that an executioner approach the martyr and put him to death with a sword. When this happened, so much blood flowed out that it completely extinguished the fire. Observing this miracle of God, the whole crowd was amazed. And the envious and malicious devil, knowing that the Christians would want to take the honorable relics of the saint, devised the following. One of the officials was persuaded to tell the governor not to give the body of the hieromartyr to the Christians, lest they begin to venerate the blessed Polycarp. So that the Christians would not secretly take the remains of the Bishop of Smyrna, the Jews undertook to guard them. After several days had passed, a certain centurion threw the holy relics of Polycarp into the fire, and they were consumed. After this the Christians took what remained after the burning of the body of the hieromartyr, and reverently and with honors buried them in a special place, to the glory of Christ our God, to whom belong all glory, honor, and worship unto the ages of ages. Amen.

The Life and Struggles of
Our Venerable Father Chariton the Confessor,
Who Was Saved from Martyric Death in the Year 276

In the year 270 after the birth of Christ, Aurelian ruled in Rome. Although he was an idolater, at the very beginning of his reign he did not hinder Christians who worshipped the True God; later, however, moved by the demons whom he served, he raised a great persecution against Christians. Throughout all the regions of his empire, Aurelian sent out an impious decree, according to which the governors were to apply all diligence and zeal in persuading Christians to renounce the faith of Christ and return to the delusion of idol-worship, and to subject those who did not submit to various tortures and shameful death. In Iconium, one of the first Christians to be seized and brought before the impious governor for trial was holy Chariton, for he was known throughout all the surrounding region as the most virtuous man.

During the interrogation, the thrice-blessed one fearlessly confessed that he believed in Christ, the True God. When asked why he opposed the imperial commands and did not wish to offer sacrifice to the immortal gods, the confessor answered with great boldness:

"I do not honor your sanctuaries because they are not true gods, but malicious demons, who have cunningly persuaded you to worship them as gods for two reasons. First, so that these deceivers might be exalted under the glorious name of deity, and they might take pride in being honored as gods; and second, to drag together with themselves into the unquenchable fire of torment all those who worship them."

"O Chariton, I should have been greatly angered with you now and immediately subjected you to the most cruel torments, because you have blasphemed the gods. But since they are longsuffering and guileless, I too wish to imitate them and advise you to choose what will be to your benefit: offer sacrifice to the gods and you will have great honor from the emperor," the emperor's viceroy tried to persuade the saint.

"Judge, if these deaf and soulless statues are gods, then you do wrong to tolerate the insults I inflict upon them. But if they are not gods, as is indeed the case, then you labor in vain to incline me to commit lawlessness, because I will in no wise ever renounce the Living and True God and serve abominable demons, since I am a follower and imitator of that famous protomartyr Thecla, who, like another Elijah, shines with the rays of martyrdom in this city of the Iconians. Moreover, I am a disciple of the great preacher of piety Paul, who inspiringly urged Thecla to endure tortures for the love of Christ. Therefore I too today say before all in the words of the divine Paul: *'Who shall separate us from the love of God? Shall tribulation, or distress, or persecution, or famine, or nakedness, or peril, or sword?'* (Romans 8:35). No, nothing shall separate me from the love of Christ," the courageous warrior of Christ replied.

"O good Chariton, if our sanctuaries, as you say, are not gods, how is it that our most august emperors, who worship them, and we, the governors, believing in them, receive glory and happiness from them?" the governor then said.

"You Hellenes are greatly deluded in acknowledging as gods carved images made by human hands, which are completely devoid of speech, mind, and living senses, as our Holy Scripture says: *'The idols of the nations are silver and gold, the work of human hands; they have mouths but do not speak; eyes they have but do not see; they have ears but do not hear, and there is no breath in their mouths. Like them will be those who make them and everyone who trusts in them'* (Psalm 134:15-18). Perhaps you doubt, O judge, that what I have said is true? Test it in practice: commit the idols to fire, command that their limbs be smashed, and then you will learn by actual experience that they are completely senseless and can neither move nor speak nor harm those who destroy them," Chariton answered.

At these words the lawless judge grew very angry and commanded that the saint be stripped, stretched out on the ground by his hands and feet, and beaten with ox sinews. At the same time, the beast-like governor said to the martyr:

"Well then, will you offer sacrifice to the gods? Or do you want even more blows to fall upon your body?"

"Not only blows, but rather a thousand deaths I would accept for the love of Christ, but I would not consent to renounce God and offer sacrifice to idols," the patient ascetic affirmed.

Hearing this, the tyrant commanded that the martyr be beaten even more severely. And they tortured him so cruelly that there was not a sound spot left on him, but his innards were exposed. From the unbearable beating, Chariton remained speechless. Then the governor commanded that he be left alone, not because he pitied the saint, but so that he would not die so quickly and thus escape greater torments. The servants lifted the half-dead confessor and, hoisting him on their shoulders, carried him and threw him into prison.

For the sake of brevity, and passing over many of the struggles of this valiant man without details, I shall say that after the Lord miraculously granted him health in prison, the martyr of Christ was again brought to trial. And again the foolish ruler tried first with deceitful flattery, and then with threats, to make Chariton agree with him. But since the latter was even more strengthened in the faith of Christ and only laughed at his foolish words, the governor subjected him to even greater tortures and commanded that the confessor's body be burned with fire, and that he then be cast again into prison.

A short time passed, and the God-fighting emperor was justly punished by God for the evil with which he had dared to attack Christians: the all-evil Aurelian died a terrible death. Tacitus, who succeeded him as emperor, was sobered by the example of his predecessor and, fearing that he too would be punished, ordered that persecutions of Christians be stopped in all regions of his empire.

Thus, by God's providence, the divine Chariton was not put to death. And many received great benefit from the long earthly life of Chariton the Confessor, which would not have been the case had he suffered a martyr's death. According to the imperial decree, he was granted full freedom. Although the saint did not receive a martyr's death for Christ, nevertheless on his enduring body there remained the marks of victory and wounds. Having almost died to this temporal life and desiring henceforth to serve the One God alone, he set out upon the narrow and sorrowful path which, according to the words of the Lord Himself, leads a person to eternal life (Matthew 7:14).

After his release from prison, Chariton decided to go to Jerusalem. On the way to the Holy Land, he fell into the hands of beast-like robbers, who bound his hands behind his back, put an iron chain around his neck, and brought the thrice-blessed one to the cave where they themselves dwelt. Leaving him bound there, they went out to the road to lie in wait for other travelers. And the divine Chariton, reflecting that the trial that had befallen him was permitted by God for the benefit of his soul, first gave abundant thanks to the Creator, and then, turning to the malicious devil, he began to revile him thus: "O vile and unclean one, why have you delivered me to these robbers? To have them kill me, or to prevent me from reaching my goal? Even if you were to strive diligently to put me to death, you would labor in vain, because you have clearly seen that I, by the grace of my Christ, despise every death. And if you wish to turn me from the path, so that I would not live in imitation of the Lord, you will accomplish nothing. Because, being merciful by nature, the Creator seeks every slightest pretext to generously grant His blessings to those who desire to live in a manner pleasing to God."

During these reflections, a viper crawled into the cave, which the saint did not see, and disgorged all its venom into the robbers' vessel filled with wine. When the robbers returned, suffering from thirst, and drank this poisonous wine, they immediately died. Thus wickedness was punished, and the wondrous Chariton was invisibly freed from his bonds at that very hour. However, the confessor did not leave this deserted place; it was very suitable for stillness, and the saint decided to remain there. With the silver that the robbers had collected through sin, he dealt justly: part he distributed to the poor and to venerable desert fathers, and with the remaining money he built a church of God in the cave, as well as the Holy Pharan Lavra, the main church of which was later consecrated by the Patriarch of Jerusalem Macarius, who was among the three hundred and eighteen God-bearing fathers of the First Ecumenical Council.

While struggling in the cave, the venerable one very soon and against his will became known to very many people. Every day he performed wonderful miracles. As a result, countless Hellenes and Jews began to receive Holy Baptism and, marveling at his ascetic labors and virtues, wished to imitate him as far as possible, and many became monks. Truly it was an astonishing miracle to see how the most blessed one struggled with incomparable desire in his life according to God, how he considered abstinence a delight, non-acquisitiveness an inexhaustible wealth, and how he loved lying on the bare ground. From vigils he received greater rest than lovers of pleasure receive from much sleep and rest on soft mattresses, so much did he love all-night prayers and the singing of psalms. From wearing a hairshirt, the touch of which scraped his martyr's wounds, the ever-blessed one received greater pleasure than those who wear bright and soft garments. All this was because hope for eternal bliss gave strength to his soul to endure with thanksgiving every pain and every labor.

The blessed Chariton was very merciful to the poor and compassionate toward sinners, hospitable and kind, meek and simple, guileless as a child and at peace with all, affable and courteous, instructive and enriched with words of wisdom, with which he gladdened the hearts of his visitors. Therefore people came to him every day to hear his soul-saving teaching. Because of the crowds, the desert became a city. Seeing that great disturbance arose from the crowds of people coming, by which his stillness and conversation with God were disrupted, and even more so striving to flee from human glory, for the saint knew that, blowing like a strong wind, it could destroy any virtue, the venerable one decided to leave the Pharan Lavra. During the farewell, Chariton commanded his disciples everything necessary for the monastic life. The rule consisted of the following: to eat once a day, preferably in the evening, and not to consume much rich food, but to abstain at the moment when one would still want more. Their food was to be bread and salt, and their drink pure water, which, for the sake of acquiring dispassion, the monks were also to use for quenching thirst very moderately. The venerable one also appointed for them times for psalmody and prayer, both day and night. At the same time, he commanded them to hate idleness as the cause of all evils, and always to give work to the hands, like the Prophet David, who said: *"I have cried unto Thee, O Lord, all the day long; I have stretched out my hands to Thee"* (Psalm 87:10). In fulfillment of these words, the ascetic advised the monks under his obedience always to pray with uplifted hands.

The holy father commanded them to cut off from the heart by fasting and by the divine sword of unceasing prayer the evil thought sown by the common enemy, so that it might not find a place of rest in a brother's heart and bear the poisonous fruit of sensuality: *"This kind does not go out except by prayer and fasting,"* it is said in the Gospel of Matthew (Matthew 17:21). Furthermore, Chariton commanded them not to send the poor who come to the gates of the monastery away empty-handed, lest they miss Christ, who, testing us, very often puts on a beggar's rags.

After the venerable one gave these precepts to the monks of his monastery and, with the common consent of the brethren, appointed the most virtuous and experienced brother as abbot over them, the abba began to prepare for his departure. However, unable to bear this, the brethren were extremely grieved and with fervent tears asked Father Chariton not to part from them. The saint would not listen to them, because he sought benefit not only for his own soul, and to console the brethren he said: "Do not grieve, my children, over separation from me, because if I depart from here, no one will come to seek me any longer and disturb you. So my departure will be beneficial both for me and for you. You and I must practice stillness in our cells, for only thus will we, with God's help, bring forth the honey of virtue." Bidding them farewell and commending them to Christ the Master, Chariton departed. After one day's journey, the venerable one discovered an empty cave in the region of Jericho, very suitable for stillness. Here he remained hidden for a long time, known to absolutely no one, conversing alone with the One God. For food the blessed one used grass, which he happened to find.

However, the Savior of the world did not allow the treasure to remain hidden and revealed His servant to the world through the miracles that were performed through him. For example, Chariton healed those suffering from bodily and spiritual diseases. After his soul-profitable instructions, many wanted to renounce the world. They became monks and remained to live near holy Chariton. For their sake he built a second Lavra, which he later expanded and named Elpidius. The Lavra flourished greatly in ascetic labors and received the nickname Douka (governor), since a certain duke, a governor, defended this holy Lavra from raids by the Jews who then inhabited the village of Noeros, adjacent to it, who out of envy sought an opportunity to destroy the monastery.

But to this monastery also a large number of people began to come every day, so that neither the saint nor the brethren had any peace. Then Father Chariton again left the brethren of the Lavra with his precepts and, having appointed a superior over them, departed to another part of the desert called Tekoa. Our Lord, who seeks the salvation of all, arranged for the saint to change places of residence, on the one hand, to make his virtue even more manifest, and on the other, so that different people, especially idolaters, might come to him and receive benefit. Some of them gained faith in Christ and received Baptism; others came to a life according to God, leaving worldly vanity and cares, became monks, and strove to imitate the venerable one in all things.

For the sake of the people who gathered there, Chariton built a third Lavra, called Souka. But since he himself greatly loved stillness, for he knew from experience its sweetness and benefit in acquiring virtue, not far from the newly-created monastery the holy father found a God-built cave, "suspended" high above the ground, on a steep and inaccessible mountain. It could only be reached by means of a ladder. Having once ascended to this cave, the courageous Chariton settled there.

Chariton spent a long time in stillness, but being unable because of old age and many years of ascetic labors to serve and fetch water, and not wishing to assign this obedience to any of his disciples so as not to be a burden to them, the grace-filled one conceived the following. He knew that at the prayer of a righteous man God can make the impossible possible and what is difficult very easy. And, O miracle! immediately after the confessor's prayer, a spring of the purest water gushed forth in the cave. And to this day it flows from one side of the cave, not only quenching thirst but also healing every infirmity. This is the best testimony to the holiness of the venerable one and to that boldness before the Creator which the grace-streaming Chariton had.

This narrative lacks the account of the repose of the venerable one, which he foreknew through divine revelation.

After the venerable Chariton learned of his approaching death, he descended from the cave to the holy Lavra of Souka and, together with the abbot and brethren, came to the monastery of Elpidius, from where, accompanied by the pastors and flock of both monasteries, he arrived at the holy Pharan Lavra, where he had first poured out the sweat of his ascetic labors. Here he left his disciples a testament as their inheritance. Its essence is as follows:

"Since the time of my death is approaching, I shall go to God, whither you too, my children, beloved in the Lord, must strive to come with all diligence, preparing yourselves well now, while there is time. For you know that after death no repentance will avail. This present life is the time of repentance and struggles for the acquisition of virtue, while the future life is the time of recompense. All sorrows and difficulties of this world will soon pass, and likewise all joys and pleasures. But in the future, both the enjoyment of blessings and the torments of hell are eternal and endless. Therefore I command you, above all, carefully guard the God-given faith, not deviating or wavering in the least from circumstances of the time or from danger. Because in a short time, as the Lord has revealed to me, a great disturbance will arise in the holy Churches of Christ from heretics, who will lead many astray into their heretical opinions. But you, stand firm in the doctrines of the Church even unto blood, if the times require it. Furthermore, take care that no one condemn you for your life, and keep yourselves blameless from every sin. If you have not yet attained this, purify yourselves from sins with great diligence every day. Guard virginity and holiness of body, that you may be undefiled temples, and that the Most Pure God may desire to dwell in you and fill your souls with His holiness and ineffable fragrance.

"Anger and irritation are the greatest evils; no passion can cause such harm to brotherly love as this one. But you, my true children, guard with much diligence concord, peace, Christ-like meekness, and love of mankind. If, through the temptation of the hater of good, a scandal should arise among you, strive as quickly as possible to call upon all-honorable love and brotherly affection for help, lest it happen that the sun sets while the scandal still operates among you and you are darkened by the hatred of rancor. For if we should happen to die this night, then without love it will be impossible to see the Sun of Righteousness, our Teacher Christ, who said in the Holy Gospel: *'By this all men will know that you are My disciples, if you have love for one another'* (John 13:35). And if the devil, the sower of the soul's perdition, should plant in your souls a thought of evil desire, strive with great diligence to uproot and remove it immediately. If you make haste, you will be able to expel it easily, but if you leave it for a long time in your heart, then only with great difficulty will you be able to uproot it. As weapons employ fasting, prayer, tears, the remembrance of death, and the recollection of the unquenchable fire of torment, using this remembrance as the destroyer of all sin. Remember also the most powerful and most terrible weapon against our enemies: the garment of Jesus Himself, victorious humility: *'Learn from Me, for I am meek and lowly in heart...'* (Matthew 11:29), the Savior tells us.

"The guarding of the mind and of all the senses, especially sight and hearing, is a safe harbor so that we may not be enslaved by thoughts that separate us from God, because through these two senses almost all evil desires enter our heart. As the Prophet Jeremiah says, through the windows of inattention, that is, the senses, spiritual death enters us. Most precious for a monk is non-acquisitiveness, freedom from care, non-attachment to the desire for perishable things. A monk must be moderate in bodily needs, as Paul advises: *'Having food and clothing, let us be content with these,'* without murmuring rashly against our Benefactor (1 Timothy 6:8).

"The greatest of all other evils is high-mindedness and pride, since they kill every good thing in a person. This passion very often seizes upon and accompanies those who are rich in virtues, but sometimes it attaches itself to one who is devoid of every good. Pride causes a terrible shipwreck for him who is possessed by it. Therefore the divine Paul, stretching out his hand to help us, shows how we can be delivered from it: *'Therefore let him who thinks he stands take heed lest he fall'* (1 Corinthians 10:12), that is, let him who thinks he stands well in virtue watch carefully lest he suffer shipwreck in virtue, so that he cannot rise again from his fall. We must be very careful not to judge our brother, but to have compassion on him and correct him, because judgment is the offspring of a proud soul, which in its thoughts judges all people and seeks, through the condemnation of others, justification and glorification of itself, saying like the Pharisee: *'I am not as other men are... or even as this tax collector'* (Luke 18:11).

"If you like to judge yourself and examine yourself, brother, you are very close to yourself. Never cease to judge and examine all your secret thoughts, words, and deeds, correcting your faults, because if we judge ourselves here, in this life, and correct ourselves, then we will not be judged by God in the other life to eternal torments, as the blessed Paul says: *'For if we would judge ourselves, we would not be judged. But when we are judged, we are chastened by the Lord'* (1 Corinthians 11:31-32). If anyone gives excessive pleasure to his belly, he easily suffers shipwreck and falls into fleshly passions, receiving evil recompense for this. But labors and vigils dry it up, fasting completely tames it and prevents the arising of disorderly movements in it.

"Love hospitality and always practice it, because this is pleasing to God. When you receive strangers, wash their feet, since this washing is Christ's service and His commandment. For He was the First to wash the feet of His disciples and commanded that we also do likewise. This act not only gives rest to the weary, but can even heal more than any other occupation the most harmful disease of the soul: vainglory.

"The means that cleanse the soul from the defilements of sin are: tears, groans, contrition of heart, fasting, prayer, lying on the ground, and everything that heals the penitent. They are not too burdensome, though they bring great benefit to the discerning. I know only one very easy but very powerful means for cleansing the defilement of the soul: compassion for sinners. By means of it not only is forgiveness of sins granted to the compassionate, according to the saying: *'Forgive, and you will be forgiven'* (Luke 6:37), but it often brings the sinner to his senses better than punishment, and turns a free man into a slave of him who showed him compassion, as is evident even among unbelievers, who say that forgiveness is better than punishment."

Teaching his disciples this and similar things, the divine Chariton wished them salvation of soul, and then, having tasted no sickness whatsoever, having experienced no ailment in any of his limbs, he fell upon his bed and, stretching out his legs, at once joyfully surrendered his holy soul to the Angels. Thus he passed into endless bliss, to that place where rest comes to those who, pouring out sweat, labored in the vineyard of the Lord, to those who walked the narrow and toilsome path of virtue.

And so, all the deeds and miracles of the ever-blessed Chariton, which, despite their antiquity, have escaped oblivion, we have conveyed to you, dear inquiring listeners, through this narrative, to the glory of the Father, and of the Son, and of the Holy Spirit, One Godhead and Kingdom, to whom belong all glory, honor, and worship, now and ever and unto the ages of ages. Amen.

The Life and Struggles of the
Holy and Glorious Martyr Thalaleaus,
Who Suffered Around the Year 284

This great martyr of Christ Thalaleaus came from a place in Phoenicia called the Forest of Lebanon. The son of the Christian bishop Beruchius and a descendant of a noble family of his city, he was raised *"in the training and admonition of the Lord"* (Ephesians 6:4) and was also taught divine and sacred letters. When he came of age, Thalaleaus desired to study the medical art, as the most necessary and most philanthropic of all other arts. He found a remarkable and extremely devout physician and in a short time mastered medicine to perfection.

The young Thalaleaus was very pious and devout, and had a soul adorned with all virtues and God-pleasing deeds. Thus, in his home he received all people without distinction: strangers and locals alike, serving them with love in every need. His house was an inn for all: poor and rich, because the saint greatly loved the virtue of hospitality and rejoiced when many were healed through him. However, he showed greater compassion and mercy to the poor; he cared for them most of all, considering their diseases and sufferings as his own. Very often, to spare these people effort, he would take them in his arms and carry them to his house, standing before them like a servant, preferring to serve them rather than to do any other good. The saint made every effort to care for and treat the poor from their diseases. And he showed such mercy to those in need of help that they did not seek him, but he himself ran to them and helped them in all their needs, restoring their health without any payment. Along with love of mankind and mercy, the saint was distinguished by non-acquisitiveness; he never took money or any other things of this world.

With such a selfless life, Thalaleaus soon became worthy of apostolic gifts. By the mere bold proclamation of the name of Christ, without medicines and plasters, he healed every disease, striving with all diligence to bring all idolaters to Christ. He made no distinction between believers and unbelievers, but healed all, obtaining a twofold healing: of soul and body. For the saint was merciful and compassionate to all, fervently imploring the Creator on behalf of all: for Christians, that they might repent and erase their transgressions; for pagans, that they might leave their errors and believe in the True God. He even rebuked those Christians who did not have compassion on unbelievers in their misfortunes and diseases.

Thus, once a certain Christian was angry at a certain idolater and rejoiced at his misfortune. Seeing this, the saint was greatly grieved and rebuked his fellow believer for his hard-heartedness:

"One should not rejoice at an enemy's misfortune, because misfortunes and sufferings are common to all. For no one knows what will happen to each of us in this life," Thalaleaus instructed.

One Christian, thinking that the destruction of the impious would be a blessing for all people, did not understand Thalaleaus, who spent his entire life in prayer for enemies, and asked himself what benefit there could be from them, since they had grown old in impiety and sins... However, the blessed one never rejoiced, but had compassion on the misfortunes of others. In this way he softened their unbelief and often led them to faith. In like manner, many Christians were also delivered from cruelty and strengthened in mercy.

Having a strong zeal for the faith, the saint strove earnestly to uproot pagan delusion. For this purpose, every night he went and cut down the tall trees in the Forest of Lebanon, where the Hellenes gathered and offered sacrifices to their gods, defiling their souls with fornication. There also drinking bouts and dances with women took place, accompanied by playing on all kinds of musical instruments. Having cut down the trees, the saint weaned them from offering sacrifices to idols and committing lawlessness, and attracted many to himself, healing them of bodily and spiritual diseases and instructing them in the Christian faith.

Once a certain man was bitten by a venomous serpent on his chest. From its poison, the chest and sides began to rot, so that the sick man was at the point of death. Having spent all his means on physicians and receiving no healing, and now utterly despairing, the sick man awaited death. However, the blessed physician willingly undertook to cure him, asking only that he believe in Christ. And as soon as he agreed, the saint prayed to God and traced the sign of the Life-giving Cross on his chest. Soon no trace of the disease remained. The sufferer glorified God for the twofold healing of soul and body, which he received from Thalaleaus.

At another time, a serious disease, the loss of speech, befell a certain physician. Having lost all hope of healing, his relatives brought the sufferer to the saint and asked him to relieve his torments.

"If you wish to be healed," the merciful Thalaleaus said to the sufferer, "believe in Christ, and He will immediately make you well."

Hearing this, the sick man fell at his feet and, bathing them with tears, indicated by gesture that he would believe in Christ with his whole soul if he received healing. And, O miracle! at that very hour Divine grace descended upon him, his tongue was loosed from the bonds of muteness, and the man spoke as before.

From that time on, the saint began to go about the city in search of the sick, or the hungry, the poor, or those in error, that he might heal their soul and body. Thus, he took pity on a paralytic lying naked on the ground, approached him, and asked what ailed him.

"Once I was walking along a steep road. Stumbling, I fell and broke my leg," the sufferer began his account. "For a long time I tried various remedies, but nothing helped; nor could I find healing from physicians. And now I lie in despair, the most wretched of all men. But you, who are more merciful than any natural father, have mercy on me, wretched as I am, and heal me."

"So that you may become well, I shall apply to you the plaster of faith in Christ, that you may be healed. Only believe in Christ, and His grace will immediately be granted to you," Thalaleaus said to him.

As soon as the sick man declared that he believed in the Savior with his whole soul, the saint set the leg. As soon as the joints touched each other, the sinews immediately came together, the wound healed, and the weak lame man rose up and ran. However, Thalaleaus did not seek human glory, and therefore asked the former paralytic not to reveal this miracle to anyone. But he did the opposite: he began running through the roads proclaiming to all the healing he had received from the saint.

When a certain demon-possessed woman heard of the miracle, she immediately came to Thalaleaus and, telling him of her misfortune, begged him with tears to deliver her from the evil and unclean spirit. At that moment she had a fit: the demon threw her to the ground and began to torment her. Seeing how the demon was tormenting her, the saint took pity on the sufferer and, signing her forehead with the sign of the Precious Cross, called upon the name of Jesus Christ. And, O miracle! immediately the demon left her and fled. As soon as this woman was delivered from the unclean spirit, she went home with great joy, loudly proclaiming the greatness of God. On the way she met an acquaintance, a blind man, to whom she said: "Why do you sit here without benefit? Have you not heard that there is a wonderful physician who heals all the sick in a wondrous manner, casting out demons, delivering from leprosy and other sores? He accepts no gifts, but teaches and commands all people to do good deeds, receives all the sick who come to him, places each one on a separate bed, finding consolation for all. Let me lead you to him, that you may receive healing."

With these words, the woman took the blind man, who was blind not only in his bodily eyes but also in his spiritual ones, for he worshipped idols, and brought him to the saint. The blind man fell at the healer's feet and said:

"Until now I was wretched and miserable, but from now on I shall be happy, because you will give light to my eyes," he said, hoping to receive healing.

"O man! The sleepless eye of God sees the hearts of all, their thoughts and deeds. Therefore, believe in Christ, the Creator of all creation, and your eyes will be healed. If you come to know Him who is the Physician of souls and bodies, He will heal you," the divine physician answered.

"With my whole soul I shall believe in Christ, as soon as I see light in my eyes," the sufferer exclaimed, and taking the thrice-blessed hands of the saint, he placed them over his eyes, and immediately he saw. After this, glorifying God, he remained with the saint.

The fame that Thalaleaus was healing the sick in a wondrous manner spread throughout the whole world, and people began coming to him from everywhere. Under the guise of healing, but in reality for the preaching of the name of Christ, the blessed Thalaleaus passed from place to place. Thus he also came to Edessa. However, the hater of good, the devil, could not bear to see the faith of Christ multiplying, and incited certain malicious people to go to Tiberianus, the governor of that region, to betray the saint. At that time, at the head of the Roman Empire stood Emperor Numerian, who was wholly devoted to the delusion of idolatry and raised a great persecution against Christians. Therefore, when Tiberianus heard that holy Thalaleaus was preaching the name of Christ, he immediately sent soldiers to bring him. After conversing with the Christian physician, the Governor of Edessa decided that the saint was mad and released Thalaleaus, ordering him not to go about the region entrusted to Tiberianus any longer.

Then the saint went to Cilicia, where, under the pretext of healing, in the same manner as before, he preached the name of Christ. But the idolaters slandered him before the governor of the land of the Aegeans, lying near the sea. They reported that this physician was deceiving the people and boasting that he healed the sick in the name of Jesus Christ, who was crucified by the Jews. Besides this, Thalaleaus dishonored the gods and cut down the sacred trees of Lebanon.

Hearing this, the governor immediately sent servants to bring the saint to him. The soldiers bound him, beat him, and brought the blessed one before the governor. The trial began the following day in the Temple of Hadrian. Here the governor asked him to tell about himself.

"My homeland is Phoenicia; I am the son of free parents, and my name is Thalaleaus. I practice healing, and I am a Christian, a servant of Jesus Christ," the physician replied. "I pass from place to place to preach faith in Jesus Christ and deliver people from the delusion of idolatry, because no other work is so pleasing to God as this."

Hearing this, the governor grew angry and commanded that his ankles be pierced and then that he be hung upside down by ropes. But by Divine power the soldiers' minds were confused, and instead of Thalaleaus they pierced and hung some piece of wood, truly thinking that they had hung the saint. Seeing the wood hanging and thinking that the soldiers were mocking him, the governor severely punished them and commanded other servants to beat the martyr with ox sinews, hoping that by this torment he would break him. However, the courageous warrior of Christ remained unconquered; the cruel soldiers wounded his body with severe blows, but could not shake his faith in Christ in the least. It seemed that the martyr felt no pain whatsoever, but courageously endured the torments for the sake of his great love for God. The tyrant was amazed at this Christian's endurance and addressed him with lawless words:

"Thalaleaus, how do you heal the sick? If you wish to know my love, tell me the whole truth, even if you heal them by sorcery, let me know about it. But if you heal them by the power of the gods, then I too shall believe that it is they who can deliver from every disease, and not Christ, who was crucified by the Jews, who promised people no blessings, nor any joys of this world, but only sorrows, dangers, and death. Our gods have pleasures: games, dances, songs, laughter, and every joy. It is they, not Christ with His Cross, which is the most terrible punishment in the world, who drive away every disease."

The blasphemies against Christ uttered by the impious one pained the martyr more than the torments inflicted upon him. And he said:

"I am not a sorcerer, and I do not heal the sick by sorcery, nor with the help of your gods, those soulless, deaf, and senseless idols, which can help neither others nor themselves. In the name of Jesus Christ they fall and are shattered. But if you wish to be convinced of what I actually heal with, question those who have received healing. They will all confirm that the Lord Himself and the sign of His Life-giving Cross healed them. He alone can cast out demons, raise up the paralyzed, restore sight to the blind, raise the dead, and heal every disease. The Only-begotten Son of God, seeing that His image, man, through disobedience had been expelled from paradise, deprived of all the blessings given to him, enslaved to the devil, and had fallen into idolatry and all the sins that the devil devised, took pity on His creature, descended into the world and became Man to save all people. And finally, for love of us, He was crucified and with His Most Precious Blood redeemed us and freed us from slavery to the devil. And how much good He did for the world!.. During His earthly life, Jesus Christ healed the paralyzed, the deaf, the blind, those with dropsy, the demon-possessed, and those suffering from various other diseases; He even raised the dead. He granted people every kind of blessing, and when He ascended to Heaven, He gave to the apostles and to all who believe in Him and keep His commandments His grace and power to heal every disease by His holy name and the sign of His Precious Cross. Therefore you should have believed in Jesus Christ, the Deliverer and Savior of the world, and left your vain gods, in order to inherit eternal life, rather than uttering blasphemies against Him. Listen to me, O governor, if you wish yourself well: believe in the True God, and then you will know His mercy and love for mankind, and His power, by which He heals not only bodily but also spiritual diseases of sinners, for He desires the salvation of all people."

"O good avenger of Christ, who have become condemned, I shall now show you that you hope in your God in vain," the tyrant said with anger, and immediately rushed at Thalaleaus to punish him with his own hands. But, O wonders of Thine, O Christ the King! at that very moment both his hands withered. But not even by this was the thrice-accursed one sobered, and he commanded the soldiers to torture the martyr with various torments: to scrape him with iron claws, burn him with fire, cut him with knives, and subject him to many other torments.

The confessor endured all things with courage and joy, because Christ was with him, easing his torments. And although the martyr's whole body was covered with countless wounds, the ascetic himself remained firm in his thoughts and, despising all the tortures, said to the Governor of Cilicia:

"Do not think that I shall be frightened by your punishments and the death with which you threaten me. With great boldness I shall fight against it, because it is better for me to die in the faith than to live in impiety. Even if you crush my earthly fleshly vessel, you cannot take the treasure of my soul. Even if you cast me out of my bodily tabernacle, you cannot deprive me of the noetic dwelling of the Heavenly Kingdom. I have praised the victories of other courageous martyrs before, and now that I am in battle myself, how can I cast away the weapons of my Christ and not win the victory? Christ does not give gifts to the cowardly and negligent; He does not crown those who sleep. Therefore the burning of your fire is a mockery to me, for the dew of my Savior refreshes me. All your torments are to me as leaves of trees, because my mind has become stone, and I am ready to offer my body to Christ as a sheep, because I must offer it as a sacrifice, as He also was offered as a sacrifice for me."

"I, in my kindness, have given him the opportunity to speak such words. He is not yet eighteen, yet he makes speeches before us better than any rhetor. I thought that by torments I would make him agree with me, but he does not fear them at all; he does not deviate in the least from his purpose. Perhaps I should bring him into agreement with me by wealth? But he counts it as nothing. Perhaps I should flatter him with pleasant words? But even by this he cannot be conquered. What other method then should I try? I shall put him in a boat and leave him in the middle of the sea; if he is a pious and good man, Divine Providence will preserve him, but if he is evil, he will drown by Divine sentence, but he will not receive death at my hands," the judge reasoned thus.

After this, the martyr of Christ Thalaleaus was placed in a boat, which was tossed violently by the sea. But the fearless preacher stood in it as if on dry land, and prayed: *"Unto Thee have I lifted up my eyes, O Thou that dwellest in the heavens"* (Psalm 122:1). Often have I called upon Thee, and Thou hast had mercy on me. Have compassion on me now also, and bring me to the saving harbor, that the depth of the sea may not swallow me up, that I may not lose my martyrdom for Thee, but may fulfill to the end my desire to offer my body in sacrifice to Thee, my Christ. The eyes of my soul hope in Thee, O Lord, and my patience will help me to appear with boldness at Thy Dread Judgment Seat."

And, O miracle! the sea, as if taking pity on the saint, immediately grew calm and carried the boat to shore. The tyrant learned at once of the miracle that had occurred and again commanded that the martyr be brought before him. Many idolaters, and especially the physicians who envied the saint, came to look at Thalaleaus. They all shouted vile slanders and called upon the judge to pronounce the death sentence.

"And you, Thalaleaus, what do you say to these accusations?" the governor asked the confessor.

"God, whom I worship and serve, will help me, even if the whole world rise up against me, because I know that my God gives life even after death. Therefore I must endure this suffering, not thinking of any bodily torments, and accept death for the love of Christ."

"Since no evil demon drowned you in the sea, I shall put an end to your life. I shall command that you be nailed to a board with four nails and doused with boiling pitch from head to foot, covered with stones and burned with fire until you die," the enraged governor exclaimed.

When the blessed one heard this, his face broke out in sweat like a weary athlete, and he wept.

"The demons have left him, and therefore he is frightened of the torment. But I too should have mercy on him," the tyrant thought, deciding that the confessor had become afraid.

"Thalaleaus, if you worship the gods, I promise to give you wealth and glory, and besides this you will have the mercy and gentleness of the gods. But if you do not listen to me, you will lose even your very life," the judge said aloud.

"I laugh at your mercy and at your gifts. Why do you try to deceive me and make me impious instead of pious? Your wealth is as dust to me. Nothing is a greater gain for me than the pure sacrifice of my body. In the beginning of the torment my will was firm and unshakable, and now, when I am already approaching the end and awaiting victory, do you, most lawless one, persuade me to do your will? Torments are joy to me, wounds are glory, dangers are a crown, and the putting off of my body I count as the putting off of a garment, because I am strengthened by hope in my Christ," the courageous ascetic of Christ said.

"I have spoken much with him, shown great mercy, tortured him with terrible torments, and could not convince him by anything. So many soldiers labored without benefit, inflicting wounds on him and tormenting him. He desires to be slain, he desires death. Why speak to ears that do not listen to you? Therefore I shall sentence him to death," the emperor's viceroy grew angry. And at that very moment he commanded that four terrible lions be released to tear the saint to pieces.

But God again did not leave Thalaleaus without help: the beasts became gentle as lambs, settled near the martyr and played with their tails. The shamed tyrant did not know what to do. Finally, he took a stylus and signed the death sentence. The Christian physician was to be put to death by the cutting off of his head with a sword. This happened on May 20 / June 2. Holy Thalaleaus, having endured many sufferings, received the crown of martyrdom. And many then, observing the courage, patience, and miracles of the confessor, believed in our Lord Jesus Christ and also ended their lives with a martyr's death for Christ. Among them were: Macarius, the teacher of holy Thalaleaus in the medical art, Asterius the wood-bearer, the soldier Alexander, Sterona, Philegrius, Timothy, Theodula, Macaria, and many others. Through their intercession may we also be granted the Heavenly Kingdom. Amen.

The Struggles of the Holy and Glorious Venerable-Martyr Paphnutius the Egyptian, a Hermit, and the 540 Martyrs Who Suffered with Him in the Year 303

In the times of the most impious Emperor Diocletian, a certain idol-worshipper named Arian became governor of Misyria—a fierce persecutor of Christians. He learned that in the region of Gentiria there lived a hermit named Paphnutius, a righteous man revered throughout that whole area. Unable to bear such people, Arian ordered two of his centurions to bring him in chains of iron.

Saint Paphnutius knew nothing of this and, according to his custom, had gone up onto the mountain to spend the night. Here, after prayer, an Angel of the Lord appeared to him.

"Rejoice, Paphnutius, ascetic of Christ," the Heavenly inhabitant greeted the saint.

"Rejoice also, my lord," the abba greeted him with praise.

"Follow me, Paphnutius, I will put a roof on the house that you began to build while still a child," said the Angel to the venerable one, showing that the time had come for Paphnutius to complete the ascetic struggle of virtue, undertaken from earliest youth, and to accept martyrdom for Christ. "So then, go to your cell, put on the priestly vestments in which, as a priest of God Most High, you offer to Him the Bloodless Sacrifice, and arm yourself. Today I have come to call you to enjoy the eternal blessings of God and to have no more cares. Impious haters of Christ have slandered you before the governor Arian, and he has ordered two hundred soldiers to bring you in chains to his tribunal. But take courage and do not be afraid, for I am an Angel of the Lord, and as I was formerly with your parents, so now I will be with you. And our Lord Jesus Christ will strengthen you and through you will put to shame Arian and his idols," thus spoke the messenger to the saint.

After these words, the blessed Paphnutius entered his cell, put on his priestly vestments, and came out with such joy as if he had been invited to a feast. When he set out on the road to Misyria, the Angel took him by the hand and walked beside him, conversing with him about Heavenly mysteries until they came to the Nile. Here the Angel left him and ascended into Heaven.

At that same hour Paphnutius saw boats coming to shore, and from one the governor Arian disembarked accompanied by his nobles, while from the others soldiers came ashore.

Then the divine Paphnutius approached Arian, who had already taken his seat upon a throne near the mouth of the river, and with boldness cried out in a loud voice:

"I am that Paphnutius whom you seek. Do not trouble your soldiers to go looking for me. You have armies that seize Christians and spill their blood, but Christians have holy Angels who gather us into the Kingdom of God. I too am a Christian—do with me what you will."

"So you are Paphnutius the apostate, who despises the imperial laws and dishonors the gods?" asked the governor with fury. "Why then, godless one, do you blaspheme the great gods?"

"I am not godless, but from childhood I have served and worshipped the Living and True God. But you, who have so many gods, are truly godless," answered the confessor.

"I swear by the great gods, I will subject you to painful and cruel punishments," raged Arian, and immediately ordered Paphnutius to be bound hand and foot in iron and held together with other prisoners—thieves and evildoers. Unable to walk freely, the blessed Paphnutius covered the distance with great difficulty and, encouraging himself, said:

"Paphnutius, think about the lot that has fallen to you, and remember that our Lord also was hanged between robbers."

When the governor arrived in the city and took his seat on the judgment seat, he immediately demanded that the blessed one be brought before him. As soon as the saint entered the court, his chains loosed themselves and before Arian's eyes fell from both his hands and feet.

"Paphnutius, why are you so mad that you do not offer sacrifice to the great gods, but prefer to die an evil death?" the governor began to question.

"For us Christians, such a death is not death, but eternal life, and I will offer sacrifice to no one else except the Almighty God, King of the ages."

Then the judge ordered the instruments of torture to be brought and placed before the martyr.

"Paphnutius, if you do not obey me and offer sacrifice to the great gods, you will be tormented with all these instruments that you see before you."

"Tyrant Arian, do you really think that I will be frightened by your tortures and renounce my God? May it never be! For I tell you that our life is above your torments, and we do not fear them at all, because we have been tested and hardened by many struggles and sufferings. And the Lord and Deliverer, Who gives us strength to conquer Satan in hidden warfare, will also give us strength to overcome your worthless persecution," said the soldier of Christ with a smile.

"You talk too much, Paphnutius, but the court will not tolerate your talkativeness," the governor threatened the saint, and then ordered the soldiers to hang the martyr and scrape his body so that all his entrails fell out and dropped to the ground, and the earth around that place turned red with blood.

"Lord Jesus Christ, I will not escape Your decree concerning me, and so I am ready to die for Your holy name. But I beseech Your goodness, do not let me die until I have put to shame Arian with his gods—*that at the name of Jesus every knee should bow, of those in heaven, and of those on earth, and of those under the earth, and that every tongue should confess*" (Philippians 2:10–11), Paphnutius prayed all this time.

And as soon as he finished his praise, an Angel was sent from Heaven, who took him down from the hook and, gathering all his entrails, placed them back in their proper place. Then he signed him three times with the Life-giving Cross and made him completely whole, as if he had not been subjected to any torment at all. The two soldiers who had been scraping the saint, seeing that the Angel had made him completely whole, believed in Christ and, removing their belts before the judge, cried out loudly with boldness:

"Know, Arian, that from now on we too are Christians."

"Tell me the truth, thrice wretched ones, what miracle did you see that you believed? Or have you come to such madness that you have despised the court and renounced your gods and the worship of the emperors?" the tyrant was astonished.

"What we have seen, governor, we cannot tell you, for thus it is written in the Christian Scripture: *'Do not give what is holy to the dogs; nor cast your pearls before swine'*" (Matthew 7:6), the soldiers cried out with one voice.

"So you have compared me to dogs and swine?"

"You are even worse than they, because every speechless animal is more righteous than you, for each of them glorifies God with its natural voice. But you, who possess reason and were created in the image of God, renounce and dishonor your Creator God. What could be worse than this?" answered the Christians.

Greatly angered, the judge immediately ordered them to be beheaded outside the city. Thus the two soldiers, Dionysius and Callimachus, completed their martyric struggle. At this time the martyr Paphnutius was confined in one of the darkest cells of the prison.

On the following day Arian began dealing with cases involving high-ranking debtors to the state. Since some of them had nothing with which to pay their debts, the governor also ordered them confined in the prison. There were forty such men. On the night when they were imprisoned, a bright light shone in the jail, as if the sun had risen. The forty nobles thought that the guard had set fire to the prison and wanted to release all the prisoners. However, the prison guard had nothing to do with it; he himself was amazed at such a bright light appearing in this dark and wretched place during the last two nights, ever since the Christian Paphnutius had been confined here.

Then the nobles went to that part of the prison where the martyr was being held and heard him praying for the salvation of the city. Opening the door, they entered and saw him with his hands stretched out toward heaven, shining like lit torches, and an ineffable fragrance was poured out all around. At that moment they fell at his feet and thus spent the whole night in his cell. Only when dawn broke did the saint ask them for what reason Arian had imprisoned such high lords in the dungeon. Learning the reason, the ascetic said to them:

"Why do you not listen to me and believe in my God, so that you will no longer be troubled? For if you confess His holy name, you will be freed from all your sinful debts, and the handwriting of your sins will be blotted out; you will become citizens of Heaven and your names will be forever inscribed in the book of life."

"From now on and forever we believe with all our soul and confess that God in Whom you also believe," the nobles answered with enthusiasm.

"So then, my children, arise. Let us go to the governor, for your names are already written in Heaven," said Paphnutius, and together with the forty nobles he went out of the prison.

"Tribunal, tribunal, I have come to contend with you, for you are with Apollo, but I am with our Lord Jesus Christ," he said as he approached the judgment seat.

Then Arian ordered him to be seized, but as soon as the soldiers rushed toward the confessor, he became invisible. The nobles then came forward and cried out with boldness:

"We too are Christians, do with us what you will."

"What has happened to you? Perhaps you are offended that I imprisoned you for debts to the state?" asked the tyrant.

"We pay no heed to your words, but have chosen the Heavenly hope, and leaving behind what is temporal, we hope for what is eternal. And so that you may know our firm intention, we renounce in your favor all our possessions. Now our incomes are in your power, and our wives and children, if they wish, let them follow us. If they do not wish, then let them forgive us."

"I see that this is madness! Like the apostate Paphnutius, you are possessed with insanity!"

"Shut your mouth and be silent, do not blaspheme the man of God," the nobles cried out.

At these words the governor was inflamed with anger and himself became like a madman. First he ordered the former courtiers to be tortured for a long time, and then to be taken out to a deserted place and thrown into a huge blazing fire. Thus all of them, holding one another by the hand, ended their lives in the fire and received martyrs' crowns.

After his disappearance from the tribunal, Saint Paphnutius wandered through the city and, seeing the door of a wealthy house open, entered there and asked the doorkeeper:

"Give me a little water to drink."

"Father, come into the house," replied the servant, and ran to her mistress so that she might come out and see the blessed one who had performed many miracles before the governor Arian.

Learning the news, the mistress immediately came down into the courtyard of the house and bowed before him, who was like an Angel of God.

"Truly, all my wealth is not worthy of your entering my house. Oh, if only I could be glorified today with Divine glory, because you have come to us," she said, led the martyr into her house, and seated him on a silver throne.

"My daughter, why do you need so much gold and silver, like one who boasts of vain hopes? Listen to me, my child, choose for yourself the angelic and immortal way of life, instead of these earthly and corruptible goods," the venerable one said with a smile.

These words surprised the mistress's daughter, who was in the adjoining room, and she, dressed in precious garments with a golden crown on her head, immediately came into the reception room to see who had spoken them. Then Saint Paphnutius rose from the throne and sat on the floor, and the mother and daughter did likewise, sitting at his honored feet.

"Children, leave that vain and corruptible wealth that you have, for it is written: *'Your riches are corrupted, and your garments are moth-eaten. Your gold and silver are corroded, and their corrosion will be a witness against you and will eat your flesh like fire'*" (James 5:2–3). Only the glory of the Lord and His Kingdom shall abide forever," the abba began his teaching. Before the divine Paphnutius had finished these words, the head of the household came, and his wife immediately went out to him to announce Paphnutius's arrival, but before she could say even a word to him, he himself began speaking:

"Why was I not deemed worthy of the honor of being together with the other nobles who were granted eternal life? How good it would be if I found that man called Paphnutius and brought him to my house, so that he might pray for us, that we too might be called by God and be granted His glory."

"Your desire has been fulfilled, my lord, for in your house is the servant of God Paphnutius, adorned with every virtue and wisdom," the wife answered her husband Eustorgius, who immediately entered the house with joy, saw the confessor, fell to the ground, and worshipped him.

"Truly, my beloved son, the Lord has sent me to you today, for you are truly chosen vessels. So then, do not delay, arise, and let us go to the judge to boldly confess the name of our Lord Jesus Christ, so that you may receive the Heavenly crown," the martyr summoned them, and rising, went first, followed by Eustorgius on his right and his wife Hermione on his left, and their daughter Stephano in front.

"My Lord Jesus Christ, Son of the Living God, behold, we have left our door open for the sake of Your Holy name. And do Thou, my Lord, open unto us the gates of Heaven and show us the true light, which Thou hast promised to those who love Thee," Hermione began to pray.

"Tribunal, tribunal, I have come again to contend with you, for you are with Apollo, but I am with my Lord Jesus Christ," Paphnutius again proclaimed as he approached the judge.

Greatly angered by these words, Arian jumped up and, like a wild wolf, ran to seize the saint with his own hands. But the Angel of the Lord caught him up out of the crowd and the soldier of Christ disappeared. And Eustorgius, Hermione, and her daughter Stephano mounted the platform and cried out with boldness:

"We too are Christians, do with us what you will."

"Eustorgius, were you all made drunk with madness from the same source? Or do you not know that I judge robbers and sacrilegious people? Worship the great gods of the emperors and go in peace to your house. But if you do not obey me, you will die an evil death," the judge said with fury.

"Let that not concern you, I am not one of those who falls for your bait or is seduced by the provocations of your father the devil and your mother iniquity," Eustorgius objected.

Then Arian tried to persuade Stephano to offer sacrifice to the pagan gods. But the daughter was unyielding:

"Never will I offer sacrifice to your unclean gods, but I will offer my body as a living sacrifice, well-pleasing to the Heavenly God and the Lord Jesus Christ."

Extraordinarily angered after these words, the judge ordered the maiden to be hung and her body scraped before her parents' eyes, and while the soldiers were mercilessly scraping her, her mother encouraged her daughter with these words:

"My sweetest child, endure the torment a little longer and you will come forth victorious, you will receive from God the crown of victory. You know, my most beloved daughter, that I prepared for you a huge dowry to marry you to the first man in the city, but now, my dear child, you will receive a true and eternal dowry, for your Bridegroom is immortal, and the bridal chamber into which you shall enter gives forth an eternal and unending fragrance. Only endure to the end, and you shall be crowned and glorified."

"Be strong and take courage, daughter, for now I have known that I have been deemed worthy to be called by God into His incorruptible bridal chamber. I rejoice and am glad, because before myself I have sent you as a gift to Christ the Master," her father supported Stephano.

While the honorable parents encouraged their only child, the soldiers scraped away all her body down to the entrails, and the blessed Stephano delivered her holy soul into the hands of God. The parents laid their dead eighteen-year-old daughter before the governor, and he at once ordered them beheaded. Thus all three completed their martyric struggle and ascended in glory to Heaven.

The courageous ascetic of Christ, Paphnutius, prayed to God by night, and by day walked about the city seeking those of whom he knew that they would believe in Christ and receive the martyrs' crown. Thus one day he met sixteen youths going to school. They were the children of those very forty nobles who had accepted a martyr's death.

"My beloved children, I marvel at how you have borne separation from your fathers, who chose the delight of Christ and now reign in Heaven, rejoicing with the Angels. Oh, if only you, my most beloved children, would all together listen to me and believe in God and follow me to the governor to confess Jesus Christ, the True God and King of the ages, for if you go to Christ, the teacher of truth, you will be taught the wisdom of the holy Angels," the saint addressed them. The youths immediately heeded his words, believed in Christ, and all together said:

"Let us go, Father Paphnutius, to the governor, nothing will hinder us in our desire, for from now on we have become strangers to this vain world, for the Holy Spirit has filled our hearts, they have ascended to Heaven, to where our fathers are."

Then the divine Paphnutius, like a good shepherd, went ahead of his flock.

"Tribunal, tribunal, I have come again against you. You are with Apollo, Arian, but I am with the Lord Jesus Christ," the confessor proclaimed as before, when he reached the tribunal.

The governor again ordered the soldiers to draw their swords and surround the saint, but the martyr was immediately caught up out of the crowd and became invisible. At this moment those sixteen youths came to the court.

"We too are Christians!" they exclaimed.

"Where are your parents? For you are still youths, unable to give an account; go and play," the tyrant addressed them in perplexity.

"We are the children of the forty nobles who previously accepted a martyr's death. We are already old enough; ask us whatever you wish, and we will answer you," said the youths.

"Offer sacrifice to the gods, lest you perish from torments," Arian addressed them once more, but the youths did not obey him, but confessed Christ with equal boldness.

"My child, what will you gain from dying an evil death?" the governor persisted, addressing the youngest of the youths. "Listen to what I will advise you, as your father. You will be in great honor with me, I will give you much money, I will write to the emperor, and he will raise you to high dignity. Only offer sacrifice to the great gods: Apollo and Artemis, about whom the emperor has written, because they are living gods."

"Where is the decree of your emperor?" the thirteen-year-old confessor inquired.

The governor ordered the decree to be brought, then kissed it and gave it to the youth, who read the names of seventy glorified gods. After this the tyrant threw a handful of incense onto the sacrificial altar and called upon the soldier of Christ to do the same. But the witness of the true faith threw onto the shrine not incense, but the emperor's decree.

"There is one God, the Father of our Lord Jesus Christ," he cried out to the whole court.

The pagan priests, watching the emperor's decree burn, went out of their minds, began tearing their hair and cutting themselves with knives on their bodies. And Arian, greatly angered at the youth's deed, and at the same time marveling at his boldness, ordered the child to be thrown onto the sacrificial altar. At that moment many idol-worshippers stood frozen in amazement at the martyr's wisdom.

"Brother, remember us also at the throne of God Most High, the Creator of all, and entreat Him for us. As by reason of your wisdom you have become the firstfruits to God and the first of us to be offered to Him as a worthy gift, so may we too, following your example, become citizens of the Heavenly Kingdom together with our fathers," said his classmates and peers.

The youth, being in the fire, gazed at Heaven and thanked God, delivering his holy soul into the hands of God. The judge, having written down the names of all the remaining youths, ordered them to be pierced with spears.

And the blessed Paphnutius continued to walk about seeking others who had gone astray, strangers to the true faith. Thus he came to the riverbank, where about eighty people were gathered.

"Rejoice, children, in the Lord," he exclaimed, addressing them. "And why did you not come to the struggle, for the time for the contest has arrived and a reward awaits you for it. Listen to me now at least, and believe in our Lord Jesus Christ, King of the ages. Confess His holy name before the judge, and the Lord will grant you eternal life."

After these words all who heard the Christian preacher believed in the One God, received the Holy Spirit, and glorified the Creator. And at that same hour, leaving their boats, for they were fishermen, they headed for the city. And again Paphnutius came first to the judge and again exclaimed:

"Tribunal, tribunal, I have come again against you. You are with Apollo, Arian, but I will conquer you with my Lord Jesus Christ."

Then the judge was greatly angered and ordered the soldiers to surround the martyr. This time the Angel of the Lord encouraged the venerable one to withstand the tyrant, but did not take the blessed one away as before. Seizing Paphnutius, the soldiers bound him. At this moment the eighty fishermen mounted the tribunal.

"We too are Christians," they cried out boldly.

"Who mocked you, that you should die an evil death?" Arian asked them.

"We have come here to put to shame both you and your idols."

"Evildoers, why do you, at the moment when I speak to you gently, answer me with such shamelessness?" the tyrant was indignant and ordered the fishermen to be beaten mercilessly.

Then seventy of them came forward and smashed the judge's throne. In response the soldiers drew their swords and inflicted wounds on them, after which the governor ordered the martyrs to be put to death. They were all taken to the wilderness and cut to pieces. After this the tyrant Arian proceeded to judge Saint Paphnutius.

"O apostate, evildoer, and sorcerer. Now I will make it so that all standing here will know that Jesus Christ, in Whom you believe and Whom you invoke, will not deliver you from my hands," the governor threatened and ordered the confessor to be raised up on an iron wheel, which was sharp as a knife blade on top and like a saw on the bottom. Crushed by this satanic wheel, the saint was cut into four parts.

"Where is your God, Paphnutius, why did He not come to deliver you from my hands? Do you now know that there is no other god besides Apollo, Zeus, Artemis, and Athena? They are all living gods who have given power to the Emperor Diocletian," the impious one proclaimed in a loud voice, and then ordered the martyr's body to be taken down from the wheel and placed on the portico of the pagan temple, so that the birds might eat it.

The saint's body lay on the temple portico, but not a single bird touched it, because the Angel of the Lord covered it. After this our Lord Jesus Christ Himself descended from Heaven together with the Archangel Michael on His right hand and the Archangel Gabriel on His left, and stood before Paphnutius's body. The Angels gathered his severed members and joined them into one. And the Savior, stretching forth His right hand, said:

"The hand that fashioned the first-created man now fashions you again."

With these words He breathed into his body the breath of life. And—O wonder!—the saint immediately came back to life and began to glorify God.

"My beloved and faithful servant Paphnutius, go and expose the shameless Arian, who blasphemes My name," said the Lord and ascended into Heaven.

The saint came to the square where Arian was standing and cried out to him:

"Do you recognize me, Arian? I am Paphnutius, the servant of God, whom you cut into pieces, but by the grace of my Lord Jesus Christ I have risen again and am speaking with you. Why do you blaspheme the name of my God and the Creator of all that exists? Behold, the Lord has raised me up to expose your impiety, and so that all may know your powerlessness, for you serve deaf and blind idols made of senseless matter."

Then, seeing that Saint Paphnutius had risen from the dead, the praepositus (the emperor's trusted official) Eusebius believed in Christ and said to the four hundred soldiers under his command:

"Listen to me, brothers, and believe in the God of Heaven and earth, Who has raised His servant Paphnutius and sent him to expose Arian in his error and in his vain hope in idols, so that others too may believe that there is no other God except our Lord Jesus Christ. Just as I have made a beginning by opening to you the way of faith, so too our Lord will open to you the way to Heaven."

And immediately all with one voice confessed Christ as the True God.

"I too am a Christian," the blessed Eusebius exclaimed, presenting himself before Arian.

"We too are Christians, do with us what you will," the soldiers boldly supported their commander.

"I do not have authority to judge you, but go to another governor, higher than I, that he may judge you," the tyrant said, frozen in astonishment.

"You have been given the authority, Arian, to judge me," Eusebius insisted.

"I do not want to hear anything about Christians!" the judge cried out.

"Then acknowledge that there is no other God except the One Who dwells in Heaven, reject the idols, that you may live together with us eternally," the military commander urged him to recognize his error.

"May it never be that I should renounce the gods, for Apollo and Artemis are living gods," Arian raged in his delusion.

Then, taking a handful of sand in each hand, Eusebius threw it in the governor's face.

"Your power and the power of your gods is like sand. So do the works of your father, Satan," the defender of the Christian faith exposed the governor.

Extraordinarily angered, the governor ordered Eusebius to be beaten, promising a long and torturous death, until the emperor should hear that he had blasphemed the court.

"I swear by the power of my Lord Jesus Christ that not even one day will pass before I partake of the mystical table (that is, he will die on the same day) of my Lord, and you will not be able to do what you wish unless you sign my death sentence."

Mounting his chariot, the governor set off to where he intended, but on the way back, when he wanted to descend from it, he could not do so. However, this did not bring him to repentance: the lawless one ordered his dinner to be brought to him right in the chariot. When the cook, filling a tray with various dishes, brought them to the governor, and Arian had already stretched out his hand to the tray, it immediately withered, so that he could not move it. Then his co-ruler began urging the tyrant to leave this city, which "because of the sorcery of Paphnutius is in danger of destruction." Enraged at the misfortunes that had happened to him, Arian ordered the praepositus to be burned alive together with the soldiers in four furnaces. Thus they all fell asleep in the Lord, receiving the crown of martyrdom on that same day.

After this Arian left the city and ordered the martyr Paphnutius to follow him. On the river Nile the governor ordered a millstone to be tied around the confessor's neck and him to be thrown into the river. He himself got into a boat and sailed to another region, but soon before his vessel Saint Paphnutius appeared with the millstone around his neck and said:

"Arian, Arian, you need a boat and wind to sail, but I need neither boat nor wind, because my Helmsman is the Lord Jesus Christ. You send people ahead to prepare your lodging, but I prepare rational souls for my Lord, that they may dwell in His Heavenly mansions."

"Let us not allow this man to follow us, for he will destroy the whole country with his sorcery," said Arian's co-ruler, and the tyrant did not know what to do. Therefore he ordered everything that had happened with the martyr to be written down, and then together with Paphnutius himself gave this manuscript to four soldiers and sent them together with the venerable-martyr to the Emperor Diocletian.

Having read the records, the emperor was astonished and decided to immediately have the divine Paphnutius crucified. The soldiers nailed the saint to a dry date palm outside the city. Being crucified, the blessed one blessed and glorified God, and that dry palm, at God's command, immediately blossomed and bore twelve branches laden with fruit. Then the soldiers who had crucified the confessor believed in Christ. When Paphnutius was crucified, it was the second hour of the day, and he delivered his soul to Christ, receiving from Him the unfading crown of martyrdom, at the ninth hour.

After the soldiers with honors buried him on September 25 / October 8, they themselves went to Diocletian and confessed before him our Lord Jesus Christ, putting to shame the emperor's idols. The enraged tyrant immediately ordered their heads to be cut off.

Thus those who through the blessed Paphnutius ended their lives in martyrdom numbered five hundred and forty-six persons. They inherited the eternal Kingdom of our Lord Jesus Christ, to Whom be glory and dominion unto the ages of ages. Amen.

The Life and Struggles of Our Father Among the Saints Niphon, Bishop of Constantiana in Alexandria, Who Flourished in the Fourth Century

In the days of the great Emperor Constantine there was in Constantinople, at the imperial court, a certain dignitary named Sabbatius. He was an experienced warrior and the military commander of the city of Almiropolis, where he was received with great honors. The governor Agapitus became especially fond of Sabbatius, and began to visit him frequently together with his son Niphon, a boy of eight years.

One day the military commander asked Agapitus whether his son was acquainted with letters, to which the governor replied in the negative, since in all of Almiropolis there were no teachers. Then Sabbatius proposed that Niphon be sent to Constantinople to study the sacred sciences and permitted him to live in his own house. Agapitus was greatly delighted and, having thanked Sabbatius, entrusted the child to him, who sent him to his home in Constantinople.

Upon arriving there, Niphon was received kindly by the military commander's wife and given for instruction in the sacred sciences to an experienced and God-fearing teacher. Niphon studied with great diligence and eagerness, devoting not only the day but also the night to his lessons. Thus in a short time he mastered many sciences, but nevertheless compelled himself to study even more.

Niphon had great reverence for God and attended the Church services. Here he became acquainted with the struggles of the martyrdom of the saints and marveled at their courage and zeal for God. The youth sought out the lives of the venerable ones, saints, and martyrs and read them attentively—thus he came to love silence and stillness, meekness and humility. Even at a young age Niphon was like an elder in his deeds. He was also distinguished by extraordinary mercy and care for the poor. And having heard from a certain spiritual man that in addition to everything else it is necessary to preserve virginity, he said to himself: "Will I be able to attain this virtue, for no small effort is required to escape the burning of the flesh? But henceforth, with God's help, I will no longer gaze upon the faces of women." And from that time he began to be more watchful over himself and did not look at any woman.

After Niphon had come to a good proficiency and grown older, he remembered his parents and homeland and decided to leave Constantinople. The military commander's wife was childless and wanted to keep him in order to adopt him and make him heir of their possessions, since she saw Niphon's progress and virtue. But being unable to persuade him, because Niphon had a strong desire to see his parents, she was greatly saddened. Then the steward of their house asked her to entrust Niphon to his care, so that the pious youth would forget both his parents and his homeland. The steward introduced Niphon to other peers and began taking him to parties. The young and guileless Niphon, as if to find consolation in his sorrow over his parents, gave himself over to drinking bouts, gluttony, and reveling, for youth easily inclines toward evil. As is commonly believed, *"evil company corrupts good habits"* (1 Corinthians 15:33).

His mind darkened by dissipation, the once quiet, taciturn, meek, and humble Niphon became a talkative babbler, a reviler, a mocker; he sang songs and danced. He completely forgot his parents, relatives, and homeland and, abandoning all his studies and virtues, gave himself over wholly and completely to a dissolute way of life. Seeing what a wretched state he had come to, a certain pious and good Christian often said to him: "Woe to you, Niphon! How could you have given yourself over to these disgusting pursuits? Why do you not come to your senses and reform?" At such moments Niphon groaned and wept, reflecting on the shameful deeds to which he had given himself, but still, overcome by the bad habit, he could not abandon them.

Once he went to his friend Nicodemus, who, unexpectedly looking at his face, froze.

"Why do you look at me so? Do you not recognize me?" Niphon asked his friend.

"Believe me, brother, I do not know what to say to you: your face is disfigured and black, like a Moor's," his companion answered.

Hearing this, the youth understood: it had become so from his shameful deeds. Niphon was seized with intense shame, he covered his face with his hands and ran away.

"Woe to me, thrice wretched, that I have come to such a miserable state! What shall I do, miserable one? Will I be able to reform and repent, and if I repent, will I receive salvation? Oh, who will instruct me? Who will let me know that if I repent and reform, I will find mercy? How shall I entreat God to have mercy on me, when I have committed so much evil?" Until late at night the youth reflected on this and much else. From intense sorrow he could not eat anything and went to bed hungry. "I will get up from my bed and make at least one prayer to God," he thought resolutely. But the hater of good, the devil, knowing of this, began to stir up great fear in his soul and bring to his mind such a thought: "If you get up at night to pray, you will go mad, and everyone will laugh at you." With this thought Satan greatly disturbed and frightened the youth. But he, having overcome it, said to himself:

"When I spent nights fulfilling my evil will, I suffered no harm; shall I now, when I want to pray, suffer it? Anathema to you, evil and unclean spirit, for giving me such a thought."

And at that same hour Niphon arose with zeal from his bed to pray. But as soon as he turned to the east, a black cloud appeared before him and stood there, causing such fear that he, as if paralyzed, climbed onto his bed and lay as if dead, trembling for his sins and reflecting on the obstacle that the devil had raised against his prayer.

A little time passed since that night, and, reproaching himself, the youth went to church. Standing in the temple, he raised his gaze upward and saw above his head an icon with an image of the Mother of God.

"O Most Holy Theotokos Virgin Mary, my light, my protection, and my foundation. Have mercy on me, a sinner, and help me according to Thy great mercy," he prayed from the depths of his soul.

And at that moment the Theotokos miraculously turned to him from the icon and looked upon him with a most joyful and gentle gaze. Niphon received no small consolation of soul, and the fire of love for the Mother of God was kindled in his heart.

"See, wretched soul, how God loves us and how He accepts us, desiring our salvation, while we forsake Him. Consider, miserable one, how the Theotokos, the swift Helper of Christians, immediately helped me," the youth said and left the temple, glorifying God.

The next day on the way to church Niphon met a person who had committed a sin, and not only condemned the unfortunate one in his thoughts, but came to hate him. When Niphon entered the temple and raised his gaze to the icon of the Mother of God, he saw that the Most Pure Virgin looked upon him angrily and turned away. This greatly troubled the youth. Examining himself, he understood that the Lady Theotokos had turned away from him because of his thoughts by which he had condemned another. Immediately falling to the ground and confessing his sin, he wept bitterly and began to pray to the Most Pure Virgin for forgiveness. After some time, looking at the face of the Theotokos, Niphon again saw that She was looking upon him joyfully. Thus consoled, he left the temple. And from that time, whenever he sinned in anything, he was rebuked by the Mother of God, Who would turn Her face away from him.

Once in a dream Niphon saw himself in a large house and, standing in one part of it, suddenly beheld a multitude of black Moors rushing furiously upon him and threatening him with death. Then he fled to another part of the house, where he found a church. Running into it, he was delivered from those attacking him. After this he opened the door a little and decided to cross to another part of the house, but the Moors, who were hiding in the corners, again rushed upon him. Then Niphon again saved himself by flight into the church. He saw this dream for a whole week, and it meant the following: it is impossible to be delivered from evil demons without frequently visiting the church and constantly praying to God. That is why from that time Niphon began to frequently attend the temple and pray to the Lord for deliverance from demonic snares.

However, the wicked and unclean spirit of foul speech and reviling did not cease rising up against the blessed Niphon and did everything to make him revile people as before. But the youth prayed fervently and asked God to cast out this demon. One night Niphon saw in a dream the Protomartyr Stephen.

"I greet you, Niphon, servant of God. Your way of life is good, but you defile it with foul speech and reviling. Believe me, if you strive to cast out the demon that compels you to revile, I will help you," the holy archdeacon addressed him.

When the youth awoke, having thanked Saint Stephen, he took a small pebble, placed it in his mouth, and walked around thus for several days in silence, reviling no one. But if it happened that he was still beguiled by the devil, he immediately went to a secret place and struck himself hard with his fist, saying:

"I will make you become humble; you will learn meekness and silence from me, so as not to become angry and revile."

Thus the blessed one made it a rule for himself to strike himself with his fist forty times each day, and if on some day he happened to revile or was tempted by some passion, he struck himself a hundred or two hundred times. Mercilessly beating himself, the ascetic became very thin and very often fainted from the pain and lay on the ground as if dead.

"Woe to you, wretched Niphon! If you cannot endure even this small pain, how will you be able to bear the unbearable torments of hell? But take heart, for *even though our outward man is perishing, yet the inward man is being renewed day by day*" (2 Corinthians 4:16), the saint admonished himself at such moments.

"Wretched Niphon, why do you not have pity on your body, but beat it so mercilessly?" the devil tempted him.

"Most foul demon, have you come here to give me commands as well? If you had flesh and fell into my hands, I would show you how Niphon can punish," the ascetic put the unclean one to shame.

Once the wicked one raised up against him the warfare of gluttony.

"Go, unclean spirit, to the dung pit where people relieve themselves, and eat there yourself what you urge upon me," Niphon repelled such attacks.

But the devil, in his malice, did not retreat, and after some time rose up again, even more fiercely, acting through the same passion. But the blessed Niphon hoped in God's help:

"I will eat and drink today to show you, Satan, that even in this way you will not be able to hinder my prayer, for I have God as my helper," he said to himself. "Consider, Niphon, that as a dog, after it has eaten and drunk, barks, so you now, when you have tasted of God's gifts, must thank God who has satisfied you from His blessings," the ascetic thought after his meal.

And then he went to the temple and prayed:

"Glory to Thee, O Christ our God, for Thou hast satisfied us with Thy earthly blessings; deprive us not of Thy Heavenly Kingdom, according to Thy great mercy."

Thereby he trampled upon the devil, as if saying to him:

"See, wicked and unclean spirit, that I have eaten and drunk, yet I have not been driven out of the church, nor have I met an obstacle in prayer. Be ashamed then, and go into the outer darkness."

Then the demonic powers brought deep sleep upon Niphon. But the saint did not submit, took a stick in his hands, and struck his body with it.

"Wicked servant, I gave you food and drink, and you seek sleep besides?" he said, and struck himself even harder so that from the pain sleep would flee and he, remaining awake, might continue in prayer.

A little time passed, and the wicked demon, unable to bear being conquered, using various methods, raised up against Niphon an even more terrible warfare: he wanted to cast the saint into fornication. However, the blessed ascetic understood where it might arise from and said to himself: "Humble Niphon, again there is a need to make a beginning."

From that day he ate only stale bread—sometimes all week, sometimes once in two days, and sometimes he abstained from food for an entire week. Then he would again eat bread, but did not drink water. Often, when he was thirsty, he placed before himself a vessel of water and looked at it, so as to torment himself even more. Many times the devil tried to tempt Niphon, but during the day he did not succeed. Then the unclean one attacked him at night, in sleep, showing shameful visions and causing the ascetic an emission of seed. The divine Niphon immediately arose and, taking a stick, struck his shameful parts so hard that they turned black. For fourteen consecutive years this warfare with the demon of fornication continued. All these years the ascetic suffered greatly, very often beating himself with stones, because he was indignant and greatly grieved at the repeated appearance of shameful thoughts and desires imposed on him by the unclean one. All this time the Lord was testing his strength of spirit and finally delivered Niphon from this warfare. One day the saint saw a dream: he was standing on a plain, covered up to his chest with filth. Then there appeared a man clad in white garments who commanded him to follow him. When they reached a pit full of stench, he ordered Niphon to shake off this filth. Having done so, he felt relief and glorified God. From that time, if the demon of fornication attacked him, he no longer harmed him at all.

Once, praying at night, Saint Niphon saw a bright light, which filled him with great joy and ineffable gladness. And at that moment the venerable one heard a voice:

"I will give you power over malicious demons. Only do you, Niphon, take good heed to yourself, not to be exalted, but to remain in great humility, for I greatly love the humble, but I hate and turn away from the proud. Therefore, if you wish Me to love you, cultivate humility, do not slander anyone, do not laugh at anyone, do not have hatred toward anyone, even if you see your neighbor sinning, for terrible torments are already prepared for such people."

After this event the venerable one especially strove to observe all that had been said.

Once, at the hour of prayer, the saint saw that he was walking together with others along a road. Suddenly there appeared before them many terrible and dark demons who would not let them pass. All were frightened and stopped, and at that moment there appeared someone in radiant garments.

"Why have you stopped and are not going your way?" he asked Niphon.

"Because I fear those dark demons."

"Have you ever prayed to God that He might give you humility?"

"I always ask God for humility."

"Behold, God has sent you humility," said the ascetic's interlocutor.

And then it seemed to Niphon that the heavenly guest cut open his chest and, taking out his heart, inserted a new and wondrous one. With it the saint fearlessly continued the journey he had begun. The dark demons were greatly confounded by this and gnashed their teeth, being unable to hinder him, and Niphon's other companions turned to the one who had appeared with a request to do the same to them as to the venerable one, so that they too might be able to continue forward without fear.

"Ask God yourselves through prayer and fasting for what Niphon asked, and the Almighty will give it to you, for if you do not ask, you will not receive, and if you do not receive, you will not be able to pass this way," the radiant Angel instructed them.

Niphon always said: "Woe to me, a sinner." And if anyone bowed to him, the ascetic in his thoughts descended into hell or to the feet of that brother who had made a bow before him, and humbled himself, comparing himself to the very last sinner who had never done anything good. The saint greatly abhorred human glory. Every time he wanted to give alms to some poor person, he first bowed his own head before him, because he saw in him Christ asking for alms. It seemed that Niphon rejoiced more than that poor person, for in his image he was deemed worthy to give alms to the Lord Himself. In those days when the wicked and unclean demon of blasphemy rose up against him, the ascetic ate stale bread every evening and spent the whole night in prayers with prostrations. Thus he spent four years and, with God's help, achieved victory: this sin no longer troubled him.

Niphon had zeal and diligence in prayer. Often, walking along the road, he would turn off it and go to a secluded place, where, bending his knees, he would fall to the ground and pray for a very long time, so that because of the numbness of his limbs he rose with great difficulty.

"Lord my God, through the prayers of Thy Most Pure Mother forgive me my sins, drive away from me all wickedness, envy, slander, anger, negligence, pride, avarice, mercilessness, insensibility, contentiousness, enmity, gluttony, drunkenness, burning passion, impurity, and the most bitter glory from men. Yea, my God, drive all these away from me," thus the saint prayed to the Lord.

Every night he prepared himself as if for burial: before sleep he read the Trisagion and some troparia from the Order for Burial, two chapters from the Gospel and another two from the Epistles of the holy Apostles. Then, crossing himself and his bed three times and anointing his forehead and chest with holy oil from the lampada before the icon of the Most Holy Theotokos, he gave himself to a short sleep. Every Sunday he spent the whole night without sleep. Already in the evening on Saturday he would stand for prayer and remain in it until dawn, not once sitting down during that time. Besides this, in spring, summer, and autumn he also prayed from dawn to the third hour with his hands raised toward heaven. The ascetic greatly loved silence and, as much as possible, avoided communication with people. In silence he spent most of his time and felt great sweetness from it, which cannot be said of us: leaving silence, we hasten to converse and communicate, and are deprived of this joy, by our foolishness finding ourselves in the gullet of Satan, that is, in the disturbance and confusion of this world. Niphon also took care to guard his mind from evil thoughts and never tired of repeating:

"Take good heed to yourself, Niphon, lest the destroyer steal your senses and you be deceived again, as before."

The saint said this because at the beginning of his repentance, when he was bewailing his sins, the spirit of vainglory would come to him, bring with it a false joy of heart, and drive away all sorrow. At this time a thought would settle in him that he was a blessed great ascetic and that there was no other like him in the world. In these moments the demon spread a fragrance, as if the Angels of God were caring for Niphon's struggles and censing him with incense. Thus the saint was deceived and fell into vainglory. But God did not abandon His child, and gave him the gift of discernment. Now, when such thoughts came to Niphon, he immediately recognized them and lamented, for the person who accepts them is far from God and follows after Lucifer, who fell from Heaven because of his high-mindedness. Only in this way was he able to drive them away. In time he learned not to accept them at all and to reject them with shame. Once a brother came to the divine Niphon and said that blasphemous thoughts greatly troubled him, and especially at the hour of prayer many heresies, malice, and revilings against Christ, the Mother of God, and the holy icons came to his mind. From this the monk fell into despair; he greatly feared that fire would descend from heaven and consume him.

"Thoughts of blasphemy come from the evil one, who brings them to a person's mind in order to disturb him and cast him into despair. Therefore one should not fear them or pay attention to them: they do not proceed from the one praying, and therefore they cannot harm him in any way. They will depart if they are despised and if one approaches everything with understanding, for such thoughts are from the devil; they cannot cause any harm to a soul that does not desire them. Just as the waves of the sea beat against rocks lying on the shore and, doing them no harm, return back, so blasphemous thoughts, striking against the mind of a person firm in faith, do not harm him at all, but turn back upon the head of the demon that brought them. Then, unable to do anything, conquered and put to shame, he flees. And the monk who was subjected to temptation is not condemned, but rather is crowned as a victor. Take heed to yourself, brother, do not slander anyone, because blasphemous thoughts often arise from slander," the ascetic strengthened the brother and dismissed him in peace.

"In a certain city there lived a pious and God-fearing man who rendered many benefactions to his neighbors and loved all as Angels of God," the ascetic recounted to a certain layman. "But those whom he had benefited, through the devil's cooperation, came to hate him: some considered the righteous man impious, others considered him crafty, and still others considered him a heretic, and therefore they slandered him without restraint. The layman listened to this and, rejoicing immeasurably, thanked God and prayed to the Almighty: 'Lord, have mercy on those who hate me, slander me, and revile me, and do not punish them for my sake, neither in this age nor in the age to come, but crush the malicious demons who have raised them up against me. And as Thou dost not turn away from me when I sin, so do not forsake those who hate and slander Thy wretched servant, but save them according to Thine infinite mercy. May Thy most holy name be glorified unto the ages. Amen.' Thus the pious lord was able to escape the passion of remembrance of wrongs, and those who condemned him, seeing his love, came to their senses and reformed."

The saint did not encourage those who give money to musicians and actors, singers and dancers, for this sacrifice they offer not to God, but to the devil:

"Just as Angels of the Lord stand beside those who pray and carry their prayer to God, so too with those who sing and dance, dark demons stand beside them and bring their antics as a sacrifice to their chief, Satan. But those who wish to find mercy with God must pray often and not allow the mind to be distracted by extraneous objects, but gather it and direct it to prayer. That is why it is necessary to attend services in the church, to listen to the word of God with the greatest attention and reverence, not to talk with one another in the temple, not to laugh, not to read and sing with vainglory, making an undisciplined clamor, because by this they, instead of propitiating God, only anger Him," Niphon instructed.

People began to come to the venerable one more and more often for spiritually profitable counsel. To all of them he first bowed and then said:

"Forgive me, brothers, because I, being blind, compelled by your love, wish to be a guide for others."

And only after this, with great humility, did Saint Niphon instruct them with his divinely inspired words.

"Why did the ancients live their lives in peace, while we now live with great disturbance and many sorrows?" a certain brother once asked him.

"Because they had strong love for the Lord and their neighbor, they held to righteousness and truth, and when they wanted to offer a sacrifice to God or give alms to the poor, they offered only what was best, pure, undefiled by any deceit and unrighteousness. That is why they lived in peace—the Creator heard all their petitions. But we do the opposite: we love ourselves more than the Creator and our neighbor, we hold neither to righteousness nor preserve truth, but spend our lives in evil and deceit. We keep everything best for ourselves, having deified our belly. We serve it, but to the Almighty and to our neighbor we offer what is useless and worthless. Because of this the All-Merciful does not hear our petitions, and we are subjected to many sorrows and temptations," the ascetic answered him. "When I came to my senses regarding my sins and began the work of repentance, not even three years had passed when one evening a thought came to me that, behold, I had been asking God for so long, but He had not given me any gift. I had defiled Holy Baptism with my sins, and God does not hear me. With these sorrowful thoughts I fell asleep and saw a dream. I found myself in a beautiful temple, where our Lord Jesus Christ sat upon a Throne of glory. Raising my hands to Him, I began to pray with the words of the Psalter: *'Hear my prayer, O God, and do not hide Yourself from my supplication'*" (Psalm 55:1).

"And the Almighty, inclining His head, listened to my prayer that the wicked spirit of timidity might depart from me.

"'I have heard your prayer, it shall be for you as you have asked,' the Lord said to me in response, and a little later addressed me again:

"'Niphon, Niphon, this evening you grieved Me with your thought that you have been asking Me for so long, but I have given you no gift. But do you not also ask Me every day not to give you earthly glory? What gift then do you speak of? The gift of tongues, or the gift of prophecy, or the gift of healing, or something else? But you yourself do not want them and do not ask for them, lest people glorify you for this. Tell me, is not what you have a gift? The air that you breathe, the sky, the earth, the sea, and all that is in them and on them—did I not give you these as a gift? And what have you, people, given Me for this? Nothing. But even worse: instead of repayment you spat upon Me, struck Me on the face, beat Me, nailed Me to the Cross, gave Me vinegar and gall to drink... And My Body and My Blood, which I gave you, is this not a gift? And the riches of all the earth, what are they? The birds of the sky, the fish of the sea, and all the rest, is this not a gift? Is it not a gift that for love of you I died and was buried and delivered you from hell and brought you into My Kingdom? Who else among you has done as much good for you? How then do you say that I have given you no gift? But now look, and you will see that the spirit of cowardice is bound.'

"At that moment Niphon saw before him a bull so firmly tied to a pillar that it could not move, only furiously rolling its eyes, seeking to break its bonds. From that time, with God's help, the ascetic was freed from the passion of fearfulness, which had to a significant degree possessed him from earliest youth. For example, when he wanted to go to church at night, or when he saw a frightening dream.

A certain young man who led a righteous life came to the saint and asked him to speak a word about the salvation of the soul.

"If you, child, very strongly desire to save your soul while dwelling among people, then fulfill the following: do not be at enmity with anyone, never have hatred toward anyone, do not condemn, do not slander, never think that you are observing a holy life, do not be exalted, do not speak or think about who is virtuous and who is sinful, but treat everyone equally, with a pure heart, as members of Christ. Besides this, do not listen to those who slander, do not be quick of tongue, and do not be hasty in prayer. Do not take revenge, do not be at enmity with one who has done you evil or condemned you, but have compassion on him and love him as your benefactor. Always think about your own sins, reproach yourself and be at enmity with yourself. Be humble, pure in soul and body from every defilement, be meek, calm, peaceful, affable with all, kind, compassionate, merciful, adorned with every righteousness and truth. Truly you will be with God when you come to consider yourself worse than all people. Never think that you have reached the highest measure, but always say to your soul that it has surpassed the demons in sins, and has done nothing good even in the smallest measure, therefore great suffering awaits it. The prayer of a Christian must be like the humble and contrite sighing of the Publican. Mind and lips must be directed to things above: *'Who can understand his errors? Cleanse me from secret faults'* (Psalm 19:12)—thus it is necessary to constantly say to oneself. The sole care and concern must be the salvation of the soul, and God will care for the needs of the body, as He Himself promised in the Holy Gospel. For if you strive with all your strength to enter the Kingdom of Heaven, you must free yourself from everything earthly: whoever sails with a heavy load will quickly sink. All bodily passions are mortified by little eating and keeping vigil, since they are all demons, and to drive them out, as the Lord said, is possible only by fasting and prayer. If we want the Lord to have pity and mercy on us on the Day of Judgment, we must love, have mercy, and have pity on our brothers, using for this what God has given us," the blessed one never tired of repeating.

One night after his usual prayer the saint lay down to rest and saw in a dream a green plain where many sheep were grazing, but they had no shepherd. At the moment when the venerable one was reflecting that a wolf might attack them, there appeared before him a man of majestic appearance, clothed in apostolic garments.

"Niphon, why do you think that the sheep of the King have no shepherd? You are their shepherd, because the King has appointed you to pasture them," he addressed the ascetic.

"How can I, inexperienced and weak, pasture them?" asked Niphon in perplexity.

"The Creator has ordained this for you, and do not resist," said the messenger of God and immediately gave him a shepherd's staff into his hands, and then, showing him the sheep and the fold, departed.

Awakening, the saint began to reflect and understood that the sheep of the King are the people of God, and the fold is the Church. Greatly fearing that here in Constantinople he might be ordained as a bishop, he boarded a ship and sailed for Alexandria, where the blessed Alexander was then Patriarch. In those days a multitude of clergy and laymen from the city of Constantiana came to the Patriarch in Alexandria and told him of the death of their bishop. The people of God asked the Patriarch to set over them a new bishop. Then the primate of the Alexandrian Church began to entreat God to reveal to him whether there was anyone worthy for such a great obedience, and that same night he saw in a dream the Apostle Paul.

"Go tomorrow to the church, and the one who will be like me in countenance, but without a bald spot, ordain as bishop, even against his will," the chief of the Apostles said to Alexander.

The next day in the church the Patriarch saw the divine Niphon and said to his archdeacon (this was Athanasius the Great):

"Does not that man resemble the Apostle Paul?"

"Yes, he resembles the Apostle, and is worthy to pasture the sheep of Christ, for I see Angels who accompany him and place on his head a crown of precious stones," replied Athanasius the Great.

Then the Patriarch summoned Niphon to himself.

"You, father, God has appointed as shepherd, to pasture these rational sheep of His standing around us."

"Holy father, I am unworthy," Niphon tried to object.

"Oh, if only I were as worthy as you!... Do not contradict the decision of God," Alexander admonished the future archpastor.

The divine Niphon reluctantly bowed his head and was appointed Bishop of Constantiana. On the first day he was ordained to the diaconate, on the next day to the priesthood, and on the third day to the episcopate. During his consecration, as Athanasius the Great later recounted, the Holy Spirit descended upon him in the form of fire. In joy all the people of Constantiana kissed Niphon's right hand. Together with him the Patriarch sent to this diocese his archdeacon Athanasius and other clergy, so that they might perform the enthronement of the new bishop according to the prescribed rite. All the Christians rejoiced with great joy and glorified God, Who had deemed them worthy of having such a chosen vessel of the Holy Spirit as Bishop Niphon for the protector of their city.

Having taken upon himself the great burden of the episcopate, the divine Niphon gave himself over to even greater struggles. As a true shepherd he pastured the sheep of Christ on the salvific pastures of God's commandments, always watering them with the waters of Gospel teaching, having become for the Christians of Constantiana an example and model of all that is good. The venerable one taught with boldness not only all the people, but also found time to instruct each one: sinners he corrected, the virtuous he strengthened, the sorrowful he consoled, those threatened by danger he delivered, those acting unjustly he admonished, the offended he defended, orphans he cared for, to the poor he gave generous alms, the sick he healed. Niphon guided all both spiritually and bodily, loved all as his spiritual children, and for their salvation, according to the commandment of our Lord, laid down his life: *"the good shepherd gives His life for the sheep"* (John 10:11).

But Niphon too was a mortal man. When it came time for the hierarch to rest from his sacred struggles, in order to go to the God he longed for and to enjoy the reward for his labors, the Lord revealed to him the day of his death. Niphon had a custom of teaching the people the word of God every day. One day, when the venerable one had dismissed the flock and lay down, he saw a dream. Before him appeared a majestic royal palace, inside of which was a fiery Throne wrought with great artistry. This Royal Seat hovered in the air, and upon it sat a certain Beautiful Ruler, surrounded by radiance and ineffable glory. Around Him stood thousands upon thousands, shining like lightning.

"Michael, show Our friend the place of his repose," a voice was heard from the Throne.

And then the Archangel Michael led Niphon to a bright place, where there was a countless multitude of palaces worthy of wonder; in one of them, majestic and lofty, there was a multitude of men clothed in radiant garments.

"Master, how long until Thou givest us our beloved one?" they asked the Chief of the Heavenly Hosts.

"By the good pleasure of the Father and the Son and the Holy Spirit he will be sent to you in three days," the Archangel Michael gladdened them.

"By the boundless mercy and love of God for mankind this palace has been granted to you for your rest in it unto the ages of ages," the Archangel then addressed Niphon.

Awakening, the saint told his disciple about this dream, and from him all the clergy learned. The news that in three days Saint Niphon would depart to the Lord spread among the people, and there was great weeping and sorrow among all. However, calling them to himself, the ascetic began to console the Christians with these words:

"My beloved children, when I am nearer to God, I will always entreat Him for your salvation."

Athanasius the Great, already Patriarch of Alexandria, also learned of the approaching death of the hierarch of Constantiana. He immediately came to the saint.

"Why have you, holy Master, taken the trouble to come to me, the unworthy one?" Saint Niphon asked the Patriarch.

"I have come, father, to enjoy communion with you, and since you are departing to the Heavenly Jerusalem, then at the hour when you stand before God in worship, ask Him for my salvation," answered the primate of the Alexandrian Church.

"And you, Master, I ask, do not forget me when you celebrate the Divine Liturgy; offer a particle for me, because the offering to the Lord for the departed grants them great benefit. He who after my death does this for the remission of my sins will receive at the hour of his own death great help from the Almighty, Who will cover a multitude of the sins both of the one praying and of mine. And I too will intercede before the Creator for him," with these words he fell silent and all night performed hymns of praise, thanking the All-Merciful and praying not only for himself, but for the whole world.

In the morning hour an Angel of the Lord came to the ascetic.

"Rejoice, Niphon, and be glad, for the Lord is coming to you," he said to the venerable one.

Hearing this, the saint was exceedingly gladdened. But after some time he had a severe attack, and ordering a rush mat to be placed on the floor, he quietly lay down upon it. When it grew light, Athanasius came to him together with all the clergy and a multitude of people.

"Father, can illness bring benefit to a person?" the Patriarch asked.

"Just as gold, placed in a fiery furnace, is purified and all impurity is removed from it, so too a person, when he falls ill, if he thanks God, is purified and casts off from himself the impurity of sin," the hierarch answered and began to weep, and all those standing around him also wept. Then his face shone so brightly that all trembled.

"I thank you, my God-bearing Apostles, that you did not delay in coming to a sinful elder," the venerable one said.

"Rejoice in the Lord, O martyrs! I thank you, my honored prophets, that you have come to me, the unworthy one! Rejoice in the Lord, my holy hierarchs, and all venerable and righteous ones!" the bishop continued.

At this moment Athanasius the Great saw the saints, who one by one approached and greeted the elder.

"Rejoice, O Full of Grace, Theotokos Mary, my light, my protection, and my foundation. I thank Thee greatly for Thy benefactions toward me!" the hierarch exclaimed and was filled with great joy.

After some time an ineffable fragrance spread through the cell, and the face of the venerable one began to shine so brightly that from fear the people ran out into the courtyard.

"Come to Me, blessed soul, bearing My humility. I am Christ Thine, Whom thou hast made thine own, always repeating: 'My Christ, my Christ.' Behold I, Thy Christ, come unto Me," a gentle voice was heard.

"Into Thy hands, O Master, I commit my spirit, for Thou art my Christ, the Son of the Living God," the saint said immediately, stretching forth his hands, and delivered up his spirit.

Then all began to grieve that they had been deprived of him, but Athanasius the Great consoled them, repeating that it was necessary not to weep, but to glorify and thank God, Who had deemed the Christians of Constantiana worthy to have such a chosen vessel of the Holy Spirit as Bishop Niphon for the protector of their city. The people, out of great reverence and love for the saint, wished to take the garments that the ascetic had worn. The Patriarch performed all that was required for the burial, and the precious relics of Niphon were honorably and reverently laid in the Church of the Holy Apostles.

And to this day the sick who come to the tomb of the venerable one and with faith and prayer turn to him, quickly receive healings even from incurable diseases, to the glory of the Father and the Son and the Holy Spirit, One Godhead and Kingdom, to Whom is due all glory, honor, and worship unto the ages of ages. Amen.

The Life and Struggles of Our Venerable Mother and Teacher Syncletica, Who Labored in Asceticism in the Fourth Century

This blessed Syncletica (some say that this venerable one was the very same virgin who hid Athanasius the Great in a well for six years. — Auth.) came from the Macedonian region. Her ancestors, having heard of the God-loving and Christ-loving customs of the inhabitants of Alexandria, left Macedonia and arrived in Alexandria, where the faith was preserved in simplicity and with true love, preferring a foreign land to their own homeland. The venerable one belonged to a distinguished family and possessed every conceivable blessing of this life. From her earliest years the blessed one gave herself over entirely to love for God, took absolutely no thought for the body, and despite the fact that she was distinguished by an extraordinarily beautiful appearance, was exceedingly chaste. Many young men wanted to marry her: some for her wealth, others for the respectability of her parents, and still others for her beauty. Even her own parents urged their daughter toward marriage, so as to preserve through her the succession of their lineage. However, the chaste and firm-willed Syncletica did not yield to their persuasions, but when she heard of carnal marriage, she pondered upon the Divine, paying no attention to earthly suitors, gazing with hope only upon the Heavenly Bridegroom Christ, Whom she loved with all her soul.

For this reason neither the many garments embroidered with gold, nor the multicolored precious gems, nor music, nor feasts, nor other worldly blessings could change her intention. Neither the tears of her parents nor the entreaties of her relatives softened the venerable one in the slightest or shook her inner disposition. She was firm as adamant and was in no way distracted from the Desired One, Christ. The venerable one closed her bodily senses and conversed with the Noetic Bridegroom, repeating the words of the bride from the Book of the Song of Solomon: *"My beloved is mine, and I am his"* (Song of Solomon 2:16). If worldly conversations were held in the presence of the blessed one, she tried to avoid them. Syncletica gathered her mind in the depths of her heart, opening it during soul-profiting conversations. The venerable one was also diligent in fasting — that medicine beneficial to the body. She loved it, and she had no other virtue equal to this one. The virgin held that this virtue was the foundation for the observance of all others. When she happened to taste food at an improper time, she was changed: her face acquired a yellow hue, she visibly grew thin, and moreover, her body withered. It is known that those who take food with pleasure are tender and full of body, while those who eat with reluctance are lean and thin. The truth of these words is attested to by the sick, who, because they eat with reluctance, remain thin and weak of body.

Blessed Syncletica strove to refine her body, yet her soul only grew stronger from this: *"but even though our outward man is perishing, yet the inward man is being renewed day by day"* (2 Corinthians 4:16), says the Apostle Paul. At the same time, no one knew that the venerable one was performing such labors.

When the blessed one's parents died, she took with her her blind sister and went to a certain relative, to a place called Iroos, which was at a great distance from Alexandria. Having distributed all her possessions to the poor, the holy virgin summoned a presbyter and cut off her hair. By this she testified that her soul had been freed from worldly cares: Syncletica had become a nun.

"I have been vouchsafed to receive a great name, and I can worthily repay the One Who gave it to me. If people spend all their wealth in order to obtain the temporary glory of this world, how much more must I give to my Master Christ (together with my possessions and my body) for such great grace, that I have been vouchsafed to become a nun. But what am I saying — give my possessions and my body for Christ — when all this already belongs to Him?.. *'The earth is the Lord's, and all its fullness'*" (1 Corinthians 10:28). With these words the venerable one clothed herself in humility and gave herself over to hesychia.

Since the blessed one had prepared herself for ascetic labors while still in her father's house, upon becoming a nun she continued to advance further in the virtues. For those who enter into this divine mystery of the monastic life without prior preparation cannot advance and do not attain the goal of the monastic life, for they have not studied in detail what is required for this and what its goal is. And just as those who set out on a journey first take care to bring with them everything necessary, so the venerable one from her very youth first prepared herself through ascetic labors, and then fearlessly set out on the path leading to Heaven. Having armed herself with everything necessary to complete the building of the house of her soul, she erected a strong tower. For the creation of a perceptible dwelling, stones, mortar, wood, and other material things are required. But the venerable one did not gather but rather spent them, distributing her possessions to the poor. By this she drove away anger and remembrance of wrongs, cast off envy and vainglory, and founded her dwelling upon the rock. And therefore her tower became famous and impregnable. But why speak at length? Already at the beginning of her labors, thanks to her strong zeal and fervor of spirit, blessed Syncletica surpassed all other nuns who had already spent many years in ascetic labors. Nothing is known of her spiritual path, because she did not allow anyone to observe her: she did not want people to gossip about her ascetic feats. For the venerable one cared not so much about performing good deeds as about hiding them from people. The holy virgin did this not out of self-interest, but moved by Divine grace, so as not to seek human glory. Syncletica always guided herself by the Gospel words: *"Do not let your left hand know what your right hand is doing"* (Matthew 6:3). From early age until adolescence she avoided conversations not only with men, but also with women, and therefore she was not praised for the excessiveness of her struggle, and fellowship with the brethren and bodily needs did not hinder the venerable one from perfecting herself in virtue. All this helped Syncletica to observe the intentions of her soul at the very beginning of their appearance and not allow herself to be cast down into fleshly desires. Just as a gardener plucks fruits and prunes the branches of trees, so the venerable one by fasting and prayer cut off the thorns of the passions. And if some passion sprouted and arose in her, she cut it off by means of bodily mortifications, by various labors, and often tormented herself not only with hunger but also with thirst.

In moments of warfare with the devil, the blessed one, at the beginning of doxology, called upon the Master Christ for help, for she was not content with physical ascetic struggle alone, warding off the lion-like assault of the devil. Immediately, with her prayer, the Lord came, and the enemy fled. But sometimes the enemy rose up against her for a long time, while the Almighty left the ascetic alone, in order to temper her virtuous soul even more. The venerable one became convinced that prolonged warfare becomes the cause of greater gifts, and she was strengthened all the more against the enemy. She mortified herself not only through abstinence from a large quantity of food, but renounced everything that gives pleasure: she ate only bread made of bran, very often did not use water at all, slept on the bare ground, and that only very little. Syncletica employed such weapons as long as the warfare continued. She constantly protected herself with prayer as with a shield, and with faith joined with hope and love, as with a helmet. Faith firmly embraced her whole soul, and moreover, the venerable one was exceedingly merciful, not always in action but always in intention. When the enemy was defeated and the warfare subsided, the venerable one gave herself rest from excessive ascetic struggle. She did this so that the members of her body would not be torn from the muscles, which would be a sign of defeat. For when a warrior's weapon is damaged, what else can he hope for, how then can he win the battle? Some damaged themselves by inconceivable fasting beyond their strength, and thus, as it were, withdrew from the battle with the enemy, destroying themselves. But blessed Syncletica did everything with discernment: when warfare began, she warred against the enemy with prayer and exercises, and when it ceased, she again began to care for the body. So do sailors. When a storm overtakes them, they eat nothing, and apply all their skill to struggling with danger, but when the danger passes, they begin to care for the maintenance of bodily strength, usually taking advantage of the calm to rest from their previous labors. However, even in calm weather they do not pass the time without cares, they do not give themselves over to deep sleep. Having just endured the trial of a storm, they again think of the coming storm, and although the tempest has ceased, the sea has not diminished; although the wind has subsided, the air that gives birth to it remains.

It is exactly the same in spiritual things. Although the ascetics drive out the evil spirit of lust, the devil who has power over this passion is nearby. Since we are not certain what the sea will be like, we must pray always — on account of diabolical malice. The venerable one, well acquainted with the storms of this present life, foresaw disturbances from the demons, and therefore with all diligence steered the ship of her soul with the rudder of piety and without disturbance guided it into the harbor of salvation, having cast the surest anchor of faith.

The life of the venerable one was apostolic, because, shining with love and humility, it consisted of faith and non-possessiveness. The blessed one fulfilled in deed the saying of the Psalmist: *"You shall tread upon the lion and the cobra, the young lion and the serpent you shall trample underfoot"* (Psalm 90:13), (Luke 10:19). And again: *"Well done, good and faithful servant; you were faithful over a few things, I will make you ruler over many things"* (Matthew 25:21). These words refer to Heavenly gifts, however they can also be applied to the saint: "Since you, Syncletica, have conquered the flesh and the world in this perceptible warfare, with My help and My protection you will also conquer in that other warfare — against the spirits of wickedness. Let the principalities and powers of darkness know the greatness of your faith. After you conquer the opposing forces of the demons, you will draw near to the good Angelic powers."

Despite the fact that the venerable one practiced hesychia in solitude and labored in virtue, with the passing of time many learned of her ascetic feats: *"For there is nothing hidden which will not be revealed, nor has anything been kept secret but that it should come to light"* (Mark 4:22), says the Lord in the Gospel of Mark. Gradually some of the nuns, enlightened by God, began to come to the venerable one and received great benefit for their souls from conversations with her. Once they asked her how one can be saved. Sighing deeply and shedding tears, the venerable one kept silent. However, the sisters urged her to speak of the greatness of God, because even the very sight of her was sufficient to amaze them.

"Do not rob the poor because he is poor" (Proverbs 22:22), replied the saint with words from Holy Scripture. But the sisters continued to entreat her with even greater persistence, citing at the same time the words of the Lord: *"Freely you have received, freely give"* (Matthew 10:8), reminding her that she should not be like that servant who hid the talent given to him.

"Why do you, sisters, think that I, a sinner, do or say anything worthwhile? We all have one common Teacher — the Lord, and we all listen to Holy Scripture," Syncletica objected to them.

"We know that the Lord is our Teacher, and we all listen to Holy Scripture. But you, laboring vigilantly, have advanced in the virtues, and therefore it befits you to give counsel to the younger sisters. For our Lord Himself commands the same thing," they continued.

Then blessed Syncletica had compassion on them and, knowing that what she would say would not become an occasion for praising her, but would serve for the great benefit of the sisters, she began thus:

"My children, we all know how to be saved, but because of our negligence we let our salvation slip away. First we must fulfill what has become known to us by the grace of the Lord: *'You shall love the Lord your God with all your heart, with all your soul... and your neighbor as yourself'* (Luke 10:27). With the help of these two commandments the Law is kept, for upon them rests the fullness of grace, in them is contained great and boundless power: everything that serves for the benefit of the soul rests upon them. For, according to the testimony of the divine Apostle Paul, *'love is the fulfillment of the law'* (Romans 13:10). Whatever profitable words people may speak by the grace of the Holy Spirit, they all begin with love and have their completion in it. Therefore salvation is this twofold love. But to this the following must be added, which also proceeds from love: let each of you be able to desire the greatest thing.

Do you not know the parable of the grain that the Lord told, that one brought forth fruit *'a hundredfold, another sixty, another thirty'* (Matthew 13:8)? A hundredfold is our monastic rank, sixty are those who abstain from marriage, and thirty are those who live in marriage chastely. It is good when someone ascends from thirty to sixty, and from sixty to a hundred. Since it is profitable to advance from the lesser to the greater. But to descend from the greater to the lesser is dangerous, because one who has once inclined toward the worse cannot stand firm in the lesser, but as it were falls into the pit of perdition. Sometimes certain people make a vow to preserve virginity, but being weak in mind, they justify themselves, as if saying to themselves, but in reality to the devil: 'If we marry and live chastely, we shall be vouchsafed to be numbered among the rank of thirty. Because the entire Old Testament did not reject childbearing, but desired it.' But this justification is from the impure one, for one who descends from the greater to the lesser is deceived by him. Just as a soldier who leaves his position in a larger army and goes to a lesser one does not receive forgiveness but is punished, so also is punished one who descends from the higher rank of virgins to the lower — of the chaste. Therefore we must go from the lesser to the greater: *'forgetting those things which are behind and reaching forward to those things which are ahead'* (Philippians 3:13)," the blessed one instructed with the apostolic commandments. "But we who stand in 'the rank of a hundred' must always, wherever and however we walk, return again to the same place, never putting an end to this: *'when you have done all those things which you are commanded, say, "We are unprofitable servants. We have done what was our duty to do"'* (Luke 17:10), the Lord tells us. We who have preferred the vow of virginity must guard chastity to the highest degree. Since many married worldly wives also live chastely, but this virtue is often combined in them with folly and ignorance, so that they live by fleshly senses. This happens because they see improper things, laugh immoderately, and hear indecent things. But we nuns must leave all this behind and advance in the virtues, guarding our sight from beholding vain things, fulfilling the words of Scripture: *'Let Your eyes look on the things that are right'* (Psalm 17:2), and restraining our tongue, avoiding foul speech. It is absurd that our tongue, created for the singing of Divine hymns and the glorification of God, should utter foul and shameless words. Therefore we not only must not utter them, but must not even listen when others utter them. It is impossible to fulfill all this if we frequently leave the cell, for through our senses, against our will, thieves — demons and passions — enter into us. How can a house not become blackened if its windows and doors are open while smoke rises above it from outside? Under no circumstances should we walk about the villages and marketplaces, because if we consider it grievous and shameful to see our own brothers and parents naked, how much more unworthy and harmful to the soul is it to see naked people on the roads and in the marketplaces, conducting lewd and indecent conversations. From seeing and hearing all this, harmful and shameful images enter the soul.

But even when we are in our cell, we must not be carefree, but always ready, and therefore the Savior says: *'Watch therefore...'* (Matthew 24:42). The more we desire to preserve chastity and virginity, the more, according to the word of Ecclesiastes, we are troubled by the fiercest thoughts: *'For in much wisdom is much grief'* (Ecclesiastes 1:18), because the more the ascetics advance in ascetic struggle, the stronger opponents they find.

Therefore each of us must consider how far she stands from true virginity, and after this go forth fully armed to battle with the enemy. If a sister conquers material fornication and does not commit fornication in deed, then the devil will war against her, inclining her to fornication in the senses. But if, remaining in the cell, not seeing and not hearing improper things, she conquers sensual fornication, then the enemy will war against her again, pushing her toward fornication in the imagination, suggesting various images in sleep and while awake. This vile one, residing in the heart, makes disturbances, brings to the mind of those who practice hesychia beautiful faces and reminds them of old conversations. We must not consent to these images brought by the enemy: *'If the spirit of the ruler rises against you, do not leave your place,'* writes Ecclesiastes (Ecclesiastes 10:4). If a virgin consents to these images, this is equivalent to the fornication committed by worldly people, for *'the mighty shall be mightily tested.'*

Thus our warfare and battle with the demon of fornication is great and terrible, because this demon is the head of all the sins used by the enemy for the perdition of our soul. Revealing this, righteous Job spoke enigmatically about the devil, that all his strength is *'in the sinews of his belly'* (Job 40:11). Therefore the impure one by many and various means inclines the lovers of Christ to fornication, and often transforms even Christ's love for the brethren into this sin, having mocked those virgins who rejected marriage and every manner of the world, and casts them down into fornication by means of brotherly love for men. In like manner the demon deceives also monks who have fled everything that leads to fornication; he casts them into sin through pious conversations with women. And herein lies the essence of the evil one — to clothe himself in what is foreign, to secretly sow his own seed, passing it off as Divine and spiritual, that is, above he places the grain, but beneath it he sets his snares. The Lord also speaks of this: *'They come to you in sheep's clothing, but inwardly they are ravenous wolves'* (Matthew 7:15).

What then shall we do, how shall we be delivered from these diabolical snares?.. *'Be wise as serpents and harmless as doves'* (Matthew 10:16), that is, think with the mind about the snares that the devil sets for us. Christ therefore told us to 'be wise as serpents,' so that we would be vigilant and not forget about the wiles of the evil one. For like can be quickly recognized through like. The simplicity of the dove shows the purity of our deeds. Every good deed requires fleeing from evil and is not mingled with it. But how can we flee from what we do not know? This will become possible only when we are vigilant, learn to discern the cunning of the enemy, and guard ourselves from his snares and craftiness, for, as the divine Peter says: *'the devil walks about like a roaring lion, seeking whom he may devour'* (1 Peter 5:8); *'his food is choice'* (Habakkuk 1:16), the Prophet Habakkuk believed. Therefore we must constantly be attentive, since he too is vigilant and takes up arms against us, not only through objects of the external world but also through thoughts that secretly come to us day and night.

What do we need for this warfare? Wearisome ascetic struggle and pure prayer, which are universal remedies for every pernicious thought. However, in fleshly warfare one must also use special means: when some shameful thought comes to us, we must resist it with the opposite. And if the enemy shows us in a vision some beautiful face, we must war against it in the following manner: mentally gouge out its eyes, tear the skin from its cheeks, and cut off the lips, and it will appear before us as a bare skull, ugly and frightening. Thus we can prevent the enemy from mocking us. For that which we so desired was nothing other than blood mixed with fetid bile. With these thoughts we must drive out the vile image of sin, drive out one nail with another — the demon of fornication. We must reason in similar ways when fighting against attachment to another person, imagining that putrefaction and stench flow from him as if he were dead. However, the main victory in repelling fleshly warfare must be the subduing of the belly, which begets all the passions," blessed Syncletica instructed the sisters with her wise and soul-profiting words. And the nuns greatly rejoiced, hearing her divine and spiritual speeches.

Once a certain nun asked the venerable one whether non-possessiveness is a perfect good.

"Yes, but for the strong and courageous, for those who endure non-possessiveness have through it affliction according to the flesh, but for the soul — relief. Just as strong and new garments, when they are trampled and rubbed, are cleansed and become white, so also a courageous soul, grieving and sorrowing on account of voluntary poverty, is strengthened even more and becomes firmer. But those whose thought is unsteady become fainthearted and grow even weaker and more unsteady. Because if such a soul grieves a little on account of poverty, it becomes worse — it cannot bear the trial produced by non-possessiveness, just as a flimsy and worn garment cannot withstand washing and tears. And the strong garment and the worn one are washed in the same way. However, for both garments the end is different: the strong garment is cleansed and renewed, while the flimsy one is torn and spoiled. Therefore non-possessiveness is a precious treasure for a courageous soul; it becomes for her a bridle preventing the committing of sins in deed. Whoever wishes to acquire this virtue must first exercise himself in fasting, lying on the bare ground, and other afflictions of the flesh. One who does not do so, and without prior preparation immediately rejects money, most often later repents of this act, since for him money is a means for a life of pleasures.

Therefore one must first reject gluttony, food that brings pleasure, and other bodily comforts. Through this one can easily cut off attachment to things and money. For it is difficult when a person possesses some skill but has no tools to practice it. One who rejects the first must also reject the second. Conversing with the rich young man, the Lord asked him whether he kept the commandments of the old law, but did not immediately command him to reject wealth, just as an instructor first asks a student whether he knows the alphabet, whether he can join letters into syllables, whether he is accustomed to pronouncing words and names, and only then asks him to read fluently. Since the rich man answered that he had kept the commandments of the law, the Lord said to him: *'sell what you have and give to the poor... and come, follow Me'* (Matthew 19:21). If the young man had not kept the commandments of the law, then the Savior would not have inclined him to non-possessiveness, for how could one who cannot read syllables immediately read fluently?

Non-possessiveness is good for those who have labored, afflicting the flesh, and have acquired a habit and facility for good, because such ones have rejected all that is superfluous. Their mind and hope they place only on God: *'The eyes of all look expectantly to You, and You give them their food in due season'* (Psalm 145:15). Not cleaving in mind to earthly things, they think only of Heavenly blessings, care about them, and fulfill in deed the words of David: *'I was like a beast before You. Nevertheless I am continually with You...'* (Psalm 73:22–23). For just as pack animals that serve man are content only with the food that is given to them, so the non-possessive work only for daily sustenance, counting wealth as nothing. They firmly keep the foundation of faith, because it was to them that Jesus commanded not to worry about tomorrow, for the birds of heaven *'neither sow nor reap,'* yet the Heavenly Father *'feeds them'* (Luke 12:24). They believed these words.

Even the devil the non-possessive conquer more than others, because he can do them no harm. Most sorrows and temptations come to people because of the loss of wealth, but what sorrow can befall those who have nothing? None. And what harm can the enemy do to them? Burn their fields? They have none. Destroy their livestock? Where is it? Cause harm in something else? But they have departed from everything. So non-possessiveness is the greatest punishment for the devil and a precious treasure for the soul. As great and wonderful as the virtue of non-possessiveness is, so great and vicious is the passion of avarice, which, in the words of blessed Paul, is *'a root of all kinds of evil'* (1 Timothy 6:10). From the desire for money come false oaths, theft, robbery, greed, envy, murders, hatred of brethren, idolatry, and everything that proceeds from these: hypocrisy, flattery, mockery. The cause of all this is avarice. However, not only does God punish the avaricious, but they also destroy themselves, never being satisfied with wealth and never ceasing their cares and concerns about it. And therefore this wound of theirs is incurable. One who has nothing first desires little, then, when he acquires this, still more. Having a hundred coins, he desires to acquire a thousand, and if he acquires a thousand, he wants to acquire a countless number. And so it turns out that these people, being unable to stop in their desire and pursuit of wealth, always complain that they are poor. Besides this, avarice brings with it envy. When vipers are born, they first gnaw through the womb of their mother in order to come out, and only then do they cause harm to others. So also envy: first it darkens the one who has it, and then it causes harm to all around.

For nuns, great profit will come from labors to acquire genuine pure silver — the Kingdom of Heaven. Those who seek the vain profit of this world suffer shipwrecks and encounter pirates at sea, and robbers on land, endure storms and strong winds, and when they receive their reward, they say that they are poor, so that others will not envy them. But we monastics, in order to receive the true Heavenly wealth, do not put ourselves in any danger, and if we acquire even the smallest virtue, we immediately exalt ourselves and show others what saints we are. Moreover, very often we tell not only about this one virtue, but add to it others that we do not have. Then the enemy immediately steals from us even that little which we have received. Worldly people subject to avarice, having received great profit, desire to have still more, counting their estate as nothing and taking every care that no one learns of it. But we monastics act in the opposite way: there is nothing good in us, and we do not want to acquire anything. Being poor in virtues, we boast of our wealth. It is good if a monk who is progressing in good works reveals this to no one, otherwise he will suffer great loss.

Thus one must hide one's virtues to the extent possible, and one who wishes to reveal them to others must also tell about his shortcomings and passions. But if they hide from people all the bad that they have, so that others will not condemn them, much more must they hide their virtues as well. Thus they will not depart from God. Those who are truly virtuous act in the opposite way: they acquaint people with their small sins, adding, as much as possible, things they have not committed, in order to deprive themselves of human glory. Their good deeds they hide. For just as a candle melts in the fire, so the soul grows slack from praises and loses its strength. A candle melts from heat and hardens from cold, so also praise makes the soul weak, while reproach and reproof strengthen it and lead it to greater virtue: *'Rejoice and be exceedingly glad, when they revile and persecute you, and say all kinds of evil against you falsely for My sake... for great is your reward in heaven'* (Matthew 5:12), the Lord tells us; *'In tribulation You enlarged me'* (Psalm 4:1), wrote the Prophet David. Similar sayings can be found in great number in Holy Scripture.

There is one sorrow that is profitable, another that is harmful. Profitable is when someone grieves over his own sins, over the ignorance of his neighbor, when he fears lest he deviate from his good purpose, that is, true and profitable sorrow is when someone grieves and sighs, desiring to attain perfect holiness. But there is another sorrow that brings harm. It is from the devil, who produces in the soul a senseless sorrow full of madness, called by some carelessness. This demon of sorrow we must drive away by prayer and psalmody. Nuns who have good cares and sorrows must not think that anyone in the world lives without care and sorrow: every head abides in labors, and every heart in grief, as the Prophet Isaiah preached. In these words the Holy Spirit reveals the essence of monastic and worldly life. As the head in man is the ruling part, so the monastic life is higher than the worldly, because in the head is found the penetrating part of the soul. Every virtue is acquired by labors. But by grief of heart the prophet revealed the disorder and sorrow of the life of worldly people, for it is in the heart of man that anger and grief dwell. He grieves when he desires what belongs to another, pines when he is poor, is indignant when he is rich, is beside himself, is proud-minded, and even does not sleep so as to safeguard his estate.

Let us not be deceived, we nuns, thinking that worldly people have no cares and labors. Compared to us, they labor more, especially women, who endure great torments, giving birth to children in pain and danger to their lives and raising them in suffering. And when the children fall ill, they too suffer with them. And much else besides this they experience. And there is no end to their labors. Because their children are either born crippled, or have an evil and corrupt character and offend their parents in various ways, and very often kill them by cunning. In such a case we must not be deceived by thoughts from the enemy that married women have a calm and carefree life. They are tormented either during childbirth or pine and waste away from humiliation when they suffer from barrenness. I am telling you now about the wiles of the evil one, yet what I have said is not for all women but only for nuns. For just as the same food is not suitable for all animals, so this word does not benefit everyone: *'And no one puts new wine into old wineskins...'* (Mark 2:22), the Savior said about this.

For one must speak differently with people: with some words to the perfect, with others to those who have attained contemplation and knowledge, with still others to the ascetics and those who are in a state of active virtue, and with yet others to worldly people. As among animals: some are on the earth, others in the water, and still others in the air, so also among people: some gaze on high, like birds, others lead a moderate life, and still others are immersed in sins, like fish in water. A nun must have eagle's wings in order to fly up high and conquer lions and dragons, commanding now over those who were once rulers. We can achieve this on only one condition — if we offer to Christ as a sacrifice our entire mind and all our thought. However, the higher we ascend, the more the devil strives to catch us in his nets. If the demons envy the insignificant and worthless objects of this world, not allowing people to take treasures hidden in the earth, what is strange about them envying us who strive to acquire Heavenly riches? Therefore monastics must arm themselves against the demons with everything possible, for they wage warfare both with the help of external objects and with the help of inner thoughts, just as a vessel sinks sometimes because of sea waves coming from outside, and sometimes because of a leak in the ship. One must always watch out for the external warfare of the demons and get rid of inner impure thoughts, and constantly be vigilant, for the demons often take up arms against us. During external storms into which a ship falls, the sailors call for help from other vessels nearby and very often escape danger. But from a leak the ship goes to the bottom even during a calm, when the sailors are sleeping carelessly. Therefore nuns must be more attentive to inner thoughts: wishing to destroy the house of our soul, the enemy begins to demolish it either from the foundation, or from the roof, or he enters through the windows and first binds the master of the house, and then takes possession of everything in it. The foundation of the house of the soul is good deeds, the roof is faith, and the windows are the senses. And so through all of them the enemy makes war against us.

One who wishes to be saved must have many eyes, because we cannot be carefree in this life: *"Therefore let him who thinks he stands take heed lest he fall"* (1 Corinthians 10:12), it is written in the Apostle. We journey upon an unknown sea — our life. In one part of it reefs are encountered, in another various creatures, and in a third calm and quiet waters. Outwardly we nuns journey through the calm and quiet waters of this life, while worldly people journey through dangerous ones. We sail by day, and the Noetic Sun of Righteousness, Christ, guides us, while worldly people, not knowing the way, walk by night. However, those who sail through unknown and dangerous places can often be vigilant and cry out to God to save the ship of their soul, while we nuns, sailing through calm waters, may sink into the depths from our negligence, having let go of the rudder of righteousness. And so, *'therefore let him who thinks he stands take heed lest he fall'* (1 Corinthians 10:12), because one who has fallen cares about getting up. But one who stands must beware lest he fall, since falls are various. Let the one who stands not condemn the one who has fallen, but rather fear for himself, lest he himself, falling to the bottom of the abyss, perish, where, because of the great depth, his voice calling for help may not be heard: *'Let not the floodwater overflow me, nor let the deep swallow me up; and let not the pit shut its mouth on me'* (Psalm 69:15), says David. And so it turns out that one who fell before you remained there, therefore be attentive lest you fall into the abyss and become food for beasts. For one who fell did not close the doors of his house, that is, did not attend to himself, but you who stand, do not slumber, but always chant the psalm: *'Enlighten my eyes, lest I sleep the sleep of death; lest my enemy say, "I have prevailed against him"'* (Psalm 13:3–4), and always be vigilant, since the noetic lion roars against you. These words are profitable for those who do not strive to be exalted. One who has fallen, if he repents and returns, will be saved, but one who stands firmly, as it may seem to him, let him beware of two things: not to return again to the old passions, especially to faintheartedness, which attacks during warfare, and also not to fall into pride when he advances in virtue. For our enemy the devil, when he sees that one is lazy and careless, will pull him back to himself, or, when it turns out that the ascetic is diligent and advances in ascetic struggle, he will secretly enter the soul by means of pride and thus completely immerse the monastic in this passion. Pride is the most powerful of all the weapons of the impure one, because even Satan himself was cast down from heaven by it. Just as the most experienced military commanders, after their arrows have run out but the enemy is still prevailing, draw out their most powerful weapon — the sword, so also the devil, when he has used almost all his weapons, then as a sword applies his last means — pride.

Thus the first snares are gluttony, love of pleasure, fornication. These passions pursue man in his youth. After them follow avarice, greed, and the like. When the soul conquers them and gains mastery over the belly and all the passions that nest below the stomach, despises money, it is then that the evil one, deprived of all weapons, secretly brings pride into the soul, so that the person may exalt himself over his neighbors in an improper manner. Truly grievous and pernicious is this poisonous passion of pride, with which the enemy saturates the soul. Many saints he has darkened by it, secretly placing in the soul the false and deadly thought of superiority over the other sisters in fasting and virtues. Thus the devil makes the person forget his sins and steals from his memory the recollection of them, so that he cannot repeat after David for his own healing in a humble voice: *'Against You only have I sinned...'* (Psalm 51:4), *'Have mercy on me'* (Psalm 51:1), *'I will be glad and rejoice in You; I will sing praise to Your name, O Most High'* (Psalm 9:2), and leaves in his memory only those words which he himself said in his thought: *'I will ascend into heaven, I will exalt my throne above the stars of God'* (Isaiah 14:13). He suggests to the proud person thoughts of power, that he will sit in the first places, of teaching, of the gift of healing. Thus the person perishes, because he has received a wound difficult to cure.

If anyone has such proud thoughts, one must always remember the words of David: *'But I am a worm, and no man...'* (Psalm 22:6), or of Abraham: *'I am but dust and ashes'* (Genesis 18:27), or of the Prophet Isaiah: *'all our righteousnesses are like filthy rags'* (Isaiah 64:6). A nun who is in hesychia, during such a demonic attack, must come to her monastery and compel herself to eat food twice a day. And if this passion has gained mastery over her from excessiveness of ascetic struggle, then the other nuns of her same age must strongly rebuke her, saying that she has done nothing good at all. For such nuns it is profitable to perform every difficult obedience and to read the lives of the great saints. Moreover, those laboring together with her must for several days increase their ascetic struggle, so that the proud one may see their great labors and be humbled, considering herself lower than them. The cause of such pride lies in disobedience. This disease can only be cured by the opposite remedy — obedience: *'Obedience is better than sacrifice'* (1 Samuel 15:22), said the Prophet Samuel. The abbess must crush the vainglory of the sisters when this is necessary, and if some nun is negligent, lazy, and does not advance in virtue, she must praise her. If she has done some small good, the abbess must marvel at this and exaggerate its significance. And the serious sins of that sister the superior must present to her as insignificant and small, because, wishing to distort in the ascetics and saints the understanding of their sins, the devil tries to hide them, so that they may come into a state of pride. With the young and beginners he acts in the opposite way: all their sins he places before them, so as thereby to cast them into despair. To one sister he may say that 'because you have committed fornication, there is no forgiveness for you,' and to another that 'because of your greed you will not be saved.' However, although Rahab was a harlot, she was saved by faith. Paul was a persecutor of Christians, but became a chosen vessel. Matthew was a tax collector, yet became an evangelist. The thief stole and murdered, but was the first to open the doors of paradise.

Souls conquered by pride must be corrected and healed, instructing them with such words: 'Why are you proud, wretched soul, that you do not eat meat? Others do not even look at fish. Why are you proud that you do not drink wine? Consider that others do not even taste oil. Why then do you exalt yourself that you fast until evening? Others go two or three days without food at all. Why are you proud that you do not wash yourself? Many, because of bodily illnesses, do not wash at all. You marvel at yourself that you sleep on a haircloth mat, while in the meantime others always sleep only on the bare ground. But if you too sleep on the ground, you have done nothing great, because some place stones under themselves so as not to receive pleasure from sleep, and others hang themselves by ropes all night. Even if you do all this and have reached the extreme of ascetic struggle, do not be exalted, because the demons did and do more than you: they never eat, do not drink, do not sleep, do not marry, and even live in deserts. So you too, if you dwell in a cave, do not think that you have done anything great.'

With these thoughts one can heal the passions opposite to them — despair and pride. Just as fire is weakened and goes out both by the blowing of a strong wind and in completely windless weather, so also virtue disappears because of pride in excessive ascetic struggle if we remain in negligence and do not move ourselves so that the Holy Spirit may kindle zeal in us and help us. Just as a knife that is sharpened too keenly easily breaks on a stone, so pride quickly destroys excessive ascetic struggle. Therefore a person must guard his soul in every way. When it is inflamed with the heat of pride, he must by means of extreme ascetic struggle lead it to shady places, that is, subject it to the grace of God. Sometimes for this one must cut off the excess from one's soul, so that the root may be strengthened better, and fruitful branches may grow from it. But one who is warred upon by despair must compel himself with the thoughts we mentioned earlier, in order to strive for the heights, that is, to hope in the boundless mercy of our Man-loving God, because the soul of such a sinner abides in an extremely fallen state. One must relate to him like skilled farmers who, when they see a stunted and low-growing plant, begin to water it frequently and care for it especially, so that it may grow, but when they see a shoot that has sprouted before its time, they cut it off, since it will soon dry up — just like physicians who recommend to some patients to eat well and go for walks, and to others to abstain from food.

It is clear that pride is the greatest of all evils, just as humility is the greatest of all virtues. The latter is acquired with difficulty, because if one does not reject glory, it is impossible to acquire the treasure of humility. Humility is so great that even the devil, who imitates all the other virtues, knows nothing at all about humility. Therefore the Apostle Paul commands us to be firmly clothed in it and wishes that all who perform good works should be clothed in it as in a garment. Even if you fast, give alms, teach, lead a life in virginity and chastity, are wise, always have humility. It, like a fortress wall, protects you and holds together all your other virtues. The holy three youths in the Babylonian furnace in their song did not recall any other virtues, but numbered among those who glorify the Lord only the humble in heart, not naming the chaste, nor the virginal, nor the non-possessive. Just as without nails a ship cannot be constructed, so also is it impossible to be saved without humility. Therefore, wishing to show how beneficial and salvific humility is, the Lord Himself clothed Himself in it when He became Man: *'Learn from Me, for I am meek and lowly in heart'* (Matthew 11:29), He said. Reflect on Who it is that spoke these words, and become a perfect disciple and imitator of His humility. Let it be for you the beginning and end of all blessings. Humility means humble thoughts of the soul, and not only a humble outward appearance. If the soul is humble, then the body is humble too. You say that you have fulfilled all the commandments? The Savior knows this, yet He commands you to begin working for Him again, for He says: *'when you have done all those things which you are commanded, say, "We are unprofitable servants"'* (Luke 17:10).

Humility can be attained through the patient endurance of reproaches, insults, and beatings. When you hear yourself called 'foolish and mad,' 'a beggar,' 'sick and wretched,' 'a failure,' 'unreasonable,' 'ugly in appearance,' 'thin' — all these are the sinews and strength of humility. Our Almighty heard and endured all this. He took the form of a servant, was struck, was wounded. So we too must imitate the active humility of Christ. But there are some who outwardly appear humble and have a humble appearance, so that people may praise them. However, they can be known by the fruits of their deeds, because if they are reproved a little, they cannot bear it and immediately, like serpents, spew out their venom.

Hearing the words of the saint, the sisters rejoiced extraordinarily, and expecting to hear more, they could not be satisfied with the soul-profiting speeches of the venerable one. And therefore she again began to speak to them:

"Great is the ascetic struggle that lies before those who approach serving God in the monastic habit. At the beginning they experience great labors, but then they receive ineffable joy, like those who, wishing to light a fire, first swallow smoke and weep, and only then receive it. We nuns must labor and weep in order to kindle in ourselves Divine fire: *'I came to send fire on the earth'* (Luke 12:49), the Lord said to us. However, there are some fainthearted ones who tasted smoke but did not light a fire. They did not have patience, and their love for God — this great treasure — was weak. They did not hear the Apostle Paul proclaiming the hymn of love: *'though I bestow all my goods to feed the poor, and though I give my body to be burned, but have not love...'* (1 Corinthians 13:3), *'I have become sounding brass or a clanging cymbal'* (1 Corinthians 13:1).

As love is a great good, so anger is a great evil. It darkens and hardens the soul, leading it to folly. Our Lord, Who cares in every way for our salvation, does not leave any part of the soul without His protection and patronage. If the enemy wars against us by means of fornication, He arms us with chastity. If that one wars against us with pride, humility is near us. If the devil kindles hatred in us, then love is at hand. However many different arrows the devil may shoot against us, the Almighty, for our salvation and for victory over the enemy, protects us with great weapons. *'For the wrath of man does not produce the righteousness of God'* (James 1:20), says the chief Apostle James. Therefore we must bridle it, since it is necessary at the proper time. It is profitable to be angry against the demons, but not against people, even if they sin against us. As soon as anger passes from us, we must turn them to repentance.

However, the gravest sin is remembrance of wrongs. If anger, like smoke, darkens the soul for a short time and then disperses, remembrance of wrongs enters it like a nail, making it worse than all beasts. Even a dog, when it is angry at some person, if it is appeased with food, cools down and calms down. Similarly, other animals, if they are tamed, become gentle. But one who is possessed by remembrance of wrongs does not submit to entreaties. And even time, which changes everything, cannot heal the passion of remembrance of wrongs. Therefore such people are the most impious and lawless of all. They do not listen to Christ the Savior, Who says: Go, *'first be reconciled to your brother, and then come and offer your gift'* (Matthew 5:24), and the Apostle: *'Do not let the sun go down on your wrath'* (Ephesians 4:26).

And so, it is good not to be angry at all, but if you do become angry, the divine Paul does not allow you to remain in this passion even one day, and therefore he said: 'until sunset.' But you, O nun, why do you wait until the time of your life sets, to be reconciled with the one with whom you were angry? Do you not know the word of God: *'Sufficient for the day is its own trouble'* (Matthew 6:34)? Why should we remain in enmity after this day has passed? Why hate the one who grieved you? She did not do this, but the devil did. Hate the disease from which your sister suffers, not the sick one herself: *'Why do you boast in evil, O mighty man?'* (Psalm 52:1).

In the words: *'Your tongue devises destruction'* (Psalm 52:2), the Prophet David tells us that all the time of our life we commit lawlessness, because we do not submit to the Law of God, which through Paul commands us not to let the sun go down on our wrath. Why then do we not cease to revile and abuse our neighbor? For this we will justly be punished by the Creator: *'Therefore God shall likewise destroy you forever; He shall take you away, and pluck you out of your dwelling place, and uproot you from the land of the living'* (Psalm 52:5), warns us the royal Psalmist. Do you hear? All these are the 'gifts' and 'rewards' of the Creator to one who remembers wrongs, which he receives for his malice.

Upon remembrance of wrongs follows a multitude of woes: envy, sorrow, slander. The evil produced by these passions, although it seems small, is deadly. For often fornication, murder, greed — these great passions — were healed by the salvific medicine of repentance, but pride, remembrance of wrongs, and slander, despite the fact that they seem to be a small sin, killed the soul, entering into its most vulnerable parts, like a nail. This happened because these passions inflicted a deep wound on the soul, but those who were wounded by them remained in negligence, thinking that slander and everything like it is not dangerous. Thus, not trying to correct them, such people little by little perished from them. For some the grave sin of slander is like food and rest. Therefore one should not pay attention to vain rumors and listen to what is said about the sins of others. One must guard one's soul from them in simplicity. The stench of impure words defiles the soul with thoughts and without cause makes one hate those who converse and communicate with you. When your hearing is defiled by the slander of slanderers, then you will no longer possess discernment, but will imagine all people to be such: an eye that gazes intently at some single color is no longer able to distinguish other colors, but everything visible appears to it in one color.

We must guard our tongue and hearing, so as not to slander anyone and not to listen with partiality to the slander of others: *'Whoever secretly slanders his neighbor, him I will destroy'* (Psalm 101:5) and *'that my mouth may not sin by human words'* (Psalm 17:4), says David. But we discuss not only those deeds which people commit, but also those which they do not commit. Therefore do not believe slander against others, and do not condemn those who slander, but act as Divine Scripture commands us: *'Like a deaf man, I do not hear; and I am like a mute who does not open his mouth'* (Psalm 38:13). Do not rejoice in the misfortunes of others, even if those people were very sinful. Some, when they see that someone is being beaten or thrown into prison, in their ignorance cite the popular proverb: 'One who makes his bed poorly will sleep poorly.' But you, O nun, who have made your bed well, do you think that you will rest your whole life? But how then can this be reconciled with Divine Scripture, which says that one and the same thing can befall both the righteous and the unrighteous? For we are all people, and we walk the same road in this world, although we conduct our lives in different ways. Can not some misfortune happen to us as well? Why then do we rejoice in the misfortunes of others?..

We must not feel hatred toward our enemies, because the Lord Himself commanded us thus: 'And if you do good to those who do good to you, what credit is that to you? For even sinners do the same...' But you, 'love your enemies' (Luke 6:33, 35). No special skill or labor is required to love one who is well-disposed toward you, for this is a natural inclination. But to love an enemy requires teaching from God and great labor to overcome natural hatred. The Kingdom of Heaven is acquired not by the heedless and carefree, but by the diligent, and those who use effort for this. And just as we must not hate our enemies, so we must not avoid and despise the heedless and lazy, since some cite for their justification the saying of the prophet: 'With the merciful You will show Yourself merciful... and with the devious You will show Yourself shrewd' (Psalm 18:25–26). By this they justify their actions, but in reality they do the opposite of what the Holy Spirit says through David. He does not command us to turn away from the perverted, but calls us to correct them. By associating with them, you will attract them to yourself and direct them from evil to good. The characters of people can be divided into three kinds. The first is distinguished by an extreme inclination to sin, the second occupies a middle position: it inclines both to good and to evil, and the third, exalted in great virtue, not only strengthens itself in good, but strives in every way to bring to it also the one who is extremely inclined to sin. When people of bad character have fellowship with those worse than themselves, they grow even more in evil. Those in the middle try to avoid the bad, since they fear becoming bad themselves from association with them, for they are still unsteadfast in good. But the third, possessing a courageous character and standing firm in good, associate with the bad in order to save them. And if these third ones are reproached and mocked by those who see them associating with the bad and negligent, they accept all these accusations as praises, fearlessly completing God's work, that is, the salvation of their brethren.

'Rejoice and be exceedingly glad... when men revile and persecute you, and say all kinds of evil against you falsely' (Matthew 5:12, 11), the Savior addresses them. And the Master Christ ate together with tax collectors and sinners. Those perfect in virtue are more brotherly-loving than self-loving, for just as those who see the houses of their neighbors burning, leave their own and run to save the neighbors' houses from the fire, so too these, seeing their brethren sinning, neglect themselves, endure reproaches and condemnations, if only they may save their brethren. Those in the middle, when they see that their neighbor is being consumed by sin, in fear lest they themselves be burned by the fire of sin, run away, while the first, like evil neighbors, seeing their brethren burning, further fan the flames, throwing into it their own sins like firewood. Thus they completely burn up their neighbors, and instead of quenching with water the fire of sin by which their brother is being consumed, they throw firewood, forcing the wretches to sin even more. The third, being good, count their possessions as nothing but consider them lower than the salvation of their brethren. Herein lie the signs of true love; such people are guardians of sincere love.

Just as sins are connected one with another: after avarice follow envy, cunning, perjury, anger, remembrance of wrongs, so also the virtues are connected with love — meekness, long-suffering, guilelessness. And the perfect good is non-possessiveness. One who does not first acquire non-possessiveness cannot attain love, because God commanded us to love all people, and not just some one person. Therefore we must not leave the needy without attention, but strive to help them in every way. If we support only some, then our love is stolen and perishes, because we do not love everyone. Only the Almighty can grant to all a full sufficiency, and if anyone says that one who has nothing must labor to acquire profit and distribute alms from it, let him know: this is possible for worldly people, but not for monks. For the All-Good One commanded giving alms not so much to feed the poor as for the acquisition of love by those who show mercy. The Lord, Who arranges the ways of the rich, will also feed the poor. Was the commandment to give alms superfluous then? Let it not be so! Because almsgiving becomes the firstfruits of love for those who do not know how to acquire it. Just as circumcision of the foreskin was an example of circumcision of the heart, so also almsgiving became a teacher of love. Although for those to whom love has been given by the grace of God, almsgiving is superfluous. I say this not to condemn almsgiving, but to show the purity of non-possessiveness. Let not the lesser good, almsgiving, become an obstacle to the greater good — non-possessiveness, which is love. You, O nun, in a short time and with little labor have attained the lesser good, since you distributed all that you had to the poor. Strive now to attain the greater — love. You must with the same free voice say: *'See, we have left all and followed You'* (Matthew 19:27). You have been vouchsafed to imitate the bold tongue of the Apostles Peter and John, who said: *'Silver and gold I do not have'* (Acts 3:6). They had two tongues, but one faith. But worldly people also must not give alms carelessly: *'let not the oil of the wicked anoint my head'* (Psalm 141:5), writes the Psalmist. One who gives alms must have Abraham's way of thinking, and perform righteousness just as he did — justly. Offering hospitality, together with the dishes he also offered his character: he stood and served himself, not wanting the servants to share with him the profit of hospitality. Truly those who offer such hospitality will receive the reward for their mercy, even if they are in the second rank. Because when the Creator created the Universe, He established in it two ranks of inhabitants. For those who spend their lives in piety, He appointed marriage for childbearing, but for those who live purely, He ordained virginity, making them equal to the angels. To the married He gave laws, teaching, allowed them to take vengeance on the impious, but to the virginal He said: *'Vengeance is Mine, and recompense'* (Deuteronomy 32:35). To the first He commanded to *'till the ground'* (Genesis 3:23), and to monastics — *'Do not worry about tomorrow'* (Matthew 6:34). To the first He gave the Law, to those living the monastic life, by grace, He revealed His commandments.

The Cross for us is a memorial of victory, since our rank and our vow are nothing other than renunciation of life and preparation for death. We must be like the dead, motionless in body. Everything that we formerly did according to the flesh, we did as unreasoning children. *'By whom the world has been crucified to me, and I to the world'* (Galatians 6:14), writes the Apostle, that is, we live only by the soul, and with its help we must display the virtues, with it we must show mercy, for blessed are those who show mercy with the soul. According to the words of the Lord, one who only looks at a woman with lust, not having committed the sin in deed, has already committed adultery and secretly committed sin in his soul (Matthew 5:28). So also one who shows mercy and pities a poor person with his soul shows mercy, and his intention takes the place of the action, even if he has no money. We have been honored with a greater dignity than worldly people. Masters in the world have various servants: some they send to the field to till the land, others, the better ones, they keep in the house to serve themselves.

And so the Lord has placed the married in the world, while those who are better than them and possess a good intention He has left to serve Himself. Such are strangers to everything earthly, because they have been vouchsafed to eat from the Master's table. They do not care about clothing, for they have clothed themselves in Christ. But both of these ranks have one Lord — God. It is impossible for there to be in one rank both sprouts and grain at the same time, and therefore monastics are not called by the Lord to clothe themselves in worldly glory. An ear of grain is ready for harvest when its leaves have fallen off and its stalk has dried up. If we do not strip from ourselves the conceptions of earthly things, which for us are like leaves, and do not dry up our body like a stalk, and then lift up our thought to God, we cannot produce the saving fruit.

It is dangerous to teach anyone without first mastering the art of performing the virtues. If a person has a house that has rotted, and he receives guests in it, the dilapidated dwelling can fall and by its fall cripple all those in it. So also one who has not built his house on a firm foundation, that is, has not learned to do good, will destroy both himself and those whom he taught. Such ones by their words first moved people to salvation, and then by their evil actions caused them even greater harm, as if the first had not instructed them at all. Teaching alone, without practical deeds, resembles an image painted with easily-washable paints, which fade under the action of time, from drops of rain, and from the blowing of winds. But teaching accompanied by deeds is not erased forever, because the word embodied in deed is firmly imprinted on the soul and gives to the listeners an eternal and indelible likeness of Christ and His virtues. We must heal the soul not only outwardly, but adorn it, showing special care for its inner purity.

We have cut off the hair on our head? Let us cast off together with it the lice that are on the head, for if they remain, they will bite us even more. The cut-off hair signifies life in the world: honors, glory, money, fashionable clothes, baths, fine food. All this we have, it seems, rejected. Let us then also cast off the soul-destroying lice: slander, avarice, lying, oaths, and other passions found in our soul, because the head signifies the soul. While it is covered with hair, that is, worldly objects, it is not visible. But now, when the soul has been stripped of what is worldly, it has become exposed. Therefore in all monastics even the smallest sins are visible: in a clean house, if some even very small insect appears, everyone notices it. But in worldly people, as in unclean caves, huge venomous serpents nest, but they are not visible — they are hidden behind the multitude of things. Monastics must constantly cleanse their spiritual house and carefully watch that no soul-destroying creature enters it. So that the passion may not pass into the secret parts of our soul, we must always cense our heart with the divine incense of prayer. Just as with incense of the strongest scent venomous serpents are driven out, so our prayer together with fasting drives away evil thoughts.

Nuns must always guard against the thoughts that come to us. One elder of holy life acted in the following way: for several days he sat in his cell and noted the thoughts — when the first came, when the second, and how long each of them lasted. With the help of this observation the elder learned the grace of God, his own patience and strength, and was also able to gain victory over the enemy. Even merchants of the temporary objects of the world count their receipts every day, rejoicing at profit and grieving at loss; how much more must we be vigilant, who deal with true treasure and desire to acquire even greater blessings? And if the enemy steals from us a small portion, we must grieve and condemn ourselves, but not despair and not abandon everything, because this sin we committed involuntarily, on account of temptation. You have ninety-nine sheep — go and seek the one that is lost! Do not fear that you have lost it, do not depart from the Master Christ, do not withdraw from Him, lest the blood-thirsty devil by despair enslave the entire flock of your deeds and scatter it. And so, because of one lost sheep do not abandon what you have, for our God is All-Good: *'Though he fall, he shall not be utterly cast down; for the Lord upholds him with His hand'* (Psalm 37:24), says the Prophet David.

Everything that we have done or acquired in this world we must consider small compared to the eternal riches of the future life, since in this world we are as in the womb of a mother. For when we were in the womb, life was not the same as it is now: we did not eat solid food, we saw neither the sun nor any other light. And so, just as in the womb of the mother we were deprived of many things of this world, so now, being in this world, we are deprived of many blessings of the Kingdom of Heaven. Therefore let us strive for the enjoyment of the Heavenly blessings of the future life, where we will see the Noetic Sun of Righteousness of the heavenly Jerusalem — our true homeland and mother, where our God and Father abides. In order to become heirs of His blessings, let us live here prudently and chastely. Just as newborn infants are first given a little food and then offered more, so also the righteous pass from this life to the Heavenly and better one, ascending, as it is written: *'from strength to strength'* (Psalm 84:7). But sinners will be delivered from the darkness of this world to the darkness of hell, like infants who die in their mother's womb. For they, while still on earth, are dead from the multitude of sins, and therefore after death they descend to dark places.

In this life we are born three times. The first time, when we come out of the mother's womb, and the other two births raise us from earth to Heaven. The second occurs from Divine grace, which descends upon us during Divine Baptism; we call it new being and regeneration. The third birth comes through repentance and good labors — in it we now find ourselves.

Those who have come to the True Bridegroom Christ must adorn themselves as well as possible. Worldly brides, marrying a mortal, try to wash, anoint themselves with fragrances, put on various adornments, to please their future husbands. Then how much more must we adorn ourselves, who have become betrothed to the Heavenly Bridegroom? We must wash off sinful impurity through ascetic labors and clothe ourselves in spiritual garments. They adorn their bodies with earthly flowers, but we must adorn our souls with virtues, and instead of precious stones place on our heads a triple wreath: of faith, hope, and love, and adorn the neck with humility. Instead of a belt let us put on chastity, and clothe ourselves in non-possessiveness as in a garment. Let the incorruptible food of prayer and psalmody become our wedding feast. However, in this let us not merely move our tongue, but let our mind be together with the words. It often happens that people pray only with their lips, while the heart and mind think of other things (1 Corinthians 14:15) — let this not happen with us. We who have come to the Divine wedding must attend to ourselves, lest we be found without lamps, that is, without virtues. If we do not fulfill what we promised to Christ, the Master of all will hate us and not accept us. What vows then must we bring to Him? First of all, to care less for the body and more for the soul. One cannot draw up two buckets of water from a well at the same time — the empty one goes down into the well, while the full one is raised up. So it is with us: when we care only for the soul, it is filled with virtues and rises up, while the body becomes light from ascetic labors and does not drag the soul down to earth: *'but even though our outward man is perishing, yet the inward man is being renewed day by day'* (2 Corinthians 4:16), testifies the Apostle.

Being saved in a coenobitic monastery, do not change the place of your abode, lest you otherwise receive greater harm. Just as a bird destroys the eggs it is hatching by leaving them, so the faith of a monastic who moves from place to place grows cold and is deadened. Let not the luxury of rich dishes and pleasure deceive you, as if there were some benefit in this. The rich value the skill of cooks who prepare tasty dishes that give pleasure, but you conquer abundant and sweet food with simple fare and fasting, for *'a satisfied soul loathes the honeycomb, but to a hungry soul every bitter thing is sweet'* (Proverbs 27:7), said the wise Solomon. Do not fill yourself with bread — and you will not desire wine.

Lust, pleasure, and sorrow are the three chief and first sins that come from the enemy. From them all other evil proceeds. They are connected with each other and follow one after another. If pleasure can be conquered, lust cannot, because pleasure comes through the body, while lust begins in the soul. But sorrow proceeds from these two. If you do not allow lust to act in you, then you will drive out both pleasure and sorrow. But if you allow lust to arise in yourself, it will bring with it pleasure, and pleasure will bring sorrow. Then all three will surround you and give the soul absolutely no rest: *'Do not give water an outlet'* (Sirach 25:25), says Holy Scripture.

Let each one receive information from her own mind, for not everything is profitable for everyone. Some need to be in a coenobitic monastery, others need to abide in solitude. Just as among plants, some grow better in moist places and others in dry, so also people: some have good health living in high places, others in low. So also among monastics: where it is profitable for each, let her remain there. Many, being in cities but imagining that it was a desert, lived a holy life and were saved. And many went into the mountains but, behaving in a worldly manner, perished. One can live near many people and at the same time lead the monastic life in mind, and one can be in solitude and in mind be with other people.

The devil has many stings. If he does not succeed in causing harm through poverty, he offers wealth for the seduction of a person. If he does not succeed in causing harm through reproach and abuse, he offers praises and glory. If the impure one is defeated by a person possessing robust health, he sends illness. When he cannot cause harm through something joyful, he tries to do the same with sorrow and involuntary sufferings. By God's permission, he causes a person to have severe illnesses, so that the person may fall into faintheartedness and his love for God may be darkened. Therefore, if your body burns, beloved, and from intense heat is torn apart, and you suffer from an incurable and uncontrollable thirst, remember that you endure this for your sins, think of the eternal torments, of the unquenchable fire and the unbearable torments of hell. Then in your earthly torments there will be no place for faintheartedness, but only ineffable joy and thanksgiving to the Lord that He has visited you: *'The Lord has chastened me severely, but He has not given me over to death'* (Psalm 118:18), you will glorify the Creator with the hymnal words of David. Iron by means of fire is freed from rust; so you by means of illnesses are freed from sinful defilement. And if you are righteous but have suddenly fallen ill, know that you are advancing, passing from the lesser to the greater. Even if you are like gold, having passed through the fire of sorrows, you will shine even brighter. And if *'a messenger of Satan'* has been given to you, *'a thorn in the flesh'* (2 Corinthians 12:7), then you have been vouchsafed to become like the Apostle Paul, and you must greatly rejoice at this. If you are tormented by heat or suffer from cold, refreshment and rest await you: *'You have caused men to ride over our heads; we went through fire and through water; but You brought us out to rich fulfillment'* (Psalm 66:12), we read in Divine Scripture. If the first has happened to you, expect also the second. You are poor, you labor and suffer, then repeat the words of the prophet: *'Deliver me, for I am poor and needy, and my heart is wounded within me'* (Psalm 109:22). For *'In tribulation You enlarged me'* (Psalm 4:1). Let us train as much as possible in these ascetic labors, because the one who wars against us is before us. Let us not be sorry that because of illness we cannot stand at prayer or chant hymns. Standing, fasting, lying on the ground, and other bodily mortifications are established for the mortification of the most shameful lusts. But if illness has weakened all this, then this labor is superfluous. And what am I saying — superfluous? The ruinous passions from illness, as from the strongest and most effective medicine, are weakened even more. Patience in illness is the greatest ascetic labor. We must endure illness and thank and glorify God for it. Thus, if we have lost our sight, let us not be offended — through this we have been freed from the organ of insatiable lust; now we will contemplate with our spiritual eyes the glory of the Lord. If we have become deaf, we have been freed from hearing vanity. If from illness our hands have become paralyzed, the inner hands of our soul are ready for warfare with the enemy. Spiritual health will only increase even if our entire body is bound by illness.

In a coenobitic monastery, obedience must be preferred over ascetic struggle, because very often ascetic struggle leads to pride, while obedience leads to humility. All those who labor immoderately are disciples of the impure one. But how can one distinguish royal asceticism, which is from God, from tyrannical and demonic? By its measure. Therefore one must fast all one's life, but not abstain from food four or five days in a row and then permit oneself abundant dishes. In this one can see immoderation, which is very ruinous. One should not expend all one's weapons at once, lest one be found against the enemy with bare hands during battle, for then he will easily defeat you. One must always care about the weapon — our body, and the warrior — our soul. While a monastic is young and healthy, it is necessary to fast, because in time old age will come with illnesses, and abstinence may become impossible. It is for this time that one must make provisions, so that when you grow weak, you may use them. In fasting reason and strictness must be combined. Then the enemy will not interfere with foolishness in your trade and will not steal the profit from fasting. This, as I believe, the Lord had in mind when He said that we should become true money-changers, that is, know precisely the difference between the king's coins and counterfeits. The nature of gold is one and the same, but the stamp and image differ. By gold I understand fasting, abstinence, almsgiving. These virtues, placing their own seal on them, are also used by the Hellenes and the heretics. Therefore we must be attentive, otherwise, not knowing letters, we will fall into their hands and suffer harm. We must confidently accept the Cross of the Lord, sealed with right faith and pious deeds.

Nuns must manage their soul with discernment, and if they are in a coenobitic monastery, not seek their own will, not follow their own opinion, but submit to the spiritual mother — the abbess. For we have committed ourselves to exile, we have gone beyond the boundaries of worldly things, and therefore let us not seek them again in the monastery. There, in the world, we had glory, but here — reproach; there — abundance of food, here — we experience want even of bread. In the world those who commit crime are thrown into prison against their will, but here we have imprisoned ourselves voluntarily, on account of our sins, so that this voluntary imprisonment may deliver us from future torment. One should not seek justification for relaxing the fast in illness, because even those who do not fast are subject to the same illnesses. One should not abandon a good work once begun, even if the devil urges this. Having endured all his wiles, you will conquer the enemy. Those who set out on a voyage by ship, with a favorable wind unfurl the sails, but with an unfavorable one do not immediately lower them but wait a little, or, battling the storm, continue the voyage. So also we, when we meet a storm, instead of a sail let us stretch out the Cross and fearlessly continue our journey.

In these words were contained not dry teachings of the blessed one, but above all deeds. However, because of the multitude of things accomplished by Syncletica, it is impossible to recount everything that she did in her long life. It is known that throughout her life the devil constantly took up arms against her. And he was always defeated. But once, by God's permission, he did inflict harm on her. First he struck the internal organs of the saint, causing such severe pain that no one among people could help her. First the lung was affected. Then the devil assailed her with other terrible diseases and almost killed the ascetic. For a long time the accursed one tormented her with a multitude of sores: Syncletica suffered from constant fever. When the saint was eighty years old, the impure one struck her with the diseases of Job; however, in order to cause her the cruelest pain, he shortened the time: Job spent thirty-five years in sickness (Saint Cyril of Alexandria and Olympiodorus, from the texts of Holy Scripture, conclude that Job spent only seven years in sickness, which, together with all the years of his life that are enumerated in the chronology, were however added to Job by God after the sickness, for the years of the righteous one were doubled. — Auth.), while the venerable one spent eight, one year for every ten years she had lived on earth. Three and a half years the blessed one warred against the enemy. Perhaps even the courageous martyrs for Christ did not suffer as much as the ever-blessed Syncletica endured. For against them they warred from without with sword and fire, but the saint was burned as by the fire of a heated furnace from within, little by little consuming all her internal organs. This is truly a grievous and inhuman punishment. When rulers wish to punish someone severely and harshly, they burn him over a slow fire, killing him little by little. This is exactly how the enemy, increasing the heat inside the venerable one, tormented her unceasingly, day and night. The saint, with great courage, not losing heart, endured this illness and did not cease to instruct the sisters in the faith, delivering their souls as from the jaws of a lion.

"Souls dedicated to God must never remain in carelessness, because at the moment when they practice hesychia, the enemy gnashes his teeth and is grieved, having been conquered by them. Having retreated a little, he watches for when they relax a bit, and then attacks and deceives them precisely in that wherein these souls were at ease and from where they did not expect the enemy's blow," the blessed one never tired of repeating.

"Just as it cannot be that extremely vicious people do not have at least a spark of good, so it is impossible that the very virtuous do not have some sin. And so it is always: in the extremely vicious there is found a certain part of good, and in the virtuous a part of sin. Very often one can find examples where one who is filled with every kind of shameful passion is merciful, while an ascetic, the chaste, and the fasting is a slanderer and a lover of money. Therefore no one should neglect the small, as if it could not harm him, for a drop hollows out a stone. Great blessings come to a person from Divine grace, but with small passions we must struggle by our own strength. One who struggles with a great passion by the grace of God and neglects small sins will receive great harm. When we begin to walk, the Lord, as our True Father, extends His hand to us, His spiritual children, so that we may not fall. Delivering us from great dangers, He leaves us alone to deal with the small ones. Thus He shows us the extent of our freedom and the capabilities of our strength. For one who is conquered by small passions, how will he be able to guard himself against the great ones?" preached Syncletica, warred against by severe illness.

Then the devil attacked the venerable one with even greater force and struck the saint's organs of speech, so as thereby to hinder her from speaking. The demon thought that now the sisters would stop coming to the blessed one. But even in such a condition, having deprived the nuns of the possibility of hearing the words of the venerable one, he became the cause of their great benefit: seeing the illnesses of the venerable one, the sisters were even more strengthened in virtue; the bodily sores of the saint healed their wounded souls, and the courage of her soul and her patience became for those who saw her a warning and a medicine. The enemy did not achieve his goal and struck the venerable one in another way: she had a toothache, and from it the gum immediately began to rot, so that the tooth fell out by itself. The infection spread to the entire jaw, so that all the soft tissues began to rot. In forty days the entire jaw had rotted away, and after two months a hole formed, around which everything had turned black. A terrible stench began to come from her whole body, and the sisters who served her suffered from it more than the sick one herself. Most of the time the saint was alone, because the sisters could not endure this unbearable smell. When it became necessary to approach the venerable one, the nuns burned a large quantity of incense and only then entered the cell. Having rendered their service, they immediately withdrew. However, more often blessed Syncletica herself did not allow the sisters to help her, as she clearly saw the enemy warring against her. Thus she once again proved her courage. Although the sisters asked her for the sake of her own weakness to anoint the sore places with myrrh, she did not agree, because she reasoned: "If I accept help from people, I will withdraw from the glorious battle with the enemy." She did not agree to any treatment, yet the physician still persuaded her of the necessity of taking certain measures:

"We do not intend to treat you or console you, but we wish, according to custom, to commit to the earth that part of your body which has fallen away, rotted, and become dead, so that the sisters who serve you may not become ill from the stench it produces. What is done for the dead, I will now do for you: I will mix wine with aloe, myrrh, and myrtle, and anoint the rotted part with this solution," he said to the ascetic.

The venerable one accepted his counsel, and out of pity for the sisters who served her, she agreed. After this the excessive stench ceased. Who will not shudder, seeing this unbearable wound; who will not receive benefit, reflecting on the patience of the venerable one; who will not be strengthened, thinking about her victory and the defeat of the devil! The vile one struck the saint precisely in that part from which flowed the saving and sweetest source of words, and his boundless malice drove away from her all human help. Like a blood-thirsty beast he rushed at his prey wherever it was. But, preparing to devour it, he himself became food, for he was caught, as it were, on the hook of bodily weakness. Seeing that the venerable one was a woman, he despised her as weak, not knowing all her courage. Seeing that her members were weakened, the blind one could not discern her most courageous mind. Three months the venerable one labored in this ascetic struggle, while her body was sustained by Divine power, because her natural strength had been exhausted. From the excessive rotting and stench, from the severe pains, the saint could neither eat nor sleep.

Before her death, the blessed one saw the Angelic powers and holy virgins who called her to Heaven. She was vouchsafed to behold the radiance of the Divine light and the place where paradise is. After this revelation she summoned the sisters to courageously endure temporal sorrows and not to give themselves over to faintheartedness. Then the venerable one told them that in three days she would be parted from the body, indicating with precision the hour of her death. At the time determined by the Lord, Saint Syncletica departed to the Lord and received from Him the rewards of the crown of asceticism — the glory and praise of the Kingdom of Heaven. And to our God Jesus Christ, with the Father and the Holy Spirit, be glory, honor, and worship, now and ever and unto the ages of ages. Amen.

The Life and Struggles of Our Father Among the Saints Epiphanius, Archbishop of Constantia in Cyprus, Who Flourished in the Fifth Century

The holy Abba Epiphanius was from the village of Visanduki, located three miles from Eleutheropolis in the region of Phoenicia. His father was engaged in agriculture, and his mother in processing flax. The father of the blessed one died early, when Epiphanius was only ten years old, and so his mother and younger sister Kallitropa were forced to live in rather straitened circumstances: often they lacked money for food. All their wealth was an unruly ox. Once the mother said to Epiphanius that he should go to the market, sell this beast, and with the money obtained buy food. However the boy, knowing the animal's temperament, opposed this:

"You know that our ox is unruly, and if I go to sell him, then the people at the fair, seeing him, will punish me," he said to his mother.

"Go, child, and the God of our fathers Abraham, Isaac, and Jacob will make him obedient, so that you can sell him, and we may acquire with this money all that is needful," the mother insisted.

Calling upon God for help and fulfilling obedience to his mother, Epiphanius took the animal and led him to the market. There the ox calmed down, became gentle, and attracted the attention of a Jewish merchant named Jacob.

"Since we are of one faith, child, and are servants of the Righteous God, let us observe fairness in the sale of the ox, so that you are not wronged and I suffer no harm," he addressed Epiphanius. "Thus we shall not afterward bring a curse upon ourselves, and God will not be indignant with us, but we shall attract blessings, because He Himself said: *'He who blesses you is blessed, and he who curses you is cursed'*" (Numbers 24:9).

Hearing this, Epiphanius became very frightened:

"I no longer want to sell the ox, because this animal is unruly. My mother ordered me to sell him so as to buy food. Our father has died, and we are in great need. However, now I have heard from you that to harm one's neighbor is bad. I fear God and do not want you to curse me for an unruly animal," he suddenly said to the old Jew.

"Child, take this as a blessing, go to your mother and give it to her, so that you may buy food. Take the ox with you as well. If he abandons his unruly temperament, then let him serve you at home, but if he does not abandon it, then lead him out of the house, lest he kill any of you," Jacob replied to the surprised boy.

Epiphanius took the three coins and the ox and set off for home. On the way he was met by a certain Christian named Cleobius, who asked to buy the beast from him. At that moment the ox became agitated and struck Epiphanius with his hoof on the thigh, from which he fell to the ground and began to weep from pain. Then Cleobius made the sign of the Cross three times over Epiphanius's sore spot and—O miracle!—the boy was immediately able to stand up, no longer feeling any pain whatsoever.

"O unruly animal, because you wanted to kill your master, in the name of Jesus Christ the Crucified, you shall no longer move from this place," the Christian said to the ox. And at that very moment, having breathed its last, the beast fell down.

"Who is this Jesus the Crucified, in whose name such signs and wonders occur?" Epiphanius inquired in bewilderment.

"This Jesus is the Son of God, whom the Jews crucified," said Cleobius.

The boy was afraid to reveal to him that he was a Jew, but at once hastened home, where he told his mother about the events of the day. A little time passed, and his mother made the decision to send Epiphanius as an apprentice to a craftsman, so that her son might learn to earn money for food through a trade. There lived in Eleutheropolis a certain Jewish teacher of the law, a wonderful and God-fearing man named Tryphon. He had an estate in the village of Epiphanius. Once, while visiting it, Tryphon came to the mother of Epiphanius.

"Would you like to give Epiphanius to me, so that I may adopt him as a son, and you with your daughter will receive all that is necessary from my house?" he proposed to the poor widow.

Hearing such a proposal, the mother of Epiphanius rejoiced greatly and immediately gave her son to him. Tryphon began to carefully instruct him in the Law of Moses and Jewish learning, so that afterward he could become a worthy husband for his only daughter. However, the Lord decreed otherwise: the maiden soon died, and Epiphanius remained alone with him, and so Tryphon bequeathed to him all his property. Upon his mother's death the young man took his sister into Tryphon's house, and together they came to possess all his property.

Once, when Epiphanius went to look at his fields, he met a certain monk named Lucian, a wonderful and educated man, who before his tonsure had been a renowned calligrapher. Having become a monk, he earned money by this craft, which he then distributed to the poor. Epiphanius was riding in a wagon drawn by oxen, while Lucian was going on foot. Both met a poor man.

"Man of God, have mercy on me, because I have not eaten anything for three days," he fell down in supplication before Lucian.

Having nothing to give him, the monk took off his garment and handed it to the beggar with the words:

"Go to the village, sell the garment, and buy yourself food."

When Lucian took off his garment and gave it to the beggar, Epiphanius saw how a garment white as snow descended from heaven and covered him. Epiphanius felt great fear and, getting down from the wagon, also fell at Lucian's feet.

"I beg you, man, tell me, who are you?" he addressed the blessed one.

"Tell me first what faith you are, and then I will tell you who I am," the abba answered him.

"I am a Jew," Epiphanius confessed.

Being clairvoyant, Lucian understood that the grace of God had descended upon this Jew:

"How is it that you, a Jew, ask a Christian who he is? For to Christians, Jews are an abomination, just as Christians are to Jews. Therefore, having heard that I am a Christian, ask me nothing more."

"And what prevents me from becoming a Christian?" the youth dared to ask.

"What prevents you is that you do not wish it. If you wish, then you can," the monk said wisely.

Moved with compunction by these words, Epiphanius did not go to the village to look at his fields, but took Lucian, brought him to his house, and showed him all the riches that were in it.

"Father, here is my property, and here is my sister. I want to become a Christian and live the monastic life. What do you say to this?" he addressed the saint.

"Child, these things hinder you from becoming a monk. Therefore, give your sister in marriage and give her all that is necessary, and distribute the rest to the poor. Only after this will you be able to live as befits a monk."

"First, father, make me a Christian, and then I shall fulfill what you have commanded me," Epiphanius persisted.

"I cannot make you a Christian; only a bishop can do this," Lucian explained to him and left the house.

"I want to become a Christian and live the monastic life," the youth later revealed his intention to his sister.

"As you wish to do, so also do I wish," Kallitropa supported him.

Meanwhile, Lucian informed the bishop of Epiphanius's intention, and the master blessed him to instruct the young Jew in Christian doctrine and then bring him to the church for the divine service. Then the blessed one returned to Epiphanius's house, catechized him and his sister, and then led them to the bishop. When Epiphanius approached the outer gates of the Christian church and stepped up onto the first step, the shoe fell from his left foot. And when he stepped with his right foot, the same thing happened. Seeing this, Lucian was amazed, and the shoes remained lying on the stairway leading to the church. Epiphanius did not pick up the shoes that had fallen from his feet and never again wore footwear. During the reading of the Gospel the master saw that the face of Epiphanius was radiant and a beautiful crown appeared on his head. Seven days after the completion of the Mystery of Baptism, Epiphanius brought Lucian and Vernika—a holy virgin who had become the spiritual mother of his sister—to his house. Giving a thousand gold coins to his godmother, he entrusted his sister to her and sent them to the monastery where Vernika was abbess. Epiphanius himself, having sold all his property, distributed the money he received to the poor, keeping for himself only forty coins for the purchase of sacred books, and went to the monastery of Lucian, where ten monks dwelt in hesychia, practicing calligraphy and obtaining their sustenance from it. All this occurred in the year of Epiphanius's sixteenth birthday. In that monastery there was a monk named Hilarion, second after Lucian, adorned with many signs and gifts. Similarly there struggled there a monk named Claudius. It was these two whom the young monk began to imitate in all things. Upon the departure of the blessed Lucian to the Lord, Hilarion became the abbot of the monastery. His food, once every two, and sometimes three or four days, was a small quantity of bread with salt and a little water. Such a manner of life Epiphanius also chose for himself and adhered to this regimen all his life. The place where the monastery was located was waterless. The brethren had to go for water during the night, five miles away. Once some travelers passed along that road, having with them animals loaded with wineskins full of wine. Since the heat was extremely intense, they became very thirsty and for this reason entered the monastery. But there was no water in the monastery at that moment, and the travelers were threatened with death. The brethren were greatly grieved because of this and began to weep.

"Believe me, brethren, that our Lord Jesus Christ, who in Cana of Galilee turned water into wine, will make from this wine water," the divine Epiphanius addressed the monks, taking the wineskins filled with wine.

And—O miracle!—the wine at that very hour turned into water. The travelers drank, watered their animals, and revived. But this miracle caused amazement both in the brethren and in the travelers. The saint was compelled to leave the monastery, because the travelers spread the word about this throughout all the surrounding regions. Epiphanius went away to a more desolate place, and not knowing where to look for him, all the brethren were grieved.

At that time some Saracens were passing near his cell. Being malicious mockers, they began to jeer at the hermit and even wanted to beat him. However, as soon as a fierce one-eyed brigand raised a knife over Epiphanius, the blind eye of the man opened. Seized with great fear, the Saracen threw down his sword and stood motionless. His companions, noticing that he stood motionless, came up to them. Seeing that his eye had opened, they froze in amazement. Then the abba began to speak calmly and with humility to them. The brigands thought that he was a god and compelled him to go with them. Following them for three months, the saint hindered them from committing lawlessness. However, this troubled the band and they asked Epiphanius to leave them. Having instructed the Saracens to a considerable degree, the blessed one warned them in parting that if they did not cease doing evil deeds, then they would not be able to live in peace and be happy. Then the Saracens brought him to the place where he had lived before and, having built him a dwelling, left him in peace. I, being one of them, but instructed by the saint in the word of truth and the faith of Christ, remained to live together with him. After six months had passed, the saint and I went to the monastery of Hilarion the Great. The brethren greatly rejoiced at our coming, and after a few days in this monastery I too was vouchsafed to receive from the abbot the Mystery of Baptism and was named John. We spent ten days there, and during all this time the brethren asked Saint Epiphanius to remain with them in the monastery, to which he did not consent. On the way home we met a youth possessed by one of the demonic princes. The divine Epiphanius took pity on him and in a loud voice cried out:

"In the name of the Crucified Jesus Christ I command you, unclean demon, to come out of this creature of God."

Immediately the demon convulsed the youth, threw him to the ground, and cried out:

"You are driving me out, Epiphanius, from my place, but know that I shall go to the Persian king and make you come there with great sorrow."

After these words the youth came to his senses and fell at the feet of the saint, who raised him up and sent him home in peace. And that evil one did indeed go to Persia and, having entered the king's daughter, began to torment her as he had once tormented the youth.

"O King, if Epiphanius does not come, who sent me into your daughter, I shall not come out of her," the demon constantly repeated and called for Epiphanius.

Hearing such words from the demon, the king sent many people to Phoenicia to seek the ascetic. However, the labors of the soldiers were in vain: they could not find the hermit. But the unclean spirit revealed to the king that Epiphanius lived in a place called Spanidrion, and the next time the soldiers found the divine one. Coming at night to the door of his cell, they began to knock, but since the saint was praying at that hour, he not only did not open to them but did not even respond to the knocking. Becoming enraged, they wanted to break down the door; one of them drew his sword from its sheath and was about to raise his hand for the blow. But at that moment his hand froze in the air and withered. Then fear fell upon the others, and they ran far from the cell. The abba opened the door only after a long time, when he had finished his prayer rule.

"Have mercy on me, servant of the immortal gods," the soldier who had suffered cried out to Epiphanius.

"What do you want from a sinful man?" the blessed one asked in surprise.

"I came here healthy, and behold, my hand has withered."

"You came healthy; become healthy again," Epiphanius said, and as soon as he took him by the hand, it became healthy like the other.

Seeing this miracle, all fell at the feet of the saint and bowed down to him. Then they revealed to him the reason for their visit. Hearing the words of the messengers, the saint understood that the demon he had cast out of the youth had entered the king's daughter and was tormenting her.

"Let us go, child, together with these people to Persia," Epiphanius addressed me.

"Father, the king sent us for you, and so we have brought with us an animal for you to ride upon," the soldiers rejoiced upon learning of the hermit's decision; they seated us on a camel and conveyed us to their country.

After thirty days of travel we arrived in the land of the Persians and stopped at a place called Urion. Three of our escort went to the king to report our arrival, after which he commanded that we be brought to him. The saint went with such boldness as if it were not at all a matter of meeting with a king, while I, at the sight of the multitude of people standing before him, was greatly afraid. When Epiphanius approached the ruler, the king wanted to rise from his throne, but the abba calmed him and urged him not to grieve over his suffering daughter:

"My Helper is the God who loves mankind, who will drive out the evil demon; only believe in Him and you shall see your daughter healthy. Bring her here and you shall behold the grace of the Lover of mankind, Jesus," he said to the Persian king.

"Come to your senses, maiden, and bow down to your father, for the wolf shall no longer possess you," he called to the maiden, whom they brought to the divine one, and made the sign of the Precious and Life-giving Cross over her three times. "As you entered the king's daughter, so come out of her and go to uninhabited places," the saint proclaimed to the demon, and the evil one at that very minute came out of the maiden.

"Rejoice, O King, for the wolf has left your daughter," he addressed the astonished father. "And you, daughter, go rejoice with your mother. And from this day keep your body and soul pure and undefiled by sin, and then the evildoer devil will never again come near you," the abba warned the princess.

After this the amazed ruler and his retinue began to beg Epiphanius to remain in Persia and teach his sorcery to all the local magicians.

"O sorcerer, enemy of truth, learn not to utter lawless words," the saint said to the chief magus of the country. "Do not think that a servant of God is a minister of lawlessness. Come to your senses, I tell you, and remain speechless."

And immediately the magus lost the gift of speech and froze motionless. Then the king and all who were present there fell to the ground from fear, but the blessed one raised the king and gave a sign to the people that they too should rise from their knees, and then he said to the magician:

"Consider what you see and hear. Do not think that I am a sorcerer, for I am a servant of the Crucified Jesus Christ. In His name, begin to speak again, but now become a friend of the Truth."

At that very moment the magus began to speak again and started to ask the saint for forgiveness, saying that he had sinned. The king then commanded that gold, silver, pearls, and precious stones be brought and laid all this before the saint.

"Father, take all this and remember me," the ruler said to the venerable one.

"For the sake of heavenly gifts we despise all this, since these are false and worthless goods of this world. Do not burden me with this gift, because Christ has taught me to do without it. Take it back and place it in your treasury, where wealth will lie as a dead weight, always idle. You will care for it, but you will receive no benefit for your soul from it, for you will only think about how to destroy souls with the help of gold given you by the Lord for offerings to those in need.

Therefore, act justly, abide with God, and as He gave gold to you, so also give it to the poor, lest at the future judgment you be condemned and cast *'into outer darkness'*" (Matthew 8:12). Then you will remember my just words, but already without any benefit. But if you listen to me now, you will always rejoice. Have no need of this world and its goods, and the whole world will be subject to you. Yes, and carefully beware of sorcerers, lest they seduce you with the law of darkness. I wished to tell you many other things as well, but you are not attentive to me, because your thought is on the table. Therefore, go and eat everything in moderation," Epiphanius instructed the king.

"Father, let us go together, let us partake of the meal," the king invited the saint.

However, the divine abba refused his hospitality and was satisfied only with a small quantity of the bread offered. The next day the ruler summoned the saint to himself, and when the venerable one came, he rose from his throne and threw his scepter to the ground.

"O King, pick up your scepter and thank God who gave it to you," the blessed one admonished the ruler.

"I beg you, father, remain with us, and I will do everything that you tell me," the sovereign began to entreat him.

"If you keep my words, then I shall remember you wherever I may be," the abba promised him and remained in the royal palace for ten days.

After this time had passed, Epiphanius charged the king to rule his country peacefully, not to go to war against the Romans, lest he become an enemy of the Crucified Jesus Christ and perish by an evil death at the hands of his adversaries. After this the king with his court decided to escort us to our home. On the way from the palace the travelers saw a funeral procession: they were carrying the dead child of a certain Persian prince, in order to throw him to be devoured by dogs (for the Persians had a custom of throwing the dead to dogs). But the saint addressed those carrying the child with a request to set the bier on the ground, so that he might look upon the deceased.

"O King, the dead should be buried in the earth, not thrown to be devoured by dogs. Know that evildoers live in your realm, who untimely kill people, as, for example, this child. Evil people have lawlessly killed him by means of magic. But my God, who was crucified on the tree, will raise him before all," with these words he took the dead child by the hand and in a loud voice addressed God with a prayer, beseeching Him to resurrect this youth.

Taking off his cloak, Epiphanius threw it over the bier, for the Persians have the custom of carrying the dead naked, and immediately—O miracle!—the son of the eminent parents arose and thanked the saint. Then the ruler thought that before him stood a god himself, but the blessed one reassured him:

"Do not think such a thing about me, O King, because I am a mortal man like yourself, but my God, in whom I have believed, grants such signs to be performed by those whom He loves."

"How many armed soldiers do you need, father, to guard you on your way?"

"I have God, who protects me with His armed host—the Angels."

"Go in health, O Epiphanius, glory of the Romans, and remember us also who live in Persia," the ruler bowed down to the abba and let him go in peace.

Having parted, we came to our home. After three days our drinking water ran out.

"O Lord our God, who cleft the rock, brought forth water from it, and gave drink to the thirsting people, cleave this earth and cause a spring of water to flow from it beside the dwelling of the poor," the venerable one prayed, turning to the east.

And immediately in that place there spread an ineffable fragrance. The blessed one made three prostrations to the ground, took a spade and dug a little, after which a small amount of water came forth. Then he dug some more, and from the previously dry earth there came forth so much water that the earth became fruitful: many vegetables grew there, and this attracted wild beasts to our dwelling, which began regularly coming to eat these fruits. Then the saint stood by the plants and conversed with the beasts as if they were people:

"Beasts, why do you cause me so much trouble? I, a sinful and poor man, came here to bewail the multitude of my sins, and God comforted me, giving me vegetables for food, but you come here and eat them. God Himself commands you no longer to come here and harm the plants."

Hearing the words of the venerable one, the beasts, as if they were rational people, immediately left that place and from then on no longer came to us. But the Saracens learned of our return from Persia. They came to the divine Epiphanius to receive a blessing and built beside the former cell three more, and then returned to their own land. Thus throughout all of Phoenicia the rumor spread that the abba was living in Spanidrion. Other brethren gathered around him, and now there were eight of us dwelling there.

Once we went to visit the monks in the monastery of Saint Hilarion. Here, as always, they received us with great joy and kept us for several days. The devil took advantage of this circumstance: he assumed the form of Epiphanius and appeared in our monastery. Seeing the apparent Epiphanius, one of the more negligent brethren ran up to him, fell to the ground, and bowed down to the evil demon. At that very hour the demon entered into him. The brother began running about in disorder here and there. At that moment the venerable Epiphanius, sensing the danger in spirit, said to Hilarion the Great:

"A wolf has entered our monastery and disturbed all the brethren."

Having bid farewell to the brethren, the abba and I set off for our monastery. Upon his return the blessed one prayed to the God who loves mankind, and the Lord delivered that negligent brother from the demon.

Another time three peasants came to the monastery, one of whom was possessed by a demon, and his two companions asked the saint to cast the demon out of him.

"Take your brother, children, and go in peace. In the name of Jesus Christ he is now free from all evil."

Believing these words of the venerable one, they departed, and before they reached their homes, the demon left the possessed peasant, and he became healthy.

In a certain desolate place about sixty miles from the monastery there lived a lion, which often came out of the thicket onto the road and devoured the people passing along it. And so one day all who used that road gathered together and came to the monastery to ask the saint to pray to God to drive away the lion.

"In the name of the Lord let us go there and look at the bloodthirsty one," the abba called to them.

When they approached the forest, the lion, seeing the divine Epiphanius, fell down and breathed its last. Seeing the dead beast, all were amazed, and the blessed one only remarked on this:

"If you believe in Jesus Christ, then all who devise evil against you will fall in just the same way."

Along with the other gifts given by God to the saint, Epiphanius skillfully interpreted Holy Scripture: when he read the Old or New Testament to the brethren, he immediately explained the meaning of the passage read.

At this time in the region of Edessa there lived an amazing philosopher and rhetorician, also named Epiphanius. He wanted to converse with the educated wonderworker who knew how to interpret Scripture. Coming to the monastery, he bowed down to the saint.

"I marvel at you, philosopher, and am perplexed as to why you, a great orator, made such a journey to come and see me, a sinner," the abba said to him.

"Beloved teacher, do not marvel at this, because in conversation many words are spoken, and where many words are spoken, one can learn much that is new," the philosopher answered him.

Then Epiphanius opened the Book of Genesis. The philosopher did not accept some points of the Old Testament and contradicted others. And so they conversed for three days, reaching no agreement. However, observing the life and conduct of the saint, the orator came to love the venerable one, and on the fourth day he said:

"Teacher, this is a good place; if you permit, I too would like to live here."

"This depends entirely upon you; if you wish, live here."

"May I bring my books with me?"

"Bring them."

"But I shall not go out from here again, and so I beg you, send Callistus, and let him bring my books and all my belongings."

That Callistus was the son of Aëtius, the first eparch of the city of Rome, and he had once been possessed by a demon. One night in a dream he saw Saint Epiphanius.

"Callistus, do you wish me to cast the demon out of you?" he asked the youth.

"And who are you, master, that you can cast out the demon?"

"I am Epiphanius from Phoenicia of Palestine; I live in the Spanidrion monastery. If I cast the demon out of you, will you come live in my monastery?"

"Cast out the demon from me, master, and I will come live in your monastery," the young man promised.

"See that you do not act otherwise, or else the demon will enter you again."

Upon awakening, Callistus told his dream to his father, and from that day he was no longer tormented by the demon, and so after three months he asked his father to let him go to the monastery of Epiphanius. The father did not oppose his son's wish, gave him money, and blessed him for monastic life. In Phoenicia Callistus found the saint and, having told him about everything that had happened, settled with him. He it was who, together with two youths, according to the command of Father Epiphanius, set off on camels to Edessa and brought the philosopher's books to the monastery.

From that day the saint and the philosopher spent much time every day in disputes.

"The Prophet Daniel says: *The judges were seated, and the books were opened*" (Daniel 7:10). "Bring your books here, and I will bring mine, which God has granted me. Let us sit and judge between ourselves," the venerable one said one day to the orator and placed Holy Scripture on the right, while the philosopher placed his books on the left.

They began their discussion from the creation of the world. Epiphanius expounded as it is written in the Book of Genesis by Moses, while the philosopher expounded according to Hesiod. They read these two books and then began to dispute. But light was light, and darkness remained darkness, that is, the origin of the world according to Moses was true, while according to Hesiod it was false. Moses wrote the Book of Genesis by the grace of God, while Hesiod had life from God but his errors from demons. And for a whole year the thrice-blessed one was unable to convince the philosopher...

In those days seven peasants brought to the monastery a certain possessed man, and since these seven could not restrain him, they bound the unfortunate man with chains. Then the saint asked the philosopher to call upon the multitude of his gods to cast the demon out of the youth. The orator thought that Epiphanius said this because he had lost the dispute.

"Philosopher, what do you say about this youth? Either you will heal him with the help of your gods, and I will believe in them, or my God, the Crucified One, will heal him, and you will believe in Him," the divine abba said, perceiving the false thoughts of the philosopher.

However, the pagan did not believe that the words spoken by the wonderworker could be true. He thought that he had spoken them out of pride.

"Do you wish me to remove the iron fetters from your hands?" Epiphanius addressed the possessed youth.

Hearing this, the philosopher became frightened with fear and locked himself in his cell. "This monk wishes to remove the fetters from the demoniac in vain. I had better flee, lest I suffer some evil from him," the orator thought.

"I, the sinful Epiphanius, a servant of the Lord, command you in the name of Jesus Christ the Crucified, the Son of God, to come out of this man and enter him no more," the venerable one proclaimed.

The demon immediately came out, and reason returned to the youth, and he came to a normal state. Then, opening the door, the philosopher saw that the youth was healed and ran to bow down to the saint.

"O Epiphanius, victor and crowned one, I believe your words through your deeds, namely, through this miracle which I see. For words, being fruitless, shake the air, but deeds have fruit and are visible. Therefore I too wish to become a servant of the Crucified One," the pagan addressed the blessed one in confession.

"Why do you marvel, philosopher, thinking that I performed this miracle? No, not I, but the Son of God performs miracles through those who believe in Him," the abba enlightened him.

Having understood all that he heard, the philosopher asked the saint to baptize him. This glorious event took place in the monastery of Hilarion the Great. After the completion of the Mystery, the divine teacher asked Hilarion the Great to send one brother together with the newly-enlightened Epiphanius (for thus they named the philosopher) to the bishop of Eleutheropolis, where he was ordained to the priesthood.

"He who formerly thought of himself that he was a great philosopher, although in reality he was nothing, has by the grace of Christ become a true philosopher and a worthy priest. Henceforth he will be your spiritual father," the venerable one said to the monks of his monastery upon the return of Father Epiphanius.

Thus the philosopher was vouchsafed to receive a gift from God and become abbot for all the brethren. The saint, however, since many people came to the monastery and gave him no peace, decided to leave there for the remote regions of Egypt.

"Children, I want to go visit the brethren in the monastery of Hilarion the Great," Saint Epiphanius said to the brethren.

However, they understood that he wanted to leave the monastery, fell at his feet, and with weeping and lamentation begged him not to leave. Taking pity on them, the saint promised for a time not to leave them, but not even ten days had passed when he called me, and at night we departed. First we came to Jerusalem, where we venerated our life—the Precious Cross of the Lord—and then, having visited all the holy sites and venerated them, we proceeded to Egypt. On the way we met a woman possessed by a demon, who seized the cloak of the thrice-blessed one and tore it. At that very moment the demon came out of her, and the unfortunate woman began to ask the abba to forgive her deed.

"Go to your home in health, and he who tore my cloak has departed," the wonderworker comforted the woman and continued on his way, descending to Joppa, called by all Giafa, from whence he sailed to Alexandria.

There we met a Jewish teacher of the law named Aquila. The saint began a conversation with him from the Old Testament, and a fierce dispute broke out between them. The next day they began to converse again, and this continued for quite a long time. This time the words of the saint convinced Aquila, and he wished to become a Christian. Epiphanius brought him to Athanasius the Great, the Pope of Alexandria, so that he might catechize and baptize him. We then departed from that country and on the way to Upper Thebaid met one of the disciples of Anthony the Great named Paphnutius.

"Bless us, father," the divine Epiphanius addressed him.

"Blessed are you of the Lord," the venerable one answered him.

Then the saint asked Paphnutius to tell him about the struggles of Anthony the Great, and after his wondrous account, he shared his intention to settle in Nitria.

"Go in health and greet the fathers there, gather the mountain grass, and proceed to Cyprus. *'Prepare fleece for your clothing and honor your young men, that they become lambs'*" (Proverbs 27:25–26), Paphnutius said to him, and after making a prayer, each of us went his own way. (These words are taken from the twenty-seventh chapter of the Proverbs of Solomon, the twenty-fifth verse, and served as a prophecy of the divine Paphnutius concerning what was to happen to Saint Epiphanius.)

In the vicinity of Leontopolis there lived a monk named Hierakas, who fasted greatly, not even partaking of oil, and did not consume wine. Some considered him a saint who possessed the gift of clairvoyance. Epiphanius also wished to see him and came to his monastery. A multitude of people had gathered there to hear his teaching. Seeing the saint, this monk asked where he was from and what his name was. Learning that this was Epiphanius from Palestine, he became very frightened, because the rumor had spread about the venerable one as a learned man and clairvoyant, but he nevertheless continued to teach the people. Thus, reasoning about the resurrection, Hierakas said that in the future age the human body which we now have will not be resurrected, but another will be resurrected in its place, while this one—according to the saying: *"For dust you are, and to dust you shall return"* (Genesis 3:19)—will crumble to dust. Besides this he said that after the resurrection children will not be perfect in stature. Hearing this, the saint became grieved and said to the monk:

"Let your mouth be silenced, that you may learn not to blaspheme."

And immediately, at the word of the venerable one, Hierakas froze in speechlessness, and all the people were amazed. And then Epiphanius began to teach them about the resurrection for three hours, citing testimonies from Holy Scripture in confirmation of his words.

"You have heard the true faith; henceforth speak to the people only the word of truth," the blessed one said at the end of his discourse.

At that very moment the tongue of the monk was loosed, and he repented before all that he had thought wrongly about the resurrection. In Upper Thebaid the divine Epiphanius met a man wondrous in virtue named John. He received us with joy and great love. Certain inhabitants of those parts brought to John, bound, a youth possessed by a demon, to leave him there. But as soon as the demoniac saw the saint, he cried out in a loud voice:

"Why have you come here, Epiphanius, servant of God?"

He cried out thus from the sixth until the ninth hour, and then, suddenly tearing his bonds, the possessed one ran up to the wonderworker and, seizing him by the feet, cried out:

"Servant of God, let me go, for the sake of the God in whom you believe."

This happened because earlier the divine abba had already forbidden the demon to come out of the youth, so that John would not learn that he cast out demons.

"Rise, man; why do you importune me?" Epiphanius said.

And immediately the evil one came out of the youth, and he became healthy and thanked the saint. We stayed with John for three days, and then descended to Bukoloi, where we spent seven years. However, even there people caused the venerable one great disturbance. Once a certain philosopher named Eudaemon came to him and conversed with him for ten days.

The thrice-blessed one demonstrated the truth to him from the Divine Scriptures, while the pagan opposed him with useless contentions. Together with Eudaemon came a child blind in one eye.

"Look, philosopher, how you are adorned with words, with wealth; you even have a multitude of gods. Why then have you not cared for your child and healed his eye?" the wonderworker asked the learned man.

"If in the whole universe there were only my child, who has one eye, then I would have cared for him. But if in all the world there is a countless number of people who cannot see at all, why should I care about one who has one eye?" the philosopher answered him with laughter.

"But if only your child were such, what would you do to heal him?"

"Nothing, only I would often reflect and say that there is no one else in the whole world like my child."

"Philosopher, do not turn my words into a joke, because God is in our midst. Bring your child here and you shall see the glory of God."

And at that very minute the saint took Eudaemon's child by the hand, made the sign of the Life-giving Cross three times over his blind eye, and—O miracle!—he saw. Then Eudaemon asked Epiphanius to make him a Christian. The venerable one brought him to the bishop, and he baptized the philosopher.

The fame of the divine abba spread throughout all of Egypt, and many hierarchs began to seek an occasion to ordain him bishop. But God, who was guiding the wonderworker, revealed their plan to him, so that we departed from there and returned to our homeland, to the monastery of Hilarion the Great, where the brethren met us with great joy, for Hilarion, on account of the disturbance caused him by people, had also left the monastery and gone to Cyprus, to the region of Paphos. We spent forty days in the monastery and then went to our own monastery, where Epiphanius of Edessa was abbot. At this time throughout all of Phoenicia famine set in because of a prolonged drought. A multitude of people came to Saint Epiphanius asking him to pray to the Creator for the granting of rain and the fruitfulness of the earth.

"Why do you tempt me, O people? I too am a sinful man," the abba answered them.

But the people did not desist, but continued to ask him all the more.

"Command the brethren to set tables and feed the people, that they may rejoice and go their way," the wonderworker asked the abbot.

When all sat down at the table, the saint went to his cell and, bowing his knees, asked God to give rain to the thirsting earth. And at that very minute the sky was covered with clouds, lightning flashed, thunder sounded, and a heavy rain began to fall. All rose from the table and thanked God. The rain continued for three days throughout all of Phoenicia. Then the people again came to the cell of the saint and asked him to stop the rain.

"Why do you think such things about me, children? For I, like you, am a sinful man. But God the Benefactor knows what is necessary for us and gives it to us," the venerable one tried to persuade them, but the laypeople continued to ask him even more fervently.

"Command that tables be set for the people; let them eat and drink, and then let them go their way," Epiphanius again said to the abbot.

Everything was arranged according to his word, the people sat down at the table and asked the saint to bless the food. But as soon as the blessed one said: "Blessed is the Lord," the rain immediately ceased. Because of the disturbance that people caused him, the divine abba again decided to withdraw. At that time the bishops of that country assembled to ordain a bishop for one widowed see. Having sought a worthy candidate, they decided to ordain Saint Epiphanius. For this they summoned a certain very pious monk named Polybius, who knew the venerable one, and said to him:

"Take a swift ox and ride to the monastery. If you see that Epiphanius is there, return and tell us of this. Be careful, do not reveal to anyone, not even to Epiphanius, that we have sent you."

Coming to the monastery, Polybius went to greet the wonderworker.

"Child, why have you come?" he asked the monk.

"Father, I always wish to speak only the truth," Polybius answered him.

"Child, you have come because the holy bishops sent you to see if I am here. But Epiphanius passes from place to place, bewailing and trembling for his sins, and is not worthy to be a bishop. But you, my child, remain here, and let the bishops themselves seek those worthy for the episcopate," the blessed one said.

Polybius obeyed Epiphanius and, sending the ox back, remained in the monastery. The Lord enlightened our wonderworker to go to Cyprus. That same night, taking me and Polybius, the venerable one left the monastery and went to Jerusalem. After three days, descending to the sea, we boarded a ship and arrived in Paphos, where we found Hilarion the Great. Meeting him was a great joy for us, so that we stayed with him for two months. Here too people coming to him caused Hilarion great disturbance.

"Child, where are you going?" Hilarion inquired when Epiphanius decided to continue his journey.

"To Gaza."

"Go to Salamis; there you will find a place to dwell," Hilarion the Great advised.

However, the saint did not want to go there, and so Hilarion again had to instruct the thrice-blessed one:

"I have told you, child, that you must go there and live there. Obey my words, or you will not escape danger at sea."

Descending to the sea, we found two ships in the harbor: one was sailing to Gaza, and the other to Salamis. We boarded the first. But as soon as we set out, such a violent storm arose that the ship almost broke apart. For three days we remained in despair, and on the fourth we reached Salamis with difficulty and, disembarking on shore, from great exhaustion and hunger lay on the ground for three days. Then, by the grace of God, we recovered, but the thrice-blessed one still did not abandon his intention and decided to depart from Salamis.

At that time, on account of the repose of the local master, all the bishops of Cyprus assembled in the city, wishing to ordain another person as the hierarch of Salamis. However, before this great event they fervently prayed and asked God to reveal to them the name of him who could shepherd the rational sheep of Christ in a manner pleasing to God. Among the masters was the Bishop of Kythrea, a man of holy life who had been vouchsafed to suffer as a martyr for the Lord. He was very old and had already headed his see for fifty-eight years. All the bishops considered him their spiritual father. It was to this hierarch named Pappos that God revealed that Saint Epiphanius should be ordained bishop of Salamis. The event described occurred at the time of the grape harvest, and before boarding the ship to sail to Gaza, the venerable one said to me and Polybius:

"Let us go to the market and buy grapes, so that we have food during the journey."

Coming to the market, the blessed one took two measures of good grapes and asked the seller what price he wanted, for the saint had a custom of not bargaining but giving as much as was asked. The seller named the price. At that same time Pappos came to the market, supported by two deacons, with three other bishops.

"Leave the grapes, abba, and follow us to the church," the master addressed Epiphanius.

Remembering the saying of Divine Scripture, *"I was glad when they said to me, 'Let us go into the house of the Lord'"* (Psalm 121:1), the wonderworker followed Pappos and came to the church.

"Father, pray," the Bishop of Kythrea said to him.

"Forgive me, father, I am not ordained (not having a sacred rank)," the divine one answered.

And immediately one of the deacons, at the blessing of Pappos, took Epiphanius by the head and with the help of the other deacons forcibly brought him into the altar, where the venerable one was ordained deacon, on the following day was ordained priest, and on the third day was ordained bishop.

"Command that tables be set for the fathers; let us eat and rejoice on account of your hierarchical ordination," the Bishop Pappos called upon the new master of Salamis.

But our abba, reflecting on the weight of the episcopate and greatly grieving over this, only wept.

"I should have been silent, but you, child, are the cause of my becoming a fool and revealing to you the meaning of what has happened. Know then that all these bishops who have gathered here to find a worthy candidate for archbishop laid this struggle upon me, a sinner, asking me to pray to God that He might reveal a worthy one. At the moment when I shut myself in and was asking God about this, lightning flashed in my cell, and I heard a loud voice saying to me:

'Pappos, Pappos, listen!'

I was greatly frightened and said:

'What do You command me, Lord?'

'Take two deacons with you and go down to the market; there a certain monk is buying grapes, and two other monks will be with him. His face resembles the icon of the Prophet Elisha, and his name is Epiphanius. Ordain him bishop. But do not reveal this to him immediately, lest he flee.'

I have become a fool by telling you this, because you compelled me. Therefore, consider what you are doing and attend to yourself, lest you be found an opponent of the will of the Most High, because I was sent by Him and have fulfilled what I was obliged to fulfill; therefore I am guiltless in this, but you—see to yourself."

Hearing this, Epiphanius fell to the ground and bowed down to Master Pappos.

"Do not be angry with me, father; I am a sinful man, and therefore am not worthy to ascend to the height of the episcopate, on account of which I grieve," the new bishop of Salamis said, bowed down to all the other hierarchs, and commanded that a meal be offered to them.

And when all had eaten and rejoiced, each went to his own diocese. Three days later a certain good and pious Christian named Eugnomon was thrown into prison by a rich man named Dracontius because he owed him a hundred coins. Being a foreigner and a citizen of Rome, Eugnomon had no one who could deliver him from prison. Learning of this, Master Epiphanius went to Dracontius and asked him to release Eugnomon.

"Go and bring me the hundred coins that your friend owes, and then you may take him," the malicious rich man set the conditions.

Then the saint went to the bishop's residence, took the hundred coins that were kept there for the needs of the Church, and gave them to Dracontius. But a certain very troublesome deacon named Charinus stirred up all the clergy of the diocese against the master.

"Behold, this foreigner Epiphanius has squandered all the Church's property. Come, let us drive him out, so that we will not be guilty of this sin."

Charinus wanted to drive out his bishop because he himself wished to be bishop.

"Epiphanius, are you not content that you came here without a cloak and received the Church, but now, being a stranger, you squander Church property! Who can endure this! Either return the hundred coins, or go back to your homeland," the enraged deacon said to him.

After such words, Eugnomon went into the city, sold everything he had, brought the money to the saint, and remained with him until his very death. Taking the money, Master Epiphanius gave a hundred coins to Charinus, and the rest to the poor.

"Take the hundred coins belonging to the Church; Epiphanius gave them, who earlier also spent them," Charinus said to the clergy.

However, none of the clergy wanted to take the money, but all decided to give it to the venerable one, from whom Charinus had unlawfully taken it. But the deacon did not give the money to the hierarch, but kept it for himself. Although this does not exhaust all the evils done by him to Epiphanius, the bishop never became angry with the unfortunate deacon. Once during a meal in the bishop's residence, when all the clergy were at the table and the saint was instructing them—for he had a habit of never letting the Gospel out of his hands, teaching the word of God day and night—a raven cried out loudly.

"Who knows what the raven said?" Charinus asked those at the table.

But no one answered him, because all were listening to the instruction of their hierarch.

"Who knows what the raven said?" the deacon asked a second time when the raven again cried out.

But the clergy again listened attentively to the word of God, which the thrice-blessed one was teaching, paying no attention whatsoever to Charinus.

"Which of you knows what the raven said?" the deacon addressed his fellow diners a third time.

"I know what the raven said," Epiphanius answered quite calmly, with a cheerful voice.

"Tell me what the raven said, and then you shall possess all my property."

"The raven said that you will not be a deacon."

And at that very minute terror fell upon Charinus: he could neither speak nor eat nor drink; with the help of servants the deacon was brought home, placed on a bed, and the next day he died. Charinus had a wife, a very pious woman of holy life, who, since she had no children, gave all her property to the Master and became a deaconess of the Church. For ten years she had suffered from a paralyzed hand, but as soon as the wonderworker made the sign of the Life-giving Cross over her, she became healthy. From that time all the clergy began to submit to the divine hierarch with fear and trembling.

The blessed Epiphanius had the following custom: during the celebration of the Divine Liturgy, when he performed the elevation of the holy gifts to God, if he did not have a vision, he would not conclude the service. (It is possible that this vision was the movement of the dove that in ancient times hung before the Holy Table, as is evident from the documents of the Seventh Ecumenical Paterikon, or some action or manifestation of the Holy Spirit that appeared to the saint during the consecration of the Gifts. The divine Amphilochius also writes the same about Basil the Great: when he celebrated the Divine Liturgy, he saw the Holy Spirit descend upon the Gifts. In the 150th chapter of the Spiritual Meadow it is described how a pious bishop did not continue the service because he did not see, as usual, the descent of the Holy Spirit.—Auth.) Thus, once he said three times: "And make this bread," but no vision followed. Then, with tears asking God to reveal to him the reason, the Master looked at the deacon standing with the ripidion to his left and saw leprosy on his forehead. From this it became clear to all that the deacon was the reason that the saint did not have a vision. Taking the ripidion from the deacon's hands, the abba quietly said to him:

"Go, child, to your house and do not receive Communion today."

After this he gave the ripidion to another deacon and again with fear and tears pronounced the divine words. Immediately a vision followed, and Epiphanius completed the Divine Liturgy. After the dismissal he called the deacon aside and asked him about the cause of this leprosy. The priest related to him that he had slept with his wife that night. Then the venerable one, calling all the priests, quietly said to them:

"My children, you who have been vouchsafed to receive the Mystery of the Priesthood must keep yourselves in purity from all defilement of flesh and spirit, so as not to celebrate the Divine Mysteries unworthily."

From that time the saint no longer ordained married men, but only monks, venerable men, and tested widowers, and everyone truly saw the Church as a beautiful bride, adorned with a holy and virtuous priesthood.

Written by his disciples John and Polybius

****

May God the Almighty be glorified, who gives us life and glorifies, as the word of God says, those *"who honor"* Him (1 Samuel 2:30).

At that time it happened that the venerable Father John, the disciple of Saint Epiphanius, fell gravely ill. Lying on his bed, he summoned me and said:

"Since the thrice-blessed one does not wish that the miracles which God performs through him be recorded, you, child Polybius, take these papers, where I have recorded the struggles of our abba, of which I was a witness up to this day, and henceforth record everything that he shall perform. For God will prolong his time of life. And see that you do not neglect this, because, by the command of God, I have recorded everything up to this day. After my death, record them yourself. Summon for me our venerable Father Epiphanius," John asked me.

"Father John, pray to God for the sinful Epiphanius," the Archbishop of Cyprus said to him, visiting the dying man.

"Offer a prayer, father, because I wish to speak with you."

"Father, place your hands upon my eyes and kiss me, because behold, I am dying," the venerable John said.

And as soon as Master Epiphanius placed his hands upon the eyes of his disciple and kissed him, John gave up his spirit. Falling upon his neck, the bishop wept and grieved for a long time over the death of his fellow struggler. After some time had passed, our wonderworker, prostrating himself on the ground, began to ask God to send help for the building of a church, because the old temple was small in size and did not accommodate all who desired to enter. And when he was praying, a voice came to him, and since the divine teacher often heard this same voice, he was not alarmed and asked:

"What does my Lord command?"

"Begin to build the church."

Immediately the saint came to the place where he wished to erect the temple and, having made a prayer and all that follows, brought there sixty builders and a multitude of workers, who began this God-pleasing work. At that time there lived in the city a very wealthy pagan named Dracon the Great, who had a son also bearing the name Dracon and suffering from severe pain in his right side. His father had spent much money on physicians, but they could not cure him. Once the saint was passing by the house where Dracon the Great lived with his sick child and many other people, and he greeted them. Then, taking the sick boy by the hand, he said to him:

"Dracon, be healthy as the others."

And—O miracle!—the youth was immediately healed. Seeing this, all froze in amazement, while the father of the healed one, from fear and horror, could not enter the house on his own feet, but with the help of servants was carried to his bed and laid upon it. The next day the wife of Dracon came to the bishop and asked him to come to their house and pray to God that the Lord might raise her husband from his bed of sickness. The venerable one did not make her beg for long, but at once hastened to the house of Dracon. As soon as the divine Epiphanius prayed, the dignitary rose from his bed, and at dawn the next day, taking five thousand coins, he came to the abba.

"To me, child, one garment for my body, bread, and water suffice; why do you add weight to me? But if you wish to be glorified, go, give the money for the building of the temple of God and to those who work there," the thrice-blessed one said to him.

Dracon the Great did so, and then asked the saint to baptize him and his household.

Another very wealthy pagan, Synesius, had an only son of thirteen years, who fell ill with a terrible disease; a swelling formed around his throat, which eventually strangled him. On account of the death of the only heir, the whole house of the pagan was filled with weeping and grief. A certain Christian named Hermias came to console the mother of the deceased:

"If you were to summon Master Epiphanius here so that he might pray to God for your child, then he would be raised."

Believing the words of Hermias, she sent him for the Archbishop of Cyprus.

"My master Synesius asks you to come to his house and pray to the Lord, so that his dead child may be raised."

And again the bishop immediately set off and proceeded to the house filled with sorrow.

"You have come here, great Christian physician; show your skill and raise our son, so that we too may see and believe in your Christ," the mother of the dead youth addressed the divine Epiphanius.

"If you believe in the Crucified Jesus Christ, you will see your son risen."

"There is nothing else in my thoughts except to attend to the Crucified Jesus."

Then, approaching the bed, the saint placed his hand on the neck of the child, rubbed it, and said with a joyful face: "Eustorgius!" And—O miracle!—the child immediately opened his eyes and sat up on the bed. All who were present froze in amazement, and the mother of the child, taking three thousand coins, gave them to the venerable one. He answered this gesture of hers thus:

"I do not need this, but let your husband Synesius take it and bring it to the temple of the Lord, who raised your son, and give it to those who labor there."

Synesius did so, and then the master baptized him together with his entire family. Since it was necessary to ordain another priest in place of the departed Father John, the wonderworker wished to take me. But I, reflecting on the great weight of this ministry, refused, and when the time came to go to the church, I decided to leave when the time came. When we came to the church, Bishop Epiphanius took me by the hand and said:

"Stand here until the time comes."

All who heard these words, but not knowing what they referred to, were surprised. But from that minute I could no longer move or go to another place, but was bound as if with iron. At the appointed time the Master sent a deacon for me, who brought me into the altar, where the hierarch ordained me to the priesthood. After the end of the service I fell upon my bed from fear and became ill. Thus I lay until the divine Epiphanius came and offered a prayer to God for me. Only after this was I able to rise from my bed and became healthy. Once a certain deacon, returning from Jerusalem, told the thrice-blessed one that Patriarch John of Jerusalem was a lover of money, was hoarding money and not distributing it to the poor.

Master Epiphanius knew the Primate of the Church of Jerusalem very well from the monastery of Hilarion the Great, where they had labored in salvation together. Out of old friendship the wonderworker wrote a letter to the Most Holy Patriarch of Jerusalem, that he should show mercy to those who needed it, but John did not listen to him. Then, taking me, the Bishop of Cyprus went to Jerusalem. There Patriarch John received us cordially and lodged us overnight in a very good house. Every day he invited the venerable one to his table and sent us many various foods and beverages, while the poor were deprived of everything and went hungry.

"Father, give me your silver vessels; I wish to entertain my Cypriot friends and impress them with your silver. Only I beg you, give me the very best that you have, for your own glory," Epiphanius asked the Primate of Jerusalem.

John brought him much silver tableware, to which the saint remarked:

"Father, if you have more, bring more, to impress my friends even more. Only remind me that I may afterwards return to you what you are giving me."

John brought him still more silver:

"Take all of it; receive your friends as you wish," the Patriarch generously lent his wealth.

Taking the silver vessels of John, of which there were up to fifteen hundred litrae, the saint sold them to a merchant, and the money obtained for them he began to distribute to the poor day and night. Much time passed, and John demanded his vessels back, to which the saint answered:

"Be patient a little, father, because I have not yet entertained the strangers, and then I shall return all that is yours to you."

Still more time passed, and one day we were in the Church of the Lord, where the Saving Wood of the Life-giving Cross is kept, when John again asked for his silver from Bishop Epiphanius.

"Father, I shall return it to you," the wonderworker answered the Most Holy. But John grew very angry, seized the saint by his robe and, choking him, said:

"Worthless Epiphanius, you shall not leave here, you shall not sit, you shall have no peace until you return to me the silver vessels that I gave you."

And thus he held him by his robe and reviled him for almost two hours, so that all who were present were already weary of standing and hearing the harsh words of John. However, the archpastor of Salamis was not in the least troubled or upset, but was very calm. At one moment he breathed into John's face, and the Patriarch was immediately blinded. All who were present were greatly frightened, and the Patriarch fell at the feet of the Master and began to ask him to pray to the Almighty for the restoration of his sight.

"Go and venerate the Precious Cross, and then you will receive what you ask," the divine teacher said to him.

But the Patriarch did not cease entreating Epiphanius. And then the abba, having instructed John as was fitting, laid his hand upon him and opened his right eye. The Primate of the Church of Jerusalem continued to ask for the restoration of his left eye as well.

"This is not from me, father. God closed, God opened. He has done as He willed, so as to instruct us," the saint admonished the Patriarch.

From that time John changed and became merciful and virtuous in all things.

When we were leaving Jerusalem to go to Cyprus, two blasphemers conspired among themselves to mock Master Epiphanius. One of them pretended to be dead and fell to the ground, while the other stood beside him, and when the blessed one was passing that way, the second said to him:

"Father, have pity on this dead man; cover him with something."

Hearing this, the saint turned to the east, prayed for the repose of his soul in the habitations of the righteous, and then, taking off his robe, covered the corpse with it. When the divine abba had departed, the joker threw off the covering and, laughing, addressed the one who had pretended to be dead:

"Get up; that simple man has gone."

But his companion did not answer anything. Then, lifting him up, they saw that he had indeed died. The fool ran, caught up with us, and, falling at the feet of the wonderworker, revealed the whole truth and asked him not to be offended by this deed, but to raise the dead man and take back his garment.

"Go, child, and bury him, because he died before you asked for the covering," the clairvoyant pleaser of God calmed him.

Descending to the sea, we boarded a ship and set sail for Cyprus, where the brethren received us with great joy. There was a certain Jewish teacher of the law named Isaac, a very pious man who carefully kept the Law of Moses. He was struck by the teaching of Christ expounded by Epiphanius, and was soon catechized by the Master, received Baptism, and began to live among us. At that time the sister of the Emperors Arcadius and Honorius was suffering from an incurable disease of the hand, from which her flesh was rotting. Having heard of Saint Epiphanius, she sent letters together with imperial servants to Cyprus, so that the bishop might be brought to Rome to heal her. The messengers who arrived on the island stopped at the house of a very wealthy pagan named Faustianus, who was very hostile toward the Archbishop of Cyprus.

"Why do you attend to this hypocrite as if he were God! He has only cold words and nothing more," he said to everyone.

One day, when the saint was observing the work of the craftsmen erecting the church, the imperial messengers and Faustianus were standing near him. One of the builders lost his footing and fell from a great height. In falling he struck Faustianus on the head, but he himself was not injured at all, while Faustianus fell to the ground as if dead.

"Rise, child, in the name of the Lord and go in health to your house," Epiphanius said, and at that very minute Faustianus stood up and went home.

His wife, having heard of the miracle performed by the saint, took a thousand coins and gave them to the blessed one, but he commanded that they be given to those working on the construction of the temple. There was a certain very pious and virtuous deacon named Philon, and since the archpastor of Karpasia had departed to the Lord, by revelation of God, the Master ordained him bishop of the widowed see. When Epiphanius decided to go to Rome, he gave him authority over his own diocese: Philon was to visit it and when necessary perform ordinations. Together with me and Isaac the venerable one set out for Rome, where in the imperial palace there was great sorrow because of the illness of the emperor's sister. Physicians made many efforts but brought her absolutely no relief, so that from great sorrow she begged her brothers to order a physician to give her some poisonous potion, that she might die sooner and be delivered from her pains. Entering the imperial palace, the wonderworker proceeded to the place where the emperors were sitting, and nearby their sister lay on a bed. As soon as they saw him, they immediately rose from their thrones and bowed down to him.

"Render the same honor to God, your Benefactor, and then you will see your sister healthy. Put your hope in Him, and you will be delivered from all evil," the Archbishop of Cyprus exhorted them.

But the brothers doubted the words of the abba.

"Why do you doubt, children? Now you will see the grace of God," he said. "Do not doubt, child, concerning your illness, but place your hopes in God and from this hour you will acquire health. Believe in the Crucified Son of God, and at this very hour you will rise from your bed. Your bodily pain has ceased, child. Glorify God, who has given you grace, and always remember Him, and He will preserve you all your life," Epiphanius said joyfully, approaching the sick woman, taking the princess by the hand, and making the sign of the Life-giving Cross over her three times.

And immediately she was freed from her pains and was healed. For the miracle performed, the emperors loved him with all their souls and henceforth believed everything he told them. They asked him to remain in Rome and be a father to them. The Master did so, instructing them in the word of God every day and strengthening them in the faith of Christ. One day the son of the healed princess was found dead in his bed, although he had not been sick. Therefore great weeping arose in the palace.

"Father, ask God that the dead one be raised," the emperors addressed the thrice-blessed one.

"Do you believe that I can do this?"

"We believe that just as you healed the child's mother, you will be able to set him alive before her."

"And if the child is raised, will you believe in the Crucified Jesus and be baptized?"

"Yes, we will believe and be baptized."

Then the saint made the sign of the Life-giving Cross over the body and, beseeching God, said to the child:

"In the name of Jesus Christ the Crucified, arise, child!"

And at that very hour the child arose and sat up on the bed, and the emperors immediately asked for Baptism.

"I accept your pious intention, but without the permission of the local hierarch I cannot baptize you," the bishop answered them.

Then the emperors summoned the Pope of Rome and told him about everything that had happened. Hearing about the miracle, the Pope rejoiced greatly and permitted Saint Epiphanius to baptize them. When the brothers entered the baptismal font and all that precedes the Mystery of Baptism had been performed, Arcadius, since he was the first to enter the font, looked attentively and saw three men in white garments, who stood one to the right, another to the left of the saint, and the third behind him. The emperor was greatly frightened by this vision, but the venerable one calmed him:

"Attend to yourself, child, and keep the mystery that you have seen."

The wonderworker was accustomed never to baptize anyone until he first saw the troubling of the water. And this time, as soon as the water was troubled, he baptized Arcadius. Then it was the turn of Honorius as well, who also had a vision. Later the great Mystery was performed upon the risen son of the emperor's sister, and then upon Procliane, his mother, who was the wife of a certain patrician. After Baptism the abba spent seven days with the newly-baptized, instructing them in the truth. At the end of this time, when the new members of the Church of Christ changed their baptismal garments for ordinary ones, the saint addressed the emperors thus:

"Children, abide in peace; the wolf shall no longer possess you. All sorrow, grief, and sighing have fled. Reflecting that there will be a resurrection of the dead, do not grieve over those who have died, because those who have believed in Christ and been baptized have been clothed in the Lord and have Him as their Helper. But the child who died before and was raised to receive the grace of Holy Baptism will depart to the Savior and behold Him in great glory, hymned by Angels." On the next day, when Epiphanius was instructing the emperors, an ineffable fragrance spread among us. Then the divine one said to the emperors:

"Rise, sons of light; let us pray."

And when we finished the prayer, all of us who were in the room heard: "Amen," as if pronounced by a multitude of people. And immediately the child of the emperor's sister gave up his spirit, as the blessed one had foretold. We remained in Rome for an entire year, and during this time Master Epiphanius performed many miracles and signs there. When we decided to return to Cyprus, the emperors asked him to take much gold for the needs of the Church, as well as for distribution to all who were in need. But the hierarch did not wish to take anything.

"You, children, give this to me for the poor, as the Lord also commanded. I rejoice in your mercy, but you give me only extra burdens, because God rewards all with what is necessary and feeds all in the present life," the wonderworker disclosed to them.

Leaving Rome, we came to Cyprus, where the brethren received us with great joy.

The archpastor had a custom of going at night to the cemeteries where the relics of the holy martyrs were buried, and asking God for all who were sorrowing and in straitened circumstances. And just as a friend gives to a friend what he asks, so too the Creator gave His servant everything that he asked of Him. At that time there occurred on the island a severe famine, so that even in the market there was no bread for sale. And the aforementioned Faustianus, having many granaries with wheat and barley, mercilessly raised the price and sold bread at a high price, giving bread to no one without money. Therefore there was great distress and severe hunger for the poor. Then the Master came to Faustianus and asked him to lend grain for the poor.

"Go and ask this of the God whom you worship. He will give you grain for your friends," the rich man snidely refused him.

But the Archbishop of Cyprus did indeed do so.

"Epiphanius, go to the temple of Zeus, the doors of which have been closed for so many years. They will open, and entering, you will find much gold there. Take it and buy all the wheat and all the barley of Faustianus and feed the poor," the Lord said to Epiphanius during the bishop's fervent prayer for his flock.

As soon as the saint heard this, he went, took the gold, and, having bought up all of Faustianus's grain, filled the granaries with it and distributed it to the whole city. And while there was abundance in all the surrounding regions, in the house of the rich man, because of his love of money, a difficult situation arose, for he had sold everything, leaving nothing even for his own people, and to ask the divine abba for bread the pagan considered a dishonor. Then he equipped five of his ships, and hired five more, so that his trusted man named Longinus might purchase grain in Calabria. On the way back from that region, when their native city was already visible on the horizon, a violent storm suddenly broke out at sea and sank all the ships, while the cargo was cast upon the shore. Hearing of what had happened, Faustianus went to see everything with his own eyes, and then began to rail against God and utter blasphemies against the Most High and against Epiphanius.

"Oh, how can I save myself from this sorcerer! He was not content with the evil that he caused me by his sorcery on land, but now he has sent demons upon the sea as well, which have sunk the ships together with the cargo of grain for my people. Oh, what wind brought this magician here, who causes us trouble?" he cried and threatened Epiphanius, after which he proceeded to his house.

And all the poor of the city—men, women, children—came to the shore and collected the scattered grain. Thus some filled their storehouses for an entire year, and others for two. The wife of Faustianus, however, was good by nature. Secretly from her husband she sent two thousand coins to the saint, so that he would give her bread, but the archpastor answered her:

"Leave the money at home, and take as much bread as you need. When your fields yield a harvest, then return to me the grain that you took."

In the bishop's residence there was a deacon-calligrapher named Savinus, extremely meek and virtuous. Among all the eighty brethren who were in the bishop's residence, he shone more than all others by his virtues. The venerable one entrusted to him the defense of the affairs of the Church in Cyprus. Once two men came before Savinus for judgment: one rich, the other poor, and the rich man was in the right. Standing in a hidden place, the bishop heard Savinus's decision in favor of the poor man, because he took pity on him. Then the Master revealed himself and said to Savinus:

"Go, child, and occupy yourself with calligraphy; remember the saying of Holy Scripture and, in passing judgment, become perfect and listen to what God the Benefactor says: *'Judge the poor righteously'*" (Psalm 71:2), and "do not be a hypocrite before the powerful."

And from that time the divine abba himself began to judge those who came for judgment, hearing cases from dawn until the ninth hour of the day. And from the ninth hour until the following morning he did not go out to anyone.

In the bishop's residence there was also another deacon-calligrapher named Rufinus, severe in appearance and bestial in character, who was in league with the rich man Faustianus. Every day he poured forth slanders against his hierarch, who softened his insolence with his great meekness. At the instigation of the pagan Faustianus and by the action of the devil, Rufinus conceived the desire to kill Master Epiphanius. Being the last among the deacons of the bishop's residence, he had the obedience of keeping the bishop's throne in order. Once he took a knife and stuck it into the throne with the blade pointing upward, and covered it from above with a cloth. However, when the blessed one wished to sit on the throne, he asked Rufinus to remove the covering, and when the deacon refused to do this, he lifted the cloth himself. At that moment the knife fell and was driven into the right leg of the impious one.

"Cease, child, to act disorderly, lest you soon suffer. Leave the church, because you are not worthy to partake of the Divine Mysteries," the divine one admonished Rufinus.

At the word of the bishop the deacon left the church, made his way to the bishop's residence, and, falling upon his bed, died after three days.

At this very time the legs of Theodosius the Great were paralyzed from the knees down. Confined to his bed, he lay for seven months. Then courtiers were sent to Cyprus by the emperor, so that our wonderworker might come to Constantinople and heal the sick man. When the messengers came to Cyprus to take the saint with them, the inhabitants of the diocese raised a lament and grieved, preventing him from leaving. When Epiphanius was leaving the island, all the Christians wept and begged for death. Because of this the saint was compelled to say to the courtiers:

"Go, children, to the emperor; I shall come after you."

"Do not be angry with us, father, because we shall not depart without you, for we have an order from the emperor that we go together. We cannot do otherwise, because in the opposite case we will endanger our lives. The emperor is sick and awaits your coming," they answered the archpastor of Cyprus.

Then the saint asked the Most Reverend Philon to take charge of his diocese, and then, having taught all the Christians what was needful, he bade them farewell, and we set out on our journey. In Constantinople, as soon as the saint approached Theodosius the Great, the emperor was barely able to utter:

"Father, pray to God for my health, for I am very ill."

"Believe, child, in the Crucified Jesus Christ and then you will always be healthy. Have God in your thoughts, and no evil will possess you. Be merciful to the sorrowing, and you will receive mercy from God. Honor God, who has given you the kingdom, and He will give you greater grace," the Master admonished the ruler, took him by the feet, and made the sign of the Life-giving Cross over them three times.

"Rise, child, from your bed, because the pain in your legs has passed," he again addressed Theodosius.

And—O miracle!—the emperor immediately rose from his bed, and his legs no longer pained him.

"Command me continually, father, and I shall obey you in all things," he exclaimed.

"Have the words of God in your soul and keep them. Do without Epiphanius, but glorify your Benefactor—God," the divine hierarch counseled the emperor.

When we were in Constantinople, Arcadius and Honorius came there from Rome and informed their healed father that the saint had come to them in Rome, had healed the sick hand of their sister, raised her dead son, and baptized them all. It was a great joy for the emperor to hear this, and from that time he considered the blessed one his spiritual father. At this time, by order of the emperor, the malicious Faustianus was brought from Cyprus to Constantinople and thrown into prison on a charge of insulting the emperor. Learning of this, Epiphanius came to the prison and asked the prisoner whether he wanted him to intercede with the sovereign on his behalf.

"Go, flatterer, to deceive simpletons, and do not speak such words to me. You have come here to rejoice over my misfortune, not to help me. Leave Cyprus and go to your homeland, to Phoenicia, and there continually practice sorcery and devise cunning," the pagan answered with malice to the kindness of the archpastor.

Leaving the prison, the saint went to the emperor to bid farewell, in order to return to Cyprus. But the ruler asked the thrice-blessed one to stay a few more days in the capital, to which he agreed. The next day an apocrisiarius came to Theodosius and announced that Faustianus had died. At this news the saint was saddened by the twofold death of the unfortunate man. The emperor wished to take into the treasury all the property of Faustianus, also because he had no children, but the saint forbade him to do this.

"Be careful, child; do not commit a sin, because the wife of Faustianus is a pious woman; she will distribute everything to the poor. Obey my words, and leave the property to his wife; then you will receive grace from God the Most High," Epiphanius exhorted him.

Then the emperor gave the saint authority over all the property of Faustianus, but to this the saint remarked:

"I, child, have God, who gives me all that is necessary, and all this, with the consent of the deceased's wife, we shall distribute to the poor."

When we were about to depart, the ruler said to the venerable one:

"Father, ask of me all that you need, and I shall give it to you with the greatest pleasure."

"I ask of you only one thing—to keep the commandments of which I have spoken to you and always to remember me."

Going out with us from the palace, Theodosius the Great asked the Master to bless him. Having made a prayer, Bishop Epiphanius blessed him and embraced him, and thus the emperor returned to the palace, and we boarded a ship and came to Cyprus, where the Christians received us with great joy. We found the wife of Faustianus bewailing the death of her husband. The saint consoled her in this sorrow, and then baptized her and made her a deaconess of the Church. All the property of Faustianus and her own, at the counsel of her hierarch, she distributed to those in need.

At that time in Salamis there were many people who held the heresy of the Valentinians and were under the influence of Bishop Aëtius. Once the divine Epiphanius was conversing with him about this heresy, but he contested all the arguments of the wonderworker.

"Impious Aëtius, put a bridle on your lips and speak no more blasphemy," the venerable one could not endure his shameful speeches, and at that very hour Aëtius became mute.

Then all who held to this heresy, seeing the miracle, fell before Epiphanius and, anathematizing the teaching of the Valentinians, accepted Orthodoxy. Aëtius, however, lived speechless for six days, and on the seventh he died. There were also other heretics on Cyprus: sophists, Sabellians, Nicolaitans, Simonians, Basilidians, Carpocratians, about whom

Epiphanius wrote to the emperor, asking him to expel them from Cyprus, because some of them, being wealthy, acquired public offices and caused great trouble to the Orthodox. Receiving the letter from the abba, the ruler issued a decree in which he spoke of the truth of the Orthodox teaching and of the prohibition against all those who held foreign teachings from residing on Cyprus. But whoever repents, confesses his errors before the common Father, and wishes to enter upon the path of truth, becoming Orthodox, let him remain on the island. After this decree was read aloud by the emperor's man, a multitude of heretics ran to the divine Epiphanius and became Orthodox. Those, however, who did not wish to leave their errors were immediately expelled from Cyprus.

At that time in Alexandria the Patriarch was Theophilus, a good acquaintance of the saint. There also lived the three sons of Heracleon, the Governor of Alexandria, who after their father's death decided to become monks. Withdrawing into the desert, they received the angelic schema there and led a life worthy of the monastic calling in great hesychia. Knowing of this, the Most Holy Theophilus brought them to Alexandria by deceit and made the eldest of them bishop of a certain Egyptian city, and the other two deacons and stewards of the Alexandrian Church. Having served thus for three years and seeing that, having abandoned hesychia, they had been deprived of divine grace, the brethren began to ask Theophilus to permit them to return to the place where they had formerly lived. But the Primate did not wish to give them permission. Then they secretly departed from the capital and settled in their former place. For such willfulness the Most Holy Theophilus excommunicated them from the Mystery of Communion for three years. The brethren asked him to permit them to partake of the Divine Mysteries, but the Patriarch did not allow them to approach the Holy Chalice. Therefore they came to Constantinople to Saint John Chrysostom, so that he might intercede for them before the Primate of the Church of Alexandria. Chrysostom wrote a letter to Theophilus with a request to release them from excommunication, but the Patriarch did not respond to the request of the divine archpastor. Then Theophilus received a second letter from Constantinople, but he still remained with his decision. All this led to John Chrysostom himself releasing the brethren from the prohibition, and for this reason there arose great sorrow between the Patriarch of Alexandria and the archpastor of Constantinople.

At that time there lived in Constantinople a certain senator named Theognostus, a good Christian, a favorite of the emperor, who had the fear of God. There also lived another senator, the Arian Dorotheus. He envied Theognostus, slandered him for reviling the emperor, and presented two false witnesses who accused him. Then the ruler ordered Theognostus to be exiled, and his property to be confiscated for the treasury. On the way to exile Theognostus died.

However, his wife still retained one estate, from which she fed herself. Once the Empress Eudoxia went out for a walk during the grape harvest to the place where this property was located, and for some unknown reason entered the vineyard and plucked a grape. Some of those with her remarked that this was someone else's vineyard, but now it had become hers, because the emperors had a custom: if they stepped on someone else's land or plucked a fruit from someone else's tree, then from that moment it was no longer the owner but the emperor or empress who owned it.

As soon as the wife of Theognostus learned that the empress had taken her property, she wrote a letter to the divine Chrysostom, and he sent his archdeacon Eutychius, an educated man adorned with all virtues, to ask the empress to return the property to the widow. However, the empress refused to do this, citing the law. She offered to transfer to the widow, in place of her estate, a vineyard in any other region. Then Saint John himself went to Eudoxia and began to entreat her to return to the widow her very property.

"Father, first learn the reason and then say that I have encroached on the property of a widow. Do not reprove emperors to their face," the empress objected to him.

"Again I say to you, return the property to the widow, for you have heard how Jezebel is condemned in Holy Scripture for lawlessly taking the vineyard of Naboth," the teacher of the Church tried to bring her to reason.

Hearing this, the empress ordered Chrysostom to be driven out of her chambers. Leaving there, the divine John went to the church and said to Eutychius:

"When the empress goes to the church, take the deacons with you and stand at the door through which she usually enters, and do not let her enter, saying that John has forbidden her to enter the church."

Eutychius did as the saint commanded him, and from that time the empress began to seek a way to send the archpastor of the capital into exile. When Theophilus learned of this, he began to plot much against the hierarch of Constantinople. Thus he wrote and sent Saint Epiphanius many letters against him, in which he reported that he held the teaching of Origen, and that the empress wished to send him into exile. The bishop once had some urgent matter requiring him to visit Constantinople. Hearing such rumors from Theophilus about the divine Chrysostom, our hierarch wished all the more to go to the capital, but not in order to harm John, but rather to help him. He took me and Isaac with him. When we arrived in Constantinople, the streets of the city were filled with crowds of inhabitants, indignant at the prejudiced attitude of the emperor and empress toward their hierarch, whom they loved and honored. We stopped at a certain monastery that was supported by the court of the empress and therefore did not receive Chrysostom. Since there was no deacon in the monastic church, the fathers begged Epiphanius to ordain a deacon for them. Hearing that in his diocese an ordination had taken place without his knowledge, the divine Chrysostom was greatly grieved and wrote a letter to the Bishop of Cyprus, which caused him sorrow. The Master wrote a reply to Chrysostom. The empress, however, learning of the situation that had developed, invited Epiphanius to her.

"Father, the whole Roman Empire is mine and is under my authority, while all the priesthood and all the hierarchs who are in my empire are yours and are subject to your authority. Since, however, John does not observe the order proper to hierarchs but behaves disorderly toward emperors, for several days now we have planned to assemble the archpastors, so that as one unworthy of the episcopate he may be deposed, and another who can govern the Patriarchate may be appointed our Most Holy Master," the empress said to the blessed one, being in great anger. "But now, since you, father, are here, there is no need to trouble other bishops, but you yourself appoint as Patriarch whomever God reveals to you. But this one—remove from the Most Holy Throne," Eudoxia concluded.

"Listen, child, without anger and malice. If the divine Chrysostom is indeed condemned for the heresy of which you speak and will be publicly exposed as a heretic and does not repent of his sin, then he is unworthy of the episcopate. Only in this case will I be able to satisfy the desire of your authority. But if you wish to drive Saint John from the Great Church for the dishonor that he has personally caused you, then your Epiphanius will never agree to this. Besides, child, it is necessary for emperors to forgive those who revile and dishonor them, because you emperors also have a King in the Heavens, against whom you constantly sin, and He forgives you. So also forgive those who sin against you and dishonor you, as it is said in the Gospel: *'Be merciful, just as your Father also is merciful'*" (Luke 6:36).

"Father, if you prevent me from exiling John, then I shall open the idol temples and compel the people to worship idols, and the last will be worse than the first," the empress said angrily, weeping from malice.

"I, child, am guiltless of this sin," the Bishop of Epiphanius answered her speech, called me, and we left the palace (our other companion, Isaac, was sick and remained in the monastery).

While we were returning to the monastery, throughout the whole city the rumor spread that the great hierarch Epiphanius had been at the empress's and had agreed with her to exile the divine Chrysostom. Hearing this, Isaac left the saint, came to another monastery, and settled there. The blessed one was very distressed about Isaac and prayed to God that He might reveal where he was. When the Lord revealed the whereabouts of Isaac, we came to him, but he turned away from his Master.

"I do not wish to be with you any longer because of the sin that you committed against Chrysostom," he said to Epiphanius.

We spent three days in the monastery, and with difficulty the saint was able to convince Isaac that he had not participated in the decision about the exile of the saint. Only after this did he follow us to the place where we were staying. However, even the divine Chrysostom himself believed that the venerable Epiphanius had given his consent to his exile.

"Wise Epiphanius, you have given your consent to my exile, but neither will you sit any longer on your throne," Saint John wrote to him.

"In vain have you believed in my consent to your exile, but you will not reach the place to which you have been exiled," the Archbishop of Cyprus answered him.

To us, however, the Master explained that he wrote these lines by the Providence of God in order that no one might reproach Saint Chrysostom, for it is impossible that one who has performed so many good deeds should fall into such a depth of sin. When before our departure for Cyprus we went to the palace to bid farewell to the rulers, the Emperor Arcadius asked Abba Epiphanius how old he was.

"I am one hundred and fifteen years old, lacking three months. When I became a bishop, I was sixty. In the episcopate I have already spent, lacking three months, fifty-five years," the bishop answered.

Boarding the ship, the wonderworker settled in the hold, and we sat down with him. The saint had a custom of never letting the Holy Gospel out of his hands. Groaning and weeping three times, he opened the Gospel, then closed it again, wept, and prayed. Then the hierarch again made a prayer, wept, and began to speak to us:

"Children, if you love me, then fulfill my commandments, and the love of God will abide in you. You know how many sorrows I have experienced in this life, paying no heed to any sorrow, but always rejoicing, looking to God. The Creator, however, has never forsaken me, but has preserved me from all the snares of the enemy. As the Apostle Paul says: *'All things work together for good to those who love God'*" (Romans 8:28). "So, my beloved children, once, when I was in a deserted place and was praying to the Creator that He would deliver me from every assault of the enemy, demons came and, throwing me to the ground, seized me by the feet and began to drag me along the ground. Some of them beat me severely, and this continued for ten days. From that time I have no longer seen the demonic face, and only through evil people have they caused me evil. How much evil and what kind befell me from the disorderly Simonians in Phoenicia, from the unclean Gnostics in Egypt, from the lawless Valentinians and other heretics in Cyprus... Attend, children, and hear the word of the sinful Epiphanius. Never desire much money for yourselves, even if it is given to you. Avoid hatred toward any person, and you will be loved by God. Do not slander your brother, and the diabolic passion will not possess you. Turn away from heresies as from venomous and deadly serpents. About them I have written in books bearing the title 'Panarion,' which I have also given to you. Guard yourselves from the pleasures of this world, which arouse the body and thought. Know that this is a temptation from Satan, because very often, when the flesh is at rest, thought paints shameful pictures for the inattentive. But when our mind is watchful and always remembers God, then we can easily conquer the enemy."

Having said this and much else, Bishop Epiphanius summoned all who were on the ship.

"Brethren, we must ask God with all our soul to preserve us, so that none of us perish, because there will be a great storm. But rejoice, for no sorrow will come near you," he instructed all who stood there. "Child Polybius, if we arrive in Constantia, stay there for seven days, and then go to Egypt, to Upper Thebaid, to shepherd the sheep of Christ. Be careful; do not do otherwise, because if you do not obey me and do not go, then you will destroy even what you have built, and you will be useless to all. But if you fulfill my words and the commandment of our Lord Jesus Christ, which He has bidden me convey to you, you will be blessed before Him all the days of your life," he addressed me and embraced me. "And you, child, remain in Constantia until you receive an indication to go to the land of the Kittim," the wonderworker counseled Isaac. "Do not be afraid, children, that there will be great agitation at sea, but ask God, and He will help you," he encouraged the sailors. "And you, do not tempt, lest you yourself be tempted," the pleaser of God admonished one sailor.

Then it was the eleventh hour of the day, and when the sun was already setting, a storm broke out at sea. The saint lay in the ship's hold with his arms stretched out and the Gospel on his chest. His eyes were open, but no voice was heard. We were all greatly frightened, and we thought that he was praying to God that the storm might cease. However, the storm continued for two days; on the third day the Archbishop of Cyprus said to me:

"Child Polybius, tell the sailors to kindle a fire and make coals, and then bring them here."

When I gave him the coal and placed incense upon it, the blessed one asked us all to pray fervently, and he himself began to offer praise, and afterward, directing his gaze upward, he said:

"Farewell, children, because Epiphanius will no longer see you in this life."

And at that very minute the divine abba gave up his spirit, and the storm immediately subsided. Falling upon his neck, Isaac and I wept bitterly, and darkness covered our eyes. That sailor to whom the saint had commanded "not to tempt, lest he be tempted" fell at the feet of the saint and wanted to lift his garments to see whether the Master had been circumcised. But the archpastor, though dead, raised his right hand and struck him on the face, so that he flew to the stern and lay there as if dead for two days. Then the other sailors carried him to the venerable one, and as soon as he touched his feet, he immediately stood up in health, and fear fell upon all who were on the ship.

When, with God's help, we arrived in Constantia, the sailors disembarked from the ship and, going about the city, loudly proclaimed:

"Men, brethren, inhabitants of the great metropolis of Constantia, come down to the sea to receive the precious relics of our venerable Father Epiphanius, because he has ended his earthly life."

And then darkness fell upon the whole city, and the people, leading one another by the hands and making great lamentation and weeping, went down to the sea. When all the clergy and people had gathered in the harbor, they began with lamps, incense, and psalmody to lift up the relics of the saint and carry them to the church, so that all the people might take leave of their archpastor.

Hearing of the death of the Master, all the peasants of that land, almost all the inhabitants of the island of Cyprus, came with great diligence to venerate him. Three blind men from the village of Skortiki also wished to honor the memory of the hierarch, but they had no guide. Then one of them, named Prosechios, said:

"Saint Epiphanius, give light to our eyes, so that we may come and venerate your precious relics."

And immediately—O miracle!—all three received their sight and without outside help ran to venerate the Master of Constantia, thanking him and at the same time telling of the miracle that had happened to them. Many on that day glorified God, who permits such miracles to be performed by His worthy servants.

I remained for seven days in the church beside the relics of the saint, and we found no opportunity to bury him because of the multitude of people coming. On the eighth day, so as not to disobey the commandment of the bishop, with great sorrow in my heart I left his relics and boarded a ship that was heading for Egypt. Coming to Upper Thebaid, I spent one year there.

Once the Governor of Egypt, the great Heracleon, was going down to his native city of Rhinocorura, and, hearing that I was a disciple of Bishop Epiphanius, he sent soldiers who unexpectedly seized me and against my will brought me to him. The bishops who had gathered there ordained me to the then-widowed episcopate of Rhinocorura. When a little time had passed, I sent the honorable Deacon Callippus to Cyprus, who learned on what day and where the precious relics of our Father among the saints Epiphanius were buried, through whose prayers may we also be vouchsafed the Heavenly Kingdom. Amen.

This part of the life of our Father among the saints Epiphanius was written by Polybius, Bishop of the city of Rhinocorura.

The Life and Struggles of Saint Gorgonia, Who Flourished in the Fourth Century

The homeland of this blessed Gorgonia was the city of Nazianzus in Caesarea of Cappadocia; her father was named Gregory, and her mother Nonna. Her mother was a Christian for several generations, while her father was a pagan by parentage. He spent much time in idolatrous delusion, but his blessed wife Nonna, having tried many approaches, finally succeeded in bringing her husband to Christian piety. He was a good man by nature even before he knew the truth, and therefore God could not leave such a good soul without enlightenment. After Baptism Gregory so shone forth in virtues that he was ordained bishop of his native city of Nazianzus. And the wondrous Nonna was so devoted to God and had such reverence that, as her son Gregory the Theologian says, she never turned her back to the eastern part of the church, that is, to the place where the Holy Table was located; she never spat on the floor of the temple; she never conversed in church during the service nor at any other time, but only outside, and then only if there was an extreme necessity. And what more is there to say?.. It is enough that by the example of her virtues and her prayers to God day and night she was able to bring her husband from impiety to piety.

It was from such a holy mother that Saint Gorgonia was born and raised, having from childhood such a pious teacher. Naturally, she became like her mother in virtue. Another Nonna in piety. Although she was given in marriage, even in this lawful and honorable marriage she surpassed all women of her time in chastity (if not to say also all the ancient women who are so praised for chastity), for she combined with marriage the virtue of virginity and showed everyone that virginity, in itself, does not unite a person with God, just as marriage, in itself, does not bind a person to the world, thereby separating him from God. Therefore, on the one hand, it is better to avoid marriage altogether, while virginity, on the other hand, is to be praised. But it is precisely the mind that rightly governs marriage and virginity: it either unites a person with God or binds him to the world and separates him from God. But the ever-blessed one was not separated from God either by the fact that she married or by the fact that her husband was her head. She did not serve the world and nature much according to the law of the flesh, which God established, but devoted all of herself to God. Her most excellent and most honorable struggle was that she also brought her husband to good character. And he was not her lord, but a good counselor in God-pleasing matters. Moreover, not only her husband, but also the fruit of her womb—her children, and the children of her children—she made fruits of the Holy Spirit through soul-profiting instructions, showing a good example in marriage. Being married, she also pleased God by her virtues because she brought forth the good fruit of marriage—children.

Wise Solomon in the Book of Proverbs praises the wife who remains in her home and keeps silence. She loves her husband, occupies herself with domestic affairs, and in general the Wise One says much in praise of the honorable and chaste wife. But through this praise he compares her with the impious and incontinent wife who wanders about the roads in dissolute attire and by her words causes harm to the souls not only of the impious but also of respectable people. However, what Solomon says in praise of the chaste and honorable wife is insignificant for the praise of the supremely honorable and chaste Gorgonia, for what other wife was equal to her in piety and modesty? And at the same time, what other woman, besides her, kept such silence in her home and did not show herself on the street, being unseen by men? What other woman so guarded her gaze from immodest looks? Who else had such quiet and calm laughter? She smiled only when necessary, guarded her hearing from vain and idle words, listening only to divine and salvific teachings. Gorgonia did not love idle talk; she spoke only about the commandments of God.

The wondrous one did not wear gold ornaments, pearls with diamonds, did not braid the hair on her honorable head into plaits, did not wear expensive garments, did not use ablutions and cosmetics, as other shameless women do, who, though being creatures of God, cover their faces with paints and ointments. These women are not content with the face that the Lord created, but want to make it better, thereby only defiling the image of God. But the blessed one cared only about adorning her soul with Christian character and virtues. She loved the red color of the face that can be seen in modest and honorable women from shame and reverence, as well as the white color that comes from abstinence and fasting. Painting herself and excessive attention to temporal, man-made beauty the incomparable one left to those women who shamelessly wander the streets, loving not the beauty of the soul but of the body.

And such was the divine Gorgonia in all things. With what words can one worthily show her understanding, knowledge, piety, and faith in God? Few examples of such virtues can be found, perhaps only in her parents. The ever-blessed one strove to imitate them in all things and to reach the level of their holiness. Her mind was so keen that everyone consulted with her about their needs, not only relatives and fellow countrymen, but also foreigners. And her wise sayings were for all a law, which was immutably and inviolably fulfilled. She, according to the word of the Apostle, made herself a temple of God (2 Corinthians 6:16). What always distinguished Gorgonia from other women was her great honor toward priests and her reverence toward strangers; she received them in her home with great cordiality. The wondrous wife had compassion on the suffering, helped the poor with alms. Her house, like the dwelling of Job, was hospitable, and no foreigner ever remained on the street. For, like Job, she was an eye to the blind, a foot to the lame, a mother to orphans. The poor always found refuge with her; all her possessions served those in need; mercy was always on the side of widows. The only wealth that she left to her children was imitation and zeal for God, that is, her good example. Through these virtues of hers, which she performed not openly but, as much as possible, in secret, Gorgonia was vouchsafed to receive Christ.

It often happens that a person does one good deed but falls into another sin. For example, if he gives alms to the poor, he no longer has any cares and gives himself over to bodily pleasures, as if he had purchased them with this alms. But this is not how the blessed Gorgonia acted: together with alms she gave herself to fasting, together with mercy and compassion toward the poor she humbled her body with abstinence; the saint never abandoned the reading of Holy Scripture. Her prayerful vigil consisted of long standings or warm-hearted prayers on bended knees. She raised her mind to the Heavenly, and in this noetic contemplation she surpassed not only women but also many men, and was spiritually higher than all others.

If Gorgonia noticed higher virtues in others, she immediately strove to attain them. However, most often it was she who was the model for imitation. In all things she was perfect, in all things she was worthy of wonder: her unwashed garments and her body, which shone with virtue alone, her soul, which kept her body almost without food, as if immaterial. The flesh of Gorgonia was mortified even before its separation from the soul; she was free from passionate feelings. How can one not marvel at her sleepless nights spent in psalmody and standing, or at her lying on the ground, from which the members of her body, from soft, became unnaturally rough, or at her tears, sown in sorrow so as to reap the fruits of joy after death, or at her fervent spirit, which desired to pray and paid absolutely no attention to dogs, or to the cold air, or to rain, or to thunder, or to hail, or to nighttime? Struggling in the struggle for salvation, she understood that the distinction between men and women exists only by nature, not by soul. She acquired abstinence and thereby conquered the bitter taste of the foremother Eve—sin, the flattering serpent-devil, and death. By her life-giving mortification, she who is worthy of all praise honored the self-emptying of Christ to the form of a servant, who accepted great sufferings. No, no one will be able to count all the struggles of the blessed Gorgonia.

In the account of her virtues, only the narrative of the rewards that she received from the Righteous Rewarder already on earth is lacking.

Once the saint was riding in a carriage drawn by mules. Suddenly the beasts went mad and ran with such speed that the carriage overturned; the saint fell out of it and became entangled in the harness. In this condition the mules dragged her a rather great distance. As a result, she injured all her limbs and broke her bones. This incident caused great scandal among the faithful: how could God allow such a holy woman to suffer so greatly?

However, Gorgonia, although she was in extreme need of treatment, did not summon a physician, so that a stranger would not see her body. She placed all her hope in the Creator, firmly believing: "If the Almighty has permitted this, then He will also heal me." And so it happened in reality—the All-Merciful completely, without a physician, healed her in a miraculous manner. This caused amazement in all and, above all, in those who at first had been scandalized.

And another time, just as suddenly, a disease attacked Gorgonia, and the ailment was so unusual and strange that no medical art helped: first from the fever her whole body began to burn, and the blood seemed to boil. Then the blood would cool, the saint would become covered with a yellowish color, her mind would weaken, the members of her body were paralyzed. Such attacks occurred quite frequently, and all her relatives and close ones shed many tears in prayer for the blessed one. But what did the divine Gorgonia do this time? After despair set in, she began to ask for help from the Common Physician for all—God. Waiting for nightfall, when no one could hinder her, she went and with faith fell down before the Holy Altar, loudly calling upon the Omnipresent for help. Imitating the woman in the Gospel with an issue of blood, whose flow of blood dried up from touching the hem of Christ's garments, she touched her head to the Holy Table and began to pour out upon the Altar the same tears with which the sinful woman had moistened the feet of Christ, saying that she would not leave this place without receiving health. Then she anointed her whole body with these tears. And—O miracle!—at that very minute she received healing, after which she returned home. For the sorrow and hope that she placed in the Lord, the blessed one received relief for body, soul, and mind, and together with strength of soul—bodily health.

But what then was the repose of the wondrous one, if her whole life is worthy of amazement? On account of her great boldness before Christ, more than all earthly joys the blessed one desired death and union with the Lord. And the Creator did not put her to shame in this hope according to God. Once, after a long prayerful vigil, Gorgonia fell into a slumber. During sleep she had a vision, in which the day of her death was revealed to the ever-memorable one. The Almighty revealed the date to her so that she might prepare and not be troubled when death suddenly came. But the saint had no need for preparation, because not long before she had received the purification of Holy Baptism. In truth, her whole life was a purification and perfection, and she drew her assurance of salvation from virtue and God-pleasing deeds. The only thing she lacked, to add to her virtues, was to baptize her husband; then none of her deeds would have remained unfinished, and she would have gone to Christ having fulfilled her duty to the end. It was for this very thing that she prayed to the All-Merciful, who does the will of those who fear Him.

After the fulfillment of her last desire, the appointed day of death drew near. In anticipation of this moment, according to the laws of nature, the saint fell ill and took to her bed. Then she called her husband, children, friends, and gave them instructions; she also delivered to them a teaching about the Heavenly life, thus creating an atmosphere of celebration, in which the wondrous one was also vouchsafed to depart unto the Lord. Gorgonia was not old, but she no longer wished to live and remain in this world, especially since in virtues she was richer than many who had reached advanced old age.

Let us add something else that is good and profitable to our account of the death of the saint. All who stood at the bed of Gorgonia grieved greatly over their separation from the blessed one and wished to hear her divine words for the last time, but no one dared to ask her for this. The sorrow and heartfelt grief of all were incurable; tears flowed from their eyes in an unceasing stream, but no one could utter a word—it seemed unreasonable to all to honor with weeping one who was departing from this world as a pleaser of the Most High. All stood in profound silence, as if some ineffable mystery were being performed. The venerable one lay almost breathless—without movement or voice. Only her father noticed that Gorgonia weakly moved her lips and, hoping to hear her last words, bent down to her. *"I will both lie down in peace, and sleep,"* Gorgonia whispered at this moment a verse from a psalm of David (Psalm 4:8), which was a clear testimony and proof of the boldness and holiness with which the blessed Gorgonia departed unto Christ, with whom, by His boundless mercy and her prayers, may we sinful and condemned ones also be vouchsafed a good and salvific end in repentance and confession, that we may glorify together with the saved His extreme goodness unto the ages of ages. Amen.

Selected from the orations of our Father among the saints Gregory the Theologian

The Life and Struggles of Our Venerable Mother Macrina, Sister of Basil the Great, Who Struggled in the Fourth Century

This present work, on the one hand, represents an epistle, but on the other, because of the importance of that which is spoken of in it, is in fact a narrative about the life of Macrina, or a life. You, brother Olympius, remember our conversation when I met you in Antioch, from which you wished to go to Jerusalem to venerate the holy places. On that occasion, thanks to your prudence, we also recalled the life of blessed Macrina. In this narrative I rely not on what I heard from other people, but on what was revealed to me by her herself, since she was my sister, born of the same parents—the eldest of us. So that the life of a woman who by unceasing ascetic struggle ascended to the summit of virtue might not be consigned to oblivion, I consider it fitting to heed your counsel and in few words, simply and without artifice, relate her life.

Our parents named this maiden Macrina, but she also had a secret name, given to her before birth in a divine vision. For our mother, Emmelia, being of righteous life, herself desired to preserve virginity and remain pure, but since she was an orphan of both parents and extraordinarily beautiful, many wanted to marry her; had she not married of her own will, a satanic danger would have awaited her: mother could have been abducted by someone who was struck by her remarkable appearance. For this reason she agreed to marry a very modest man—I mean our father Basil—so that he might become the guardian of her life and chastity.

When the time came for our mother to give birth for the first time, she saw in a dream that she held in her arms an infant daughter. Immediately a man of majestic appearance came and called the infant Thekla—the name of her who had great glory among virgins. Having spoken this name three times, the Heavenly guest became invisible, at the same time easing our mother's labor. Thus, as soon as she awoke, she immediately gave birth to our sister. And so our sister's secret name was Thekla. I think that the Angel of the Lord, who appeared to mother, did not wish to impose the name Thekla upon the parents, but, having called her thus, indicated in advance the similarity of her will with the life of the virgin Thekla. After Macrina emerged from infancy and became capable of learning those subjects which a child can comprehend, she began to advance in those studies in which her parents wished. Mother endeavored that her daughter should study the God-inspired words of Holy Scripture, especially the book of the Wisdom of Solomon and all that contributes to the formation of good morals; likewise Macrina studied the words of the Psalter, uttering each verse at the appropriate time: both when she awoke from sleep, and when she began the performance of any task, and when she completed it, and when she partook of bread, and when she rose from table, and when she lay down to sleep—always, as a good companion, the psalms of David sounded upon her lips. Thus the venerable one grew up in the study of these sciences. After she had learned sacred handiwork and reached the age of twelve, Macrina became the most beautiful maiden in the land. A multitude of young men came to her parents with proposals of marriage. But father, being a prudent man and capable of discerning good character in people, chose one noble and chaste young man who had advanced in learning, and decided to marry them when his sister reached the proper age. This excellent young man hoped to marry Macrina and, as a wedding pledge, showed our father his advancement in affairs, defending the wronged. However, death cut off his good hopes, snatching the bridegroom from this life in the very flower of youth.

Macrina knew of her father's intention to give her in marriage and considered herself already as if in marriage. After the death of her bridegroom she resolved to remain faithful to her word and not to enter into a second similar marriage, despite the great number of proposals. In her opinion, it would have been absurd and unlawful not to agree to the marriage which her father had prepared, but it would also be strange to seek another marriage, since people are appointed one marriage, one birth, one death. She considered that the bridegroom, who by the will of her parents had been as if united with her, had not died, but had merely departed to God for the hope of the resurrection; therefore it would be strange not to preserve fidelity and chastity for the sake of her departed bridegroom.

She devised a way to fulfill her good intention as follows: never, not for a single minute, to be separated from her mother and thereby to replace a multitude of servants. Thus a good exchange was established between them—mother cared for the soul of her daughter, while the daughter served her mother in all her needs, often preparing bread for her with her own hands. Macrina considered that to engage in this sacred handiwork was worthy of the calling of a virgin. The sister shared with mother all the cares of the household, for besides Macrina mother had nine other children: four sons and five daughters, and our property was located in the territories of three different peoples, so that it was necessary to pay taxes to three different rulers. Father died early, and upon mother's lot fell many cares of the household, in which Macrina participated together with her parent, thereby greatly lightening her heavy labor. She herself led a life in purity and chastity, having her own mother as instructor in this, and at the same time became an example for her mother, who strove to imitate her struggles. Little by little Macrina drew her to the joys of the immaterial and perfect monastic life.

When mother had worthily raised her daughters, our brother Basil the Great returned from his studies, having studied wisdom for many years in Caesarea, Constantinople, and Athens. The wondrous Macrina showed him too the true goal of philosophy and ascetic struggle. Despite the fact that the holy hierarch Basil was extolled for his knowledge of philosophy and was more famous than rulers, though he regarded their high ranks with contempt, Macrina compelled him to part from worldly magnificence, to despise the praises of external wisdom and learning, to come to perfect non-acquisitiveness, and to prepare for himself an unhindered path to a virtuous life. But let the account of the life and struggles of Basil the Great, through which he became famous throughout the whole world, wait, for much time is required to write of this. We shall return to the subject of our narrative.

And so, since blessed Macrina had freed herself from the cares of worldly life, she persuaded her mother also to leave her customary life, to renounce the services of her maidservants, and to live with virgins and nuns, making her former servants equal sisters to herself. Here I wish to include one account, since through it the spiritual height of the venerable one is revealed even more.

One of us four brothers, Naucratius, second after Basil the Great, was distinguished from the others by natural gifts, bodily beauty, strength, skill, and abilities in the performance of everything he undertook. When he had reached twenty-two years of age, the fame of his industriousness reached the ears of many, but he, by Divine Providence despising all that he had, with great zeal hastened to the non-acquisitive and ascetic monastic life. One of our household servants followed him, the most beloved by Naucratius, who preferred the monastic life to the worldly. The two of them settled in an extraordinarily deserted place near the river Iris, on an elevation densely overgrown with forest. Here, far from the bustle of the city and all manner of cares, they served with their own hands the elders, the poor, and the sick who lived nearby. Naucratius proved to be a skillful fisherman and began to feed the sick with fish. By these labors he subdued his youth, not forgetting to obey our mother's instructions if she sometimes commanded him something. Thus he conducted his life, advancing in the fulfillment of the Divine commandments.

Five years after Naucratius began his ascetic struggle, a grievous incident occurred: he went to the river to catch fish in order to feed the sick elders for whom he cared, but was brought to his cell dead together with his companion Chrysaphius. It is believed that this happened from an attack of the devil, for the ever-blessed one was snatched from life without any illness and without any other apparent cause. His mother at this time was at a distance of three days' journey from that place, but when she received the news of her son's death, despite her perfection in virtue, she became breathless and speechless from grief. Then were manifested the courage and virtue of the great Macrina. She withstood the passion of sorrow with right reasoning and preserved imperturbability. Mother, who had fallen into weakness, she taught courage by the example of her own steadfastness, thanks to which mother quickly recovered from the misfortune: she did not cry out, she did not tear her garments in grief, and she did not provoke tears in herself with mournful songs, but calmly and imperturbably endured her grief, driving away the weakness of nature by her own right reasonings and by those which Macrina offered her, consoling her in her suffering.

After our mother's cares for the upbringing of her children and their future position had ended, she divided all her property among us. At precisely this moment the life of her daughter Macrina became a good example in the ascetic life. Therefore she left all her old customs and attained the same measure of humility as her daughter. She became equal with the other nuns, ate the same food, slept on the same bedding, and was like them in everything else: Macrina and our mother were separated from all worldly vanity, imitating the Angels by their life. Never was there seen in them anger, or envy, or hatred, or pride, or any other similar passion. They desired nothing vain for themselves—honors, glory, and all such things. Abstinence was for them a delight, obscurity was glory, non-acquisitiveness was wealth. All that people so strive for in the present life was for them something secondary, and what was primary was the investigation of Divine things, constant prayer, unceasing psalmody, both at night and by day, which became simultaneously both work and rest. And with what words is it possible to describe such a life, which was as if on the boundary—between the human and the Angelic? For the freedom from human passions which Macrina and her mother attained was a matter above human nature, while having a sensory body is below the Angelic nature. However, who will dare say that in this they were lower, because although they were bound by the body, yet like the bodiless Angels, they were not burdened by it. Ascending by their life, they were raised up together with the Heavenly powers.

In this manner they lived for many years, constantly advancing in virtue. This same great purpose of Macrina's life was also served by our youngest brother Peter, who was called an orphan—when he was born our father died, but his eldest sister Macrina raised him, teaching him the highest moral laws. From an early age he was instructed in the sacred sciences, which did not allow his soul to be subject to vanity. Macrina was for him both father, and teacher, and educator, and counselor in every good and holy deed. Thanks to his sister, while still a child he was raised up in ascetic struggle and became capable in every craft. Having no special teacher, he precisely learned every craft and science, though many require a great amount of time and labor for this. Thus our brother Peter, despising the study of external wisdom and having as teacher of every good science nature and the beautiful example of his sister Macrina, so advanced in virtue that it seemed he yielded in nothing to Basil the Great.

At that time a severe famine came, and many, knowing of the good deeds performed by these three—Macrina, her mother, and brother Peter—came to the place where they were struggling, and Peter, with the help of his household acumen, managed to have food in such abundance for the hungry that from the multitude of people coming the desert seemed like a city.

Our mother lived to a deep old age and departed unto the Lord, reposing in the arms of her two children. However, here it is worth including the last words which she said to her children as she was dying. Having blessed her other children who were absent, she stretched out her hands to Macrina and Peter, who sat beside her—one on the right, the other on the left—and exclaimed to God, pointing with her hands to Macrina and Peter: "To Thee, O Lord, I dedicate both the first-fruit and the tenth fruit of my womb. My first-fruit is this my firstborn daughter, and the tenth is this my last son. To Thee according to the law they dedicate both the first-fruits and the tenth part, to Thee these offerings belong. And so, may Thy sanctification and grace descend both upon this first-fruit and upon my tenth." After this, having commanded her children to bury her in the grave of her husband, she ended her earthly life. After the funeral Macrina and Peter began to struggle even more zealously and conquered their former struggles by those that followed.

At this time Basil the Great, having become bishop of Caesarea, ordained his brother Peter to the presbyterate, and then to the episcopacy of Sebastia. From that time, after the acquisition of the hierarchical rank, Peter increased his ascetic struggle and began to lead a life even more holy and exalted. Eight years later, when the great teacher of the universe Basil departed this world, his sister Macrina, who was at that time far away, though she grieved in soul over such a loss, did not fall in spirit but courageously endured the misfortune. And just as gold is purified in a furnace in order to remove from it all impurity and dross, so that it might become perfectly pure, so also the sister was subjected to trials through various sorrows, so that the purity and firmness of her soul might be shown: first was the death of brother Naucratius, then the separation from mother, and finally, when our incomparable Basil the Great departed from us. She remained for us the only and unconquered ascetic, who had not succumbed to calamities. When nine months had passed from the day of the repose of Basil the Great, a Local Council assembled in Antioch, in which I, Gregory, also participated, and upon its conclusion all we hierarchs returned each to his own diocese. After this one year passed, and there came to me the thought to go to my sister Macrina, since I had not visited her for a long time because of the constant struggle with the defenders of the Arian heresy. Counting the time, I discovered that we had not met for eight years.

Then I set out on my journey and had already covered a significant distance, being one day's journey from my sister, when I saw a dream which gave rise to terrible apprehensions for the future. It seemed to me that I was holding relics of martyrs, from which came forth such radiance as from a pure mirror when it is set before the sun. And this radiance blinded my eyes. The vision repeated three times in one night. I could not understand what it meant, yet a great sorrow settled in my soul. When I was already not far from the ascetic dwelling of the venerable one, I met one of the friends who lived there and first asked about my brother Peter. It turned out that Peter had gone to me four days earlier, but we had passed each other on the road. Then I inquired about the health of the great Macrina and learned of her illness. I made the remainder of the journey quickly—my soul was troubled by sorrow and fear for the future. No sooner had I entered the dwelling of the venerable one than word of my arrival spread throughout the whole brotherhood. The ascetics came out to meet me; they had such a custom—to meet friends; at the same time the assembly of women ascetics decorously awaited me in the church. But this time their abbess Macrina was not among them, so I took a guide and went to her cell. Though she was ill, she was lying not on a bed or a mat, but on a board on the bare ground. Another board of some peculiar shape served as her pillow. As soon as she saw that I had come to the door, she raised herself and leaned on her elbows, but she could no longer rise and come to me because she was weakened by the fever. Leaning with her hands on the ground as much as she could, the venerable one raised herself, showing me the respect due at a meeting. I ran to her, caught her as she was falling, lifted her up, and laid her back down. Raising her hands to God in prayer, she said: "This mercy also hast Thou shown me, O Lord, not depriving me of my desire, that Thou hast moved Thy servant to visit Thy handmaiden."

So as not to cause me sorrow, she restrained her groaning and concealed from me the grief of her heart, beginning her speech with joyful words and gladdening me with her questions. However, when we began to speak of Basil the Great, my heart began to be tormented and my face became sad. But blessed Macrina was so far from sympathizing with me that the remembrance of the saint became for her the cause of even greater courage. Discoursing at length about human nature, she said that in sorrows is concealed the Divine economy. Enlightened by the Holy Spirit, she reasoned so about the future life that it seemed to me that my mind was raised up by her words and, having gone beyond the limits of human nature and led by her words, penetrated into the Heavenly sanctuary.

Macrina, like Job, who suffered greatly in body while his mind was free and did not cease to contemplate things on high, was all dried up from the fever, yet suffered no harm at all from her illness. And if this would not lengthen my writing, I would relate in order all things: how the ever-blessed one was exalted by conversation, how she reasoned about the soul, about life in the flesh, about why man was created, how he became mortal, whence death came, and how he returned again from death to life. All her words, enlightened by the grace of the Holy Spirit, were like water from a spring.

"Brother, now is the time to give rest to your body, wearied from the journey," she said to me after her instruction.

And though for me the best and true rest was to see her and hear her penetrating words, I, obeying my instructor, went with my guide to a neighboring garden, where I settled under the shade of the grapevines. However, in my heart there was no joy, my soul grieved in expectation of sorrowful events. My dream was becoming reality: the blessed one truly resembled the relics of a holy martyr, dead to sin and radiant with the grace of the Holy Spirit dwelling in them. During these my heavy thoughts, I know not how, the venerable one learned my thoughts and sent me joyful news—she had grown better. She let me know of this not in order to mock me. Just as a runner on a course outstrips his rival and, approaching the end, already sees the victor's crown and begins to exult in his soul as if he had already received it, and reports this to his friends, so also Macrina, moved by the same desire, having turned her gaze to the highest reward, informed me that I should hope for the better:

"Finally, there is laid up for me the crown of righteousness, which the Lord, the righteous Judge, will give to me on that Day" (2 Timothy 4:8), because *"I have fought the good fight, I have finished the race, I have kept the faith"* (2 Timothy 4:7), she said in apostolic words.

After I had rested, she called me again and began to tell me in detail about everything she had done from her youth, as well as what she remembered about our parents, and what happened before my birth. The purpose of this narrative was to bring thanksgiving to God for all things. Acquainting me with the life of our parents, she related that their large fortune at that time had increased not so much from acquisitions as from the loving-kindness of the

Creator. For the ancestors on my father's side had been deprived of their property because of their confession of Christ, and on the maternal side one of them had been put to death because of the wrath of the emperor, and our parents were left without inheritance. But despite all this, the fortune and wealth of our parents, thanks to their faith, increased so greatly that in those times there was no one else who was wealthier than they. When the property was divided into portions according to the number of children, then the Almighty by His blessing so increased the portion of each child that the fortune of each one of us exceeded the total fortune of our parents. Macrina also said that of the property due to her she had kept nothing for herself, but gave everything to Peter so that he might dispose of it according to God's commandment. Throughout her life she never ceased to labor, never relied on anyone, and received all that was necessary not from the beneficence and alms of people, but from her own labor. However, if anyone turned to her with requests, she would send no one away empty-handed, but donated to the charities of the lovers of Christ, and her modest handiwork, which she constantly engaged in, was secretly multiplied by the Almighty.

When I began to tell of my own labors, first endured during the persecutions of the Orthodox by the Arian emperor Valens, and then about times of confusion and discord in the Churches of Christ, the ever-blessed one said:

"How long will you remain ungrateful to God for the good that He has done for you? Why do you not make amends for your ingratitude before Him? Compare the beneficence shown to you with that which was shown to your parents. Our father was distinguished by his learning and among other rhetors was the first, yet he is unknown beyond the borders of our homeland. But you have become known in all countries and nations, and the Churches of Christ send for you that you might come and help them. Yet you do not consider such mercy and do not even know the reason whence all these blessings come, for the Creator has raised you to this height through the prayers of our parents. You yourself would not have had the strength for this."

At that moment I desired most of all that the day might be prolonged and that the blessed one would not cease to gladden my hearing with her speech. But since the voice of those chanting psalms called us to vespers, I went to the church, and Macrina again returned to God in prayer. Thus the night passed. On the following day I understood that this was the last day of my sister's life, for her strength was exhausted by the fever. But she, seeing the weakness of my thoughts, was thinking how to soften for me the sorrowful expectation, and again with her good words, but now quite weakly and with labored breathing, she healed my sorrow. My soul experienced different feelings: by nature—sorrow, as was fitting, for I did not hope to ever again hear her voice, since the praise of our race was soon leaving this life. But on the other hand—joy, at the thought that my sister had truly surpassed common nature and risen above it. Already being at the very point of death, Macrina did not fear the separation of the soul from the body; her hope was in eternity, her last breath was in lofty thoughts about the monastic life. She revealed to those present the love for God concealed in the depths of her soul, for the Invisible Bridegroom Christ, and the desire to be freed from the bonds of the body in order to reach more quickly the desired Jesus.

And although the greater part of the day had already passed and the sun was declining toward the west, the zeal of the blessed one did not weaken in the least. The nearer her end approached, the more her longing to be united with Him grew, for ever more clearly she beheld His beauty. She no longer looked at me, but unceasingly beheld only Him, for her bed was also turned toward the east. She ceased her conversation with me, and henceforth in prayer conversed only with God, whispering such words:

"Thou, O Lord, hast delivered us from the fear of death. Thou hast made the end of our present life the beginning of true life. Thou dost give rest to our bodies for a time in the sleep of death and wilt awaken us again at the sound of the last trumpet. Thou dost place in the earth for safekeeping our dust, fashioned by Thy hands, and wilt again take from the earth that which was given to it, transforming our corruptible and unsightly body with incorruption and grace. Thou hast delivered us from the curse and sin, having become a curse for love of us. Thou hast crushed the head of the serpent that swallowed man for his disobedience. Thou hast shown us the way to resurrection, having shattered the gates of hades and abolished *'him who had the power of death, that is, the devil'* (Hebrews 2:14). Thou hast given to those who fear Thee the image of Thy Precious Cross for the destruction of the enemy and the protection of our life. In Thee have I hoped from my mother's womb, and Thee has my soul loved with all her strength; to Thee—from my youth and until now—have I offered as a gift my body and soul. But Thou, entrust me to a radiant Angel, who will lead me to the place of repose, to the bosom of our holy fathers. Thou Who didst set a barrier to the fiery sword and didst restore in paradise the thief crucified with Thee, who submitted to Thy loving-kindness, remember me also in Thy Kingdom. For I also have been crucified with Thee, having nailed my flesh by the fear of Thee, having feared Thy judgments. Let not the terrible abyss separate me from Thy chosen ones; let not the slanderer stand in my way, and let not my sin be found before mine eyes. And if I have sinned through the weakness of nature by word, deed, or thought, Thou, Who hast the power to forgive sins, forgive me, that I may find rest. And when I am divested of this body and my soul appears before Thee, free from spots or any blemish, receive her into Thy hands pure and undefiled, as incense before Thee."

Saying this, she made the sign of the Cross over her eyes, her mouth, and her heart, and then, since her tongue was burning and because of this she could not speak clearly, her voice broke off. Only by her open lips and the movement of her hands did we understand that she was praying.

Evening came... When fire was brought, the blessed one opened her eyes and, it seemed, wished to pronounce the customary evening thanksgiving prayer. However, since she had lost her voice, she gave thanks with her heart and the movement of her hands, and at the same time her lips also moved. At the completion of the rule, Macrina made the sign of the Cross, marking the end of the prayer, sighed deeply, and died. Then I remembered the commandment which she had given me the first time we met—to close her eyes when she died, as is usually done with the dead, and to bury her as befits. I placed my hand on the face of the saint only so that it might be seen that I was fulfilling the commandment, for there was no need to close the eyes of the blessed one; they were beautifully closed by her eyelids, as happens during ordinary sleep, her lips were tightly closed, her hands were decorously folded on her breast, and in general the position of the body was so seemly that it seemed superfluous to prepare her for burial.

I remained in a twofold stupor: from grief, from the sight of the body and the weeping of the virgins. From their bitter and unrestrained lamentations I too could no longer restrain myself, and sorrow, like a turbulent torrent, completely filled me. I surrendered myself entirely to tears, considering reasonable the cause for which the nuns wept. They bewailed not the fact of death, because the venerable one would no longer be with them in the body, as worldly people do when their relatives die, but tearfully lamented that they had been deprived of hope according to God and of the salvation of their souls:

"The lamp of our eyes has been extinguished, the light that guided our souls has been taken from us, the seal of our incorruption has been removed, the bonds of our unanimity have been torn asunder, the healing of the sick has been taken away. With you, O our good teacher, even the night seemed like day, illumined by the purity of your life, but now this day has turned into night and into darkness," they cried out.

But more than the others those lamented who considered her their mother and educator, because Macrina had found them on the road during the famine, had taken them with her, had raised them, and had brought them to the incorrupt virginal life. However, soon, looking at Macrina, I cried out to the virgins in a loud voice:

"Look at your teacher and remember her precepts by which you were taught—to maintain good order in all things. This divine soul taught us that we must weep only when we pray to the Lord; therefore let us transform our sorrowful voices into compunctionate psalmody."

I spoke loudly in order to drown out with my voice the voices of those who were weeping, after which I persuaded the virgins to go to the nearby cell, so as to leave by the bier only the few who, with Macrina's consent, had served her during her life. Among them was a certain wealthy, noble, and beautiful woman by the name of Vetiana. She had been married to a nobleman for only a short time and then became a widow, making the great Macrina the guardian and instructor of her widowhood. Spending the greater part of her time in communion with the virgins, she learned from them the virtuous life.

"Nothing now hinders us from vesting the sacred remains in fitting garments and adorning this pure and undefiled body with a bright covering," I said to her.

"We must find out whether the venerable one wished this, because we must do that which was pleasing to her. And what was pleasing to her was that which is pleasing to God."

There was here a certain virgin, first among all the others—a deaconess by rank—by the name of Lampadio. She knew exactly what the venerable one had commanded regarding her burial.

"The adornment of the saint was her pure life; it was her ornament during life, let it also be her burial shroud. But the things that serve for the adornment of the body she did not accept even during life; why then adorn her at burial? Even if we should wish to do something more for her body, we have nothing prepared," she said to us.

"Have you prepared nothing of that in which the body could be dressed?" I asked her again.

"See, she has everything prepared here: her garment, her covering, her worn shoes. This is her wealth and her possession. And besides this, you see there is nothing that would be stored in chests or in the cell. She knew only one treasury for her wealth—Heaven, where she gathered everything, leaving nothing on earth."

"And if I bring something of that which I have prepared for her burial, will it be pleasing to her?" I inquired of Lampadio.

"Certainly, and if the saint were alive, she would accept this offering from you because of your hierarchical rank and because you are her own brother. For this very reason the abbess commanded that you commit her body to burial with your own hands."

Having received agreement to vest the holy relics in what I had with me, I ordered my man to bring the garments.

"Here is her necklace," Vetiana said to me, as she was covering the sacred head of the venerable one. She showed me an iron cross and a ring, hanging on a thin thread at the heart of the venerable one.

"Let this be a common acquisition. You take the cross for yourself, and the ring will suffice for me," I answered the pious woman.

As Vetiana related to me, on the seal of the ring was engraved a cross, and within it was a particle of the Life-giving Cross of the Lord.

When it came time to clothe the pure body in garments, the blessed one commanded me to serve in this, and Vetiana, who was present, said:

"Do not pass over the great miracle performed by the saint."

And immediately she bared part of the breast of the venerable one and, bringing the lamp closer, showed me a small mark on the skin, resembling a trace from a pinprick.

"Well, and what kind of miracle is this, that there is such a mark on the body?" I asked in perplexity.

"This remained as a remembrance of the great help which God granted to the venerable one. Once in this place a strong tumor formed, which could have become incurable, therefore her mother implored Macrina to allow a physician to cut it out. But the blessed one thought that if some part of her body were seen by a stranger, this would be worse than the disease from which she suffered. When evening came and she had finished her customary service to her mother, she entered the sanctuary and remained there for the night. Falling down before the Physician of all, she prayed for healing. From the tears she shed she made an anointing and applied it as medicine to her breast. Since mother greatly pitied her and again urged her to show herself to the physician, the saint answered that if mother would make the sign of the Cross on the sore place with her own hand, she would recover. And immediately, as soon as mother made the sign of the Cross on her breast, a miracle occurred: the tumor disappeared, and only this mark remained, as a reminder of the Divine healing and as a cause for constant thanksgiving to the All-Merciful One."

After the body of the saint had been prepared for burial, Vetiana again said to me:

"It is not fitting that the saint should appear in the eyes of the virgins adorned like a bride. I have a dark covering of your mother. With it we shall cover the holy relics over the top, so that it may not seem that this sacred beauty is shining with ornamentation foreign to her."

This black covering was placed on top of the saint, but even in it her face radiated. I believe that Divine power added such grace to the holy relics that, as I had already seen in my dream, it seemed that from this beauty there proceeded certain lightnings. When we had finished, the psalmody of the virgins mingled with weeping was heard everywhere; I do not know how they had learned of her repose, but people kept coming and coming, and the monastery courtyard could no longer accommodate all who wished to enter. That night an All-Night Vigil with psalmody was performed, as on the feasts of martyrs. And when morning came, the multitude of assembled men and women interrupted the psalmody with lamentations. Though I was greatly distressed with sorrow, I was thinking, insofar as this was possible, of how not to omit anything of what is prescribed at burial; consequently I divided the assembled people: I placed the women with the virgins, and the men with the monastic order, and arranged for them to sing harmoniously and in good order, like two choirs.

When day had come and it had become very crowded from the assembled people, the bishop of that place, by the name of Araxius, who had come to the funeral with all his priests, asked me also to carry the relics to the place of burial. I was first to lift up one end of the bier of the deceased, the bishop lifted the other, and two honorable clergy lifted the two remaining ends, and we calmly set out on our way. At the head of the procession, on both sides, walked a multitude of deacons and readers—all with lighted candles. Since those walking in front and those walking behind were chanting psalms, the funeral of Macrina resembled a kind of triumphal procession.

The distance to the Church of the Holy Martyrs, where the bodies of our parents were buried, was seven or eight stades, but because of the multitude of people we barely covered it in a day. When at last we reached the church and began to pray, the lamentations of the people resumed with renewed force; before lowering the abbess into the grave one sister began to cry out in a disorderly fashion:

"Woe to us, for we shall see this sacred countenance no more!"

Hearing these words, the other nuns also began to repeat the same thing, so that a disorderly noise arose, disturbing the sacred prayer, for the hearts of all those assembled were breaking and tears were flowing. But then I gave a sign to be silent, and the deacon began to pronounce the exclamations appointed by the Church, calling to prayer. Only after this did the people with difficulty return to the performance of the burial rite, at the conclusion of which I was seized by fear that I was violating the Divine commandment: *"The nakedness of your father and the nakedness of your mother you shall not uncover"* (Leviticus 18:7). I was thinking how to escape condemnation, since I was about to see in the bodies of my parents the common unsightliness of human nature. And their bodies had already decayed and become shapeless and unsightly bones. Reasoning thus and fearing that indignation which Noah showed toward his son Ham, who saw his nakedness, I finally decided to use the same method as Noah's other two sons—Shem and Japheth. As soon as the tombstone was moved from the grave of my parents, their remains were covered with a clean shroud before we saw them. Then the bishop and I took the holy relics of Macrina and placed them next to the remains of our mother. Thus was fulfilled the wish and promise of both: mother and daughter, because both had asked of God that their bodies after death might be together, as also during life.

Having performed everything prescribed at burial, I fell upon the grave and began to kiss the earth, after which, sorrowful and all in tears, I set out on the return journey. On the way I met a certain noble man who had military authority in one town of Pontus, Sebastopolis. Having heard of the death of Macrina, he was greatly saddened because he was our relative, and then he related to me the following story, with which I shall conclude this narrative.

"Listen, what a great blessing has left this life," he began, having recovered from his tears. "Once my spouse and I wished to visit the school of virtue—for this is what that ascetic dwelling where Macrina lived ought to be called. With us was also our daughter, one of whose eyes was afflicted with an infectious disease, because of which she looked very terrible and pitiful: the iris around the pupil was thickened and had turned completely white. On the way we separated: I went to where the men were struggling, whose abbot was your brother Peter, and my spouse went to the convent of the virgins—to the monastery of the great Macrina. After some time we decided to leave, but when we gathered for the journey, we were both detained. Your brother asked me to stay and share the ascetic meal, while your blessed sister would not let my wife go because she held our daughter in her arms, saying that she would not give her back if my spouse did not share a meal with her. As was customary, kissing the child, she brought her lips to her eye.

"'If you grant me the kindness of sharing a meal with me, I will give you a reward worthy of such honor and kindness,' she said.

"'What kind of reward will you give us?' my spouse inquired.

"'I will give you a medicine with which it is possible to heal the child's eye,' Macrina encouraged.

"About this promise of the saint they sent a message to me, after which we gladly stayed. Upon completion of the meal we set out on our journey, along the way telling each other of what we had seen and heard. I spoke of what had been in the men's monastery, and my spouse related to me in detail, not omitting the slightest detail, about the venerable one, but when she came to the saint's promise to heal our child, she suddenly interrupted her story.

"'And what has happened to us? How is it that we neglected to take the promised medicine?' she wondered.

"Since I too was saddened by our negligence, I ordered her to return at once and take the medicine. At that moment the little girl, who was being held in the arms of the nurse, happened to turn around and look at her mother. The mother, looking into her eyes, joyfully said to me:

"'Do not be distressed about the medicine, because we have received what Macrina promised: this medicine was the healing of our daughter through her prayers, and in her eye not a trace of the illness remained.'"

"What is great in the fact that by the hand of the Lord sight is restored to the blind, if even His handmaiden by faith in the Creator has wrought a miracle no less than those?" concluded his narrative the relative, and from his eyes flowed tears.

I heard also of other miracles of blessed Macrina from those who lived with her and knew her life exactly, but I shall not speak of them, because to many they will seem unbelievable. For most people judge what they hear by the measure of their own knowledge, and when something exceeds this measure, they begin to suspect that it is all deception. Therefore I omit the account of the miraculous multiplication of grain during the famine, when Macrina distributed it to the poor and it did not diminish at all, and also of other cases more wondrous than this: healings of the sick and demon-possessed, prophecies about future times, in which all those possessing exact and perfect knowledge believe as true, although they seem incredible. They surpass our nature, which has a carnal mind, and think that this is impossible. Such people do not know that Divine gifts are given according to faith: to those of little faith—small gifts, and to those whose faith is great—great ones. So in order that those of little faith, who do not believe in Divine gifts, might not suffer harm, I have refrained from describing the most amazing of those miracles which God wrought through Macrina, considering sufficient what I have already written about her life. By her prayers may we also be deemed worthy of the Heavenly Kingdom. Amen.

Written by her own brother, Saint Gregory of Nyssa, and sent to the monk Olympius.

The Life and Struggles of Our Venerable and God-Bearing Father Paisius the Great, Who Struggled in the Year 370

This divine Paisius was born in Egypt of pious, virtuous parents who were rich in good Christian habits. This family, having seven children, possessed sufficient wealth for a life free of want, and therefore they always helped those in need. And the more mercy the family showed to the poor, the more abundant became their estate. After the death of the head of the family, all the care both for maintaining the estate and for raising the children, especially for Paisius as the youngest of the children, fell upon the shoulders of the grieving mother. One night an Angel of the Lord appeared to her in a dream, sent by God Himself, the Father of all orphans, and said:

"Why do you grieve so over having to care for your children, as if this were only your concern and not God's? Do not sorrow, but dedicate your son to the Almighty, through whom the most holy Name of God shall be glorified."

"All my children belong to the Creator; let Him take whomever He wishes."

"This one is pleasing to the Creator," announced the Angel, taking Paisius by the hand.

"He is not yet able to serve and work for the All-Merciful One, but rather take one of the older ones," the mother answered him.

"O most excellent of women, you say that Paisius cannot serve the Knower of Hearts because he is small, but know that the power of God is usually manifested in the weak. This one, the least of all, is the chosen one of the Father and will please the Ruler of the World more than all the others."

With these words the Angel departed, and the woman, having awakened, marveled at the command from on high and glorified the Almighty with the words:

"Let Thy mercy, O Lord, be upon us and upon Thy servant Paisius."

The divine Paisius was a God-fearing youth, in whom the grace of God increased from year to year. While still a child he desired the monastic life, and upon reaching a certain age, like a guiltless lamb, he came to the desert of Scetis to be under obedience to the renowned elder Pambo. Possessing the gift of clairvoyance, this abba knew the future of Paisius and, receiving the youth with great joy, clothed him in the holy monastic schema. The young monk struggled well in patience, with zeal fulfilling everything that his spiritual father entrusted to him. The divine Pambo helped the ascetic reach the lofty summits of virtue and taught Paisius always to walk with bowed head, so that the mind, imagining to itself the beauty of the ineffable glory of God, might unceasingly think upon heavenly things. This contemplation, as the teacher of the blessed one believed, would always help to glorify the almighty goodness of God, our great Benefactor. Thus Paisius for three years did not see a human face at all, but diligently read Holy Scripture and investigated its Divine meaning, which helped him become, in the words of the Prophet David, *"like a tree planted by the rivers of water, that brings forth its fruit in its season"* (Psalm 1:3).

"How sweet are Your words to my taste, sweeter than honey to my mouth!" (Psalm 118:103), the monk loved to repeat these lines from the Psalter.

Paisius tormented and afflicted his body with fasts and prayer vigils, thanks to which he was able to subject it to the commands of his soul. The holy Pambo so well and piously guided the thrice-blessed one that he was able to make of him an ascetic experienced and skilled in everything. Before his death Pambo blessed Paisius and uttered many prophecies about him, after which he peacefully departed unto the Lord.

From that day I, the humble John, who wrote this narrative, began to live in one cell with Paisius. Our way of life was built upon the rule received from our spiritual father; we mutually strengthened each other in virtue and cared for the salvation of our souls. A little time passed and Paisius began to struggle even more severely than before: he began to fast the entire week, partaking only of a small piece of bread with salt, and that only on Saturdays. All the rest of the time he devoted to reading the Word of God. The venerable one studied the prophecies of the God-inspired Prophet Jeremiah, who, as they say, appeared to him more than once and explained the hidden meaning of his works, thereby stirring the ascetic to love for the promised blessings.

The blessed one, according to the word of the Apostle Paul, always *"reached forward"* (Philippians 3:13), that is, he constantly compelled himself to perform still greater feats. Thus the saint began to fast not one but two weeks in a row. The most amazing thing is that no one knew of the equal-to-the-Angels life of Paisius except Him Who sees what is hidden and unknown. Captivated by the love of hesychia, he loved one thing—always to pray and converse with the One God. Once I tried to find out from the divine one whence he had acquired such a desire—from God, or by his own will:

"Brother Paisius, I see that you love hesychia," I said to him. "Know that I also long for it. But whence has this thought come to us? Let us pray to the Merciful One, that He may reveal to us His holy will, and then we shall act in accordance with it: either we shall both practice hesychia in one place, or we shall part from each other."

"You have spoken well, beloved John; let us do so, that our zeal for hesychia may be pleasing to the Creator," Paisius replied to these words.

Having said this, we spent the entire night in vigil, and the Good One heard our petition. In the morning hour an Angel of the Lord appeared to us.

"God commands you to part, and let each have a separate dwelling. You, John, remain in this place, and become for many a guide to salvation. But you, Paisius, inhabitant of Christ, depart hence and go to the western part of the desert. There, thanks to you, a countless people will be gathered: a monastery will be built and the Lord will be glorified," announced the Angel and became invisible.

Submitting to the command, we parted from each other: I remained in that place, while Paisius, coming to the western part of the desert, carved a cave in the rock and settled there. For his extraordinarily pure and lofty life God so loved him that Christ Himself often appeared to him and instructed him in virtue.

"Peace be to you, My beloved servant Paisius," the Savior once greeted the blessed one, who was at prayer in his cave.

"Behold, I am Thy servant. What dost Thou command, Master? What has moved Thee to condescend to me?" the saint asked with fear and trembling.

"Do you see this vast desert? All of it, thanks to you, I will fill with ascetics who glorify My Name."

"Thy words, Master Lord, are subject to Thy sovereign hand, and Thy desires are immediately fulfilled. However, I beseech Thy goodness, tell me, whence in this desert will the ascetics receive what they need?"

"Believe Me, if I find those who have among themselves the mother of all virtues—love, and who fulfill My commandments, then I will take all care for them upon Myself, and they will have no lack of anything."

"Once more I ask Thy goodness, how can they easily escape the nets of the enemy and be delivered from his fearsome temptations?"

"If they, as I told you, keep My commandments with meekness, righteousness, and a humble heart, I will not only deliver them from warfare with the enemy and from his snares, but will also make them heirs of the Heavenly Kingdom," the Almighty strengthened Paisius and ascended to Heaven.

The sacred Paisius was seized with great fear from such a condescension to him of the Savior Himself.

But what did the envious hater of mankind, the enemy, devise at this time? Paisius had received power from God, passed safely through the demonic snares, and suffered no harm from the attacks of the evil one. The cunning one could not approach the venerable one, so he attempted to use deception and tried to deprive the ascetic of the virtue of non-acquisitiveness, and through this of Divine grace as well. Having assumed the form of an angel, the devil appeared to a certain Egyptian rich man and persuaded him to go into the desert, to find there "a pauper named Paisius, rich in name and brilliantly adorned with virtues, a chosen vessel of Divine grace," and to offer him much money for alms to the monks who were struggling. Not knowing that this was demonic deception, the rich man took much silver and gold and set out for the saint.

However, the Lord did not abandon His servant; He revealed to him the meaning of so costly an offering from the rich man, and therefore the venerable one immediately arose and went himself to meet the archon.

"Who is Paisius, and where does he dwell?" the Egyptian addressed the ever-blessed one.

"But why do you need him?"

"I have brought him money so that he may distribute alms to the monks."

"Forgive us, O lover of Christ, why do we need money if we have resolved to settle in this desert? Take it, go into the world, and do not be troubled, because God will accept your gift if you distribute this money in the Egyptian villages, where there dwell many poor: the destitute, orphans, and widows."

The rich man heeded the ascetic and returned to Egypt. When Paisius returned to his cell, the devil appeared to him and said:

"What violence! I cannot, Paisius, do anything to you, because you have escaped my traps. I am going away from you and going to war against others; to you I shall come no more, because you have conquered me."

Hearing these words, the venerable one immediately forbade the evil one to speak:

"Be silent, because you are known for your malice," said the warrior of Christ.

Thus shamed, the unclean one was driven out and no longer dared to approach the divine Paisius. Now the ascetic settled in the inner desert and began to lead an even more severe life, in all things resembling the bodiless Heavenly Powers and often conversing with Christ the Master. The Spirit of God, Who dwelt in Paisius, was pleased to deem him worthy of contemplating the Heavenly treasures and that joy which the righteous have there. Once during prayer the divine one was caught up to Heaven, where at first he saw the beauties and delights of paradise, from which he was filled with joy and exultation, and then all the saints. Having tasted that immaterial food and having been delighted by it, he was deemed worthy to receive from God the gift of complete abstinence from food. Partaking of the Most Pure Mysteries every Sunday, the venerable one remained in fasting the whole week until the following Sunday. He lived only by Holy Communion, partaking of no other food. Let no one doubt this, because all things are subject to the Divine will: the venerable one spent seventy years without bodily food, nourished only by partaking of the Divine Mysteries. And there is nothing surprising in this compared with the boundless power of God. For bodily food is required by our nature for the strengthening of the body. But to those who are above nature, the creative power of God, being self-sufficient and in no way subject to the laws of nature, gives a gift surpassing human powers and possibilities. In the same way it is above every law of nature: without food, until the last times, it preserved the Prophet Elijah, which is quite sufficient for proof of this prenatural gift.

By the favor of God, a countless multitude of monks and laypeople began to stream to Paisius, wishing to live with him. Surrounding him like bees around a hive, they were insatiably nourished by the noetic honey of his most sweet teaching, as a result of which the number of monks constantly grew. Those who wished to practice hesychia alone he taught to converse with God through prayer. But those who wished to remain in subordination and obedience—this truly blessed way of life—he settled in community with other brethren, assigning to each suitable work, thanks to which the monks did not sit idle and exercised their bodies, making them obedient to labors, fed themselves, and also gave alms to the poor. Paisius gave the inhabitants a commandment: to do nothing, not even the smallest thing, by their own will, but in everything to be guided by the blessing of the spiritual father.

But who can accurately describe those feats which the venerable one himself performed in hesychia and solitude?

When the divine Paisius came to the inner desert, he settled there and lived for three years in one cave. During this time the hair on his head became too long, so the ever-blessed one devised the following. He drove a stake into the ceiling of the cave and prayed while tying his hair to it, thereby inflicting upon himself still greater labor. Feats became rest for the venerable one. Once during prayer there suddenly appeared before him the Savior, most beloved by him. The righteous one fell in fear and terror to the ground, since he could not gaze upon His Divine Countenance.

"Peace be to you, My servant; fear not. Thy works bring Me exceedingly great joy, and thy prayer is exceedingly pleasing and acceptable to Me. Rejoice, therefore, and receive a generous reward for thy labors. Behold, I give thee such a gift: whatever thou shalt ask in My Name shall be given to thee. And the sins of those sinners for whom thou shalt intercede to Me shall be forgiven," the Almighty said to Paisius.

"Christ the King, ah, if I, wretched as I am, were deemed worthy to receive from Thee the grace to ask for that which is necessary for me, that I might easily traverse the saving paths of Thy commandments, for without Thy Providence we cannot do any good. If Thou hast shed Thy precious Blood for our salvation, hast consented to endure death and burial, granting us eternal life by Thy Resurrection, how many deaths must we endure for love of Thee?"

From that day the venerable one indeed received from God the gift of obtaining all that he asked. A certain elder had a disciple who died, having been deceived by the envious devil. He not only fell into disobedience but also did not repent of such a sin before his repose to his spiritual father. The elder many times asked God to reveal to him where the soul of the lazy disciple was, and the Creator revealed to the abba that the monk was in hades and was undergoing terrible torments. Then the elder, greatly stung in heart, began to fast strictly and pray for forty days, at the expiration of which the elder heard a voice:

"This soul, for which you fervently pray, must remain in hades until I come with Angels and trumpets; only then will it receive a fitting reward for its labors."

This grieved the spiritual father even more, and he decided to prolong his fast for another forty days.

"Let it remain in hades until I come on the clouds," was said to the abba when these days too had ended.

Since he could not persuade the Man-Loving God to have mercy on the disciple (perhaps the Savior did this so that the elder would seek the intercession of the blessed one), the desert-dweller ran to Paisius for help. Knowing by Divine grace of the elder's coming, the venerable one came out to meet him.

"Why have you, father, come to me, wretched and sinful, subjecting yourself to such torment?" the ascetic asked him after their mutual greeting.

Having related to the saint the misfortune of his disciple, his own prayers to God for him, and the answer he heard, that the disciple must endure punishment in hades until the Coming of the Lord, the elder replied:

"For this reason I have come to ask your reverence that you might have compassion on me, wretched as I am, and beseech God for my poor disciple, for I believe that if you ask Him, He will hear you. Do not leave me in sorrow, but ask Him; otherwise I shall not depart hence."

The good elder persuaded the great Paisius to pray to God and to appease the Ruler of the World more with his tears than with his words.

"O, it is impossible for me to undertake such a task, because it is your concern, although, for reasons known only to God, He does not hear you now. His judgments are *a great deep* (Psalm 35:7); however, so as not to disobey you, behold, I will ask the Creator together with your reverence, and whatever seems pleasing to Him, let it be so. You remain in this place and pray to the Creator here, while I will go to ask Him in the inner desert."

In that place Paisius stood at prayer and, raising his hands and mind to Heaven, said:

"Creator of all things, look upon our prayers, of us Thy unworthy servants, and as Thou art good, free from the bonds of hades the soul of the elder's disciple."

When he was thus praying to God, and also with other words, it was impossible not to hear him, according to the true promise given to him by the Master. Immediately Christ, invisibly present everywhere, appeared to him and said:

"What are you asking for, My servant Paisius?"

"Thou, Lord, Who knowest all things, knowest that I ask to have mercy on the disobedient and sinful disciple who is in the torments of hades. I beseech Thee, hearken unto Thy servant, and as Thou art Compassionate and Most Merciful, deliver him."

"I have appointed him to the torments of hades for his disobedience and sin until I come on the clouds together with the Angels."

Then God's chosen one Paisius again began to ask the All-Merciful One:

"Master of all things, all things are subject to Thy commands. It is easy for Thee, Creator of all that exists, to descend now in exactly the same manner as then, at the time of Thy future Coming."

After these words the Savior ascended to Heaven, and then descended on the clouds in great glory with Angels and Archangels, with trumpets and the choirs of the righteous, together with all those with whom He will descend to earth on the last day of Judgment. After this, thrones and fearsome seats were set up, and the soul of the deceased disciple was summoned to judgment. It came forth from hades and, having appeared before the Judge, was given into the hands of Paisius, and then to its elder, who at that moment was intensely praying, as had been agreed between them.

"Take from the hands of My servant Paisius the soul of your disciple, delivered from hades. You will see it no more in torment, but in repose," the Lord announced to the spiritual father great joy, and at that same hour the soul of the disciple came and appeared before the elder, acknowledging that it had endured many torments in hades for its disobedience, "because this very thing was the cause that I fell into sin and was subjected to torments. But through your prayers and the prayers of the divine Paisius the Man-Loving One had mercy on me and freed me from the bonds of hades. And now I go to the place of rest of the righteous."

All this was revealed to the elder during prayer. After he received news of the salvation of his disciple, he immediately went to the great Paisius and disclosed the vision that had been granted to him. Then the venerable one related to the abba the terrible appearance of the Lord and all that he himself had seen, after which they both thanked God, Who had wrought such wonders.

"I thank you greatly, divine Paisius, that by your prayers you have saved not only my despairing disciple, but my own soul, which was subjected to great danger while remaining in sorrow. But I ask you, tell me, what wondrous deed have you done, what struggles have you undertaken upon yourself, that you have been deemed worthy to receive such gifts?" the elder asked Paisius.

"Forgive me, honorable father, because no deed worthy of such recompense is found in me, humble as I am, but Divine Providence, Which arranges all things for those who ask with their whole soul, heard your prayers and did not disdain your great love for your disciple. For by your deed you have imitated the Merciful One, Who for us men, who were expelled from paradise by disobedience and through the deception of the evil one had become enemies of God, was born of the Ever-Virgin Mary, was raised as an ordinary Child, suffered as a Man, and by His death delivered us. He showed us that there is no other greater good than pure love. For its sake one lays down one's life for one's friends, as you, father, have laid down yours for your disciple. Therefore the Almighty heard your prayer and saved your disciple. But I am a sinful man and know no good in myself, and therefore am unworthy of any gifts from the Creator. Forgive me, sacred soul, and let us thank and glorify the One Compassionate Lover of Mankind." After these words the humble one and the abba praised the Giver of all gifts, and then, having blessed each other, each returned to his own place.

After this the great Paisius went into a waterless desert. He did this, on the one hand, to hide from people who observed his feats, and on the other hand, to enjoy in peace the honey of hesychia. However, God did not allow this lamp to remain unnoticed in the desert, but, wishing that he might enlighten and bring others to salvation, commanded him to go out into the outer desert and strengthen the local monks in the equal-to-the-Angels life.

"But I, Lord, what shall I gain from leaving the desert, where I rejoice in Thy visitations, and going to others, whom I cannot guide? I fear, Master, that while instructing them, I myself will not be able to fulfill Thy commandments as I ought and will be condemned for my negligence," the ascetic humbly asked the All-Merciful One.

"No, for the labor which you undertake for the salvation of others you will receive a reward incomparably greater—a generous recompense in the Jerusalem on High," the All-Good One encouraged the righteous one.

Submitting to the Divine command, Paisius went out into the outer desert, where the monks received him with rejoicing. "I also wished to see him," says the venerable John, "and insofar as possible to enjoy Divine grace from his very appearance alone; therefore I went to him and, before knocking on the door of his cell, heard that he was conversing with another person. Being too shy to knock, I stood outside, yet made a small noise. Then, having heard it, the righteous one came out into the courtyard and, seeing me, joyfully embraced me, kissed me, and invited me into the cell, inside which there was no one. I began to wonder with whom the venerable one had been conversing a little before this.

"'Why do you look here and there and are perplexed, as if you saw something strange?' the great Paisius asked me.

"'Indeed, I see something strange and am perplexed. A little before this I heard the voice of another person conversing with you, but now I see no one. What this is I do not know. I ask your reverence to reveal to me this strange mystery,' I answered.

"'O John, a strange miracle will God reveal to you today, and I must show you the love which His goodness has for us. O best of friends, the one whom you heard conversing with me was Constantine, the first Christian emperor. Sent by God, he descended from Heaven and said to me: "Blessed are you who have been deemed worthy of the monastic life, for it was of you that the Savior spoke in one of the commandments of the Beatitudes." I asked him: "Who are you, sir, who say this and greatly bless us monks?" He replied: "I, Constantine the Great, have descended from Heaven to tell you of the glory which monks enjoy in eternity and of the boldness which they have before Christ. I bless you, Paisius, that you incline them to this sacred ascetic life, but I reproach and condemn myself that I did not attain to this most exalted rank." Then I say to him again: "Why, O wondrous one, do you blame yourself? Have you not tasted of that eternal glory and Divine sanctification?" To this he replied: "Yes, I have tasted, but I have neither the boldness that monks have nor equal honor with them. For I saw the souls of certain monks which, upon separation from the body, soared like eagles and ascended to Heaven with great boldness, and none of the demons dared to approach them. Then I saw how the gates of paradise were opened for them, and they entered in and, having appeared before the Heavenly King, stood at the Throne of God with great boldness. This is why I bless you monks, and condemn myself, who was not deemed worthy to receive such boldness. Ah, if only I had left the temporal kingdom, the royal attire and crown, had become poor, put on rags, and fulfilled what the monastic life requires." And I answered him:

"'O most sacred emperor, all that you say is good, for it serves for our consolation. But such are the judgments of our God, and it is unjust to reason differently about His righteous judgments, for He is a Righteous Judge and renders to each according to his worth and gives reward in accordance with his labors. Your life was not filled with such labors, and was in no way similar to the life of monks: you had a wife as helper, children, servants, various enjoyments and pleasures. But monks, having despised all the joys and pleasures of temporal life, have accepted God in place of all these worldly goods, and He was their joy and their wealth, and the fulfillment of His pleasing commandments they counted as enjoyment and great pleasure, enduring, according to the Apostle, "destitution, affliction, torment"' (Hebrews 11:37). So you, O emperor, cannot be equal with them.'

"At the time when we were conversing about this, you also came, my brother John, and he immediately ascended to Heaven. But now, when thanks to this mystery you have clearly understood what great blessings ascetic labors bring, strengthen the brethren," Paisius concluded his account.

"I, John, gave much thanksgiving to God, and then, having conversed sufficiently with the holy Paisius, returned in joy and gladness to my monastery."

In a certain village there lived an elder who, through ignorance having fallen into error, said that Christians should serve only the Father, and should neither honor nor even call God the Son and the Holy Spirit. A considerable number of people followed this false teaching, but the Almighty did not want all these people to perish and the ascetic labors of the erring elder to be lost. It was revealed to the venerable one where this village was located, and he came to it. With him the ever-blessed one brought many baskets with three handles. The people who came running did not recognize Paisius and were very amazed at such a peculiar construction, asking the venerable one what this was and what he intended to do with it.

"I wish to sell them," the great one answered.

"But why have you made them with three handles?"

"Since I worship the Holy Trinity, I must also show in practice the three Persons of the Holy Trinity, praise Her, and glorify the Tri-Hypostatic Godhead, holding in my hands the sign of the Trinity. Just as the Holy Trinity is one Nature in three Persons (if anyone thinks otherwise, he is greatly mistaken), so also one should reason about these baskets. Each of them has one nature, contemplated in three, since in its three handles the entire nature of the basket abides equally. So also the immaterial nature and the prenatural Godhead abides equally in the Three Hypostases, that is, in the Three Persons—the Father, the Son, and the Holy Spirit—and is present in each of the Three Persons, and therefore is called not a Quaternity, and not a Duality, but a Trinity. One Person of the Holy Trinity is not greater than the Second, nor is the Second less than the First."

After this, when the divine Paisius had briefly recounted all this, the elder and all those who were there came to know the truth.

"Teach us further, O wondrous one, the pure Orthodox teaching, using similar clear proofs, because by your first words you frightened us," they said to him with reverence.

Then the thrice-blessed one with a bold voice overthrew all the blasphemous words of the heretics, showing that they were no stronger than a spider's web, and explained to them the foundations of the Orthodox faith more expansively, with a greater number of examples, by which he brought his listeners to the true knowledge of the Holy Trinity. Then, having instructed them all, having taught them to confess their errors and repent of their former false teaching, the righteous one gave thanks to the Creator and returned to his desert. When he was already approaching it, a light suddenly shone forth before him, which came from a multitude of Angels who had filled the desert. At that moment he heard the voice of his Heavenly Guardian:

"Both when you were here, Paisius, and when you departed, we, according to the promise of God given to you, guard the monks dwelling in this desert."

After these words the ascetic glorified the All-Knowing One even more, Who has care for all people.

The fame of the saint spread almost throughout the entire world and moved lovers of virtue to go to him in order to receive his blessing. Being at that time still young, the great among the fathers, the venerable Pimen, also had a strong desire to see Paisius, and therefore he came to the venerable Paul and began to ask him to go together with him to the illustrious one. Paul was a friend of Paisius and often visited him.

"I am embarrassed, child, to take you to him, because you are still young, and he is exalted in virtue; therefore we do not go to him casually, but with great deliberation and reverence, and even then not always. Most often, for the common benefit, we meet with him at an appropriate time," Paul instructed Pimen.

"When we arrive, I will remain outside the door. It will be an extraordinary joy for me even just to do this, and I will consider it a great gift if I merely hear his divine voice. But if even this is impossible, I agree only to touch the cell of the great Paisius, and then, I believe, I shall already be saved. And when you come out of it, I will receive abundant blessing by embracing your feet, which trod the same ground as the beautiful feet of the ever-blessed one," Pimen humbly entreated.

Paul marveled at the strong faith of the young monk and, taking him with him, set out for the venerable one. When they arrived at the place, only Paul entered the cell. After their heartfelt meeting, the divine Paisius asked him about Pimen and said to his friend:

"It is not good to hinder those who come to us and to leave them on the street. They, as our Savior says, easily enter into Heaven."

With these words the saint embraced the youth and, blessing him, prophesied that "this youth will save a multitude of human souls, and many through him will be deemed worthy of paradise, because the hand of the Lord is clearly with him, which preserves him and guides him to the Divine commandments."

Once, when the sacred Paisius had already been fasting for twenty-one days, Christ appeared to him.

"O My chosen one Paisius, you have suffered much for Me," He said to the desert-dweller.

"What is great in my paltry suffering, my good Master? For Thou, by Thy goodness, dost Thyself give me strength," the ascetic wondered sincerely.

"Every good deed is pleasing to Me, and to those who perform it I wish to give a reward equal to their labors. Follow Me."

Thus Paisius followed the Savior. When they reached an unknown cave, the Redeemer asked the blessed one to enter inside, to where a true ascetic was. He saw a man who was rolling on the ground and rubbing his face against it. Wondering at the excessive asceticism of this man, the venerable one came out of the cave and began to beseech the Sweetest Jesus to tell him about such a great feat.

"Have you seen My ascetic, what labors he bears for Me?"

"I have seen, Master, and was horrified by his labors. I ask Thy goodness, reveal to me what kind of feat this is?"

"He fasts for only two days, but you see how he is tormented by hunger and thirst?"

"But how is it that I fast for twenty-two days, and nothing similar happens to me?"

"Because My grace strengthens you, and you are able to fast without pain. But that abba fasts by his own will and, burning with great love for Me, endures with many labors beyond his strength."

"What reward will he receive from Thy goodness for his two days?"

"For these two days he will receive a reward equal to that which you will receive for twenty-two days. And to you, who received five talents, I will also say: *'Enter into the joy of your lord'* (Matthew 25:21), and to him who received two, because you have equally done good, and both have shown zeal according to your strength." With these words the Savior became invisible.

Having returned to his cell, Father Paisius increased his struggles and prayed to God to allow him to rise above food, and his food, as we have already said earlier, was the weekly Sunday Communion of the Most Pure Body and Precious Blood of our Lord Jesus Christ.

"Why do you ask again about food when you eat nothing at all? If you need something else, ask for it," the Savior instructed the great abba.

"I beseech Thee, Lord, when I go out of the desert to visit the brethren, allow me to return again to the desert as quickly as possible, because I cannot bear the delay in visiting others when I myself am deprived of Thy visitation."

"Do not be troubled about this, because when you go out of the desert, I do not withdraw from it, and I do not forsake you, but am always with you."

"I beseech Thee, my Christ, deliver me from anger," Paisius continued.

"If you wish to conquer anger and wrath, take heed not to reproach, revile, or despise anyone. If you fulfill all this, then you will not become angry."

"O Master, Lover of Mankind and Long-Suffering One, if someone fulfills Thy commandments and visits those who love Thee in order to serve their needs, what does such a one receive—reward or harm?"

"Just as a farmer working in a field receives wages from the owner of the field, so also those who do good and help or teach others will receive generous rewards in Heaven."

"Lord, what is the difference between one who struggles in virtue and serves others, and one who only struggles but does not serve?"

"He who struggles himself and also serves others is a son and heir of Mine."

"And if he who strives to serve others and also struggles according to his strength, but this service hinders him and he does not attain the measure of struggle of those who have no such hindrances—will he receive a reward equal to theirs?"

"Yes, such a one will receive a reward equal to theirs," Christ proclaimed and ascended to Heaven.

In the regions of Syria there lived an ascetic adorned with various virtues. Once, when he was praying, there came to him a thought: had he attained the measure of God's saints? At that moment he heard a voice:

"Go to Egypt. There you will find an ascetic named Paisius, who has humility and love for God equal to yours."

Without thinking for a moment about the great distance, the honorable elder immediately set out for Egypt. Having reached Mount Nitria, he began to ask about Paisius, who was known throughout the whole region, and the Syrian monk easily found the desert where our righteous one dwelt, and the venerable one himself met the guest from Syria. The venerable ones joyfully embraced and gave each other a kiss in Christ, after which they came to the cell of Paisius and, having made a prayer, sat down. The elder was the first to speak, and he spoke in the Syrian tongue, but Paisius knew only Egyptian. Grieving that he did not understand the soul-profitable words of the elder, the thrice-blessed one immediately arose and, raising his hands to Heaven, exclaimed:

"Son and Word of God, grant me, Thy servant, Thy grace to understand the meaning of the elder's words."

And—O miracle!—the swift visitation of the Lord! Paisius immediately began to speak and understand the Syrian language.

During this long conversation, one told the other about the visions which each had been deemed worthy of, with which fathers each had associated, and what virtues those abbas had. After six days, when the Syrian and Egyptian desert-dwellers had told each other everything, the elder began to prepare for the journey. Then Paisius summoned his disciples and addressed them with these words:

"Behold, beloved children, before you is a righteous one, perfect in virtue, filled with the Holy Spirit and Divine gifts of grace. With reverence take a blessing from him, which will be for you like a tower protecting you from enemies."

And at that very moment the monks fell to the ground and, having made a prostration before the venerable elder, fervently asked him for prayers and blessing. Having prayed for them, the honorable monk departed for his own country.

After some time a certain hermit came to the great Paisius, and the disciples of the venerable one began to say to him:

"Father, if you had come a little earlier, you would have acquired great profit for yourself, for a man of God came to us from Syria, radiant in mind and heart, who, having instructed us with saving words, departed shortly before your arrival. If you wish, you can still catch up with him, because he should not be far from our parts."

The ascetic was already about to run in order to catch up with the Syrian, but blessed Paisius stopped him:

"Wait, do not go, because that guest is already at a distance of eighteen miles from here, being carried to his home by a cloud."

Hearing this, all were amazed and glorified God.

A certain brother came to Abba Paisius and found him sleeping. An Angel of extraordinary beauty was guarding his repose. Marveling at this, the monk said:

"Truly the Lord guards those who hope in Him," and glorifying the Creator, Who exalts those who love Him, he departed.

The sacred Paisius had a disciple, very simple in his thoughts, but obedient to the venerable one in all commands. Once, when he went to Egypt to sell his handiwork, along the way he met a certain Jew, with whom he continued his journey. Having understood the simplicity of the monk, the Jew began to pour upon him with his vile tongue the poison of the soul-destroying serpent:

"O monk, how can you believe in the Crucified One, Who was not the Messiah? For the Messiah is another, and not He in Whom you Christians believe."

"Perhaps it is so, as you say," by his guilelessness and heartfelt simplicity the monk was deceived by these words, and at that very moment—O woe!—he suffered misfortune, being deprived of the grace of Holy Baptism. When he returned to the desert, the divine Paisius not only did not receive him but did not want to look at him, or approach him, or converse with him, but only turned away from him.

The disciple was greatly grieved, wondering why his spiritual father had so changed toward him, and, falling at his feet, he asked:

"Father, why do you shun me, wretched as I am, not wishing to see me, loathing me as something abominable, although before you did not treat me thus?"

"Who are you, man, I do not know you!" Paisius answered to these words.

"Father, what strange thing have you seen in me, that you do not recognize me? Am I not your disciple?"

"My disciple was a Christian and had received the Mystery of Holy Baptism, but you have not. If you are that disciple, then why do you not have Baptism? Tell me, what happened to you on the road?"

"Nothing."

"Go away from me, because I cannot hear the speech of one who has denied Christ. If you were my disciple, I would see you as you were before."

Then the apostate groaned and began to shed tears, moving the elder to mercy and saying that he (and no one else) was his disciple, that he knew absolutely no sin of his own, and had done nothing evil.

"With whom did you speak on the road?" the venerable Paisius then inquired.

"Only with one Jew, no one else."

"And what did the Jew say to you, and what did you answer him?"

"He said nothing else to me except that Christ is not the One Whom we Christians worship, that One is yet to come. And I agreed with his arguments."

"Wretched one, what can be worse and more abominable than what you have said? For by this very thing you, miserable one, have denied Christ and divested yourself of Holy Baptism. So go and lament yourself as you wish. You have no part with me, because your name is written with those who have denied Jesus, and with them you will be tormented."

"Father, have mercy on me, wretched as I am, for I know not what will become of me. Through thoughtlessness I have divested myself of Baptism and gladdened the demons. After

God I flee to you; do not despise me, wretched as I am," the monk lamented and cried out after the rebuke of Paisius.

Entreating thus, the disciple appeased the elder more with tears than with words, and he said to him:

"Wait, child, I will ask the Man-Loving and Merciful Creator on your behalf."

With these words he began to fervently ask the Creator to forgive his disciple, and the Lord did not delay in granting him forgiveness and deeming him worthy again of the grace of Holy Baptism. As a sign of this the divine Paisius saw how the Holy Spirit in the form of a dove entered the mouth of the disciple, and the spirit of blasphemy came out like smoke and dissolved in the air.

"Glorify the Almighty, child, and thank Him together with me, because the unclean spirit of blasphemy has come out of you, and instead of it the Holy Spirit has entered. The gift of Baptism has again been given to you; so take good heed to yourself, that you do not fall once more into the nets of dishonor through your negligence and inattention, and do not consign your soul to the fire of eternal torment for some other sin," the ascetic said to his disciple, instructing him.

Once a certain elder by the name of John came to the sacred Paisius, and from the long journey through the desert he was greatly fatigued and needed food and rest. When they had conversed sufficiently, Paisius ordered his disciple to prepare a meal so as to share it with John. The disciple fulfilled what the elder had commanded; however, the visitor, pleading his many sins, refused to partake of the brotherly meal. Marveling at John's resolve, the blessed one immediately arose and from the depths of his heart said:

"Lord, visit Thy servant John, who subjects himself to extreme asceticism for Thy Name's sake."

And with the conclusion of the divine one's prayer, a wondrous gift was given to John: a certain beautiful youth extended to him food and drink. Having come to himself, John was filled with joy and was satisfied, having no need of servile food; he was satisfied by Angelic food. Rising, he thanked God and the divine Paisius, then returned again to the desert, having tasted nothing at all of the prepared meal. Adding to his former fasts others, he said to himself: "You have eaten sumptuously, John; now you must also fast with all zeal." Thus the courageous one continued to struggle, conquering his flesh through the prayers of the sacred one.

A certain novice monk lived in the desert, who was strongly troubled by demonic thoughts, and therefore he decided to come to Paisius the Great and ask for his help:

"Pray to the All-Merciful One for me, wretched as I am, for I have a cruel warfare from the demons."

Knowing that he followed his own will and followed the demon of fornication and vainglory, the venerable one decided to prevent this and answered:

"Child, it is not from the demons that you have warfare, as you think; they have not even noticed that you came to the desert. But you have warfare from your own thoughts; therefore go and struggle properly, asking God to visit you, although the demons will sorely tempt you. Then you will come to know well their wiles and will learn what those experience with whom they fight." With these words he dismissed the youth to his place, and then from his whole soul began to ask God to preserve the monk unharmed.

"What have you against me, Paisius? Why do you persecute me by your prayer and protect by it those dwelling in this desert? How wretched am I, and how much more must I suffer if I remain here! Therefore I am going far away from here," roared the chief of the demons at this moment at the venerable one.

"Apostate and enemy of the human race, tell me, why do you trouble and tempt the young monk, raising against him a cruel warfare? Why do you rise up with such fury and cruelty against those who are only beginning the ascetic struggle?" the thrice-blessed one began to interrogate the unclean one.

"I do not approach beginners when they are only setting out on the path of virtue, because the grace of the Lord does not permit me to torment those who struggle with great fervor. But after, because of their own negligence, Divine grace departs from them, I approach them and take possession of them as prey, making them a laughingstock. Therefore at first I do not war against them, but afterward I war against them without hindrance. And when I see that they have become zealous again and are advancing spiritually, then I wage an even greater war against them, so that by means of their constant struggles and good deeds they might not unite with Divine grace and become unconquered and invincible."

From that day the monk was freed from demonic harassment, and the envious demon could no longer war against him. Strengthened by the prayers of the sacred Paisius, the youth completed his ascetic life in a God-pleasing manner and was deemed worthy of a good end.

"At the time when I," continues his narrative the venerable John, "once again set out to the divine Paisius, several monks came to him to hear his profitable teachings.

"'Preserve the traditions of the fathers, and do more than what has been commanded to you,' the righteous one answered them.

"Then the monks again began to ask him:

"'Tell us something more for the benefit of our souls.'

"Discerning with spiritual eyes their thoughts, the ascetic began to tell each one what he had been thinking, and which of his thoughts were good, and which were bad, and whence these thoughts had arisen in them. Marveling greatly at this, each of the monks said to me privately:

"'Father John, truly all our soul's passions, which are known only to God, the venerable one revealed to us one by one.'

"'Believe me, everything that I thought about or did in private the elder revealed to me more than once during our meetings.'"

Following his own will and fulfilling his own desire, a certain brother left the desert and settled near a certain city. Since he often had to go to the settlement to sell his handiwork, he met a Jewish woman who burned with satanic love for him. With the assistance of the demon, having been deceived by his own thoughts, the monk fell into the snares of the Jewess and fell. But the worst thing was that he denied the Christian faith, accepted the Jewish faith, and began to live with that Jewess; she so worked upon him that he soon became like her in impiety. And this thrice-accursed woman fell into such a pit of perdition and attained such shamelessness that she would often take the wretched one by the head, open his mouth, and with a thin stick clean between his teeth so that not the slightest crumb of the Holy Communion of the Most Pure Mysteries would remain. O godlessness! I know, brethren, what sorrow you experience hearing this, and what heartache. And I marvel at the great longsuffering of God. But I shall tell you also the strange thing that happened to him, so that you may marvel at the boundless loving-kindness of the Ruler of the World, with which He deems us worthy from on high.

That man, who by disobedience was cut off from Christians for his impiety, after the passage of time was enlightened by the light of Divine providence, came to himself, and repented of what he had done. Certain monks from among those dwelling in the same desert where he himself had formerly lived, having gone to the city on their own business, stopped at the house of that crafty Jewess. Seeing them, he was pierced in his very heart, remembering the old and sacred brotherhood of the monks, after which he asked where they were from, what their names were, and why they had come to the city. The brethren replied that they were from the desert of Nitria, disciples of the divine Paisius, and had come to the city on their own business. Then the one who had sinned began to entreat them fervently that they would ask their abba to pray to God for him and to appease the Creator by his doxology, so as to deliver him, wretched as he was, from the wiles of the enemy.

The monks promised the brother that they would fulfill his request and ask Paisius to become an intercessor before the Savior. When they returned to the desert, they revealed to the elder everything that had happened to that wretched one, conveying his request. Hearing this story, the venerable one groaned from the depths of his soul:

"Alas, my beloved children! How many great men whom we find mentioned in Holy Scripture were deprived of Divine grace because of women, for the enemy has no more convenient weapon for the destruction of men than a woman. Using her, he is accustomed to conquer great men. You know that with the help of a woman he conquered the great David, his ancestors and descendants. Therefore we must always pray to the Creator that He deliver us from the traps of the demon."

After the instruction, the ascetic began to intercede for the fallen one:

"Lord Jesus Christ, Son and Word of God the Father, do not allow the creation of Thy hands to perish utterly, but look down, O Guileless One, upon him from Thy heavenly dwelling and receive the prayers offered by me for him who at first denied Thee but now has again come to himself and recognized the evil he committed. I beseech Thy goodness, call him to repentance."

The ever-blessed one prayed in this manner for many days in a row and asked the Merciful God to have compassion on His creation. Finally the Savior heard his request and, appearing to the righteous one, asked for whom he was interceding:

"Perhaps My servant Paisius is praying for him who denied Me and left My rank, going together with those opposed to Me? For him who was once a monk but has now become a Jew?"

"Yes, Man-Loving Lord, I pray for him, placing my hopes in Thy mercy. For Thou dost call all and always to repentance, and dost not desire the death of the sinner but dost await his repentance; therefore I have dared to beseech Thy goodness for him. I ask Thee, hearken unto Thy servant, be merciful, and call back Thy straying sheep."

"If you wish Me to have mercy on that lawless one and apostate and call him to repentance, you must consent that I take from you most of the rewards and recompenses which you were to receive for your struggles and, by My loving-kindness, bestow them on him who is worthy of a thousand punishments," Christ replied to the desert-dweller.

"Yes, Lord, I agree with joy; however, I do not know whether I have any deed pleasing to Thee. But by Thy goodness, through which I also receive beneficence every day, pour out Thy mercy upon him, for I would rather be punished for him, so long as he is saved, than enjoy Thy beneficence while he is tormented."

"Worthy of wonder are thy good desire and love for thy neighbor, Paisius, by which thou dost resemble My love for mankind. Since thou hast chosen to be deprived of the honor due to thee for the sake of the sinner's salvation, thou shalt not be deprived of this honor, and the sinner shall be saved according to thy petition."

After some time, because of Divine wrath, that evil woman died, and Isaac (for so the fallen monk was called) returned again to the desert. Instructed by the great Paisius, he again accepted the Christian faith and began to struggle with great zeal in the monastic life, spent the remainder of his life in obedience, piety, and virtue, and peacefully reposed in the Lord. That monk, through the prayers of the sacred Paisius, was deemed worthy of salvation, and we who hear of the wondrous miracles of the venerable one must glorify and magnify God.

In the monastery of the blessed one there lived a certain priest who constantly thought about worldly things. And when other monks went to the venerable one to hear profitable teachings, this priest also went with them. But even while listening to Divine words from the lips of Paisius, he received no benefit from them because he did not set before himself a good aim; his heart was not directed in the ways of the Lord. Moreover, the priest not only received no benefit but also distorted the words of the venerable one with his worldly talk and mocked them.

Indignant at him, the other monks came to a certain God-loving elder and began to complain about this clergyman. Then the abba went together with them to Paisius the Great, and that priest also followed them. Going in to the righteous one, the elder said:

"Know, Father, that this priest is a cause of harm and scandal for the brethren. You must prevent him in this and correct him by rebuke."

"For a long time now I have wished to do what you tell me, if I were certain that he would receive benefit. For the devil is already prepared to drag him to perdition, and if this man hears a harsh word from me, he will leave the brotherhood and go into the world. Then I will be found guilty of his perdition because I could not bear with a brother upon whom the enemy has set himself. But we must ask God to deliver him from this passion," the great one answered and prayed to the Creator for the priest, and immediately drove out of him the demon of shamelessness and self-will.

The priest at that very moment was pierced with the desire for repentance and, convicted by his conscience, was greatly grieved. Confessing his former transgressions more with tears than with words, he asked forgiveness for all he had done and promised to abstain from evil and to amend his ways in the future. From that time he became pious and meek, listened with reverence to the divine words of the venerable one, and joyfully fulfilled them. With the assistance of the prayers of the blessed Paisius and thanks to the longsuffering of the Lover of Mankind, he surpassed many in virtues and became an experienced hermit.

Once, when the divine one was praying in his cell, Christ came to him with two Angels, as once to the Patriarch Abraham, and said:

"Rejoice, Paisius; today you must receive Us."

Imitating the Patriarch, Paisius willingly offered hospitality and, not concerning himself with the preparation of food and drink as that one did, he received the Omnipresent One with pure thoughts. Then, pouring water into a basin, he washed—O wonder!—through the extreme condescension of the Lord, His most pure feet. Paisius diligently cared for the reception of his guests, and the Savior showed him His great love. Since to wash the feet of guests is the best part of hospitality and most pleasing, and since Paisius had done all things, Christ announced to him:

"Peace be to you, My chosen servant," after which He became invisible.

Burning with Divine love and imitating Cleopas, for his heart burned and beat strongly in his breast, Paisius hastened to the water with which he had washed the feet of the Lord and with strong desire drank it, leaving a little for his disciple, who was at that time in Egypt. When he came, greatly fatigued from the journey, the venerable one sent his child to the basin to drink the water that remained there, so as to quench his thirst from the scorching sun.

The disciple replied that he would fulfill his command. However, in his mind he began to reproach the elder because he had sent him to drink not pure water from the spring but dirty water in which feet had been washed. While the disciple was reasoning thus, the ascetic again sent him to the basin; the disciple answered, "I am going," but did not go. The righteous one commanded him a third time to drink that water, but he did not obey. Then Paisius said to him:

"Behold, child, you have received the reward for your disobedience, having been deprived of Divine mercies."

Hearing this, the monk was greatly grieved and ran to the basin but found nothing there.

"Father, there is no water in the basin," he then said to the abba.

"And how can it be found when you have shown yourself unworthy? For disobedience deprives the disobedient of Divine mercies, just as obedience is the cause of them for the obedient."

"And what was this great gift of which I was deprived, and how did it disappear from the basin?" asked the disciple in sorrow.

And the venerable one told him all that had happened to him, adding also the following:

"Since you persisted in disobedience and did not agree to drink the water, which you were commanded to do three times, an Angel of the Lord descended from Heaven and, taking that sacred water into his hands with reverence, ascended again to Heaven."

Then the monk began to tremble all over and remained speechless for a long time. Then, coming to himself, he began to lament and bewail his misfortune, weeping aloud:

"Woe is me, wretched one, what a blessing I have lost! What envious demon prevented me from enjoying it!"

Taking pity on him, the elder consoled the monk:

"Adam, my child, was deprived of paradise for disobedience, acquiring death instead of eternal life. Being unworthy of that glory and the blessings of paradise, he was expelled. In the same way you too have been deprived of the grace which you could have enjoyed, because you disobeyed my commandment. But since you are so grieved and repentant, arise from disobedience, obey, and fervently appease God, asking Him to forgive you, for God is merciful to the penitent and has compassion on those who entreat Him."

After these words the disciple calmed down a little, but, remembering again that evil which he had suffered, he began once more to grieve greatly.

"Father, I am completely inconsolable from my thoughts, and as soon as I remember that grace which I lost, I lament my misfortune, not knowing what to do. I am being plunged by my thoughts into despair. Allow me to go to some experienced elder; perhaps there I will be delivered from sorrow."

Taking a little bread, the divine Paisius gave it to his disciple.

"Take the bread and go to the city. There, near the city wall, on the right, you will find a certain beggar sitting on a dung heap, at whom children throw stones and laugh. Give him the bread and you will hear what will be of benefit to you," the ascetic said to him.

Having found that man of God, the disciple began to wait until the children stopped playing, so as to approach. But that one, seeing him, addressed him:

"Come and give me the blessing, that is, the bread which your elder has sent."

The disciple handed it to the homeless one, and the beggar began to kiss this bread.

"How is Paisius? I very much wished to learn about him. But you, child, why do you delay in carrying out what he tells you and not obey his commands? Do you not know that it was precisely for your disobedience that you were deprived of that Divine washing and the grace which you would have received from it? But not only do you not listen to the advice of your spiritual father, but you come to another! You are like one who has pure, cold water in his hands but does not drink it, instead wandering everywhere in search of water to quench his thirst. So go and obey Paisius the Great, for he who does not do this will not submit to the commands of our Savior Christ either," the beggar addressed the monk.

After this the disciple, glorifying God, returned to the desert, and from then on began to obey the commands of the venerable Paisius without question in all things.

A little time passed, and that disciple, having remembered the grace of which he had been deprived, began to bewail his perdition and again to ask Paisius the Great for permission to go to that man who sat on the dung heap. But the venerable one did not advise him to go, and since because of the thoughts troubling him the disciple did not obey, the elder said to him:

"Child, that man has reposed in the Lord. But since I see that you place your hopes only on him and obey his counsels, I allow you to go. Go to the northern part of the country and you will find a huge tomb. Enter it; there the bodies of three holy men are buried, who were deemed worthy of prophetic gifts. Having foreknown their end, they came to this tomb and lay down there. So then, say to the one who lies in the middle: 'By the power of Jesus Christ, Who raised four-day Lazarus, the servant of Christ Paisius commands you to arise and tell me what will be of benefit to me.'"

After these words the disciple hastened with zeal and, coming to the northern region of the country, found the tomb, entered it, and said to the departed one what the elder had commanded him. And—O miracle!—the dead man immediately arose and said:

"Why did you not obey me when I counseled you to submit to your spiritual father? Go, and without doubt submit to him, listen to his words, if you wish to be saved, because he who does not listen to his words truly resists the commandments of Christ." With these words the dead man fell asleep again, and the monk, marveling at what had happened, returned to the sacred Paisius.

From that time his thoughts were calmed, and, perfecting himself in virtue, he strove through obedience to acquire what he had lost by disobedience.

Once two brothers by blood came to Paisius the Great. They settled in his monastery and, having spent sufficient time in obedience, began to ask the saint for permission to live in solitude in the desert. Seeing their zeal, he released them. Having gone to the desired silence, the brothers struggled much, repelling the attacks of enemies, but the devil through other monks raised warfare against them. With the assistance of the evil one a certain thief robbed one of the hermits, and that one, wishing to find the malefactor, heard about a certain elder who possessed the gift of clairvoyance and could identify him. When he came to this abba, who was clairvoyant in reality not from Divine grace but from demonic action, that one addressed him:

"Those two monks who have settled in this desert have robbed you. Do not release them until they return your belongings to you."

After these words the hermit went to the abbot of the Lavra, the brothers were seized, brought with beatings to the monastery, and cast into prison, having been condemned to death as criminals for theft. Learning by Divine grace of the temptation which had befallen the brothers, Paisius immediately went to the Lavra. All the fathers came out to meet him, among whom was also that deluded elder who was considered clairvoyant. After all had given the venerable one the proper greeting, he asked them:

"Brethren, what have you done to those two young men who went to practice hesychia?"

"Father, they are thieves, and for their unworthy deed have been cast into prison."

"And who told you that they are thieves?"

"This clairvoyant here."

"If the gift of prophecy were in you from God and not from manifest demonic delusion, a demon would not be seen at your mouth," the venerable one rebuked the elder.

These words caused confusion; the brethren were frightened because the words of the sacred Paisius were true and not subject to any doubt. Reproaching that monk, the fathers made him ask forgiveness for his sin, and he, frightened, fell down at the sacred feet of the venerable one:

"Forgive me, holy Father, and pray for me, who have been deluded."

The venerable one prayed to God for him, and immediately from the mouth of the elder, in the form of a swine, which furiously and angrily threw itself at the ever-blessed one, threatening to tear him with its tusks, the demon of vainglory came out. But the divine one rebuked it and sent it into the netherworld. And that elder, who had been deluded before, began to accuse himself, repented, and, greatly bewailing his fall, entreated the venerable one, rolling on the ground, to forgive him his past sins committed while in a state of delusion. Likewise the other monks who had been deluded through him, accusing themselves, first asked for forgiveness and then, having invited the two slandered young men, repented of the disgrace they had inflicted and asked forgiveness for the blows they had given them.

Taking compassion on them, our Father Paisius instructed them properly, and then led aside the one who was in charge of the monastery and, without naming the thief, revealed to him the place where the stolen things of the hermit were, after which he returned to the desert.

Having learned how God helps people through the venerable Paul, Paisius set out to him. Having met, they began to remain inseparable, helping each other, and were like a fortress wall. Receiving with joy the blessings of hesychia, each day they devised new feats. Being already an elder and a contemporary of the divine Paul, and having a most zealous soul, the sacred Paisius said to him:

"Let us always struggle and labor while there is time, because on earth one cannot cease to work at virtue; otherwise it is impossible to please the Lord. It would be fearful and shameful for us if the hour of death should find us in negligence."

"Behold, O most excellent of fathers, I follow your good counsel, because, hoping in your prayers, I believe that God will deem us worthy to end this life working at virtue," the venerable Paul replied, listening with joy to the counsel of Paisius the Great.

And so both of them were wonderworkers, experienced physicians of souls and bodies, entreating the Almighty for all and for all being the cause of salvation.

Since we would have much to tell about the divine Paul, we leave this task to another. However, concerning the sacred Paisius, very much that is incomprehensible has come down to us. Something of what is known, so as to move listeners to imitate them, is also in our narrative, but there are not enough words to describe exactly the lofty life of the divine Paisius, and he himself, through extreme humility, did not wish to reveal his struggles; he always said that the highest virtue is that which is hidden from human eyes. He also said that the highest of virtues is to follow the counsel of others and not one's own will.

The venerable one, both when he practiced hesychia and when he associated with someone, always strove to please God. In hesychia he loved the ascent to God, and in association he desired the salvation of others. The ascetic's way of life was wondrous: even while in the monastery, he hid it from others. When they wished to praise him, Paisius the Great would immediately abandon what he had done and take up another task, so as not to harm the previous one by praises. For truly human praises present great danger. And those who chase after them gain little from this. Therefore the Lord also commands us: *"Do not let your left hand know what your right hand is doing"* (Matthew 6:3).

And now the time has come to tell also of the blessed end of the venerable one.

And so this warrior of Christ was called by God to Heavenly blessedness when he had reached a deep old age and, like a bright star, had shone with all manner of virtues. His body was honorably buried, and his spirit ascended to eternal life.

A little time passed, and the all-praised Paul also departed unto the Lord, being of the rank of the divine Paisius. However, not only were the souls of these great ascetics united in Heaven, but also their very bodies, having been laid in different places, after a short time were united in the following manner. And you, readers, must be very attentive, listening to this account, because it will tell you of one strange miracle.

When the most wondrous Paisius died, the divine Paul went into the inner desert and after some time there reposed, after which he was honorably and reverently buried. Having heard of the death of Paisius the Great, our Father Isidore on a small vessel set out for the place where the holy relics of the venerable one lay. Taking them with all honors, he placed the sacred remains in a shrine prepared for them and set out on the return journey, wishing to enrich his homeland of Pisidia with them. He had already sailed a considerable distance when he reached the desert where the relics of Abba Paul lay: not far from the shore the vessel stopped and would not move forward, but, being as if alive, of its own accord turned toward the land. Those on the ship applied all their efforts for two days to make the ship sail forward. Having understood that the delay came from God and not knowing what to do, the people calmed down and let go of the rudder. Then the vessel, guided by an invisible hand, sailed on its own and stood motionless at the shore so as to take on cargo. At that moment the renowned Father Jeremiah, an elder of that desert, came out to the seafarers.

"People, why do you resist the miracle of God, seeing that it is above nature? The great Paisius is calling his friend, the divine Paul, wishing that his precious relics be brought aboard the ship, so come out quickly and seek the place of repose of the fellow-ascetic of the righteous one."

The honorable Isidore and those with him went all over the desert in search of the relics of the divine Paul, and after they had found them, they brought the sacred remains onto the ship. And—O miracle!—both great fathers—Paisius and Paul—were truly the helmsmen who guided the ship through the sea and delivered it from all difficulties until the vessel reached Pisidia.

A triumphal procession, with psalmody, led by the great Isidore, transferred the precious relics of the saints to the monastery built by him. And those who were afflicted by demons, and those who suffered from other diseases, immediately received healing at the shrine of the venerable ones. From that time God has wrought through them so many miracles that it is impossible even to enumerate them. But I, the humble John, have told only a small part of them, to the glory of the Father, and of the Son, and of the Holy Spirit, now and ever, and unto the ages of ages. Amen.

Written by our venerable Father John Kolobos

Part 2

The Life and Struggles of Our Father Among the Saints Martin, Bishop of Gaul, Who Flourished in the Fourth Century

Saint Martin lived in the times of the Roman Emperors Gratian and Valentinian and was a skilled military man. In the year 381 he was appointed to the rank of archstrategos, and fifty thousand soldiers were under his command. Once this numerous army set out on a campaign against the barbarians, who had begun a war with the Romans for the possession of their territories. When Martin and his army approached the enemy encampment, the countless multitude of foes frightened the Roman legionaries. While Martin remained in perplexity and sorrow, not knowing what to do, a certain beggar in tattered clothing appeared before him and began to ask for alms. The merciful and compassionate archstrategos took pity on the wretched man and brought him into his tent. There he cut off a piece of his chlamys (an expensive officer's garment) and clothed the beggar, then gave him bread, wine, and money to acquire the most necessary things. That day, from intense sorrow and heavy thoughts, Martin lay down to rest without supper. In his sleep, in the image of that beggar to whom the commander had shown mercy during the day, our Lord Jesus Christ appeared to the archstrategos, clothed in the piece of his chlamys.

"Why are you so sorrowful, Martin?" the Savior asked him.

"Because I cannot withstand such a multitude of enemies, and I do not know what to do," replied the warrior.

"Take courage, be not sorrowful at all, and do not fear the enemies, for because you, seeing Me naked, clothed Me, and when I was hungry, you gave Me drink, and when I was thirsty, you fed Me, I shall repay you and preserve you from your enemies. When they see My face, they shall be greatly afraid, shall fall at your feet, and with many promises and gifts shall beg for peace. Thus you shall return to Rome with great glory and honors. Moreover, throughout your entire life I shall help you, and after death I shall deem you worthy of My Kingdom," the Almighty encouraged the commander, who immediately awoke.

In the morning Martin ordered all the soldiers to arm themselves and go out to battle, but in fear they said to him that they could not withstand such a multitude of barbarians.

"I shall go out to battle alone, but you remain here, and then let us see whether you can save yourselves from the enemies without the leadership of a commander," the archstrategos said to them with anger.

Not expecting such a reply, the soldiers fell at the feet of their commander and began to entreat him to cease being angry, because the entire army was ready to follow him to certain death. The soldiers took up their weapons and went out to battle. But as soon as the enemies caught sight of them, they became greatly afraid, because they saw around the Roman army armed and fearsome giants sitting upon countless chariots and horses—these were the ranks of the Heavenly Powers, whom the Most High had sent to help Martin, so as to guard him from his enemies according to His promise. The barbarians immediately sent envoys to the archstrategos to conclude peace, but the commander did not agree. Then other envoys came to him with many gifts and promises to be in submission to the Romans. They barely managed to persuade the archstrategos to conclude peace and end the military operations. Having subjected the barbarians to Roman rule, Martin returned to Rome with great joy, where the emperors themselves, together with a multitude of their nobles, met him with glory and honors as a victor.

Having recounted to the emperors his vision and the glorious victory, blessed Martin said:

"That terrible war was ended not by me, but by Jesus Christ—the Invincible Power of Christians. He secured the victory for us, therefore I ask you, allow me to spend the remainder of my life laboring for God, Who helped me."

"We desire that you remain with us, and we shall reward you with great dignity and honors for your victory," the emperors, saddened by this request, tried to dissuade their favorite.

"Permission to depart into stillness, to care for the salvation of my soul, will be for me higher than any rewards and honors," Martin remained resolute.

Marveling at his praiseworthy and God-pleasing aim, the rulers permitted the archstrategos to act according to his heart's desire. The ever-blessed one distributed all his possessions to the poor and, having renounced the world, came to a quiet place, where he received monasticism. Throughout entire days he studied Holy Scripture and after seven years, through his exercise in ascetic struggles, attained the highest virtues. By divine revelation and against his own will, the sacred Martin was ordained bishop of the city of Constance in Gaul.

Having accepted the heavy burden of the episcopate, the saint, as a true shepherd tending the rational sheep of Christ in the saving pastures of His commandments and giving them to drink of the waters of His Divine teaching, became for all an example of virtue. To Martin was given the grace from God to foretell the future, to raise the dead, to cast out demons, to work signs and miracles worthy of wonder. Of these, for the sake of confirming the truth of the many others, we shall recount only some.

Once the venerable one was walking along the road and encountered a funeral procession. But a certain lawless slanderer would not allow the dead man to be buried, claiming that the deceased owed him three hundred gold coins.

"Why do you not allow the deceased to be buried, when I have heard that he returned this money to you with interest?" the blessed one asked the impious man.

"He gave me nothing, because if he had returned his debt, then I would have given him the receipt," the liar insisted.

"Master, he lies, because he received his money with interest. However, wishing to slander us, he did not return the receipt to us, making the excuse that he had lost it," the widow of the deceased objected to these words.

"You have received your money, so now allow the dead man to be buried," Martin tried once more to bring the man who had lost his conscience to reason, but he continued to insist on his position. "But if the dead man rises and proves that you received your money, what shall be done with you?"

"If he rises, as you say, then let me die, and let him live."

Of course, he said this because he did not believe in the resurrection of the dead man.

"There was no need either for the dead man to rise, or for you, wretched one, to descend into Hades, but since you yourself, in your shamelessness, have preferred death to life and do not allow the deceased to be buried, let it be as you wish," Bishop Martin replied to these words, approached the dead man, and prayed thus:

"O Lord our God, True Witness and Savior of the wronged, Resurrection of the dead and Guide of life, Who alone knowest the depths of the heart and givest life to those who hope in Thee, command in Thy holy and awesome name that this dead man rise unto the knowledge of the truth and the conversion of those present, that beholding Thy wonders, they may glorify Thee, the only True God, unto the ages. Amen."

Then, taking the dead man by the right hand, he pulled him slightly and—O miracle!—the dead man immediately rose, sat up on the bier, saw the slanderer standing opposite him, and said:

"Depart, evil man, to the dark place of torment prepared for you because you have troubled me who had reposed in peace. But the righteous and holy Martin by his supplication to God has taken me from thence, that I might convict you concerning the money which I gave you, and you would not return to me the receipt, awaiting my death. Righteous is God, Who repays each one for his deeds, and swiftly avenges the wronged."

With these words he rose from the bier and, approaching the ascetic, bowed down to the ground before him, while the slanderer, falling to the ground at that same hour, gave up his spirit. And his wife cried out:

"Woe is me! What a terrible and bitter exchange has taken place! Holy one of God, return my husband to me alive, and I shall give back both the receipts and the three hundred gold coins with interest, and even more."

"You cry out in vain, woman, for the Lord Himself, Who raised this one, commanded that one to die, even as he himself wished," the bishop replied, and all the rest glorified God.

Another time, passing through the city, Martin saw a certain youth who had hanged himself.

"This evil befell him through the action of the devil," the venerable one said to those present, and turning toward the east, began to pray at length to the Almighty, and then pronounced:

"Unclean and crafty spirit, who moved this youth to hang himself, in the name of our Lord Jesus Christ appear before all, that they may see you."

And immediately the demon appeared in the form of a little Moor, who held a rope in his hands. His eyes flashed with fire, his lips were black, his teeth white, his hands long, his legs crooked, and his tongue hung from his mouth like that of a rabid dog.

"Unclean and crafty spirit, what is your occupation?"

"By my chief, Satan, I am appointed to drive people to hang themselves."

"And why did you move this youth to hang himself?"

"This man was formerly an idolater, and then became a Christian, but he did not live according to the commandments, but followed his own will, giving no thought whatsoever to eternal torments. He bowed his neck under the yoke of sin and, being wounded from head to foot, lost hope in salvation. Then I found the opportunity to push him to hang himself, and to drag him with me to torment, therefore great is my labor."

"Crafty murderer, enemy and accuser! You yourself inclined him to surrender himself to the power of darkness and to destruction, brought him to such a miserable state, and now you accuse him? For this, Jesus Christ commands you through me, a humble one, to depart to the edge of the universe and to remain there until the end of the age, and then to descend together with your minions into the Hades prepared for you."

At that same moment the demon became invisible, and the saint approached the dead man and made prayer:

"O Lord my God, Who hast boundless compassion and an ineffable abyss of mercy, forsake not the work of Thy hands, but as Thou art Good and the Lover of mankind, look down from Thy holy height and raise this dead man, that Thy most holy name may be glorified unto the ages of ages. Amen."

At that same instant the dead man arose and, falling at the feet of Bishop Martin, began to thank the thrice-blessed one because through the prayer of the hierarch the Lord had not abandoned him in terrible and sorrowful Hades.

"Child, since this night you have tasted of the torments of Hades and seen that great evil which deeds of unrighteousness produce in a man, repent worthily, bewail your sins, be disgusted by them, and henceforth abstain from them," the ascetic consoled the one he had saved, gave him suitable instruction, and having set him upon the deeds of repentance, dismissed him in peace.

Once Saint Martin was summoned to come to another city and teach its inhabitants about salvation. Setting out from his diocese, he went on his way and along the road found a man whom a dragon dwelling in that place had killed.

"This evil was done by our enemy the devil," Martin pronounced. Since that night the wondrous one had seen in a dream how a terrible dragon had risen up to the Heavens, and he had prayed to God and cast it down to earth, he left his path and went to where it dwelt. Seeing the blessed one, the dragon rose into the air, arching like a vault, and opened its maw, wishing to devour the wonderworker. But the saint spat in its face, and—O miracle!—it fell to the earth and gave up its spirit.

"You shall tread upon the asp and basilisk; the lion and the dragon you shall trample underfoot" (Psalm 90:13), the ascetic said, stepping on its head, then approached the dead man and, taking him by the hand, prayed:

"Jesus Christ, Who rose from the dead and gives life to the dead, may He raise you also."

After this miracle was accomplished, the risen man asked the hierarch to make him a Christian, because he had been an idolater. Having instructed him, Martin baptized him in the name of the Father and of the Son and of the Holy Spirit, and then communed him of the Most Pure Mysteries and, having taught him all that was necessary, dismissed him.

The ascetic continued on his way, and on the road to the appointed city he met a beggar who asked alms from him. The bishop commanded the deacon appointed to distribute alms to give all the money he had, but the clergyman gave the sufferer only half, and decided to distribute the other half to other beggars. They stopped for the night at the house of a very wealthy woman who was an idolatress, whose house was situated near the road.

Seeing the saint with his companions, she received them with joy and set a rich table. But the blessed one touched nothing, but prayed all the time for the salvation of her soul. At midnight the woman came to the venerable one and, falling at his feet, asked him to make her a Christian, saying that she had seen in a dream a certain Fearsome Judge seated on a high throne, surrounded by many soldiers. A multitude of bound condemned persons were being brought before Him, and some He commanded to be cast into fire, others to be cruelly tormented. Among them, bound and trembling, she herself also stood, but one of the soldiers of the Judge approached her and asked:

"For what have you been condemned and bound?" "I do not know," answered the woman.

"And what will you give me if I free you?" he asked.

"All my possessions."

"I do not need them, but give me your promise that you will become a Christian, and then I shall deliver you from the bonds and from the torments to which you are to be subjected."

And the woman, to avoid punishment, promised and swore by the God of Christians to receive the Sacrament of Baptism. Only after this was she freed from the bonds and released.

"Therefore I ask you, make me a Christian and teach me how to be saved, so as not to fall into the hands of that Fearsome Judge, Who judges righteously and regards neither gifts nor persons."

Hearing this request, the saint rejoiced and, having instructed her and all her household, baptized them in the name of the Holy Trinity. Having taught them all that was necessary, he was already preparing to depart, but the woman began to ask him to accept from her as a gift a golden vessel of four litrae and four hundred gold coins. So as not to grieve her, and for the sake of the poor, the blessed one accepted these offerings, and then, blessing her, departed. Along the way Martin asked the deacon how much money he had given to the beggar whom they had met on the road.

"Two hundred gold coins," replied the companion.

"And how much did you have?"

"Four hundred."

"O you of little faith, why did you not give four hundred, as I commanded you? Therefore now you have received from the woman four hundred gold coins and four litrae of gold, but had you given him four hundred, you would have received eight hundred coins and eight litrae of gold. By your disobedience you have harmed the woman as well, depriving her of a fourfold reward, and yourself."

When they finally arrived in the city, they heard songs and music. The ascetic listened for a long time, and then spoke with sorrow:

"Behold what the devil does: he does not wish to appear cruel, but always and in everything pleasant, therefore he devises deception through which he destroys a multitude of souls. By means of melodies drawn forth by musical instruments, and by songs, he carries away the mind of man from the remembrance of God. Many abandon spiritual chants and come to listen to demonic songs. Having the sweetest psalms of David, the God-inspired words of the prophets, apostles, and hymnographers of our Church, they forsake this spiritual aid and run to fulfill the will of the devil by means of instruments and songs."

At this time a certain woman adorned with many jewels and fragrant with myrrh and perfumes was passing by him. With great shamelessness she stopped on the road and, smiling, was inviting passersby to debauchery with gestures.

"If this harlot adorns herself like a bride, striving to seduce people and draw them to destruction in order to please the devil, how much more should we adorn our souls with virtues and keep ourselves undefiled by every sin, so as to please our Bridegroom Jesus Christ? Thus we shall be deemed worthy to enter His eternal bridal chambers and shall reign with Him without end," the hierarch said with tears.

From these words that woman was moved to compunction and, approaching, fell at the feet of Martin.

"Lord, do not turn away from me, miserable and wretched, do not leave me in the mire of my iniquities. I, unworthy even of this life, burdened with an infinite multitude of sins, condemned to the eternal bitter and cruel torments of Hades, beg you to have mercy on me, sinful and despairing, and save me," she began to pray.

Raising the woman from the ground, the wonderworker set her on the right path and called her never to despair, because the mercy of God the Lover of mankind is boundless.

"I shall fervently entreat Him for your salvation, but only repent from all your soul and from all your heart. I promise you that the Much-merciful God shall receive you as His prodigal son, and as our Physician shall heal all your spiritual wounds." From that day on, the woman not only turned away from her sins and came to hate them, but renounced the world altogether, confessed her sins to Bishop Martin, distributed all her possessions to the poor, after which she enclosed herself in a small cell and began to bewail her former iniquities.

"What springs and what rivers can wash away my countless impurities? What lamentations and tears can beseech the Righteous Judge God to forgive me my iniquities?" the woman reproached herself.

From all her heart she asked the Almighty to forgive her former sins:

"O God, be merciful to me, a sinner, and destroy me not, O Master, with my iniquities. Lead me not down into the depths of Hades for my sins, but as Thou art Good and the Lover of mankind, save me by the abyss of Thy mercy, for Thou art He Who takest away the sin of the world."

And such repentance did blessed Zoe (for so was this woman named) display that for a full twelve years she strove unceasingly with tears in fasting, lying on the bare ground, vigils, prostrations, and prayer, leading many to salvation by her example. The Much-merciful Lord granted her the grace of healings, and through the intercession of the venerable Zoe many sufferers received healings. Having lived in a manner pleasing to God, she reposed in the Lord with joy.

And Saint Martin, while he was in that city, unceasingly sowed the seeds of the Divine word in the parched and embittered hearts of the citizens, both publicly before all the people and in private conversations. The bishop gathered many and great fruits: he made the coarse gentle, the wrathful meek, the merciless merciful, drunkards and the debauched chaste, the impious pious, and he taught the ignorant Divine letters so that they began to strive to attend the divine services, and in general he brought all sinners to repentance and corrected them. After this, rejoicing and blessing God, he returned to his diocese.

One day, going through the city, the saint saw a poor man who was being greatly oppressed by creditors: he owed them three hundred gold coins. Taking pity on him, the bishop asked the creditor to wait a little, after which, raising his eyes to Heaven and lifting up his hands, he pronounced:

"O Lord, Who rained down manna from above in the wilderness and for forty years fed Thy people, and through Thy apostle Peter drew a stater from the mouth of a fish, send down also now from on high to this poor man his debt, to the glory of Thy holy name, for Thou art One God, glorious and wondrous throughout all the universe, and to Thee belongs glory unto the ages. Amen."

And—O miracle!—immediately a dove flew down from Heaven and settled on the shoulder of the thrice-blessed one. And when he took it into his hands, it turned to gold. The venerable one brought it to a goldsmith:

"Take it as a pledge, and give me three hundred gold coins. Tomorrow I shall return them to you."

Marveling at the skill with which the dove had been made, the jeweler gave him three hundred gold coins with great joy, hoping that the dove would remain with him. Taking the money, Saint Martin gave it to the creditors and freed the poor man from his debt. On the next day Christians came to the ascetic from afar to receive instruction in the faith and gave him much money for the distribution of alms. Receiving the Christians with joy, the bishop taught them the word of God and set them on the path of salvation, after which, blessing them, he dismissed them in peace.

"Take, child, three hundred gold coins and thirty more in addition for the good you have done for us, and return to me my pledge," he said to the jeweler.

Saddened, the craftsman took the money and returned to him the golden dove.

"I thank Thee, O Lord, that Thou hast heard my supplication," Martin addressed the Most High, and then released the dove to where it lived. When the dove flew up, the jeweler fell at the feet of the praiseworthy one and began to ask him to accept the three hundred thirty gold coins for the poor:

"It is enough for me that I was deemed worthy to see this great and strange miracle."

Accepting the money, the saint blessed him:

"May the Lord have mercy on you, child, on the Day of Judgment."

After this Martin set out for a country where a multitude of Hellenes lived, to teach them the word of God and bring them to the knowledge of God, but along the way he met a Hellene who was standing over his dead donkey:

"In vain do Christians preach the resurrection of the dead. How is it possible that a person who has died, whose body has decomposed in the earth, can rise?" the pagan was pondering.

"Friend, why do you think that the dead cannot rise?" the ever-blessed one addressed him.

"How is it possible for those who have died, decomposed, and become dust to rise?"

"With God all things are possible, and for Him nothing is impossible."

"If you raise this donkey, then I shall believe that the dead too will rise, because He Who raises this animal can raise the dead as well."

"God will not raise brute beasts, because they will not go to the Judgment and will not be deemed worthy of resurrection, but He will raise only men, in order to judge them and require an account for their good or evil deeds, and to repay each one for them."

"And Who is this God of Whom you speak, Who will do all this?"

"Jesus Christ, the Son of God, Who was crucified for the salvation of mankind."

"And why did He not take vengeance on those who mocked Him?"

"He did not take vengeance immediately because He was awaiting their repentance, on account of His extreme goodness and longsuffering, but He will take vengeance in the future."

"What is the use of many words? If you raise this donkey, then I shall believe your words."

Raising his hands to Heaven, the saint began to pray with these words:

"O Lord my God, Who hast become the Cause of salvation for all men, raise this animal also for the conversion and knowledge of this man, for by means of this miracle he shall know Thy omnipotence and believe in Thee."

As soon as blessed Martin pronounced these words, the donkey arose and began to walk. Seeing this strange miracle, the Hellene fell at the feet of the ascetic.

"Now I have come to know that this is the True and Almighty God. I beg you, servant of God, show Him to me, that I may hear His voice and believe in Him."

"He who hears us, His humble servants, hears Him, because God is seen not by bodily eyes, but is understood by the eyes of the soul, which are the mind and thought. But you, child, if you wish to see Him, believe in Him, and then with your noetic eyes you shall see Him and shall live forever."

"I beg you, master, come to our country and guide us onto the true path."

This was precisely what Martin wanted, therefore he set out for that country together with the Hellene and the risen donkey. Hearing the word of God preached by Martin and learning that the venerable one had raised the donkey in the name of Jesus Christ, the idolaters believed in Christ, up to a thousand men, not counting women and children. Having instructed them, the hierarch baptized them in the name of the Father and of the Son and of the Holy Spirit. He remained with them for a long time and constantly instructed them until the remaining idolaters were also moved to compunction and were baptized together with their wives and children in the name of the Holy Trinity. Bishop Martin conducted conversations with them about death, resurrection, the future Judgment, torments, and the eternal blessings of the Kingdom of Heaven, and returned to his native land.

Martin also worked a miracle at the hour of his death. This event became a great joy and consolation for the inhabitants of his entire diocese. A severe drought occurred in their region, so that all were in sorrow and perplexity. Assembling his flock, the bishop gave the people many instructions and called upon them not to despair.

"Do not sorrow, my children, on account of the drought. Tomorrow the Lord shall send you such rain as you desire."

Then, having prayed to God and committing them to His protection, the saint departed to the Lord on the 10th of November. Then all the bishops, priests, the entire clergy, and Christians assembled from the surrounding regions and held an All-Night Vigil. At dawn, taking up the body of Martin, they went out of the city with candles, incense, and the singing of psalms and buried the ascetic at a distance of one mile, in a church of the Martyrs. And when they returned, the sky filled with clouds, lightning began to flash, and in that region such heavy rain poured down as the blessed one had promised. From that time until now there have been many healings at his grave for those who approach him with faith, to the glory of God, to Whom be glory and dominion unto the ages of ages. Amen.

The Life and Struggles of Our Father
Among the Saints Cyril, Archbishop of Alexandria,
Who Flourished in the Fourth Century

The great teacher of the Church, the hierarch Cyril, was born in Alexandria and came from a pious and noble family. He was the nephew of Patriarch Theophilus of Alexandria. Cyril received an excellent education and became very skilled in philosophy. The future hierarch always exercised himself not only in external wisdom but also in spiritual wisdom, and the beloved occupation of the venerable one was the reading and study of Holy Scripture, which also caused the most blessed Theophilus to number his nephew among the church clergy and ordain him archdeacon.

Upon the repose of Patriarch Theophilus, all the clergy and the flock unanimously decided to appoint the divine Cyril as their primate. And as soon as he assumed the Patriarchal throne, all heretics and schismatics called Novatians, who considered themselves pure and righteous like the Pharisees, were expelled from Alexandria. As a sign of their "pure" life, they wore white garments.

The Novatians maintained that whoever fell into mortal sin after Baptism was no longer a member of the Church, and that the sin committed could be forgiven only through a new Baptism. The heretics did not allow second marriage, calling it fornication, yet they baptized a second time those who had already once been immersed in the font. Holding to other heretical ideas as well, they were called Novatians after a certain Novatus, the founder of this schism. Once, during the reign of Emperor Decius, this man was a priest serving in Rome. He wanted to become Pope of Rome, but contrary to his wish and hope, after the martyric death of Pope Fabian, the blessed Cornelius was chosen as the head of the Roman Christians.

Then the proud Novatus broke away from the Catholic Church and began to wage war against the divine Cornelius, who received back into the Church those Christians who, during the time of persecution, had denied their faith out of fear of tortures. In this, Cornelius imitated Christ Himself, who, after sincere repentance, restored Peter to his apostolic rank. The proud Novatus condemned Pope Cornelius, calling him a "companion" and "comrade" of idolaters and, having united with those of like mind, proclaimed himself a second Pope of Rome.

Besides the expulsion of the schismatics along with their bishop Theopemptus from the bounds of the Alexandrian Orthodox Church, the hierarch Cyril waged unceasing warfare against the pagan demons. Not far from Alexandria there was a place called Canopus, and near it Menuthis, where from ancient times there stood an altar that served as a dwelling place for demons. Patriarch Theophilus had more than once wanted to cleanse this place by building a monastery here for the glorification of God, but because of many obstacles and his early death, he was unable to bring his dream to fruition. The thrice-blessed Cyril, the successor of Theophilus, took this care upon himself.

Once an Angel of the Lord appeared to him in a light sleep and said that the demons would depart from Menuthis after the translation thither of the precious relics of the unmercenaries Cyrus and John. And as soon as this command was fulfilled, the unclean spirits retreated, and the former pagan shrine became a source of healings. After the hierarch had driven out the invisible demons from Alexandria, he took care to drive out the visible demons as well—the Christ-hating Jews, who had made their home in the ancient city since the days of Alexander the Great. With the passage of time, they had greatly multiplied and never ceased, according to the custom of their race prone to rebellion, to secretly and openly plot evil against Christians. Because of their irreconcilable hatred for the Savior, they became the cause of many disturbances, uprisings, bloodshed, and murders.

Having summoned the rulers of the synagogues to himself, the most blessed Patriarch Cyril counseled them to restrain their people from vile deeds and to come to their senses, but they began to act with even greater malice. Thus, in Alexandria there was a beautiful large temple called the Church of Alexander, since it had been built by Bishop Alexander. Having conceived the plan to slaughter Christians, the impious Jews armed themselves and one night began to run through the streets with noise, shouting under the windows of houses where Christians lived that the Church of Alexander was on fire. Hearing the cries, the Christians immediately rushed out in haste to extinguish the fire, but as soon as a person ran out into the street, the evildoers would attack and kill him—some with swords, some with knives, some with spears... Many citizens perished during this slaughter.

In the morning, upon learning what had happened, the hierarch Cyril was greatly grieved and called upon Orestes, the eparch of the city, to judge the Jews according to the law. But he, although he was himself a Christian, out of hatred for the venerable one helped the Jews and concealed the murderers. Then, filled with Divine anger, the primate took with him a multitude of Christians and himself drove the Jews from Alexandria, destroyed their houses, and closed their synagogue. The eparch became angry with the Patriarch for this act of self-governance and began to do evil to the relatives and friends of the hierarch. For example, he ordered that the garments be publicly torn from Hierax, secretary of the most blessed one, a man well-known and respected by all, and that he be beaten mercilessly.

From that time a great discord and disagreement arose between the eparch and the ascetic: the hierarch defended the Christians, while the eparch defended the Jews. Both of them separately wrote to Emperor Theodosius the Younger about this matter and awaited what command would follow. Meanwhile, there was also another circumstance in Alexandria that became the cause of murders and great disturbance.

There lived in the city of Alexandria a virgin-philosopher named Hypatia—the pious and virtuous daughter of the philosopher Theon. Bishop Synesius of Cyrene writes that in her wisdom she surpassed all the philosophers of that time. She preserved the purity of virginity, not wishing to marry, on the one hand, primarily for love of Jesus Christ, and on the other, so that she might calmly devote herself to reading philosophical books. Every day priests and nobles came to her in Alexandria from various countries; the whole people honored her and lovingly listened to her soul-profitable counsels and instructions. The virgin-philosopher wished to reconcile the Patriarch with the eparch and with humility and meekness came now to the one, now to the other. With her reasonable words she persuaded both to be reconciled, although the most holy Patriarch had already sought peace with the eparch several times before, but the latter, because of his evil disposition and vindictiveness, would not hear of anything.

One day, when the virgin-philosopher was returning home in a chariot, certain insurgents who did not want peace between the eparch and the hierarch suddenly attacked her, dragged her from the chariot, and, tearing her garments, began to beat her mercilessly until they killed her; but even with this they did not satisfy their malice. What inhumanity and bestial cruelty! Falling upon the body of the virgin, they cut it into pieces and burned them in a place called Cinaron.

Upon learning of this tragedy and misfortune, all the Alexandrians were greatly grieved, and the monks living on Mount Nitria, filled with zeal, descended into Alexandria to help and defend their primate. They numbered about five hundred. Happening to meet the eparch on the road as he sat in his chariot, they began to make noise, reviling him and calling him an idolater—for he had formerly been a Hellene and had received Baptism in Constantinople not long before. One of the more agitated monks, Father Ammonius, threw a stone at the eparch and struck him on the head. The assembled people dragged the monks away from the eparch. Suspecting that it was the hierarch who had sent the monks against him, the eparch was inflamed with anger and subjected Ammonius to such cruel tortures that he died. Upon learning of this occurrence, Cyril was grieved and sent for the body of the monk, whom he buried with honors.

These events emboldened the Jews. They built themselves a new synagogue and then, for the mockery and shaming of the Savior and Christians, dared to commit the following lawless deed: they fashioned a long cross, caught a Christian child and, having stripped him naked, crucified him on it—not with nails, but with thin rods. Having mocked him, they spat in his face and derided him, just as their fathers had mocked the Lord, and they beat him so severely that the child died. Thus that blessed child became a partaker and imitator of the Passion of Jesus.

The divine Cyril reported this attack and impiety to the emperor, and the ruler, although with delay, pronounced a just judgment. He commanded that the Jewish leaders be severely punished, and he removed the eparch Orestes from his office. After the disturbances and scandals had ceased, the hierarch diligently and in a God-pleasing manner tended his rational flock, enjoying peace for a certain time. The next trial for the Alexandrian Christians and the whole Church was the blasphemous heresy of the impious Nestorius, who became Patriarch of Constantinople after Sisinnius. At the beginning of his patriarchate, he preached nothing contrary to the faith and outwardly appeared pious. But in his soul this wretch was a heretic, calling Christ the Master only a "High Man" and not God, and the Lady Theotokos not the Theotokos but "Christotokos."

The first to begin sowing this heresy like tares among the wheat were Bishop Dorotheus and Presbyter Anastasius, who shared Nestorius's views and lived with him. Once, when instructing the people in the cathedral of Constantinople, Dorotheus pronounced this blasphemous word: "Whoever calls Mary Theotokos, let him be anathema." And Anastasius during his sermon said: "Let no one call Mary Theotokos, because Mary was a human being and a woman. And how can God be born of a human body?" When the people heard these blasphemous words, they became indignant and came with their perplexities to Patriarch Nestorius. Then this vile one, of one mind with the Jews, could no longer conceal the heretical poison in his heart and openly spewed forth such blasphemies against Christ and the Mother of God: "I do not call God the One who was conceived in the womb of a Woman, and awaited days and months until He was born. And that Woman who gave birth to a fleshly Man from her own nature, I do not call Theotokos."

From that time disputes and divisions began among the people, because some opposed the heresy of Nestorius and turned away from it, while others had communion with him and agreed with his impiety. But these divisions occurred not only in Constantinople, but almost throughout the entire world, since Nestorius, together with his followers, recorded his heresy in books, which he distributed everywhere, even in the deserts where monks dwelt. And he led astray so many clerics, monks, and laymen into this delusion that, as Arius had formerly rent the seamless garment of Christ, so also Nestorius divided the whole fullness of the Church into many parts.

Upon learning of all this, the hierarch Cyril of Alexandria was greatly grieved and, as a faithful servant of Christ and the Mother of God, armed himself for battle for Their honor. As a true shepherd, he prepared to drive out the noetic wolf from the fold of the rational sheep. First, the primate of the Alexandrian Church wrote a letter of instruction to Nestorius, in which with brotherly love he advised him to renounce these heretical opinions and, having turned to piety, to correct those whom he himself had led into impiety. However, upon receiving the letter of the thrice-blessed one, the impious Nestorius not only was not corrected but became even worse, and strove still more to spread his false teaching, and he tormented in various ways the clerics and monks who opposed his delusion. He became very angry with the divine Cyril and slandered him before all the people.

When the hierarch Cyril saw that Nestorius was not being corrected, he wrote him another, already more severe letter, in which he exposed his heresy; likewise the venerable one addressed letters to the clergy of Constantinople, to the emperor, and then to Pope Celestine and other patriarchs. In like manner, Cyril wrote to various cities and countries to bishops, rulers, and archons, to many hermits and other monks. The First Hierarch of Alexandria proved on the basis of Holy Scripture how terrible and soul-destroying was the delusion of Nestorius, and urged everyone to guard against this heresy as against a deadly poison.

Finally, since the heresy of Nestorius was multiplying day by day and already many bishops had been perverted by it, the pious Emperor Theodosius, wishing to quiet the scandals and cleanse the Church of Christ and the wheat of faith from the thorns and tares of Nestorian delusion, commanded that the Third Ecumenical Council be convened at Ephesus in the year 431, at which more than two hundred bishops assembled from the entire world, and those who because of some obstacles could not come themselves sent their representatives in their place.

The Patriarch of Alexandria Cyril represented Pope Celestine of Rome at the Council—he was the first leader (the second was Juvenal of Jerusalem, the third was Memnon of Ephesus). The blessed one, together with the other fathers, preached and taught that our Lord Jesus Christ is One according to hypostasis, and that one and the same is Perfect God and Perfect Man, and not one and another. And the Most Pure Virgin who gave birth according to the flesh is Lady and truly Theotokos. And there was great joy among all the Orthodox, and all the people of the city of Ephesus triumphantly applauded and said not as before: *"Great is Artemis of the Ephesians!"* (Acts 19:28), but "Great is the Most Pure Virgin Mary, the Theotokos!"

As for the vile Nestorius, as a blasphemous heretic, the fathers of the Council anathematized him and deposed him from his rank, but since he did not quiet down and again began to preach his heresy, he was first exiled to Thas, near Theophani, and then to an Egyptian oasis, called in Turkish Ibis. While there, the impious one experienced upon himself the Divine wrath, because, as Evagrius writes, the blasphemous tongue of the schismatic rotted and was eaten by worms; likewise, as Cedrenus and Nicephorus affirm, his whole body also rotted. The wretch, like Arius in Upper Thebaid, underwent a terrible death: an Angel of the Lord struck him, and all his entrails fell into a vessel of filth when he went to relieve himself and began to blaspheme Christ and the Theotokos. There, as Saint Germanus of Constantinople relates, the evil one gave up his spirit. Such is the disgrace and punishment to which the Jewish-minded heretic Nestorius was subjected.

The hierarch Cyril received great honors and privileges from the Third Ecumenical Council. The wondrous John Zonaras, in a laudatory discourse dedicated to this ascetic, describes the following awards: the fathers of the Third Council granted the divine one the right to be called "Judge of the Ecumene" and during the divine services to wear on his head a thin cloth in the form of a veil.

The title "Judge of the Ecumene" indicates the wondrous ecumenical judgment exercised by the primate of the Alexandrian Church, who through Orthodoxy united the whole world that had been divided into many parts by the heresy of Nestorius.

The thin veil signifies the subtlety of mind of the venerable one, for he composed the teaching on the hypostatic union of Christ. By means of this term is represented simultaneously both the one Person in Christ and His two natures.

Moreover, the divine Cyril was also called "Pope." Perhaps this occurred because he represented Pope Celestine at the Council. Others, however, interpret the aforementioned privileges differently, for all the Patriarchs of Alexandria, successors of Saint Cyril, retained the title of "Pope" and "Judge of the Ecumene," as well as the right to wear two crowns and two epitrachelia, perhaps indicating that thin cloth granted by the Council.

It is known that before the convening of the above-mentioned Council, which was called to strengthen the Orthodox faith, the ever-blessed one endured many labors and temptations, and was subjected to lawless slander and attacks by the heretics who shared Nestorius's views. Having secured the help of secular rulers, they assembled their own meeting and falsely proclaimed the hierarch Cyril a heretic like Apollinarius, who denied the true humanity in Christ and considered Him only Divinity. The slanderous letters aroused the emperor's anger against the ascetic, and he, together with Memnon of Ephesus, was thrown into prison and bound in irons. Having examined the matter in detail and having learned of the false accusations of the heretics and of the innocence of the saint, the emperor humbled the heretics with exile, and the most blessed one together with those who shared his mind he confirmed on their primatial thrones, praising their patience and meekness.

To understand how hateful the blasphemous heresy of Nestorius was to the Mother of God, against which the hierarch Cyril so struggled, we shall here cite as a digression a story related by the fathers of the "Spiritual Meadow"—Sophronius and John. Once they visited Abba Cyriacus, a presbyter of the Lavra of Calamon on the Jordan, and the venerable one related to them the following.

—Once in a dream I saw the Lady Theotokos with a radiant countenance, clothed in purple, accompanied by two God-befitting men, standing at my cell. I recognized that this was the Lady, the Mother of God, and the two men with her were Saint John the Baptist and Saint John the Theologian. Then I came out of my cell and, having bowed down to the Most Pure Virgin Mary, began to ask her to enter and bless my cell, but She would not agree.

—Let not Thy servant return, O Lady, shamed and reproached by Thee, I besought the fervent Protectress.

—You have My enemy in your cell, so how can you ask Me to enter? the Theotokos answered me and became invisible.

When I awoke, I began to weep and grieve, but since there was no one else in my cell, I wondered whether I had sinned against the Most Pure One in some thought, for which reason She had turned away from me. However, I found nothing, and continued in perplexity and grief. To console myself, I began to read a book of Hesychius, the presbyter of Jerusalem, which I had requested from him some time before. At the end of this book I discovered two blasphemous words of the impious Nestorius. Then I understood that he was the enemy of the Theotokos who had been in my cell.

—Brother, take your book, for I have received from it more harm than benefit, I said to Father Hesychius. When he learned the reason, for I told him about the vision, he was filled with Divine zeal and that very hour tore those two blasphemous words from the book and burned them, so that in his cell too there would be no enemy of our Lady the Theotokos.

"It belongs to God alone to be without sin and free from every passion," writes Gregory the Theologian in his funeral oration for Basil the Great, and therefore we must not be silent here about the sin of the great Cyril of Alexandria. The Saints of God, however holy they may be, are, like all people, subject to human weakness and certain minor passions. The hierarch corrected his passion in a wondrous manner.

Since the great Cyril was the nephew of Patriarch Theophilus, the enemy of John Chrysostom, he believed in the truth of the false accusations against the hierarch, not out of malice but out of simplicity: *"A guileless man... believes every word"* (Proverbs 14:15), and he formed an unfavorable prejudice against our divine father Chrysostom. He was angry with him not only during the life of the archpastor but even after his death, and he did not want, as is customary, to commemorate the blessed John among the other pious patriarchs in the diptychs.

Atticus, the primate of the Church of Constantinople after Arsacius, wrote to Cyril that he himself had also been an enemy of Chrysostom, but afterwards, upon reflection, he understood that the holy man was innocent, and therefore he repented, numbered the hierarch among the saints, unfailingly began to commemorate the departed one, and fraternally advised the Pope and Patriarch of Alexandria to do likewise. But the divine one did not listen to him, apparently not wishing to condemn the Council against Chrysostom held under Theophilus. Then Saint Isidore of Pelusium, his relative and elder in age, also addressed the ascetic. He boldly and with great courage rebuked Cyril for his unjust and unreasonable anger against the innocent John Chrysostom. "One ought not to condemn a man," wrote the Pelusiot, "before his guilt and transgression have been thoroughly investigated, for even God, who although He knows all things before they happen and foresees the future as the present, according to Holy Scripture, came down from Heaven to the cities of Sodom to see whether or not it was true that the Sodomites had sinned: *'Because the outcry against Sodom and Gomorrah is great, and because their sin is very grievous, I will go down now and see whether they have done altogether according to the outcry against it that has come to Me; and if not, I will know'* (Genesis 18:20–21). All this the Lord did in order to show us an example: one should not immediately believe the words of accusers, but one must first personally examine all the circumstances and verify the reports."

—So also you, he said to the divine Cyril, must first think, and then, if you find a reasonable basis for anger, be angry, because many of those who were with you at the Council in Ephesus openly accuse you of unjustly opposing the innocent John, and that, being a relative of Theophilus, you imitate him in everything. And as he publicly displayed his madness by driving from his throne the innocent, holy, and God-beloved John, so also you act, accusing and slandering the persecuted one, even though he has already died. The examples from Holy Scripture frighten me and impel me to write to you. If I am a father to you, as you yourself call me, then I fear the condemnation that the priest Eli received under the Old Law because he did not admonish his sinning sons as he ought. But if I am your son, as I myself also know, then I fear lest the punishment of Jonathan, the son of Saul, should befall me, who could have prevented his father when he turned to the sorceress but did not restrain him from sin. For this reason he was also killed first in battle. Therefore, lest I too be condemned, I tell you what serves to your benefit, that you also may not be convicted by the Impartial and Righteous Judge. Listen to me, lay aside your anger against the departed one, and do not trouble the Church of the living, causing disturbances in it, the Pelusiot admonished the hierarch. —You ask me, for what and how was John exiled? But I will not answer you in detail, lest I be found reviling and condemning others, but I will only say that many lawless men unjustly vented their malice upon him. I will briefly tell you about Egypt. Egypt rejected Moses and served Pharaoh. It scourged the humble and tormented the Israelites who labored. They built cities for him, and he gave wages to the workers. Engaging in such deeds, Egypt raised up Theophilus, who worshipped gold as god. He, together with those of like mind with him, hated and persecuted John, the beloved of God and preacher of God. But the house of David, as you yourself see, grows ever wider and stronger, while the house of Saul diminishes and declines, the Pelusiot addressed the First Hierarch of the Alexandrian Christians.

Thanks to such epistles, the divine Cyril began to become aware of his sin and to be corrected. However, he clearly realized and expiated it fully only after a vision in which he found himself in a beautiful place filled with ineffable joy, where Abraham, Isaac, Jacob, and other wondrous and glorious men of the Old and New Testaments dwelt. When the blessed one entered a radiant temple filled with people, he saw the Lady Theotokos praying and shining with ineffable glory, surrounded by a host of Angels. Near the Mother of God, in great honor, stood John Chrysostom, holding in his hands the Book of his homilies. With him were many glorious men, ready to avenge the slandered archpastor. When the great Cyril wished to bow down to the Ever-Virgin Mary, Saint John with his guard fell upon him with anger and not only prevented him from approaching the Theotokos but drove him out of the temple entirely.

While the primate of the Alexandrian Church stood in terror, reflecting on what had happened, the voice of the Mother of God was heard. The Queen of Heaven asked John Chrysostom not to drive Cyril of Alexandria from the temple, because he had had an unfavorable prejudice against him not out of malice but out of ignorance:

—For love of Me, forgive him, for he labored much for My honor, having put to shame My reviler Nestorius, and proclaimed to the people that I am the Theotokos.

After these words, Chrysostom immediately calmed down and, embracing Saint Cyril, kissed him in a friendly manner. Thus, through the mediation of the Most Pure One, the two saints were reconciled with each other in the vision.

Upon awakening and carefully reflecting, the thrice-blessed one repented and began to accuse himself for having been so long subject to a vain and unreasonable passion toward such a God-pleasing holy man. He immediately gathered all the bishops of Egypt and arranged a great celebration in honor of Chrysostom. He entered his name in the diptychs and began to commemorate him among the great saints, glorifying his memory each year with laudatory discourses. Cyril wrote the first life of John, which formed the basis for the life of the hierarch John Chrysostom composed by George of Alexandria.

From that time, the divine Cyril tended his rational flock in life-giving pastures for the rest of his life, always leading believers on the path of salvation, wisely delivering the wayward from diabolical delusion. To demonstrate his skill, let us cite the following account for the delight of listeners, and with this conclude our narrative.

Abba Daniel relates in the "Paterikon" that in Lower Egypt there lived a certain venerable elder. He was righteous, but rather simple and even coarse in mind. Thus, he thought and said that Melchizedek is the Son of God. This was reported to Saint Cyril. The Pope and Patriarch of Alexandria invited the monk to himself, and having learned that he performed signs and wonders, and that whatever he asked of God, He revealed to him, he employed his wisdom, gently saying to the elder:

—Abba, doubts assail me. One thought tells me that Melchizedek is the Son of God, and another that he is a simple man and a high priest of God. Therefore I have summoned you; ask God that He reveal to you the truth, and you will tell me.

—Give me, Master, three days for this, and whatever God reveals to me, I will tell your holiness, the abba answered boldly, trusting in the holiness of his way of life.

The monk departed and, having shut himself in his cell for three days, fervently besought the Lord to reveal to him concerning Melchizedek.

—Master, Melchizedek is a simple man and not the Son of God, the elder proclaimed at the end of the appointed time.

—How do you know this? the great Cyril inquired.

—God showed me all the patriarchs from Adam to Melchizedek, who passed before me, and when Melchizedek passed by, the Angel of the Lord said to me: "You see, this is Melchizedek." Thus, Master, I learned that so it is.

Then, giving thanks to the Lord, the hierarch greatly rejoiced that he had delivered the elder from delusion and dismissed him in peace. From that day the abba began to preach to everyone that Melchizedek is a simple man and not the Son of God. Thus through his wisdom the ever-blessed one, renowned for his struggle for the purity of Orthodox teaching, brought the simple one to the knowledge of the truth.

Having remained on the Alexandrian throne for thirty-two years, the hierarch Cyril composed many soul-profitable books for the Orthodox, of which the most well-known are the "Thesaurus" and his Commentaries on the Old Testament. His memory is celebrated on June 9—the day of his repose unto the Lord, and also on January 18, when the day of his arrival from Alexandria in Ephesus is commemorated. This flight of the hierarch was considered worthy of celebration because it served as the cause of many blessings for the Church of Christ, for thanks to it the Third Ecumenical Council was convened, the heresy of the blasphemous Nestorius was condemned, and the Orthodox faith was proclaimed throughout the world. Other historical documents also testify to this, in which under the date of January 18 the following verses are written:

"Of the flight of Cyril the memory is now celebrated,

And not the repose of the ever-blessed one is the occasion."

If in printed Menaia we encounter "silence" instead of "flight," this is a typographical error, for in the manuscripts of the Synaxarion under the date of June 9 is written:

"Cyril died, the Pope of Alexandria,

To the Lord of all lords he departed.

Cyril was found in an earthly grave on the ninth day."

At the death of the great Cyril of Alexandria, the Lady and Sovereign Theotokos Herself was present. The Mother of God visited Her servant because he too had faithfully served Her during his life, struggling for Her honor. And now he abides in Heaven and rejoices together with the choirs of Angels, patriarchs, prophets, apostles, hierarchs, and all the saints. With his beloved friend, the divine John Chrysostom, he stands before the Throne of Christ God and His Most Pure Mother, whom he defended and for whom he suffered. He unceasingly beseeches the All-Holy and Consubstantial Trinity on behalf of all Christians, that they too may be deemed worthy of the Kingdom of Heaven, which may we all attain by the grace and love for mankind of our Lord Jesus Christ, to whom belong all glory with the Father and the Holy Spirit, now and ever and unto the ages of ages. Amen.

(From the writings of Nicephorus, Sozomen, and other church historians)

The Life and Struggles of the Venerable Andronicus and His Wife Athanasia, Who Labored in the Fifth Century

This our venerable father Andronicus was by birth from Great Antioch. He was most virtuous, God-fearing, and wealthy not only in worldly goods, for the whole region knew him as a silversmith, but also in spiritual ones. He took for himself an equally modest and God-loving wife named Athanasia. After taking counsel together, they decided to divide their wealth into three parts: from one they gave generously to the poor, from another they lent without interest to all who were in need, and the third they kept for themselves to live on. After giving birth to two children, a boy and a girl, they no longer wished to unite with one another, but lived a chaste life and always cared for their salvation as much as possible. They often prayed, attended church services, visited the sick, cared for strangers, clothed the naked, freed prisoners from dungeons, and performed other good and God-pleasing deeds.

After twelve years of life together, their children, being at that age when parents take their greatest delight in them, suddenly died on the same day. The blessed Andronicus showed no faint-heartedness at this, nor did he wail in an unseemly manner, as most people usually do in such cases. Rather, having grieved in moderation, as is fitting according to the laws of nature, he endured this tribulation, crying out in the blessed words of Job: *"Naked I came from my mother's womb, and naked shall I return"* (Job 1:21). But his wife Athanasia mourned for her children inconsolably, and after they were buried near the church of the holy martyr Julian, she did not want to leave the grave, saying that she too wished to die and be buried together with her children.

To console Andronicus, the Patriarch took him to the Patriarchate. But Athanasia, in her grief, could not leave that place and remained near the church of the holy martyr Julian, weeping and wailing with many sighs and cries. And behold, in the middle of the night, the martyr Julian appeared to her in the form of a monk and asked:

"Woman, why do you weep and give no rest to those who are here?"

And she answered him:

"My lord, do not be angry with your servant. My heart aches greatly, for I had two children, and now I have buried them, and so I weep."

"Do not weep for your children. I assure you that just as the body needs food and will not be at rest until it is given nourishment, so too your little children who have died ask God for Heavenly blessings, saying: 'Lord, Righteous Judge, instead of the earthly blessings of which we have been deprived, grant us Heavenly ones.' And it is impossible that God would not grant them."

Hearing this, Athanasia came to her senses and, being moved to compunction, she changed her sorrow to joy, saying:

"My children are alive and rejoice in Heavenly blessings; why then do I weep and grieve?"

She turned around, seeking the monk who had spoken with her, but having searched the whole church, she found no one. Then the woman turned to the sexton with a question:

"Where is that monk who just came in here?"

"You see, all the doors of the church are closed. How can you ask where the monk is?"

However, the sexton understood that the woman had seen a vision. Athanasia, filled with fear, went home and told her husband everything, and then began asking to enter a monastery. The blessed Andronicus received her words with joy, because he himself desired the same thing, which he also confessed to her. And so they both resolved to renounce the world and become monastics.

Andronicus immediately distributed the greater part of their possessions to the poor and set all their servants free. The remaining portion of their property he left to his father-in-law, directing that hospitals and hospices be established with this money. And having taken a small amount of funds for the journey, they left their home by night. Looking back at their house from afar, the blessed Athanasia lifted up her eyes to Heaven and said: "O Lord my God, Thou Who didst say unto Abraham and Sarah: *Get out of your country, from your family and from your father's house... to a land that I will show you* (Genesis 12:1), lead us also in Thy fear, for we too have left our home for Thy name's sake. We beseech Thee, do not shut against us the doors of Thy Kingdom." They wept and departed from their native city. Coming to Jerusalem and having venerated the holy places, they met the holy Fathers and conversed with them for many days. Departing from there, they came to Misirius to the renowned Abba Daniel and told him of their intention, asking him to set them on the path of salvation.

Abba Daniel placed Athanasia in the women's Tabenisiot monastery, and kept Andronicus with himself. After testing him for some time, he tonsured him, clothing him in the angelic habit. Thus Andronicus remained with the elder for twelve years, showing him obedience in all things. After twelve years had passed, Andronicus began asking Abba Daniel to let him go to Jerusalem to venerate the holy places. Having bestowed a blessing, the elder released him. As he walked along the road, the venerable Andronicus sat down under a tree to rest from the heat, and at that time, by God's providence, his wife also came there, in the guise of a man, having been renamed monk Athanasius. She too was traveling to the holy places. When they greeted each other, she recognized Andronicus, but he did not recognize her, because from her excessive labors her beauty had faded, and she resembled a Moor. She asked him:

"Lord Abba, where are you going?"

Andronicus replied:

"To the holy places."

"I too wish to go."

"If you wish, let us go together? As you desire, only let us travel in silence along the way, so that it is not apparent that I am traveling with you."

"As you wish, let us go in silence."

Then Athanasia asked him:

"Are you not a disciple of Abba Daniel?"

"Yes, I am a disciple."

"And are you not called Andronicus?"

"Yes, I am called Andronicus."

"May the prayers of the elder accompany us."

"Amen. So be it."

Thus the two came to Jerusalem together, venerated the holy places, and returned to Alexandria in silence. There Athanasia asked Andronicus:

"Do you wish for us to live together in a cell?"

"As you wish, but first I will go to my elder to ask permission and a blessing."

"Go, I will wait for you at the place called Octocaedecaton. If you can live with me without speaking, as on the journey to the Holy Land, then come. But if you cannot, do not come."

Andronicus came to the elder and told him everything, asking, if he deemed it reasonable, to allow him to live with the monk Athanasius. From Andronicus's words, Abba Daniel understood that Athanasius had greatly advanced in virtue, and therefore gave permission, saying at last: "Go, embrace stillness and dwell with that brother, for he is a true monk." Thus Andronicus returned to the appointed place and lived together with Athanasius for twelve years, not knowing that this was his wife. How many and what kind of struggles they took upon themselves is impossible to describe worthily. Many times Abba Daniel visited them, conversing on spiritual topics and discussing the salvation of the soul. Once, when Abba Daniel had come to them again and, having conversed sufficiently, had said farewell and set out on his return journey, Abba Andronicus ran after him and, catching up, said:

"Abba Athanasius has fallen ill and will soon depart to the Lord."

Hearing this, Abba Daniel returned and found that the sick one was having a terrible seizure. Seeing Abba Daniel, Athanasius began to weep, and the elder said to him:

"Instead of rejoicing that you are going to God, you weep?"

"I weep because Abba Andronicus remains alone. I ask you, father, show love. After my death, you will find a small tablet by my head. Read what is written there, and give it to Abba Andronicus to read."

Then all three prayed, the blessed Athanasia received Communion of the Most Pure Mysteries, and reposed in the Lord. Then Abba Daniel read the tablet, and they learned that the ever-memorable Athanasia was the wife of Andronicus. This became known throughout the Lavra. Abba Daniel sent word to the brethren, and all the Fathers living in the inner desert, from all the Alexandrian Lavras, from that whole region, and from Scetis, gathered for her burial. Those from Scetis put on white garments, for they had such a custom—to put on white garments for the burial of the brethren, as ones who had conquered the three enemies: the flesh, the world, and the devil the ruler of this world. The precious relics of the venerable Athanasia were brought out with palm branches and, glorifying God who had given the saint such endurance, they buried her with great reverence and doxologies.

And Abba Daniel remained there to perform the seven memorial services for the venerable one, after which he wanted to take Abba Andronicus with him, but Andronicus did not wish to leave that place, saying:

"I wish to die here, together with my lady Athanasia."

Then, having bid him farewell, Abba Daniel set out on his way, but a certain brother caught up with him on the road and said that Abba Andronicus was having a seizure. And again Abba Daniel returned and sent word to Scetis that the venerable Andronicus was following the venerable Athanasia. Again all the brethren gathered and found him still alive. After they received his blessing, he reposed in the Lord. And between the brethren who lived in Octocaedecaton and those from Scetis, a dispute arose over the precious relics of the venerable Andronicus as to who would take them. With difficulty Abba Daniel managed to quell this dispute, and the venerable Andronicus was buried together with his co-laborer, the venerable Athanasia, glorifying and blessing God Who is over all. Amen.

The Life and Struggles of Our Father Among the Saints Andrew, Archbishop of Crete, a Native of Jerusalem, Who Flourished in the Eighth Century

The homeland of this divine father of ours Andrew was the renowned Damascus, now called by the Turks "Siam." The venerable one was born of God-fearing and virtuous parents, George and Gregoria, and until the age of seven was mute, so that they grieved greatly, thinking he would remain so forever. When seven years had passed, one day he went with his parents to church and partook of the Most Pure Body and Blood of the Lord, and a miracle occurred. His tongue was immediately loosed from its bonds, and the boy began to speak freely.

Then his parents gave him to a school for instruction in the sacred sciences. Possessing a keen mind, Andrew devoted himself to his studies with great eagerness and zeal, and exercising himself with extraordinary desire in his subjects, he excelled in all sciences. Having experienced teachers, he mastered everything perfectly. His tongue was purified, and Andrew began to speak skillfully and pleasingly. He made his soul capable of acquiring virtue and truth, and his mind capable of advancing in contemplations of things above. Then, having studied Holy Scripture, he was so enlightened in mind that he fervently loved truth and Divine wisdom, striving wholly toward it alone.

Reflecting that by no other means is it possible to be united with Divine wisdom except by freeing oneself from earthly material things, he asked his parents to dedicate him to God, for he had no inclination or love for anything worldly. Moved, of course, by God, his parents brought him to the Life-giving Tomb of the Lord and dedicated him as a pleasing sacrifice to God. The Patriarch of Jerusalem at that time was Theodore, a man of holy life, who received the youth with great joy and made him his spiritual child (for like always loves like). Clothing him in the monastic habit, he ordained Andrew to the diaconate and began to care wholly for his advancement, striving to nurture him in virtue and bring him *"to a perfect man, to the measure of the stature of the fullness of Christ"* (Ephesians 4:13).

Having before him the youth's soul as good soil, the patriarch also had good hopes that with the help of the Divine word and the good example of his own virtue, his soul would bear a hundredfold fruit. But the elder could not perfectly enjoy him, because he was released from the bonds of the body and, having died joyfully in the arms of his spiritual child, went to Christ the Master to receive bright crowns for his good governance of the Church. And upon his death, he appointed the divine Andrew (besides making him steward of the Church) as administrator and guardian of the whole Church, because due to his young age he could not leave him as successor to the Patriarchal throne. Notwithstanding his age, in virtue, care, oversight, and the benefit he brought, Andrew yielded to no other protector of the Church, but was for the Church of Jerusalem both father and teacher, and steward and servant, and a shining example of every good thing.

By order of the pious Emperor Constantine, grandson of Heraclius, the Sixth Ecumenical Council was then convened in Constantinople, which solemnly rejected the Monothelite heresy and composed a sacred compilation of dogmas. Letters were sent to all the Churches from the emperor, in which the Conciliar canons were approved by him and all the faithful were called to follow them. When this letter came to the Church of Jerusalem, it filled her with spiritual joy and was a testimony that piety, which had previously been assailed by heretics, had gloriously been strengthened again. The best people of Jerusalem decided that they needed to send to Constantinople a man who could prove that they too agreed with the dogmas of the Divine Council; at a general assembly they resolved to send for this purpose the great Andrew together with two other clerics, since he was educated in the dogmas of piety and excelled in them more than any other by the power of his word and by the Holy Spirit.

And so, taking with him two distinguished clerics, whom he himself had chosen, Andrew came to Constantinople. He did not find the emperor still alive, but the heir to the kingdom was his son Justinian II, Rhinotmetos. To him he delivered the confession of the Church of Jerusalem, and whatever was lacking in it he supplemented with an excellent speech. Having aroused admiration by his holiness and wisdom, he well managed the affairs of the embassy entrusted to him and sent the clerics back to Jerusalem to announce to the rest how the embassy had concluded, while he himself remained in Constantinople in order to be free from ecclesiastical affairs and to lead a solitary life in stillness.

Having prepared himself inwardly and free from all cares, both seemingly good and not good, he devoted himself entirely to the study and contemplation of Divine things, struggling with fasting, vigils, and tears. Thus he was purified in body and soul, enlightened in mind, and, having become in all things like unto God, he was mystically united with Him, receiving a foretaste of the blessings to come. Having spent a long time in stillness, the saint was able to contain the perfect measure of virtue and subsequently brought much benefit to all who came to him. But since this man, glorious in deed and word, could not long be hidden under the bushel of stillness, he became known both to the emperor and to the Church. Forcibly separated from stillness, he was appointed against his will to the service of the Great Church. Then he was entrusted with the care and administration of the orphanages. Having performed this obedience splendidly, he became a father and nurturer of orphans and the poor. Diligently caring for both orphanages of Constantinople, he not only achieved an increase in the funds for their maintenance, but also built new and spacious quarters for the orphans. Having proved himself worthy in all things, he also received a greater charge, being elevated to the lofty hierarchical throne of the metropolis of the renowned island of Crete, and it was precisely his service on this island that enabled him to become a shepherd and teacher of the whole Church of Christ.

In his diocese he immediately set to work, applying all his strength to increase and save his flock. First he wisely addressed the priests with a most gentle word concerning order in divine services, showing what a priest must be who is not only himself deemed worthy to approach the First and Unapproachable Light—God—but is obliged to enlighten others as well, reconciling them with God; that is, a priest himself must shine and be pure as a mirror in order to receive in himself the rays of Divine light and shine upon others. Then the venerable one brought order to the convents and monasteries, writing a Rule for them. After this he began to care for the laity, teaching them to cleave to God and not to the flesh and the world, to despise worldly pleasures, to keep the commandments of God, and to struggle for their salvation. The young he instructed in chastity, sinners he returned to repentance, to the repentant he gave hope of Divine mercy, those who struggled he inclined to feats of virtue, he helped those assailed by passions, he supported those in danger of falling into sin, the fallen he raised up, for the weak he was strength, for the sorrowful he was consolation, for widows he was a defender, for orphans he was a father, for the poor he was a treasury, for the hungry he was a nurturer, for the naked he was a covering. And why say much?... *"I have become all things to all men, that I might by all means save"* all (1 Corinthians 9:22). And just as in the age to come the Lord will be for the saints both Light, and Life, and Glory, and Food, and Raiment, and Joy, and all the other blessings of beatitude, so also was this great Andrew for the inhabitants of his diocese every good thing—not only spiritual but also bodily, with which they could pass through the present life without sorrow.

He opened the good treasury of his heart and brought forth from it good words, and, having opened the mouth of his understanding, filled it with the grace of the Holy Spirit (Psalm 44:2). By wisdom, understanding, and Divine inspiration, the venerable one composed books, through which he presents himself as a capable orator and a divinely inspired sacred speaker. In his "Homilies" on various feasts of the Theotokos, he solemnly praises the Most Pure Mother of the Son and Word of God; he praises the Life-giving Cross of the Savior, on which the Impassible God endured blessed sufferings and voluntary death, making us partakers of His Kingdom and glory; and he also praises many other feasts of the Lord. Furthermore, the venerable one rendered praise to certain saints, making their sufferings as it were his own through his praises. He especially honors the great John the Forerunner with his praises. The venerable Andrew also composed many canons and troparia, by which he not only adorned the feasts and moved Christians to spiritual gladness and joy, but also evoked compunction, causing those who sing and read them to pour forth fountains of tears; he composed that praiseworthy Great Canon, the reading of which evokes not only repentance and compunction, but also provides extensive knowledge, since it teaches Christians the disposition with which they should read the histories of Holy Scripture, and how to make them the cause of higher moral contemplations (the Great Canon of Andrew of Crete).

The venerable Andrew adorned his flock not only with words, but also with deeds and great labors, and gladdened the other Christian Churches. He restored ruined churches of God, providing generous help to the builders, and in honor of the Most Holy Theotokos and Ever-Virgin Mary he erected a beautiful church, calling it Blachernae. The venerable one also built hospices, where they gave rest to the aged, healed the sick, and provided shelter for strangers and the poor. To all those in need he not only generously distributed necessities, wisely and in a manner pleasing to God expending money, but, as in everything else, so also in this, imitating his Master and Teacher Christ, he served the infirm and the strangers with his own hands, washing their hands, feet, and head, cleansing the wounds of the sick—so did the love for God and neighbor burn within him.

It is fitting to mention here two of the saint's miracles, in order to show the holiness and boldness that the divine Andrew had before God. Once an army of barbarians attacked Crete, wishing to capture and destroy the saint's flock, for which purpose they employed all military means, subjecting the island to a prolonged siege. But the God-pleasing prayers of Saint Andrew not only protected his flock from danger, but also instilled such fear in the barbarians that they fled of their own accord, with no one pursuing them. Moreover, because of this hasty and disorderly flight, many of them perished either in the sea waves or at the hands of Christians.

Another time, it was early summer. The sun scorched the earth, there was no rain, and all the crops withered, so that the danger of famine appeared. From fear of death by starvation, parched, without water, scorched by the sun, the people had already completely despaired. But how did the compassionate and merciful soul of the saint act in such misfortune? Perhaps he despised his flock, which was threatened by mortal danger? No. Raising his hands to heaven and lifting up his eyes, he called upon God with all his soul to pour rain upon the earth. And—O miracle!—the sky filled with clouds and rain poured down. The plants were nourished with moisture and brought forth abundant fruits, so that the people were calmed and comforted.

And at another time a plague broke out in his diocese, which destroyed many. The prayers and tears of the saint to God prevented the spread of the deadly disease. The great Andrew also performed many other miracles, which, if one were to tell them, would not suffice for an entire lifetime, because, having God in his soul, he was for the inhabitants of his diocese the cause of all blessings from Him, delivering them from every evil. And to God, as a pleasing and precious sacrifice, he offered the souls of the people saved by him.

Once the saint, out of necessity, had to travel to Constantinople. Arriving there, he was received with great honor and respect by the whole Church, and by the emperor, and by all the officials. Having spent some time there, he distributed to those who thirsted the Heavenly bread—the words of teaching—and gave drink to the thirsty with the life-giving water of the Holy Spirit; nor did he neglect material goods—he offered bodily food to the hungry, helped the wronged, defended widows and orphans, and consoled the sorrowful. Finally, he prepared to return to his diocese, and although he already knew that he would not see his flock again, nevertheless he gave himself over to the Holy Spirit who moved him. Boarding a ship, he sailed for Crete, but upon reaching Mitylene, the vessel stopped. When the saint asked what this place was called, they told him it was Eressos. Then he said: "Here I must give back to God that image which He gave me; here I shall die." And so it came to pass. Released from his bodily bonds, he ascended in joy to the Desired God, and, radiant with the Unapproachable Light of His Divinity, he enjoys the ineffable blessings of His Kingdom. And his sacred relics were laid in the church of the holy and victorious martyr Anastasia, as a treasure that cannot be stolen and a fountain of miracles ever-flowing, to the glory of the Father and of the Son and of the Holy Spirit. Amen.

(Written by Macarius Makres)

The Life and Ascetic Struggles of the Holy and Righteous Eudocimus, Who Shone Forth in the Ninth Century

The narrative of the life of the righteous Eudocimus brings great benefit to both the narrator and the listener. This is not only because the saint ardently loved virtue, as many other ascetics have done, but even more because, while in the midst of worldly cares, borne like a ship upon the sea of life, plunged into turbulent waves and assailed by the devil through various visions, he imperturbably preserved himself from all the passions arising from anger and kept his soul pure and undefiled, both from passionate desire and from even the slightest thought. And the blessed one acquired all the virtues, by which he wounded the demons more than those who struggled in the deserts for fifty or sixty years, and for whom he became an example of virtue. But he became the highest model for emulation for those virtuous ones who live in the world, and they, turning their gaze upon him, could safely pass through their earthly sojourn and be saved. And now the fitting time has come to offer to pious listeners an account, as it were a table upon which are served spiritual viands that never diminish and never spoil.

This wondrous Eudocimus was from Cappadocia by birth, the son of pious parents. His father was called Basil, and his mother Eudocia. They were of noble lineage, possessed great wealth, and held high offices. The father of Eudocimus, Basil, was a patrician. Although Eudocimus was of such illustrious lineage, he was not so much honored for his renowned origin as he was glorified and admired for his ascetic struggles, to which the ever-blessed one zealously devoted himself of his own will. The offspring of noble parents, in order to become famous (and perhaps even to attain high positions), for the most part remain in the world. But to be in the world and to lead a virtuous and extraordinarily chaste life where people indulge in pleasures and luxury is exceedingly difficult. This blessed youth, when given by his parents to study letters, did not need to be compelled to study by fear of punishment with rods, for he himself compelled himself to learn with all diligence, reading Sacred Scripture day and night. In the study of this, that thrice-blessed soul rejoiced more than those who sit at a sumptuous table and feast with dancing and timbrels. To this saint the prophetic saying was fitting: *"How sweet are Your words to my taste, sweeter than honey to my mouth!"* (Psalm 118:103). He loved to go to the churches of God, to hear the sacred services and the words of God, striving in every way to become a pure temple of *"the living God,"* according to the expression of the great apostle (2 Corinthians 6:16).

And the enemy of truth inclined many youths, peers of Eudocimus, to urge him to go with them to feasts and to spend time pleasantly in hunting and amusements, but this ever-praised one had for himself only one feast, luxury, and delight: prayer and the reading of soul-profiting books. And not as some do, who pray though their mind does not attend to the prayer, and read without grasping either what they themselves read or what others read to them. But this true servant of the Lord, both when praying and when reading, clung with all his mind and all his thought to the sacred words.

And chastity and purity, the most precious of all other virtues, which makes a person equal to the angels, the blessed one so loved in his soul that with boldness he could say together with the righteous and most-victorious Job, that never *"did my heart follow my eyes"* (Job 31:7). But the greatest thing is that the ever-praised one resolved not to look upon women's faces while he remained in this life. And throughout his entire life he did not look at nor speak with any women or maidens other than his mother.

Together with chastity he also combined mercy, accompanied by gentleness. By chastity a person is adorned before God, and through mercy the soul is nourished by the grace of the Holy Spirit. The venerable one was distinguished by such mercy that he even distributed to the poor what was necessary for his own life, and not only money but also everything that others needed. He helped the poor so much that if it had been necessary to sell himself into slavery in order to free others, he would have agreed with joy, for the blessed one knew that mercy is the fruit of love. He was a father to orphans, a protector of widows, clothing for the naked, sustenance for the hungry, and comfort for the sorrowing.

This wondrous man, on account of his virtues, and against his own will, was deemed worthy even of imperial dignity, but for all that he did not in the least cease to think of heavenly beauties. Moreover, thinking that this dignity was given him as a gift from God, he began to labor even more and devoted himself to divine love. This saint was even appointed stratopedarches (military commander, field marshal) of Cappadocia in the eparchy called Charsianon. As a prudent steward, he did not spend money for his own honor and glory, as most do, for having received some rank they strive to become famous through foolish deeds and enjoy privileges, and the wretched ones do not think of the dread Judgment which the Righteous and Terrible Judge will render upon them. But the blessed Eudocimus placed all his diligence and care on ruling both small and great in holiness and righteousness, and he would have laid down his very soul, if it had been required, for his subjects.

And what is the use of saying much? The blessed Eudocimus was perfect in every virtue: fervent in love for God, inimitable in love for neighbor, for the sake of which he avoided all slander. And not only did he himself guard himself from condemnation, but he also in every way hindered others from speaking anything against their neighbor. He taught that everyone should be able to listen more than to speak. Living such a blessed life, Eudocimus was a chosen vessel, a teacher by word and an example by deed, a living model for those who associated with him. And this continued until he approached the blessed end of his life in that same Cappadocia, having lived thirty-three years, being young in age but an elder in understanding and knowledge.

Having foreknown his approaching death, the righteous one was not troubled, because his whole life had been a meditation on death. The only thing he lacked was his mother, who was far away at that time and could not be present at his repose. And so his last hour came before going to the Lord. Many came to visit him at that hour. After speaking words about the remembrance of death, he bequeathed that he be buried in the garment he was wearing, and that nothing be done over him that is usually done for other departed ones. Then he gave a sign, and as soon as all had gone out, he began to pray to God with these words, which some heard and later related: "Lord my God, just as during my life I did not wish to show others how I lived, so also at my death, I pray, let there be no sign, so that no one would think that I have pleased Thee." After his words, *"Into Thy hands, O Lord, I commit my spirit,"* his holy soul departed. Those present there, out of reverence for the saint, preserved not only the garments that were on him but also the bed on which he slept (it was made of roughly hewn boards), placing it in the tomb.

However, the sun could not be hidden behind a cloud, nor the lamp under a bushel, because the more the thrice-blessed one concealed himself, the more the Lord revealed him for the benefit of many. A certain Elias, possessed by a terrible demon, many days after the saint's repose was passing near the place where his relics lay, when the demon suddenly began to torment him and, shaking him violently, threw him to the ground as though dead. And so the demon departed, and that man was set free. The Lord glorified His servant, and the report of the miracle that occurred with Elias spread everywhere like the sound of a trumpet. Multitudes of people began to flock to the relics of Eudocimus, bringing those ill with various diseases, who were healed at the saint's tomb.

A certain woman had a child whose hands were paralyzed. As soon as they approached the tomb of the saint, on that same day the child was healed. And another child had not only paralyzed hands but also legs. Coming to the tomb with the same faith as the previous ones, he too received healing. Even the lampada over the tomb of the saint was a source of healings, because all who suffered from any ailments, anointing themselves with oil from it, were healed. And a certain woman had an unclean spirit within her. As soon as she approached the tomb of the saint, the demon departed. Another woman had suffered long from a terrible and incurable disease. Coming to the saint's tomb with faith, she took earth, mixed it with her tears, and anointed the wound with this mixture, immediately receiving the health she desired. And the earth from the saint's grave helped not only those who came there but also those who were far away and could not come. It was sent to the sick, and they, anointing themselves with it, according to their faith received health. It is impossible to describe all the miracles of the saint.

And now the time has come to tell also of the translation of his honorable body from Charsianon to Constantinople. The fame of the saint's miracles spread to all cities and countries, so that many marveled and wondered how one young in age, living amid the temptations of the world and holding high rank, could attain virtues that ascetics in the deep desert barely attain, and could preserve such purity and chastity. Hearing of the countless and swift miracles, all were amazed, and most spoke only of the saint. When the report of his death and the miracles at his grave reached his parents, they were grieved by the first but received consolation from the second and greatly desired to see it for themselves. Overcome by love for her son, the saint's mother did not hesitate to think about the length of the distance, nor the labors and dangers of the journey, but, moved by strong desire, she set out for the grave of her dear and holy son. Seeing there the multitude of people coming with great reverence, and the miracles that were wrought at the sacred tomb when those possessed by demons and suffering from other diseases were quickly healed, she fell to the ground and embraced the tomb. The mother wept for the deceased, at the same time marveling at the grace of miracle-working which he had received from God. Mixing lamentation with praises, she spoke thus: "My sweetest child, light of my eyes, unspeakable beauty of us your parents. Whence have you received such grace of healings? Surely this grace is given by God to those who live in purity and ascetic struggle, concealing their labors and virtues. This grace is given by God to His true servants as a foretaste of the future blessings of the Heavenly Kingdom. For your sake, my child, I too am called a blessed and thrice-blessed mother. No longer shall I weep and wail as a mother, but as to a friend and beloved of God I shall offer songs and spiritual hymns. No longer shall I call you the fruit of my womb, but a son of God by grace. I gave birth to you according to the flesh, and now I myself am born from you according to the spirit, and I am not ashamed to call you my father. For on account of your virtues, the Heavenly Father Himself is your Father, the holy angels and the choirs of saints are your kinsmen. Show mercy, beloved one, to us your parents as well, whom sorrow for you oppresses more than old age. Repay the recompense for your upbringing to me, your mother according to the flesh, and unite me with your Heavenly Father. Repay also the father who begot you according to the flesh, and grant his old age rest in Abraham's bosom. This supplication is addressed to you, my blessed child, by our aged parents, and by the pangs of your mother's womb, and by the breasts with which you were nursed, and by your kinsmen. I know that if you ask God on behalf of your parents, who have the commandment to honor their children, He will hear you, for honor given to parents for their children ascends to God, Who is the Father and Creator of all."

With these words, the pious mother of the saint ordered that the tombstone be raised and the coffin with the holy relics be brought out. And a strange miracle appeared, sufficient to confirm all that has been said. Since the time the saint was buried, eighteen months had passed, and having been in the earth for so long, the honorable relics had in no way undergone what usually happens to the bodies of the deceased. Neither had the color of the face changed, nor were there any signs of decay or the slightest corruption of any member. The most holy body had not even darkened at all, but the face of the venerable one was joyful, blooming, and pleasant, like the face of one who had not died but was asleep. Only the absence of movement prevented it from seeming that the saint was alive. Not even the garment in which he had been placed in the coffin had decayed. And we all know what happens to the bodies of the deceased: besides the stench of the body, a heavy smell of mold and decay comes from the garments as well. But from this thrice-blessed one, both the body itself and the garments gave off a wondrous fragrance. It was pleasant both to look upon him and to breathe in. It seemed that they had opened not the coffin of a dead man but some most beautiful garden with fragrant plants and flowers.

There was present a certain hieromonk named Joseph, who took up the holy body to set it on its feet. And as soon as he touched the saint, he rose by himself as though alive. In great fear, Joseph fell at the feet of the saint and asked him, as though he were alive, to allow him to remove his garments. First he removed the tunic and put on another, then he removed the footwear from his feet, and so easily that it seemed the saint himself was helping in this. Having finished all this, Joseph again returned him to his former position, together with those present glorifying God, Who glorifies those who glorify Him.

From this one may conclude that the saint's tomb was opened providentially, so that the great grace might be revealed with which God glorified him, preserving the saint's body incorrupt in a manner beyond nature. When it was revealed, the demons trembled and fled, driven away as by lightning. Of course, even when it was hidden in the earth they feared it and departed from people, but how much more did they fear when it was revealed, radiant in the glory of holiness.

After this, a dispute arose between the saint's mother and the local inhabitants, because the mother wished to take the holy relics with her to Constantinople, saying, "This star shone forth from my womb," while the locals in response maintained, "Indeed from you it shone forth, but among us it reigned. How can you deprive us of such grace, which has spread the rays of so many miracles precisely here? Yes, the vine is from you, but it brought forth its grace-filled fruit among us. So it has pleased God, and do not contradict God's decision. Do not envy us because of God's benefactions, do not deprive us of so much benefit for soul and body. It is enough glory for you that you are the mother of such a saint." Hearing this, she wisely departed to her own home. Many days passed after this, and that hieromonk Joseph, being in that region, found an opportune moment and stole the treasure, departing so that the locals did not notice him. Although Joseph was departing with the holy relics secretly, this became known through the myrrh that flowed from them and through the miracles that were performed along the way. Thus, a certain woman possessed by a demon, who was being led along the road by several people, found herself near the holy relics. Then the demon flew into a rage, and she, impelled by him, began to cry out, reviling the saint and leaping about indecently. The demon departed, driven out by the grace of the Holy Spirit, and the woman recovered and returned home, glorifying the Lord. And another certain maiden, having a terrible disease, as soon as she approached the holy relics with faith, immediately received healing.

Thus by miracle-working the saint repaid his parents with a precious gift. The God-loving and child-loving mother made a silver reliquary for the holy relics, which she placed in the beautiful church of the Most Holy Theotokos that they had built before. And every day there occurred countless... Such grace did the holy Eudocimus receive from God for his extraordinary mercy, because his desire to give was far stronger than the desire of those who asked to receive. The blessed one sowed temporal things abundantly here, and now he reaps thousandfold eternal fruits in the Heavenly Kingdom, which may we also be deemed worthy of through the intercession of this thrice-blessed Eudocimus. Amen.

(Written by the divine Symeon Metaphrastes)

The Life and Struggles of Our Venerable and God-bearing Father Paul, Called Xeropotaminos, Who Flourished in the Ninth Century

This venerable father of ours, Paul, came from Constantinople. His father was Emperor Michael the Curopalate, also called Rhangabe, who, being a peaceful and God-fearing man, could not calmly look upon the daily disorders occurring at that time, renounced his throne and was tonsured a monk in the monastery of Myrelaion, which he had founded. Having lived in a manner pleasing to God, he reposed in the Lord. The mother of the venerable one was Procopia, a woman wondrous in virtue, daughter of Emperor Nicephorus and sister of Emperor Stauracius. When she was pregnant with the saint, on the night before the birth, she saw in a dream that she gave birth to a lamb upon a sheaf of wheat. When it descended from the sheaf, two lions came and wanted to tear it apart. The lamb began to fight against them. Seeing this, the empress rushed to help him, and when she drew near, she saw that it was not a lamb but a boy holding a cross in his hands, by the power of which he had slain the lions. Rising from sleep, the mother gave birth to the blessed Procopius, for so they named him in Holy Baptism. The dream had the following meaning: the lamb signified the guilelessness and meekness of the child, the male gender signified courage, and the slaying of the two lions figuratively showed the mortification of the passions, that is, that he would become a monk, taking upon his shoulders the Cross of Christ and many sorrows, and by them would conquer and slay two fearsome lions and two of the greatest enemies of a monk—the devil with all his powers, and the world with its glory and its enticements. The sheaf of wheat signified that by his instructive word and the example of his angelic life he would nourish many hungering souls, and would make many who were useless, resembling chaff, worthy of the Heavenly granaries and pleasing bread unto God.

And there was great joy throughout the entire city at the birth of the child, for even from his earliest years it was evident that he was destined to become great. The infant had barely been weaned when his father renounced his throne, and Leo the Armenian began to rule in his stead. Fearing that Procopius, when he came of age, would want to take the throne from him, he sent servants to make the child a eunuch. When Procopius reached the age of twelve, diligently laboring with the abilities natural to him, he gave himself entirely to the study of sacred sciences, so that he surpassed all the wise men of that time, as is evident from his writings: his "Discourse on the Feast of the Entrance of the Most Holy Theotokos into the Temple," eight canons in the eight tones to the Forty Martyrs, and an iambic canon to the Precious Cross. Emperor Romanos also testifies to this in his discourse, calling him the best of philosophers. When the venerable one reached such perfection, he also attained blessed contemplation, which followed from the virtue in which he had labored from childhood. Reflecting on the vanity of the world and turning his mind to the saying of Saint Macarius: "The soul, if it does not free itself from worldly cares, can neither truly love God, nor worthily abhor the devil," he resolved to leave home. Besides this, there was yet another reason: every day the wondrous Procopius was on everyone's lips. Some praised him for his love toward all, others for his humility, still others for his wisdom, others for his temperance, mercy, and disdain for worldly glory and splendor. Daily and hourly praises of Procopius were heard. And so, in order to flee the praises of men, the blessed one departed from Constantinople. Putting on an old, torn robe, in the guise of a beggar, like a thirsting deer, he hastened unrecognized to the Holy Mountain. Having traversed all of Athos, he came to the monastery of the ever-hymned Empress Pulcheria the Virgin, the one which is now called Xeropotamou. Shortly before these events, the Arabs had destroyed it when they came as brigands to the Mountain; they also destroyed other monasteries and put many monks to a martyric death, as in ancient times on Sinai and at Raithu. Seeing the beautiful location of the monastery and the stillness of the place, the venerable one built a small cell on the ruined monastery wall and began to live alone, conversing with God alone. Not far from this place there lived a remarkable hesychast of holy life named Cosmas, from whom he received the monastic tonsure with the name Paul. From that time the venerable one established for himself an exceptional order and discipline as his rule. He fasted, he prayed, he slept on the bare ground, placing a stone under his head. His handiwork was compunction, tears, love for all, and boundless humility. The venerable one believed that for a monk to come to perfection, he must acquire the fruits of the Holy Spirit, as the Apostle Paul says: spiritual love, *"joy, peace, longsuffering, kindness, goodness, faithfulness, gentleness, self-control"* (Galatians 5:22–23). Laboring to attain these qualities, the venerable one became known to all the fathers, and all marveled at him and praised him. The venerable Athanasius of Athos also praised him, as is evident from his life. And although the most wise Paul pretended to be an illiterate barbarian and rustic, it turned out that everyone noticed him, like a city set on the top of a mountain, and finally his fame reached the protos (the head of a group of monasteries). The venerable Paul had a custom of going three times a year, on the three Great Feasts, to the kelliote monastery called the Protaton. When once he came to this monastery, the protos, according to custom, asked him in private who he was and from whence he came. In a quiet voice and with a pleasant countenance, Paul answered: "I am a poor monk, as you see, holy father, from an old settlement called Xeropotamos." For this reason he was called Paul Xeropotaminos, and from him the monastery of Pulcheria, which he renewed, also came to be called Xeropotamou. It was renewed in this way.

During his reign, the ever-memorable Emperor Romanos the Elder, who was a kinsman of the saint, sent his people to find the saint, and they discovered him on the Holy Mountain. After many requests and even the urgings of the protos, Paul obeyed and came to Constantinople. Oh, who can describe the joy of his relatives and of the entire city upon seeing an angel in the flesh and a master of words! The archons cast aside their royal regalia and bowed down before that poor man who had nothing except a worn robe and a cross. Such is the virtue worthy of wonder, and such does it make those who labor in it. It happened at that time that Emperor Romanos lay ill with a mortal sickness, but as soon as the venerable one came and laid his hands upon him, a miracle occurred! The emperor recovered, as he himself writes in his imperial charter. This glorified the saint even more, and after many entreaties from the emperor he remained in Constantinople, but continued to follow his monastic rule and performed his ascetic labors while simultaneously teaching the emperor's children. When the time he had decided to stay in the capital came to an end, Paul came to the emperor and said: "Just as a fish taken out of water perishes, so too a monk, if he leaves his cell, finds it impossible to labor in the commandments of God. Therefore I am leaving you and returning to my cell, to abide always with my King, God." Hearing this, the emperor was greatly grieved, yet he could not hinder him because he had great goodwill toward him. He only said: "I would wish, father, that we would never be separated while I live, so that you might comfort me and be my teacher in salvation. However, I cannot detain you. I ask only one thing: take as much wealth as you desire to distribute to the poor for the salvation of my soul." The saint answered him: "I have no need of wealth, and I do not even know how to distribute it, and you have plenty of poor people here—distribute as much as you wish. I shall only say one thing to you: if you wish to have eternal commemoration for yourself, renew the ruined monastery of the ever-blessed Empress Pulcheria." The emperor received the words of the venerable one with great joy, and immediately sent people, providing them with means, to rebuild the holy monastery from its foundations in beauty incomparable with what it had before. Then he also sent his own son Theophylact, who was patriarch, to consecrate the church. When Saint Paul was about to leave the city, the emperor brought him to the treasury. It is fitting to cite the emperor's own words, as they are written in his charter: "I entered with some of the senate into my imperial treasury, where there was kept the greatest of all and most wondrous of relics—a portion of the Precious Wood of the Life-giving Cross of the Lord, which to this day preserves the memory of the Passion of the Master—the holes from the nails with which the Divine flesh of the Lord was pierced, and upon which, for the cleansing of our sins, His Most Pure Blood was poured out (the height of this portion is approximately one cubit and one hand-breadth, the width approximately two fingers, the thickness one finger, the full weight one hundred drachmas). Taking into my hands this holy treasure—the dread standard of the Heavenly King, which appeared in Heaven as the sign of the Son of Man who shall come to judge the living and the dead—I reverently handed over this Divine instrument of our salvation into the holy hands of the most reverend Paul Xeropotaminos, that until the coming of the Lord it may be an inalienable gift to the above-mentioned most honorable imperial monastery of ours, giving it both ecclesiastical and civil escort, so that they might place this gift in the holy altar of the monastery for its sanctification and confirmation." Taking the Precious Wood, the blessed Paul came to the Holy Mountain, and after the monastery had been completely renewed and consecrated, the patriarch placed the Precious Wood, according to the imperial command, in the holy altar. Since the fame of the venerable one had spread throughout all the earth, many monks laboring in virtue began to come to the monastery. Fleeing disturbance, the venerable one left the oversight of the monastery to another brother of virtuous life, and himself went to the foot of Athos, where in stillness he began to live his life. However, many followed him there as well, so that the wilderness became like a city. Around the elder there gathered this time about sixty disciples. Fearing that the Arabs, who often attacked the Holy Mountain, might enslave or kill them, the venerable one, with the help of the pious emperors, built another monastery in honor of Saint George, which to this day preserves the name of the venerable one, being called the Monastery of Saint Paul.

When the construction of this monastery was completed, Paul was already very old. Having foreknown from Divine revelation the time of his departure, the venerable one summoned all his disciples—both from the Xeropotamou monastery and from the new one—and began to teach them with soul-profiting words: "Little children, in two days I shall depart from my wretched body. You know how I have lived in this holy place and how I have kept all the commandments of my fathers from my youth. So also I ask you, my dear ones, to keep them until death. During my youth, when there was the heresy of the iconoclasts, I struggled so much that I was ready to shed my blood for the love of Christ, and I endured many beatings and wounds until this foul heresy was destroyed with the help of proofs from Sacred Scripture and patristic testimonies. I tell you this not out of pride, but so that, awaiting crowns from God, you might magnanimously endure every temptation and affliction." Hearing this, all the brethren were bitterly grieved and said with tears: "Father, do not leave us orphans, deprived of your spiritual teachings. We, experiencing great love for your holiness, thought that you would never die, but now, hearing these bitter words, our hearts grieve, for you were our comfort in sorrows and helper in temptations; we knew you as father, and mother, and brother." Hearing such words, the venerable one wept, for he was easily moved to tenderness and all his life had the gift of tears. Thus, once, when a brother asked what he should do to acquire tears of compunction, Paul answered: "Always reflect on the Dread Judgment Seat of Christ and on your sins, and then tears will never fail you."

Having wept, as we have already said, the venerable one addressed those present: "Do not weep, brethren, but forgive me, for the time has come which my soul has always awaited, while my flesh feared." Rising, he put on his mantle, and after long prayer he communed of the Most Pure Mysteries. In an instant his face shone like the sun, so that all those present fell to the ground, unable to bear the radiance emanating from the venerable one. After communing, he sat and said the customary prayer which he always recited: "My hope is the Father, my refuge is the Son, my shelter is the Holy Spirit, O Holy Trinity, glory to Thee," after which he again began to instruct his disciples, saying: "Have, children and brethren, love, prayer, humility, and obedience, for that monk who does not have these virtues must be called not a monk but a worldling." And at the end he said: "Woe to that monk who associates with the beardless, for such a one shall never see the face of God." Then the venerable one stretched out his legs, assumed a dignified posture, and raising his hands and eyes to heaven, gave up his blessed soul into the hands of God. This occurred on July 28. The monks of the monastery, with hymns and spiritual songs, carried his sacred relics to a ship in order to send them to Lonkos for burial, as the saint had commanded. It was evening, and the vessel, which was heading to Lonkos during the night, in the morning—O wonders of Thine, O Christ the King!—found itself in Constantinople. Learning of this, the emperor, the senate, the patriarch, and all the clergy of the Church, vested in priestly garments, with candles and much incense, took up the relics of the venerable one and, with hymns, placed them in the Great Church, having venerated them with great reverence and thanking the Lord who had enriched them with such a treasure. The disciples of the saint, having venerated the relics of the saint and invoked him in their prayers, bought hot bread and went aboard the ship to sail back. During the voyage they conversed about the saint, when suddenly, after a short time—for how wondrous are Thy works, O Lord!—they found themselves already at the monastery pier, and coming to the monastery, they told the fathers what had happened, also showing the loaves, which were still hot. Those who heard this marveled at the great boldness that the ever-hymned Paul had before God, to Whom is due all glory, honor, and worship, now and ever and unto the ages of ages. Amen.

The Life and Miracles of Our Venerable and God-Bearing Father and Healer Theodosius the New, Who Was Born in the Year 862

The homeland of this thrice-blessed father of ours Theodosius was the renowned city of Athens, where he was born in the year 862 to parents who were noble and God-fearing, and he was raised *"in the training and admonition of the Lord"* (Ephesians 6:4). When he was sent to school to learn the sacred sciences, being naturally capable, he quickly mastered them. This blessed one was distinguished by great reverence toward God, and attending the church services and hearing about the struggles of the saints, he marveled at their zeal and patience. Wherever he found them, he attentively read the lives of the saints, and greatly desired to imitate their struggles, so as to attain the same virtues as they, which indeed happened afterward.

A short time passed, and his parents reposed. After the burial, blessed Theodosius without delay distributed all his possessions to the poor and, renouncing the world and all that is in the world, left his homeland to visit a certain spiritual elder. From the elder, after various trials, he received the monastic way of life and gave himself over to spiritual struggles. Theodosius so excelled in his life according to Christ that after a short time he desired to depart into stillness, so as to converse alone with the one God in noetic prayer. Passing from place to place in search of stillness, he found himself in the Morea. In the diocese of Argos the venerable one finally found a solitary place suitable for stillness, where he remained. And immediately this good laborer began to add labors to labors, struggles to struggles, living an almost immaterial and incorporeal life in extreme abstinence: prolonged fasts, all-night vigils, prostrations, lying on the bare ground, unceasing prayers during which he stood like an immovable pillar, constant weeping, superhuman non-possessiveness leading to the height of humility, meekness, purity of soul and body, firm faith, steadfast hope, and the crown of all virtues—love. The venerable one was a stranger in this world, a heavenly man and an earthly angel

For this he was also deemed worthy of a Divine vision. One night the Prophet, Forerunner, and Baptist of the Lord John appeared to Theodosius and, greeting him, encouraged him in his spiritual struggles, commanding him to build a church. He promised that he would help in this and would be his companion throughout his entire life. Finding himself filled with spiritual joy, the venerable one glorified God from his whole soul, thanked the Honorable Forerunner, and was extraordinarily encouraged for the struggle that lay before him. Having begun the work, with Divine help he built a monastery in the name of the

Honorable Forerunner, which, by the grace of God, has been preserved to this day in the same place, pouring forth spiritual fragrance and causing tenderness of heart in those who come here with faith.

Having established a school of asceticism, he waged war not against flesh and blood, that is, not against fellow men subject to passions, but, as the divine Paul says, *"against principalities, against powers, against the rulers of the darkness of this age, against spiritual hosts of wickedness in the heavenly places"* (Ephesians 6:12). On account of brevity of exposition, I do not describe all his struggles, but it is easy to understand what a battle the courageous Theodosius endured with the terrible and crafty enemies, how all his life he afflicted his body, so as to subject the lesser to the greater, the body to the soul, and to enslave the flesh to the spirit. Truly he achieved this goal, and with the help of Divine grace he both conquered the demons and subdued the body. Having become spiritual, entirely divine, the venerable one was also deemed worthy to receive from God a pledge of future blessings: the grace of wonderworking and healings, on account of which he was called wonderworker and healer. News of his virtuous life spread everywhere, since God also desired to reveal and glorify His servant, as He Himself says: *"I will honor those who honor Me"* (1 Samuel 2:30). The more the saint avoided the world and its glory, the more, with God's cooperation, he evoked wonder and veneration, for people tormented by various diseases came to him from everywhere and quickly received healing. Some of them, having heard the spiritual instructions of the venerable one, which healed the infirmities of the soul, that is, sins (for from them in most cases bodily illnesses also arise), took care to heal these as well. Having received a twofold healing—of soul and body—they greatly thanked God, and returning home, solemnly proclaimed the Divine grace and the boldness that the saint had before God. Others, under the influence of the saint's instructions, together with their bodily infirmity also cast off their carnal love of pleasure. Renouncing the world and all that is in the world, they became monks, and having before them the example of the venerable one's way of life, zealously walked the narrow and strait path, listening to his soul-profiting teachings and imitating his Divine virtues. Thus, under the guidance of the saint, by the grace of Christ, a fold of rational sheep was gathered there.

But the originator of evil and envious devil, the enemy of our salvation, could not endure this. Using as the instrument of his malice several hypocrites who outwardly appeared pious and virtuous, but in reality were envious and corrupt, he persuaded them to go to the then Bishop of Argos, the most holy Peter the Sign-Bearer, whose memory is celebrated on May 3, and to slander the venerable Theodosius before him, saying that he was a sorcerer and deceiver, and by his sorcery was seducing people who venerated him, which could become a cause of destruction for many. Hearing such opinions about the saint and carried away by the deceitful words of the envious ones, the hierarch decided to banish the venerable one from the diocese, but at this time he received a letter from Constantinople from the patriarch, who summoned him to come as soon as possible to a Council and resolve an urgent Church matter. Divine Providence prevented the exile of Theodosius, for the patriarch immediately departed for Constantinople, having decided to exile the venerable one immediately upon his return. But God again hindered him from doing this and arranged things so that the virtue of

His servant Theodosius and the boldness that he had before Him would be revealed even more to his greater glory.

After examining the Church matter together with the patriarch and the Holy Synod, Peter prepared to return to his diocese, but at night in a dream vision the venerable Theodosius appeared to him and said: "Master, why are you unjust toward me and wish to drive me from the diocese, although I have done nothing wrong either to your holiness or to anyone else? Know then, if you drive me out, you will cause me no harm, but you yourself will fall into sin and will destroy those guilty of this slander, and those being saved, by the grace of God, will suffer great harm, because those terrible slanderers falsely accused me out of envy. But do not act unjustly toward me, because I too am a servant of our Lord Jesus Christ, I serve Him alone, and from childhood I place all hopes for my salvation in Him. If you cease this senseless persecution, it will be well. But if not, the Lord will avenge me upon you." Hearing such words, the hierarch asked: "Who are you, that you speak thus with me?" Theodosius answered: "I am Theodosius, a servant of Christ, living in your diocese." Blessed Peter awoke in fear and, reflecting on what he had seen in the dream, repented of the decision he had made. At this time a patriarchal servant came to him and summoned him to the patriarch, because Theodosius had also appeared to the patriarch in a dream, told him everything, and said: "Command Peter not to act unjustly toward me, lest he anger God and cause harm to many Christians." When the patriarch asked who he was, he answered: "I am Theodosius, a servant of Christ, living within the bounds of the diocese of Argos." Upon awakening, the patriarch commanded that Peter be summoned immediately and asked him whether there was a certain Theodosius in his diocese, and whether he had offended him in any way. "Yes," answered Peter, "holy Master, there is in my diocese a servant of God named Theodosius," and he related to him everything in detail, including what he had seen in his dream. Then the patriarch also told him his dream. Thus they both learned that Theodosius was holy and had great boldness before God, after which they glorified God, Who worthily glorifies those who glorify Him. Then the patriarch commanded the divine Peter to depart for his diocese and, in the name of the patriarch, to bow before the saint and ask him to intercede for him before the Lord. The patriarch repeated his command also on the day when blessed Peter was preparing to leave Constantinople.

Having reached the Morea, the divine Peter decided first of all to visit the venerable Theodosius, in order to fulfill the patriarch's command and to ask the saint's forgiveness for his intention to exile him on the basis of the slanderers' accusations. The saint foreknew of the hierarch's coming, because he was deemed worthy to receive from God, along with other gifts, also the gift of foresight. He placed burning coals in his cowl and, taking incense in his hand, went out to meet him. Approaching, he placed the incense on the coals, and an ineffable fragrance spread forth, while—O miracle!—the cowl did not burn at all, but the venerable one began to cense with it, and Peter, marveling at this strange miracle, understood that before him stood the venerable Theodosius. Dismounting, he rushed to embrace the venerable one, who, releasing the cowl from his hands, bowed low before the hierarch of God and received him with reverence. Then, glorifying God, the divine Peter asked the venerable one for forgiveness for the past and, bowing in the name of the patriarch, conveyed all his words to Theodosius. The latter answered with great humble-mindedness, both in words and gestures, which kindled in the hierarch an even greater love for him according to God. Without delay he ordained him a deacon, and then a priest, although the venerable one, on account of his extreme humble-mindedness, declined the ordination. From that time on, for the wise hierarch Peter and those around him, after they had learned in deed how much eyes are more reliable than ears, the venerable one became an example of virtue.

The fame of the saint spread ever more throughout the world, for those healed by him of various illnesses recounted this everywhere, and the divine Peter and even the Ecumenical Patriarch himself praised the sanctity of the venerable one and his boldness before God. There was not a single sick person who, having with faith called upon the venerable one for help, did not receive swift healing. Thus the venerable one became known to all and loved by all, proving to be a most necessary helper in their illnesses and needs, and a cause of the salvation of their souls.

But when the saint came to a very old age and as a man was obliged to pay the common debt (that is, to die) and receive the reward for his many struggles and labors, three days before his death God revealed to him that he was departing from this world. Having summoned his disciples, he instructed them at length in the life according to God, and then, informing them of his imminent death, began to console them, promising that in spirit he would always be with them. But they wept greatly and grieved that they were being deprived of converse with an angel. When the third day arrived, he embraced the disciples, gave thanks to God and glorified Him, and finally, raising his hands to Him, said: "Lord, into Thy hands I commend my spirit." With these words Theodosius delivered his blessed soul into the hands of God on the seventh day of the month of August.

Learning of his death, the divine Peter came together with all the clergy and a great multitude of people. They prepared everything necessary for the burial and reverently buried his sacred remains before the church of the Honorable Forerunner. And from that time all the sick who bowed before the tomb of the saint and with faith called upon him for help rose up already healthy, glorifying God and thanking the saint, in whose name they also erected a church. From that time until this day miracles and healings constantly occur in that church of God; I shall recount only some of them, for the spiritual joy of those who love virtue.

After a long time had passed, the number of monks laboring there began little by little to decrease, because the disciples of the venerable one had departed to the Lord, and others did not settle there for the reason that one could not find there what was needed for the body. The place became deserted, and no monks remained there at all. However, the Christians who lived nearby, having strong spiritual love for the saint, constantly came here and every day glorified the Lord and the venerable one with hymns, psalmody, and spiritual songs, and celebrated the Divine Liturgy.

Once a priest and devout Christians from Nauplia, having taken all that was necessary, went out early in the morning from their village and came to the church of the saint.

Approaching the church, they saw from afar a venerable-looking elder standing at the church door with a staff in his hands. Deciding that he was reading the sequence of the Hours and was preparing to serve the Liturgy, they were saddened, thinking that the elder had preceded them, but in the church they found no one and thought that this was a vision from God, for the church was full of ineffable fragrance. Thanking God and the saint, they greatly rejoiced, but while the priest was preparing for the service, other Christians came, in greater number than the first, and demanded that their priest serve the Liturgy. Those who had arrived first, moved by zeal for the saint and inflamed by the vision, began to resist. They quarreled for a long time at the entrance to the church, and then two youths, one from one group and the other from the other, drew their swords and rushed at each other. But by God's help and by the grace of the venerable one, a dove flew up between the two swords, as if intentionally released by someone for this purpose. It received the blow, and two small lumps fell to the ground between the youths, while they themselves remained whole and unharmed. Seeing this miracle and reflecting on the visitation of the saint, the youths threw their swords to the ground and, embracing one another, exchanged kisses, glorifying the saint who had miraculously delivered them from danger. Both priests and the people were also moved to compunction, and with warm tears thanking God, they reached an agreement that one priest would serve in the church of the venerable one, and the other in the church of the Honorable Forerunner. After this, in harmony, love, and common thanksgiving to God, they returned to their villages. And this strange miracle that happened to them became an example for others, and if thereafter two groups of Christians with two priests came there, they no longer quarreled with one another, but in love agreed that one priest would serve in one church and the other in the other.

A certain nobleman from Nauplia named Nicholas was one day at his house when he suddenly became half withered. Half of his head withered, together with his ear, eye, shoulder, arm, half of his body, and his leg. And these members of his became completely insensible and immovable, so that he presented a pitiful sight. His wife, brother, and other relatives, pitying him, invited the best physicians, but whatever they did, they could not cure him. Finally, after consulting with pious and virtuous men, the relatives decided to have recourse to the healer Theodosius. Placing the sick man on a bed, they brought him to the church of the venerable one. Having performed an All-Night service of prayer and praise, and in the morning the Divine Liturgy, they called upon the saint for help with faith. In the evening they carried the sick man back to Nauplia. But when they set the bed on the ground to rest a little, the sick man suddenly rose from the bed himself, saying: "Saint Theodosius, help me!" Standing on his feet—O miracle!—he understood that he was completely well, and not a trace of the illness remained. He entered Nauplia on his own feet. Glorifying God and the saint, he remained in good health to the end of his life, having traveled many paths both by land and by sea in various places, proclaiming to all the wonderful miracle that the great Theodosius had worked upon him.

A devout priest from Nauplia named Antonios became seriously ill and for a long time lay bedridden, from which a severe swelling formed in his right side, causing him terrible pain.

From the swelling his leg also began to rot, and the priest became lame. Having despaired of human help, he had recourse to the help of the venerable one, but since he was unable to go to him on his own feet, he was carried to the church on a stretcher. After the customary All-Night Vigil and the Divine Liturgy, the relatives were already ready to return home, when suddenly the sick man felt some strength within himself and, trusting in the grace of the venerable one, reluctantly, little by little, began to step on his feet. Strengthened by faith in the venerable one, he walked on his own feet to Nauplia, and the farther he went, the more he was strengthened, until he felt himself completely well. He who shortly before had been paralyzed walked without hindrance a distance of more than six miles from the church of the venerable one, constantly glorifying God.

Another pious and God-loving inhabitant of Nauplia named Michael was once sitting at table with his wife and children when he suddenly saw that his wife's eye had become red and the upper eyelid had swollen. He asked what had happened to her, but she did not know what it was. After some time the swelling increased and began to hang from the eye, resembling a red grape, which impaired her vision. The experienced physicians who were summoned could do nothing to help her. Michael, having despaired of receiving help from them, ran to the church of the healer Theodosius together with his wife and other laymen and clergy, where they performed an All-Night service of prayer and the Divine Liturgy. After the service, the husband immediately fell asleep at home, while the wife, looking at the icon of the venerable one that was opposite her, called upon him for help with all her soul. And at that same moment the wonderworker Theodosius, swift to help, appeared to her, coming forth from the icon and holding a staff in his hand. Approaching, he wiped the swelling with the edge of his cowl and said: "Woman, you together with your husband came to my church with faith to ask for help, and so I have come to your house to grant you healing." With these words he became invisible, and she immediately felt that the swelling had completely disappeared. Touching her eye with her hand and finding it completely well, she called her husband. When he awoke and asked what had happened, she answered: "The great Theodosius has just appeared to me and healed me." Michael immediately leaped from the bed, lit a light, and seeing the miracle worked by the saint, immediately ran to tell the priest about it, after which he asked that the church be opened. Together with many priests and laymen, bringing candles, oil, and incense, they thanked the saint all night long. In the morning, after they had celebrated the Divine Liturgy, Michael invited everyone to his house and generously treated them, distributing abundant alms at the same time, telling everyone of the miracle of the venerable one and glorifying God.

A certain Albanian suffered greatly from dysuria and for many days could not relieve himself, from which his bladder swelled, causing unbearable pain. The unfortunate man tried many remedies but received no benefit from them, and the more time passed, the stronger the pains became. Then he came to the church of the saint and, remaining there three days and three nights, prayed with warm tears to the venerable one for healing. On the third night the wonderworker Theodosius appeared to him in his sleep and, touching the afflicted place with his staff, said: "Quickly go out of my church and urinate." Awakening, the sick man ran out of the church in fear and relieved his natural need for a long time. After this the swelling subsided, the pains ceased, and the former patient, thanking God and the saint, returned home in health.

Another man had diseased legs, but having with faith called upon the saint for help and prayed to God, he received healing, and in gratitude he made silver legs (the size of his own) and donated them to the church of the venerable one, so that everyone would always remember the miracle.

A certain noble Venetian who held a government position, having learned of the numerous miracles performed by the saint, came to Nauplia with his barren wife. Grieving greatly over their childlessness, he and his wife came to the church of the venerable one and, having prayed to God with faith, asked the saint to give them a child, promising to name him Theodosius. The saint heard their supplication and gave them a child. They named the child Theodosius, to the glory of God Who is glorified in His saints, and he was the only one among the children of the Venetian nobility with such a name.

And in our days (says the author of the life) a certain nobleman of Nauplia, George, of the house of Puzikios, a courageous and experienced warrior, terrible to enemies but beloved by the Venetian aristocracy, became famous for wonderful and great victories. During the war of the Venetians against the kings of the West, he was awarded the rank of general for his exploits. Once during dinner, when both armies were resting after battle, an enemy general, a German of enormous stature, strong, full of envy and malice against Puzikios, rode in full armor into the Venetian camp and shouted: "Who is George Puzikios here? Come out and let us fight!" As soon as George heard this challenge, having strong faith in God and in Saint Theodosius, he immediately rose, bared his head, crossed himself three times, and said from his whole soul: "My great Theodosius, come at this very hour from Nauplia and help your servant." After this, arming himself and mounting his horse, Puzikios rushed into battle. The German, unlike Puzikios, lowered the visor of his helmet, and they charged at each other. Seeing that Puzikios's forehead was exposed, the German struck there with his lance, scraping off the skin at that place and slightly grazing the bone, but he could not knock him from the saddle. Puzikios cried out: "God, Theodosius, help me," and with these words struck the German in the chest, throwing him to the ground. Dismounting, he cut off the German's head and, tying it by the feet to his horse, ordered his servant to drag the German along the ground so that both armies could see. He himself, holding in his hands the remaining part of the lance, which had broken from the blow against the German's chest, rode in triumph on horseback before both battle lines. Later he ordered a silver lampada to be made the size of the remaining piece of lance and, together with other suitable gifts, sent it with great gratitude to the monastery for the adornment of the church of the venerable Theodosius.

There lived in the environs of Argos a certain Hagarene called the Voivode. Once in summer, going about the sown fields with his scribes, he was collecting the tithe and recording everything in books. When they came to a small village called Zalevis and had done all that was necessary, the time for dinner arrived. But since the place for eating and rest was unsuitable, seeing the church of the venerable Theodosius, the Hagarene said to his scribes (and they were Christians): "Let us go to your church, eat and rest until the heat subsides, and in the evening we shall return to work again." They entered the church, set the table, and began to eat. The Hagarene greatly admired the beautiful lampada that hung before the icon of the saint, and he said to his servant: "Take that glass vessel, wash it well, and bring it to me; I shall drink wine from it." One God-loving scribe named Gavros, having strong reverence for the saint and moved by zeal for God, said to the Hagarene: "Do not take anything that belongs to the saint, lest some evil befall us." To this he answered: "What can this dead monk do to me, a living man, and moreover a lord?" Gavros objected even more, but the Hagarene justified himself by saying that he had the authority to take it. Then Gavros rose from the table and said: "If you have firmly decided to take it, then allow me to go home, and then do what you will, for I am certain that the saint will not let us depart peacefully." Seeing that Gavros was defending the lampada of the saint with such fervor, the Hagarene said mockingly to his servant: "Let it be; we shall not scandalize our scribe." However, when they were already about to leave, the Hagarene secretly ordered his servant to take the lampada, so that no one would see, and bring it to his house. The servant did as he was commanded. But when the Hagarene, having returned home and eaten supper, lay down to sleep, he saw in his dream that dead monk, that is, the venerable Theodosius, alive, with a radiant face and a fearsome appearance, standing over him, holding a staff in his hands. Touching the Hagarene's chest, the saint asked: "How does it seem to you: did you take this thing from a living man or from a dead one? Behold, I have come to show who you are and what your strength is, and who are the servants of my Christ, who though dead are alive, by the grace of Jesus Christ, and can put to death you who think you are alive, but are dead in soul." With these words he squeezed his throat, the Hagarene's eyes swelled, his face turned black, his tongue fell from his mouth, and he began to squeal like a pig at slaughter. Hearing the cries, his household immediately ran to him, and seeing such a pitiful sight, asked: "What is the matter with you?" But he could say nothing except, with great difficulty, to call for Gavros. The servants ran for him and brought him to the Hagarene. When Gavros came, he asked: "What happened?" The Hagarene, barely coming to himself, answered: "I took the monk's lampada, and he came to kill me with his staff. Take a vessel of oil, candles, and the lampada, and go quickly to him and ask him not to come here anymore, not to be angry with me. And I henceforth will always help his church."

"Did I not tell you not to take the lampada, lest some evil befall us? But you took it, and behold, now you are in danger."

"That I acted wrongly, I understood from what happened to me. But now, I beg you, take what I told you about, and together with your companions go quickly to the church."

"How can I go now, when it is night? I shall go at dawn."

The Hagarene began to tremble all over and cried out:

"Woe is me! This night he will come to kill me!"

Seeing that inordinate fear had seized the barbarian, Gavros took the oil, the candles, and the lampada, and at that same hour placed everything in the church of the venerable one. Thus the impious one was delivered from his fear and from danger, and from then on, even catching sight of the honorable church from afar, he would bow to it as he passed.

"I wished to conclude my discourse with this, but my debt to the saint," says the holy Malaxos, "compels me to add to these also those miracles that the wonderworker Theodosius worked for me and my family. I had a son Andronicus, who suffered severely from his throat. It swelled so much that it was difficult for him to breathe. Since no medicine helped, his mother, praying to God with warm faith, decided to have recourse to the help of the saint. Reverently taking his icon that was in our house, she placed it at the child's head and with tears begged the saint to visit her child. After some time the child started and called his mother. She heard his voice and asked: 'What happened?' With weeping he answered: 'A venerable-looking monk came to me and lightly struck my throat with his staff. He burst the swelling, and all the pus flowed out.' The mother immediately lit a light and—O miracle!—discovered that the swelling was as if cut with a razor, and the child's clothes were soiled with pus mixed with blood. The boy himself, who previously because of his illness could not speak, could now talk freely. Thus, by the grace of God and the saint, he was delivered from a mortal illness. Once I had to sail to Venice. As soon as we set sail, a strong storm arose, which kept growing stronger. Having despaired of human help, we called upon God, the Most Holy Theotokos, and all the saints with weeping. And I, going to where I slept, began to read the canon to the Mother of God and to call upon the saints, one after another. Remembering the countless miracles of the venerable Theodosius, I asked with warm faith and a contrite heart for his help as well, that he would work a miracle over us also. Thus with my requests I fell asleep, and in my sleep I saw that I was in a beautiful church together with other priests. We were performing a service of prayer to God with reverence and tenderness of heart. There I saw a certain child with his mother, who were selling lampada oil for the church. Approaching me, the child gave me a vessel of oil and said: 'Pour this oil into the lampada of the venerable Theodosius, and by his intercession he will help both you and your companions, and the storm at sea will cease.' Suddenly awakening, I beheld a miracle. The most violent storm had subsided and turned into a calm. Glorifying God, I thanked the saint who had miraculously delivered us from mortal danger. And at another time the saint by his swiftest intercession unexpectedly delivered my elder son Stauracius from an unjust death."

These and other countless miracles this wondrous and great Theodosius worked and continues to work, for which he was worthily called by all the faithful a healer and wonderworker, to the glory of the Father, and of the Son, and of the Holy Spirit, the one God of all, to Whom belongs glory and dominion, unto the ages of ages. Amen.

(Written by the holy Nicholas Malaxos, Protopriest of the city of Nauplia)

The Life and Struggles of Our Venerable Wonderworking Father Luke the New, Who Struggled on Mount Stirion in Greece in the Tenth Century

This divine father of ours Luke was an offspring, or better to say, an adornment of Greece. The ancestors of the venerable one came from the island of Aegina. Unable to endure the frequent raids of the Hagarenes, they left their homeland and resettled in Greece, in the region of Phocis, which is now called Salon, in the village of Kastorion, where the blessed Luke was born. His father was called Stephen, and his mother Euphrosyne. In childhood, Luke did not love, as other children do, to play, laugh, or run about in disorder, but conducted himself quietly, decorously, and in all things displayed a firm and mature mind. He so loved abstinence that from childhood he did not taste meat, cheese, eggs, or any other rich food that brings pleasure, nor fruits, but ate only barley bread with water, vegetables, and beans, and on Wednesdays and Fridays he fasted until sunset. And the most astonishing thing is that no one taught him to fast in this way or to live such an ascetic life, but he himself turned away from all food that delights the palate, and loved hunger, labors, and everything that serves to afflict the flesh. Once, when the divine Luke was dining together with his parents, they, thinking that he abstained from food not for God's sake but out of vainglory and the ignorance proper to children, decided to test him. In one pot they cooked meat with fish and served it at the table. Not knowing this, and thinking that his father was giving him fish, Luke began to eat. But sensing the taste of meat in his mouth and understanding his parents' cunning, he was greatly grieved and spat out what he was eating. As proof of his patient endurance, the venerable one spent three days without food, all this time lamenting his involuntary sin. Since his parents understood that his intention was not from man but from God, they allowed him to live as he wished.

Luke greatly respected his parents and, submitting to them, in imitation of Abel, Jacob, and Moses, he tended his parents' livestock. The blessed one was so merciful and compassionate to the poor that he cared nothing for himself. When his parents sent Luke to do the usual work, upon meeting the poor along the way, he would give them his food, while he himself remained hungry, for his food was to feed his hungry brethren. In like manner he acted also with clothing: if along the way he found the naked, he would take off his clothing and give it to them. Often returning to his father's house unclothed, the venerable one cared nothing for the cold he endured, nor for the shame, nor for the condemnation and reproach from his relatives. Several times his parents even beat him for this, but the thrice-blessed one did not even grieve, but when they beat him, he was confident that he was receiving honors, crowns, and gifts.

Many times they left him naked for a long time and did not give him clothing, so that he might renounce that blessed love of mankind which he showed to the poor. However, the blessed Luke counted all these punishments as Heavenly rewards, because when the soul is captivated by the bonds of Divine love, it counts as nothing the punishments it has endured for the God it loves, but rejoices in sufferings. And when it suffers for the One it loves, then it thinks even more about suffering, and flees rest and pleasure as torment. The love of mankind of the venerable one was also clearly manifested in what I wish to tell now. When the venerable one was sent to sow his father's fields, more than half of the grain he distributed to the poor, but for the mercy shown to the poor there followed a reward from God, because the less seed Luke sowed in the ground, the more fruit it bore.

A little time passed and the father of the venerable one departed to the Lord, and the blessed one dedicated himself to the Heavenly Father.

Renouncing the cares of livestock and lands, he devoted himself only to prayer, reading, and the study of Holy Scripture. The venerable one made great progress in prayer, as many testify, and especially his mother, which is no small thing, for her words bring amazement to all who hear her account. Wishing with her own eyes to see how her son prayed at night, she once hid near the place where the venerable one prayed, in such a way that she herself could see but would not be seen by others. And she beheld something fearful and great, as she herself later affirmed under oath, that her son was praying standing before God with extraordinary reverence and concentration, and his feet did not touch the ground at all, but were at a distance of one cubit from it, and in some manner were ascending to God. This strange vision the mother beheld not once or twice, but three times. This miracle was also seen by other witnesses, and they have announced this to us.

Since the saint had long desired the quiet monastic life, having chosen a convenient time, he set out for Thessaly. Along the way he was seized by soldiers who had been ordered to catch runaway slaves and put them in prison. Noticing that the saint differed almost in no way from a runaway slave, both in his poor clothing and in his movements, they asked him whose slave he was, whence he came, and where he was going. The saint answered them that he was a slave of Christ and was going where he had promised God to go. Thinking that he was mocking them, concealing his slave status, they beat him severely, forcing him to say whose slave he was. But Luke, out of love for the truth and out of genuine magnanimity, thought that it would be faintheartedness to tell a lie, that he was someone's slave, only so as not to be beaten. As a result, they put him, beaten, in prison. The devil thought that in this way he had taken revenge and punished the venerable one because during the warfare, by means of which the vile one with great shamelessness had armed himself against the venerable one through thoughts and passions, the latter had strongly resisted him and conquered. Soon some of his friends, who knew the venerable one well, testified that he was not a slave; he was released from prison and returned again to his relatives. However, they began to reproach and condemn him severely, which was much harder than the blows of the soldiers. Knowing that the devil was hindering him from going to God, the venerable one did not cease to beseech His Mercy to fulfill the desire of his soul, which the One who ever cooperates unto good accomplished in the following manner.

Two monks from Rome stopped for the night at his mother's house. When the venerable one saw them, then, full of love for God, he again desired the monastic life. Conversing with them, he asked them to take him with them to the monastery. But they did not agree because of his youth and inexperience, and also because if his parents and relatives found out, the monks would be subjected to punishment. But after the venerable one informed them that he was a stranger and no one would seek him, they agreed to take him with them. Secretly leaving the village, they set out for Athens and stopped at a monastery there. Entering the church of the Most Pure Theotokos, they prayed, and entrusted Luke to the abbot so that he might tonsure him after some time and number him among the rest of the brethren, while the monks themselves departed for Jerusalem.

Many times the abbot of the monastery tried to find out where Luke was from and who his parents were, but having learned nothing, he clothed him in the small schema. However, the mother of the venerable one, unable to bear the separation from her dear son, grieved and wept bitterly. From great sorrow she complained to the Master of all, God, saying: "Woe is me, O Lord, Witness of my widowhood and loneliness. Thou, who didst first deliver to death my husband, whom Thou Thyself didst give me, and didst make me a widow, which for a woman is harder than death itself, hast again taken from me him who was my consolation in this grief. I see no longer the true light in my wretched life. Why hast Thou removed from me my beloved son? Perhaps I hindered him from devoting himself to converse with Thee and to prayer? Perhaps I compelled him to leave the service of Thee and to care for me? Perhaps I taught him to prefer the material to the immaterial, and the temporal to the eternal? Could I have acted thus, I who was well taught by my parents to be to my children a mother not only according to the flesh but also according to the soul? Could I have acted thus, I who prayed that my son would love his soul more than his body? I only wished always to see my most beloved son, or at least to see him once in so many years. It would be enough for me if I heard of his good deeds, so that my soul would rejoice and I would become more diligent about it. O King of all, despise not my tears, but place them before Thee, as the divine David says, and dispel the darkness of my grief, which Thou canst do if Thou wilt return my son to my eyes. Then I will summon people from everywhere and will glorify Thy greatness and praise Thee all the days of my life."

Praying thus, the mother of the venerable one inclined the God who loves mankind to mercy and compassion, and what happened? God, who creates all things by His command, helped her as well. The mother of Luke appeared in a dream to the abbot of the monastery and began to accuse him sternly: "Father, why hast thou caused me, a widow, such torments and added wound upon another wound of mine? Why hast thou, merciless one, deprived me of the only consolation of my widowhood? Why hast thou stolen my son, the reposer of my old age? Return him to me quickly, return my light and my only hope. If not, I will not cease to beseech God, the King of all, and will call thee to judgment, because I have suffered great offense from thee." This vision greatly troubled the abbot. At first he thought it was a phantom and a temptation from the enemy, but since twice, thrice, and many times he saw the woman who cruelly reviled him, he decided that the vision was from God and should not be disregarded.

And so, after some time, the abbot summoned the youth and sternly said to him: "Why didst thou not tell me about thyself when I asked so many times? Answer me, why didst thou say that thou hast neither parents nor relatives? How didst thou dare to receive this holy monastic schema while being full of cunning and hypocrisy? If thou hadst openly disclosed all the truth about thyself without guile from the very beginning, then it would not have been revealed now against thy will. Depart then from us and from the bounds of Athens, go to thy mother, who for three nights in a row has caused me great disturbance." During this speech, the blessed Luke stood in fear with his gaze lowered to the ground, he said nothing, but his tears and his whole appearance showed that he was deeply grieving because he was being separated from the monastery and the brethren. Noticing this, the abbot softened his anger, moved by the great humble-mindedness of the divine Luke, but said to him: "At the present time it is impossible for thee not to return to thy mother. But after thou hast fulfilled this, no one will any longer be able to hinder thee from caring for the salvation of thy soul in any place. By all appearances, thy mother's prayer is very pleasing to God and has prevailed over thine own." As soon as the divine Luke heard this, he did not object, since he was very modest and out of his reverence honored everyone. Making a prostration and requesting the prayers of the abbot, he reluctantly departed from the monastery and set out for home to his mother.

When he entered the house, his mother was sitting on ashes in great sorrow. Seeing her son, she was filled with amazement and at the same time with joy, and rose from her place. Consider the virtue of the woman, for it was fitting for such a tree—the mother—to bring forth such fruit—the son. For this blessed one, suddenly seeing her son, did not immediately rush to embrace or examine him, considering this a secondary matter, but first turned her eyes to God and, raising her hands, confessed to Him this benefaction by which she had again found her lost son. She embraced him whom she loved with the words: *"Blessed be God, who has not turned away my prayer nor His mercy from me"* (Psalm 65:20).

Returned to his mother in this manner, the blessed Luke served her and showed her the honor and obedience befitting a mother from a son, but after four months an irresistible love for God and stillness again took hold of him, causing him to forget everything and become his own only for God. Then his mother too did not hinder him, not considering this contempt for herself, because she knew that although every son should prefer his parents to everything else, yet he should prefer God even to his parents themselves. Having received his mother's blessing, he went to Mount Joannitsa. Walking around that part of it which descends to the sea, he found a church of the holy unmercenaries Cosmas and Damian and there built a hermit's cell. How many battles and combats the venerable one endured there, struggling with hunger, sleep, and the inhuman demons who wage war on us through these passions, no one can either verify or recount, because of the surpassing nature of this subject. But if one must demonstrate the struggles of the venerable one by a few examples, as one can describe a lion by its claws and the quality of a spring's water by tasting a small amount of water, then it will not be a sin to add the following accounts to the narratives of his virtues.

One disciple of the venerable one did not believe him and suspected that the venerable one only pretended to devote himself to prayer and vigil, but in reality spent the greater part of the night in sleep. This suspicion arose in the disciple because the venerable one did not devote himself at night to the study of sciences and did not read books of Holy Scripture, but was allegedly very ignorant. So said that disciple about the venerable one. Wishing to verify whether everything was really so, once, when the door to the cell of the saint was closed, the disciple came close to it and pressed his head against it to listen to what the venerable one was saying. Standing thus until morning, he returned to his cell, filled with amazement and free from the former thoughts of unbelief that had tempted him. What he learned while at the door of the venerable one was the following, as he himself related after the death of Luke: "I heard that the venerable one, making prostrations and touching the ground with his face, each time said: *'God, be merciful to me a sinner'* (Luke 18:13). The more the venerable one warmed himself, the more prostrations he made, until he exhausted all his bodily strength and could no longer follow the desire of the spirit. Then he would fall to the ground and lie motionless for a long time. But even on the ground he was not idle, he did not simply lie there and did not sleep, but raised his hands and lifted up his noetic eyes to heaven, fervently crying out: 'Lord, have mercy.' Having given his body a little rest, he would rise again and pray until dawn." Such are the proofs of the secret struggles of the venerable one and of his ardent love for stillness.

Once the venerable one came to a friend of his who led a holy life, the abbot of a monastery. Having stayed with him for three days, he felt a strong desire to return again to stillness in his cell. Luke began to ask leave to go, but the abbot did not release him, because he loved the venerable one and could not bear to be parted from him, for the love of friends in God is stronger than natural love. Since the venerable one did not agree to stay, wishing to return to his cell, the abbot, on the pretext that a great feast was soon coming, said: "How long wilt thou thus oppose in a peasant-like manner and prefer the desert to the church assembly, and besides, a universal feast is soon coming, and if thou dost not hear the sacred words and hymns, thou wilt bring the greatest harm upon thyself." To this the God-bearing Luke with his customary blessed simplicity answered: "Good teacher, blessed shepherd, thou dost command well, but what benefit do canons, readings, and the Church service bring to a man? What is their purpose?" Hearing the question, the abbot did not know what to answer. The venerable one, noticing his perplexity, again with his characteristic simplicity answered: "Good teacher, blessed shepherd, psalmody, readings, and every service lead the virtuous to the fear of God, as thou teachest. But for one who zealously strives to acquire this fear of God in his heart, does he need all that of which thou speakest?" The abbot of the monastery was greatly amazed to hear this, and no longer detained the venerable one, but allowed him to return to his cell.

Near his cell the venerable one cultivated a small garden, in order to labor with his body and to distribute to the brethren what was necessary for their needs. In the garden there were various trees, and he also grew vegetables, which he distributed every day to those who came to him. Sometimes, having gathered the fruits of his garden and loaded them on a mule, he would take them to nearby villages. Having secretly unloaded them, he would leave the fruits in the middle of the village and return to his cell. Thus the venerable one generously distributed the other fruits of his labors.

However, deer from the mountains began to frequent this garden of the venerable one, trampling the plants with their hooves. The venerable one drove them away sometimes with stones, sometimes with shouting, but they continued to come and damage the plants. Once, seeing one deer that was larger than the rest, the venerable one began to speak softly to it, as if conversing with a man: "Why do you offend me and spoil the fruits of my labors, although I have not offended you in anything? Both I and you are servants of one Master and Creator God, but I, created in the image of God, have authority over all His creatures. Therefore God commands thee, do not come down from this place where thou standest, but receive due condemnation from Him." And at that very moment the deer fell and remained motionless. Hunters who were nearby, seeing the deer lying motionless, came running and wanted to slaughter it. This displeased the venerable one. He pitied the unfortunate deer and, approaching the hunters, meekly said: "Brethren, you have no right to kill this deer, because you did not chase it and did not labor. It is clear that this animal, which has fallen, needs rather mercy and help." With these words he persuaded the hunters, and they not only left the deer but also helped the venerable one lift it up, after which they set it free. The hunters only marveled at the great compassion and meekness of the venerable one.

One must also tell the following case. Although the venerable one subjected his body to torments with so many labors, constant vigils, countless prostrations, meager food, because he ate only barley bread and water, and that with abstinence, sometimes he ate vegetables and such beans as came his way, he froze in winter from cold and in summer was scorched by heat, he suffered from a multitude of lice (I pass over all the other hardships he experienced: nightly standings, unceasing prayer, solitude, the desert, which usually makes a man rough and hardens his soul), he nevertheless offended no one, but was always affable, cheerful, and meek with those who came to him. He offered them both bodily and spiritual food, eating together with them until they were satisfied, hiding nothing of the food and leaving nothing in reserve, because he knew that God, who feeds the cattle and birds, would not leave without His care those who unceasingly call upon His Divine name in truth.

Since the venerable one greatly desired to receive the great angelic monastic schema, he was deemed worthy of this by Divine Providence in the following manner. Two monks of comely appearance and holy life, elderly in years, on their way to Rome passed through those places where the venerable one lived, as if someone had sent them. Receiving them with great friendliness, the venerable one revealed to them his strong desire to become a great schema monk and fervently asked them to tonsure him. Seeing that the venerable one was a vessel worthy of the schema, the monks did not delay, but, having performed the appointed sacred rites, clothed him in this angelic habit with new and most strict vows of self-denial on the narrow and sorrowful path that leads to life. All rejoiced at this: God, the Angels, and men. Only the devil grieved greatly and was frightened, because he saw a new soldier of Christ and a true ascetic, clothed in the armor of the Holy Spirit and breathing courage and nobility, preparing to war against him with even greater zeal than before.

For the hospitality of the monks, who had become for him the cause of great good, the venerable one had nothing except the usual meager food. Because of this the venerable one was greatly saddened. But God, who opens His bountiful right hand and satisfies every living thing from His bounty, here too worked a miracle. When at dawn the monks were sitting on the shore and admiring the gently lapping waves and the sight of the bright sun, suddenly a huge fish leaped out of the water and fell right at their feet; it thrashed softly, as if asking to be taken. Seeing this, the monks marveled at the Providence of God and thanked the Lord, but He, the Generous One, as if not satisfied with one fish, sent them yet another. And immediately another fish, the same as the first, leaped out of the water onto the land, as if asking to be taken as well, and to give even greater thanks to God. In this way God revealed to the monks how great Luke was, and they, having received more benefit from him than they had brought him themselves, departed.

Having received the spiritual weapon of the great angelic habit and having reflected that now for the first time he was enrolled as a soldier of Christ and must fight against the devil, and for this still greater struggles than before were required, the venerable one added fast to fast, tears to tears, lived in even greater stillness, and spent his time in even warmer and more prolonged prayer. For this he received from God greater help, the grace of healings, and knowledge of the past and future, and of what happens in secret in the present. Thus, the Bulgarians, who had captured almost all of Epirus, he delivered to destruction by his prayers to God, but many days in advance he predicted that they would cause much evil. He said this obscurely, so that people would not glorify him for his foresight, for some heard him say: "Hellas will be captured, and there will be war against the Peloponnese."

The cell of the venerable one was built simply, but not in order to protect him and to store anything in it, because he had nothing except his own body, but in order to conceal his ascetic labors, of which he did not want anyone to know except God. In order always to remember death, he dug a deep pit in his cell and entered it as into a grave. Snatching a little sleep, he would rise and pronounce the words of David: *"I rise before the dawn and cry for help"* (Psalm 118:147), and then: *"My eyes are awake through the night watches, that I may meditate on Your word"* (Psalm 118:148).

With what words is it possible to speak of the great compassion and kindness of the venerable one? Although in the previous accounts we did speak of these qualities of his, for he showed mercy and was a benefactor not only to people, but also to cattle, birds, and even venomous creatures. This ever-blessed one for a long time fed two serpents, remembering the commandment of the Lord, which says: *"love your enemies, do good to those who hate you"* (Luke 6:27), and these serpents caused him no harm. Many times he also fed the small birds of the field, being merciful, as the divine David says: *"He is ever merciful, and lends"* (Psalm 36:26).

Since the fame of the saint had spread everywhere, two brothers once came to him. After the venerable one had received them and they had enjoyed conversation, the brothers related that their father before his death had buried money in the ground, but they did not know exactly where, and therefore asked the venerable one to reveal this place to them. They were poor, lacking the most necessary things, and what was worst, because of this money they were fighting with each other, each accusing the other of having stolen the money. Having heard all this, the venerable one, out of his humble-mindedness, reflected that their words required no answer at all, and therefore immediately withdrew. But they, still hoping to find the money with his help, went to him a second time and again began to ask. The venerable one refused, saying that he did not have such Divine grace. But since they asked him for a long time, promising not to leave until he satisfied their request, he reluctantly agreed to help them, but did so in a skillful manner. Just as one who wishes to conceal what he knows would act, he said to them: "You know the place where your father hid the money (by such and such a sign). Why then do you come in vain and disturb me?" Hearing the answer, they immediately went to the place indicated by the venerable one. There they found confirmation of his words, and, taking the money, divided it between themselves, and proclaimed the miracle to all the people who were there.

Once certain people came to the venerable one. Aloud he said: "A man is coming to us with a heavy burden." After these words the venerable one left everyone and went up to the mountain. Those who heard his words began to wonder who might be the one coming with a heavy burden, and what this burden was. And behold, as the venerable one had predicted, a man came to them, but without a burden. He began to ask about the venerable one, saying that he needed his help. The people invited him to wait, since not long before this the saint had left. The man began to wait, saying that he would not leave from there until he met the venerable one. Thus seven days passed, and as soon as the venerable one came out of his secret retreat on the mountain and saw the man, he said in a stern voice unusual for his meekness: "Man, what hast thou come to seek in the desert? Why hast thou left the cities and come here, to the mountains? Why hast thou left archbishops, teachers, spiritual fathers, and seekest unlettered hermits? Dost thou not fear Divine condemnation, being guilty of so many sins?" Hearing such words, that man trembled, and from fear his tongue was bound so that he could not speak, but only wept. The saint continued: "How long wilt thou keep silent and not confess thy sin before all, revealing the lawless murder committed by thee, and at least somewhat propitiate God, who hateth evil?" And that one, as it turned out a murderer, forcing himself, with failing breath, said: "Man of God, what else dost thou wish to learn from me, for thou hast already learned everything from the grace dwelling in thee, even before I have told thee about everything? However, I submit to thy command and before all will confess the evil I have done, and all present will be witnesses of my secret sin."

With these words he openly confessed his sin, indicating in detail the place, manner, and cause of the murder of his companion, accusing both himself and the sower of sin—the author of all evil. Then he fell at the feet of the venerable one and began to ask him for correction and deliverance from the snares of the enemy. Feeling compassion for him, the venerable one raised him from the ground, consoled him, gave him counsel and a rule to perform wherever possible. Together with this he commanded him to go to the grave of the one he had killed, to shed streams of tears, and to make three thousand prostrations, generously performing the appointed commemorations. All his life he was to lament his sin and constantly remember it. After this, having instructed him a little more, the venerable one placed in his mind the condemnation of sin and commanded him henceforth to show strong repentance and to confess his sins before a spiritual father in order to receive forgiveness.

Once a ship-owner named Demetrius, who was a friend of the venerable one, was fishing near the place where Luke lived, and decided to send him fish. He labored much but caught nothing. Finally he cast his nets into the sea, calling upon the name of the venerable one for help, and—O miracle!—immediately on the hook, as if someone had drawn it, there was caught a large fish. Seeing this, Demetrius was amazed, but again tried to cast his hook in the name of the venerable one; with the same ease as the first time, another fish was caught, only a little smaller than the first. But here the father of envy, the devil, did to the ship-owner the same thing that he had once done to Cain. He persuaded him to keep the larger fish for himself, and to give the smaller one to the venerable one, which he received with gratitude and good wishes, pretending that he did not know of the deception. However, so that the ship-owner would not remain without correction, and would henceforth offer gifts to God with discernment (for what he gave to the saint, he thought he was giving to God), the venerable one quietly said to him: "Why do we men sin of our own will and unreasonably anger God, as Cain once did, and then Ananias and his wife? Cain preferred his own pleasure to God, and Ananias and his wife stole money that they had dedicated to God. Perhaps something similar has happened with this fish, for a man has been shown greater preference than God." From these words the ship-owner understood that the venerable one had the gift of foresight and knew of the sin he had committed. Immediately repenting of his unworthy act and asking forgiveness, Demetrius promised not to act so in the future. Having received the forgiveness of the venerable one, he returned home.

Having prepared the fish, the disciple of the venerable one offered it to his teacher as something very desirable. But God, who knows that for the venerable one delight and comfort is care for his neighbor, sent at that hour several Christians. Seeing them, the saint said to the disciple: "This fish God commanded to give as food to the brethren, and not to me, so serve it to them at table." Thus those Christians ate the fish, and the venerable one was nourished by his love for them.

Having spent seven years on Mount Joannitsa, the venerable one was compelled to leave it, because the Bulgarian prince Symeon, in violation of the treaty with the emperors of the Romans, began war in Epirus: from some inhabitants he took their lives, from others their freedom. Out of fear of the Bulgarians, some took refuge in cities, others went to Euripos and the Morea. The peasants who were neighbors of the venerable one sailed to the nearby islands. But even there the envious enemy subjected them to danger: the Bulgarians noticed them sailing in a boat and, suddenly attacking, killed almost all of them; only those few who knew how to swim were saved. Among them was also the venerable Luke. Later, with relatives and acquaintances, he sailed to Corinth. There he wished to learn to read and enrolled in a school, but this brought him little benefit, because, seeing that the children were mischievous, he left there, preferring rather to remain unlettered than to learn what is not good. Hearing that in Patras of Achaia there was then a venerable stylite of lofty life, he wished to meet him.

At that very time, that stylite, who was in Zemena, sent a man to Luke with a request to come to him, to be his companion, and to serve him, if this would not be too hard for him. Receiving this word with great joy, because the venerable one loved rather to submit than to rule, for this is more profitable for the young, and knowing what great acquisition comes from submission and humility, he went to the stylite to serve him. And from that time the thrice-blessed one strove to perform every service for him, because he considered it a great dishonor and harm to himself if anyone else did this instead of him. He carried wood and water, cared for the table and kitchen, mended nets, caught fish, and did all this not one, not two, not three years, but for ten whole years, imitating the humility of Jesus Christ, who, as He Himself says, *"did not come to be served, but to serve"* (Matthew 20:28). The venerable one showed the stylite not only obedience but also a love that surpasses the love of a carnal son for his father. Once he heard how one of those who loves to condemn others was reviling and condemning his elder; this seemed to him very offensive, and he was kindled with such zeal that he forgot the meekness and modesty proper to him and was compelled to speak harsh words against that shameless one. However, that one, being inhumane and cruel, having not a few grievous passions difficult to heal, needed greater admonition. Unable to endure the reproofs of the venerable one, he struck the saint with his foul hand, but at the same time received a blow also from a demon, fell to the ground, began to shake and foam. But the most fearful thing, worthy of tears, is that he remained possessed by the demon until the end of his life, being punished by Satan *"for the destruction of the flesh, that his spirit may be saved,"* as Paul says (1 Corinthians 5:5). This should be remembered by all who do not restrain their tongue. Thus the one who should have been a teacher and instructor of others, because he was a priest, and should have given counsel to others both by word and by his life, proved to be so unreasonable that he became an example of spiritual harm and an open disgrace to the priestly dignity.

But the hater of good, unable to endure that the divine Luke remained to the end in submission to the stylite and was acquiring from this much benefit for his soul, made every effort to lead him away from there. The chief of the ports of that locality did not permit ships to sail to Central Greece because of the invasion of enemies. And it happened that in one of the boats he encountered the venerable one, who wished to sail there. For this the chief beat him very severely. From that time the venerable one decided to live alone and went to the monastery of Saint Procopius, where he began to practice stillness. But once there was heavy rain, which destroyed the small cell where the venerable one lived, and he was compelled to leave there. Perhaps God arranged it so that, staying in the Morea, he would not be deprived of his homeland for long, because not much time passed before the impious Bulgarian Symeon died, and the power passed to his son Peter. Hating wars and bloodshed, the new emperor concluded peace with the Romans, and all the refugees returned to their homeland. The divine Luke also returned to his desired stillness on Mount Joannitsa, continuing his struggles and undertaking still greater labors of virtue, caring for the relief of the labors of travelers, out of love of mankind showing them hospitality.

Once, on his way to Constantinople, the Bishop of Corinth stopped to rest not far from this place. The venerable one came to him, bringing the very best of the vegetables that were in his small garden. Learning who he was, where he lived, and what his life was like, the bishop wished to go himself and see his cell. Seeing the voluntary and unprecedented poverty of the venerable one, he was amazed and ordered the one closest to him among his people to give him gold. The venerable one did not want to take the gold, saying that "I desire to receive prayers and instructions, Master, and not gold, for what use is it to me, who lives so poorly? Give me that which I greatly thirst for and that which I so need, teaching me, rough and uneducated, about salvation." Then the archbishop was saddened, thinking that the venerable one had scorned him and had not taken the gift not because it was not needed, but because he did not like it. With pain in his heart the bishop said: "Why hast thou turned away from my gift? I too am a Christian, though a sinner, and a bishop, even if unworthy. How then dost thou, who in everything imitatest Christ, not imitate Him in this? For He received the intent and gifts of those who wished to receive Him in their house, as the money box bears witness. But if thou dost not need my gift, give it to him who has need of it. But now it seems to me that the commandment about alms is for thee a vain and senseless thing, for thou art harming thy God-loving and man-loving disposition. In short, thou art overthrowing that which can console the poor and become for many a path to salvation."

As soon as the venerable one heard this, he no longer resisted, so as not to appear proud and not to grieve the archbishop. He accepted the gift and repaid him with the riches of his prayers. Then with great humble-mindedness he said: "Tell me, Master, how are we to commune of the Divine Mysteries, because, for our sins, we are in the mountains and deserts. We are deprived not only of the Divine Liturgy, but also of a priest." Praising the venerable one for his question, the archbishop answered thus: "Father, it is good that for the sake of a good thing thou askest about a good matter. For good will not be good if it is done in a way that is not good. There must be a priest to impart to thee the Most Pure Mysteries. But if there is no priest, then, of necessity, place upon the Holy Table the Communion vessel with the Presanctified Gifts—this if in a church. But if in a cell, then spread on a clean bench a small cloth and place upon it the particles of the Most Pure Mysteries, then cense, recite the customary psalms, the Trisagion, and the Symbol of Faith, make three prostrations, and, folding thy hands, commune of the Divine Mysteries, saying 'Amen.' Instead of water, drink a cup of wine, but this cup must not be used for anything else. Gather the remaining particles into the cloth and place them in the Communion vessel, taking care that not a single particle falls to the ground and is trampled." Having heard this, the venerable one greatly thanked the archbishop.

The venerable one had a custom on the Feast of the Entry into Jerusalem to take in his hands the divine weapon of the Precious Cross and to ascend in the morning to the summit of the mountain, crying out all the way: "Lord, have mercy." When he was thus ascending once, the hater of good envied him and, wishing to hinder him, caused a viper to crawl out of its nest, which bit Luke on the toe of his foot. Out of his goodness and love for God, the venerable one immediately bent down and, taking the viper, said: "Neither dost thou offend me, nor I thee, but let each of us go his own way, because we are creatures of one Creator, who, if He does not will something, we ourselves cannot do it." After this the viper crawled back into its nest, and the venerable one suffered no harm from its bite.

Once a special official was sent by the emperor to the regions of Gaul, but when he reached Corinth, the money issued for his official expenses was stolen from him. He sent people everywhere to search for the thief; all the suspicious ones who were caught he subjected to interrogation and punishment. However, all was in vain, and there remained no hope that the money would be found. The envoy grieved so much that from sorrow he wished to die. The princes consoled him in various ways, saying that he should hope in God, who often provides a way out of hopeless situations. With this they tried to bring to his senses the one whose life was threatened by grief. And one of the princes, standing in the midst of all, said: "No one can discover this theft except the divine Luke, who shines in our times with a multitude of miracles." All the Corinthians confirmed his words and greatly praised the venerable one. Hearing about the venerable one, the imperial envoy was encouraged and somewhat calmed. That very hour he sent for him, but he, fleeing the glory of men, did not want to go; however, learning of the excessive grief of the unfortunate man and feeling compassion for him, he went with those who had been sent. When he entered the house, the imperial official himself came out to meet him and, having shown him due honor, said that he himself should have gone to the venerable one, but because of his great sorrow he could not. Then he told the saint about the theft. In order to calm him a little and to lay a good foundation for joy, the venerable one said: "For now let us give due care to the stomach and rejoice together. God is mighty, who has given us to drink of the wine of compunction and sorrow, and He will also give us to drink of the cup of joy." The official received the word of the venerable one with joy and commanded his servants to prepare *"a table in the presence of his enemies,"* according to the divine David (Psalm 22.5). After they had eaten enough and delighted in remembrances of God, the venerable one suddenly raised his eyes and, looking at one of the servants standing there, beckoned him to himself, calling him by name. When he came, the venerable one asked: "Why didst thou wish to bring death upon thyself and danger upon thy master, daring to steal the emperor's money? Go then quickly and bring it here, if thou wishest to receive mercy and forgiveness." Hearing this, he became speechless, because his own conscience also accused him. Immediately falling at the feet of the venerable one, he confessed his sin, asking forgiveness. Having received it, he immediately went out and brought the money, placing it in the sight of all.

And now, beloved, consider how many good things followed from this one miracle of the venerable one: the grieving one rejoiced, the one who sinned was corrected, the dark deed was exposed and from this evil ceased. The author of all evil, the devil, was put to shame, and Christ was glorified through His servant.

Once the venerable one went to the God-loving Antony, who was abbot of a monastery outside the city of Thebes (the venerable one had a custom of visiting God-fearing and pious men). It happened then that the son of the first nobleman of that land fell mortally ill, and there was no longer any hope that he would survive. Around him stood his parents in sorrow, all relatives and friends, expecting his imminent death. One of them told them about the venerable one and suggested calling him, for if he visited the sick man, he would be able to deliver him from the illness. The father of the sick man immediately ran to the venerable one, who was in the monastery, fell at his feet, and with fervent tears asked him to visit the sick man. But since he alone could not persuade the venerable one, he made a sign to the abbot, that he too would assist him in this. The abbot fervently asked the venerable one to visit the sick man, but he did not agree, saying: "Who am I, and what good is found in me, that you have such respect for me? You are deceived; God alone is powerful to deliver from death, but a man who is corruptible and subject to sin cannot work such a miracle." After such words, the father of the sick man returned in grief and despair. When evening came, conversing with the venerable one, Antony said: "I think, honorable father, that we have acted badly and contrary to the commandments of God by not visiting the sick man, especially after we were asked to do so with many tears. Therefore we will justly hear: *'I was... sick... and you did not visit Me'* (Matthew 25:43). Imagine what sorrow the parents and relatives of the sick man have fallen into? In my opinion, our refusal is very merciless and far from love of mankind."

To this the divine Luke answered: "To heal the sick is proper only to God and His grace; to console the sorrowing is proper to those who have the gift of the word and reason, but I am deprived of both the one and the other. What benefit will I bring to the one who asked me to come? But if thou, father, considerest this deed good and pleasing to God, then go thou first, and I will follow thee." After this they got up and, when they entered the house of the sick man, it was already late evening. They found the sick man speechless, senseless; only his breathing was heard, showing that he was still alive. Those present wept quietly; only the father of the sick man said to the venerable one, who sat beside the bed: "Pray, honorable father, for the servant of God, my son, and work upon him a sign for good, only that I might see him healthy by the power of thy prayers to God." To this the venerable one answered that he could not work such miracles. But the father of the sick man again began to ask him, and the abbot joined in his requests. With great difficulty they were able to persuade the venerable one. Rising, he raised his hands and in the hearing of all began to beseech God for the sick man, and after the prayer departed with the abbot to the monastery. In the morning the venerable one went away to the mountain, fleeing the glory of men, for he knew what his prayer had accomplished. But the abbot, wishing to know whether the prayer of the venerable one had brought benefit to the sick man, sent his man to ask about this. The one who was sent returned and related what is fearful to tell, but evil to suppress, for he whom they had recently numbered among the dead, he saw on horseback; in full health he was riding to the baths.

Another time, when the venerable one was singing Matins together with the brethren who were with him and the service was already drawing to a close, he said to the refectorian: "Take care, child, to prepare food and set it out for the brethren who are coming to us." The refectorian kindled the fire but fell into perplexity, wondering who would come to them, about which he also asked the venerable one: "Thou hast commanded me to prepare the meal, but there is no one here. Who has come and told thee that brethren are coming?" Then, pretending not to know, the venerable one answered him: "Forgive me, child, demons have deceived me, that is why I spoke thus." Hearing such an answer, the monk did not prepare anything, but when it grew light, those brethren came of whom the venerable one had told him earlier. Seeing them, the monk began to condemn himself for unbelief and marveled at the gift of foresight of the venerable one. He prepared food for the guests, but secretly set aside a portion for himself also, which, however, did not escape the notice of the venerable one. Having sent him for water, the venerable one took this portion and placed it on the table with the rest of the food. The brethren ate everything and departed. When the refectorian wanted to eat what he had hidden, he found nothing and, upset, accused the saint of having wronged him. At the same time the refectorian said: "Am I not worthy of being cared for, as the guests were? And if thou hast no need of food, then why dost thou deprive us of what is necessary?" To this the saint quietly answered him: "Brother, this food God prepared for the brethren who came to us as guests, and not for us. Of course, if it had been for our benefit, then God would have nourished us also with this food." Hearing this, the refectorian repented of his words and, falling at the feet of the venerable one, asked forgiveness.

Since in that place where the venerable one dwelt he was greatly disturbed by people constantly coming to him, troubling his stillness, he decided to go to another, more deserted place. However, not wishing to do this by his own will, he sent his disciple Herman to Corinth to the then-famous teacher in virtue and wisdom, Theophylact, to ask what he should do. He commanded him to tell that he should follow the example of holy Arsenius the Great, to whom God said: "Arsenius, flee and thou shalt be saved." And again: "Arsenius, flee, be silent, practice stillness." Hearing these words, the divine Luke left Mount Joannitsa and went to another place, peaceful and healthful, called Kalamion, struggling as he desired, in complete stillness, spiritually rejoicing and being glad.

Three years had passed since the venerable one had settled there, and the Hagarene people rose up and began to devastate Greece with raids. Therefore the venerable one, together with other local inhabitants, crossed over to the nearest island of Ampelon, which lacked water and was covered with dried vegetation. His stay on the island became for him a school of virtue and a cause of good fruits. The venerable one in a small boat distributed water, gave it to the people, and when he had wine and food, he distributed those as well. Sometimes he caught fish and also distributed it. The inhabitants, hoping that Greece had already been freed from the Turks, asked him to take them across to the Morea, but he hindered them, saying: "Brethren, this spring storm will soon disperse, and peace will shine for us again," as indeed happened later. Greece became free from the Hagarenes, and the people returned to their homeland. The venerable one spent three years on the island and often had neither bread nor water, because when strong winds blew, he could not cross in the small boat to the mainland and remained on the island, burning with thirst. Besides this, the enemy brought upon him an illness: he developed an unbearable and terrible itching in the genital organs, so that he was already ready to cut them off. The venerable one began to ask God and the saint whose relics were on the island to heal him. Once in a dream that saint appeared to him and pointed to a plant, saying: "With it thou shalt find healing, but know that in doing so thou shalt lose the reward for patience." Awakening, the venerable one preferred rather to suffer from his illness for a time than to lose the eternal reward. So, seeing his extreme patience, God healed him.

The sister of the venerable one, a nun, once brought him, who was suffering on the island, loaves of bread. Taking them, the venerable one praised her for her good intention, but said: "I must not eat any of them, because God has prepared them not for me, but for other brethren, and after some time thou shalt see them and marvel at how necessary these loaves will be." She was perplexed and waited to see the brethren of whom he had told her. The venerable one himself after some time began to be troubled and seemed to be feeling compassion for certain brethren who were threatened with danger. Then it seemed that he was straining his ear to hear a voice that addressed him from some place. And finally, it became noticeable that he had taken heart, greatly rejoiced, and was thanking God.

The reason for such behavior of the venerable one was the following. From the West came a ship, which was overtaken by a storm and was threatened with sinking, from which it was delivered by the intercession of the venerable one, and, sailing to the island, it cast anchor. And since the sailors knew where to look for the venerable one, they came to him and told of the danger that had befallen them, and how they had already despaired of salvation, not knowing that they were telling this to one who knew of their danger and by his prayers to God had delivered them from it. Out of his love of mankind the venerable one offered them the loaves brought by his sister and showed every care for the sailors, consoling them by word and deed. He had such zeal that if it were possible, he would have opened his heart and placed them there, so extraordinary was his love for people. This is the precept: to give with cheerfulness and to have the soul of Abraham, that is, to receive guests without any grief and with greater desire to give than to receive.

The time has come to tell also how the venerable one left the island and settled on Mount Stirion, where his holy relics now repose. The Christians who had found refuge on the island together with the saint, after they had returned to their homeland, remembered his benefactions and, knowing how great he was in virtues, wished the venerable one to settle near them. Leaving the island, they prevailed upon him to go with them, just to look at the locality and, if it did not please him, to return again to the island. When the venerable one saw that the place was peaceful, with a moderate climate, delighted the eye, was free from people, and abounded in water, he decided to settle there. Having cleared the approaches to the water from the forest that grew around, and having cultivated the land, the saint arranged a beautiful garden, planting various trees. But his cell he built not near, but at a distance, so that it could not be seen. His aim was always to cut off all vainglory, so that people would consider him as if dead.

However, the envious devil did not cease to wage war upon the venerable one: sometimes in thoughts, sometimes by temptations from evil people, sometimes appearing to him in the form of phantoms in a sensible manner. Once he appeared at the door of his cell in the form of a black, vile little man and said: "Thou hast burned me, monk, but wait a little, and thou shalt know who burns more fiercely." Making the sign of the Precious Cross, the venerable one answered: "May the Lord destroy thee." And at that moment he became invisible. After this, a monk acquaintance and friend of the venerable one, Gregory, came to him, to whom he said: "Did Konidarios meet thee on the road?" (by this name the venerable one usually mockingly called the devil). Gregory, perplexed, asked: "And who is this Konidarios?"

"A short Moor came and threatened me that he would soon burn me, after which he went away."

Then Gregory understood of whom the venerable one spoke and said to him:

"Father, may God deliver us from his snares by thy holy prayers. He will not be able to do anything to thee, because God guards thee."

Spending the holy days of Lent with the venerable one, this Gregory did not cease to ask him to deliver him from his illness (he suffered greatly from his stomach). And although the venerable one assured him that this was beyond his powers, Gregory with pain and boldness (for he knew what boldness the saint had toward God) kept asking him, until the venerable one could no longer resist him. And then he said: "Humble Gregory, because of thee the demons mocked me this night; I do not know what to tell thee." Believing that the vision of the venerable one was from God, Gregory began to ask him to reveal what he had seen. The venerable Luke then related the following: "It seemed to me that I saw a man, fearful in appearance, who stood beside me and was adorned with golden and bright garments. Beside him stood thou and looked at me. Pointing to thee, I asked the one who had appeared: 'Why does he trouble me? Have mercy on him, I beg thee, or deliver me from the trouble which he causes me.' The one who had appeared answered: 'Leave him, because he wishes to become a monk.' I then said: 'He, as thou thyself seest, has already become a monk,' and at the same time I pointed with my finger at thy schema. The one who had appeared objected: 'I am speaking to thee of the measure of monastic perfection, and not of the schema, for a true monk is known not by his clothing, but more by his deeds and by his progress in virtue. If the true sign of perfection in virtue is crucifixion and mortification of oneself to the world, it is clear that bodily infirmity also leads a man to perfection and is the chief school of virtue. Bodily infirmity is very beneficial for one who wishes to become a true monk.' This is what the one who had appeared meant when he said: 'Leave him, because he wishes to become a monk.'" After this Gregory said nothing, but only began to sing the thirty-ninth psalm: *"I waited patiently for the Lord; and He inclined to me, and heard my cry"* (Psalm 39:1). However, the saint did not despise him to the end, but appeared to him in a dream in the guise of a physician and pretended to give him medicine for the stomach, and then said: "Go, humble Gregory, in health, and no longer will thy stomach ache from food." And so it happened in reality, because he is alive to this day and testifies to this case.

At that time a rebellion was being planned against Emperor Constantine Porphyrogenitus, and therefore in Constantinople they were detaining all who were members of the seditious organization or were under suspicion. But the wife of Pothos, the chief military commander of Greece, in a letter asked the general to return quickly to the capital, for the emperor greatly desired his presence there, and besides, mortal danger threatened their child. The general was greatly grieved and did not know what to do, because the danger threatening the child compelled him to set out for Constantinople, but the disturbances there frightened him and he did not want to go. He was especially troubled by the fact that it was not the emperor but his wife who had written the letter. While the general remained in doubt, one prince advised him: "If thou tellest the divine Luke about thy matter, thou wilt have no doubts about what to do, and thou wilt clearly learn what will serve to thy benefit." Hearing this, the general immediately arranged a meeting with the venerable one, who said to him: "Go, lord commander, to Constantinople without grief and without fear, and all the unevenness and difficulties God will correct and make easy, for the emperor wishes to see thee, and moreover he will bestow upon thee great honors. And thy child thou shalt see healthy." Not hesitating at all after these words of the venerable one, the general set out for Constantinople, and everything came to pass exactly as the saint had predicted, which he announced to all with amazement.

Another famous archon, Crinites, set out to govern Greece and reached Larissa. Hearing of the struggles of the venerable one, he wished to see him and converse with him. Coming to Thebes, he sent people for the venerable one, and he immediately followed those who had been sent. He found the archon at table, for it was mealtime. The venerable one also sat down at table, and when all rose from the table, together with them the venerable one also rose, not having been deemed worthy to hear a single word from the archon who had so called him to come. The venerable one was grieved, but not for himself, because no one else so loved dishonor as he, but for the archon, who had despised the honorable monastic habit and his name. Saint Luke was about to leave, but on his way out he addressed a servant: "Without any embarrassment, convey to thy master the following words from me. 'Why didst thou make me leave my cell and come here, why did I take upon myself so many useless labors because of thee? Why didst thou compel a lover of the desert to come to the city, not deeming me worthy of a single word and not greeting me. Thou hast not acted as a pious man who loves virtue. Didst thou call me only to dine, thinking that for me this is a pleasure? With what spiritual speeches or what profitable readings didst thou gladden us at thy meal, which was full of laughter and unseemly words? How didst thou show thyself before those whom thou wert entertaining? Why didst thou not sit upon a throne or upon something else, in a seemly and orderly manner, but lay upon a carpet ungirded, having cast thy belt far away, in no way differing from a pagan? Or are all things the same for Christians and for those who have not God in their mind and desire not salvation?'" Having left the meal, the venerable one went to the monastery of the venerable Antony, which was a little farther in that same region. The servant told the general everything, and he immediately understood that he had not treated the venerable one worthily and began to blame himself for negligence where diligence was required. And since he truly was humble and meek, he leaped onto his horse and, taking no servants with him, galloped to the venerable one. First he confessed his sin with fervor and pain in his heart, and then, having received forgiveness, he commanded all who were there to leave, after which he conversed with the venerable one until evening. The saint became so close to him that his soul clung to him according to the word of David, and he did not want to be parted from him even for a short time. Therefore, in any need that arose for the saint, the archon readily helped, assisting him and spending means on the construction of the church of Saint Barbara. When Crinites' time in power ended, he came to the venerable one, requested his prayers, and asked him never to forget him. The venerable one, by Divine revelation, predicted to him that at present he would not see the Imperial City, because God wished him to be ruler of the Western regions, which later came to pass. When the archon was returning to Constantinople and reached Larissa, the prediction of the venerable one was fulfilled. Crinites had to turn back, since he received an imperial letter and was appointed ruler of the Morea.

All the predictions of the venerable one are worthy of amazement, but the prediction about Crete seems almost incredible, all the more since it proved to be most true. Twenty years before the prediction was fulfilled, Luke, by Divine revelation, predicted that the island would be liberated during the reign of a certain emperor. He clearly said that Emperor Romanos would take Crete. Since at that time the elderly Romanos Lekapenos was reigning, someone asked the venerable one whether this was the Romanos who was now reigning. The saint answered that it was not this one, but another, the grandson of the elderly Romanos.

A certain rich and noble woman from Thebes fell gravely ill, and her husband, having spent much money on physicians, could not help her in any way. Their last hope was the divine Luke, who prayed to the Lord and, feeling compassion for her husband and consoling him, called his disciple named Pancratius, saying to him: "Take this vessel of oil and go to the sick woman, anoint her whole body with it." The monk without reasoning, because he was simple and adorned with the good habits of his elder, set out for the woman. At first she considered this improper and did not agree to be anointed. But then, having discussed with her husband how great was that saint who had sent him, and compelled by necessity, they agreed. Pancratius, as a son of obedience, obeying the command of his elder, anointed her from head to foot. Consider what fruit he received from his obedience, because he did not harm himself even by a defiled thought from touching the body of a woman. Consider also the power of faith of those who asked the venerable one for help, because as soon as the sick woman was anointed, she immediately received health and glorified God.

This Pancratius told me: "At that time, when those places were invaded by pagans, I and my spiritual father hid together in a cave, and at sunset two women also came to us to take refuge. Pitying the frozen refugees, the venerable one received them and showed every possible care. When the time for sleep came, he commanded me to sleep on one side, he himself lay on the other, and them he settled in the middle. And just as a child touches its mother, or as someone touches a stone or a tree, and no carnal thought comes to him, so also the venerable one was embraced by simplicity and dispassion."

Another disciple of the venerable one, Theodosius, had a brother who was a layman named Philip, a spatharius (bodyguard of the emperor), who often came to the venerable one. Once, when Philip wanted to come, the saint said to Theodosius: "Prepare everything for the meeting, because thy brother is coming to dine with us." Hearing this, Theodosius rejoiced and at the same time marveled at the foresight of the venerable one. Waiting for his brother, he looked at the road. With the coming of evening Philip also came, bringing with him all the most necessary things. The meal was prepared, and together with the venerable one all sat down and for the sake of common love equally partook of it. After they had finished the meal and had read Small Compline, they went to sleep. However, after a short time the venerable one awakened them for Matins, and they began to read Matins, and Theodosius, knowing that his brother was unaccustomed to vigils and standing, let him sleep until the end of the hymns of Matins. Philip, however, during this time did not sleep because of his thoughts, for he began to consider the venerable one a glutton and drunkard, only pretending to be pious, but in reality deceiving people. These thoughts were, of course, from the cooperation of the devil, who sows wicked seeds in our souls, and also from his fainthearted mind, which judges everything only by appearance, being unable to think of anything greater and higher, for the taking of food was not a sign of gluttony, but of the greatest economy. On the one hand, the venerable one, out of exceeding love, despised what was small in order to acquire what was greater, for what is abstinence from food compared to love? Naturally, it is nothing. And on the other hand, the venerable one showed people still more his extreme humble-mindedness. But Philip was led astray by his thoughts, sinning against the truth, as was shown by testimony from Heaven. While he was tossing in bed trying to sleep, he was caught up and saw two beautiful and most radiant youths, who, looking at him with a stern and hostile gaze, said: "Why dost thou trouble thyself with such thoughts, why dost thou condemn the innocent? Lift up thine eyes upward, thou who seest only downward, and thou shalt see what glory he whom thou considerest a deceiver, hypocrite, and reviler of the monastic habit has been deemed worthy of from God." Lifting his eyes upward, he saw spread on the ground a precious purple robe, and on it stood the venerable one. His face and garments emitted a wondrous and ineffable light, and he himself was truly light. Philip awoke in fear and went to where the fathers in assembly were glorifying God. Having told the venerable one everything—both about his thoughts against him and about what he had supernaturally seen in his dream—Philip asked forgiveness and received it.

Having spent seven years on Mount Stirion, the venerable one by Divine revelation foreknew that his end was approaching, but he told no one of this. Going out of his cell, he went around to all his friends and neighbors and bade them farewell, kissing each one and saying: "Pray, brethren, for me, pray, because we do not know whether we shall see each other again." Then, returning to his cell, he lived another three months: at first he was a little ill, after which a more severe attack followed, and after eight days all learned that he was departing to God, whom he had so loved.

As soon as all the Christians who lived in the vicinity learned of this, they, although it was winter and so much snow had fallen that the roads were blocked, all came to the venerable one. They remained beside him until the ninth hour, not even remembering food and not going home, but all looked at the joyful face of the saint, listened to his sweetest voice and his last words, not wishing to be parted from him. From their eyes tears flowed like rivers, which testified to the sorrow that had seized them because of the separation from the venerable one. After he had bidden farewell to all and wished them every blessing, they departed. Then the venerable one asked the presbyter Gregory, who was standing beside him, what time it was, and hearing that the sun would soon set, he understood that he too, like a bright star, was now setting. The venerable one asked Gregory to read Vespers quickly, after which Gregory asked him where he wished to be buried. The venerable one said: "Art thou not ashamed to ask me this, dost thou not know that I should be bound by the feet with a rope and thrown into a ditch to be devoured by wild beasts?" Gregory, not restraining his tears, began to fervently ask him to say where he wished to be buried, since he did not want to do anything contrary to his will. Then the venerable one said: "Dig in this place where I lie, and thou shalt find a stone. Lift it up and commit my remains to the earth. Then place the stone on top, because God, by paths which He knows, will glorify this place until the end of this world. A multitude of Christians will gather here and will glorify His holy name." With these words, having kissed the presbyter and those who were with him, he lifted his eyes to heaven and said: *"Into Thy hands, O Lord, I commit my spirit."* And thus he delivered his blessed soul to God. In the morning, having summoned Christians from the neighboring villages, Gregory asked them to dig a grave. Having prepared the body of the saint for burial and having read the appointed service, he buried the holy relics of the venerable one. Then, having closed the grave with a stone, he departed.

After six months had passed, a certain monk, a eunuch from a village of the Paphlagonians, by the name of Cosmas, decided to go to the Western lands. His path lay near Mount Stirion, and behold, during a brief stop, he saw a strange dream, which he also told to the local inhabitants. The inhabitants of that place explained that the will of God commanded him to remain there, and for this reason the Lord had brought him here. Not hesitating at all, the monk came to the cell of the venerable one, as if led by someone by the hand. Seeing that the place was peaceful and pleasant, he promised God to settle there. Immediately the monk began to care for the grave of the venerable one, raised it from the ground, faced it with slabs, and around it set up a fence, so that no one would enter there except those who came for the sake of piety. Then, after two years, the disciples of the venerable one, observing the healings and miracles constantly occurring at the grave of the venerable one, judged that they would be bad children of a good father if they did not pay their debt to their spiritual father to the end, and with zeal they set about building a church and cells. First they completed the construction of the church of Saint Barbara, adorned it, and then built a sufficient number of cells and various buildings necessary for the needs of the community and for receiving guests. Then they gave a completely different appearance to the cell where the tomb of the venerable one was, building a beautiful cross-shaped church. So the prediction of the venerable one about the glorification of this place was fulfilled: both about the Christians coming to it and about the miracles performed daily. Of several of these miracles we must tell, to the glory of God and the venerable one.

A certain woman's hands and feet were completely immobile and she could not move them. The most grievous thing was that her son, who should have consoled her in her illness, was himself possessed, and the demon often threw him to the ground. Out of compassion, her relatives placed her on a donkey and in that position brought her to the grave of the venerable one, left her there together with her son, and themselves departed. But wondrous are the judgments of the Lord! The venerable one left her unhealed for a long time. The woman grew weak from the long wait and completely despaired of her healing. But—O inexplicable is Thy goodness, O Lord!—not long before this, fragrant myrrh had flowed from the grave of the venerable one. The sacristan came and poured it into a lampada, hanging it directly over the grave of the venerable one. But the son of the paralytic, seizing the moment when no one was near, said to his mother: "I want to drink the myrrh from the lampada." But his mother did not allow him, saying: "Child, do not do this, because the sacristan is irascible and may drive us out of here." But the son repeated: "I want to drink." Immediately he took the lampada and drank the myrrh. At that very moment he fell to the ground, began to roll about and foam. The mother, pitying her son and wishing to help, suddenly—O miracle!—she herself, on her own feet, ran to her son, took him by the hands, and lifted him up. At that same moment the son came to his senses and was freed from the demonic activity. Marveling at the double wonder-working, the woman glorified God and the venerable one and, falling upon his grave, reverently and with tears began to kiss it, singing hymns of thanksgiving and proclaiming to all the double miracle of the saint.

Another woman had two children: a boy and a girl. They could not walk, since they were lame. Because of this the mother constantly grieved and wept, not knowing what to do. Hearing of the miracles of the venerable one, she came with her children to his tomb. With warm tears the mother began to beseech God and the venerable one for help, expecting that He would heal her children. Eight days passed, healing did not come, and the woman, in despair, decided to return home, saying out of great humility: "For my many sins I have proved unworthy to be heard by the venerable one and to have God heal my children." For this humility she received the benefaction in a wonderful manner, for at that very moment when she entered her house, a miracle occurred. She saw that both her children were healthy and walking on their own feet. This caused amazement in others, and filled the mother with immeasurable joy. With fervent tears she thanked God and the saint, then summoned friends and relatives, and all together with doxologies and praises they sang to the Lord.

Yet another woman had an incurable ulcer on her face, causing her the most severe pains and shame. Physicians tried to help her, but nothing came of it, and she only spent on them her time and wealth. Despairing, she came to the tomb of the venerable one and, washing it with her tears and praying to the Lord, asked to be healed. Having anointed the diseased place with oil from the lampada over the tomb of the venerable one, she was completely healed of her illness, so that not the slightest trace remained on her face.

There lived in Boeotia an elderly woman, rich and noble. Her eye pained her greatly, causing not only terrible pains, but from it, as from an evil spring, fluid constantly flowed. The woman tried many medicines, and they brought her no benefit. Having tried all remedies, the woman went to the monastery of the venerable Luke. Falling upon his tomb with warm faith, she prayed fervently to God and anointed her eye with oil from the lampada mixed with myrrh from the tomb; after several days she recovered her sight—the eye was completely cleansed, and not even a trace of the disease remained.

A certain man named Nicholas suffered from leprosy, being afflicted by it from head to foot. From his wounds foul-smelling pus constantly flowed, so that everyone turned away from him. Despairing of receiving help from people, he came with faith to the sacred tomb of the venerable one, prayed to the Lord, and anointed himself as with medicine with the oil from the lampada of the saint and the myrrh from the tomb. Once, sitting by a vessel filled with the Divine myrrh and joyfully watching the blessed myrrh flow from the tomb, he, without wishing it (yet not without Divine will), fell into this vessel and, as soon as he fell, a miracle occurred. Who would not rejoice, or who would not marvel at this new miracle? The sick man was cleansed from leprosy as easily as from ordinary bodily uncleanness.

Another man, who for many years had suffered from demons and was grievously tormented by them, since they often threw him to the ground, came to the tomb of the venerable one and remained there for several days. Understanding that God was not hastening to grant him healing, what did this lover of God, who honored God, devise? He returned home, but again and again came and asked the Lord and the venerable one for healing. Spending three or more days at a time in waiting, he would return home again. Thus, once, when he was again asking the venerable one together with the fathers of the monastery, the saint appeared to him in a dream and, calling him by name, said: "Open thy mouth." When he opened his mouth, the saint breathed into it and said: "Go in health and tell all of the wonders of God." Awakening, the sick man understood that the dream was true and that he had been delivered from the demon. Telling of the miracle, he moved all to glorify God and His servant.

A certain John suffered for many years from a dark demon. He also came to the tomb of the divine Luke for healing and used the same medicine—the oil from the lampada and the myrrh flowing from the tomb of the venerable one, with which the monk Pancratius anointed him (he felt compassion for the suffering and anointed them). Meanwhile, many days passed and the sick man was still not healed; however, showing great patience, he prayed to the Lord and did not waver at all, but came to the tomb without thoughts of unbelief and faintheartedness. He waited six months, until the venerable one appeared to him in a dream and drove out of him the unclean and wicked spirit. Moreover, the venerable one revealed to him something which he commanded him not to tell anyone until his death.

Another man, also named John, also suffered for many years from the activity of demons. He came to the tomb of the venerable one and called upon him with tears. At night in a dream the venerable one appeared to him, touched his head, opened his mouth, and placed there a hook, which went down to his very throat. He pulled on the hook and drew out the demon, after which he said: "Behold, thou hast received healing according to thy faith. Having been delivered from the wicked spirit, go in peace." And immediately the word became deed, because as soon as the sick man awoke, he found himself free. Thanking God and the saint, he returned home with joy.

A certain lover of Christ was blind in both eyes. He came to the saint and, entering the church, began to fervently pray, saying: "O Saint of God, dissolve the darkness of my eyes. Heir of the True Light, deliver me from the dark night, that I may see Thy holy icon and the sacred tomb of the venerable one; allow me to delight in the beauty of the divine church, and fill my mouth and tongue with joy and gladness. I will proclaim Thy wonders to all." He prayed for a long time, but not receiving healing at once, that man lost heart and went home. However, the divine Luke did not despise him, and on the way home granted him the light of his eyes, and this not at once, but gradually; the light became ever brighter for him, and the darkness retreated. Therefore the blind man at first did not believe that this was really happening, but then, when he began to see as clearly as others, he was filled at once with joy and amazement, and greatly thanked God and the venerable one.

John from the island of Terbenia, because of severe pains in his legs, was confined to bed. Hearing of the wonder-working of the great Luke, he wished to visit his tomb in order to fall down before him, but for this there was no possibility at all. What then did he do? He mentally went to the monastery, mentally came to the wonder-working tomb, and called upon the venerable one, crying out: *"Let my supplication come before You; deliver me according to Your word"* (Psalm 118:170). "If thou healest me by the power received from God, then I will come to thank thee and to bow down before thy holy tomb on my own feet." With such a request the sick man addressed the venerable one, and he quickly healed him, freeing him from the paralysis of his legs and making him healthy, so that after some time he came to the monastery on his own feet and fell down before the wonder-working tomb of the venerable one with the words: *"I thank thee, O Saint of God, that thou hast delivered my eyes from tears and my feet from falling"* (Psalm 114:8). Then, having told the fathers of the monastery about his illness and how the venerable one had quickly healed him, he returned home with joy, glorifying God and the venerable one.

Demetrius Kalonas, a young man strong in body, was digging a pit in his house for storing grain. The pit was already deep when he encountered a huge stone. Having decided to pull it out, Demetrius took hold of the stone with both hands. But since the weight of the stone exceeded his strength, he developed a hernia in the groin, so large that he could not move. His relatives with great difficulty pulled him out of the pit and placed him, languishing with pain, on a bed. No one among men could help him, but God sent him mercy in the form of the compassion of the venerable Luke. Just at this time there came to Demetrius an acquaintance from Mount Stirion who had myrrh from the tomb of the venerable one. He gave it to the sick man, who anointed the hernia with it, and after three days was completely healed. When health returned to him, he began to glorify God and the venerable one and to proclaim His miracles to all.

Constantine, a native of Thermopylae, was troubled by a demon who not only threw him to the ground and shook him, but also filled his soul with darkness and fear, tormenting the sufferer in every way. What then did Constantine do? Scorning help from men, he had recourse to God and to the divine Luke, the servant of God. Going to his church, he fell upon the tomb and began to wash it with fervent tears, and then anointed himself with myrrh—the medicine for every illness. Day and night he prayed constantly, made prostrations, wept, and in expectation of the love of God for mankind anointed himself with myrrh mixed with hot tears. But the God who loves mankind delayed and did not bestow the benefaction, evidently for the sake of some benefit for his soul and salvation, for God does everything for us for our own benefit. But the good Constantine all this time did not waver, did not quench the warmth of his soul, did not despair in faith and hope, did not think of returning home, which would have been understandable, but unworthy of amazement. The healing of Constantine was delayed for a full six months, as much patience as was in his heart, so that he might be delivered not only from the demon but also be deemed worthy of the salvation of his soul. After six months Constantine was freed from the tyranny of the demon, and the reward for his patience and faith he will receive in the age to come.

The same thing happened to another man, a native of Euripos: he was troubled by a most cruel demon, and therefore he also came to the wonder-working tomb of the venerable one. One of the government officials, named Christopher, out of reverence came to the church of the venerable one and, having venerated his precious tomb, asked the fathers to allow him to spend the night at the tomb. The fathers allowed him, but said that the one possessed by a demon would also sleep here. Christopher objected: "Let the demoniac sleep in another place this night, because I wish to sleep at the tomb alone." The fathers allowed this also, and Christopher remained at the tomb alone. But the sufferer, who was assigned another place for sleep, was very grieved that he would not receive the grace of the saint, and considered this a dishonor to himself. But the Lord, who comforts the sorrowing, not only consoled him but also miraculously delivered him from the wicked demon. Surrounded by radiant light, the venerable one appeared to him in a dream, looked at him with a joyful gaze, and, calling him by name, commanded him to open his mouth. When he put his fingers into his mouth, it seemed that he pulled out from there a black hair, on which hung a dung beetle. Having driven it away, the venerable one asked the sufferer: "Dost thou see thine enemy? Behold, thou art freed from him who tormented thee." Thus the saint showed him both his love of mankind, and represented the demon in a fitting manner in the form of a dung beetle, and in the form of a hair he showed its powerlessness. Health returned to the man, and he departed home with joy, proclaiming to all the miracles of God and the venerable one.

A certain cleric from Diavlia, by the name of Nicholas, fell ill with dropsy and spent a great deal of money on physicians, but received no healing, and the illness kept increasing, so that death threatened him. Leaving the physicians and medicines, he turned with a request to the common benefactor of Greece, to the free and true healing—the wonder-working tomb of the venerable Luke. The monk Pancratius, who was there, saw Nicholas sitting at the tomb and had compassion on him, deciding to render him some help. He moistened a sponge with water and wiped the sacred tomb with it, and then with the same sponge anointed the sick man from head to foot and—O miracle!—he became healthy.

Moreover, another Nicholas, who came from a village in Coroneia, called by all Rastamites, for an unknown reason had blisters all over his face resembling smoldering coals. From the pus that flowed from them his face was not only dirty but burned as if on fire. Nicholas spent a great deal of money on physicians, receiving no benefit, because as long as he gave them money, they said he would recover. But if he gave still more, then he would hear from them that very soon his illness would disappear and his health would fully return. But when he had spent almost all his money and ceased spending it on physicians, then they told him the truth. Those who earlier, for the sake of profit, had assured him of recovery, now finally said that his illness was incurable by earthly physicians, and that Divine help was required, surpassing all human skill, for only to God is possible what is impossible for men. Hearing this, the unfortunate Nicholas began to accuse himself of madness and was greatly grieved, because together with his money he had lost hope of recovery. Unexpectedly, being in such grief and perplexity, he met an acquaintance who had oil from the lampada of Saint Luke. Knowing of the Divine power contained in the oil, he told the sick man about people who had been healed with its help from illnesses. The acquaintance ran home, brought the oil, and with prayer and strong faith in healing anointed the face of the sick man, and also his own. During this anointing both called upon God and the divine Luke for help. What followed from this? After several days the force of these blisters weakened, and the flow of pus from the wounds completely ceased, and soon not the slightest trace of the wounds remained on his face.

As it is impossible to count the sand of the sea, so it is impossible to count exactly

The Life and Struggles of Our Venerable and God-Bearing Father Euthymius the New, Who Labored in the Tenth Century

This our venerable father Euthymius was by birth from Iberia, from the city of Tao, the son of pious, renowned, and wealthy parents. When the father of Euthymius renounced the temporal and passing nobility and glory of this world, preferring the poverty that enriches in Christ and having clothed himself in the angelic monastic habit (with the name John), he set out for Constantinople. Euthymius, being still very small, remained with his grandfather, a man renowned in glory and virtue. And his grandfather raised him in *"the training and admonition of the Lord"* (Ephesians 6:4). A little time passed and the grandfather, taking Euthymius with him, came to Constantinople to find his son John. Having found him, the grandfather, weeping, tried to persuade his son to return to his homeland, but not only did he not listen, but he tried in every way to keep his son Euthymius with him, which caused the father to grieve greatly.

Since a dispute arose between them—John wanted to keep his son with him, while the grandfather would not allow it—Emperor Nicephorus, having learned of the quarrel, ordered both to come before him and to bring Euthymius with them. When the three of them stood before the emperor and he heard the whole story, he commanded them not to pull the child by force, each to himself, but to leave the judgment in this matter to God. Whichever one the child wished to go to of his own accord, let him go to that one. As soon as the child was released, he immediately ran to his father, whom he had never seen and had not known until that hour. The child's action caused astonishment and tears among those present.

Having received his son as though from the hands of God, the blessed John immediately clothed him in the monastic habit and gave him over for instruction. The good Euthymius possessed not only a keen mind, but also great fervor and diligence, so that in a short time he learned both external wisdom and inner divine wisdom, having absorbed spiritual teachings. Soon he fell gravely and seriously ill, but through the care and help of our Most Holy Lady the Theotokos, after some time he was delivered from the illness. He continued to advance in virtue, wisdom, grace, and in many other things worthy of wonder, from which it became clear to all what a wondrous man he would become. Therefore we shall relate one of the miracles of Euthymius as confirmation of the truth of many others.

Once a certain Jew came to Euthymius to converse with him about the faith. But the blessed Euthymius did not at all wish to speak with him, since he was convinced that it was useless to converse with Jews. However, yielding to his father's entreaties, he nonetheless agreed and was compelled to refute the words of the Jew with proofs from the Old Testament. Unable to endure his defeat, the vile Jew began to blaspheme our Lord Jesus Christ, and the blessed Euthymius burned with divine zeal and said: "Let the mouth be stopped that speaks blasphemies against our Lord and God." And—O wonder!—immediately the Jew became mute, fell to the ground, foam issuing from his blasphemous mouth, and lay thus, presenting a pitiable sight. On the following day he breathed forth his vile soul. This miracle caused fear and wonder in all, making the wondrous Euthymius famous throughout Constantinople.

Hating human glory as contrary to the glory of God, the blessed one immediately left the capital and set out together with his father for the Holy Mountain of Athos. Meeting there the venerable Athanasius, they all wished to settle with him in the Sacred Lavra, but the divine Athanasius, foreseeing with clairvoyant spiritual eyes, by God's revelation, the grace of the Holy Spirit dwelling in Euthymius, persuaded him to receive the priestly rank. At first he did not wish to, citing his unworthiness, but later he obeyed the venerable one and was ordained to the priesthood.

After this, the saint added struggles to struggles, abstinence to abstinence, and multiplied in himself all the good things he possessed, becoming a divine vessel of the Most Holy Spirit. He translated the Holy Scriptures into the language of the Iberians, wrote many instructive books, built numerous churches and hospitals, and adorned the entire Holy Mountain with monasteries. Who can worthily recount his noble treatment of people, his incomparable humility, by virtue of which he cared for his infirm father for fourteen years and assisted the great Athanasius? When both of them departed to the Lord, the blessed Euthymius cared for the Sacred Lavra, and not only for it, but for all the monasteries of the Holy Mountain. He was zealous and swift in caring for the souls and bodies of the brethren, and his divine lips always poured forth rivers of wisdom and teaching to the glory of God. However, the love of utmost stillness prevailed, and he appointed his kinsman George as abbot of the Lavra, while he himself began to labor in solitude, pleasing God day and night. And no one knew of his spiritual struggles and their fruits, because the venerable one strove to accomplish them in secret, so that only God would know of them—He Who also made his struggles known, as will be told further.

Once the venerable one came to Thessalonica and was received with great kindness by the local hierarch, who was wondrous in virtue but was himself in turn amazed at the life of the venerable one. The hierarch was friends with a certain Jew who served him, and therefore the hierarch, as a reward for their friendship, always counseled him and tried to persuade him with many teachings to believe in Christ. However, he would in no way listen. All the time that the venerable one was with the hierarch, the Jew also came to him. The bishop gave him saving counsel, which did not convince the Jew, and during conversations about the faith, he used words full of shamelessness, despising and counting as nothing the words of the hierarch. Once the hierarch asked the venerable one to refute the arrogant Jew with his wise words, but the true disciple of the meek and humble Jesus Christ said that he was earth and ashes, and that it was fitting for the hierarch, not for him, to persuade the Jew. But the bishop asked him again and again, and the venerable one was compelled to agree. The blessed Euthymius refuted the words of the Jew with proofs from the prophets, forcing him to fall silent, and clearly proclaimed concerning the dispensation of our Lord, so that the Jew, unable to endure the shame, began to speak blasphemous words against Christ. Looking at him, the saint pronounced: "Let your impious mouth be stopped, which speaks lies and blasphemy against Christ, the Creator and Master of all." At that very moment the Jew became mute and fell to the ground, while his eyes became crossed and his mouth twisted to the side. Seeing this, all the Jews and Christians who were there were amazed and greatly frightened. Falling down in supplication before the venerable one, they began to ask him to have mercy on the Jew and heal him. Hearing their pleas, Saint Euthymius took pity on the Jew and, having signed him with the sign of the Life-giving Cross, healed him, making him healthy as before. After this the Jew began to proclaim aloud that Jesus Christ is the True God and Creator of all, the Guardian and Provider of all living creatures, and then was baptized, not only he himself together with his household, but also all the Jews who were there, who had been present at this miracle, and many other Jews believed in Christ. In gratitude, the one who was healed brought the venerable one much money, but he did not accept it and commanded that it be distributed to the poor.

Once there occurred on the Holy Mountain a severe drought, and all the fathers were gripped by sorrow on account of the lack of rain. They began to ask the venerable one to pray to God and only with great difficulty were able to persuade him. The venerable Euthymius went up to the Chapel of the Prophet Elijah, which is near the Iveron Monastery, and with tears began to pray to the All-merciful God, offering to Him the Spiritual and Bloodless Sacrifice. And—O wonder!—immediately such heavy rain began to fall that it satisfied the earth, and all glorified God, Who glorifies those who glorify Him.

From ancient times it had been the custom among the Holy Mountain monks on the radiant feast of the Transfiguration of the Savior to ascend to the summit of Mount Athos, to serve the All-night Vigil, and on the following day, after the celebration of the Divine Liturgy, to descend. Once, on this feast, the divine Euthymius also ascended to the summit together with many other brethren. When they wished to celebrate the Divine Liturgy, they began unanimously to ask the venerable one to do so. Euthymius with great humility obeyed and began to serve. When he pronounced: "Singing, crying, shouting, and saying the hymn of victory," and the brethren answered: "Holy, Holy, Holy, Lord of Sabaoth," suddenly an unbearable light enveloped them all and the earth shook. All the brethren immediately fell to the ground face down, only the blessed Euthymius stood without moving, resembling a pillar of fire. This miracle made him even more renowned everywhere.

Therefore, when the Archbishop of Cyprus departed to the Lord, the then-reigning emperor of the Romans sent people to the saint with a letter, earnestly asking him to take charge of the archbishopric. But the venerable one did not wish even to hear of this, saying that he was unworthy of such responsibility, and that he only deserved to be shepherded, not to shepherd others, for rooted in his heart was the mother of all virtues—humble-mindedness.

The apostate devil, who always envies and wars against good and God-pleasing works, could not calmly look upon the God-pleasing struggles of the saint, which he performed every day to the glory of Christ our God, and from envy and malice burned all the more. Having found a monk who was such only in outward appearance, but in heart most vile and impure, worthy to be a dwelling place of the devil, he entered into him and inspired him to kill the venerable one, whispering to the monk as once in ancient times he whispered to Eve: "If you kill the venerable one, you will receive a great reward." And that wretched man undertook the work with zeal, having prepared a knife and ascended to the tower where the cell of the venerable one was located. The disciple of the saint, noticing that he was completely controlled by the demon and held a knife in his hand, closed the door of the cell and did not allow him to enter. Not finding the venerable one on whom to satisfy the madness which he aroused in him, the murderer plunged the knife into his blessed disciple. Fleeing from there with wild cries and noise, he encountered another disciple of the venerable one, whom he attacked in the same manner. Then, having run a short distance, the monk fell face down on the ground and, with demonic words on his lips, breathed forth his vile soul. But the saint, having learned by the grace of the Holy Spirit what had happened to his disciples through the working of the devil, hurried down from the tower and tonsured both of his disciples into the great schema, after which both of them soon departed to the Lord.

But the shameless and filthy dog, the devil, could not look upon the struggles of the venerable one to the glory of God, and again incited a certain gardener to stab the saint. He prepared a knife, approached the saint, and struck him in the stomach. But—O wonder!—the saint suffered no harm, the point of the knife became as wax, and the hand that struck the venerable one withered and remained without movement. Then the gardener, falling with tears at the feet of the venerable one, confessed to him the devil's design and asked for forgiveness and healing. Taking pity, the saint prayed to God for him, and health was granted to his soul and body.

With what words can one worthily recount the virtues of the venerable one? He was compassionate, cheerful, without anger, humble, spending all nights in ceaseless prayer and standing before God, observing frugality both in food and in clothing, treating his body harshly, for he wore heavy chains. To speak simply, he was an angel in an earthly body and a light in the world, holding forth the word of life.

But since temptations pursue us everywhere, for the earth is preeminently a place of temptations, some occurred even on the Holy Mountain. For this reason the fathers asked the saint to go to the reigning city, so that by imperial decree he might root out the temptations from their midst and establish firm peace in that place. Having obeyed them, the venerable one set out for Constantinople. The emperor with the entire synod of nobles received him with reverence, greeted him in a friendly manner, and immediately fulfilled his request.

While in the capital, the venerable one once rode with a certain monk on a mule on some errand to that part of the city which was called Plateia. Along the way they encountered a beggar asking for alms. Seeing him, the saint took pity and wished to give him something, but suddenly the mule became frightened and enraged and, jerking the venerable one violently, ran wildly clattering its hooves and did not stop until it threw Saint Euthymius to the ground, from which he was badly injured. Christians ran up, lifted him, and took him to where he was staying. After several days the venerable one committed his holy soul into the hands of God on the thirteenth day of the month of May. At his burial many healings and miracles occurred as proof of the holiness and boldness of the venerable one before God.

Subsequently, the holy relics of the venerable Euthymius were translated to the Holy Mountain and placed in the monastery of the Honorable Prophet, Forerunner, and Baptist of the Lord John, which he himself had built, and which was named Iveron, to the glory of the Father, and of the Son, and of the Holy Spirit, one Godhead and Kingdom, to Whom is due glory, honor, and worship, now and ever and unto the ages of ages. Amen.

The Life, Struggles, and Accounts of the Miracles of Our Venerable and God-bearing Father Lazarus, Who Struggled on Mount Galesion in the Twelfth Century

This venerable Lazarus came from a certain village in Asia, near Magnesia. His noble, God-fearing, and virtuous parents were called Niketas and Irene. At the moment of the venerable one's birth, an extraordinarily bright cloud appeared in the house, which indicated that the infant was destined to become a son of light and a vessel of divine illumination. The women who had come to visit the new mother were so frightened at the sight of this strange spectacle that they ran out of the house. Later, another miracle occurred. After a sufficiently long time had passed and the cloud had already risen up and the women had again entered the house, they saw that the infant, with his arms crossed upon his chest, was standing on his own feet, turned toward the east. From that time, everyone began to say that this infant would be very famous and renowned in all things.

When the venerable one had grown up, his parents gave him to study the sacred sciences, which he mastered with ease. However, the boy was repulsed in his whole soul by the character of his teacher, because the instructor was enslaved to the passion of avarice. For this reason, whatever item or money belonging to the teacher that came into his hands, Lazarus would give to the poor. And although the teacher constantly scolded and beat him for this, the venerable one continued to give gifts to the poor, for his mercy toward the poor and hatred of avarice caused him to endure the insults and beatings. Despite the reproaches and beatings with which the teacher rewarded his pupil for taking his things and money to give to the poor, he admired his mercy and praised him before all.

Having reached a more mature age and attained more perfect knowledge, Lazarus desired to leave his homeland and go to venerate the Holy Tomb of the Lord and the other holy places of Jerusalem. However, no matter how many attempts he made, each time his relatives prevented him. So that he would not run away secretly, his parents sent him to the nearby Orovos Monastery, where he could devote himself to the sacred sciences and exercise himself in virtue, but most of all because there he was under supervision. Inflamed by love for God, the blessed Lazarus did not rest, but always thought about escape. Having once found such an opportunity, he, together with one of the monks, unnoticed by his parents and relatives, set out for Jerusalem with all zeal.

Passing through Chonae, the place where the miracle of the Archangel Michael occurred, he entered the church dedicated to the Archangel and asked for his help on the journey. Then the travelers headed for Attaleia. However, the monk accompanying him on the journey devised a plan to sell Lazarus into slavery to the Saracens. When the monk (if such a one can be called a monk) was already bargaining with the Saracens in Armenian over the price, a certain Christian who knew this language happened to be passing by, which was none other than an act of Divine Providence. The Christian understood the monk's intention and informed Lazarus of it, who immediately left that place. There was a monastery nearby, and Lazarus found there a certain honorable hieromonk, advanced in age and understanding, to whom he told about his homeland, about his parents, about his desire to venerate the holy places of Jerusalem, about the scheme of the monk accompanying him, and about all that had happened to him on the way. After this, the hieromonk inquired whether Lazarus still intended to go to Jerusalem. Learning that the venerable one greatly desired this, the honorable elder said that a youth, who could easily be overcome by the devil, ought not to go wherever he wishes, since following one's own thoughts is a great evil, for one who follows his own will becomes a victim of the enemy, who has everywhere set his nets of destruction. But if for the benefit of his soul the youth would heed his advice, he should remain in this monastery, where the elder was abbot, become a monk, live for a long time until he reached maturity, and only then would he be able to go out without danger.

Having heard this good counsel, the divine Lazarus received it with great joy and remained in the monastery. Having put off the old man together with his worldly garments, he clothed himself in the new, in Christ, donning the monastic habit, and from that time devoted himself to ascetic struggles.

Fasting, which refines the body and calms the passions that war against the soul, the blessed one loved as much as lovers of the flesh do not love pleasure and overeating. Struggling diligently, Lazarus acquired obedience—the foundation of the monastic life—and humility—the highest of all virtues, becoming for all a pattern and example of these two virtues. And what shall we say of vigil, of the drying out of the body, and of the other severe struggles he undertook for the refinement of the flesh? Let us say only that, being healthy by nature, he also acquired a good struggle, and therefore possessed in himself every virtue, as though he were not earthly but heavenly, for a good nature gives strength to the soul, and a good struggle brings the soul's strength to a good completion.

There was no one who did not marvel at the struggles of the divine Lazarus, who did not praise him and tell others about him. But more than all others, his spiritual father, the abbot of the monastery, held him up as an example to others—the one whom the venerable one served and who taught him the spiritual struggle. The venerable Lazarus had already spent a sufficiently long time in the monastery when one day the elder said to him: "My child, in a short time I shall depart to the earth, the common mother of all, and I dedicate you to Christ, the common Master of all; He will care for you." At these words, the venerable one groaned from the depths of his soul and wept bitterly, because he did not want even to hear about separation from his elder. But a little time passed, and his elder departed to the Lord. Having mourned his death, the divine Lazarus after three days left the monastery and, coming to a certain cave located in an inaccessible place, remained there to converse alone with the One God.

It is difficult for human tongue to convey how many struggles and bodily hardships this patient soul subjected itself to. But the more he tried to hide his virtues from people, the more he became known to all, because virtue reveals to the eyes of people the one who labors in it, no matter how carefully he may hide. Crowds of people came daily to see the venerable one and to receive his blessing. Neither the distance of the journey, nor the impassable terrain, nor other reasons stopped the people. To make the path to his cave easier, they even built a road: they gathered brushwood and firewood in great quantity, lit a fire on the rocky path, then poured vinegar on it to soften the hard stones, and broke them with metal tools. After this, the road leading to the venerable one became easy, for the desire for good in God moves people to undertake what is nearly impossible.

Such was the love that many people had for the venerable one, and when the local bishop heard about him, he desired to ascend to Lazarus in the cave to converse with the venerable one. Because of the multitude of those coming to him, the saint decided to build in that place a church in the name of the Most Holy Theotokos and cells for the brothers who wished to receive monasticism, for many were renouncing the world and wished to live with the venerable one. And since many readily responded and helped this God-pleasing work with all their strength, the venerable Lazarus built there a remarkable monastery, and each of the Christians there experienced great joy at the thought that he was fulfilling the command of the venerable one.

Once a certain man came to him and said that he wanted to go to a steep cliff to gather wild honey there. The venerable one, by the grace of the Holy Spirit, could foresee and understood that that man might perish (and the place was indeed precipitous), and he said to him: "My child, for your own benefit you should not even see that place, because a great danger hangs over you, and you may perish if you do not go away from it. If you wish to escape danger, abandon your intention." However, that man did not heed the advice of the venerable one and went to the cliff with his companions. Having tied himself with a rope, he began to descend with the help of his friends. Consider how bad it is not to listen to the advice of those who give it for our benefit. The unfortunate man had not even descended halfway when the rope broke, and he fell down, having expired even before he touched the ground, from the many blows against the protruding rocks. Thus he reaped the deadly fruit of his own senseless intention. From that time, all began to heed the words of the venerable one as the words of a prophet, never contradicting them.

Once a man came to the venerable one who confessed his sins, and at the end said that he earned his living in a convenient and clever way, requiring no knowledge of a trade. He would go into other people's houses at night, take whatever he found, and hide it in a secret place. When the owners began to look for what was missing, he would tell them that the saints, revealing to him many secrets, had also revealed the place where the thieves had hidden their things. Placing the Precious Cross or an icon of some saint upon his shoulders, he would go with the owners, show them where to dig. Thus all would find their things, and they honored him as a friend of God, worthy of beholding Divine revelations, and as a reward they gave him part of the things found. Having heard this, the venerable one said: "And using such a wicked trade, you, my child, say that you earn your living in a clever and skillful way? Woe to you, whose mind is darkened, because you are deceived and mocked by the devil, considering as clever his teaching, which you have learned for the destruction of your soul, taking darkness for light. If you do not cease from this sin, then woe to you, as the Prophet Isaiah says (Isaiah 3:11), who takes bitter for sweet, because soon punishment and the wrath of God will come upon you." Having heard all this, the man fell at the feet of the venerable one and with tears began to ask forgiveness of his sins, promising that henceforth he would not believe the devil's flattery, but would cease from sin and work at virtue with all his strength. Having received forgiveness from the venerable one, he, with the help of God and through the prayers of the saint, kept his promise.

And although by his instructions and deeds the saint brought great benefit to many, raising up those who had fallen into sin and strengthening those who stood in virtue, he very much wished to leave that place for Jerusalem, in order to flee the glory of men (for the venerable one knew what a great obstacle it is for those who travel the higher and heavenly path), and thus fulfilling the desire he had had from his youth to venerate the holy places of Jerusalem. Having announced his intention to the monastery brotherhood and consoling them as much as possible (for they were very grieved at their separation from him), he commanded them to keep the vows of the monastic calling, and also to care with all their strength for their salvation, after which he departed for Jerusalem.

Having venerated the wondrous shrines there and the Tomb of the Lord, the venerable one after several days came to the Lavra of Saint Sabbas, where he decided to remain for a long time in order to struggle in ascetic feats together with the venerable fathers living there and to receive great benefit from them. Nothing so moves people to virtue as good rivalry with those who live in virtue. Just as stone is rubbed against stone and as a result becomes smooth and shining, so also one who is virtuous, vying with one who is virtuous, comes to greater progress and becomes more radiant. Received joyfully by the brethren, the venerable one remained in the Lavra and was given the obedience of paraecclesiarches (one of the lower ranks in the degree of sacristan). This obedience he fulfilled for six years, struggling equally with the foremost and chosen monks of that monastery, who constantly strove to attain the state of the bodiless angels. But the divine Lazarus not only struggled equally with them, but surpassed them in all things, and his labors aroused admiration. He was deemed worthy of the rank of priest, and the abbot of the monastery urged him to accept the rank. At first the venerable one refused, saying that he was unworthy of such a rank, but since the abbot continued to urge him (for he knew what Lazarus was like in virtue and what rank he was worthy of), the venerable one, so as not to appear insolent, reasoned that it was senseless to resist further. He obeyed and was ordained to the priesthood by the Patriarch of Jerusalem at that time, after which he spent another six years in the monastery. Then, seeing that the monks most advanced in virtue, in the first week of Great Lent, according to an old custom, would go out from the monastery into the wilderness and return to the monastery on the Sunday of Palms, bearing the good fruits of their struggle, he also desired to go into the wilderness. Not revealing his desire to the abbot, he secretly left the monastery—not because he disdained the abbot (for who else showed greater obedience to his superiors than the blessed Lazarus?), but because he was overcome by the sweetness of stillness, which he had desired for many years already and for the attainment of which he had employed so many means. Having spent in the wilderness the appointed days of the Forty Days, he returned to the monastery together with the other brothers. But while all the others were received and cared for, because the monks were tired from long wilderness labors, the divine Lazarus alone, by order of the abbot, was driven out of the monastery and not permitted even to cross the threshold. Lazarus wept for a long time at the doors of the monastery, asking forgiveness, but not receiving it, he went to Jerusalem to the steward of the Great Church of Jerusalem, who was his old friend, so that he would intercede for him with the abbot. As soon as the steward heard him out, he immediately went to the Lavra and long entreated the abbot to forgive his friend Lazarus, after which the venerable one received forgiveness from the abbot and was again numbered among the brethren of the Lavra.

When the following Great Lent arrived, seeing how other monks again departed for the wilderness, the venerable one thought neither about the anger of the abbot, nor about possible expulsion from the monastery, nor about other consequences, but also went, for to one who has but once tasted the sweetness and honey of stillness, it becomes forever desired, causing him to despise all else and to strive for it alone. Having once tasted this honey, the venerable one was not able to remain in the monastery and be deprived of so great a good. Therefore, having come to a place of stillness, he no longer wished to return to the Lavra and devoted himself entirely to stillness. On a very high place he built a pillar and, having completely renounced all things material and earthly, he ascended it as a soldier free from all burdens, to wage *"warfare not against flesh and blood... but... against spiritual hosts of wickedness in the heavenly places"* (Ephesians 6:12). He spent many years on the pillar, courageously struggling against the demons and achieving great victories over them.

Once, having come down from the pillar and walking across the plain, the venerable one heard a voice saying to him: "Lazarus, you must return to your homeland." Surprised, he looked around, and seeing no one, he thought that a demon had said this. But the next time, when he happened to pass by this place, he heard the same voice and thought that this might be Divine Providence. To ascertain this precisely, he remained there for some more time and heard the voice again. Then the venerable one went to the ascetics living nearby, who had spent their whole lives in the wilderness, from youth to old age, and told them about the voice he had heard and asked what he should do. When they told him that the voice was from God, he went to Jerusalem and, taking as a companion a monk of virtuous life named Paul, came to Sebasteia. There they parted ways: Paul went to Trebizond, and the venerable Lazarus went to Rome, where he had long wished to go to venerate the two chief apostles.

Passing along the road through some thickets, he encountered enormous bears. Very frightened and not knowing where to flee from danger, he had recourse to the help of God. Raising his eyes and hands to heaven, he uttered words from the Psalm of David: *"O my God, 'be not far from me, for trouble is near, for there is none to help'"* (Psalm 21:12). Save me, O Lord, from the mouths of bloodthirsty beasts and from death deliver my soul." As soon as he uttered these words (O miracle!), he saw that the bears bowed their heads and, humbly turning aside to one side of the road, yielded the way to the venerable one as to their master, for virtue inspires respect even in wild beasts.

Although the man of God remained unharmed by the sensible beasts, the noetic beast, the devil, unable to bear this, transformed himself into a huge black dog and ran after the venerable one. Sometimes he would run ahead and threaten to tear him with his teeth, and sometimes he ran behind and barked maliciously, pretending that he was about to grab him by the legs. Thus did the thrice-accursed one act for three days. When the venerable one needed to enter a village to buy food for the journey (he had no bread with him, for he never cared for the morrow), the dog began to hinder him. By prolonged barking he attracted the village dogs, and inciting them, he was the first to attack the saint, and all the rest attacked him after him. The venerable one was forced to remain hungry all day and all night, because he could not approach the village on account of the demons troubling him. However, with the help of God, the venerable one was delivered from this temptation; the enemy grew tired of opposing the great soul and, shamed in his weakness, was driven away as if by a whip.

Having by God's Providence risen above the temptations of the enemy, the venerable one reached Ephesus, where he came to the local bishop and in conversation with him revealed his intention to go to Rome.

Marveling at the meekness of the venerable one, his simplicity, the sweetness of his words, and the grace of the Holy Spirit that shone through him, the hierarch was captivated by love for him and began to object to his journey to Rome. Then the venerable one, on the advice of the Bishop of Ephesus, abandoned his intention, but to abandon stillness and live with the hierarch he would in no way agree. Having departed from the bishop, he came to the Orovos Monastery, from which he had once set out for Jerusalem. At the beginning of his stay there, the venerable one concealed who he was, but then the brothers began to ask him to tell them about himself, for they themselves had not recognized him. Then the venerable one said that he was that very same Lazarus who some time ago had departed from them. Immediately the news that Lazarus had again returned to the monastery spread throughout the area, and everyone rushed to the monastery to look at him, especially his mother, who had already mourned the death of his father.

The gentle face of the venerable one and his soul-profitable words evoked in people a spiritual rapture, for alongside his other virtues, his speech, according to the Apostle, was *"always with grace, seasoned with salt"* (Colossians 4:6). And the blessed one spoke tenderly, with great kindness, so that he could soften even a soul as hard as stone. Therefore, many of those who heard the divine discourses of the wondrous Lazarus wept for joy. However, the crowds of people disturbed his peace, and Lazarus decided to leave the monastery for a quiet place. Having stayed in his homeland for a few more days out of gratitude to his mother for her love (for he saw how she grieved at separation from him), he left in search of a quiet place. Learning that opposite Mount Galesion there was a small monastery with a church of the holy Martyr Marina, he went there. The place was very quiet, and in the monastery he found two of his own brothers. The Bishop of Ephesus was very glad when he learned that his beloved Lazarus had come there, for he had always wished to have fellowship with him. Coming to the monastery, he joyfully greeted Lazarus and appointed him abbot, and to the brethren he commanded to obey the venerable one as a father and never, even in the smallest thing, to oppose him.

In stillness, the divine Lazarus began to devote himself to even more severe struggles and with still greater zeal he cared for the acquisition of all virtues. He preferred that no one know about his struggles, for he rightly reasoned that to perform the labors of virtue for show and for the sake of pleasing men is the same as not performing them at all. He said that those who practice virtue for the sake of acquiring human glory will receive no reward, as the Holy Gospel says: *"you have no reward from your Father in heaven"* (Matthew 6:1). Many people, if there were none to praise them, would of course not even attempt to be virtuous; but those who practice virtue secretly from people and are known only to God, such shall receive manifold glory. Therefore, as much as the glory of God is higher than the glory of men (because the first is eternal and incorruptible, while the other is temporal and corruptible and does not accompany a person constantly, for before the death of such people their hypocrisy is exposed), so much higher is the one who practices virtue in secret. And although the venerable one for this reason concealed his virtues, showing himself to be the lowliest of all in words and deeds, everything turned out just the opposite. Just as one standing on a market platform summons all with trumpet sounds and thereby becomes noticed, so also the divine Lazarus, although he hid himself, was still visible to all, not because of trumpet sounds but because of his labors of virtue.

And in the monastery, countless crowds of people constantly came to the venerable one. And always his first task was to nourish with the saving word the souls of those who came to him, and then with bodily food as well. And thus he acted always, even if there was not enough food for himself and the brethren, even if there was only one small loaf for all, and this aroused amazement in everyone. The venerable one was distinguished by such love for mankind that he surpassed the most famous men in this virtue. Those gave alms from their abundance, or gave a little from what they needed and distributed it to the poor, but only so much as was necessary to give so as not themselves to depend on others. But only the venerable one magnanimously gave to others the food that he himself needed to strengthen his body weakened by fasting and wearied by labors, not caring for himself and considering it his food to feed those in need. This is, in the proper sense of the word, almsgiving. For a loving disposition of heart consists not in giving from one's abundance, but in giving what is necessary to oneself and voluntarily distributing to the poor what one lacks oneself.

Two brothers could not endure such love for mankind from the venerable one, and they were very grieved and constantly grumbled, believing that the venerable one was giving to visitors the food that was intended for them. They tried to convince Lazarus, but having achieved nothing, they left the monastery, leaving the venerable one with a few disciples. The disciples, with the consent of the venerable one, sowed beans not far from the road, and since the soil was good and fertile, the beans produced abundant fruit; however, all who passed by the field picked the fruit, ate it, and even took some home. Noticing that the fruits of their labors were being eaten by travelers, the disciples of the venerable one were very grieved, but the saint himself did not grieve, but consoled his disciples, trying to cheer them with joyful words. When the time came to harvest, he sent them to gather the beans, but they did not want to go and labor in vain, because they knew well that almost no fruit remained, for they had checked the pods by touch. But the venerable one, partly by force, partly by entreaties, persuaded them to go to the field. They gathered the remaining fruit and brought it to the threshing floor, but when they read the prayer appointed during the winnowing of grain, a miracle occurred. There were so many beans in the winnowing basket that one might have thought that all the stalks had turned into beans. Greatly rejoicing at this and remembering the words of the venerable one, which he had spoken to them in consolation, they ran to him to tell of the miracle, at the same time asking forgiveness for having shown opposition, not wishing to gather the beans. The venerable one immediately forgave them, because he knew that they had done this not out of malice, but because they did not know what could happen through prayers to God.

After some time, the venerable one, understanding that he received no benefit but only harm from the constant disturbances, went to a certain elder of virtuous life living opposite Mount Galesion, who told him that on the summit of the mountain there was a cave very suitable for ascetic labors, since that area was deserted due to the inaccessibility of the mountain, devoid of every comfort, and demons fiercely attacked all who came there. In that cave, Paphnutius, great in virtue, had performed his ascetic labors. Then the divine Lazarus decided to settle in that cave. But as soon as he began to ascend there, the demons, understanding that their destroyer and warrior was coming, decided to frighten him and began to disturb the area with strange and terrible sounds. But the venerable one fearlessly chanted psalms and walked with even greater boldness, knowing that all demonic enterprises are only phantoms that do not really exist. When he finally ascended the mountain, he found the cave. He finished chanting the psalms, made the sign of the cross over himself, and also made the sign of the cross over the stone that was in front of the cave. And—O miracle!—on the stone there immediately appeared a cross, which was carved so deeply and beautifully that it seemed as if some skilled stonecutter had carved it. From this miracle, the venerable one concluded that his coming here was providential, and that after a good beginning there should follow a good end, and he thanked God and entered the cave. Seeing that it was suitable, as he had wished, and that water even dripped from one stone above, with which he could quench his thirst, the venerable one decided to remain here in stillness in order to converse constantly with God.

Who can describe the unbearable temptations that the venerable one endured from the demons while in the wilderness without brothers? All the days that the venerable one was in the cave, the accursed ones did not cease tempting him in various ways, frightening him with various phantoms, just to force him to leave. But the saint courageously accepted the battles, never tiring of conquering their temptations. Thus he spent many years in stillness, conversing alone with the One God. After this, six monks (no one knew how they had learned about the venerable one, because no one except that elder knew where he was struggling, and that elder, at the request of the venerable one, revealed this to no one) came to him and with tears asked permission to remain and live together with him. Seeing their strong desire, the venerable one received them and gave them rules for the monastic life. For a long time already he had wished to build near the entrance to the cave a small church in the name of Christ the Master, but he could not do this alone; and now, having found helpers, he decided to accomplish what he had planned. The venerable one had no means for the construction, but by Divine Providence there was found in Ephesus a certain wealthy woman of virtuous life who paid the expenses, and the church in the name of Christ the Savior was built.

After this, six more brothers came, and in all there were twelve. But the place was narrow, which did not allow for the construction of either a house, or even simply a canopy or anything else, so that they lived under the open sky. Then the venerable one ascended with the brothers to the summit of Mount Galesion and built there a church in the name of the Theotokos, and around it sufficient cells for the brothers. Then he built cells outside the monastery, at a great distance from one another, so that the brothers could enjoy stillness in them. Once in summertime, when there was intense heat and the venerable one was in one of these cells, reading the order of the Sixth Hour, he became so intensely thirsty that he nearly died from thirst. Not finding water, the blessed Lazarus fell to the ground in a faint and lay with his hands raised to God, asking Him for help. The God Who loves mankind, quick to console and swift to help, did not despise His servant who was in danger; He sent His Angel to a disciple of the venerable one who lived there, with a vessel filled with water, commanding him to run to his elder. Running up, the disciple revived his spiritual father with the water, thereby delivering him from death. But our enemy the devil did not rest at this, but, taking the form of a huge black serpent, crawled into the venerable one's clothing to frighten him. Knowing the wiles of Satan and having experience in fighting him, he was not at all frightened, but made the sign of the Precious Cross over it, and it immediately disappeared.

From that time the monks began to multiply in number, but the monastery could no longer contain them all (when the venerable one built it, he did not think that so many would gather, for the place was harsh, lacking water and everything else necessary for life). For this reason, the venerable one once for many days in a row with tears besought God to reveal to him whether it was His holy will that a larger church and monastery be built, capable of containing all the brethren who came, and where to lay the foundation for the future church. While he was praying thus, one night he heard a voice commanding him to go out of his cell. The venerable one went out and saw a pillar of fire reaching to the heavens, and Angels of

God descending to earth and sweetly singing: *"Let God arise, and let His enemies be scattered"* (Psalm 67:2). He immediately understood that it was pleasing to God that he build a church in the place where the pillar had appeared. The venerable one set about the construction with great zeal, building around the church also a monastery, no worse than any other, both in size and in the beauty of the construction.

It would be well to tell how the venerable one, having not even an obol to his name, found the means for the costly construction, completing such an extraordinary and great work in a short time. The Emperor of the Romans at that time, Romanos, was at enmity with Constantine Monomachos, one of the chief archons of Constantinople. For various reasons, but most of all because he suspected him of intending to seize the kingdom, Romanos was greatly angered at Constantine and exiled him to the island of Mytilene. Having heard of this, the divine Lazarus out of compassion for Constantine was very grieved, because punishment had befallen one who had done no evil. The venerable one sent men to Constantine to console him in his sufferings and to give him good hopes that he would become the successor to the kingdom of the Romans, for Lazarus foresaw this by Divine grace. After a short time, Romanos died, and, according to the prediction of the venerable one, Constantine became emperor. Then he sent Lazarus much money, precious vessels, holy objects, and gifts, so that he could completely finish building the monastery. With these means the venerable one erected the Church of the Resurrection and a huge, renowned monastery. The construction of the monastery began after the Divine vision, and by Divine Providence the means were found as well. Thanks to the fame of the venerable one, monks constantly multiplied, and soon there were already more than seven hundred of them. One of them was the own brother of the divine Lazarus, who, having learned from him the monastic way of life, made such progress in virtue that he surpassed all the rest, except his brother. After the death of the venerable one, by the decision of all the brethren, it was he who took over the governance of the monastery, laudably succeeding in the position of superior.

Upon completion of the construction, the saint built near the church, behind it, a pillar without a roof, difficult to ascend and very narrow, because its width was only three spans. He ascended it in a leather garment, with uncovered head, with bare feet, and with heavy chains on his body. There the venerable one endured all the hardships of winter: heavy rains, snows, cold, fierce frosts, from which the ever-memorable one became almost transparent. Likewise he endured the heat and unbearable scorching, leading a life on the pillar as one without a body.

Once there was such heavy rain that the water carried away huge stones, destroyed many animals, and damaged the crops. A certain goatherd, who was not far from the monastery, unable to endure such a deluge, ran to the monastery, fleeing from the danger. Approaching the saint and asking him for help (O who can worthily tell of the greatness of Thy wonders, O Christ God!), he saw the Most Holy Theotokos standing in the air over the pillar, protecting the venerable one from the rain. Who has ever seen or heard of such a miracle? Although a Cherub guarded Abba Macarius the Egyptian, and an Angel of the Lord guarded Paisios the

Great, such a miracle, I think, no one has seen or heard—that the Queen of the Angels Herself covered Lazarus like a cloud, preserving Her servant and slave unharmed.

Listen also to another miracle similar to this one. The rumor spread through all the surrounding areas that neither rain, nor hail, nor snow touched the pillar of the saint, and the vagaries of the weather caused him no harm. While some believed this miracle without any doubt, the governor of that region did not believe it until he saw it with his own eyes. In winter, when the snow fell in flakes and struck his face so that he could not even breathe freely, greatly forcing himself, the governor with great difficulty climbed up to the monastery and, approaching the pillar, saw an amazing miracle. The snow, which was falling with such force, as it approached the pillar divided in two and fell to the ground, so that not a single snowflake touched the pillar.

Marveling at this miracle, the governor asked the venerable one for forgiveness for his former doubts. Having received forgiveness, he returned home, telling everyone about the miracle he had seen, and all believed what was said about the saint.

A disciple of the saint once went on some necessity to a nearby village, and a harlot followed after him, who by various means tried to seduce him. But he—O easily crushable human nature!—conceived the thought of falling into sin. And at the very moment when he was already ready to commit it, he heard the voice of the venerable one, which frightened him with eternal torments. The disciple was so frightened by this voice that he trembled and turned away from the harlot, thereby being delivered from sin. The venerable one knew nothing of this miracle until the disciple himself told him. God, Who glorifies His servants, called to the disciple with the voice of the venerable Lazarus, delivering him from danger.

During a war between the Romans and the Persians, an old friend of the venerable one, Philippikos, was taken captive. Together with others, he was led into slavery to a barbarian land and, bound in iron, was thrown into prison. Suffering greatly from hunger and other misfortunes, he begged God to send him death in order to be delivered from such an unfortunate life. Suffering and receiving no help from anywhere, the unfortunate man spent many years in prison. But one night, remembering the great Lazarus and the miracles he had performed, he began with warm tears to ask the venerable one to deliver him from his bonds and misfortune. And—O miracle!—in the middle of the night the venerable one appeared to him, and as soon as he touched his chains, they fell off his feet by themselves, after which he commanded him to follow him. Thus, together, they set out on the journey and walked for the rest of the night. When dawn came, it turned out that they were both ascending a mountain. The venerable one immediately became invisible, and Philippikos was left alone. When he came to himself and realized that this was Mount Galesion, he glorified God for the freedom he had received. Coming to the monastery and relating the miracle, he gave thanks to the venerable one for a long time. Not wishing to return to his relatives anymore, Philippikos became a monk and spent the rest of his life pleasing God.

Once, having quarreled with the venerable one, the steward of the monastery built with the monastery's money a monastery in another locality, pleasant and healthy: in winter it was not cold there, and in summer it was not hot, and water was in abundance. The steward wanted to attract monks with the beauties of the place and lead them away from the monastery of Lazarus, in order to deprive the saint's monastery of people, and himself gain glory. This deed could not be hidden from the venerable one, although the steward made every effort to conceal his action. Having learned of the construction, the venerable one summoned the steward, asked him to stop the building and not quarrel with him. But the steward not only did not want to listen to his spiritual father, but also answered him rudely, continuing the work with even greater zeal, or rather, ignorance. After the venerable one had asked him two and three times, and he still held to his position, Lazarus said: "My child, God Himself will take care to correct you." And immediately, by the word of the venerable one, God chastised the disobedient man. Before he reached his cell, he miserably gave up his soul, thus reaping from his wicked disobedience the worst fruits. There is no worse passion than disobedience, since death follows after it. Proof of this is the transgression of Adam and Eve, which gave birth to death.

Another time, certain brothers were transporting wine to the monastery on mules. Arriving at an inn, they unloaded the animals and sat down to eat. When the time came to drink, one of them, lifting the vessel, said: "Bless, father." And—O miracle!—he immediately heard the voice of the venerable one answering him: "God bless you, my child." This same voice was also heard by another brother sitting nearby. The next day, when they brought the wine to the monastery, the saint told them to drink a little of it. The same brother lifted the vessel and said to the venerable one: "Bless, father." The venerable one answered him: "My child, you already received a blessing yesterday, but your companion did not." And at that moment they understood that the voice they had heard yesterday actually belonged to the venerable one. Thus, thanks to the eyes of his soul, the saint knew everything, and nothing could be hidden from him, for those whose spiritual eyes are purified from the passions can gaze upon the Noetic Sun—Christ—and from Him be illumined with the knowledge of mysteries hidden from others.

Once a certain old friend of the venerable one sent him two vessels of good wine with his servant. The servant hid one vessel along the road and brought the other to the venerable one. Knowing of the theft, the venerable one said to him: "Beware, my child, do not approach that vessel which you hid on the road, lest you be subjected to danger." But the man paid no attention to the words of the venerable one and joyfully went to take the hidden vessel. At that very moment, a huge and terrible serpent leaped out of the vessel and attacked him. If he had not called upon the saint for help, he would not have escaped the danger.

Once a severe drought occurred in those regions: the earth dried up, the springs and rivers dried up, the plants withered, the fruits perished, and everything that grew on the earth. In the monastery of the venerable one, the drought was even more severe, because due to its location on the summit of the mountain the monastery was deprived of water not only during drought, but also during rain. When the venerable one saw how severe the drought was, his eyes did not dry from the streams of tears he poured forth, so greatly was he grieved because of the calamity that had befallen everyone. He fervently asked God to have mercy on His creation and to give drink to the earth that had dried up from lack of rain. And what did God, Who arranges all things for good, do? He did not despise the prayer of the saint, but neither did He fully grant his request, because the saint asked for rain for the whole earth, and God did not want to pour rain on the whole earth, perhaps in order to bring sinners to repentance by this punishment. He poured rain only on the monastery, and in a most wondrous manner. When the night had passed and the sun shone forth, suddenly from one side of the sky a cloud appeared, which stood over the monastery and poured rain only on the monastery; but all the land around continued to languish without rain. Only the brethren of the monastery enjoyed the water and filled their cisterns with it; then the sky again became cloudless.

Seeing this miracle, the inhabitants of the nearby villages ran in sorrow to the venerable one and with warm tears asked him to have pity on them and to entreat God for mercy. Having compassion on them, the venerable one began to ask the Lord more earnestly than the first time, and the Lord heard His servant and ended the drought, and the fields after the rain began to grow green again. By the prayer of the venerable one to the Lord, a most severe downpour also once ceased.

There was a case when the monastery experienced a severe shortage of bread. The venerable one blessed only three small loaves that remained with him and satisfied with them more than seven hundred monks, for to the venerable one who was pure in faith all things were possible, and nothing was impossible for him.

After this, the venerable one, who was dead to the body, suffered a severe and terrible illness. Suffering grievously, he joyfully awaited death, because he had long been ready for it, and he himself, according to the Apostle, desired to be released from the bonds of the body *"and be with Christ"* (Philippians 1:23). Around him gathered a multitude of disciples, grieving and mourning the death of their spiritual father, and ready for his sake to give even their own lives. Their groans and weeping could evoke tears even from the most hardhearted. Therefore their divine father, although he was already at his last breath, himself wept out of pity for his children. Grieving because of their future orphanhood, he asked on their behalf the Mother of God, his customary Helper, Protection, and Refuge. The venerable one prayed to Her that life might be granted him—not for himself (for how could one who had died to the world and always wished to die in order to be with Christ ask for himself?), but for his spiritual sons. And the Virgin Mother, Who gave birth to Life Itself, the common Salvation of the human race, Who had protected the venerable one from all misfortunes, at the end of his life also became his Helper and prevented death. She asked of Her Son, Who has power over life and death, to add to the life of the venerable one fifteen more years. Being in ecstasy during his illness, the venerable one saw the Theotokos asking this of Her Son, and this was fulfilled, because the venerable one lived for another fifteen years.

After this event, fourteen years passed, during which the venerable one struggled and afflicted himself even more intensely than when he was young and strong of body. For seven days in a row he could eat nothing, and then consumed only vegetables. Having exhausted himself by such labors, he could no longer stand on his feet and sat on his pillar, for he no longer had control of his legs, which ached and were covered with terrible sores. Although he sat on the pillar and his legs touched nothing, he experienced even more severe pains than before. Pus flowed from him and covered the surface of the pillar. The venerable one suffered in this way for an entire year. Thus the fifteen years passed that God, through the intercession of the Theotokos, had granted him. He learned of his death from the Lord, but did not reveal it to any monk (for they would have wept and wailed greatly). With his own hands the venerable one composed a testament and hid it in his bosom. Thus at the end of his life, having cast off the earthly man and parting from this lower prison and sufferings, he departed to God, being seventy-two years of age.

Following his death, wondrous phenomena occurred: as soon as his divine soul was separated from his body and ascended to the heavens, a bright cloud descended from above, similar to the one that had appeared at his birth, indicating the death of the most blessed one and by its strange light summoning all to the pillar of the venerable one. It also summoned a disciple of the saint, Gregory, who was then practicing stillness in that church of the Theotokos which the saint had built for the twelve monks. All who saw the cloud ran to the pillar. At the sight of the dead body of the venerable one, they began to weep and wail inconsolably, calling him father; they mourned their orphanhood and, unable to endure separation from him, wished to die together with him. They wept bitterly, thinking that he had died without leaving a spiritual testament. But Gregory grieved more than all, and, owing to his closeness to the venerable one, addressed him as if he were alive: "Father, why have you so inconsolably grieved us? Why have you caused us sorrow that we are not able to bear? Why did you not wish to compose a testament with a command as to what we should do, but hid your death from everyone? Do you not pity us, your children? Do you not see what grief over you has done to us?" Weeping thus, Gregory addressed the venerable one—and a miracle occurred. The breathless corpse, as if alive, raised his hand, lowered it into his bosom, took the testament, and gave it to Gregory, after which he again became breathless. Gregory began to read the testament attentively and saw that it was not signed, as was customary, with the name of the saint. Then he again addressed the dead man: "Father, if with your signature you do not confirm what is written, then we, your children, will not be able to bury you as befits." Then the venerable one—O fearful miracle!—rose again and before all signed the testament with his name, confirming what was written, and then fell asleep with a sweet sleep. His body was buried near the pillar where he had performed his supernatural struggles, so that this place and the grave of the ascetic might be a clear testimony and proof of his struggle in the name of the Lord. Thus the venerable one was, as it were, divided in two. To those below and earthly were left his holy relics—as an inexhaustible source of healings, a remedy for various diseases, a refuge from demons, a generous gift of saving blessings, and deliverance from every harm. But his divine soul, accompanied by Angels, flew to the heavens, there where is the Church of the firstborn, where are the ranks of Angels, the choirs of Apostles and Prophets, the hosts of Martyrs, the assemblies of Teachers, the multitudes of Ascetics, the company of the Venerable, and unceasing song to the Holy Trinity, to Whom belongs all glory, honor, and worship, now and ever and unto the ages of ages. Amen.

(Written by Gregory, Most Holy Patriarch of Constantinople)

The Life and Ascetic Struggles of
Our Venerable Father Cyril Phileotes,
Who Struggled in the Eleventh Century

This blessed Cyril was from the regions of Thrace, from a place called Philea, in the Eparchy of Derkos. He was born of noble parents and at Holy Baptism was named Cyriacus. Having studied the sacred letters from childhood, he surpassed all his peers in sharpness of mind and understanding, for this child was enlightened by God Himself. When Cyriacus grew up, he was ordained as a reader by the local bishop, and from that time, having been dedicated to God, he meditated day and night *"in the law of the Lord"* (Psalm 1:2). He constantly read the sacred books, chanted psalms, and prayed to God, while performing many prostrations. The youth avoided association with dissolute peers and by his silence healed and corrected loquacity, and by stillness corrected the turmoil that the soul experiences after unprofitable fellowship. During the Divine Liturgy he stood with extraordinary reverence, directing his gaze downward, while in his thoughts he turned to God, with faith and hope asking help from Him. And fervently believing, he received help from the Lord.

This youth, in mind like an elder, was seen pouring forth streams of tears, keeping silence according to God, which is the mother of wisdom, for sorrow not only contributes to progress but through humility preserves what has been attained. Sorrow is mourning according to God, which is begotten by repentance. Therefore, seeing a youth who led such a life, the virtuous rejoiced and honored him immensely, calling him a young elder, as once they called Saint Sabbas. Hearing such comments, the youth would say: "Flee, Cyriacus, from praises and be ashamed of censures, then you will not think of vanity, seeking the praises of men, for such a one should not hope for a reward from the Lord." But the wicked accused him, trying by their accusations to cool his zeal, yet the blessed one looked only to God, neither rejoicing in honors nor being offended by the dishonor inflicted upon him. Just as a dead man does not feel either honor or dishonor, so also a Christian should not perceive either glory, or praise, or contempt, or insult. It is impossible not to become angry when you are insulted and accused, or to overcome by longsuffering the temptation that occurs in sorrow, unless you consider yourself lower than all and possess extreme humility. Asking God to grant him patience when he is censured, the youth would say: *"Set a guard, O Lord, over my mouth; keep watch over the door of my lips. Do not incline my heart to any evil thing, to practice wicked works"* (Psalm 140:3–4). Seeing his good intention, the Lord, the Knower of Hearts, added to him desire upon desire and zeal upon zeal, so that the venerable one was *"like a green olive tree in the house of God"* (Psalm 51:8), trusting in the mercy of God.

It was the custom of the blessed one to come to the church services before everyone else and to leave after everyone else. He read and sang with such a pleasant voice, and served God with such diligence, that all the lovers of God asked him to become a priest, because from the All-seeing One neither the fragrance of virtue nor the stench of sin can be hidden. Thus the Bishop of Derkos often asked him to accept ordination, for he wished to have such a watchful cleric, chaste, capable of teaching, knowledgeable in Sacred Scripture, attentive, not covetous, calm, gentle, God-loving, a lover of the poor, not prone to anger, not bearing grudges, not vainglorious, inaccessible to flattery, steadfast and diligent in instructing his neighbor. But the humble-minded Cyriacus, although his conscience did not accuse him of anything, considered himself unworthy of the high priestly rank and continued to remain in the degree of reader, to which he had been called. He spoke thus: "It is good to extend a helping hand to one who is falling, if you yourself can avoid falling together with him. But if afterwards the one who showed compassion to another suffers, then let him prefer his own benefit to the benefit of the other, because no one is closer to a person than himself. Let the one who can correct others associate with the wicked and correct them. But the one who, like me, is weak, let him flee from the wicked, so as not to become a partaker of their wickedness and a cause of harm to others. The hierarch Basil the Great says that the one who wishes to lift up one who has fallen must himself be stronger than him. But if he too falls, then another is needed to lift him up. One of the fathers said that if you have no deeds, do not speak of virtue, because just as Jesus began to do and to teach (John 7:14–17), so we also must, while progressing in words, have a life to match. Since we are passionate, we must submit to others and ask God to cleanse us from the passions, for only with God's help can we anticipate the passions. *'A poor man's wisdom is despised, and his words are not heard,'* says Ecclesiastes (Ecclesiastes 9:16). How can one who cannot rule himself rule others in accordance with the Divine ordinances? Not all of us must save others, but certainly all must save themselves."

When Cyril reached the age of twenty, he took a lawful wife, but not for pleasure but for childbearing. She was a helper to him and a zealous, courageous co-worker on the path to virtue. And they were both one in mind and in manner of action, spurring one another to the fulfillment of God's commandments. After a son was born to them, the blessed one began to speak to her about chastity: "It is unjust for us to prove ourselves more unreasonable than the irrational animals, because they mate with females once a year at a certain time, while we, being rational, often do this for the sake of sensual pleasure, which I call licentiousness. If we cannot lead a chaste life, then let this be two, three, or four times a year. Although even this is not fitting for those who practice self-restraint, yet I hope God will forgive us as weak and will not condemn us for licentiousness. Chaste is not the one who abstains from forbidden pleasures, but from permitted ones. Since we have been made alive through Holy Baptism, let us make our members weapons of righteousness and sanctification, because God Himself is holy and rests in His saints. We ought not to fear the height of continence, but rather fear the depth and abyss of incontinence. Sensory continence is when a person abstains from all unreasonable actions that work through the body. Mental continence is when the mind withdraws from indulgence in passionate thoughts. But it is impossible to achieve continence of the senses without thinking about and keeping continence in the thoughts, which must be inseparably bound to the soul." Having heard his arguments, his wife agreed with him, and from that time she remained in abstinence and chastity, no longer tempting him with her outward appearance, for the beginning of carnal love is sight. Hope of pleasure increases passion, recollection nourishes it, and habit preserves it. Thus from sight is born passionate love, from which comes consent, followed by the sin itself.

Knowing that it is impossible for one who is himself conquered by gluttony to conquer the carnal passions, the venerable one, according to the Divine canons, began with xerophagy on Wednesdays and Fridays, eating food late and drinking only water. Then, after some time, he also began to eat dry food on Mondays, Tuesdays, and Thursdays, while on Saturday and Sunday he ate all kinds of food and drank a little wine. Both food and wine the venerable one consumed in moderation and at a set time, keeping the ascetic rule even on the Lord's feasts. Then the venerable one began to abstain completely from wine, because wine, according to Gregory the Theologian, never makes the nature chaste but inclines it to pleasure. He avoided filling the belly, for it is impossible to acquire dispassion for one who fills himself with food. Dispassion is not the state when someone abstains from committing sin in deed (this is called abstinence, not dispassion), but when someone uproots passionate thoughts from his heart. This is also called purity of heart. All his time, and especially on feast days, the venerable one strove to spend in vigils, psalmody, prayer, and reading, for he knew that vigils refine the mind, which becomes capable of contemplating what is profitable for the soul, while long sleep dulls it. Seven times a day the saint sang the psalms of David with many prostrations, and often would say, "Alas," "Woe," shaking his head, strongly striking himself on the cheeks and pulling his hair, because his heart was set ablaze by the grace of God. Therefore this courageous one did not feel pain during the ascetic labors he performed, but in his sorrows according to God he rejoiced more than those subject to the passions rejoice in carnal pleasures.

His chaste wife strove according to her strength to follow him in his ascetic struggles, and the ever-blessed one urged her to press forward and not to look back, contemplating the path of virtue already traveled, but to endure the struggles for the Lord's sake to the end. Seeing that she followed him with zeal, the venerable one thanked God.

Hearing of the struggles and virtues of true monks, he extraordinarily loved monasticism and greatly desired to renounce the world and what is in the world, so as to serve God in the monastic life and stillness. Since the beginning and foundation of monastic life is obedience, Cyriacus wished to test whether he would be able to keep it and cut off his own will. For this reason, he delivered himself into complete obedience for three years to a certain ship-owner, so that, fulfilling the commands of the shipmaster and his companions without murmuring and with zeal, he might know by actual experience whether he could obey a spiritual father and keep the rules of the monastic life. It is better to be subject to a disciple than to live as you please, reaping the worthless fruits of your own will. The blessed Cyriacus served the shipmaster and his companions as angels of God, fulfilling everything they commanded him, whether honorable or dishonorable, being to all as a slave who does not contradict, does not argue, does not show disobedience. And although the foolish mocked him and often reviled him, he endured everything with joy, and on the contrary, when he was not reviled, he grieved, as if losing a treasure, because he looked with hope to the future recompense. Considering reviling and dishonor to be medicine for pride, he prayed to God for those who dishonored him, as if they were actually his physicians. And although the unwise condemned him for hypocrisy, false piety, and fasting, he never broke his fast. They ate rich meat and fish, enjoying all kinds of food, while the venerable one, looking at them, experienced joy as he ate onions with bread, or garlic, or wild greens. Content with this, he would say: "I, brethren, am weak and cannot tame my flesh with rich food, because it kindles in me the flame of the passions."

Every time the ship put to shore, the blessed one would go onto land to gather wood or fetch water, or for some other necessity, and then would go to a place where no one could see him and would pray to God, performing many prostrations. Then he would mercilessly beat himself on the thighs and shoulders, sometimes with a rope, or a stick, and sometimes with thorny brambles. After such beatings, the blood from his lacerated thighs would flow down even to his ankles, as he himself told the author of this life, yet by the grace of God his wounds did not become inflamed. When he beat himself, he would weep plaintively, calling upon God for help. And he did this whenever some passionate thought of lust or anger tormented him.

Once, when they were returning from the cities along the Danube, where they had sailed on some trading business, the saint was sitting in a corner of the ship. Reflecting on his sins, he said mentally: "How long will you delay pleasing God, O wretched one? What age are you waiting for? You are not a youth of twenty years but a grown man, and if you neglect this now, putting it off from day to day, you will never make progress. Thus you will deceive yourself until your end comes. Hasten to the struggle, because the struggle is here and now, and delay is not permitted." Reasoning thus, he could no longer restrain himself but began to weep loudly, striking himself on the face and scratching himself mercilessly, because his heart burned as if from fire. The sailors began to ask what was happening to him and what he was thinking about, if he was weeping so. Being unable to silence them, he said: "If you had as many sins as I have and remained unrepentant, you would weep even more than I." They answered him: "We too are sinners, but none of us weeps like this, so we thought you were sorrowing about something else." Groaning from the depths of his heart, the venerable one said: "This river that you see flows out, as I have heard, from paradise and encompasses the whole earth. I imagined it as paper upon which all my sins are written, which fill and defile the universe. That is why I weep." When the unwise heard this, they began to mock him, but the sensible ones said with groaning: "Woe to us! If you, who fast, keep vigil, and unceasingly pray to God, serving us unworthy ones as a slave, are in such affliction because you have sins, and weep thus, then we, hard-hearted and unrepentant, who every day add sin to sin, how will we suffer on the dread Day of Judgment? Woe to our insensibility, for we spend our days in vanity!"

Once the blessed one was ordered to climb the mast. Being exhausted from fasting and cold (for he wore only light clothing and was barefoot), worn out from the unbearable beatings and wounds, he tried to climb but could not. Bowing to his companions, the venerable one said: "Forgive me, brethren, for the Lord's sake, because even if I force myself to climb the mast, not being able to hold on, I will fall into the sea, because I am sick and have lost the last of my strength." The sailors pitied him and offered: "Go away from us, O man of God, we are afraid that God may drown us in the sea, seeing your humility. But if you do not leave the deck, at least sit quietly and pray to God for us. He will give us the strength to do your work." They managed to persuade him not to work until the ship arrived at the home port. There Cyriacus went home and, having told his wife what had happened, said: "I must do one of two things: either go to a monastery, or remain here, but then I will be useless because of bodily illness." His wife answered him with tears: "Remain here, with us, my lord, and I will feed the children with the little that we have. I believe that God will not allow us to lack what is necessary for life."

Cyriacus arranged for himself a tiny cell in the house, in which he made prostrations and prayed, and spent many years in it in stillness, devoting himself to fasting, psalmody, and prayer. He engaged in handiwork, weaving nets for the neighbors, but did not take payment for them. At the same time, the venerable one would say: "If your hands are occupied with work, your tongue should chant hymns, and your mind should pray, because God requires from us as a debt that our mind and thoughts always be occupied with Him. But if you want the works of your hands to be pleasing to God, and not to earth, then give them to the poor." The venerable one wore iron chains on his body, which pressed upon him so that from the wounds came an unbearable stench. Yet he endured everything with joy, saying: "For those who love toil and truly wish to repent, this is insignificant and easy, though it seems heavy and laughable to lovers of the flesh and the carefree, for the apostle says that *the sufferings of this present time are not worthy to be compared with the glory which shall be revealed in us*' (Romans 8:18). To console him in his labors, the Lord gave the venerable one the gift of tears, through which he received rest and consolation.

Since he greatly loved stillness, he would go out at night from his cell and go to a deserted place near the lake, where he would remain fasting for two or three days, and sometimes for a whole week, eating nothing at all, though sometimes he would satisfy his hunger with grass. From excessive fasting, extreme stillness, and many tears, he mortified the bodily senses in himself, awakening the inner powers of the soul. Since his mind shone from unceasingly remembering God and constant prayer, he was caught up into the contemplation of God, from which the venerable one experienced delight.

Often, leaving the noetic contemplations, he would say to himself: "Leave the things above, O impure one, because every lawless and proud man is impure before God. Descend in mind to hell, that you may contemplate there those like yourself, to whom you, wretched one, will soon be numbered, and their terrible torments. Behold, at the door is the Angel sent from God; what then are you sitting for? O, how will you be able to endure the worm that sleeps not and suffer the fire unquenchable? How will palpable darkness envelop you, how will God separate you from the righteous and place you with the demons, whose deeds you have done? You did not fear God, you did not feel shame before men, you did not have mercy on yourself, so who will have mercy on you? God is righteous, and righteous are His judgments, so He will repay you according to your deeds." And again and again, sorrowing, with tears and wailing, he would offer such a prayer: "Have mercy, have mercy, have mercy, O my Christ, Knower of hearts, I have sinned, do not condemn me. Accept my wailing from the bitterness of my soul. By Thy Passion heal the passions of my soul, by Thy wounds heal the wounds of my mind, by Thy Blood cleanse me, as Thou knowest, and make me a partaker of Thy Divine Body. From the gall of bitterness with which Thou wast given to drink by the enemies, O my Christ, deliver me quickly. By Thy Body stretched out upon the Tree of Thy Cross, stretch out my mind to contemplate Thee. By Thy head, which Thou didst bow on the Cross, may this my head be exalted over my adversaries. By Thy nailed most pure hands, raise me up to Thyself from the pit of destruction. Being struck and spat upon by the accursed, may this my face, defiled by lawlessness, be illumined by Thy holy countenance. By Thy Soul, which on the Cross Thou didst deliver to Thy Father, may this lead me to Thee by Thy grace, that I may be delivered from the joyful-sorrowful food. May Thy holy will, O my Christ, be my food always, now and unto the ages of ages." Praying thus, lamenting and reproaching himself, he did not wish to gaze upon things above, but day and night he reflected upon his sins. When it was not winter, he often went out into the desert and struggled, as we have already said, and then returned again home, to his wife and children.

It was the custom of the venerable one to care for the sick. Once, having come to a certain bedridden old woman and finding her in great sorrow, he asked her the cause of such a condition. She answered that in another village, eighteen miles away, she had a daughter who had fallen ill and was at the point of death. The old woman had decided to send her other daughter to her, but since that one was still young, she was afraid to let her go alone, lest someone cause her harm. Hearing this, the venerable one also became sorrowful and said to the old woman: "Do you want me to lead your daughter to her sister?" She answered: "Yes, I do, because I am entrusting her not to a man but to an angel of God." Cyriacus together with the maiden came to her sister, who was still alive. Having joyfully greeted her sister and the venerable one, the sick woman surrendered her soul into the hands of God. After three days, Cyriacus returned with the girl to her mother. Such was the compassion and love for mankind of the blessed one. And on that night when he brought the girl back to her mother, he saw in a dream a beautiful maiden dressed in bright garments. Her mantle covered almost the entire sky. In amazement he asked her: "Who are you, Lady, and why have you come here?" She answered him: "I am called the grace of God and have come to you." The maiden embraced him and covered him with her mantle. Having perceived an ineffable fragrance issuing from her, the venerable one was filled with joy and gladness, for he understood that God thus glorifies those who glorify Him.

The venerable one was so merciful to his brethren that he gave away even the most necessary tools to those who had need of them, and with such joy, as if he were receiving them. As for bread and other food, it is superfluous even to speak of how generously he distributed them, especially when the sick needed them. His wife rejoiced at this as if she were distributing them herself. At the same time the venerable one would say that one must show mercy with discernment, and only to those who are worthy of mercy, but one must not give what has been acquired through injustice. But if someone does not show mercy, then let him at least bear the injustice of those who wrong him, entreating God on their behalf. The one who has been shown mercy must himself be merciful. And if he sees or hears something that grieves his brother, and his heart is also grieved by it, then God accounts this as mercy. If someone reviles or strikes another, and that one, being ashamed, does not turn against him or grieve him, but treats him with meekness and longsuffering, then this is the same as true mercy.

To his wife the venerable one would speak thus: "He who does good to others makes himself like God. Love for neighbor is known not only in the distribution of money, but much more in a word of consolation and bodily service. It is good to do good to all, but most of all to those who cannot repay. Abraham, sitting before his tabernacle, invited travelers without any distinction and showed them hospitality. Therefore he was deemed worthy to receive not only angels but also their Master. If someone can do good to another and does not, then he wrongs him and brings himself under the condemnation of the Master. Therefore we must do good to all with zeal."

Once there was a storm: lightning flashed, thunder rumbled, heavy rain poured, and the venerable one at this time was sitting before the house. A certain traveler approached him, exhausted from the road and the cold, and looking at him, asked: "Sir, where is the house of Cyriacus the Merciful?" Surprised by his words, he said: "I am Cyriacus, but who the merciful one is, I do not know. Tell me for the Lord's sake, why did you say that?" And that pious man answered: "Since I unexpectedly fell into many temptations and in my folly sank into the depths because of self-loving thoughts, I asked God to overlook my sins and show me a means of protection and salvation. Immediately there appeared to me a warrior, beautiful in appearance, on a horse, and he said: 'Do not sorrow, because God will take care of you. Go to the village and ask for the house of Cyriacus the Merciful; he will give you rest.' This is what the warrior said to me, and beyond this I know nothing; therefore, my lord, I asked you." The venerable one went into the house, poured water into a basin to wash the guest's feet, but the guest, understanding his intention, would not allow it. The venerable one remarked to this: "Consider, brother, Who washed the feet of His disciples, and what fearsome words were said to Peter, who out of piety did not allow the Lord to do this." After these words, the guest obeyed, and the venerable one washed his feet, as he was accustomed to do for guests. He also gave him a change of clothing and, setting the table, entertained the guest and rejoiced with all his family, glorifying God.

Once the venerable one was practicing stillness in his cell, and his daughter was playing with a friend. Not without the instigation of the devil, the girl threw a stone and knocked out his daughter's right eye. Her mother, being greatly frightened, became indignant and began scolding the girl and her parents. Coming out of the cell, the venerable one did not utter a single bad word but thanked God with warm tears, considering himself the cause of such a misfortune. His wife called him hard-hearted, but the wondrous Cyriacus began to instruct her, citing many sayings from Sacred Scripture and the lives of the saints. Thus, with God's help, he managed to soften his wife's anger and bring her to a peaceful state. He persuaded her to be reconciled with the parents of the one who had blinded their daughter and to forgive the girl, who had done it unintentionally.

The venerable one loved to visit churches. Throughout the entire year, every Friday he walked on foot to Constantinople to venerate the Blachernae Church of the Most Holy Theotokos and to kiss Her holy icon, and at the end of the night doxology would return home again, walking approximately thirty or forty miles. "The venerable one told me," says the author of the life, "how he rejoiced to walk along that road in spring and autumn, and how he suffered in wintertime. He added the following: 'Woe to the one who suffers from two winters, from cold and from hunger. But if chains press upon him and he exhausts himself with vigils, then this woe becomes three times worse.'"

Once in the land where the venerable one lived, a great famine began, from which many died. Soon he too was deprived of what was most necessary, and only a little bread remained for his wife and children, and Cyriacus set out hungry for Constantinople. Having walked eighteen miles, he grew weak from his previous fasting and the difficulties of the journey. Then the venerable one began to ask God to give him strength to live not by bread alone, but also by the spiritual word of God. And the loving Lord, Who said: *"Behold, My servants shall eat and drink and rejoice,"* showed the venerable one fresh bread lying on a stone, and a vessel of water. Having offered a prayer, he sat down, partook of the bread, and drank the water, after which he rose and thanked God. Coming to the Blachernae Church of the Theotokos, he gave thanks to Her and to the Son with tears and spiritual joy.

The venerable one had a custom of assuming the guise of a fool for Christ. Once, returning from the Church of the Theotokos, he came to the city of Neapolis. To the question of the governor, who he was and where he was coming from, the venerable one kept silent, pretending to be mute. The question was repeated two and three times, and the governor, receiving no answer, struck Cyriacus, saying: "Will you tell me who you are?" The venerable one pointed with his head and hands toward heaven. Growing angry, the ruler struck him again and then, deciding that he was a spy, threw him into prison, ordering that wooden stocks be put on him. After two days spent by the saint in prison, by God's providence a friend of his happened to pass by. Visiting the venerable one in prison, he asked with amazement: "Man of God, what evil have you done, that you are in such a place?" To this the venerable one answered: "It is not the place that magnifies virtue, but virtue the place, for God is not ashamed to seek an ardent spirit and a chaste soul. I have committed no evil, but by the will of Christ and the governor I sit here. When my Christ wishes, He will lead me out of here." Hearing this, the governor fell on his knees before the venerable one, asking forgiveness, after which he released him in peace.

At another time, having heard that in Constantinople there lived a monk of virtuous life and discernment named Hilarion, the venerable one came to him to ask whether he was following the path of virtue in vain. Hilarion received him with joy and, having heard his account, praised all his deeds except for the wearing of chains, concerning which he said that although some of the fathers did wear chains for the mortification of the flesh, they were stylites, desert-dwellers, hermits, but not those who live in cities and villages. Although such ones try to hide the wearing of chains from people, they cannot do this for long, and therefore they are called "chain-bearers." And indeed, the venerable one was called this by everyone until his death. Abba Hilarion also said to him that the virtuous greatly honor those who wear chains, but from this honor is born vainglory, which steals away virtue. The careless, in turn, condemn those who wear chains, and from this condemnation of those who do not have self-reproach are born other condemnations and all that follows from them. But those who are courageous in soul endure all condemnations and look only to God, avoiding any accusation or praise of men. However, many, being unable to bear dishonor from people, were deceived and fell, because not everyone is able to pay no attention to those who revile and mock him.

Having heard such most wise words from Abba Hilarion, the humble-minded Cyriacus at that very moment fell at his feet and asked him to command him to remove the chains, saying: "I hate the labor that brings harm." Having removed the chains and cast them at the feet of the abba, the venerable one said again: "Behold, the dog has been loosed from his bonds. Pray, Father, that I may find protection from diabolic cunning, so as not to harm either myself or my brethren. But if you find it right, allow me to bind myself with a cord, so as not to leave the flesh free." With the consent of Abba Hilarion, he did so. The elder, seeing the unbearable wounds on the body of the ascetic, marveled at the humility which God had granted him, for humble-mindedness is not the accusation of conscience and self-reproach, but the knowledge of God's grace. Reflecting on the zeal of this holy man and his guileless character and simplicity, Abba Hilarion said to him: *"God gives grace to the humble."* May He see your humility, your labors, and exalt you above carnal thoughts and bring you to *"a perfect man, to the measure of the stature of the fullness of Christ"* (Ephesians 4:13), for the freedom of your soul, and may He give you the Holy Spirit to endure all things with thanksgiving." After this, he asked Cyriacus to go with a letter to a certain most renowned lady of the Comnenian family, who at that time was not yet empress, because at that time the pious Michael Ducas was reigning.

And the blessed one went with this letter to the addressee. The lady, having read the letter, recognized Cyriacus by his clothing, gait, look, and the yellowness and dryness of his face. Falling at the feet of the venerable one, she asked his blessing, but the venerable one also fell on his knees, asking her blessing. The lady insisted, and the venerable one blessed her with these words: "May the Lord God deem you worthy to see the sons of your sons, and may your children possess cities and nations, and may their name become famous and fearsome to all their enemies." And this blessing was later fulfilled. And the Comnena addressed him with these words: "Tell me, servant of God, a word of salvation." And the venerable one answered: "As long as someone is enslaved by the passions, he is not considered a servant of God, because the prophet says that all *'shall be taught by the Lord'* (Isaiah 54:13). Hear what Daniel said to Nebuchadnezzar: king, *'let my advice be acceptable to you; break off your sins by being righteous, and your iniquities by showing mercy to the poor'* (Daniel 4:27), and David says: *'He has dispersed abroad, he has given to the poor; his righteousness endures forever'* (Psalm 112:9), and Solomon: *'He who has pity on the poor lends to the Lord'* (Proverbs 19:17). And the hierarch Basil the Great teaches: 'If you did not show mercy, you yourself will not be shown mercy; if you did not open the door of your house, you will be expelled from the Kingdom; if you did not give bread, you will not receive eternal life.'" Then the Comnena said to him:

"I wish to reveal my thoughts to your holiness, but I fear that I will not fulfill your words and will sin before God."

"It is impossible for one who truly fears God to feel fear. As Solomon writes: 'Besides Him (God), fear no one else.' If someone reveals his thoughts to spiritual men, this is a sign that he wishes to correct his life. Concealment of thoughts means that the person is subject to the passions, for he who associates with thieves will never betray them, because he loves the passion. But he who asks, listens, and when he shows disobedience yet condemns himself for it, such a one is humbled, and from humility obtains some mercy. But he who does not ask, does not listen, and does not show disobedience, does not humble himself and does not obtain mercy. Just as a sick person is repelled by the food brought to him, yet later such food is found that he accepts with pleasure, eats, and recovers, so also a fearful soul, although it listens many times and shows disobedience, after a certain time comes to shame. Thus, having heard a good word that pleases her, she acts according to it and is saved."

Having heard this, the Comnena said:

"This is indeed so. But know that I fear the sins that seem small, that is, idle talk, slander, mockery, and the like, more than the great ones."

"Do not believe that one who neglects small sins cares about great ones. That sin is called great which conquers a person, and that is called small which the person himself conquers. If the devil neglects small sins, he will not be able to cast a person into another greater sin, since great sins are born from lesser ones. And why are great sins born? Because the small ones were not properly corrected. But guard yourself from small sins, and by the grace of Christ you will not fall into great ones."

Hearing this, the Comnena was moved to compunction and confessed to him most of her most pressing thoughts, asking counsel as to how, when, and which thought should be preferred over others. Since the blessed Cyriacus answered all her questions fittingly, she greatly rejoiced that she had found such a God-wise counselor. Loving monks, she gave him a little money, which the venerable one did not want to accept. However, she adjured him by the name of God, and he obeyed and took it, because he greatly feared the name of God. Having blessed her and her children, the venerable one left them, and he distributed most of the money to the poor on the way home.

Once the venerable Cyriacus wished to go to Chonae, where the Archangel Michael had performed a miracle, to venerate his holy icon. On the way, Cyriacus stopped for the night at an inn. The innkeeper, however, was a thief and began to ask him many questions:

"Who are you, and where are you coming from, for your eyes are like the eyes of a thief, and your speech also betrays you? And what do you have in your bag?"

"I, by the grace of Christ, am not a thief, and I am going to Chonae to venerate the Archangel Michael. In my bag I have the necessary means from home for the journey, so as not to beg for alms."

Being a thief, the innkeeper took his bag and began to remove his clothes. Calling upon God for help, the venerable one said to him:

"Man, fear God, do not strip me in the sight of these women, but if you wish, strip me in a corner of your house, so as not to expose my shame."

But that beast-like and cruel man stripped Cyriacus anyway. However, when he saw the wounds from the cord with which he was tightly bound and smelled the strong stench issuing from the wounds, he took pity, dressed him again, and let him go.

The venerable one said to himself: "If you, Cyriacus, endure this robbery with thanksgiving, you will receive the same reward as if you had given these means to the poor. When he had already gone some distance, the innkeeper began to cry out after him. Hearing the cry, the venerable one stopped. The innkeeper approached and returned the money he had taken. Asking the venerable one for forgiveness and blessing, he said: "Now I know that you are a man of God." Taking the money from the innkeeper and forgiving him, the venerable one instructed him thus:

"Brother, are you not a Christian, and have you not heard the Lord's words: *'I was a stranger and you took Me in; I was naked and you clothed Me'?* (Matthew 25:35-36) And again: *'Depart from Me, you cursed, into the everlasting fire... for... I was a stranger and you did not take Me in; I was naked and you did not clothe Me'?* (Matthew 25:41–43) But you, stripping those who are clothed, how will you enter the church of God, how will you kiss this holy icon of Christ? Are you not going to die? Will not the Lord repay you according to your deeds? Listen to me, repent and confess your sins to your spiritual father. Fulfill the rule that he gives you and refrain from your sins."

Having given him many other counsels and blessing him, the venerable one set out on his way, rejoicing and thanking God for the unexpected change in the innkeeper. Coming to the Church of the Archangel Michael and venerating his holy icon, he asked him to continue to preserve him unharmed from visible and invisible enemies, and so he returned again to his home.

Once he wished to inspect those few vineyards that he had and the workers who were then working there. Seeing from afar that they were not working but lying on the ground, he too fell to the ground and lay thus for three hours. Then a thought began to trouble him to shame them somehow, but the venerable one resisted it, saying: "If you believe that God provides for you, why then are you caring for yourself, for *'one thing is needful'* (Luke 10:42). Wretched one, you are concerned that the vineyard bear fruit, but you do not care that your soul not remain fruitless. Why then do you live and *'use up the ground'*? (Luke 13:7) *'Cast your burden on the Lord, and He shall sustain you'* (Psalm 54:23), *'Trust in the Lord, and do good'* (Psalm 36:3). But since the thought reminded him again that from his property were fed the strangers who came to his house, and that if he remained negligent he would deprive them of food and shelter, he spoke thus to himself: "Let the apostle console us, who said: *'I do not seek yours, but you'* (2 Corinthians 12:14). If we cannot benefit the brethren bodily, let us then benefit them spiritually. Then God will certainly account this to us as virtue, for He Himself says: *'Do not labor for the food which perishes, but for the food which endures to everlasting life'* (John 6:27). True food that endures to everlasting life is meekness, humility, freedom from care, guilelessness, brotherly love, and the like." Speaking thus to himself, the venerable one did not rise from the ground until he saw the workers themselves get up and go to work. The blessed one did this because he did not wish to shame them by accusing them of laziness. For this reason I have also recounted this story, to show the self-reproach, meekness, freedom from care, and love of the venerable one for his neighbors, even before he became a monk.

The venerable one had a younger brother, completely unlettered but enlightened by God, zealous, brotherly-loving, a lover of stillness, God-loving, chaste, and more pure than anyone else. He wished to go to Rome to venerate the honorable relics of the holy apostles. The venerable one went with him. Both brothers went together barefoot, taking with them neither staff, nor bag, nor change of clothes. They ate in the evenings, and even then only bread and grass. On the way they decided not to greet other travelers but to keep stillness. From the severe labors of the journey, the venerable one fell ill and collapsed not far from a certain village, under a tree, waiting out the daytime heat and burning sun and having no other consolation besides God, on Whom he had cast all his hopes. His brother with tears asked him to agree to a visit from a physician who would take care of him, and begged him to eat something cooked, or to drink a little wine. But the thrice-blessed one would not agree to any of this, saying: "Brother, if you wish, anoint me with oil from the lampada before the icon of my Christ, for the Lord will not allow us to be tempted beyond what we are able to bear, as the divine Paul says" (1 Corinthians 10:13). Several days after he was anointed with the holy oil, the venerable one, by the grace of Christ, was strengthened, and they set out again on their way. Coming to Rome, they venerated the tombs of the holy apostles and, having brought great benefit to many through their conversations, returned again to their village. And there was near their village an ancient church, old and abandoned, consecrated in the name of our Savior Jesus Christ. Having received the monastic tonsure in it and been renamed from Michael to Matthew, the brother of the venerable one, with God's help and his own labors, transformed it into a monastery and gathered brethren there. The venerable one also came to this monastery to visit the brethren, and he arranged their manner of life and put in order the psalmody with prayer. Cyriacus himself had an open character, forced himself in everything, and had a conscience that did not accuse him, and he counseled the brethren to be the same. From the monastery he would return home, where he practiced stillness in his cell together with his wife and children, which was, to tell the truth, quite strange and alien to monks.

Once those regions were attacked by pagans who caused harm to Christians. Out of fear of them, everyone took refuge in the cities. So did the brother of the venerable one, who together with the monks of his monastery took refuge in the city of Derkos. But the blessed Cyriacus did not wish to go with everyone else, because he avoided the disturbance caused by the multitude of people. He went to a deserted place near the lake and, having built a small hut, remained there until God drove away those barbarians. From that time he no longer wished to return to his home but went to the previously mentioned Monastery of Christ the Savior, and there received monasticism and was given the name Cyril. The place where the venerable one wished to build himself a cell was overgrown with thorns, but among the bushes he saw a column. He asked what this column was, but the brethren answered that they saw nothing, and were greatly astonished. Since this happened two and three times, the venerable one understood that it was a sign from God. He gladly built himself a cell and, entering it, said: *"This is My rest forever; here I will dwell, for I have desired it"* (Psalm 131:14). In the beginning he chanted the hymns and prayed together with the brethren. Together with them the venerable one went to the refectory, but he ate nothing, reading the lives of the saints. After three years he began to come to the church only on Saturdays, Sundays, and the Master's feasts. Near the cell the venerable one fenced off a small place to grow vegetables, and except for the cell he stopped going anywhere, because he greatly loved stillness and solitude. Solitude is the mother of stillness, and stillness, in turn, is the mother of thoughts about God and contemplations, through which the mind is united with God.

For three years the venerable one remained in silence, speaking to no one except the monk who served him, for in his mind he conversed with God. The saint constantly reproached himself for his solitude, saying: "And now, whom should you serve, whose feet should you wash, whose inferior should you become? To whom should you show mercy, how should you exercise patience, when no one opposes your will? Woe to the one who falls into negligence, carelessness, or something else, because there will be no one to raise him up. For this reason, before you are condemned by the righteous judgment of God, condemn yourself and your thoughts at the tribunal of your heart, examining them as to which of them are your own and which are from enemies. Your own good thoughts, keep as a treasure in the depths of your heart, but the opposing ones strike with the rod of your mind and drive them from your heart, leaving them absolutely no place or refuge there. Better yet, cut them down with the sword of prayer and reflection on the Divine, so that the chief thief, the devil, may become afraid when he sees that his other accomplices, the thieves and crafty thoughts, have been put to death. Our judge is conscience, so do not neglect it, because when it does not accuse you, it teaches the knowledge of the Divine. But if you neglect it, then you will be filled with darkness." Thus the venerable one reflected in his cell, lamenting himself day and night.

The venerable Cyril also worked with his hands, weaving woolen kamilavkas (a headcovering of the priestly rank), some of which he sold, others he gave away, and still others he simply gave to the monastery for the brethren, so as not to be a burden to them. Sometimes he also worked in order to drive away negligence and carelessness, for negligence is born when the mind is scattered everywhere. The scattering of the mind comes from idleness of the hands, from vain conversations, from abandonment of reading, from overeating, and from great ascetic struggle and labors according to God. Patience shown in labors drives away negligence.

And if anyone wished to come to him for benefit, the venerable one would give him his handiwork and say that rest and idleness are perdition for the soul and can cause more harm than demons. To the monastic brethren he counseled, according to God's commandment, to receive with cheerfulness the strangers who came to them, not considering the disturbance they caused an obstacle to their stillness, so as not to violate the law of love. It is absolutely necessary to care for them as much as possible, and indeed in such a way as if we were receiving mercy from them and not ourselves showing it. However, one should not set out various dishes for guests or speak to them in elaborate words, but care for them with scantiness of food and words. If those prove wiser, the brethren should remain silent; if equal to them, they should speak in moderation. However, the best thing is to consider everyone greater than oneself. But those who wander from place to place should not be received at all, not out of hatred for them (God forbid!), for *"whoever hates his brother is a murderer"* (1 John 3:15), but in order to avoid harm from their presence. *"Evil company corrupts good habits"* (1 Corinthians 15:33). One should not be bold with them, since such ones harm not only themselves but also the simpler brethren. There are, however, those who travel for the Lord's sake or for some spiritual reason or for the desire of pilgrimage to the saints. He who receives such people receives Christ Himself, for *"inasmuch as you did it to one of the least of these My brethren, you did it to Me"* (Matthew 25:40).

Once the venerable one gave a certain merchant from Anchialos eleven kamilavkas so that he might sell them and bring him wheat. The merchant forgot about the request and did not sell them, but in sorrow brought them back, asking forgiveness. The venerable one told him that this happened not because of him, but Christ willed it: "For I saw in a dream a man in bright clothing, fearsome in appearance, who said to me: 'Abba, why did you give your kamilavkas not to me but to the merchant? If you had given them to me, I would have fed you without difficulty.' I asked him: 'Who are you, sir?' And he answered: 'I am called Elpidius.' Then I again said to him: 'I hope in God that if you will accept them, from now on I will give them to you and to no one else.'" From that time this became customary: all the kamilavkas he made, the venerable one would give to the poor, saying to himself: "Give in order to receive." But if he made a kamilavka and had no one to give it to, he would throw it over the wall of the monastery so that passers-by might take it, for the saint's desire to possess nothing was as great as the desire of others to possess.

Once he hung his clothing outside the cell and saw a certain poor man secretly take it. The venerable one hid so as not to put the brother to shame, saying to himself at the same time: "I should have given the clothing to some poor man myself for the sake of Him Who said: *'He who has two tunics, let him give to him who has none'* (Luke 3:11), but since I did not fulfill the commandment, God sent a poor man to help me fulfill another commandment: *'from him who takes away your goods do not ask them back'* (Luke 6:30). But even now I did not fulfill the commandment, because the clothing was not mine but belonged to that Christian who gave it to me." Such was the humility of the venerable one, for he always considered his own will erroneous and mistaken.

When the saint was still in the world, he would recite the Horologion that the monks on Mount Olympus read. When he came to the monastery, he diligently strove to learn the Psalter by heart. Having learned half by heart, he gave the book to a poor man who was asking for help. That night, having chanted half the Psalter and performed five hundred prostrations, as was his custom to do every night, the venerable one, pressed by the cord and suffering unbearable wounds because of this, lay down on his mat. However, he was sorrowful only because he had not managed to learn the whole Psalter. It seemed to him that he fell asleep and saw in a dream that someone in white garments appeared to him and said:

"Abba, why are you not singing?"

To this the venerable one answered:

"God knows that all the psalms and prayers that I knew, I have sung."

"Why are you not singing the Psalter?"

"I do not have a Psalter."

"Rise, let us sing the Psalter together."

And so they sang the whole Psalter twice. Then the one who appeared vanished. Whether that vision was in waking or in a dream, and who it was that taught the venerable one the Psalter, he could not say for certain, but from that time he knew the Psalter so well that he could explain many psalms to certain brethren.

When the venerable one received the monastic tonsure, his son was fourteen years old. Once he came to the monastery. Seeing him, the venerable one said:

"I am with God, I am a monk. If you too, child, wish to become a monk, good; but if not, then the next time you will not see me."

Then the son asked him:

"If I become a monk, will I see you?"

"Yes. And from that time you will be together with me and with Christ."

"But will I never see my mother and sister again?"

"You will see them at the gates of the monastery when they come to the monastery. But if you fulfill my word, you will be with Christ both in this life and after death, for He Himself said: *'Let the little children come to Me, and do not forbid them; for of such is the kingdom of heaven'* (Matthew 19:14)."

And then his son agreed to become a monk. That night the venerable one saw in a dream that a man in white garments with a shining face came to him and asked for the sacrifice that he was holding in his hands. And the venerable one gave it to him. Coming to himself, he understood what that dream meant and wished to test his son two and three times, to find out how attached he was to his relatives. His mother and sister called him to return home with them, but he would not go, saying: "I wish to be with my Christ and with my father, not with you." The venerable one left his son in the monastery for another forty days, and the boy, when the time elapsed, again did not wish to return to his mother. Only after this did the saint order that he be tonsured as a monk; the youth began together with the other brethren to eat dry food without oil on Mondays, Wednesdays, and Fridays, and he went nowhere outside the monastery. After eighteen months the youth, having been slightly ill, surrendered his blessed soul into the hands of God. The venerable one glorified the Creator that his son had departed to the Lord as a monk.

It once happened that the venerable one was conversing with a certain Armenian; with his God-wise words he tried to persuade him to renounce his heresy and unite with the Catholic and Apostolic Church. He said to him that "a person must have not only faith but also virtue, must avoid all evil, conquer the passions, and follow the commandments of Christ. For only such a one is a true person." Having thus strengthened him in the Orthodox faith and given him many instructions, the venerable one sent the convert away in peace. After some time, it so happened that the children of the Armenian together with his wife, by God's allowance, were sold into slavery. The Armenian, coming to the elder, told him of his misfortune. Taking pity on him, the venerable one asked certain Christ-loving people for money to ransom those who had been enslaved. Taking the money, the Armenian wished to return quickly to his homeland by land, but the venerable one advised him to sail by sea with acquaintances who were believing shipmen, so as not to fall on the way into the hands of robbers who would not only take the money but kill him as well. But the Armenian insisted that the voyage would take a long time since there was no favorable wind and hastened to return home by land. The venerable one did not wish to let him go, protecting him from the danger revealed to him by God's Providence, but the Armenian said:

"Pray for me, Father, and may the Lord's will be done."

"The Lord's will is His commandments. The will of the rational nature is to do God's will. The will of the flesh is the violation of God's law. The will of God is also called the will of His servants, from which you have deviated, and may I be innocent in this. If you wish, go, and God will arrange everything for the benefit of our souls. However, I know that every judgment and manifestation of one's own will in a person is unreliable."

Having gone down to the village, that Armenian happened to meet two soldiers who were about to travel the same route. On the way they began to question him as to who he was, where he was from, and why he was in such a hurry. And he told them the whole truth. Learning that he had money with him, the soldiers killed him and took the money for themselves. Such are the fruits of disobedience. And if someone should say that the venerable one uttered a prophecy, he would not be wrong at all.

At that time the Scythian tribe was attacking and ravaging the Thracian lands, and therefore all the inhabitants of those lands took refuge from danger in the cities. The venerable one, however, did not wish to take refuge in the city of Derkos because of the disturbance from the crowd and went to a monastery located by the Black Sea, where the brethren received him with joy, and especially the abbot, who was distinguished by a virtuous life. Many from near and far villages, and even the Constantinopolitan nobility, came to this abbot for the benefit of their souls. The abbot assigned the venerable one a cell where he could practice stillness. However, the fame of the venerable one spread everywhere, and those who came to the abbot also went to the venerable Cyril. After conversing with him, each one began to regard him with great reverence and love. But the all-evil devil aroused envy against the saint in the abbot (for there is no righteous man without sin, just as there is no sinner without some virtue). Unable to overcome this envy within himself, the abbot went to the saint and, as if concerned about the observance of God's commandments, said to him: "It seems to me, Father, that you do everything in your life for the sake of pleasing men. Why do you wear rags, go barefoot, eat dry food without oil, drink only water, refuse to eat cooked food, and are called a 'chain-bearer'? I do not know whether you wear chains, but your name is so famous that a multitude of ignorant monks consider you better than me, me who have labored for God for so many years. It is strange that you do not agree to eat with me, although I have invited you so many times, fulfilling the Lord's commandment. Do you not know that by your life you distinguish yourself from us, and this testifies to your haughtiness? Therefore accept my advice, become like all the brethren, because, as the fathers say, what is lofty is from demons. Keep to the middle way, seek neither what is above nor what is below, and then you will be delivered from your insensibility, which is born from not fearing God, from extreme inattention, and from sin. It is not I who say this, but the divine fathers. I ask you, come to yourself, in order to live a blessed life, because to know that you do not know is already knowledge. But if you wish to know God, first know yourself. He who considers himself nothing knows himself more than others. Do you not know that he who does not rebuke his brother's sin is cruel? For God says: *'You shall rebuke your neighbor with a rebuke, and so you shall not bear sin because of him.'* Rebuke is twofold: that which is with malice and revenge, and that which is with fear of God and truth. But I, God forbid, do not rebuke you with malice. Seeing how you exhaust your body and do not receive a reward from God, I pity you so much because of your obstinacy that I will pray to God to bring you to the knowledge of the truth. But you cannot come to the knowledge of the truth unless you abandon self-will and cease to trust yourself. Because whoever is firm in his own will is infected with pride, and *'God resists the proud'* (James 4:6). It is better to be called the disciple of a disciple than to live by your own will and reap its worthless fruits."

Having heard such words, the venerable one humbly threw himself at the feet of the abbot and said: "I thank God and your holiness that you have not only perceived the impurity of my soul but have also rebuked me in a fatherly way and instructed me as you should. For I have listened to your words as words of God, not of man. Besides, you said that you will pray to God to bring me to the knowledge of the truth. I ask you, fulfill this, according to the commandment of the Lord, Who will give you a hundredfold reward for your love, for He says that *'he who brings out the worthy from the unworthy shall be as My mouth.'* That is, he who turns a person from error to truth, and from sin to virtue, imitates Him. But you, Father, have fulfilled your whole duty, leaving me without answer." Seeing that the venerable one was not troubled by his instruction but with self-reproach and humility fell before him, asking his prayers in order to come to the knowledge of the truth, the abbot was moved to compunction and fell silent. Praising the God-given patience of the venerable one, he returned to his cell, accusing himself and saying: "Woe to me, hypocrite, having a beam in my own eyes, I instruct the servant of God in small things and judge him, being myself condemned! I do not reflect that he who judges and severely investigates the actions of others will not receive forgiveness for his own transgressions, because God will judge us by the same judgment with which we judge others. Woe to me, insensible one!" Having reflected on all that had happened, the abbot went to the venerable one and bowed to him, asking his forgiveness. The venerable one also said to himself: "To be condemned by many wicked people is an injustice that brings no harm, but to be condemned by a righteous man is a truth that brings benefit. Woe to you, that the darkness of deeds darkens the hearts of saints." Praying to God, the venerable one said: "My God, do not forsake me. I have done no good before Thee, but grant me, by Thy goodness, to make a beginning, because my salvation rests upon Thy mercy and love for mankind, for Thine is the glory unto the ages of ages. Amen."

That night the venerable one saw in a dream that he was standing on a high tower, and beneath him stretched a plain without end or boundary, and an enormous dragon was attacking him, with hissing and open mouth, wishing to devour him. Not knowing what to do, the venerable one looked around and saw a stick under his feet. He took it and struck the dragon. Immediately it fell and died. As it fell, the dragon split in two, and from it came such a stench that, unable to bear it, the venerable one came to himself. Reflecting, he understood that the dragon was the demon of pride, the stick was humility, and since he had endured the abbot and bore his rebuke with self-reproach, he had been delivered from the dragon's jaws by the commandment of Christ. The venerable one glorified God, because if he had contradicted the abbot, he would have been swallowed up by pride. From that time, all the time that the venerable one spent in the monastery, he would fall at the abbot's feet with great humility and, as much as possible, watched himself so as not to give cause for scandal. After some time, having made a prostration before the abbot, he left the monastery. Returning to his cell, the venerable Cyril continued to practice stillness, struggling in ascetic labors of prayer, so that his conscience would not accuse him, for the ascetic labors of fasting, vigil, and patience cleanse it.

Near the cell of the venerable one there was a spring with slightly warm and murky water, which was not very good to taste, yet he drank precisely this water. Many came to the spring for water, and once the venerable one made the sign of the Cross over the spring and prayed, and all who drank that water began to be healed of various diseases. "This water, or rather this holy thing and Divine gift, I once tasted," says the author of the life, "because from an attack that befell me I could neither eat nor speak for seven days because of severe stomach pains. On the seventh day I sent to the venerable one to tell him of my illness and asked him to send me some water as a blessing from him. Toward the end of the day they brought me the water, and as soon as I drank it, at that very hour, God is my witness, I was delivered from my illness."

At another time, when I was together with the venerable one in his cell, a certain monk came, his friend, and recounted: "Abba, when I was in my cell sorrowing over the multitude of my sins and my lack of repentance, suddenly and unexpectedly, without effort, weeping and unceasing tears were given to me, so that for two days I did not remember bread, but with a burning heart, with sweetness and ineffable delight, with sorrow and joy I grieved bitterly over my sins. Sometimes I confessed to God, sometimes I entreated Him, thanked or glorified Him. Being in such a state and constantly thinking about my sins, I turned to my Guardian Angel: 'Most holy Angel, I adjure you by God our Creator and beseech you, protect me, for you see what danger threatens me. I have lived my life in vanity, and you, perhaps, guard me in vain.' Thus I said three times, and from weariness I sat down; my mind was at that time in deep stillness, peace, and remembrance of God. Therefore I cannot say exactly whether I was caught up in sleep or not, but suddenly I saw a delicate hand, white as snow, which struck me on the right cheek, not strongly but not weakly either. The fragrance of that hand remained on my face for seven days, and during those seven days I did not wish to partake of any bodily food. I ask you, abba, tell me how to understand what happened to me—is this from God or from demons?"

Having listened attentively to the account, the venerable Cyril answered him thus: "Usually a good and child-loving father, having two children—a mature, courageous, and father-loving man and a lisping infant—if he is compelled to go away, entrusts the younger brother to the care of the elder, so that he may protect the little one from any danger until his return. And the elder brother, out of respect and love for the father, out of his own good intention, and out of love for his brother, guards him with all his strength. But the younger brother runs everywhere, stumbles, and cuts his feet until they bleed. However, the elder one tries to protect him from falls and watches that no beasts attack him. Not wishing to bind his brother's will, he only gives advice, allowing him to walk according to his own will, hoping that with age he will become sensible. But the younger brother, not realizing his own ignorance and not recognizing the wisdom and knowledge of the elder brother by which he tries to keep him unharmed, or his love for him, says: 'I adjure you by the father who begot us, guard me well, because you see what dangers threaten me,' and shows him the few wounds he has. But the good brother, who has honestly guarded him, loving him and wishing to bring him to his senses, strikes him on the cheek and says: 'Adjure yourself and command yourself not to walk in steep places, and I am innocent of this.' The same story happened to you, brother, and the hand that appeared to you was not demonic. This is clear from the fact that it was whiter than snow and fragrant, and that you changed and did not wish to eat for seven days. Changes that occur by demonic action do not bring peace to the spiritual and bodily senses, nor can they produce supernatural feelings." Such was the discernment according to God that the divine Cyril possessed, that he could instruct even the weak in virtue.

Once, when the venerable one was praying, he perceived a fragrance as if from burning incense. Reflecting on this fragrance, he suddenly heard someone singing with a pleasant and tender voice: *"When I pass through the place of the wondrous tabernacle, even to the house of God, with the voice of joy and thanksgiving, the sound of those who keep the feast"* (Psalm 41:5). He immediately struck the semantron, because he was accustomed, when he called, to use a wooden semantron instead of his voice, and his disciple came, whom the venerable one asked: "How is our sick brother? It seems to me he has departed to the Lord, because I heard such a voice. Go quickly and see." The disciple went and found that the brother had reposed at precisely that hour. At this news, the venerable one said: *"Lord, now You are letting Your servant depart in peace, according to Your word; for my eyes have seen Your salvation"* (Luke 2:29–30); *"O Lord, how manifold are Your works! In wisdom You have made them all"* (Psalm 103:24). This brother who had fallen asleep in the Lord had come to the monastery three years before and with meekness and unfeigned humility had served the brethren, obeying the venerable one in everything. Once the relatives of this brother came to him in the monastery to consult on a certain worldly matter, but that blessed one answered them: "I cannot simultaneously be a dead man and manage the living." Truly, he who does not act according to his own will is dead to everything worldly, and his soul, freed from attachment to the world, cries out together with David: *"You have put off my sackcloth and clothed me with gladness"* (Psalm 29:12). Such was the divine Cyril, for he could in a short time make spiritual people out of carnal ones, as happened with this brother.

At another time, when the venerable one was sitting on his mat, he heard a voice: *"If riches increase, do not set your heart on them"* (Psalm 61:10). Reflecting in the morning on these words, he saw Constantine, a butcher, coming to him, who had great reverence for the venerable one. After a greeting, they talked a little about the salvation of the soul, and he said to the venerable one:

"My lands, which are near the monastery, I give over to your holiness together with all the animals. Let everything belong to the monastery. If you yourself do not wish to possess them, sell them and distribute the money to the poor for the salvation of my wretched soul."

The venerable one answered him thus:

"We have promised God to be free not only from our possessions but from our very bodies, in order to acquire purity of soul. Therefore we must not accept another's property and bind ourselves with heavy material bonds, because those immaterial ones who hunt us are swifter than eagles. If we burden ourselves with worldly things, we will move more slowly, and consequently the enemy will easily catch us."

Having heard these and other divinely-wise words, the Christ-loving Constantine marveled and glorified God, Who protects and grants wisdom to His servants, after which he said to the venerable one: "And truly you have no need of my riches, because he who has acquired true wealth hates and turns away from these false and deceptive goods." Having asked for a blessing, he departed.

When the pious Emperor Alexius Comnenus went to war against the proud Latin Bohemund, some said that the emperor would be victorious, while others said Bohemund would win. The author of the Life, who was with the saint all this time, asked him: "Who truly deserves to be victorious in this war?" The venerable one answered: "Only God knows who is worthy and what is true, but what I saw several days ago, I do not know whether it was from God or from demons, yet now I shall relate it to you. As soon as I, unworthy one, completed my nightly doxology, following my custom of commemorating the emperor in prayer, I began to beseech God for him with tears (for who would not pray for such a Christ-loving man?). I said the Trisagion, the subsequent prayers, then aloud I said: *The king shall have joy in Your strength, O Lord; and in Your salvation how greatly shall he rejoice!* (Psalm 20:1) and, while meditating, I sat down on my mat. Soon I fell asleep, and I saw that in my dream I was walking across a bright plain. Looking around, on my right I saw the imperial tent, which had the appearance of a church. Around the tent stood a great multitude of soldiers, and inside, upon a high throne, sat the emperor himself. On his left side was an immense sea, and in it floated many small ships. The sea was breaking them apart and casting them onto the shore. There was also a huge black dog with bloody eyes, looking toward the emperor. A certain radiant warrior held it on a chain. Shortly afterward, he forcibly dragged it and threw it at the emperor's feet. I think the emperor will conquer Bohemund." And so, with God's help, it actually came to pass.

Once a monk from a coenobitic monastery came to the venerable one and said: "Abba, what should I do about my sins, how can I be healed, how can I be delivered from evil, and what must I do to become worthy of God?" And the venerable one answered him: "My lord (for so he was accustomed to address everyone), you must pass through evil days and nights, and even after this, I do not know whether your ship will reach the harbor of salvation. If you seek a remedy, attend to your conscience and do what it counsels you, and then you will find profit. Know that wickedness or passion is not inherent to human nature, because the Lord created in us not passions, but a multitude of virtues, among which are the following: mercy, for even the Hellenes show mercy and love, just as irrational animals often weep when separated from one another; faith, since by our words we inspire trust and believe in the words we hear; hope, because when we lend, or travel, or sow, we hope that we shall receive. Thus, love for us is a natural virtue, *love is the fulfillment of the law* (Romans 13:10). Virtues are inherent to our nature, so let those who say they have no strength to practice virtues be ashamed. Besides these natural virtues, there are also virginity, freedom from anger, humble-mindedness, prayer, vigil, fasting, and constant compunction of heart. But you, if you wish to be delivered from evil, fight against your enemies to cut off the passions, and then strive to acquire the virtues and preserve them. This is the meaning of the saying: *'Blessed is he who watches and keeps his garments'* (Revelation 16:15). And if you wish to become worthy of God, do nothing unworthy of Him."

Having heard these and many other instructions from the venerable one, but not coming to his senses, the brother after some time left the coenobium, because he did not want to submit and cut off his own will. He came to the desert and settled in a small prayer house, as if for work according to God. After yet more time, he befriended robbers and, becoming their leader, committed murder. This is exactly how demons repay those who do their own will.

Once, when I happened to be with the venerable one, some irritation arose between the abbot and the brethren, so that everyone began to shout loudly. Summoning them, the venerable one said to the abbot: "Is this how you teach your children? A father is called a father because he protects his children. But he who does the opposite should be called something else. If you acquire all virtues but neglect the souls of those given to you by God, your virtues will bring you no profit, but you will be condemned for the negligence with which you treat the brethren. Do not be harsh in your threats, because neither severe rebuke nor complete lack of punishment brings profit. Do not be quick to reprove and do not do so with passion, for this is shamelessness. Do not judge the brethren severely in small transgressions, but correct those who sin in a fatherly manner, as the Apostle says: *'Brethren, if a man is overtaken in any trespass, you who are spiritual restore such a one in a spirit of gentleness, considering yourself lest you also be tempted'* (Galatians 6:1). Compel the disorderly not to violate proper order and established rules." The abbot answered:

"I am a sinner, *'But to the sinner God says: "What right have you to declare My statutes, or take My covenant in your mouth?"'* (Psalm 49:16) For this reason God gave us you, so that you might guide us, because if it were not for you, I would certainly not have been able to establish this small monastery. According to the will of God and your holiness, lead us, because you know that we listen to your words."

"Brother, you have said that you are a sinner, yet in your deeds you do not consider yourself such. He who considers himself a sinner and guilty of sins does not argue with anyone, does not fight, is not angry at anyone, but regards all as better and wiser than himself. But if thoughts mock you, how can you consider yourself a sinner? How can they move your heart against those who are better than you? Attend to yourself, brother, for what you say is not true. We have not yet attained the measure of considering ourselves sinners. If you were a sinner, how would you accuse your brother? You say that because of him you have sorrow, but do you not know that each person is tempted by his own conscience, and it is precisely this that causes sorrow? Leave aside your justifications, and if you do say something, do not say: 'I said well.' If you think of something, do not say: 'How well I thought.' Well is well, but where is this well? One must think about not saddening anyone by word or deed, and God will help us in this. As our brethren who serve for the sake of God, so we too must *'bear one another's burdens,'* in order to *'fulfill the law of Christ'* (Galatians 6:2). When someone is troubled, grieves, and is angry at his brother for a supposedly good and soul-profiting reason, it is already clear that this is not from God. Everything that is from God brings peace and leads a person to humility and self-condemnation, not to condemnation of his brother by arousing anger against him."

These and many other things the venerable one said to the abbot, and then he turned to the brethren and said: "A monk who has obedience imitates Jesus Christ, and he who submits imitates the Angels. But he who contradicts and resists makes himself foreign to Jesus and becomes a friend of the devil. I ask you, my children, acquire unquestioning obedience, for obedience is the mother of eternal life, just as disobedience is the mother of perdition. Let none of you be a babbler, or a gossip, or a slanderer, or a reviler, or a murmurer, because all this and the like are fruits of the devil. If you wish to please God, you must cut off all self-will and submit to the superior placed over you by God as to Christ Himself. And let there be no Judas among you, but be like the apostles who submitted to Christ. Those who resist will bring upon themselves great condemnation. Do not judge one another, and even more so your spiritual father, because he who judges will go to perdition. Love the elder as your father, but also fear him as one who has authority over you. You should neither treat him carelessly because of great love, nor fear him to the point that from great fear you do not love him. He who is a true disciple loves his elder and obeys him unto death, is edified by everything he does, not daring to reason about what he does, not asking questions about why and wherefore. If you ask in this way, then you are not disciples, but judges of your elder. All evil comes from accursed self-will. Do not be deceived, brethren, doing your own will, for self-will never leads to good. But when you leave your will to God, then God acts as He wills." With these and other counsels to the abbot and brethren, the venerable one, with God's help, brought them to agreement and reconciled them.

Another time, when I was conversing with the venerable one, a certain brother from a coenobitic monastery came to him and said:

"Father, I have heard from a physician that figs are beneficial to eat in the morning, and therefore I eat them."

"Woe to that physician who moved you to this, and you will hardly receive profit. If you do not conquer your belly, brother, then why do you *'occupy the ground'* (Luke 13:7) and weaken the ascetics? Have you not heard what Saint Basil the Great commands monks: of the twenty-four hours in a day, they should spend one hour on food, and occupy themselves with noetic work the rest of the time. For what you give to the body, you immediately lose, but what you give to the soul, you will have forever. Therefore, without bodily necessity, do not eat or drink, and let this commandment not seem heavy to you, for in truth it is not so. Leave your own will and do the will of your superior. Cut off attachment and bind yourself to the love of God, the true Physician of souls and bodies. He who follows his own physician will not only be enslaved by gluttony and eat like a pig, from morning to morning, but together with gluttony will fall into all impure passions."

Then, since it was Friday, the venerable one asked the monk:

"And what did you eat today?"

"Today we ate 'holy' broth."

"And what is this 'holy' broth?"

"Onions and other vegetables with aromatics are put in water, and this is called 'holy' broth."

Then, groaning, the venerable one said:

"Woe, brother, you have not noticed that this is not simply 'holy' broth, but 'holy' broth for gluttons. Have you not heard the story from the Paterikon? A certain elder came to a brother and saw that he was eating. When the eating brother saw the elder, he hid behind the door what he was eating. When the elder asked what he was eating, the brother answered: 'Forgive me, father, I was cutting dates, and from the heat my throat became dry. Therefore I put a little salt in water and moistened the bread, for I could not eat it dry.' Hearing this, the elder cried out: 'Come and see Isaiah, who eats broth!' And to the brother he said: 'If you want to eat broth, go to Egypt.' You see, brother, what 'holy' broth that monk ate, and even that with shame. I think that brother was a novice. But woe to us, gluttons and pleasure-lovers, yet we think we have preserved the way of life of the ancient fathers. I ask you, brother, if you cannot discontinue this custom, then at least do not call this broth 'holy,' because thereby you reproach the saints. But if we reproach ourselves, we do not feel it. An abundance of foods gives birth to a multitude of thoughts and impure dreams."

Such were the words of the venerable one, and it is not surprising that he spoke thus, for he himself for more than fifty years did not taste food cooked on fire, nor grapes, nor any other fruits, nor did he drink wine, and only sometimes ate quince. I asked him: "Abba, why do you not allow yourself to taste food with oil even on the Lord's feasts?" He answered me: "I am weak, and if I allow myself, I will no longer be able to restrain myself. Those who can loose and bind themselves are free from the passions and from servitude to the belly." Thus spoke the venerable one with humble-mindedness.

He also said: "Satiation with bread and water arouses in a person the desire for various foods. He to whom bread tastes sweet and who drinks water with restraint will never desire various foods and drinks, for from hunger and thirst, taste is forgotten. But I am troubled not so much by hunger as by thirst." The venerable one not only experienced hunger and thirst, but he did not wash his feet or face, nor did he have two garments, even when he was in the world. On his feet he wore only shoes, and that only in winter. He slept leaning on his right side, and sometimes dozed a little where he sat. Instead of a mattress he had a thin mat and a soft bearskin. When the venerable one went to sleep, he would say: "My God, do not forsake me, but deliver me from this mortal body." And he repeated the instructions of Basil the Great: "You sleep, yet time outpaces you; you are awake, yet your mind wanders in vanity; life is shortened, though you do not understand this. Of course, what we lack most is time, because our life is short, and the art of salvation must be studied long and much, while the end of our life is near. Be watchful then, O careless one, do not lie down to sleep before you have examined what you have done during the day: which commandments of God you have transgressed, what deeds pleasing to God you have done, and which you have not performed as you ought. If you have acted badly, then grieve and torment yourself with sighing, tears, and bitter repentance. But if you have acted well, then rejoice and thank God, Who helped you. If you wish to flee evil, you must first hate all that is in the world, because it is impossible to love the world and at the same time not participate in the evil that comes from worldly things."

He also spoke these beautiful words every day: "I beseech you, my feet, do not run to evil, but until the time when you can no longer stand and move, and before you are bound and become immobile, stand with zeal in prayer to God. You, my hands, do not be filled with blood and iniquities, but stretch out to God in holiness and righteousness, because the hour will come when you will be immobile, bound one with the other. You, my eyes, do not look upon evil, but before your eyelids close, look upon the works of God to His glory. You, my ears, do not listen to what is vain, but only to all that is salvific and profitable. You, my mouth, do not utter what is wicked and venomous, but *meditate on His law day and night,* that the grace of God may be poured out upon you, and you may rejoice when you sing to God. You, my tongue, do not become a sharp knife, but become *the pen of a ready writer,* meditating on the righteousness of God. And you, my body, before we are separated and depart from one another, for I shall go to Hades, and you shall crumble into dust and stench, stand manfully and worship God. Before others carry you, who are dead, carry me, that I may glorify God and confess to Him. If, as though desiring to lie down, to rest on a bed and sleep, you have not condemned me to eternal torment, for the time will come when the present sweet sleep will be turned into eternal bitterness. If you, my body, will listen to what I tell you, then we shall inherit eternal life together. But if not, then why have you been joined to me? Woe to me, because my soul has been joined to you for so long. Woe to me, for because of you my wretched soul will be condemned! If you will listen to me, you will become a temple of God, and God will give us greater knowledge and lead us into all truth. But if you do not listen to me and do not submit to me, I tell you truly, then know that I shall not cease to war against you and shall subject you to torments by all means until, with God's help, I mortify your death-dealing deeds and by pain raise myself from the passions. Although God will resurrect us at the time of His second coming, yet He requires of us also another resurrection, a new way of life in the present life, which can be attained by a change of our behavior and character. When a negligent and drowsy person becomes zealous and vigilant, and from a doer of lawlessness and evil becomes a doer of righteousness and virtue, then he already here rises and receives the resurrection, which will serve as a threshold to eternal resurrection. And how can this resurrection occur? Through the mortification of sin and the resurrection of virtue, when the old life is destroyed and a new, angelic life begins.

But you, body, cannot keep vigil all night singing psalms. Keep vigil, singing troparia, making prostrations, saying prayers. Keep vigil, grieving and weeping over your sins. Keep vigil, glorifying God and spending time reading the Holy Scriptures. If you cannot keep vigil all night, keep vigil half the night, only do not become lax and darken me with long sleep, do not fatten my mind: *'Consider and hear me, O Lord my God; enlighten my eyes, lest I sleep the sleep of death'* (Psalm 12:3-4), that I too may boldly say like David: *'I lay down and slept; I awoke, for the Lord will help me'* (Psalm 3:5); *'The helpless commits himself to You; You are the helper of the fatherless'* (Psalm 9:35); I will sing and greatly glorify Your most holy name, now and unto the ages of ages. Amen." Then he would say to sleep:

"Come, evil slave of a slave."

Having snatched a little sleep, the venerable one immediately arose and glorified the much-hymned name of the Father and of the Son and of the Holy Spirit. He also said to me:

"Since I became a monk, I do not remember spending even one day without psalmody, prayer, handiwork, and tears, which are a gift of God."

To this I asked:

"Can you have them whenever you wish?"

"Yes, but know that tears are evoked by zeal, desire, mortification of the body, and pure, undistracted noetic meditation. Tears purify the soul from the passions. It is now eighteen years since God gave them to me, according to the saying: *'My tears have been my bread day and night'* (Psalm 41:3), because after the completion of Compline, the Midnight Office, and Matins, I weep. During the day, with God's help, I weep as much as I wish."

"Forgive me, father, but what do you remember when you weep?"

"Sometimes I remember my sins, sometimes the sorrows of the poor and orphans, sometimes the Passion of Christ, and very often I remember the sorrows endured by irrational animals, because they too have an irrational soul and therefore feel pain. Do you not know that the more the heart of one who grieves and weeps is warmed by tears, the more it is purified from the passions and enlightened? Then such a person begins to pity and grieve for all rational and irrational creatures, and even plants. But how can one convey in words the sweetness of honey to one who has not tasted it? There are servile tears and at the same time tears of gratitude arising from fear of wounds and torments, there are tears from love, and there are tears from demonic activity. And these latter I call not tears of gratitude, but only servile tears, may the Lord abolish them. First come tears from fear, as the fathers say. They warm the heart, sometimes moderately, and sometimes excessively, and dry out the body. If a person preserves a good disposition (which is life according to reason and knowledge, for it is precisely this that generates and preserves a sorrowful state), and will strive intensely in hesychia and labor according to God, then, whether he has these tears or not, the door of the mysteries of His love is opened to him by God. That which is from God will come to him of itself; such a person will not need to think about this beforehand, if his heart is pure.

From love proceed supplicatory and consoling tears: *'Blessed are those who mourn, for they shall be comforted'* (Matthew 5:4). Consolation is the grace of God, which comes to the hearts of those who weep from the divine illumination of the Holy Spirit. The face of such a person becomes inflamed with joy, as if from intoxication (so once someone thought that I, a wretch, was drunk), because together with the heart, the body also becomes inflamed. Such a person then no longer has fear, but love. *'There is no fear in love; but perfect love casts out fear'* (1 John 4:18)."

"And how can one know whether one has attained this love?"

"When a person remembers God, his heart is immediately penetrated with love for Him, and tears flow abundantly from his eyes (for in love it is natural to shed tears from remembrance of the beloved). He who loves God always has tears, because he has the reason that makes him constantly remember God, so that even in sleep he converses with Him (for he who loves also acts thus with the beloved: he desires to kiss him with a holy kiss and is ready to sacrifice even his very life for his friend). He desires to remain in solitude in order to converse alone with God, and then a power rises in him that gathers his mind and brings him as if into ecstasy. And although a person contemplates heavenly things, the sweet contemplation and the frequent exercise of that ineffable conversation are not interrupted in him. But his outward senses remain outside this world, because he is intoxicated with divine love and considers even the most terrible death as nothing. *'Oh, taste and see that the Lord is good; blessed is the man who trusts in Him!'* (Psalm 33:8) It says: 'taste,' not 'be satiated,' because now we see truth only in part, as if reflected in a mirror, *'in a riddle'* (1 Corinthians 13:12), but the time will come when the present betrothal and taste of grace will be transformed into the perfection of delight. These are the fruits of hesychia according to God and of frequent abstention of the belly from bread and water, and also many conscious sorrows, in which patience is strengthened. Patience, in turn, is strengthened by unfeigned self-reproach, and from self-reproach, as from a spring, flow tears according to God, which whiten us more than snow. It is precisely those who are whitened in this way who have entered into the Sabbath and into rest, for the true rest for Christians is freedom from sinful passions and the fullest and most active indwelling of the Holy Spirit in a pure heart, and therefore the Apostle says: *'Let us therefore be diligent to enter that rest'* (Hebrews 4:11). Many have found this grace of weeping and tears, and then lost it, because they acquired boldness in their hearts, drew near to the world before the proper time, and were conquered by its flattery and pleasures, suffering justly. Everything acquired without labor is not valued, and therefore remains in reproach, whether it be an active or contemplative gift, for such a person thinks he will easily acquire it again. But his mind does not watch over the senses, and therefore through them he falls into sins."

I asked the venerable one again:

"Abba, why did you not speak about tears that come from demonic activity?"

"Is there a need to speak of what is useless? But if you wish to know, I will tell you all that I know. These tears occur differently in worldly people than in monks. When people are deprived of something from the goods of this world, they lament and weep because of the love they have for them, and sometimes they weep from intoxication. Monks who pride themselves on their virtues (though in reality they are nothing), and unreasonably justify themselves, exalt themselves over negligent monks because they supposedly have zeal according to knowledge, and sometimes they even reprove and forbid the saints, weeping and grieving over them, though they themselves are worthy of many tears. Very often they weep over their own sins, but do not feel them, because if they felt that their sins are heavier than a kantarion (about 57 kilograms) of lead, then they would not weep over the sins of others. Such people think they have Divine love. But when the devil inflates them with conceit and pride, bringing them to compunction in order to kill them, and multiplying their tears, they are ready to weep while unceasingly fulfilling their rule, which in no way hinders the demon, but assists him until he casts them into some transgression. Happy is he who is not conquered by such tears, but has been deemed worthy to delight in servile tears of gratitude, and in those that come from love."

Another time I came again to the venerable one and found him greatly afflicted and weeping. When I asked what had happened to him, he answered:

"Demons have burned my heart, and I have burned them with the help of my body. I had almost burned the sinews that hold my members together and begun to crawl on the ground like a serpent, as befits me, had not God protected me."

"For the Lord's sake, tell me the cause of all this."

"You know that I have a disciple who is a priest and receives confessions. Once he related to me, without naming names, the thoughts of certain pleasure-lovers, and I immediately understood, and my heart together with my body took pleasure in them. Therefore I was grieved and, becoming angry with myself, took coals and placed them on my shameful members. As the wise Nilus says, 'A spiritual father who desires to cleanse the deeds of those who confess to him necessarily receives from them a certain defilement. He who converses about carnal passions and cleanses others from defilement cannot himself remain undefiled, for naturally, even the remembrance defiles his mind.'"

With these words he bared his members, and I saw a terrible sight, because the first wound he had made was so large that a hand could fit into it, and the other wound was smaller, since from the intense pain he had fainted.

Seeing this, I asked:

"Is it possible that God rejoices in this?"

"Of course He rejoices, because, according to Gregory the Theologian, a person can serve God by nothing else as much as by suffering, and can repay Him for His loving-kindness with tears. Martyrs are not only those who accepted death for the faith of Christ, but also those who died fulfilling the commandments of Christ. We must treat sorrowful thoughts without resentment and enmity, but resist and war against pleasure-loving ones. But no one can conquer if he is afraid, just as a soldier, if he fears death, cannot perform a feat. As Saint Isaac says: a small sorrow for God's sake is better than a great deed without sorrow, because by voluntary sorrow our faith and love are tested. And I believe, for this is the truth, that the martyrs of their own will gave themselves over to being scraped, burned, and to sufferings for the love of Christ, than which there is nothing stronger in this world. And Christ Himself voluntarily suffered for us, so we too must suffer for ourselves, lest we be deprived of His love, as the Apostle says: *'If we endure, we shall also reign with Him'* (2 Timothy 2:12)."

Hearing this, I said:

"Woe to us who love the flesh! For because of love for the body we become enemies of God."

Smiling, the venerable one said:

"When the demon caused me to take a little pleasure, he laughed at me for a long time and appeared in the form of a fattened pig. But now the accursed one has been put to shame and sighs bitterly, being burned more than I. At the same time, he again frightens me, gnashing his teeth like a dried-out and weak boar. But now I laugh at him and rejoice and say that my Christ has angered you now, and again may His will be done."

"You speak well, father, that you laugh at him and rejoice, because he who conquers the passions that attack him in fury, rejoicing in victory, forgets his pain from joy."

Another time, when I again came to the divine Cyril, I saw him leaning on his elbow and gathering grass. Having gathered an armful, he knocked with his staff and a disciple came, to whom the venerable one said:

"My lord, take this grass and give it to some animal" (the venerable one was accustomed to do this sometimes).

"I am amazed that you have mercy on irrational animals, but are unmerciful to yourself. Do you not experience bodily suffering?"

"Act thus, and you will be called righteous, as the Holy Scripture says: 'Blessed is he who has mercy even on beasts.'"

Once there was a severe famine, from which many people perished. And the venerable one gave half the bread he received from the monastery sometimes to an orphan, sometimes to someone else, and thus saved many from hunger and death, saying:

"If you have only one loaf of bread and a poor man comes to you asking for alms, take that bread in your hands and, looking up at heaven, say: 'Lord, You see that I have only one loaf of bread and I am perishing from hunger, but I consider fulfilling Your commandment more important than preserving my life. Therefore, as I give this bread to my hungry brother, so give You to me. I know Your goodness and trust in Your power, for You do not delay in Your grace, but generously distribute Your gifts.' If you act thus with the bread that you give from your poverty, it will become for you like a seed producing abundant fruits."

Many of the orphans considered the venerable one their provider, and one of them told me that once, when they came to him for alms, they found him weeping and striking his face with his hands, while the venerable one kept saying: "Woe to me, woe! I, who am an enemy of God, eat every day, while the children of God eat once every two days." After this account, I said: "Saint Isaac says: 'Consider that person a man of God who, from great mercy toward others, gives them what is necessary for his own survival, and by his own choice mortifies himself, giving greater preference to his brother's need than to his own. Such a one has Christ, Who cares for him.' He who has become poor for Christ's sake finds for himself an inexhaustible treasure. Although God has no need of anyone, He rejoices when anyone gives rest to His image, the human being, and honors him for His sake. To Him be glory unto the ages."

The venerable one had a custom, whenever he wished to partake of food, to address a greeting to the Most Holy Theotokos and the Precious Cross with these words: "Rejoice, O Cross of my Christ, scepter of the King of kings. Rejoice, O Cross that has sanctified the ends of the universe. Rejoice, O Cross, more honorable than the Seraphim and Cherubim, because it was not upon them that my Lord was stretched out naked during His Passion, but upon you. Rejoice, rejoice, rejoice, because he who takes you upon his shoulders and with a sincere heart believes in your power shall not walk in darkness, but shall have the light of life." And to the Theotokos he spoke thus: "Rejoice, my praise, my hope, my refuge, my strength, my strong tower that protects against enemies, *'I will abide in Your tabernacle forever,'* for with You *'the poor is not forgotten forever'* (Psalm 9:19), and You are my song always! How fearful You are to enemies, O my mighty help, fill my mouth with Your praise, that I may sing Your glory in all the few days of my life, for most glorified is Your most holy name, with the Father, the Son, and the Holy Spirit."

Speaking these words, he would leave his food and continue to greet and glorify the Theotokos. And if his heart was warmed still more, he would immediately rise, make many prostrations, and praise God at length. Sometimes he cried out for a long time, because he could no longer restrain himself, glorifying the most holy name of God, for the Spirit of God dwelling in him did not allow him to be silent. When the venerable one finished his doxology, he sometimes sat down and ate his bread, and sometimes forgot about food from the sound of his sighing and was satisfied with spiritual food alone. And his face at that moment was like the face of an Angel. The venerable one avoided acquaintance with people, especially with rulers and princes. As great as he was, so much did he humble himself, yet God, Who gives grace to the humble, so glorified him that He brought even emperors to him

The pious Emperor Alexius, who loved monks, once came to a certain monk who was a close friend of the venerable one. In conversation with the emperor, the monk happened to recall the words of the venerable one, and then the emperor asked:

"And who is this Abba Cyril of whom you speak, and why do I not know him?"

The monk answered:

"Who am I, a foolish one, to speak to you about him. Eyes are more reliable than ears. As for me, I believe, and God is my witness, that Cyril is a true servant of His."

Having listened to the monk, the emperor rejoiced greatly and immediately sent to the venerable one his brother-in-law Michael Augustus, who was also distinguished by love for monks and was God-fearing. Michael came to the monastery where the venerable one was laboring late in the evening. At his knock, the gatekeeper opened the doors and immediately, taking him by the hand, led him along so that none of the brethren would hear that a dignitary had come and be troubled. Coming to the cell of the saint, Michael knocked on the door and said:

"Father, give a blessing."

"May God not bless you."

He knocked again and said:

"Father, give a blessing."

"I told you, may God not bless you."

Then Michael knocked a third time:

"Father, open."

"May it never be that you should be my son, accursed one. Go to your father, satan."

"Abba, I am a man, not a demon, and I have come to you for a blessing."

"I know well who you are, and I marvel at your shamelessness, for despite my curses, you continue to bark."

"Lord Jesus Christ, Son of God, have mercy on us. Abba, I am Michael Augustus."

Hearing these words, Cyril immediately rose and opened the door. Having said a prayer, the venerable one said:

"If you are a man, make the sign of the cross and say a prayer."

When he had done everything, the saint greeted him and, after they sat down, asked:

"Who are you and why have you come here to a sinful man who has no spiritual work whatsoever, but acts according to his own will, which is foreign to God?"

"If only I, abba, could have the same work as you and a will 'foreign' to God, and were not of noble birth and did not have power, ranks, and other vanities of this world."

"I am unworthy of heaven and earth, but may the Lord give you according to your heart, and according to your faith be it unto you. If you wish to be saved, always concern yourself with eternal glory, because the glory of this world is false and has led many astray. Since you are a man, remember the common misfortune of all people, that there is nothing reliable in the human race, no one lives the life he wants, and strive always to remember your end. Truly noble is he who despises pleasure, wealth, glory, life, and loves the opposite of these: pain, poverty, dishonor, and death. Truly rich is he who has many friends: the holy Angels and all the saints, and truly poor is he who abandons his friend, his Guardian Angel. The greatest rank is not the one in which you have many honors, but to be worthy of honors. And a ruler and governor is he who rules over himself and subjects his soul and body to reason. But if some passion gains mastery over a ruler, he cannot render just judgment. Know also that he who is worse than his subjects should not rule over others. And you, if you wish to be a friend of God, do not be overcome by gifts, friendship, enmity, or anything else when you render judgment, which is the judgment of God, but judge rightly and according to the laws. Therefore David says that *'Your friends are exceedingly honored, O God'* (Psalm 138:17). The pious man is not he who shows mercy to many, but he who offends no one, and he who does not punish the wicked is unjust to the good. Those who punish those who commit violence do not allow others to act unjustly. So be a judge to those who commit violence against others. But to those who commit violence against you, be compassionate. From the former you will acquire a name as one who keeps the laws, and to the latter you will show your loving-kindness and compassion. But today we see that everything happens the other way around. If you wish to have that 'foreign' will of which I spoke at the beginning, and if God wills, He will make you a monk, for nothing is impossible for Him. But now serve God with fear, according to your strength, which you must always compel to do good. If my Christ sees this, He will come to you as to Zacchaeus and say: *'make haste and come down'* (Luke 19:5), and so you will leave the sycamore tree and follow Him. And if, to your great joy, He stays in your house, then you will give half of your possessions to the poor, and if you have defrauded anyone, you will repay fourfold. Then you too will hear: *'Today salvation has come to this house'* (Luke 19:9), and you will be able to hate this world."

Having heard these and many other soul-profiting words of the saint, Michael wished to see his face and said: "Abba, command that a light be brought." The venerable one knocked with his staff, and a disciple came, to whom he commanded that a light be brought. But the disciple remarked:

"For forty years you have not brought a light into your cell, and now you tell me to bring one?"

"Do you see what a disobedient person you are? Go and bring a light."

Marveling that the venerable one abstained even from light, Michael asked:

"Why do you not light a lamp? Does it not help with reading and psalmody?"

"The Church for each person is his mind and heart; it is there that we must perform the services. In the same way, you too, wherever you may be, if there is a service in church, go, but if not, read psalms, the Apostle, or the Gospel. If I had a light, I would start counting the beams on the ceiling of my cell. Moreover, light is a sign of those who have a bright life, but I sit in darkness, praying to God for my sins, since I have done and continue to do deeds worthy of darkness. But if instead of the temporal light that I do not see, I am deemed worthy in the future age to behold a ray of that never-waning light, which I hope for, may glory be to the Holy God. But if not, all the same, may glory be to His righteous judgment. For me it is already much to see the light of the sun, and therefore I do not cease to thank God, Who *'makes His sun rise on the evil and on the good'* (Matthew 5:45)."

After the light was brought and Augustus saw the venerable one, he began to ask him about many things that he did not know. The venerable one answered everything with knowledge and the wisdom of God, instructing him throughout the night with many soul-saving counsels. When dawn began to break, Michael rose, kissed the hands and mouth of the venerable one and, having received his holy prayers, departed from him. Having asked the brethren whether the venerable one had any relatives still living, Michael learned that his daughter and mother were alive. He immediately ordered that all necessities be sent to them, after which he departed with joy, thanking God, Who had deemed him worthy to converse with such a wondrous man.

When Michael Augustus came to the emperor, he said to him thus:

"Truly, holy emperor, all that we have heard, we have seen. The venerable one is a sacred-looking elder, a good man, peaceful in character and balanced. And why say much? He is adorned with all good things and is filled with divine love. In appearance he resembles the Prophet Elijah."

Such and many other praises did Michael Augustus lavish upon the venerable one to the pious emperor, who, as soon as he had heard everything, was filled with great joy and soon came to the venerable one with his whole household. After they had exchanged a kiss in Christ, the venerable one asked:

"Why have you come here, most pious emperor, to an old man who has nothing good to his credit? Has a report of my hypocritical words and deeds reached your majesty, and is that what has brought you to my lowliness? But you, in your Divine humility, honor me, an unworthy one, as you do our holy fathers. A pitiful hypocrite I am; how shall I justify myself before the All-Good God, how shall I repay your majesty for such labor?"

The emperor answered him:

"Abba, *'the lesser is blessed by the greater'* (Hebrews 7:7). Since such power has been entrusted to me by God, though undeservedly, I constantly devote myself to cares for it and remain in such confusion that I do not remember God. How then can I not honor those who fear Him, not go to them for their holy prayers for the enlightenment of my darkened soul and for a successful military campaign? You know that *'the effective, fervent prayer of a righteous man avails much'* (James 5:16), and I, through my negligence, although I do not act according to your holy prayers, yet I believe that they contribute to my strengthening. I am certain that those who live the solitary and monastic life are preferable to those who live in the world with many people, even if they are more modest than others. Monks by their stillness calm those passions which in worldly people, from constant spectacles, are inflamed and make them worse, though they do not feel their harm, because over a long time they have become accustomed to them, as to a long-standing warmth that secretly consumes them."

"I agree with your words, but know that, as Saint John of the Ladder says, it is impossible for all to become dispassionate, but it is possible for all to be saved and reconciled with God. As the divine John Chrysostom says: 'I promise and assure you that if a sinner leaves behind his past sins and from all his heart promises God not to sin anymore, God will require nothing else from him in return, because He loves mankind. Just as a woman experiencing the pains of childbirth desires to give birth, so God desires to pour out His mercy upon all.' As Gregory the Theologian says: 'He who remains in the world and has attained small virtues has far surpassed him who is free but has not attained all. It is stranger to see a man bound with chains who travels a short distance than one who, having no burden, travels a great distance; and more wondrous to see him who walks persistently through mud and is only a little soiled by it than him who is clean and walks on a clean road. Proof of this is the harlot Rahab, whom hospitality alone justified, though for all her other deeds she received no praise; the publican was exalted by humility alone, and there is no evidence of whether he had other virtues. And why? So that we may learn not to despair. You have said, my lord, that from worldly cares you do not remember God, but I tell you that, by the grace of my Christ, you always remember Him.'"

"How can you know this, abba?"

"The remembrance of God is a pain of the heart arising from piety, as Saint Mark says, and therefore the care that you have for the strengthening of our faith, the churches, monasteries, and the world entrusted to you by God, is a pain of the heart arising from piety."

"You speak well, father, and I, with God's help, care for the empire according to my strength, but I do not know whether I have the remembrance of God, because I am enslaved by love of pleasure, love of glory, love of money. How can I be delivered from them and please my Lord?"

"And truly these are the three firstborn daughters of satan and brides of his spouse, malice, which give birth to every wickedness in us. By them satan thought to tempt our Lord after His Baptism, but our Lord conquered them and became an example and model for us, according to His own words: *'For I have given you an example, that you should do as I have done to you'* (John 13:15); *'learn from Me, for I am gentle and lowly in heart'* (Matthew 11:29). Meekness calms the wrathful part of our soul, and humility frees us from vainglory. He who has these virtues will not be enslaved either by love of pleasure or love of money. A true emperor is recognized not by his purple, belt, and crown on his head, but by his imperial virtue. But he who is commanded by the passions and is a slave of sin is unworthy to rule over others. A true emperor is he who conquers the passions and governs according to the laws of God and guards the freedom of his soul. The signs of a free soul are simplicity, meekness, loving-kindness, courage, justice, chastity, condescension, magnanimity to judge not by favor but by right. Such an emperor will not say to one who asks: 'Go away now, and come later, and then I will give you,' but gives to each according to his need. And so you, by the grace of God, have acted and continue to act, especially with the orphanage of Saint Paul. You feed the hungry, give drink to the thirsty, give shelter to strangers, clothe the naked, visit the sick, ransom captives, and not only from the sensible pagans, but from the noetic ones, the demons. Because many, being enslaved by the pagans, have handed over their souls to eternal death together with their bodies, because they mingled with the pagans and learned to perform their deeds. But he who ransoms these captives not only visibly fulfills the commandments of Christ, but also in a noetic manner, for they are truly those who hunger and thirst as hearers of the word of God. They are strangers, deprived of the Christian way of life, whom God desires us to clothe and warm. They are the sick who are in danger of losing their life-giving faith. They sit in the dark prison of godlessness and desire to escape from it and see the light of the Sun of Righteousness. He who fulfills this, by the grace of God, is equal to the apostles.

And if I recall those whom you have brought to God from every nation by your divinely-wise tongue, I will not have time to recount them. Especially the Scythians, because by the help of God and victory over them, you made sheep of those who were formerly wolves, and through Holy Baptism numbered them among the flock of Christ. And one soul gained, as Saint John Chrysostom says, can often blot out the burden of sins and become a means of salvation for us on the Day of Judgment. And if alms are given with money, then this serves as the cause of so many crowns, so many rewards, and how will all these blessings not be there where souls are benefited? For such a person will be a mouth of God, according to the saying of Holy Scripture. Acting thus, O Christ-imitating emperor, do you still say that you do not remember God? But in general, you do well to speak thus, so as to teach us, miserable ones, not to think highly of ourselves, for which you will also receive a reward on the Day of Judgment."

Concerning this and much more about the salvation of the soul did the all-blessed emperor converse with the venerable one. Rejoicing at such a pleasant and sincere conversation, the emperor said:

"Just as one who carries spices, even if he does not wish it, is known by their fragrance, so too one who has the Spirit of the Lord is known by his words and humility. Whose monastery is this, abba?"

"This church we inherited from our forebears. Before me, this monk lived here," said the saint, pointing to his brother, "who, with God's help and by his own labors, established this small monastery, where we, the unworthy, now dwell, praying to God for our own salvation and for the dominion of your holy majesty, and for the whole world."

"To whom does the place where the monastery stands belong?"

And, hearing that it was state property, he said:

"From this hour I grant it to the monastery, for your holy prayers, and whatever debts are recorded against the monastery, I forgive and will issue my chrysobull, so that this place may remain free."

And this happened later. Then, having received the blessing of the venerable one, the emperor gave him five litras of gold to be distributed to the poor and one litra for the monastery, and thus, rejoicing that he had been deemed worthy to see such a holy man and converse with him, departed.

This emperor greatly loved monks and honored them, and therefore very often, when he sat on his throne and was told that a certain virtuous monk had come, he would immediately ask for his belt, gird himself, and go out to meet the monk. Having bowed, he would kiss him and remain standing with crossed arms. And if the monk did not sit down, he too would not sit on his throne. And if it happened that he was eating when a monk came, he would say: "Remove, remove the table," after which, having washed, he would rise and kiss the monk. And during illness, if a monk sat at his feet, the emperor tried not to stretch them out too much, so as not to touch the monk, as if he were a holy icon. But if sometimes, forgetting himself, he touched a monk with his feet, he would immediately draw them back as if burned by fire. The emperor said: "I believe that all the good things that God has granted me have been granted to me through the prayers of my holy elders, and because of my love for them, as I have repeatedly been convinced." But let us return to our narrative.

After the emperor, with the pious empress and children, bade farewell to the venerable one, they experienced such joy that they gave all their garments to the poor, and not only they, but all those who accompanied them. The poor then sold these garments back to them, for who could buy such expensive garments? And there was great joy in that land, because at that time there was a severe famine, and a rumor spread throughout the land that Abba Cyril was distributing money. A multitude of poor people immediately gathered at the monastery, and after the five litras of gold had been distributed, the crowd of poor who had received nothing began to shout, asking the monks for money. The venerable one commanded that the litra given by the emperor for the monastery be distributed, but other poor continued to shout. Then the venerable one asked the brethren:

"Does anyone have money from the sale of handiwork?"

And they answered:

"We have eighty coins."

"Give forty to the poor."

But when these forty coins had been given, other poor continued to shout. The venerable one commanded that another twenty coins be given, but the poor still shouted; then ten, but other poor still shouted. Then the venerable one addressed the brethren:

"If you wish, accept my sinful prayers and give the remaining ten coins; perhaps Christ is testing us."

But the monks did not want to give the money, because it was needed to buy oil for the church. The venerable one remarked on this:

"The passion of love of money is manifested when one receives with joy and gives with sorrow. The divine Maximus says that 'there are three causes for the love of money: love of pleasure, vainglory, and unbelief, which is worse than the other two. The pleasure-lover loves money to pay for his evil desires, the vainglorious one loves it to be glorified, and the unbeliever, to keep it from fear of poverty, or old age, or sickness, or wandering, and hopes in it more than in God, the Provider even of the smallest animals. There is also a fourth, who saves money to distribute to those in need. He who considers another's need as his own will never be deprived of money.'" So I ask you, be economical so as to be delivered from love of pleasure, vainglory, and unbelief. Do you not know that God, by His providence, brought the emperors and their retinue here so that even they would give their garments to the poor? But we, though we have seen emperors who acted thus, do not want to give to the poor what does not belong to us. We brought nothing into this world, so we can take nothing out of it. As I have already told you, give the remaining ten coins, and God will give you a hundredfold alms."

After the brethren had given these coins as well, other poor still continued to shout. Then the venerable one called some of them and said: "Believe me, brethren, there is no more money, for they have given even what they had from the sale of their handiwork." And so the poor departed, thanking the saint of God. Several days later, the monks began to experience need. They came to the venerable one and said:

"Where, abba, is the hundredfold alms of which you spoke?"

"Why do you speak like madmen? I believe in my Christ that He will send us all that is necessary."

After some time, a relative of the emperor came to the venerable one and gave him a large bag of money. Then, calling the monks, the venerable one said:

"You see, O you of little faith, you wavered in vain! Take, earthly ones, what belongs to the earth, and having satisfied your needs, distribute the rest to the poor, that you too may be shown mercy and receive the grace of our Lord, to Whom be glory unto the ages."

In the village of the venerable one there lived a certain pious and virtuous man named Melimauras, who was his friend. Once he went to another region and spent the night at an inn. As soon as the innkeeper's wife learned that he was from the homeland of the Venerable Cyril and was also his friend, she began to exclaim: "Glory to God that I have found an opportunity to tell of the miracle that occurred in my house by the righteous judgment of God, for if I remain silent, I shall have no part with truth and with God. Several days ago, a soldier spent the night here, young in age and in mind, who did not cease to revile the Venerable Cyril. And the reason for this was, as he said, that he went to venerate the venerable one, but he did not wish to see him. I and my husband long asked him to stop reviling the saint, but he would not listen, grew angrier, and continued to curse. Seeing his utter shamelessness and audacity, I do not know how, but I said to him: 'Man, stop insulting Abba Cyril, because you revile not him, but God, Whom he serves. The whole world proclaims him a true servant of God; beware lest God not endure you and strike you through His Angel.' After some time, the soldier developed a terrible pain in his stomach; he cried out, and not even an hour passed before (O miracle!) all his intestines fell out, and the soldier died." Melimauras told me about this incident, and I considered it worthy to record it for the sake of Him Who said: *"What I tell you in the dark, speak in the light, and what you hear in the ear, proclaim on the housetops"* (Matthew 10:27).

At the age of ninety, the venerable one became ill, and although he was worn out by old age and exhausted by sickness, he did not abandon his former ascetic struggle, but lay like adamant, as if someone else were suffering, or as if he were bodiless. The venerable one had conquered the dominating belly and attained the utmost dispassion, for sixty years eating bread, grass, water, and even this sparingly. He himself said: "Since I became a monk, I have not drunk water to satiety. And since my tongue clung to my palate, before putting bread in my mouth, I moistened the edges of my lips with one or two drops of water so that I could swallow it." When the emperor heard of his illness, he came to him with his whole family. Seeing his sufferings, the empress with her own hands began to feed him (she had brought food with her) and gave him a little wine to drink. Since the venerable one was now somewhat hard of hearing, the emperor commanded his servant to ask whether he would be acting rightly if he now went to the East to wage war against the godless Turks. Having thought a little, the venerable one said: "You will accept my counsel and will not go to the East now, but when God wills, you will go, and He Himself *'will prepare your way'* (Mark 1:2)." Hearing this, the emperor rose and, bowing to God, said: *"Amen, let it be to me according to your word"* (Luke 1:38). Then, having received his holy prayers, the emperor left the cell of the venerable one. Seeing that the monastery church was falling apart, he ordered it to be demolished to the foundation and rebuilt anew, which was done. And God fulfilled the prophecy of the venerable one when the emperor, after some time, went to the East and subjugated the so-called Solimopolis.

After the church was built, as the venerable one wished, he commanded that a sheep be given to the builders. One of them, while eating it, began to complain that it was supposedly not very fat and pushed away his portion. The other builders told him that in this way he was rejecting the blessing of the venerable one. But that ungrateful soul was displeased. And then a miracle occurred: under the influence of a demon, he turned his face backward, fell to the ground, went into convulsions, began to gnash his teeth and foam at the mouth. Seeing this, his companions ran to the venerable one and told him what had happened. The venerable one answered them: "My lords, God bears all human sins, but the sins of a murmurer and an ungrateful person He does not bear, and punishes him." Then he filled a cup with water and gave it to them, saying: "Go and pour it on his head, or give him to drink, and then, in the name of my Lord Jesus Christ, he will be healed." As the venerable one said, so they did. When the murmurer came to his senses, he fell at the feet of the venerable one, thanked him, and asked forgiveness. Having given him instruction, the venerable one finally said: *"Sin no more, lest a worse thing come upon you"* (John 5:14), and thus from that hour, by the grace of God, he was healed.

There lived in the monastery a young monk, the nephew of the venerable one. Since young people have much zeal at the beginning, he too wanted to imitate the venerable one not only in food and clothing, but even to surpass him. Cyril often advised him to refrain from all excess and not to try to place his foot on a higher rung of the spiritual ladder of virtues, but to begin from the first, for thus, little by little, one can ascend to the summit, which is the love of God, whereas that which is beyond measure is from demons. After many instructions, the venerable one commanded the young monk to follow the middle path and to eat once a day, so that he would not afterward begin to eat many times a day, and thus cut off his will. However, the youth answered the Venerable Cyril:

"Father, it befits me to fast all week, and eating every other day is nothing to me."

"Brother, he who wishes to preserve true humility must not rely on himself in anything, for this is true humility. But he who does not wish to cut off his own will and fasts a week, then, having become fainthearted through the assistance of demons, reaches the point of eating many times a day without discernment. This happens to those who do not wish to preserve patience and humility, but trust in themselves."

And now the time has come to tell also of the repose of the venerable one. The Venerable Cyril was thirty years old when he began his ascetic struggle, in which he spent more than sixty years, and up to ninety-three years he never had pain in his eyes, teeth, or any other members. But in the last three years of his life, he sometimes became a little ill. At ninety-three years of age, the venerable one was bent from deep old age and many years of ascetic labor, because of which he rarely rose. Seeing him in this state, our enemy the devil was envious, lest he end his life in a good old age. So listen to what this vile one devised.

The nephew of the emperor, John Augustus, often came to the venerable one for a blessing. Knowing this and seeing that the venerable one was bedridden, the devil showed him in a vision that a tent was pitched in the monastery next to his cell; in it stood a bed spread with red carpets; John Augustus was sitting on it, and around him was a multitude of servants. After this, as if in continuation of the vision, Augustus entered the cell of the venerable one and began a conversation with him. And as soon as he began to speak, the mind of the venerable one was darkened, and the more the accursed Augustus spoke, the more the mind of the venerable one was darkened, until the venerable one almost lost his mind. The poisonous words of the devil, by God's permission, can do not only this, but even more. Then the demon said to the venerable one: "You know what reverence I have for you; therefore I wish that the Liturgy be celebrated in your cell and that you receive Communion." The venerable one, not understanding what he was saying, replied: "Here is the cell; do as you wish." Immediately there appeared in the cell of the venerable one, as it were visibly, a Holy Table, a table of oblation, a diskos with a chalice, and covers, and there entered as if priests, who began to celebrate the Liturgy. The venerable one stood in another corner of the cell and listened to what the celebrants were saying, but he could not understand what they were saying. They read both the Apostle and the Gospel, but from the responses the venerable one heard nothing except "Amen," "Amen." Then, when these impious priests said: "Approach,"

Augustus from the vision approached and communed from their shamelessness and impiety. All those who were with him did likewise. The venerable one wondered whether he too should go and commune. But he did not go, saying to himself: "If it is the will of God, then Augustus will tell me, but if not, who am I, unworthy, to commune?" The All-Merciful God did not despise his humility, but delivered him from his enemies and did not allow him to commune, for if he had communed, he would have completely lost his mind. When their accursed liturgy ended, Augustus (who was actually a demon) went out and went to the tent.

The venerable one, exhausted from meaningless standing, sat down with a greatly troubled and darkened countenance. He knocked, and at his knock a disciple came, whom he asked:

"Are you not Christians, and do you not need to die? Why do you not pity my old age and do not see my torments? Is it right that worldly people should disturb me so and celebrate a liturgy in my cell?"

The disciple answered:

"Forgive me, abba, I do not know what you are speaking of."

"If you do not believe my words, then believe the deeds."

"What deeds?"

"Did you not see Augustus with his people and the tent?" And he told the disciple everything that had happened.

"I saw nothing of what you speak of." The venerable one pointed with his hand to the corner of the cell:

"Do you not even see this diskos with the chalice and covers?"

Picking up the cup, the disciple asked:

"Is this not the cup from which you drink?"

"Yes."

Then the disciple began to strike him on the face, saying:

"Woe, you have lost your mind, abba."

"It is you who have lost your mind, but I am fine."

"No, you are not."

Thus they argued for a long time, and sometimes the venerable one came to himself. During one such moment, the brethren suggested to the venerable one:

"Do you want us to bring that monk to you (possibly the author of this Life), so that he may help you?"

"Yes, bring him."

That monk came and, making a prostration, asked the venerable one:

"How are you, father?"

"As my brethren say, badly."

When the venerable one told of all that had happened, the monk said:

"Glory to the Lord, Who helped you, because if you had communed from their filth, then you would have completely lost your mind."

"But is it certain that what I saw was deception and a vision? I cannot believe this."

"With God's help you will believe, and do not say no. But if you do not believe, then I will bring to you the real John Augustus, and he will confirm my words. Do you not remember, father, how many stories there are in the Paterikons about people who were deceived by satan in one way or another?"

"Yes, I remember, but what should I do now?"

"You need only believe our testimony, because we, the witnesses, are many, and we know for certain that Augustus did not come here at this time, and nothing of what you saw in the vision happened. Being unable to deceive your noetic eyes, as the demon deceives my eyes and those of people like me, he deceived your senses, and this is proof of his weakness. Believe that you saw all this through the activity of demons. Sometimes even a good captain's ship is wrecked, and very rarely does one walking on a road not stumble. But you know, father, that the virtuous, if they sometimes fall into sin, can rise again and not become fainthearted."

Having heard this and much else, the venerable one came to himself and began to weep, repeating:

"Woe, woe to me, for my soul would have settled in Hades, had not the Lord become my Helper. Woe to me, for I could have lost everything without gaining anything. My Christ, my Christ, do not forsake me. You know that I am not afraid of the torments of Hades, but I am afraid of being separated from Your Sweetest Face and from the brethren, and that it will be impossible to venerate Your Precious Cross and Your holy icon, and impossible to partake of Your Most Pure Body and Blood. All this is worse for me than any death and eternal torment. All this I would have experienced in the present life if I had been abandoned by You in the company of demons, and in the future life I would have been condemned with them to the dark and unquenchable fire and separation from You, my Christ. Forgive me, Lord, my transgressions, that I may rest with assurance from You, before I depart from here. Have mercy, my Christ, on my old age; take pity on my suffering; pity me, gone astray, and deliver me from the manifold wiles of the enemy, for You are the God of those who repent, and on me show all Your goodness. Save me, unworthy, according to Your great mercy, and I shall praise You always in all the few days of my life."

Having thus confessed to God with tears, the venerable one rose and made a prostration before the brethren, saying: "Forgive me, gone astray." And the brethren, moved with compunction and tears, urged him to commune of the Divine Mysteries on the morrow, because he had not communed for a long time. I told him that this Mystery is called Communion because it unites us with Christ and makes us partakers of His Kingdom. A certain Jewish magician named Daniel, when they wanted to burn him, cried out: "Behold, the Angel of the Lord is tormenting me to make me say to Christians what I did not want to say. I swear by my mortal hour that my magical art never worked on a Christian who communes every day."

Hearing this, the venerable one said to God: "I thank You, my Lord, that *'You prepare a table before me in the presence of my enemies; You anoint my head with oil; my cup runs over'* (Psalm 22:5). Having prayed thus, the venerable one communed of the Divine Mysteries, and his face became like a flame. Shortly afterward, with a smile and spiritual joy, he said: *"Weeping may endure for a night, but joy comes in the morning"* (Psalm 29:5). Truly the Lord humbles and exalts, *'and raises up all who are bowed down'* (Psalm 144:14). Woe to me, as long as I have communion with the enemies of God, what communion do I have with God? I commune to my own condemnation, and therefore the priest says: 'Holy things are for the holy,' and not 'for the unclean.' But if I am holy, then who are these enemies who labor for my destruction? Blessed is he who approaches the Divine Mysteries with fear and trembling, thinking that he receives eternal life. I marvel at how, by the permission of God, demons can present one thing to people as another, and I think that if it were not for the protection of God over people, then because of the fierce rage that demons have against us, they would cast us all into the sea like a herd of swine."

After some time, the demon in the form of Augustus again came to the venerable one, who, looking at him, immediately recognized the demon and wanted to strike him, but the demon became invisible. The venerable one struck his hand against the wall and afterward showed everyone his hand, blackened from the blow. Having been completely delivered from this temptation with God's help, the venerable one received bodily health for a time. Then he became ill again, and I came to visit him. Seeing that he was lying on a bare mat, I asked him to put at least a little grass underneath, to have some small comfort. He obeyed and placed grass underneath, and we covered it with a hairy covering. The venerable one lay down and said with a groan: "O Cyril, what have you come to, lying on a soft bed and eating exquisite food," calling the grass a bed and the boiled beets exquisite food. When he reached the age of ninety-five, he became even weaker and more sickly. We barely persuaded him to eat fish and drink wine, because only at ninety did he begin to eat cooked food on the Lord's feasts, but without oil. At ninety-two he began to eat oil as well. At ninety-six the venerable one was completely infirm, both from illness and from deep old age. Having foreknown the approaching end of his life, he commanded us not to bury him in the Lord's temple, considering himself unworthy, but to bury him in his brother's grave. On his head we were to place a stone, and his body we were to cover with earth. Struggling still many days in fasting, he surrendered his blessed soul into the hands of God, and his holy relics we buried with honor and reverence in the year one thousand one hundred and eleven from the Nativity of Christ, on the second day of the month of December.

Eleven years after the repose of the venerable one, out of great reverence for him and a desire to kiss his holy relics, I dared to open the tomb and, with God's help, found his holy head filled with divine fragrance. Placing it in a reliquary, I set it in the monastery church for the healing of soul and body of those who with faith kiss it, to the glory of our Lord Jesus Christ. Melimauras, of whom we spoke earlier, having heard of the repose of the venerable one, came to the monastery and, seeing his holy head, with great faith kissed and embraced it with much love. Rejoicing and exulting, he said:

"Wherever it may be for me, unworthy; I could not even hope to see the holy head of my good father, all of whose benefactions to me I cannot even enumerate, not only during his life, but even after his death."

Then he said, addressing me:

"Abba, have you heard of the miracle he worked for me?" And he began to tell:

"Once I lifted up a large anchor from my boat to put it inside, and I developed a hernia. I barely made it home and, from severe pain and boundless grief, wished for death. Remembering the venerable one, I came to the monastery and fell upon his grave, asking with faith that he have mercy on me. I took earth from his grave and placed it on the sore spot, when suddenly a miracle occurred. Within a day I was well, by his holy prayers, so that no trace of the illness remained. And so I glorified God, Who glorifies His servants."

Once the following occurred. A certain widowed woman named Phoca wept day and night because of her widowhood, the orphanhood of her children, and severe poverty, and from her tears she lost her sight. Continuing to weep day and night, she called for death to be delivered from all these torments. Phoca went to a physician, but her desired sight did not return; she suffered greatly. But one night, Phoca saw in a dream a woman of modest appearance who told her that she could be healed only by the head of the venerable one. Phoca immediately came to the monastery, and as soon as the priest began to celebrate the Liturgy (O ineffable are Your judgments, O Christ the King!), the holy head of the venerable one, by Divine grace, adhered to the woman's eyes (before this, the head had been placed on top of her eyes) and until the end of the Liturgy remained on her eyes, to the amazement of all who witnessed this miracle. After this, the blind woman began to see a little, until her sight was fully restored, after which she glorified God and the venerable one.

The grandson of the aforementioned Melimauras, eighteen years of age, once saw a fly fly into his nose, and immediately a demon entered him. The youth fell to the ground, began to roll about, foam at the mouth, and gnash his teeth. Thus he suffered for a whole year, calling upon many saints for help. Finding no healing, he turned for help to the Venerable Cyril. His holy head he immediately placed on his forehead. And, O miracle! It adhered to his forehead, and then, under the influence of the Divine grace dwelling in it, descended by itself to the chest of the sufferer, who from that hour was healed.

One of the inhabitants of a village near Derkos, together with his wife and children, was paralyzed due to the action of the sorcery of a certain evil-minded man (by the permission of God, demons can do this too). Having prayed to God, they resorted to the help of the venerable one and, having received sacred oil from his head, anointed themselves with this oil, after which the paralysis passed and they glorified the much-hymned name of God and the grace given to the venerable one by Him. Many say that miracles are not for believers, but for unbelievers, and that present-day Christians cannot become saints and perfect, because of which the grace of miracles has diminished. And a clear proof of this is found, for we have no Christian deeds, since we are negligent, think on worldly things, and therefore the grace of God does not act. But Grace is the Holy Spirit, Who is not powerless, but all-powerful. He does not withdraw from us, but is present everywhere, and is manifested and acts according to our faith and according to how we keep the commandments of Christ, to Whom belongs all glory, honor, and worship, with His Unoriginate Father and the Life-giving Spirit, now and ever, and unto the ages of ages. Amen.

(Written by the Venerable Nicholas Kataskepeinos)

The Life and Struggles of Our Father Among the Saints Gregory, Bishop of Assos, Who Flourished in the Twelfth Century

This father of ours among the saints, George, came from the island of Mytilene, from a village called Akorni. His pious parents, George and Mary, long besought God with tears to give them a child. The Lord heard their prayer and gave them this divine Gregory, whom in Holy Baptism they named George, like his father. The child was raised with great diligence, being taught sacred letters.

At that time the emperor issued a decree that children of noble parents should be sent to the palace, where they would be educated for three years and then returned to their homeland, from where others were brought in their place. Therefore, at the age of fourteen, this good George was sent together with other children to the palace. The emperor at that time was Manuel Porphyrogennetos. During his three years of education at the palace, the blessed George did not give himself, like the other children, to vanity, nor to indecent games, nor to carnal soul-harming lusts, but strove to give no rest to his body, mortifying and afflicting it with fasts and severe treatment. Very diligently devoting himself to the study of the sciences, he sufficiently advanced in them, having the great Agathon as his teacher. However, the venerable one was diligent not only in the sciences, but strove with all his might to acquire the necessary virtues. Even the weekly provisions he received he distributed to the poor, leaving for himself to eat exactly as much as was necessary to sustain life in his body.

When the time came for the children to return to their homeland, the praiseworthy George, while others were preparing for the reunion with their parents, began to reflect on the inconstancy of the world and the vanity of all temporal things, and on the disturbance and care connected with them. Constantly thinking about this, he wisely resolved to choose a quiet and tranquil life, in order to be free from the cares of the world and with his whole being attend to the eternal and unfading Heavenly blessings, to think only of them each day and strive to taste them. This Heavenly citizenship can be attained in no other way than by the narrow and sorrowful monastic path. Renouncing his homeland, parents, wealth, worldly vanity, and all carnal pleasures, he departed from Constantinople together with his teacher, the wondrous Agathon, and went to the east, to the monastery built by his abba. Becoming a novice there according to the rules of monastic life, the venerable one settled on a mountain near the monastery, where he spent three years, struggling with all strictness in all the virtues. Then, since his heart was burning with divine love, he conceived the idea of going to Jerusalem in order to venerate the holy places and to enjoy conversations with spiritual and virtuous men, to learn from them the strict monastic life and to be clothed in the holy angelic schema.

Having announced his intention to the holy Agathon, the venerable one understood that he was in agreement. And so with great desire he set out for Jerusalem. Coming there with God's help, he reverently venerated the Holy Sepulchre of the Lord and the other holy places, and then went into the wilderness of the Jordan. Finding there wondrous ascetics, he conversed with them at length on spiritual topics, communed with them, and beheld their superhuman struggles. Amazed, George became fearful and began to think about not even attempting to live such a life. Then he went to one of the most virtuous and experienced elders and revealed his thoughts to him. Having in turn heard from him all that was necessary, the venerable one cast out all fear from his heart and with hope in the Lord gave himself over to this elder, becoming his disciple. He was clothed by him in the angelic schema, renamed Gregory, and remained with him, feeding on the grass of that wilderness. Who could tell of the ascetic labors and struggles which the blessed one undertook there? Seeing his struggles, the haters of good, the envious demons, began in various ways to wage fierce warfare against him. But in vain did they labor, for, intensifying his struggle even more and unceasingly beseeching the Lord with faith and tears, the divine Gregory, by the grace of God, repelled all demonic attacks. Having become a conqueror of the malicious demons, the venerable one clothed himself in the garment of joy and was lifted up in spirit, having acquired the fruits of the Most Holy Spirit, as the divine Paul says.

Having spent fifteen years in the wilderness, Gregory again remembered the divine Agathon. Departing from there, he came to the aforementioned monastery and settled in his old cell on the mountain, exercising himself in superhuman struggles, through which he shone for all like a most radiant star, illuminating all with his deeds and appearance. Therefore both monks and laymen—all came to him to hear his salvific and soul-profiting teachings. And the divine Agathon, seeing and hearing of the struggles of the sacred Gregory, rejoiced in spirit, glorifying the Author and Perfecter of all good things—God, and testified before all that Gregory had already come *"to the measure of the stature of the fullness of Christ"* (Ephesians 4:13) and had become perfect in virtue.

At that time a certain episcopal see in the east, called Assos, became widowed, and the clergy together with the archons of that diocese requested from the hierarchy of the Great Church a worthy pastor. When the patriarch and the hierarchs began to seek someone worthy of serving in that see, the great Agathon happened to be in the capital. Being acquainted with the patriarch and the entire Holy Synod, he told them of the struggles of the divine Gregory. And then the emperor and the patriarch sent letters to the great Gregory, inviting him to come to Constantinople. Not knowing why he was being summoned to the capital, Gregory came there and against his own will was ordained Bishop of Assos by the Metropolitan of Ephesus, after which he was sent to his throne with great honors from the emperor and the Great Church.

Having accepted the great burden of the episcopate, the venerable one devoted himself even more to his struggles. As a true pastor, he shepherded his flock in a manner pleasing to God, considering it necessary constantly to teach it the word of God, while at the same time commanding all to keep the commandments of God and to abstain from every evil. From his belly, as it were, flowed rivers of living water, because he had only one care and one concern: how to gain human souls and bring them to God. Sometimes he employed severity with spiritual discernment, fulfilling the commandment of the apostle, who says that a spiritual steward must know the disposition of each one: one to comfort, another to rebuke and reprove *"in season and out of season"* (2 Timothy 4:2). He applied himself greatly to spiritual governance and ordained no one without careful examination, so as not to become a partaker in the sins of others. Thus, honoring the Mystery of the Priesthood and showing how great its dignity is and what a priest must be, the hierarch multiplied the talent given to him by God. He taught not only by word but also by deeds, having become for all an example and a good pattern of all the virtues.

But seeing such struggles of the venerable one, the hater of good, the devil, could no longer endure them. He raised up against Gregory restless and idle clergy and priests. The protopope of the diocese had a son named Leo, whom he gave to the divine Gregory. The saint, taking him under his care, constantly taught him the fear of God. And since he proved to be prudent, faithful, tested in all things, and lived virtuously, the hierarch entrusted to him the management of the church property. Moved by envy, the aforementioned clergy wrote a document full of lies and slander with accusations against the saint and sent it to the council of the holy hierarchs. But no one believed these accusations, because all knew of the virtuous life of the venerable one. Meanwhile, the divine Gregory also came to the council. As soon as his enviers saw him, all the accusations were scattered like spider's webs. Convicted by their own conscience, the accusers repented and fell at the feet of the saint, asking forgiveness for their unjust accusations. As a true disciple of Christ, the righteous one forgave them and returned in peace to his diocese together with the adversaries who had slandered him, who, following his instructions, obeyed him for a time. But the wicked demon, who had gone out of them at their repentance, wandering through waterless places and finding no rest, returned to them again. Finding them careless, he entered into them together with seven spirits even more wicked, and again raised up even greater warfare against the saint through these clergy. Having completely given themselves over to Satan, these men again wrote a document against the saint with accusations greater than the former. This document they brought to the Great Church and, having submitted it, cried out against the saint. But the patriarch and the hierarchs drove them away, rebuking them for their manifest lies and slander.

But what did the good ascetic, the divine Gregory, do, he who knew how to fight only with demons and not with men? He ordered his disciple Leo to take his robe and book and follow him. Going out from the diocese by night, they boarded a ship and sailed to Tenedos, where there was a most beautiful monastery with many monks. There the venerable one remained in stillness for some time, and there also he tonsured his disciple a monk, renaming him from Leo to Leontios. Then they crossed over to Mytilene and ascended a mountain.

Wishing to see his parents, the venerable one went to his village of Akorni. There he happened to meet his mother, who was on her way to the bathhouse. Not recognizing him, she greeted him and asked for a blessing. The saint answered her: "May God bless you and grant you to see the one who is abroad." Having fulfilled his desire, he immediately departed from there and, ascending Mount Priant, kept stillness there together with Leontios. Finding a hard-to-reach and forested place called Little Leukopedi, by Divine inspiration the venerable one went to the owners of that land and asked permission to clear it of forest and establish a monastery there. The owners were glad at such a proposal and gave him these lands, attaching a written document of the transfer. This land was completely useless to them, because it was filled with demons.

The saint made a prayer, and as soon as he set about the work, the demons rose up against him, producing great disturbance and noise: "You wrong us, Gregory; leave our dwelling!" Raising the noetic eyes of his soul to heaven, the saint besought the Most High God to deliver him from the malicious spirits. Receiving help from Him, the venerable one drove them away by prayer. But these accursed ones came to the owners of that land and threw them into confusion, for having seen that the place was carefully cleared and put in order, they regretted having given it with a document. They drove the saint out of there, although he had labored and endured so much while clearing this place. Some of them, being malicious heretics, having heard that the saint was preaching the Orthodox faith, treated him with hostility and, falling upon him with sticks and stones, beat him half to death. Taking him by the feet, they threw him at the foot of the mountain. And at this place (O wonders of Thine, O Lord!), where they threw the venerable one, nothing has grown to this day, but it appears as though burned.

The divine Gregory was miraculously healed by the Lord and glorified God. Once, entering a certain garden together with his disciple, he thrust into the ground his hazel staff, upon which he had leaned for twelve years, and said: "Brother Leontios, if God grants us the Kingdom of Heaven, then let the staff sprout and become a tree, and bring forth fruit, like the other trees." And a miracle occurred! It was the month of September when he planted the staff, and all winter it was dry. But when March came, the staff sprouted and bore fruit, and its fruit healed every disease, to the glory of Christ and in honor of the saint. A certain fool named Michael said that all this was sorcery and not a miracle. Running to the tree, he shamelessly cut off all the branches of the staff, but his own limbs immediately became numb. He fell to the ground and presented a pitiful sight. His relatives picked up the unfortunate man and brought him to the house, where, punished by illness for his unbelief and shamelessness, he lay bedridden as long as the saint was alive. After his death and burial, many sick people came with faith to the tomb of the hierarch, which exuded blessed water, and having drunk of it, were healed. Michael also was brought there by his relatives, and with faith and warm tears he prayed to God and invoked the saint for help. And a miracle occurred! As soon as the sick man drank of that holy water, he immediately became well, glorifying and blessing God and the saint, and proclaiming to all the miracles that had happened to him.

But let us return to our narrative. Having learned of the miraculous healing of Gregory by the Lord and his great patience, the owners of that land changed their cruelty to gentleness, and (O wondrous God!) changed their disposition and repented of what they had done. They fell at the feet of the saint, asking forgiveness, which they immediately received. Henceforth they allowed the saint to do peacefully with that land whatever he wished. Having conceived the idea of building a church but not having animals for transporting all that was necessary for construction, the saint once met a woman in a gorge, a widow. Having told her of his need, he gave her three gold coins as a blessing. And then she said to him with respect: "Father, I have many animals, but they are all wild. If you can, gather the whole herd, and I shall give them to your holiness." Having made a prayer, the saint ordered his servant to go up the mountain where the animals were grazing and choose the two best ones, which, submitting to the word of the saint, immediately calmed down and followed the servant. With their help the saint brought the timber and built a most beautiful church in the name of the Most Holy Theotokos, and then built cells and founded a monastery. People who had learned of the struggles of the saint, having gathered here in great numbers, then accepted monasticism and entered into obedience to Saint Gregory, for he was a sleepless shepherd and in all things a wise steward. However, there was no water in that place, and the monks grieved greatly. Then, raising his hands and lifting up his mind to the Heavens, the saint with faith and tears prayed long to the Most High God to give water. An Angel of the Lord descended to him from heaven and revealed his impending departure to Heaven. Showing the saint the place of his burial, the Angel said that from it sweetest water would flow. Having spoken these words, the Angel ascended to Heaven. Summoning his disciple Leontios and the other brethren, the divine Gregory announced to them what he had heard from the Angel. Having sufficiently instructed them, he commanded them to do all that befits the monastic life, after which he gave himself to prayer and thus departed to the Lord. His sacred and all-honorable remains were committed to burial in the place designated by the Angel of God, where later a church was built in the name of the saint. In the middle of the church is his tomb, from which flows a spring of sweetest water, which to this day heals every disease in those who come with faith, to the glory of God and the saint, through whose intercession may we also be delivered from every evil and be granted the Kingdom of Heaven. Amen.

Part 3

The Life and Struggles of Our
Father Among the Saints Leontius, Patriarch of
Jerusalem, Who Shone Forth in the Twelfth Century

The homeland of our venerable and God-bearing father Leontius was a city called by all Strumica (formerly known as Tiberiopolis). He was born to wealthy and pious parents and, regenerated in Divine Baptism, was named Leo. When the venerable one grew up, he was sent to school to study sacred letters. Reading the lives of the saints, he greatly desired to renounce the world and become a monk in order to labor for the Lord. When his father died, he left his homeland and, coming to a small village, found there a certain pious priest who was a friend of his father. Knowing Leo well and loving the youth for his virtue, he received him into his home. Seeing the holy icons in the priest's house, Leo approached them and began conversing with them as if they were alive, asking them to direct his path and lead him to salvation.

Then he lay down to sleep in order to rest from the labors of his journey. Awakening at night, Leo took a small icon depicting the Lord as an infant and, unnoticed by anyone, went up the mountain. Placing the icon before himself, he knelt and began to pray: *"Cause me to know the way in which I should walk, for I lift up my soul to You"* (Psalm 142:8). Plant me in Your holy mountain, in Your prepared dwelling-place. Cover me with the shelter of Your wings, for behold I have fled far away, and I know not where I shall dwell, but in You have I hoped from my mother's womb, forsake me not unto the end." Praying with these and other words and conversing with the holy icon as if it were alive, he stood thus until evening, having tasted nothing. When darkness fell and he wished to sleep, he gathered a great quantity of thorns and, stripping himself naked, lay down upon them. The thorns pierced his tender body, which began to bleed, causing him severe pain. Suffering without food, and lying naked upon the thorns to sleep while shedding warm tears, Leo spent three days thus. Then he descended from the mountain and came to the priest's house. Bidding him farewell, he set out for Constantinople without a single obol or piece of bread.

Approaching Constantinople, Leo entered the monastery of the Theotokos called Ptelidion, and there received monasticism. And thus, being a monk both outwardly and according to the inner man, the venerable one came to the capital, known by no one and a stranger both to the city and to its inhabitants. He wished to greet no one, he wished to become acquainted with no one, neither small nor great, but immediately began to struggle against the powers of darkness. Feigning madness, he appeared before the inhabitants of the city. And some struck him on the cheeks, others with fists, and still others mocked him.

Desiring to test whether he had acquired any benefit from his holy folly, he took burning coals in his hands and, running through the marketplaces, censed everyone he met on the road, especially the holy icons of Christ and the Theotokos which were at the crossroads. And a miracle occurred, because these coals did not burn his hands at all. Wishing to test whether this was not a diabolical deception for the seduction of people, he repeated the same thing when he was alone. But even then the coals did not harm him. He decided to try once more and, gathering up the hem of his robe, placed many burning coals there with his bare hands. But neither did his garment burn, nor did he burn his hands. Upon the coals lay incense, which, burning, gave off fragrance. The venerable one marveled greatly at this and thought that perhaps he had already attained a great measure of holiness. But immediately Leo drove away these thoughts, calling himself earth and ashes, pulling himself by the hair, shedding many tears, covering his head with earth, and calling upon God for help.

But the venerable one did not stop at this test and, being in the bathhouse, removed the cloak from his shoulders and threw it into the bathhouse furnace, but the same miracle occurred: the garment suffered nothing at all from the fire. Then, thinking that the demon of pride was mocking him, he began to weep even more and beat his head against the wall, fearing that he would become proud and lose all that he had acquired from his holy folly. The venerable one continued his holy folly all the time that he was in Constantinople. He aroused amazement in some, and they testified that he was a servant of God, while others beat him, considering him mad.

Later there came to Constantinople a bishop of Tiberias renowned in virtues, and the divine Leontius immediately attached himself to him, submitting to him in all things. And he too pleased his spiritual father, who rejoiced and blessed Leontius for his prudence and obedience, for at such a young age he had taken upon his shoulders with all his soul the yoke of Christ. His obedience was made manifest in the following miracle.

It should be said that his elder did not reside in Constantinople, but in a certain mountainous place, in a harsh location suitable for hesychia, where he instructed his disciples in all that serves the benefit of the soul. Once the elder sent Leontius on an errand to the capital, commanding him to return that same day after completing it, so as to avoid the temptations that occur in cities. The bishop also added the saying that even for fish it is harmful to remain on dry land for a long time. Having heard this instruction, Leontius set out for Constantinople. There he endeavored to complete the task entrusted to him as quickly as possible. Having finished everything while it was still day, the youth went down to the shore, but discovered that there was no ship to take him to where the elder lived. For a long time he ran along the shore as if someone were chasing him, seeking a suitable ship. But since the sun had already set, there was no one on the shore who could ferry him to the elder. Meeting a certain priest, a friend of the elder, he asked him to quickly take him to him, because he did not have a blessing to spend the night outside his cell. The priest replied that it was already late, everyone had gone to their homes, and persuaded him to come to his house to have supper and sleep. But the blessed Leontius, learning that the priest had two beautiful daughters and considering the danger to which his soul might be exposed, preferred rather to fulfill the elder's blessing and drown in the sea than to violate the blessing and fall into temptation. Placing all his hope in God and in the prayers of his elder, he threw himself into the sea. And—O miracle!—God, who once helped Peter to walk on the waters, now also helped His servant, delivering him from the sea current, for while being in the water, the venerable one began to walk as if on dry land. Realizing that he could walk on the water, he went forward, but did not understand how this was happening, for the waters completely covered him, and some were even a span above his head. Thus he walked until he reached the opposite shore.

With what words can one convey the great faith in God that the youth had, or the miracle wrought for him by God? If anyone should ask why God did not allow the venerable one to walk upon the sea as on dry land, or upon the sea floor, as Israel did of old, but immersed him in the water, we shall answer thus: Since the venerable one was still young and unestablished in virtue, this happened to him so that he would not be exalted, thinking he had attained perfection in holiness, and so that he would understand that only one who has poured forth much sweat and struggled greatly in virtue can walk on the sea as on dry land. The venerable one came to the elder in the deep of night, completely wet. Seeing him and learning of the miracle wrought by God, his spiritual father rejoiced, marveling at his disciple, and glorified him for his love and faith in God, and his perfect obedience to his teacher. And the disciple, in turn, was pleased to have such a teacher, who could deliver his disciples from death.

Having decided to return to his diocese, the teacher took Leontius with him. But because of a storm that arose at sea, they arrived at the island of Patmos. Going up to the monastery of the holy John the Theologian, they rested there for several days, and then again boarded a ship and arrived in Cyprus to spend the winter, intending to go to Jerusalem and to Tiberias, the diocese of the father, in the spring. But God, who knew beforehand the future struggles of Leontius on Patmos, did not allow him to go to Jerusalem from Cyprus. Knowing that it was not beneficial for him to remain in Cyprus, the youth asked the elder to allow him to return to Patmos, to the monastery of John the Theologian, because he had greatly loved that place and the life of the fathers there. God, who had moved the disciple to this, also moved the soul of the teacher, who gave him permission. Thus the venerable one returned to Patmos with all diligence, having with him nothing except the old clothing that he was wearing.

Coming to the monastery, he was received by the abbot of that time named Theoctistus, who was truly a spiritual man and servant of God, able to discern what lies within a person by the outward and apparent. Having received Leontius, the abbot commanded the venerable one not to associate with the brethren, not to attend the common church services, but to keep hesychia in his cell and fulfill the rule which he himself assigned him, because Leontius was still a beardless youth and might cause scandal. Remaining in his cell, the youth underwent monastic life with all strictness: he prayed unceasingly, read Sacred Scripture, chanted psalms, had zeal for the virtues, tears flowed from his eyes like streams, and when the other brethren slept and it was difficult for him to produce tears, he would take a strap prepared for this purpose and strike himself on his naked body. From the severe pain, the venerable one wept even against his will. Many nails were fastened to the strap, so that when he struck himself, the nails, piercing deeply into his flesh, tore away skin, blood flowed from the wounds, and the cruel pains caused abundant hot tears. Because of the wounds, lying on the ground was even more painful for the venerable one. To those who saw him, he appeared dry and emaciated from the beatings and wounds, but no one knew the true cause of this.

In order always to have remembrance of death, very often at dawn Leontius would secretly leave his cell and go to the brotherhood cemetery. There he would remove his clothing and, without any fear, boldly enter some tomb where the remains of the departed lay. He would fall to the ground as if dead, of his own will, and lie there the whole day, weeping and sobbing so intensely that he drenched the bodies of the departed with his tears, while no one knew that he was there. Leontius did this not one, not two, not ten, but many years, as the brethren later understood when they learned of it.

The abbot appointed the venerable one to assist the ecclesiarch, and while performing this obedience, he did not cease his secret labors of unceasing prayer, meditation, contrition of heart, tears, vigils, and standing, so that his body became weak from the many afflictions, and he began to be subject to blameless bodily passions, especially sleep. Seeing that Leontius was drowsing during the service and leaning his head against the wall of the church, the abbot would approach and push him in the chest; the venerable one would strike his head against the wall, wake up, and the other brethren would become more attentive. The abbot did this until he learned of the venerable one's secret labors, and then he ceased troubling him. Having learned of Leontius's ascetic life, the abbot decided to test him in other ways as well, to see whether this adamant could be overcome by anything. Sometimes he elevated him to the dignity of superior and ecclesiarch, sometimes he demoted him from this dignity, making him a humble servant, but the blessed one paid no attention whatsoever to these changes; never did a word of complaint come from his mouth, as though he were completely without soul. And although the venerable one was always humble and considered himself worse than a dog, he never ceased inflicting beatings upon himself, doing this sometimes at night when the other brethren slept, and sometimes during the day, going far from the monastery to a quiet place so that no one would see him. When he beat himself, he would say: "Open the eyes of my heart, O Lord, and enlighten them with the light of Your knowledge, *for with You is the fountain of life; in Your light we see light*" (Psalm 35:10). Speaking thus, he implored God with warm tears, and one night he saw a hand up to the elbow, holding bread, and heard a voice: "Take this bread and eat it." And that bread resembled a pita made from flour with spices and honey. As soon as the venerable one ate that bread, he came to himself, and from that time he began easily to understand the meaning of Sacred Scripture. There was not a single spiritual book that did not seem sweet and pleasant to him, or that he did not understand. His tongue became sharper than the tongue of rhetoricians, and he eloquently expounded all that the good Spirit of God spoke to him. Leontius easily memorized entire books by heart, and not only those that contain the lives of the venerable ones and martyrs, or the writings of the divine fathers with moral teachings, but also those in which the lofty dogmas of the faith were expounded, which few understood because of the theological concepts they contained. Leontius remembered them so well and cited them when he spoke, that some thought he was reading from a book; Leontius thoroughly mastered the theological book called the "Dogmatic Panoply." Thus enlightened in the lofty knowledge of theological dogmas, the venerable one became a beacon of knowledge and a most God-inspired mind, but the more the gifts of the Holy Spirit abounded in him, the more the thrice-blessed one multiplied his labors. To his daily beatings he resolved to add even greater humility and to abstain completely from all food. But since he was in a coenobitic monastery and went to meals together with everyone, it was difficult to refuse food entirely, and so that the brethren would not learn of it and be scandalized, he devised the following. The venerable one sat down at the table together with everyone, took food, put it in his mouth, but did not swallow it; instead, he secretly spit it into the sleeve of his garment. There he kept it until the end of the meal, and then gave it to the birds. Thus he left the table hungry.

Having reflected on all this, the abbot deemed Leontius worthy to receive the priesthood. But when he informed him of this, Leontius at first did not even want to hear of it, but then, being strongly pressed by the abbot and so as not to be found disobedient, he reluctantly allowed himself to be persuaded and received the great and full monastic schema and the priestly rank. And although through the Mystery of the Priesthood the venerable one became a teacher and enlightener of others, he did not behave as a teacher and despise the lesser brethren, but was for all an example of humility, laboring with those who labored, consoling those who sorrowed, correcting those who were falling, and healing those who were scandalized. After this, under pressure from the abbot and by the decision of all the brethren, Leontius became steward of the monastery. Being bound by cares and labors beyond his strength, he nevertheless did not abandon his secret labors and his customary beatings, which he manfully endured in his cell. The venerable one spent all night in reading the word of God, prayers, psalmody, and purifying tears, and only for the last hour of the night, at dawn, did he sleep. Therefore the Lord also visited him with His grace, which is clearly seen from the following account.

On the feast of the holy John the Theologian, after the vigil, the venerable one went to rest a little in his cell. There he took a book in his hands, and... a miracle occurred! Under the guise of the abbot, the apostle of Christ John the Theologian appeared to him and said: "Child Leontius, go quickly and begin to serve earlier than the usual time, because I wish to go to Ephesus." Unable to contradict the abbot's command, he went to his cell, pondering along the way why he had not told him beforehand that he wished to go to Ephesus, and why he was not taking him along. Making the customary prostration, the venerable one asked for a blessing to begin the Divine Liturgy. The abbot asked him:

"What is the matter with you, brother? Do you wish to serve now?"

"Father, did you not yourself command me to quickly perform the Divine Liturgy, because you wish to go to Ephesus?"

Hearing this, the abbot understood that it had been John the Theologian, and therefore said:

"Go, child, and do what you were commanded, for the beloved John will invisibly celebrate together with both us and the Ephesians."

Thus the venerable one was deemed worthy to see John the Theologian and hear his voice. The monastery of John the Theologian received a yearly imperial allowance, which came from the island of Crete. At that time, these funds on Crete were administered by John Stravoromanos. Being the second superior of the monastery, the venerable one together with other brethren went to him for the allowance and to acquire all that was necessary for the brethren. When he was on Crete, one evening a certain Constantine Scanphis, who pretended to be mad, although there were testimonies that he foresaw and predicted the future and healed spiritual and bodily passions of some, began to cry out loudly: "Lord, have mercy!" and did this repeatedly. Thinking that by this unusual cry he was warning that a great evil was coming upon Crete, many ran to him to find out what was happening. However, to the question of why he was crying out and what had happened, he gave no answer, but only continued to cry: "Lord, have mercy!" The divine Leontius also wished to go to him to find out the reason for his cries. As soon as Leontius set out on his way, Scanphis stopped saying: "Lord, have mercy!" but began to cry out even louder: "Make way, make way, he is coming, he is coming! Woe to you, O pious ones, at this hour. If he had not come, what would have happened to you?" When the venerable one approached him, Scanphis said: "Welcome, welcome, my Chrysostom." He fell down at his feet, began to kiss them, and cried out even more fervently: "Welcome!" But why Scanphis spoke thus and acted thus, no one learned, nor did he himself tell anyone, except that by his actions and words he showed that Leontius was great before God and holy.

On another occasion, the abbot fell ill with a terrible mortal disease and took to his bed. The venerable one was greatly grieved because of the illness of his spiritual father. After the Liturgy, Leontius went with the brethren to the common meal and inquired of the attendant what the abbot would eat and whether he had an appetite. Learning that the elder not only had no appetite, but was suffering terribly from a frightful attack, the venerable one was greatly grieved and, sighing from all his heart, began to pray. Rising from the table, he went to the abbot's cell. Making the customary prostration and asking for a blessing, he understood that his elder was suffering so intensely that he could not even speak. Then the venerable one found a small gourd with wine, filled a cup with it, and wanted to give it to the sick man to drink. The sick man refused and said in a barely audible voice that as soon as he drank this wine, he would immediately die. But the venerable one still persuaded him to drink, saying that Christ had blessed this and as soon as he drank, he would immediately recover. With these words, the venerable one made the sign of the Cross over the cup, secretly calling upon the Lord for help. Seeing that the elder did not want to drink, Leontius called upon the Lord aloud, speaking such simple words: "My beloved Christ, my desired Master. If You love Your Mother, my Lady, hear me, Your poor servant, and grant healing to my spiritual father." Hearing this and being moved by this simple prayer, the elder obeyed and drank the wine. And—O miracle!—his illness passed at that very moment, and so much bile came out of him that they filled an entire vessel with it. This also confirms the extraordinariness of the miracle, for undoubtedly the abbot could not have lived with such an amount of deadly matter.

Learning what great boldness Leontius had toward God, the elder from that time urged him to become abbot and himself gladly submitted to the one who by his prayer to God had granted him life. But the venerable one did not even want to hear of this, but remained in his former obedience, submitting to his spiritual father. He continued diligently to heal the sick and to kiss the rotting members of the infirm.

Having once come to Constantinople on monastery business, the venerable one, being the second person after the abbot, fulfilled all that had been entrusted to him, and then went up to the monastery of the venerable Daniel the Stylite. Seeing that this place was deserted and peaceful, he greatly desired to spend the rest of his life there in hesychia. Sharing these thoughts with the brethren who struggled there and receiving their agreement, he promised first to go to Patmos to give an account of his affairs to the brethren, and then to return here. But God, who arranges all things, at this time took the abbot of the monastery on Patmos to the eternal dwellings, having commanded him to appoint Leontius as abbot, of which the abbot left a written instruction.

Returning to the island and seeing that the monastery was in such a distressed state, the venerable one did not know what to do. He remembered the promise he had given to God and to the venerable Daniel—to become the successor of his virtue—and was more inclined to go to the monastery of the Stylite. However, the tears of the brethren, who were orphaned like sheep without a shepherd, and the written decision of the abbot, or rather the unwritten one from God, prevailed upon him, and he reluctantly accepted the brethren's proposal to remain. Then he began to add labors to labors, vigils to vigils, explaining to all that the vigilance and care of superiors for their subordinates compels subordinates to respect and obey their superiors: "If I keep watch, it is not only for myself but also for those subordinate to me, so as to make them obey my commands." Therefore, everyone who disobeyed the venerable one's instructions received appropriate correction, but not from men, but from cruel demons, as will become clear from the following account.

Opposite Patmos lies a small uninhabited island called Lipso, on which the monks kept their animals. In summer the monks would slaughter the surplus animals, dry the meat in the sun and sell it, obtaining funds for the monastery. A monk named Prochorus was sent for this obedience, a malicious and inhuman man. Prochorus constantly pestered the venerable one with requests for new shoes. Learning from the monastery's cobbler that the shoes were not yet ready, the venerable one gently told Prochorus that he would receive the shoes when he returned from Lipso. But the obstinate Prochorus, feeling no shame before the venerable one, behaved insolently and demanded the shoes at once. The venerable one gently said to him: "Go in peace and fulfill your obedience, lest something you do not want befall you." But the other did not listen and kept refusing to leave. Then the venerable one decided that he was worthy of correction like a disobedient ram, and said: "Go, and *let your way be darkness and slippery places, and let the Angel of the Lord pursue you.*" No sooner had the saint uttered these words than God confirmed his holy words with a deed. As soon as the disobedient Prochorus got into the boat to go to Lipso, stones suddenly began to rain down upon him, as thick as hail. But the most amazing thing was that the stones fell only on Prochorus, not touching anyone else who was sailing, while everyone heard voices: "For stubbornness, for stubbornness." Then the wretched man understood that these were demonic forces sent to punish and teach him what an evil thing disobedience and disregard for the requests of one's spiritual father are. Getting out of the boat in sorrow and somewhat freed from the stones, he came to himself and began to reflect on why such an evil had happened to him. If the stones had continued to fall, he would have become completely exhausted or gone mad. When Prochorus prepared to have dinner, stones again began to rain down on him, the bowl was smashed, the food was spilled, the vessel of wine was also broken, and the demons who were throwing stones at him called him by name and kept saying: "For stubbornness, for stubbornness."

The wretched Prochorus lost his mind because of the extraordinary calamity that had befallen him and did not know what to do. He forgot about food and drink and returned from Lipso with wounds on his body from the stones. Showing them to the venerable one, he told him of the misfortune that had befallen him. One of the monks, having listened to his story, gathered courage and proudly said to the brethren: "This monk suffered because he does not know his letters, with which to drive away the demons. But I always rely on God and on my knowledge of letters, and therefore suffer no disturbance from the demons." Taking the Psalter, he made the customary prostration to the venerable one and set out for Lipso. However, the same thing happened to him: stones began to fall upon him from nowhere, and the one who had previously considered himself brave and had hoped in his knowledge of letters suddenly became a coward and ran back to the monastery. Then, judging that these two monks had been sufficiently punished by righteous correction, the great Leontius took with him several pious brethren and set out for Lipso. There he prayed to God and drove away the demons, and those who had been righteously punished, one for disobedience and the other for pride, ceased to be afraid.

Once pirates came to the monastery, and the venerable one received them with all friendliness. But since they were barbarians, they demanded the food that was customary for them: bread, wine, sheep's meat, and other things. The venerable one ordered that everything the monastery had be given to them, but the pirates demanded still more. The venerable one at first calmly persuaded the pirates to take what was offered, because the monastery had nothing more. However, they did not want to take lenten food, but, insulting the abbot and frightening the brethren, went down to the shore and burned the monastery's ship, of which the monks who saw this informed the venerable one. Grieving with all his heart, the venerable one took in his hands the icon of John the Theologian and said loudly before all the brethren: "O beloved Theologian, if you do not avenge these evildoers for the damage they have caused us, your servants, then know that I shall remain here no longer and shall not be abbot, if you do not hear me." No sooner had the venerable one said this than his words immediately became a deed. When the pirates were leaving Patmos, the sea was calm. But as soon as they dropped anchor at Ikaria, a strong wind arose and raised enormous waves, which sank the ship together with the pirates. Those who managed to get ashore half-dead were killed by the Ikarians. Only one woman survived, and she told the people about the miracle. Learning of this incident, other pirates from that time began to honor and respect the great Leontius. And that the venerable one also knew the secrets of the heart will be clear from the following account.

The venerable one took from Crete a disciple named Antony, whom he commanded to confess every evening the thoughts that had come to him during the day. And so he did. But once a thought came to him which he did not reveal to the saint, considering it insignificant. Having made a prostration, Antony wanted to leave the venerable one's cell, but the blessing of his spiritual father compelled him to confess this thought as well. A twofold feeling struggled within him: on the one hand, he wanted to confess the thought, and on the other hand, he wanted to go to his cell. Then the venerable one said to him: "Speak, child, also this thought that has come to you, and do not disdain it, considering it insignificant and harmless. He who despises the small, as we know, will later despise the great as well." Hearing these words unexpectedly, Antony became afraid because the venerable one had revealed to him both what the thought was and its power. Falling at the feet of the venerable one and accusing himself of negligence, the disciple asked forgiveness, which he received.

The venerable one was also informed of matters that occurred far from the monastery, as the following account attests. There lived on Crete a monk Athanasius, a native of Constantinople. Wishing to bring repentance to God for the sins he had committed, he came to the monastery on Patmos and received the great schema, also making large donations to the monastery. However, the envy of the hater of good did not allow him to struggle peacefully in the monastery, but made him go again to Crete and remain there. When Leontius came to Crete, Athanasius promised him that if he sent Antony there the following year, he too would return with him to the monastery. Having returned to the monastery, one day when Antony came to his cell, the venerable one said to him:

"Know, child, that Athanasius has died on Crete."

"How do you know this, holy father?"

"Today a ship came from Crete, and those on it informed some inhabitants of the island of this news, and they transmitted it to me."

That Athanasius had died, there was no doubt, but as became clear after inquiries, no ship from Crete had put in to the island either then or later. Antony alone heard this news from the venerable one and told the others.

Once the demon of blasphemy began to attack Antony, and the warfare was terrible, for the blasphemy was directed against the Lady Theotokos. Antony was greatly troubled and confessed his blasphemy to the venerable one, asking for his help, and in reply heard:

"Take courage, child, and do not be afraid, let the dog bark, and you say to him: 'Be silent, accursed one, and do not make noise.' Because it is impossible to revile and blaspheme Her, on whom alone is the hope of my salvation, and whom I cannot but glorify and honor worthily—my Sovereign Lady and Mistress."

With such a weapon did the venerable one arm Antony against the demon of blasphemy, but the impious demon began to trouble him even more. When Antony went with the brethren to the services, he received respite and deliverance from the warfare, but as soon as he entered his cell, he was again subjected to the fiercest attacks from the enemy. And he had no other refuge except the venerable one and his counsels. Since this warfare continued many years and the enemy did not retreat, Antony was finally overcome by fear, and once, leaving the church, he did not dare to enter his cell, fearing the warfare from the blasphemous thoughts. Running to the venerable one's cell, he again told him of the temptation, and the latter again commanded him not to worry about these thoughts, but to drive them away with words of contempt. Possessed by fear, Antony said:

"Father, I shall not leave your cell unless you deliver me from this enemy temptation. How can I go to my cell? For it is a refuge of temptation for me."

After this, the venerable one rose from the bench on which he was sitting and, standing before the analogion, asked God and the Lady Theotokos, whom the demon was blaspheming, to help the brother. Then, taking Antony by the hand, he placed it upon his own neck and said:

"Let this sin, brother, be upon me, upon my neck. If the enemy attacks you again, then say to him: 'By the prayers of the humble and sinful Leontius, I consider you, enemy of truth, a black and unclean dog.'"

Having been thus taught by the venerable one and armed by him for battle, Antony made a prostration and left his cell. After these words, the warfare immediately ceased, and the blasphemous thoughts completely disappeared as if they had never existed. That same night Antony heard some voices reviling the venerable one and threatening him: "You are fortunate that you turned to Leontius and placed your hope in him, but if you had not done this, you would have learned what was to happen to you."

Next we shall recount how the great Leontius conquered the passion of anger. In the Patmos monastery there were many monks from different nations and of different dispositions. Due to human weakness, they sometimes became angry with one another, disobeyed, and treated the monastery's obediences with negligence. Therefore, the venerable one often sternly corrected and rebuked them for their neglect of duty, but he said and acted thus only outwardly, while in his heart he was not disturbed at all, but remained imperturbable. When the time came, he approached the Divine Mysteries without hindrance, as if nothing had happened, entered the holy altar with imperturbability, and celebrated the Divine Liturgy. Once, when Antony asked him whether the discord with the brethren did not trouble him, and whether it was possible after this to serve the Liturgy, the venerable one answered in such a way that to simple people this may seem supernatural and difficult to accept: "Believe me, child, that my anger is feigned and entirely in words only, for how can one correct those who sin unless one shows that one is angry with them?"

Once the saint set out for Constantinople, but a storm arose at sea, and his ship put in at a certain small island where there lived a rich man named Mavros. Learning that the divine Leontius was on the ship, Mavros greatly rejoiced (for he had already heard of him), desiring to converse with this wonderful man. Therefore, Mavros asked the venerable one to come to the city and bless his house. Taking with him two disciples—Antony and Andronicus—the venerable one came to the house of Mavros. Having prayed for him and his wife, he blessed their house and instructed them with soul-profitable teachings. When he was preparing to leave, the couple fell at his feet and asked him to pray that the Lord would give them a child, for they were childless, and grieved greatly because of this. The venerable one answered: "I am a sinner and, like you, need the help of God. But according to your faith, so be it to you. May the Lord give you a child the following year," which indeed occurred according to the venerable one's prediction. The following year, Mavros's wife bore him a daughter, whom they named Leonto in honor of the venerable one.

On another occasion, the venerable one again prepared to set out for the capital on monastery business. However, a strong wind forced the ship to return to port. Waiting on the ship for the storm to subside, Leontius became seriously ill and, gravely suffering, was carried on a bed to the monastery. During the fourteen days of his illness, he could neither eat nor drink nor speak. Only a faint breathing showed that the venerable one was still alive. His bodily strength was failing, he was approaching death, and therefore everything had already been prepared for the burial. However, the Lord, who both breaks down and heals, granted him another thirteen and a half years of life, that is, according to the number of days of his illness, and at the end of the fourteenth day he received a revelation from God about the extension of his life. After this, Leontius began to come to himself and to partake of food little by little.

During this time, the storm at sea subsided, and the sailors decided to sail. Going up to the monastery, they asked the venerable one whom he would send in his place. In a weak voice he answered that he was appointing Antony. But the latter received these words like an arrow to the heart, saying: "In what have I sinned before you, father, that I should be deprived of your final prayers, for you will soon die and leave us orphans. Separation from you is unbearable for me, just as I cannot remain without your final prayers, and therefore I do not wish to hear or think of this."

When the distressed Antony had expressed all this to the venerable one, the latter called him to himself and said: "Did you truly think, Antony, that the time of my life had come to an end?... No, my Christ has extended it according to His ineffable love for mankind, as He is accustomed to do with me, and has added to me fourteen and a half years of life. Depart with joy and remember that I shall be conversing with you for another fourteen and a half years." As the venerable one said, so it came to pass. And during the time that was granted him by God, he performed other wondrous deeds and became Patriarch of Jerusalem, of which we shall recount below.

The following year, the Lord willed that the holy Leontius with Antony should again sail to Crete for the customary allowance for the monastery. But the tax collector on Crete did not issue them the appointed allowance, and the venerable one returned to Patmos empty-handed. Being in need, the brethren began to ask the venerable one to go to the capital and report this matter to the emperor, so as to receive the customary allowance. The venerable one, however, answered nothing, hoping that the Holy Spirit would reveal to him whether he needed to go to Constantinople. Since the brethren insisted, he said, as if with irritation, so that all might hear: "Leave me alone and do not compel me, for if I go to the capital, I shall only pass through Patmos afterward." But no one understood what he meant until the venerable one's prophecy was fulfilled. Having prepared for the journey, the venerable one set out for Constantinople. There he met and conversed with a certain man wise not only in divine matters but also in human affairs, who was a close friend of the emperor and held the office of droungarios. This man respected the venerable one as a father and honored him as a man of God. He presented him thus to the emperor Manuel Comnenus: "O Emperor, here is a man of God who can be an intercessor for your realm; I believe that when he wishes, he can entreat the God who loves mankind." Believing that the divine Leontius was exactly as the droungarios said of him—for his face, dry and yellow, testified to this, as did the simplicity of his speech, his readiness to answer questions and resolve difficulties of Sacred Scripture— the emperor understood that he had found a great treasure, and therefore planned to make him a hierarch and pastor of the people.

At that time the patriarch of the Russians had died, and the emperor decided to appoint him patriarch among the Russians in place of the deceased. He conveyed this news to the venerable one through the droungarios, but Leontius did not wish to become pastor of the Russians. Later, the island of Cyprus became widowed, and again the emperor tried through the droungarios to learn whether the venerable one wished to become Bishop of Cyprus. But he again refused, for by the grace of the All-Holy Spirit he knew that he was to become a hierarch. But his disciples urged him to agree, and especially Antony, who said: "It seems to us, father, that you do not wish to bestow a benefit either upon yourself, or upon us who after God and the Theotokos hope in you alone, or upon your monastery. Will the emperor hear your request concerning the monastery if you yourself have twice refused his request? If you were to become Bishop of Cyprus, you would be a helper to us throughout your life, and our monastery would be exalted and flourish." Having listened, the venerable one replied:

"Child, why do you compel me to reveal to you that which God has wished to reveal to me alone, the humble one? Neither the emperor knows this, nor you."

"What is it, honorable father?"

"If the Heavenly King wishes me to be a patriarch, how can an earthly emperor make me a bishop?"

"To which throne, holy father, will God appoint you as patriarch?"

"That I shall become patriarch, I have learned precisely from the Lord, but upon which throne I shall exercise the patriarchate, He has not revealed to me."

After some time, in accordance with this prophecy, the divine Leontius became Patriarch of Jerusalem. Moved by the Holy Spirit, he appointed Antony as steward of the monastery on Patmos, telling him that he would become abbot after the one he was now appointing, which later came to pass. Having become Patriarch of Jerusalem, the great Leontius on his way to Jerusalem stopped at Patmos. The venerable one went up to the monastery and, having blessed the abbot he had appointed, sailed away after two days. Then the brethren remembered the prophecy of the venerable one, which he had uttered when they were urging him to go to the capital, when he said that afterward he would only pass through Patmos.

Arriving at Rhodes at the beginning of winter, the venerable one decided to remain there until spring. He sent a man to the monastery to the steward Antony to inform him that his necessary provisions had run out and he had nowhere to obtain them, unless Antony would take care of him and send food. Maintaining obedience to his elder, Antony purchased all that was necessary and prepared to sail to Rhodes; however, a strong contrary wind arose and carried the ship to another place. All, together with Antony, asked God for help through the prayers of the venerable Leontius—and a miracle occurred. The wind ceased, and after some time the ship entered the port of Rhodes. Enlightened by the grace of the Holy Spirit, the venerable one at this very time commanded his companions to go down to the shore, saying that the steward of the monastery had arrived with provisions. Believing him, they went with the Patriarch to the port and were greatly amazed to find Antony and those with him with the provisions; such was the clairvoyance of the saint.

When spring arrived, the venerable one sailed to Cyprus, where there was a monastery under the jurisdiction of the Patriarchate of Jerusalem, where one could stop for a brief rest. However, this monastery proved to be in great neglect, since there were only two monks in it whose behavior was unmonastic. These monks lived with wives and occupied themselves only with licentiousness. Being greatly grieved, the venerable one advised them to abstain from sins in the future and to repent now, lest sudden death overtake them and they go to hell. But the monks continued to remain in sin, excusing themselves by saying that habit had overcome in them both the law and the canons. Groaning from the depths of his heart, the holy Leontius said: "Children, I have fulfilled my duty and counseled you in what is good, but since you have despised both me and my words, God shall now judge you." A day later, Divine judgment punished these wretches, and being completely healthy, both of them suddenly died. This is how unrepentant sinners are punished by His judgment.

A certain Cypriot monk named John decided to become a disciple of the venerable one, but fell into fornication, and thinking that the saint did not know of this, remained unrepentant. The spiritual father revealed this sin to him and, giving him a penance, inclined him to repentance and correction, but he did not want to repent, for which he received a double punishment from God. When the saint raised his hand in the air to make the sign of the Cross over the sinful monk, the wretch immediately went blind, and not six days passed before he died. Such was the wretched bodily and spiritual end that befell him.

From the time that the former Patriarch of Jerusalem had reposed, the imperial tax collector named Kyriacus, who was assigned to Cyprus, had been appropriating for himself all the revenues, including those of the dependencies of the Patriarchate of Jerusalem, and therefore the venerable one found nothing for the maintenance of himself and his people. Such a great hierarch, the Patriarch of Jerusalem, being in the heart of the land of the Romans, had not only no surplus of provisions, but even lacked the necessities of life. However, the holy Leontius manfully endured all misfortunes. The devil, wishing to test the venerable one to see whether he would lose heart in the temptations that had befallen him, raised up against him the servant of the tax collector named Triandaphyllos. Coming to the house of the Patriarch, he angrily demanded that all the revenues from the real estate of the Patriarchate of Jerusalem in Cyprus be handed over, threatening that if he did not receive them immediately, he would throw the Patriarch and his people into prison. The saint asked him to wait a little, but the other rose up in anger and left. However, Divine wrath overtook him; becoming deranged, he began to beat his head against the walls. Deciding that this was an accident, he ordered his servants to take away the Patriarch's mule, and he himself rode after them on a horse. Unexpectedly, his horse reared up, he fell from it, and striking the ground, was blinded. Only then did he understand that he had sinned and commanded his men to take him to the saint. Falling at his feet, he confessed his sin and asked forgiveness. The compassionate venerable one made the sign of the Cross over him and kissed him with a holy kiss. At that moment, the wretched man regained his sight and began to see better than before.

Once Leontius went to the dependency of the Holy Sepulchre to visit the brethren who were there. And since he was well known in those parts, a multitude of Christians came there to venerate the saint and receive his blessing. There also came a certain monk who was living contrary to his vows and was possessed by the demon of fornication. Although the wretched man knew of his passion and grieved, he was constantly overcome by evil habit. Looking him in the face, the venerable one said before all: "Brother, you are suffering from a spiritual illness which will lead you to death." Struck by the words of the venerable one, the monk fell at his feet, asking for healing. The venerable one prayed to God, laid his hands on him, and blessed him, after which the monk was healed and began to abstain from sin. Answering the questions of his countrymen who were interested in what the Patriarch had exposed him for, the monk boldly confessed that he had suffered from the passion of fornication and had fallen into sin the previous night. As this monk, so also all those who confessed their sins and sincerely repented received healing.

The steward responsible for the property of the Holy Sepulchre in Cyprus reported to the Patriarch that the Bishop of Amathous had branded with his seal the sheep, oxen, horses, and almost all the animals belonging to the dependency of the Holy Sepulchre, and had appropriated them. The holy Leontius summoned this bishop to himself, but the proud bishop did not want to submit. Only after the Patriarch summoned him a third time did he reluctantly come. The venerable one received him and asked him not to brand with his seal the animals belonging to the dependencies of the Church of Jerusalem, so as not to experience the wrath of God upon himself. Paying absolutely no attention to the Patriarch's words, the bishop rose up in anger and left without returning the appropriated animals. But several days later, God avenged him for his falsehood. When the bishop was crossing a small river on horseback, he fell from his horse, was injured, and died, presenting a spectacle worthy of lamentation.

The Most Blessed Archbishop of Cyprus Barnabas, greatly honoring the great Leontius, once came to him with a request to serve the Liturgy together with him and his bishops, saying: "We wish to be sanctified by your presence, holy Master." Leontius responded to Barnabas's request. When the Divine Liturgy was being celebrated and all the priestly order stood in their places (O great purity of Thy servants, O Lord!), the holy Leontius noticed that the faces of the Archbishop of Cyprus and the Bishop of Trimythous shone more brightly than the sun, from the abundance of the Divine grace dwelling in them; the faces of other hierarchs were somewhat darker, of others still darker, and of some—both light and dark at the same time. Among these latter was also the Bishop of Lapithos, a cousin of Antony, the disciple of the holy Leontius, to whom the Patriarch recounted the vision when, meeting him in the capital, Antony asked about his cousin.

Then the venerable one departed from Cyprus and arrived in Acre. Learning of his arrival, a multitude of people came to him. Some he blessed, others he sprinkled with holy water, and through the prayers of the venerable one, many were healed of their diseases. The fame of the holy Leontius spread throughout all Syria and Phoenicia. And each one tried to outstrip the other in order to venerate the venerable one and receive his blessing. Since the Latins were then the rulers in Palestine, they did not allow the venerable one to go to Jerusalem, and he remained in Acre.

A certain deacon, having been married for three years, could not know his wife because he was bound by a demon. Coming to the venerable one, he told him of his misfortune and asked for his help. Having prayed and sanctified water in the name of the Holy Trinity, the venerable one gave it to both spouses to drink, after which the deacon was loosed from his demonic bonds.

Once, passing through Nazareth, at midday the saint ordered a brief halt to rest from the heat and the labors of the journey and to partake of bread in a garden that they encountered on the way. When they began to look for the gardener so that he might give them fruit from the garden, a certain woman came out. To the saint's question whether she had a husband, she answered with bitterness that her husband had been bedridden for many years, and his bed had become a tomb both for him and for her, the wretched one, who suffered together with him. Having heard her account, the saint pitied her and sighed from the depths of his soul. Before leaving, he went in to the sick man and, turning toward the east, called upon the Physician of souls and bodies to help the sufferer. Then, touching the head of the sick man, he blessed him and departed. And—O miracle!—after some time the sick man rose from his bed in complete health, as if he had never been ill. When the venerable one was returning to Acre, they brought him from that garden a multitude of vegetables and various fruits as a small token of gratitude for the priceless help he had rendered.

Once the venerable one secretly came to Jerusalem by night and entered the Church of the Holy Resurrection to venerate the Life-giving Tomb of the Lord. And although he did everything in secret, the miracles that occurred from his presence revealed his presence. At that time there was a terrible drought in Jerusalem, and the Christians were calling upon the prophet Elijah to resolve this calamity; God also sent them the great Leontius. Through his prayers, a heavy rain fell which filled all the wells with water, watered the fields, and those who shortly before had been suffering the most severe thirst received water in abundance and gained hope that the harvest would be saved and they would receive bread and fruit in plenty. Everyone spoke only of the wondrous Leontius: "By his coming and prayers, the great holy hierarch of God has delivered us from the danger of dying from thirst. Come, let us fall down before him, that he may continue to be our helper."

Learning that Leontius was in Jerusalem and that the people were glorifying him, the Latins, and especially their bishop, out of envy conceived the plan of killing the saint, who had done them no evil. The Latin bishop at night sent armed men to the house where Leontius was staying, but God preserved him from the murderers, punishing them with blindness. They saw that a light had been lit in the venerable one's house, and running up to the house, they wanted to enter, but did not find the door. They searched for the door all night, thinking that they would be able to enter the house by the light which they saw, but the impious ones were put to shame. Returning empty-handed to the one who had sent them, they said: "The righteous Leontius is guarded by God, and no one can harm him." This miracle became known everywhere, and many marveled. The report of this incident even reached the capital, and the emperor Manuel Comnenus, learning of it, invited the saint to come to him. The ruler of Damascus also heard of this miracle, and though he was a Hagarene, he honored the virtue of the venerable one. He sent him a letter in which he invited him to come to him, promising to issue him a chrysobull, to appoint sufficient provisions for him and his people, and to hand over to the Christians the church of the Theotokos, which was under the dominion of the Hagarenes. The saint sent him a reply letter with thanks for his good disposition and explained that he would not be able to come to Damascus, since the emperor had invited him to Constantinople. The venerable one only asked the ruler to send him a document commanding the pirates sailing on his ships not to cause harm either to him or to his companions. The ruler immediately sent the safe-conduct document, considering that the venerable one had done him a favor. This document Leontius brought to Constantinople and showed to the emperor as a reproach to the Latins, who, calling themselves Christians, had not shown him such favor as the impious ruler of Damascus had shown.

The divine Leontius made great efforts to obtain permission to serve at the Life-giving Tomb of the Lord, but was unable to achieve anything. He was only permitted to enter and venerate, like any of the pilgrims, and therefore the venerable one decided to depart from Jerusalem. On the return journey to Rhodes, a most violent storm arose at sea, so that the ship was in danger of sinking. All the passengers cried out and wept in expectation of death, and when the rope on which the lifeboat was secured broke and the boat fell into the sea together with the people, they began to weep even more. Seeing such grief, the saint took pity on them and, shutting himself in the cabin at the bow of the ship, began to entreat God for help. The Lord heard his prayers and granted salvation both to him and to the people who were on the ship and in the boat. When the holy Leontius, exhausted from prolonged prayer, dozed off, God revealed His benefaction to him. Immediately shaking off sleep, the venerable one said to the weeping people: "Take courage and do not fear, none of us shall drown, but by the grace of God we shall all be saved, even the people in the boat, whom you think have perished. Tomorrow we shall find it with all the people who were in it." All those who knew Leontius as a holy man believed his words, but many did not believe, among them even the captain. The venerable one comforted him, saying: "Fear not, O man, by the grace of God we shall all be saved, with the ship and the boat." However, thinking that the venerable one's words were merely a consolation, the captain continued to bewail his misfortune, for judging by the strength of the wind and the distance of two miles that separated them from land, shipwreck could not be avoided. And yet the ship, driven by the strongest wind, drew near to land, where everything that the venerable one had predicted came to pass. The storm ceased, a calm ensued, the ship was delivered from danger, the boat was found at the shore unharmed; all marveled and glorified God and the Patriarch, calling him a holy and clairvoyant man, and considering themselves fortunate to have been deemed worthy of the honor of traveling with such a holy man. After this incident, they began to regard Leontius as an angel of God.

When the travelers arrived in Constantinople, the emperor, learning of what had happened, greatly blessed the saint, kissed his hands, placed them upon his own eyes, and greatly rejoiced at that mercy by which the King of all, the Lord, had gladdened him with communion with such a great saint. But not much time passed before the emperor Manuel departed to the Lord. At this very time, the steward of the Patmos monastery, Antony, having come to the capital, asked the Patriarch to intercede with the emperor that he might issue him a chrysobull so that the monastery would not pay tax for owning a ship. The Patriarch sternly answered Antony:

"What are you talking about, Antony? That which I have acquired from childhood to old age, must I lose in a single minute, despise God and His commandment for the sake of your monastery? Depart from me, O man, I shall never prefer a corruptible emperor to my Immortal One."

Hearing this, Antony was greatly grieved, but the venerable one, encouraging him, said:

"Why do you grieve, Antony, and why has your face grown dark? Know that after my death and the death of the present emperor, which will soon follow, you shall receive what you are now asking."

"When you die, this will not happen."

"Do you not believe me, Antony? By the grace of the Holy Spirit I assure you that you will resolve this matter by your own means, simply by paying for the chrysobull."

All this came to pass as the venerable one had predicted, during the reign of Isaac Angelos.

This same Antony the holy Leontius healed from a disease of the tongue, for a growth had formed on his tongue the size of a pea, because of which Antony could not speak normally and ate with difficulty. Having consulted physicians, Antony learned that he could be healed only by removing the growth. The Patriarch said to Antony:

"Come, be my canonarch for a while, and I shall sing to my God, and after that I shall examine your growth."

Taking the book, Antony, overcoming the pain, began to canonarch in a lisping voice, while the venerable one sang. When the service ended, the saint, turning to him with a smile and a joyful face, said: "And now show me what illness you have." Opening his mouth to show the growth, Antony—O miracle!—discovered that no trace of the illness remained, and it seemed that someone had cut out the growth while the saint was singing. To this Antony the venerable one predicted many things that were to happen in the future. Among other things, he also told him of two monks who were in the Patmos monastery. Outwardly it seemed that they were leading a life like all other monks, but in reality they had plunged themselves into perdition by their sins. Groaning from the depths of his soul and weeping, Antony asked the venerable one who they were, whether they would recognize their sins, and whether they would repent.

The saint named the monks and said:

"O that they would repent, otherwise woe to them."

Hearing this, Antony wept bitterly, and I weep with him, the author of these lines, because truly worthy of lamentation is the conduct when someone sins all his life and does not repent.

The great Leontius had from God authority even to command angels, of which we shall tell further, so that truly did the Apostle Paul write to the Corinthians: *"Do you not know that we shall judge angels?"* (1 Corinthians 6:3). The Patriarch of Antioch Cyril became extremely gravely ill. He was bedridden, and in his face there remained not even a trace of life. A multitude of hierarchs and dignitaries came to visit him and bid him farewell, among whom were also the Patriarch of Constantinople Theodosius, a man full of virtues, breathing goodness more than air, and the great Leontius. All stood around the bed of Cyril, but could not help him in any way, could not even converse with him, because, being at his last breath, he was without consciousness. What then did the two patriarchs decide to do? They decided to hasten his death in order to spare him the sufferings caused by the slow separation of the soul from the body. One urged the other to command the angel to take the soul of Cyril as quickly as possible. The divine Leontius said to the Patriarch of Constantinople that he should command the angel, because his rank, according to the canons, is higher than that of the Patriarch of Jerusalem. The Patriarch of Constantinople replied that greatness yields to virtue, for virtue is more valued by the Lord. Finally, so as not to waste time and torment the sick man, the great Leontius obeyed, read a prayer, raised his hands, made the sign of the Life-giving Cross in the air, and said to the angel: "By the dread name of the Consubstantial and Life-originating Trinity, I command you, O Angel of the Lord, a servant like us humble ones, to separate without delay the soul of our brother from the body and present it to the Master God, and do not fulfill any other commands until you have finished this." And the Angel of God, obeying the command which came from a man great both in rank and in virtues, immediately separated the soul of the Patriarch of Antioch from the body and carried it to the place appointed for it.

Once the divine Leontius, having fallen ill, decided to visit the bathhouse. After the bath he felt better and, sitting on a bench, said in jest to his servant Eulogius: "Well, Eulogius, shall we not go to Cyprus to inspect the property of the dependency of the Holy Sepulchre?" Eulogius answered nothing, but thought to himself: "Indeed, Eulogius, this decrepit and half-dead man wants to go to Cyprus too." And at that very moment the venerable one said: "Eulogius, do you think that I, sick and a half-dead old man, cannot go to Cyprus? No, Eulogius, and do not hope that the thoughts of your heart are hidden from me." After these words, Eulogius was dumbfounded and was silent for a long time, marveling at how Leontius knew of his thoughts, and no longer said anything and drove away base thoughts, lest the saint again begin to expose him. Of many other similar incidents that happened with the great Leontius we shall not tell, so as not to weary those who listen, and we shall proceed to describe the venerable one's repose.

When the thirteen and a half years granted by God to the saint came to an end, he became ill and took to his bed. Knowing that the time of his repose had come, he hastily bade farewell to all, as if he were hurrying to depart more quickly to the desired Lord. But those around him sorrowed over his departure, because they were no longer destined to see him. On the fourteenth day of the month of May, he surrendered his blessed soul into the hands of God, leaving no instructions concerning his burial. Those who were with him placed the sacred remains in a wooden coffin and left them in the Church of the Archangel Michael until instructions should come from the emperor.

All the clergy of Constantinople sang the funeral hymns, while the venerable one's disciples, especially Eulogius, commissioned a skilled painter to paint an image of the saint on a panel. Standing opposite the bier where the sacred remains lay, the artist gazed with curiosity at the divine countenance in order to capture it. He approached from the right side and from the left, went farther away and closer, but labored in vain, because he could paint nothing. Even after death, the saint did not want an icon to be painted of him. Therefore his divine countenance appeared to the painter as different—O miracle!—and constantly changing. Even after death, the venerable one strictly preserved his humility, in order to teach us how we must struggle to escape the snares of the envious devil. But what happened after the burial of the venerable one is truly a miracle of miracles.

Under the coffin with the relics of the venerable one, they placed a quantity of crushed tiles to absorb the cadaverous fluid, should it flow from the coffin. After four days had passed, those who approached the coffin smelled an ineffable fragrance issuing from the holy relics. But the most amazing and awesome thing was that blood flowed from the holy relics as if from a fresh wound made by a knife. Blood was also on the marble slabs covering the floor and, it seemed, sparkled against the whiteness of the marble. It is also amazing that the wooden coffin with the relics of the venerable one was placed inside another coffin, but there was so much blood that it overflowed both and flowed onto the floor. From this miracle one may conclude that the saint was, as it were, alive among the dead, numbered among the martyrs for the voluntary suffering which he had endured when he beat himself with the strap studded with nails.

Learning of the extraordinary miracle, the emperor Andronicus constructed a magnificent reliquary and with honor placed in it the most honorable relics of the venerable one. Thus the righteous one was gathered to the righteous, the venerable one to the venerable, the voluntary martyr to the martyrs, the great hierarch to the hierarchs. Now he abides where God is and receives worthy rewards for his labors, to the glory of the Father and of the Son and of the Holy Spirit, one Godhead and Kingdom, to Whom is due all glory, honor, and worship, now and ever, and unto the ages of ages. Amen.

(Written by the monk Theodosius of Constantinople)

The Life and Ascetic Labors of Our Venerable Fathers Symeon and Sabbas, the Ever-Memorable Founders of the Sacred Monastery of Chilandar, Who Flourished in the Twelfth Century

These saints were from Serbia by birth. Symeon was the father of Sabbas and king of Serbia, and his wife, the mother of Sabbas, was named Anna. Both of them were Orthodox and pious Christians of the royal line. They had two children: a son and a daughter, then the queen fell ill, and they had no more children. Being rulers of the kingdom and possessing many riches, they prayed with tears to God that He might give them another child. Hearing their entreaties, the Lord granted them a third child as well — the ever-memorable Sabbas, whom his parents from an early age gave to learn the sacred letters. Soon he had studied all the church books in the Serbian language and displayed such understanding, humility, good conduct, and meek disposition that all who associated with him loved and respected him. The more he grew in body, the more the love of God was kindled in him. Having given himself entirely to this Divine love, Sabbas thought of nothing else than how to please his Creator and Maker, his God. Being seventeen years of age, he prayed unceasingly, day and night, labored in fasts, vigils, and other ascetic hardships, asking God to vouchsafe him a life according to Christ, for he had greatly come to love virginity. And the Man-befriending God granted him what he asked in the following manner.

Having learned of the virtues of Symeon, the father of Sabbas, who was most merciful to the poor, certain fathers from the Holy Mountain came to Serbia for alms. Among them was also a Russian from the Russian monastery, a man of holy life. Conversing with him, the blessed Sabbas asked him about the monasteries on the Holy Mountain, about their rules, about how the fathers live in them, and about everything that was useful for achieving his goal. Having learned all that he wished, Sabbas burst into tears, and then said: "I see that God, who knows the depths of my heart and my purpose, has sent you to me, a sinner, that you might guide me onto the path of God. My soul has greatly rejoiced at your Divine words, and I can no longer remain in this deceptive world and behold its false glory and splendor. I ask you, therefore, teach me how to escape worldly vanity and be vouchsafed that life which your holiness lives. My parents wish to marry me off soon, and therefore I have resolved to depart to the Holy Mountain and ask your counsel." The elder replied to him: "I see, child, that your intention is pleasing to God, and that the love of God possesses your soul. Therefore, do quickly what you have conceived. I shall be your companion and guide until I bring you to the Mountain." After this, the blessed Sabbas devised a way to escape. He sent the elder ahead to wait for him at an agreed place, while he himself went to his father and said: "I have heard that near this mountain there is good hunting, and therefore I ask you to bless me to hunt and walk about a little. If I am delayed, I ask you not to be angry with me." His father gave him permission, provided him with as many servants as he wanted, and blessed him. Departing with great joy, Sabbas came to where the elder was waiting for him and ordered the servants to wait for him there. He himself, together with the elder, went to a nearby village and, exchanging his royal garments for the clothing of a poor man into whose house they had entered, set out for the Holy Mountain to the Russian monastery. There Sabbas began to learn the monastic life from the elder, which he pursued with great zeal through obedience, extraordinarily honoring his elder. The parents of Sabbas, however, wept inconsolably and sent people everywhere to search diligently for him, for they could not calmly endure the disappearance of such a fine and prudent son, whom his father wished to make heir of the kingdom. Those sent by the king searched everywhere; even to the Holy Mountain came three archons. Having carefully searched everything, they discovered Sabbas in the Russian monastery and wished to take him away with them. But Sabbas secretly at night climbed to the monastery tower and compelled his elder to clothe him in the angelic monastic habit. Then, having written a letter about the vanity of the world, about the end of the age, about the blessedness of the saints and the unending torments of sinners, he sent it to his parents. From the letter of Sabbas, his parents were brought to such compunction that both resolved to receive monasticism. Having departed to a women's monastery, his mother was clothed in the angelic habit and in God-pleasing ascetic struggle departed to the Lord. And his father, having renounced everything that is in the world and left as heir to the kingdom his son Stephen, came to the Holy Mountain. Having met with his beloved son Sabbas and rejoicing in spirit, he remained there, asking to be clothed in the angelic habit, so as to live with his son, which indeed came to pass. After the customary period of testing, the son became the sponsor of his father in the Divine and angelic schema and, being his son according to the flesh, Sabbas became a father according to the spirit to his father according to the flesh, Symeon. Both of them lived for a long time at the Vatopedi monastery (for there his father had found Sabbas, since the protos of the Holy Mountain — that is, the representative of the first-ranking monastery — had directed him there beforehand so that his father would not find him), laboring in the good struggle of daily fasting, all-night vigils, and prayers. In a short time they attained the highest level of virtue, having completely freed themselves from the carnal passions, and became worthy vessels of the All-Holy Spirit.

Since the report of their virtue moved many other Serbians to come to them, who then received monasticism, the ascetics were compelled to begin building their own monastery, because those coming to them increased more and more each day. Having undertaken a many-day fast and performing vigils, they fervently entreated the Lady Theotokos to show them a place pleasing to her for the future monastery. Inspired by a revelation and vision from God and moved by Him, father and son built with their own funds a most beautiful monastery in the name of the Most Holy Theotokos, called Chilandar, in honor of the Entrance of the Theotokos into the Temple. Having served in a venerable and God-pleasing manner in this monastery, Symeon reposed in the Lord on the thirteenth of February. After some time, when the day of commemoration of his repose arrived, the blessed Sabbas called the protos and the pious fathers to perform a vigil for the repose of the blessed soul of his father. During the doxology, an ineffable fragrance spread from the tomb of the saint, filling the entire monastery. Approaching the tomb, all saw that myrrh flowed forth from it, and they glorified God, who glorifies those who glorify Him.

Having become convinced of the blessed repose of the soul of his father and the sanctity of his relics, the blessed Sabbas greatly rejoiced in soul. From that time he increased his fasting, vigil, and other ascetic labors, which it is impossible to describe. The virtue of holy Sabbas could not be hidden; it became known to all, and numerous pilgrims began coming to him each day seeking teaching and spiritual guidance. Even for the protos himself, a man of virtue and Spirit-bearing, the blessed Sabbas was the first counselor, and the other abbots of the monasteries did not begin any undertaking without his blessing, because the grace of the Holy Spirit dwelling in him enlightened him, and he spoke wondrous words that were soul-profitable and salvific. The protos and the brethren loved him greatly and urged him to accept the priesthood. But the humble-minded Sabbas said that he was unworthy of the rank, and therefore, when they continued to urge him, he often hid himself.

Finally, so as not to be found disobedient and foreseeing that such was the will of the Holy God, he said: "May the Lord's will be done," after which he was ordained by the then Bishop of Ierissos, Nicholas, to the diaconate, and then to the priesthood. Having learned of the virtues of the saint, Metropolitan Constantine of Thessalonica, after long persuasion, was able to bring Sabbas to his city. Constantine conversed at length with the venerable Sabbas, and the bishops with the clergy and all the people received great benefit from his soul-profitable teachings, and on one of the Sundays the metropolitan, with the agreement of the bishops and the entire clergy, suddenly and against the will of Sabbas, elevated him to the rank of archimandrite. Because of the excessiveness of the honors shown to him, the saint secretly departed from Thessalonica and returned to his monastery.

In the time of Emperor Theodore Laskaris, the blessed Sabbas together with the superiors of other monasteries was sent by the protos to the emperor on matters concerning the Holy Mountain. The emperor with the syncletos and the patriarch with the clergy were then in Nicaea, because the Latins had taken Constantinople from the Romans. In this city, holy Sabbas met with the emperor, to whom he was also related, for the nephew of the saint had married the daughter of the emperor. The emperor had long wished to see the saint, not so much because of their kinship as because of his virtue. Having finally seen him, the sovereign greatly rejoiced and received him with great cordiality. Having conversed with him, the emperor was struck by his virtue and from that time felt great reverence for the saint. Sabbas told the emperor about his homeland, Serbia, that there was no bishop there, and asked the emperor to persuade the patriarch to appoint someone as bishop of Serbia. Summoning the patriarch, the emperor spoke at length with him about holy Sabbas and about Serbia, and then the patriarch questioned Sabbas at length. Having become convinced of his virtuous life, the patriarch decided that Sabbas was worthy to receive the apostolic rank of bishop. After a corresponding meeting and conversation between the patriarch and the emperor, it was decided to ordain holy Sabbas, against his will, as Archbishop of Peć and all Serbia. For many days in a row, both of them persuaded him to accept the rank, until finally the patriarch ordained him; on that day the emperor rejoiced with great joy. After his consecration, the saint devoted himself to even greater ascetic labors and set out for his diocese, where each day he instructed his flock in the word of the Gospel and in life according to Christ. The Orthodox he strengthened in piety and virtue, and heretics he converted to Christ by the grace and sweetness of his teaching. In a short time, all the unbelievers and heretics who had been in his diocese he made Orthodox. To all he was not only a shepherd and teacher, but a deliverer and savior.

Having set in order the affairs of his diocese, the hierarch again came to the Holy Mountain, where he enjoyed communion with the fathers of his monastery. Several days after his arrival there, he gathered all the brethren and disclosed to them his long-held desire to go and venerate the Holy Sepulcher of the Lord. Having asked for the prayers of the brethren, he sailed to Jerusalem, where he was received by Patriarch Athanasius of Jerusalem, who served the Liturgy together with the saint on Sunday. The patriarch asked him to bless the people and deliver a sermon. The patriarch, the clergy, and all the people so loved holy Sabbas that they did not wish to part from him, but came each day to hear his soul-profitable teachings. Having venerated the holy sites with great reverence and compunction and having shed rivers of tears at the Holy Sepulcher, Sabbas left the city and after some days came to Emperor John Vatatzes, who was related to him. The emperor received him with great respect and honors, glorifying God that He had vouchsafed him to receive the blessing of the saint. In like manner the empress also treated him, so that both of them chose him as their spiritual father. Having stayed there many days, the saint resolved to set out again for the Holy Mountain. Since he was a kinsman and spiritual father of the emperor, the latter gave him a portion of the Wood of the Precious Cross, portions of the relics of the saints and precious vessels, after which he sent him on an imperial ship to the monastery. Having arrived there with God's help, the saint donated to his monastery all the gifts of the emperor. Having remained there a long time and instructed the fathers in the proper manner, he appointed as their abbot a virtuous man, and then again returned to his diocese. Shepherding his flock in a God-pleasing manner, he enlightened all of Serbia through his virtue and knowledge of divine teachings and, preserving it unharmed from the noetic wolves, wisely led it to the Heavenly fold.

Since many heresies were then arising in those lands, the saint set out to visit other dioceses as well. Traveling to various places, he continued, in imitation of the apostles, to teach the flock the Divine laws and brought many heretics and impious people to piety. Later he went a second time to venerate the Holy Sepulcher. In the Holy Land he again went through the cities, teaching and performing many miracles, about which we, for the sake of brevity, shall not expand. We shall say only that once, together with three of his companions, he came to Great Tarnovo, where he was received with honors by the then tsar Asen, who was related to him. When the saint was celebrating on the Feast of Theophany, during the blessing of the water a miracle occurred. As soon as the saint immersed the Precious Cross in the water, the water divided in two and stood like a wall. Those who saw this glorified God. The tsar, greatly honoring the saint, asked him to remain in Tarnovo until Pascha, because he needed to depart on business. The saint remained, and after a few days fell ill. Having foreknown by Divine revelation of his death, he summoned his disciples and began to teach them how to save their souls, and then gave them portions of holy relics and all the church holy things that he had with him. Having heard of the illness of the saint, the Bishop of Tarnovo came to visit him. Seeing that Sabbas was very ill, he decided to inform the tsar of his illness. The saint, however, with his characteristic humility, said: "Brother, I ask you, do not inform the tsar, and may your holiness not undertake the further labor of coming here. Go in peace and pray for me, and the Merciful God will meet us in the Heavenly Jerusalem." On Saturday evening, before the onset of Sunday, the saint communed of the Most Pure Mysteries. His face shone radiantly, he was filled with joy and gladness, and having said three times: "Glory to Thee, O God," he gave his holy soul into the hands of God. After his repose, the bishop with the clergy and all the people came to commit to burial his holy remains, from which an ineffable fragrance issued. All were amazed and did not know where to bury the saint. They sent word of this to the tsar, and he commanded that the saint be buried in the Monastery of the Forty Martyrs, which was honorably carried out. Several days later the tsar came to the tomb of the saint and with tears asked him to forgive him for not having been with him at the moment of death. The tsar ordered the tomb to be faced with marble and lit an inextinguishable lampada above it. From that time, every sick person who came there with reverence received healing.

The saint had two nephews: Rostislav, son-in-law of Emperor Theodore Laskaris, and Vladislav, who then ruled Serbia and was son-in-law of the Bulgarian tsar. Vladislav and Archbishop Arsenius of Serbia, whom the saint had previously ordained as his successor, upon learning of the death of the saint, were greatly grieved. Having heard of the miracles being performed at the tomb of holy Sabbas, they resolved to request his holy relics to be brought to Serbia. The Serbian tsar Vladislav wrote to his father-in-law and sent several nobles to him, asking him to give up the holy relics. But the Bulgarian tsar refused. Then the son-in-law wrote to him a second time, fervently asking him to return the relics, and sent precious gifts with the nobles. But even then the Bulgarian tsar would not give up the relics, replying thus: "Since God has arranged that the saint reposed here, He has also granted this treasure to us. Who am I to oppose the will of the Lord?" So the nobles returned again to Vladislav with nothing. Then Vladislav himself with chosen nobles went to ask for the return of the relics of the saint. Coming to the place of burial, he first approached the tomb of the venerable one and with fervent tears said: "O Saint of God and our most honorable father, why have you left us sinners and do not wish to come to your homeland, for which you are not only a shepherd but also a savior? You delivered us from the deception of the devil and led us to the truth; you freed your ailing flock from heresies, healed it, raised up those who were in danger of spiritual death, adorned it with divine services, sacred orders, and soul-saving statutes. Why now, O saint, do you deprive us of sanctification by your divine relics? Why do you deprive your homeland of the inexhaustible source of your divine grace and your miracles? O most merciful father, have pity on me, look upon my sins and the sins of my people, by which we have sinned against you. Come to us, although we are unworthy sinners, but do not leave us without your presence and protection." Vladislav prayed at length and with compunction, then went to his father-in-law. That very night, the father-in-law saw in a dream holy Sabbas in the form of a radiant angel, who commanded him to give his relics to his son-in-law, so that he might bring them to his homeland. Having gathered the people and the clergy headed by the metropolitan, the tsar related to them all that had happened, and then with singing, candles, and incense, both tsars opened the tomb of the saint. Immediately — O Christ the King, O Thy wonders! — all that place was filled with ineffable fragrance, the face of the saint shone like the sun, and all in amazement prayed: "Lord, have mercy!" After this, with a great procession and cross-procession, both tsars (father-in-law and son-in-law) carried the holy relics on foot out of Tarnovo, and tsar Vladislav with great joy transferred them to his homeland. Who can describe what joy there was on that day? And the miracles that occurred were like unto this, to the glory of the Father and the Son and the Holy Spirit, the Most Holy Trinity, to Whom belong dominion, honor, and worship unto the ages of ages. Amen.

The Life and Struggles of our Venerable Father Gregory, Who Labored Near the Gulf of Nicomedia in the Thirteenth Century

This God-bearing father of ours Gregory came from the regions of Bithynia. His parents were pious and renowned, noble by birth, and still more notable for their character and virtue. Having been raised by such parents, the venerable one paid no heed to childish games, which so delight the young, but at every hour was instructed in the words of Divine Scripture. Not stopping at this, he wished to study also the Hellenic sciences, choosing from them those that are free from sin. By virtue of his natural sharpness of mind, constant reading and exercises, he soon mastered all the good and beneficial sciences, by means of which he could escape the snares and wiles of the opponents of Orthodoxy, warring against them either from afar with his winged words, or striking them with the weapon of his remarkable tongue, if such people came to converse with him.

Gradually, having studied all possible external sciences, the venerable one approached the knowledge of God. He began to seek teachers and instructors in the struggles of virtue, knowing that to live virtuously by oneself, without having an example before one, is dangerous, for such a person is beset by many snares and calumnies of the enemy, whereas life with those experienced in virtue and their example incline one toward the struggles of perfection, kindling within a person the fire of zeal, which increases the desire for the knowledge of God and always leads from small to great and still greater. For this reason, the venerable one came to one of the best monasteries. Having been clothed in the monastic habit, he devoted himself to spiritual struggles, learning to wage the secret, invisible warfare against the devil, but in such a way as not to receive blows and wounds from him, but rather to inflict them himself. The ascetic studied the provocations of evil thoughts that war against the wretched human race. Thus he learned what the peaceful mind is, the guarding of thoughts, which of the thoughts belong properly to man and which are sown by the enemy, which thoughts stir up and trouble the firm thoughts and against which thoughts one must constantly struggle, and which ones should be disregarded, which should be despised, and to which one should respond with outward feigned friendship.

In the monastery he learned to reject the sensible together with the senses, beautiful colors, bodily tenderness and all the pleasures by means of which the ruling mind is cast down, beguiled and poisoned. The venerable one was trained in psalmody, prayer, guarding of the mind, fasting and abstinence, which are only in their proper balance when there is humble-mindedness among them. Having received all this, the divine Gregory brought forth fruit thirtyfold, sixtyfold, and a hundredfold more (Mark 4:20). No one else could compete with him in these things, which he fulfilled with meekness and humble-mindedness, without any compulsion of himself. His non-acquisitiveness, humility, meekness, going unwashed, lying on the bare earth are worthy of all praise. What struggles did this venerable one not perform with all fitting zeal? What virtue did he not acquire? And who could surpass him in these struggles? But even that which he had acquired, the saint counted as nothing, and that which he had not yet acquired, he strove to obtain. Thus was the apostolic saying fulfilled in him: *"Not that I have already attained, or am already perfected; but one thing I do, forgetting those things which are behind and reaching forward to those things which are ahead, I press toward the goal for the prize of the upward call of God in Christ Jesus"* (Philippians 3:13–14).

Since envy always follows one who possesses virtue, the devil, unable to bear the sight of such a young saint adorned with knowledge, chastity and courage, invulnerable to his wiles, and indeed serving as an example and beneficial model for all, devised the following: having found several corrupt, worthless and lying little men, he induced them to declare that this divine Gregory had stolen sacred vessels, which had in fact gone missing at that time. These people slandered the man of God; wandering everywhere and swearing oaths, they insisted that they could confirm their false testimony. The simple and foolish thought that the demon had already conquered the venerable one, while the sensible and discerning considered this game worthy of laughter. However, foreseeing the intentions and stratagems of the devil, the divine Gregory departed from there to another monastery, so as not to become the cause of greater punishment for the slanderers. After a few days the real thief was discovered, and the demon who had tried to mock the saint was himself made a laughingstock. Striving to deceive others, he was himself deceived, and the sin was thus made manifest to all. How could the venerable one teach others not to steal and not to commit sacrilege if he himself were a sacrilegious thief? Such a thing is simply impossible.

But let us return to our subject. Having come to another monastery, where his own brother lived in obedience and struggle, Gregory began his struggles anew. Submitting to the abbot, respecting the brethren who struggled together with him, he continued his fasting, vigils, chanting of psalms, prayed with genuflections, served and humbled himself before everyone. All the brethren came to love the venerable one, for humble-mindedness, simplicity of character, and undemandingness in food give rise to love for the one who possesses these qualities, while pride and a stubborn character become the cause of anger and hatred. Having lived in this monastery for quite a long time, the venerable one was clothed in the great angelic habit, becoming a great-schema monk. After this, the abbot and all the brethren insistently urged him to receive the priesthood, but the venerable one would not agree, because he knew what pure and highly moral life a priest must lead. However, when they began to urge him again and again, he judged that compliance and obedience are the foundation of all virtues and agreed to receive the rank, which he regarded not as something befitting himself, for he always crushed this vainglorious thought in himself, but as service to people and to God.

After three years, the venerable one withdrew from the monastery, having decided to lead a life in hesychia, because he knew that one who dwells in hesychia and devotes himself to prayer can, through the stripping of the senses, enter into the contemplation of the noetic world, and by means of this contemplation, love for God abides in a person, and he is permeated by it, and through love of God he delights and rejoices in the glory and beauty of God. He grows in love for God and through love contemplates the glory of God. So that the love and glory of God are to each other as mother and daughter. Having left the monastery and his brother, Gregory went to a certain village that was convenient for hesychia. Having lived there for a sufficient time and somewhat freed his senses from worldly disturbance and turmoil, the venerable one resolved to seek still greater hesychia, since the mind, by nature, has the habit, when freed from external things, of returning into itself and seeking greater hesychia and freedom. By means of this freedom it more purely apprehends the hoped-for blessings of the age to come, and the more it is freed from earthly things, the more it ascends to God by the ladder that this freedom and hesychia become for it. Conversely, disturbance and care are a departure from God. For this purpose the venerable one ascended the mountain that was near the village called Ilinsky, where he found a place very suitable for hesychia. Gregory said aloud: *"This is My resting place forever; here I will dwell, for I have desired it"* (Psalm 131:14).

He set up his poor kaliva on the mountain and settled there. Freeing his mind from the external senses, and his senses from wandering among earthly objects, the venerable one strove to unite himself more closely with God, from Whom he was never separated anyway. Having been purified from all external thoughts, he became a friend of God, a second Moses, forgetting what lies behind and reaching forward, toward the prize of the great upward call of God, learning what is "behind" and what one may ask for and what one may not (Philippians 3:13–15). To anyone who has been purified or is still being purified, it is permitted to seek the mysteries of God, that is, to learn about Divine Providence, how the world is governed, about the wisdom and goodness of God, about His power and boundlessness. For to those who are purified or are being purified, it is permitted to investigate these things. But it is not permitted to them to investigate the Essence of God, since this is utterly unconquerable, incomprehensible and ineffable to man. Speaking of His essence, God therefore said to Moses: *"No man shall see Me, and live"* (Exodus 33:20).

Gregory united himself with God, became His friend, and God made His friend, the divine Gregory, a partaker of His mysteries. Thus he became a contemplator of the Divine mysteries, meditating on the dark and secret words, receiving revelations about the future as a gift worthy both of God who gave it out of His goodness, and of the venerable one who received it for the purity of his mind and his love for God. Gregory not only received the gift of foreseeing the future as a reward for his virtue, but also began to work wondrous miracles. Just as kings and princes entrust their treasures to faithful friends, appointing them guardians and stewards of their possessions, so also does Divine Providence act, inexplicably arranging all things. Since this venerable one loved God as is fitting, with all his strength, he was also beloved by God, Who promises in the Gospel: *"He who has My commandments and keeps them, it is he who loves Me. And he who loves Me will be loved by My Father"* (John 14:21). Therefore the spiritual mysteries of God are entrusted to the worthy for abundant sweat and many struggles, and not freely and without labor. The venerable one, as it were upon a rich table, set out that spiritual food which each one required, and to those who needed counsel, he wisely provided it. And if there was need of a prophetic word, he would with humble-mindedness and restraint reveal the future to those who needed it. The sick and maimed he healed with great humility, lifting his eyes to Heaven and laying his hands upon them. For this reason the venerable one became widely known; he was called a foreteller of the future and a teacher, a corrector of morals and a healer of diseases. For his love of God he was deemed worthy to receive from Him great and abundant gifts, and it is time to tell of some of them, so as to delight the readers.

It is the custom of the cunning devil to make war and trouble people often. If he succeeds in something, then he achieves his purpose; but if not, he provokes laughter in those who have experienced his warfare upon themselves. Wishing to take away the prophetic gift of the venerable one, the vile demon persuaded certain little men, worthy only of pulling carts, plowing and digging the earth, that the saint foreknew the future not by the grace of the Holy Spirit, but by the working of the devil, with the help of the magical art. Testing the venerable one, they dragged thieves, sacrilegious men and evildoers to him and asked about each one, what sort of person he was. Knowing their wicked intentions, the venerable one did not remain silent, so as not to give them occasion to accuse him and mock the divine gift, but told about each one who he was and with what intention he had come to him. Thus he told about one man who had suffered shipwreck, that he had made it to shore at a place where there was a vineyard, and due to the sufferings he had endured and terrible hunger, had picked and eaten another's grapes. The saint related this not so that people might glorify him for the gift of foresight, but in order to expose their unbelief and shame those who accused him of sorcery.

However, the malice of these people did not diminish and they hired a certain harlot, that she might incline the venerable one to lust and thereby defile him. This harlot came to the venerable one and began to tempt him, shamelessly contorting herself, laughing, flirting and speaking lewd words. But the venerable one strove with instructions and counsel to bring her to chastity, that she might be ashamed of her behavior and words. Yet the harlot paid no heed to the saint's words: she suddenly fell under the attack of a demon, who threw her to the ground; foam flowed from her mouth, she began to gnash her teeth and to behave as those possessed by a demon usually behave. Seeing what had happened to the woman, those who had sent her repented and asked the venerable one to have pity on her and heal her. Immediately the saint, not waiting to be asked a second time, raised his hands to Heaven and, having prayed fervently to God, healed the woman, charging her henceforth to preserve chastity, lest she experience a worse evil, for a person must purify the soul created in the image of God through fasts and prayers, striving toward every possible virtue. Having set her on the path of repentance, the venerable one dismissed the woman in peace. Thus the harlot became chaste and, having repented of her former impiety, spent the remaining part of her life in purity and good repentance.

But let us also tell of other machinations wrought by the devil against the venerable one. Wishing to disturb the saint and cause him harm, the vile demon incited certain clerics to envy against the venerable one. They came to the Bishop of Nicomedia and raised many accusations and slanders against the divine Gregory, using everything to arouse the bishop's anger. Being simple in character (for an innocent man believes every word), the bishop believed the words of the clerics and, becoming greatly angered, sent men to the saint so that they might bring him to the bishop as quickly as possible. The venerable one perceived the devil's cunning and the slander raised against him. He offered the messengers dinner, and after this told them to return quickly to the bishop, assuring them that he would be at the bishop's before them. Being almost dead in body from his many struggles and afflictions, the venerable one mounted a horse and went directly across the sea to the bishop. And—O miracle!—the water became firm as dry land, and the venerable one was able to cross to the opposite shore, where Nicomedia was located, without even wetting his feet. Seeing that the venerable one was riding on horseback across the sea as on dry land, the bishop remembered the Apostle Peter walking on the waves and, falling to the ground, worshipped God, saying: "Blessed art Thou, O Lord, and most glorious, for today Thou hast shown us another Peter. How wondrous are Thy works, how many servants Thou hast, of whom we know not, but of whom Thou knowest before their birth." As soon as the venerable one approached the bishop, the latter fell at his feet with reverence. Having rendered many honors to the venerable one, the bishop was almost grateful to the slanderers for having seen such a holy man, a wonderworker. Afterwards the bishop asked the venerable one to forgive these slanderers. Seeing this miracle, they themselves repented and with tears asked the venerable one for forgiveness. From that time they began to honor him as a heavenly man, as a servant and friend of God. And all who heard of this unheard-of miracle were amazed and astonished, while the venerable one again returned to his cell and continued his usual labors.

Once a certain married couple was sailing on a ship with a favorable wind, but suddenly such a strong wind arose that the ship was wrecked. Those good spouses, finding themselves in the water, called upon the venerable one for help. Swift to help, he appeared to them, stretched out his hands and delivered them from perishing in the depths of the sea. Those who were saved rendered great thanksgiving to God and to His servant Gregory.

And upon fishermen the venerable one bestowed benefactions. Many times, casting their nets into the sea, they drew them out empty. At last, remembering the venerable one, they called upon him with faith and cast their nets again. And—O miracle!—so many fish were caught in the nets that the fishermen could not haul them in until their companions came and helped them. Glorifying God and the venerable one, they told everywhere of the miracles of this friend of God.

Hear also of another miracle. A certain noble and wealthy woman, very merciful and virtuous, by some means I know not, swallowed a serpent into her belly. Days passed, and her belly kept increasing, evidently because the serpent also increased in size. Having lost all hope in the skill of physicians, she came to the venerable one and with tears fell at his feet, asking with faith that he deliver her from the misfortune that had befallen her. Having compassion on her, the venerable one raised his hands to Heaven and with great humility and contrition of heart asked God, praying for a long time. And—O miracle!—the serpent died and came out, and the woman, delivered from the danger, gave thanks to God and the venerable one.

At that time a certain she-bear in the vicinity of the village near which the venerable one labored began to cause harm to the villagers. Having forbidden her, the venerable one drove her out of those places. Similar to this she-bear are all those who transgress the laws of God and harm their neighbor. Such people the venerable one admonished with instructions and made them refrain from their lawlessness.

Having completed his ascetic labors, the venerable one, according to the Holy Scripture, *"being made perfect in a short time, fulfilled a long time"* (Wisdom 4:13). When he reached fifty years of age, he desired to depart from this world and go to Christ. Sick, lying on his bed, he charged his disciples always to guard the precepts of the faith, never to abandon the struggle of crucifying and mortifying the flesh, for they had promised this to God in the present life. Having imparted these and many other spiritual teachings to them and bidden them farewell, his soul departed from the body, which was already dead even before, and went to the desired Christ, to Whom is due all glory, honor and worship, now and ever and unto the ages of ages. Amen.

(Written by Monk Joseph Kalothetos, the Most Honorable Among Monks)

The Life, Ascetic Struggles, and Account of Certain Miracles of Our Venerable Father the Confessor Meletius of Gallisius, Who Lived in the Thirteenth Century

This venerable father of ours, Meletius, hailed from the regions of the Black Sea coast, from the village of Theodotu. His parents were named George and Maria. They were God-fearing, virtuous, and exceedingly merciful and hospitable people. The more generously they distributed their wealth to the poor, the more God increased it, and besides wealth He made them very well-known. Thus, the saint's father was a commander of no small portion of the imperial armies, while his mother, a most virtuous and pious woman, spent her entire life in prayer and in glorifying God. From their virtues they reaped good fruit, having begotten this wondrous Meletius, whom they named Michael at his Baptism. He was named Meletius later, in monasticism, when together with his name he also changed his life, which was entirely devoted to spiritual training, and therefore he rightly received this name, consonant with his life and deeds.

After the infant's Baptism, his father saw a prophetic dream in which God foretold what his child would become in the future. In the dream a certain venerable man, a messenger of the king, came to him and asked for a golden brooch. Upon awakening, George understood that the dream was about his son, who would become a golden adornment, a chosen vessel of the Heavenly King, and therefore he was being asked from his father, for God loved his son more than his own father did. But the father also did everything necessary for the child to receive a good upbringing. He entrusted his education in the virtuous life to a teacher; the boy not only studied the sacred sciences but also virtue, yet since instructing one's own children is nonetheless the duty of parents, George himself also instructed his son to do what is pleasing to God, and endeavored to take him twice daily to church: to Matins and to Vespers, so that he would hear the teachings from Holy Scripture and grow in the fear of God. The prudent and modest youth did more than his father commanded him, and therefore he surpassed all his peers in virtue and learning. One day this youth, who was advancing in good deeds, had a vision in which, as in ancient times to Abraham, he was commanded to leave his country and his kinsmen and go wherever God would lead him.

Without losing time, Michael renounced everything: his homeland, his relatives, his peers, his wealth, and with zeal followed after God, Who had called him. Taking up the Cross of Christ upon his shoulders, he went to Jerusalem to venerate the holy places where the Son and Word of God and the Father had dwelt, where He became incarnate, endured the Cross, death, and burial, rose on the third day, and ascended to Heaven. When the venerable one set out on his journey, it was January, the very height of winter. But good Michael went on foot, without a pack animal, without companions, without a cloak or other necessities for the road. He manfully endured the rains, snow, mud, and the flooding of rivers that he encountered on his way, and burning with strong love for Christ, did not consider them a hindrance. It happened that Michael was passing through Lydia at the place where the river Pactolus flows. A swift and difficult current to cross at any time of year, it flooded even more in winter, raising waves as on a sea. Seeing neither a ford nor people to ask how to cross the river, the man of God did the following. He turned for help to Him with Whom all things are possible. Raising his hands and fervently praying to Him, the venerable one sighed from the depths of his soul and asked for help to be sent from above. And—O miracle!—the youth was immediately lifted into the air and carried to the opposite bank. Glorifying God, Who had helped him in such a wondrous way, he continued his journey with even greater zeal. Having come to Jerusalem and venerated all the holy places with great reverence, Michael desired to converse with the venerable fathers who struggled in those deserts, in order to learn from them the patterns and rules of the ascetic life.

Coming to Mount Sinai, he saw remarkable venerable fathers, some of whom had labored in ascetic struggle for more than eighty years, and others for their entire lives. Having marveled at their supernatural manner of life, he asked them with tears to receive him. Having been received by them, he immediately cast off his worldly garments, and with them his worldly name, becoming Meletius. Having clothed himself in monastic garments of haircloth, the venerable one immediately set about severe ascetic labor, exercising himself in every kind of virtue. By day he served the brethren, and he spent the night in prayers, doxology, and reading of Holy Scripture. Sometimes he went entire weeks completely without sleep, and at other times, yielding to necessity, he slept a little while standing, holding onto a rope, or directly on the bare ground, because he had neither a bed, nor a mat, nor a second garment. So it was during the Holy Week of the Saving Passion of the Lord and on other great feasts of the Lord.

Having spent sufficient time with the divine fathers in ascetic labors of virtue, the venerable one was deemed worthy of the contemplation of the heavenly world and received spiritual gifts. Everyone who knew the saint marveled at his spiritual struggles, and his virtues became known even in distant lands, and his name was on everyone's lips. Growing sorrowful (for Meletius feared lest through the praise of men he might lose the reward from God for his labors), the venerable one wished to leave Mount Sinai. Departing from the monastery by night, Meletius came to Jerusalem to spend some more time at the Lord's Tomb and himself see the miracle of the descent of the "Holy Fire." Having been deemed worthy to see the fire, as he desired, he went to Misiri, to Alexandria, and from there, returning to Syria, he came to Damascus in order, like a diligent bee, to gather the honey of virtue from different fathers. Having left Damascus (for he could not remain there in the midst of the ungodly [Muslims]), the venerable one came to Mount Latros. Having lived there a sufficient time, he came to

Mount Gallisius, which is in Asia Minor, a little beyond ancient Ephesus, where there was a very large monastery. The great Lazarus of Gallisius had founded it, and God extraordinarily expanded and glorified the monastery, for from this monastery came forth venerable men who, shining like lamps, illumined the whole world.

Having come to this monastery and conversed with the fathers dwelling there, the venerable Meletius marveled at the strictness of their manner of life and desired to settle with them. He was received into the number of the brethren and tonsured into the great schema, after which Meletius also gave himself into obedience to an elder named Mark (surnamed Amisellis). Who then can recount his extreme patience, his zeal in fulfilling obediences, who can describe his indefatigable character? Meletius spoke little but did much, obeyed his spiritual father in everything, and did not exceed his customary ascetic labor. He kept vigil in prayer at night, and by day shed tears in repentance, and there was not a single minute when he did not think of Jesus Christ in his heart, and there was not a moment when he did not utter aloud the name of Jesus Christ, but he always prayed thus: "Lord Jesus Christ, Son of God, have mercy on me."

All the long time that the venerable one lived with the elder and remained in unquestioning obedience, both the elder himself and all who associated with him praised Meletius and marveled at his ascetic struggles. When speaking of the virtues of the divine Meletius, the elder called upon all the brethren there to take him as an example, for Meletius was a model of life according to God.

I almost forgot to tell of a wondrous struggle of the venerable one, the truth of which no one calls into question. The divine Meletius had the custom of shutting himself in his cell and, imitating Moses and Elijah, and especially the example of our common Savior and Teacher Christ, spending forty days in fasting. The servants of the monastery would place in his cell a vessel of water and figs, but after the forty days had passed they would find them untouched. The entire Mount Gallisius marveled at him, and crowds of people from all over Asia flocked there to look upon such a wondrous ascetic, which disturbed the stillness and the struggle of Meletius. Because of this, the venerable one was greatly saddened and intensely considered how to escape human glory and praise. Day and night he entreated God to show him a way to attain what he desired. And one night, when he was fervently praying to God, his cell was suddenly illuminated with heavenly light. Christ Himself appeared to him, clothed in wondrous and radiant garments, surrounded by beautiful youths in white garments with scepters in their hands. Seeing all this vision, the venerable one froze in amazement and fell to the ground. One of the youths, taking him by the hand, raised him up, and the Master Christ said: "Meletius, what are you afraid of? You called Me, and behold, I have come." The venerable one, still experiencing fear, not only gave no answer but did not even dare to look at the Lord. Then the Lord said to him: "Go to Constantinople, you will help defend the truth against which war has been raised." With these words Christ ascended to Heaven together with the youths. Filled with ineffable joy, Meletius resolved to fulfill the Divine commandment, yet considered that first he should consult with his elder. He revealed his

351

desire to him, but did not tell him about the vision, and asked permission to leave. But the elder, knowing what a wondrous man he was losing, did not wish to let him go and tried by various means to dissuade him, mentioning that in cities there is turmoil and temptations contrary to the monastic calling.

What then happened? The divine Meletius grew sorrowful and again began fervently to pray to God. His prayer was heard, and a Divine voice came to the elder: "Do not hinder, but release My servant to Constantinople, for he will bring benefit to many souls." After Mark heard this Divine voice, he blessed Meletius and sent him off to Constantinople. Thus the venerable one came to the capital, where he was most concerned that no one should learn of him, to avoid human glory. However, he was unable to do this, for he was a true lamp of virtue. Just as it is impossible for one who walks with a lit lamp in the midst of night to remain hidden, so it is impossible for one who is a model of virtue to remain unknown, even if that person lives in the desert, in mountains, in caves and chasms of the earth. So also the divine Meletius, although he did everything possible to remain unknown and without glory, could not hide from the leading men of the city, and he became known to emperors, archons, senators, and all others.

Numerous inhabitants of Constantinople came daily to the venerable one to receive great benefit from his teachings. And indeed, it is difficult to enumerate all the virtues of the venerable one, for he was humble of character, his clothing was poor, his head was unwashed and unshorn, his feet were bare, his words were fruitful, his mind was attentive, but remarkably, his behavior and even his movements brought great benefit to those who saw him. It is difficult to say how many people came to him each day, for among other qualities the people of Constantinople have one good virtue. They find out whether there are wise and virtuous men anywhere, and learning of such, they go to them, inscribe their words on the tablets of their hearts, and some of their listeners even on paper, so as always to receive benefit from them. Thus to this day, in remembrance of the venerable one, his words have been preserved in writing by many.

But the divine Meletius was saddened by such renown more than before, for he loved to keep stillness rather than be glorified by people. Only through stillness can the human mind, being purified, receive God; by no other path can this Divine grace be attained. The venerable one left Constantinople for the mountain of Auxentius the Great and, finding there a small natural cave, settled in it and lived there for a long time, having no other shelter, no clothing, and no light. Then, having built a small hut before the entrance to the cave, he began to struggle with such zeal as if he had only just begun his spiritual struggle. He fasted for many days in a row, kept vigils, performed multitudes of prostrations, and so afflicted his body that one monk, seeing how the saint struggled in this manner, told him that he need not so openly mortify himself with labors beyond his strength. To this the saint replied: "Child, have you not heard that even Abraham will repent that he did not struggle more when on the Day of Judgment he sees the extraordinary gifts of God?" Having heard these words, the monk was amazed, and having respectfully received the saint's answer, fell silent. Going away from there, he began to proclaim to all monks and laypeople the wondrous life of the venerable one.

And again a multitude of people began to flock to the venerable one, disturbing his desired stillness. Again growing sorrowful, the venerable one cried out to God. After prayer, he opened the book of the Prophet Isaiah, to learn by what path the Lord would lead him, and read the following saying: *"I will keep You... as a light to the Gentiles"* (Isaiah 42:6). The venerable one understood what these words meant and remained in his former place, receiving those who came to him, healing the sick, resolving the perplexities of those who questioned him, offering teachings profitable to the soul, and helping those in need in every way.

Once again the fame of the venerable one grew considerably, and there was not a single Christian who did not ask for his holy prayers. Sailors and travelers, the infirm and the healthy all called upon him equally: the sick—to be healed of their diseases, and the healthy—to preserve their health. The saint left neither soldiers nor farmers without help, he extended benefactions to shepherds, and to hunters he gave what was necessary. Even the fishermen bore witness to the good that the venerable one did for them, for as soon as they uttered the name of Meletius, immediately a countless quantity of fish fell into their nets. Even domestic animals and wild beasts expressed gratitude to the venerable one for his benefactions, for toward them also he had sympathy and compassion.

However, the venerable one not only worked miracles but was also a hospitable host. From the meager bread that he had, he fed all who came to him, and everything that was brought to him he generously distributed to the needy, while at the same time extending spiritual alms, for he generously nourished their souls with his divinely wise teaching.

It is impossible to recount the remaining part of this narrative without tears. Like a storm cloud with hail that threatens to bring many calamities, Latinism besieged the Orthodox Church of Christ. The chief of evil, the devil, after numerous wars raised against the flock of Christ, finally also raised war against the Church. He altered the Creed and captured the first Church in the world—the Church of ancient Rome, and therefore all the other Churches wept and groaned that they had lost their first sister—Rome. With them wept the Guardian Angels of the Churches: *"A voice was heard in Ramah, lamentation and bitter weeping"* (Matthew 2:18), as the Scripture says, while the common enemy rejoiced and was glad, observing the Division of the Churches and the disunity of Christians. The Latins also taught other impious inventions, for example, that the Holy Spirit proceeds from the Father and the Son, and during the Liturgy they proclaimed: "Glory to the Father, and to the Son, and to the Holy Spirit proceeding from Them Both," and to the Creed they added: "Who proceeds from the Father and the Son." This new teaching began in ancient times and took possession of old Rome and the western countries. In the time of Emperor Michael, called "the Unleavener" (1261–1282), this heretical teaching also reached the eastern lands and long tormented the Eastern Church. But even then there were warriors of Christ who fought for the truth, for other fathers and theologians also opposed this impiety, and their shepherd and teacher became Joseph, the pillar of Orthodoxy. They strengthened the Church of Christ as much as was possible, giving themselves over even to death from the persecuting Latins and the Latin-minded, and showed themselves to be strict guardians of the Divine teachings. One of these fathers was the great Meletius, who, leaving his stillness, went with his preaching through all of Bithynia, strengthening the Christians in Orthodoxy and commanding them to keep the faith and carefully refrain from accepting the new perverted teaching, meaning Latinism.

Once, when the venerable one had spent the whole day traveling, the sun was already setting, and there was no lodging nearby, his companion said to him: "Father, it is already evening; let us stay here, since the village is still far away and we will not manage to reach it." But the venerable one raised his eyes to Heaven and prayed thus to the Lord: "O God my Savior, Thou who art the Light of the world, Who in ancient times stopped the sun for the sake of the people of Israel, stop it today also for our sake, that we may manage to reach the village." And—innumerable are Thy wonders, O Christ the King!—the sun did not set below the horizon until the holy Meletius so desired. Let no one doubt this, because if a word is spoken with faith, it is able to move unmoving and enormous mountains (Matthew 17:20). And if we know that those who believe in Christ can perform even greater miracles, what is strange if the venerable one worked such a miracle, and can anyone doubt this? In this case one should only marvel at the boldness that the great Meletius had before God and glorify God, Who does not cease to perform ancient miracles even in these last times. By this miracle God showed that if anyone by his life becomes like Moses or Joshua, he will be able, when necessary, to dry up the sea, to stop the sun, and to perform all those miracles that they performed.

But let us return to our narrative. Not far from the mountain of Auxentius the Great there was a small island of Saint Andrew, small in size but very beautiful. On this island the venerable Meletius built a monastery with a beautiful church, and around the monastery were located the dwellings of hermits and other buildings. In this monastery Meletius again gave himself over to fasts and the excessive labors of all-night standing, vigil, prayer, fasting, and tears, but God continued to manifest miracles here as well. Witnesses to them were the multitudes of people who came here and experienced their effect upon themselves. Because of the numerous crowds of Christians, the peace of the venerable one was disturbed again, and he decided once more to go away to the mountain of Auxentius the Great. But after this decision a wondrous event occurred! When the venerable one had already prepared to leave, during the day Auxentius the Great appeared to him visibly and, having greeted him and thanked him for the church he had built, told him that he would repay him for his labors with a great reward, like that which the Venerable Martyr Stephen the New had received, who had struggled on that same mountain. What the saint predicted came to pass, for the divine Meletius received the confessor's crown, as will be recounted below.

When Emperor Michael "the Unleavener" openly began to preach the Latin teaching in the Ecumenical Church and demanded that the Eastern Church be united with the Western, the Orthodox Patriarch of that time was driven from his throne, and the defender of falsehood, John Beccus, was elevated to the throne. After this the Orthodox began to be thrown into prisons, violence was committed against them, and they were tormented with various punishments. Then the holy Meletius, on the advice of the divine Galaction, came together with him to Constantinople. Having struggled on Mount Gallisius together with the venerable Meletius, the hieromonk Galaction had greatly advanced in word and virtue, for which he was revered. In the capital, both of them appeared before the Latin-minded Emperor Michael and declared with boldness: "We are defenders of Orthodoxy and will not commune with the Latin heresy, which, even before it appeared, was refuted by the divine Fathers of the Ecumenical Councils, who decreed in the Creed that the Holy Spirit proceeds from the Father, and that those who dare to add or subtract anything, even the slightest thing, should be anathematized. So why have you, O Emperor, despised the words of Christ Himself, with which He addresses His apostles in the Holy Gospel, and the testimonies of the divine Fathers, and the sacred canons of the Catholic Church, giving yourself over to this error? Not only that, but you wish us also to follow the heresy and reject the traditions of the apostles? This shall not be; do not try to move what cannot be moved, because we would sooner choose to lose our minds than to lose our Orthodox faith."

Considering these words a personal insult, the emperor threw them in prison, where these valiant warriors of Christ joyfully endured many other sufferings. After several days of imprisonment, the emperor ordered that they be brought from the dungeon, hoping that after their torments the saints would become more compliant. But the saints, who had not become softer from torments like wax, but had been tempered like iron, with even more ardent faith and even more sharply began to denounce the evil speech of the emperor. Since they displayed even greater boldness, they inflamed the emperor's anger even more. He ordered them to be exiled to Skyros, an island under the jurisdiction of the Metropolis of Athens. From Skyros the divine Meletius was sent to Rome for conversations about the faith with the wise men of the Pope of Rome, and there he was again thrown into prison and kept in chains for seven years. Then, by the emperor's order, he was sent back to Skyros and placed in the same prison with Galaction.

Of course, imprisonment conceals within it many dangers and evils, which increase even more if the inhabitants of that place are wicked in character. The prison in which the saints dwelt was very harsh and gloomy, like the shadow of death; the hunger to which the venerable ones were subjected continued for many days, for the ruler of Skyros resolved to kill them by starvation. But the venerable ones, and especially the divine Meletius, remembered the ancient and familiar path of many days of fasting and exchanged the compulsory torment of hunger for a voluntary act, regarding it as a ladder to God, and for forty days they remained without food. The prison guard was so amazed that he repeated to his wife the words spoken in ancient times by Manoah: *"We shall surely die, because we have seen God!"* (Judges 13:22). The prisoners are so holy that they seem not to be men but far above men." After this he told his wife about their many days of fasting, about their frequent prayers with genuflection, about their all-night vigils, thereby bringing his wife to astonishment. At dawn the woman, together with her only daughter, visited the saints in prison, and both, falling at their feet, received a blessing.

Enduring the most severe sufferings, the saints rejoiced and constantly glorified God, while the emperor exerted great efforts to spread Latinism, trying to attract some by intimidation and torment, others by ranks and titles, and others by various other methods that made it possible to conceal the truth. Many became his friends by accepting Latinism, and those Orthodox whom the emperor did not persuade he subjected to disgrace, confiscated their estates, exiled them, and put them to death. Uprooting in such a tyrannical manner all who disagreed with Latinism, the monarch was certain that he had already conquered all the Orthodox. Once, while conversing with his nobles, he said with a laugh: "It seems to me that great peace has now come to the Church, and the Patriarch owes this to me, since there are no more of those who disturb the people." Many approved of these words of the emperor, but one of the nobles remarked:

"The exiles on the island of Skyros are still disputing, claiming that they are the most knowledgeable of all, and thus they oppose your authority."

"Who are they?"

"Meletius and Galaction of Gallisius." These words wounded the emperor to the very heart, because these men were known and famous for their virtue. Immediately a ship was prepared for the imperial messenger. The saints were brought to Constantinople and placed in the prison called the Noumera. Many days passed, but the emperor, citing other urgent matters, kept refusing to examine the case of the saints. All this time the hierarchs and especially the Patriarch (O judgment and longsuffering of God!) diligently slandered the saints before the emperor and strove with all their might to compel them to accept either Latinism or death. Finally the valiant venerable ones appeared before the emperor, but confessed their faith with even greater boldness and courage, for which they were subjected to even greater punishments. They were beaten for many hours until their lifeless bodies lay upon the ground. As soon as they had recovered a little, Galaction was thrown into prison, while the divine Meletius was suspended by ropes on a high pillar. And—O miracle!—this dry pillar immediately came to life and was covered with leaves.

Having heard of such a miracle, the emperor changed his mind and through intermediaries began to converse with the venerable one again and again, urging him to accept Latinism. The saint, scorning the emperor's request, was like an eagle soaring in the clouds, according to the expression of the proverb, uncatchable and unconquerable by any art or means of man. Not knowing what else to do, since he could not persuade them, the emperor decided to conquer their bodies by means of torments. He cruelly blinded the sacred Galaction, and from the holy Meletius he tore out his tongue, so that Galaction would no longer be able to serve, and the divine Meletius would no longer be able to theologize concerning the Holy Trinity. However, everything turned out differently than the emperor wished. For after Andronicus became Emperor of the Romans, boldly preaching the

Orthodox faith, the divine Meletius spoke clearly even without a tongue, and the good Galaction continued to offer the Bloodless Sacrifice as before.

As soon as the emperor was elevated to the throne, he immediately strengthened Orthodoxy, because he considered nothing more necessary. His first act was the restoration of Joseph, the unshakable pillar of Orthodoxy, to the Patriarchal throne and the expulsion of the adulterer and usurper John Beccus, the corrupter of the rational sheep of Christ. Then the emperor summoned the saints from prison with great honor. At that time many of those who had not accepted Latinism received high ranks. But the venerable Meletius neither the emperor, that ardent zealot of piety, nor the archons, could persuade to accept the priesthood, because he guarded himself from human glory, considering it harmful.

Already in deep old age, the venerable one fell ill, and he was ill for three years, and all this time he ate only vegetables, and even those with extreme abstinence and strictness. When the time came for him to depart to the Lord, he gathered all the brethren and spoke words of consolation to them for the last time, and gave each one instruction concerning the spiritual life. Then together with all he glorified God, and raising his hands to heaven and directing his eyes upward, he said: *"Into Your hands I commit my spirit."* And at that very hour he fell asleep with the sleep of the righteous, departing to the Lord whom he loved.

A monk named Gerasimus was sleeping in his cell and saw in a dream the divine Meletius with his hands raised upward, ascending to Heaven with joy. When he came to the cell of the venerable one, the saint had already died, and his face was shining with heavenly light.

Another hieromonk, Theoleptos, who greatly respected and loved the venerable one, served the Liturgy for forty days from the day of his repose. This period ended on the Sunday of the Triumph of Orthodoxy. After the service, Theoleptos began to ask God to reveal to him in what mansions the soul of the divine Meletius had found rest. Having fallen asleep after prayer, he saw in his dream that he was in a great and beautiful temple, facing east and reaching up to heaven. This temple was illumined with ineffable light. Within it, the holy fathers were singing to God a wondrous angelic song. There was also a preacher who told him that Meletius had built this temple in honor of the Holy Trinity while he was still alive. Theoleptos greatly rejoiced at what he heard and saw there. Then, still in his dream, he approached the tomb of the saint and saw that it was open, and inside it stood two men clothed in white, who held in their hands censers of wondrous beauty and were censing with them. Then Theoleptos also noticed Meletius himself, who began to reproach him: "You, dear Theoleptos, have left my tomb without care, and God has sent to me those whom you see." And while Theoleptos was marveling at how the holy Meletius could speak if he was dead, he suddenly heard a voice from Heaven: *"He who believes in Me, though he may die, he shall live"* (John 11:25). This is all concerning that.

And now I wish to recount to the glory of the saint some of the miracles he performed during his lifetime. Once, when the saint was walking along the shore, he met some fishermen who had spread out their nets on the sand. Having inquired whether they had caught anything, they answered that they had fished all night but had caught nothing. Having compassion on them, the saint said with boldness: "Children, cast your nets again in the name of our Savior God." Obeying the venerable one, they got into the boat and, having sailed out a little, read a prayer and cast their nets. O Thine indescribable mercy, my Christ! So many fish were caught in their nets that the fishermen had great difficulty pulling them into the boat. Marveling at the boldness that the venerable one had before God, they glorified God and thanked Meletius.

After the saint had built on the small island the church of Andrew the First-Called, as we already said, the cellarer once told him that there was nothing to feed the builders. Then, taking his staff, the saint ordered him to follow. They went down to the sea, and the venerable one gently struck the water with his rod, saying: "In the name of the Master Christ, give us today what we need!" And—O miracle!—at that very hour a large fish leaped out of the water onto the land. When the cellarer approached to take it, a second fish, no smaller than the first, leaped out of the water. Having taken both, the cellarer prepared a meal and fed the workers.

When the Orthodox Emperor Andronicus was reigning, he once invited the great Meletius to his palace to consult with him on a certain ecclesiastical matter and received the venerable one with great honor. One of the archons, named Sirmurinus, a protovestiarios by rank, began mentally to accuse the saint of loving temporal glory, and therefore said to one of those sitting near him: "This monk, it seems, has abandoned the heavenly glory which he should have sought and is now seeking human glory and rejoicing in it." Having returned home in the evening, Sirmurinus lay down on his bed and saw a dream. He found himself in the imperial palace, where a fearsome King sat enthroned, clothed simultaneously in royal and hierarchical vestments, and around Him stood innumerable hosts. Being greatly angered at Sirmurinus for insulting His servant, the King commanded His bodyguards to take vengeance on him. They wished to bind him hand and foot and cast him into the place of condemnation for blasphemers, but the great Meletius interceded for him before the King and delivered the unfortunate nobleman from punishment. Frightened by this terrible dream, Sirmurinus, as soon as he awoke, went to the saint. Falling at his feet, he confessed his condemnation and then recounted his dream. Having sought forgiveness with warm tears, which he immediately received from the venerable one, he departed with joy and thereafter spoke of the struggles of the saint with many praises.

Such, my beloved brethren, was the life of the venerable Meletius, such was his extraordinary zeal for Orthodoxy, and such were the miracles he manifested. Having lived seventy-seven years, he left all this that is temporal and departed to God, where he entreats the Most Holy Trinity on behalf of us all, to Whom is due glory, honor, and worship unto the ages of ages. Amen.

(Written by Macarius Chrysocephalos of Philadelphia)

The Life and Ascetic Struggles of Our Venerable and God-bearing Father Cosmas, Who Struggled in the Honorable Monastery of Zographou in the Thirteenth Century

This our venerable father Cosmas was a Bulgarian, and was born according to a vow, from pious and noble parents. He received a good upbringing, and in school he learned Greek and Bulgarian letters. After school his parents decided to have him married, however the youth, having a strong desire to become a monk, secretly left his homeland and came to the Holy Mountain. On the way to the Holy Mountain he was subjected to temptation from the hater of good, the envious devil, who, wishing to prevent him from reaching the Holy Mountain, in a vision showed him the Holy Mountain as an island, situated in the midst of an ocean. Wondering how the monks reach the Mountain, whether they use ladders or boats, the blessed Cosmas, having no one to ask, turned to God with this prayer: "Lord Jesus Christ, through the prayers of Thine All-Pure Mother, show me the path by which monks come to the Holy Mountain." Immediately the phantom sea vanished, and the youth, realizing that this was the cunning of the devil, gave thanks to God and the Mother of God.

Having entered the Holy Mountain without hindrance, Cosmas came to the honorable monastery of Zographou. Received with joy by the abbot and all the brethren, the youth spent sufficient time there, after which he was clothed in the monastic habit by the abbot of that time, who appointed him together with others to serve in the church.

When the feast of the Annunciation drew near, the youth received permission from the superior, and together with other brethren set out for the Vatopedi Monastery, in order to venerate the Precious Cincture of our Most Holy Sovereign Lady the Theotokos and the relics of the saints who reposed there. Upon entering the church, Cosmas saw a certain woman who was serving in the church, at the refectory, and participating in all the monastic obediences. Not knowing that this was the Most Holy Virgin, the venerable one was greatly grieved that the monks allow women into the monastery, for this is dangerous.

When he returned again to the Zographou monastery, the abbot, seeing his sorrow, asked what was the matter. The venerable one told him everything, and the abbot said: "Know, child, that that Woman Whom thou sawest was the Most Holy Theotokos, the protectress of that monastery and of this whole Mountain." Having learned everything, Cosmas gave thanks to the Most Holy Virgin, Who deigned to appear to him. After some time had passed the venerable one was ordained to the diaconate, and then to the priesthood, and from that time he struggled even more, fulfilling all the monastic obediences without complaint and with great zeal.

Once, when Cosmas was alone in the church, he addressed the Theotokos on the icon with these words: "Most Holy Theotokos, entreat Thy Son and our God, that He may guide me on the path of salvation." And at that very moment he heard a voice from the icon: "My Son and my God, guide Thy servant on the path of salvation." And Christ answered the Theotokos: "Let him leave the monastery and go into stillness." Coming out of the church, the venerable one told the abbot everything that he had heard, and the abbot settled him in a quiet cell near the monastery. Keeping stillness there for several years, the venerable one, with the help of God, attained all the virtues, and was even deemed worthy to receive the gift of clairvoyance, so that many came to him for confession.

Once two hieromonks from the Hilandar Monastery came to him who had hidden along the way a gourd with wine, in order to take it on their return journey. Having received a blessing from the venerable one, they were about to leave, when the clairvoyant elder said to them: "Break the gourd that you hid near the road, because a serpent has crawled into it; and do not drink that wine, lest you be poisoned." The hieromonks did so: breaking the gourd, they found a serpent inside and glorified God, Who had delivered them from death, and they also thanked the venerable Cosmas.

There was a certain monk of virtuous life by the name of Damian. He struggled near the Esphigmenou Monastery in a place called Samaria, and had a blessing not to spend the night in another's cell. Once Damian came to a certain acquaintance on some urgent matter, and since that person was not home, he was compelled to wait for him until evening. Having finished his business, Damian prepared to return to his own cell, but his friend urged him to stay, because it had already grown very dark and rain had begun to fall. But Damian, on account of the blessing that he had, did not remain with his friend. Since it was very dark and heavy rain was falling, he eventually became lost. Not knowing what to do, he cried out to the Lord: "Lord, save me, I perish." After this supplication, he immediately found himself in his own cell. Later, coming to the venerable one, he told him what had happened, in order to learn why this occurred and whether he had unknowingly sinned in anything before God. The saint answered him: "Brother, thou didst fulfill the commandment, and God preserved thee from death." Thus comforted, Damian returned to his cell, glorifying God.

Once the venerable one fell ill and, as a simple man, desired some fish. At that very moment (O wonder!) an eagle brought him a fish. Now nearby there struggled a certain spiritual elder, Christophoros, who had also fallen ill and asked a certain person to send him fish. When Christophoros was already washing this fish, an eagle flew down and snatched it from the elder's hands. This fish it then laid before Cosmas. Having given thanks to God, Cosmas fried the fish and was already preparing to eat it, when he heard a voice: "Leave a portion for Christophoros, that he too may taste of it." Soon Christophoros came to the venerable one and knocked on the door of his cell. The venerable one answered: "Enter, for I am waiting for thee, that thou mayest eat thy portion of fish." Christophoros asked the saint with astonishment how he knew whose fish it was. And the saint related everything to him in detail, after which both rejoiced, and Christophoros returned to his cell. Once on Great Thursday the venerable one saw in the air a soul being tormented by demons. Learning that it was the soul of the Hilandar abbot, he sent his disciple to the monastery to tell the brethren that they should pray to God for this soul. The disciple came and announced to the brethren the vision of the venerable one, but they did not believe him, and said: "The abbot has just come out of church and went to his cell to bring everything necessary for the Liturgy, and that deluded one bids us pray for him." Nevertheless they went to the superior's cell, where they found that the abbot had indeed died.

On another occasion the same Christophoros came to the venerable one to converse about the word of God. Knocking on the door, he heard voices and thought that someone was confessing in the cell. He waited a long time until the conversation ended, and after that knocked on the door. The venerable one met him, embraced him, they went inside, made the prayer, and sat down. Since Christophoros saw no one, he asked the saint with whom he had been speaking. The elder could not conceal this and answered that he had been speaking with Christ: "He told me what the demons will soon do to me, and that in a few days I shall depart this life and pass into His Kingdom. But do thou go in peace, but on such-and-such a day be sure to come here again." Christophoros departed and on the appointed day came again to the venerable one, whom he found lying in bed and dying. Asking the reason, he heard in answer:

"The chief of the demons came this evening with many demons, wept and said: 'O powerless and negligent ones, not one of you was able to kill this dread enemy of mine, who has so grieved me that in the end he has taken my throne from me.' With these words the malicious demon took a rod and beat me severely, as thou seest."

Christophoros remained there and cared for the sick man. After two days the venerable one asked to commune of the Most Pure Mysteries and, having received them with reverence and given thanks to God, committed his spirit into His hands in the month of September, on the twenty-second day, in the year 1233 from the Birth of Christ.

Learning of his repose, the hieromonk fathers and monks came to bury the sacred remains of the venerable one. And God, Who glorifies those who glorify Him, glorified this saint after death in the following manner. When the brethren were chanting the Order for Burial, all the animals of the wilderness gathered and stood quietly until he was buried, after which each cried out loudly in its own way, and all dispersed again. After forty days the brethren came to the cell of the venerable one and served the All-night Vigil, after which they opened the tomb to take his precious relics to the monastery, but (O ineffable are Thy wonders, O Christ the King!) they did not find his body there, and to this day no one knows where it is, save God alone, to Whom is due glory and dominion unto the ages of ages. Amen.

The Life and Struggles of Our Venerable and God-Bearing Father Gregory of Sinai, Who Labored in the Fourteenth Century

This divine Gregory was by origin from the village of Koukoulis in Asia Minor, near Klazomenai, and came from parents who were rich and noble, and at the same time God-fearing and virtuous. Diligently raised by them, he was given to teachers, from whom he learned the divine and sacred sciences. At that time (the great Andronikos Palaiologos was then reigning) the Hagarene race attacked Asia, plundered it, and reduced to slavery almost all the Christians there. Together with them, the divine Gregory was also enslaved along with his parents and brothers. They were brought to Laodicea and, by the Providence of God, the barbarians permitted them to attend church. During the customary psalmody and doxology, the local Christians, seeing that they stood with great reverence, sang beautifully, and were trained in music, marveled at their piety and singing. Immediately after the dismissal they came to the Hagarenes and, giving them much money, ransomed Gregory and his family from slavery. After this, the divine Gregory set out for Cyprus. He lived there but a short time, yet everyone came to love his virtue and natural gifts. His pleasant countenance indicated the interior state of his divine soul, and his modesty, piety, and reverence toward God amazed everyone, and the people greatly honored Gregory.

At the time when the venerable Gregory was living on the island, God, Who knew the fervent love for virtue dwelling in his heart, showed him a certain virtuous monk who was laboring in hesychia. Gregory immediately came to the monk with joy, was clothed by him in monastic garments, and became a novice. Having spent some time with the elder, he conversed with him repeatedly on spiritual topics, and then departed for Mount Sinai, where he was tonsured as a monk. Together with the tonsuring of his hair, Gregory cut off all desires and movements of the flesh and with great courage of soul continued his ascetic labors. A short time passed, and the fathers there were amazed at his almost immaterial, incorporeal life in fasting, vigil, all-night standing, unceasing psalmody, and prayer; a little more, and they would have begun to think that he was truly bodiless.

In obedience—the root and mother of the virtues—and in humility that leads one upward, he was so skilled that it is difficult to describe them separately, lest the lazy should think that for the sake of exaggeration I am speaking of things incredible. At the same time, precisely because of the lazy, I do not intend to conceal the truth and shall write about what I heard from his closest disciple, Saint Gerasimos. This blessed one told me that the divine Gregory fulfilled with diligence and every zeal the obedience assigned him by the abbot, as if he were seen by God on high, and never neglected the usual common rule of the brethren either. In the evening, having made the customary prostration to the abbot and received a blessing from him, the venerable one would enter his cell. Having shut the door, he would raise his hands and nous to God and, completely withdrawing from this material world and striving to draw near to God, would begin the rule with extraordinary zeal. All night he would chant psalms to God and pray with fervent heartfelt desire and genuflections, until he finished all the Psalms of David, the singing of which gave him joy. Then in the morning, when they struck the semantron, the venerable one was, according to custom, the first at the doors of the church. He was always so strict with himself that he never left the temple before the service ended. Thus Gregory entered the church first and departed last. His food was only bread and water, and that in such quantity as merely to sustain life in the body. For more than three years Gregory fulfilled the obedience of cook and baker, and not once did he even think that he was serving men; on the contrary, he was certain that he was serving the ranks of Angels, and he considered the place of his obedience a true altar and sanctuary of God. Moreover, almost every day he would ascend to the peak of Mount Sinai to venerate the place where the well-known great wonders had been wrought. The venerable one was highly skilled in calligraphy, and he devoted himself so much to reading that day and night he diligently selected sayings from the Old and New Testaments and strove to commit them to memory. I do not know whether there was another father who had so studied the Holy Scriptures as he, and who in his knowledge surpassed all the fathers there. However, the malicious devil could not calmly observe the struggles of the venerable one. He secretly led the monks into the passion of envy and, being a sower of tares, sowed in them strong confusion and agitation. Gregory, a disciple of the meek and peace-loving Jesus, understanding that the monks envied him, secretly left the monastery, taking with him Gerasimos, who was originally from the island of Euripos and was a relative of the ruler of the island, the Riga. Having despised wealth, glory, and noble birth, having renounced the world and the things in the world, Gerasimos came to Mount Sinai, where he made the acquaintance of the divine Gregory. Having been astonished at his extreme virtue, Gerasimos became one of his disciples and, with God's help, attained a high level of practice and contemplation, becoming after the great Gregory an example for others.

Having left Sinai, they came to Jerusalem to venerate the Life-Giving Tomb. After visiting the holy places, the ascetics boarded a ship and sailed to Crete, to a place called Fair Havens, where the venerable one with great zeal began to search for a calm and quiet place to dwell. After long searching, they finally found secluded caves and with joy settled there. Immediately that good laborer began to add labors to labors, struggles to struggles, in some way striving against himself with even greater courage. His food was bread and water once a day, and nothing else, although there was the danger of perishing from thirst. The face of the venerable one took on a yellow hue from dry eating, the members of his body dried out and were worn out by many labors, weakened from physical exertion and incapable of any other activity. Moreover, the blessed one strove to find such a spiritual man who could instruct him in that which he himself could not understand in Holy Scripture and in which he had not been taught by the Spirit-bearing divine fathers.

God, in answer to his entreaties, sent him such a man. In a divine revelation He showed the divine Gregory and disclosed his desire to a certain hermit named Arsenios, who was practicing hesychia in those parts and was adorned with pious deeds and Divine contemplation. Moved by the Spirit of God, Arsenios came to the cell of the venerable one, knocked on the door, and was received by him with great joy. After the customary prayer and greeting, Arsenios began to speak as if from some divine book, speaking of guarding of the nous, of nepsis, of prayer, of prayer of the nous, and of how the nous is purified through the fulfillment of the commandments and becomes like light. Having spoken of this and much else, the elder, addressing the venerable one, asked: "And you, child, what labor do you perform?" Then the divine Gregory told him everything about himself from the very beginning: about his departure from the world, about his love for the solitary life, and about all his deeds. The divine Arsenios, knowing well the path that leads a person to the height of virtue, remarked with a smile: "Child, all that you have told me is called by the God-bearing fathers practice, but not vision." Upon hearing these words, the blessed Gregory immediately fell at his feet and began fervently to beg, imploring him by God, to teach him what prayer of the nous is, what hesychia is, and what guarding of the nous is. That divine father, accepting the request of the venerable one as a certain treasure, without delay taught him everything, omitting nothing of what he himself had abundantly received with the help of Divine grace. Moreover, the elder revealed to him what happens to those who labor in the struggle for virtue, for on the right and on the left they are attacked by enemies of the good—demons, and envious people whom the evil one uses as instruments of his malice. Arsenios told Gregory about all of this in detail.

After this conversation, Gregory immediately resolved to sail to the Holy Mountain. Having gone around all the monasteries, cells, sketes, and even the difficult-to-reach cells of hermits, he considered it right to meet all the fathers and render them due veneration for the sake of prayer and blessing. And, as he himself related, on Athos Gregory met a multitude of ascetics adorned with prudence, modesty, and many other virtues. They all applied all their diligence to the labor of practicing virtue. But when he asked whether they practiced prayer of the nous, whether they gave themselves to nepsis and guarding of the nous, they replied that they did not even know what prayer of the nous was, what guarding of the nous was, or what nepsis was.

Having gone around the entire Holy Mountain, the venerable one came at last to the skete of Magoula, opposite the venerable monastery of Philotheou. There he met three monks: Isaiah, Cornelius, and Macarius, who practiced not only the practical virtues but to some extent the contemplative as well. Having labored much together with his disciples, he built cells there. At a small distance from them he built for himself a hesychasterion, so that he might converse alone with the One God through prayer of the nous and propitiate Him through the practical virtues. It was then that the venerable one recalled the instruction of the honorable Arsenios, and what he had told him concerning guarding of the nous, nepsis, and prayer of the nous. Having subjected all the senses within himself, having united the nous with the spirit and nailed himself to the Cross of Christ, he repeated again and again: "Lord Jesus Christ, Son of God, have mercy on me a sinner." Praying thus with tenderness of heart and heartfelt compunction, with sighing from the depths of his soul, he wept constantly, and tears flowed from his eyes like a river. For these tears the Lord did not despise his prayer: *"A heart that is broken and humbled God will not despise"* (Psalm 50:19), for *"the righteous cry out, and the Lord hears"* (Psalm 33:18). Under the action of the Holy Spirit his soul and heart were inflamed and, having been changed with a good and wondrous change, being enlightened by Divine grace, the venerable one saw that his cell was filled with light. Filled with joy and ineffable gladness, again pouring forth streams of tears, he was wounded by Divine love, for truly in him were fulfilled the words of the one who said: "Practice is the way to contemplation." For the venerable one had left the flesh and this world and was wholly filled with Divine love. From that time the light continually illumined the righteous one, according to the saying: *"Light is always for the righteous"* (Proverbs 13:9). When I (the blessed Kallistos) and other disciples asked the ever-memorable one about the meaning of these words, he answered: "He who by the grace of the Holy Spirit is exalted in God, beholds as in a mirror all creation in the world, *'whether in the body I do not know, or whether out of the body I do not know,'* as the Apostle Paul says (2 Corinthians 12:2), until someone hinders this, causing him to come to himself."

Simply and completely without any curiosity I would ask him various questions when Gregory came out of his cell with a joyful countenance and looked upon me meekly. You, spiritual fathers, know how much more you love your last spiritual children than the first. In like manner my ever-blessed spiritual father showed more love toward me as his last spiritual child, and I would whisper to him as to a loving father. And he answered me thus:

"The soul that cleaves to God and is wounded by His love will rise above every creature, will live above all the visible world, and will be united with the desire for God. It will not be able to hide, as the Lord Himself promised it, saying: *'Your Father who sees in secret will reward you openly'* (Matthew 6:4). And again: *'Let your light so shine before men, that they may see your good works and glorify your Father in heaven'* (Matthew 5:16). For the heart trembles and rejoices, the nous overflows, the countenance becomes joyful and radiant, as the wise man also said: *'A merry heart makes a cheerful countenance'* (Proverbs 15:13)."

And I again asked him:

"Divine father, teach me, for the love of truth, what is the soul, and what do the saints say about this."

With his characteristic meekness he answered:

"My beloved spiritual child, do not seek what is beyond you, and do not investigate what is deeper, for in order to understand what you have asked me, you must cease to be an imperfect infant who cannot digest solid food. It is not within your power to comprehend lofty concepts, just as the food of mature men does not benefit tender infants, who require only milk."

Falling at his feet and firmly grasping them, I fervently asked him to answer. Yielding to my urgent request, Gregory said: "He who does not see the resurrection of his soul cannot know exactly what the noetic soul is."

"Tell me, father, have you attained this degree of ascent, that is, have you come to know what the noetic soul is?"

"Yes."

Then I asked him, for the love of the Lord, to teach me as well that which could bring great benefit to my soul. The divine and most honorable Gregory praised my zeal and gave me this teaching:

"When the soul employs all its zeal and labors with understanding and discernment in the practical virtues, then, repelling all the passions, it subjects them to itself. And when it conquers the passions, only the natural virtues will surround it, which follow it as a shadow follows a body. These very virtues will not only follow it but will also teach and guide it toward what is supernatural, as if ascending a spiritual ladder. And when the nous, by the grace of Christ, ascends to the supra-natural state, then, being enlightened by the radiance of the Holy Spirit, it extends itself brightly into contemplation as well. Having become above itself according to the measure of grace given by God, it clearly and purely beholds the nature of beings, their connections and order—but not as the external philosophers babble, who resort only to the shadow of things and do not strive to follow, as they ought, the essential energy of nature, because, as Scripture says, *their foolish heart was darkened; professing to be wise, they became fools* (Romans 1:21–22). Then that soul which has received the betrothal and grace of the Holy Spirit, little by little, by virtue of the multitude of contemplations which it has, leaves behind the former things and ascends to the heavenly and Divine, as the Apostle Paul says: *forgetting those things which are behind and reaching forward* (Philippians 3:13). The soul that has been truly purified in this manner lays aside all fear and timidity and, having cleaved in love to the Bridegroom Christ, sees that its natural thoughts completely cease and fall away, as the holy fathers also command. Having attained to unseen and ineffable beauty, it converses alone with the One God, being brightly illumined by the radiance and grace of the Holy Spirit. Enlightened thus by the infinite light, it moves only toward God Himself, and through this wondrous and new change it no longer perceives the low, earthly, and material body, because the soul appears transparent and luminous, without any additions or earthly attachment—a nature that is noetic above all else, such as was our forefather Adam before his transgression. In the beginning he was clothed with the grace of that infinite light, and then for his hateful transgression (O woe!) was stripped of his luminous glory and sanctification. Thus this precious creature, man, was found naked."

The venerable one also related to me that the person who has attained such a height through the toilsome practice of prayer of the nous, and has purely seen and come to know his own state to which he has come by the grace of Christ—has seen the resurrection of the soul before the general resurrection for which we all hope. The soul purified in this manner can say, together with the divine Paul: *"whether in the body I do not know, or whether out of the body I do not know"* (2 Corinthians 12:2), but it is itself perplexed and amazed at this, and cries out in wonder: *"Oh, the depth of the riches both of the wisdom and knowledge of God! How unsearchable are His judgments and His ways past finding out!"* (Romans 11:33). This is what that divine father related to me.

But concerning his disciples, who under the guidance of the venerable one ascended to the height of virtue, I do not know how to speak worthily or how to recount their battles and struggles. The first among them was Saint Gerasimos, who came from Euripos, as I have already said. Afterward he became a disciple of the most holy Patriarch Isidore, brought enormous benefit, and earned his praise, for from the very beginning he had been well taught by the divine Gregory in virtue and the life befitting a monk. This wondrous man imitated the venerable Gerasimos of old (of the Jordan), and as that one traversed the apostolic path and tamed the wilderness of the Jordan, raising venerable monasteries in it, so also this new Gerasimos, filled with Divine grace and enlightened by God, came to Greece. Like the apostles he traversed it and fed all who hungered and thirsted for the word of God with the sweetest teaching of virtue, enriching them, as much as was possible, with the wealth of sanctification and piety. But Gerasimos himself also, thanks to his striving and diligence, gathered around himself a multitude of disciples and, with God's help, founded a heavenly dwelling and monastic community, handing on to the brethren the rules of the strict angelic life. He taught them, being an example of virtue, as in ancient times the venerable Gerasimos. In like manner, this new Gerasimos was also counted worthy to behold Divine visions in hesychia and lived a life of spiritual struggles worthy of wonder, after which he reposed in the Lord.

The second disciple of the venerable one was Joseph, a countryman and companion of Gerasimos, who courageously struggled for Orthodoxy, opposing the Latins, and extracted many from this impiety, bringing them to Orthodoxy by the grace of Christ. Few among those known and accomplished in the external wisdom were able to do so much for Orthodoxy as Joseph did, for he had the inner and true wisdom—the grace of the Holy Spirit—with the help of which those fishermen, the divine apostles, also were glorified and put the external philosophers to shame. So also the wondrous Joseph was glorified by God and put the Latins to shame. But who can worthily recount his other virtues and renowned and modest life? I too shall be silent about this.

But you, O listener, consider another disciple of the saint—the wondrous Abba Nikolaos, an elder eighty years old, from Athens, who was worthy of honor not only for his venerable age but also for his prudence and modesty of character. He courageously endured numerous persecutions for Orthodoxy from the Latin-minded Michael Palaiologos: he was exiled, his estates were plundered, and many times he was cast into dark prisons. At the time when the divine Nikolaos was preaching the word of God in his homeland and teaching the people to keep the Orthodox faith and not accept the corrupt teaching of the Latins, the emperor sent his cruel and inhumane Latin-minded servants to punish him. Obeying the emperor's command, they bound Nikolaos tightly with ropes, put chains on his neck and hands, shaved off his beard to shame him, and, having beaten him cruelly with rods and kicked him, led him everywhere along the roads for all to see. The vain-thinking ones did not know that by this they were only displaying their own malice, while for Nikolaos they were the cause of greater glory. But since, by the mercy of God, peace came to the Church of Christ at that time and the persecutions of the Orthodox ceased, the Ecumenical Patriarch, the most holy Joseph, tried various ways to ordain the divine Nikolaos as a bishop. But that humble-minded one would by no means agree to become a bishop, and desiring hesychia, he came to the Holy Mountain. The then protos of the Holy Mountain greatly loved Nikolaos, who was adorned with all virtues and piety, and appointed him, against his will, ecclesiarch in the venerable monastery of Karyes. After some time, Nikolaos met the wondrous Gregory and, having heard his sweetest teachings, desired with his whole soul to become his disciple.

As a magnet by its great natural power attracts the hardest iron, so also our divine teacher Gregory, by his soul-profitable words (which every prudent person would justly call words of eternal life, and truly the Divine voice), attracted to himself all who saw him or conversed with him. As Andrew once saw Christ and immediately left John the Forerunner, after which he followed Jesus inseparably, so also the disciples of the divine Gregory constantly accompanied him, observing what extraordinary reverence he had attained, into what imperturbability and peace of soul he had come, because his meek and joyful countenance indicated the interior illumination and grace of his soul. Many virtuous monks left their elders and, striving to hear his instructions and join his brotherhood so as to receive benefit for themselves, went to him in obedience. Thus Abba Nikolaos also acted, who not only left the honors and glory of men as vain and unnecessary burden, but despised even his own old age, throwing himself at the feet of the venerable one. He received with joy the struggle and labor of obedience as if he had acquired some great treasure. Heeding the sweet words of the venerable one, absorbing his instructions, he became experienced in every virtue, and especially in humility, surpassing in this all his fellow-brothers.

One ought also to marvel at how the divine father dealt with his novices. When he wished to correct a disciple who had sinned, having considered with the clairvoyant eyes of his soul how to bring benefit to the novice, he would suddenly begin to reproach him, calling him evil and wicked, saying that he had grown old in wickedness and had done nothing good. The venerable one called him a slothful man who neglected the salvation of his soul, and often commanded some monk to drive the one who had sinned out of the trapeza with a stern countenance. In all this the venerable one cared in every way for the salvation of the brother's soul. Having heard all this, the ascetic of Christ, Abba Nikolaos, fell with great humility at the feet of the saint and began to weep. And even my own heart, as I relate this, is constricted, and abundant tears flow from wonder when I picture the venerable elder prostrate at the feet of the teacher. But you, listener, consider and marvel at this story. Having thus rebuked the disciple who had sinned, Gregory would instruct him and, having forgiven him, would send him away with great profit for his soul. What I have now related is only a tiny part, since there is no possibility of recounting in detail all the struggles of the venerable one.

But you, beloved, look at another disciple of the divine Gregory, the most wondrous Mark, who was originally from Klazomenai. Having come to Thessaloniki, he was tonsured as a monk in the monastery called the monastery of Lord Isaac. Coming to the Holy Mountain, he struggled with great zeal and diligence, acquiring prayer of the nous and nepsis, and he greatly loved unceasing prayer. Although Mark became a precious treasury of all virtues, he so loved humility and obedience that he wished to serve zealously, as much as possible, not only the abbot but all the brotherhood in Christ as well. He was very displeased if he was unable to serve, like a slave, all the monks who came there. Truly by his deeds he fulfilled without hypocrisy the commandment of Christ: *"whoever desires to be first among you, let him be your slave"* (Matthew 20:27). There was no one who did not marvel at and praise the divine Mark, and who did not perceive his spiritual fragrance. Having seen him but once, any person received sanctification into his soul from him and took from him an example of humility. This divine ascetic, having come to deep old age, wished with great joy to perform the same struggles as in his youth, not at all considering either old age or weakness or anything else that might hinder him. He zealously fulfilled the obediences in the kitchen and never once neglected his duties under any pretext. Therefore God also, Who blesses the humble in heart, seeing such humility in him, raised him to such glory that, radiant with Divine grace, he became a most brilliant instrument of the Holy Spirit. Having reached the tranquil and quiet harbor, he was united in his striving with God, conversing with Him alone and ineffably rejoicing in His radiance, bringing to many spiritual benefit from his teachings and holiness. Such I knew him to be, and I had the opportunity to experience this over a long time, because I came to live together with him, having one thought and one desire in all things, by the grace of the Holy Spirit. From the very beginning, when I first became acquainted with him, I loved him with my whole soul, extraordinarily treasuring his friendship. And although he commanded me not to divulge the virtues which God had granted him, yet since the praise of the saints pertains to God, I thought it right not to conceal his struggles at all—those about which people speak and listen with joy and gratitude, and which incline the hearers to imitate the ascetic. When the divine father our Gregory resolved to return to the venerable Lavra, he so united us, one with another, by his teachings and instructions that it seemed we had one soul in two bodies. Having commanded us to remain inseparable until the end, being moved by the grace of the Holy Spirit, he told us much that was good, including that if we remained in unity, we would be counted worthy of the Heavenly Kingdom. We then made the customary prostration and received the blessing of his prayer, and we remained together and were inseparable, thinking and doing everything alike. We did not know what "mine" and "yours" meant, and we lived together for a full twenty-eight years. If someone called Kallistos, Mark was also with him. If someone called Mark, Kallistos also came. All the fathers who lived with us in the skete saw in us a praiseworthy example because of the good harmony that was between us, by the grace of Christ. And if sometimes, through the envy of the devil, disagreements and disputes arose among certain brethren, they often recalled our God-pleasing example.

Then, I do not know how, a bodily illness occurred in Mark. For this reason we came to the holy Lavra for healing. Having come to know his great virtue, the fathers there did not wish to let him go, for this would have been unbearable for them. But I, being moved by God, came to the venerable Iveron Monastery, and although it seemed to some that we were separated from each other bodily, being in different places, yet in soul, by the grace of God that unites and preserves what is good, we continued to be together. Wherever we were, we were always united with each other, and each of us preserved the remembrance of the other with great love. The blessed Mark was glorified by God, receiving each day greater glory with the gifts and illumination with which he was honored by Him.

And now let us tell also of another disciple of the saint, the most praiseworthy Iakov. With the help of the teachings and instructions of the divine Gregory, he ascended to such a height of virtues that he was counted worthy to receive the hierarchical dignity as well, becoming Bishop of Servia.

A little later Aarōn came to the Holy Mountain and was received by the venerable Gregory, who pitied him greatly because he was blind. The saint told him that in His extreme goodness God became Man in order to call back our forefather Adam, who had fallen through disobedience, to free him from the tyranny of the devil, to bring him to the first original state of nobility, and to raise him from the corruption of death. Bodily blindness not only purifies the eyes of the soul but also grants eternal light to those who bear it with thanksgiving and undoubtingly hope in God. When we, with God's help and by His grace, purify our hearts through fervent prayer and unceasing supplication, then our nous and thought are enlightened, which are like the two eyes of the soul. When the eyes of our soul are enlightened and opened, then the person who has become spiritual in God sees naturally, as Adam also saw before his transgression.

Having heard such instructions and understood them with his mind, Aarōn began with heartfelt compunction to entreat God: "O Lord my God, Who raised up her that was bowed down to the ground, Who healed the paralytic by a single word, Who opened the eyes of the blind man, look upon me with Thine indescribable compassion and despise not with despair my wretched soul, bowed down with the mire of sin and lying upon the earth. As the Lover of mankind, open the eyes of my heart, that Thy fear may dwell in it, that I may understand Thy commandments and do Thy will." Praying thus to God from the depths of his soul, Aarōn was heard, and the eyes of his soul were opened, so that not only did he no longer need a guide, but sitting in his cell he would sometimes foretell what was to happen, for example: "Let us go out into the street, because such-and-such an elder or such-and-such a brother is coming to us." Remarkably, just as he foretold, so it came to pass. When the day of the commemoration of some great saint or a feast of the Lord was to come, he would speak of it well in advance, having been taught by no one and having received such information from no one. When asked how he learned of this, Aarōn answered that before the feast a great sanctification and glory descends into his soul from God, and all his knowledge is from God. Thus once, when they were going together with Iakov to a certain monk and were at a distance of two miles from his cell, Aarōn, enlightened by God, said to Iakov: "The monk to whom we are going is holding in his hands the Holy Four Gospels and is reading from it this verse." When they came to the cell and questioned the monk, they discovered that he had indeed been reading that verse of which Aarōn had spoken.

We must also tell of the other disciples of the venerable one: Moses, Longinos, Cornelius, Isaiah, and Clement. They began their life according to God with great zeal and labored much in sweat and toils to acquire all the virtues. Continually practicing the salvific labor of prayer of the nous and having acquired a multitude of disciples, they peacefully fell asleep, committing their souls into the hands of God. Since I have remembered the wondrous Clement, it will be right to tell something of what God granted him.

This Clement was a shepherd of sheep, originally from Bulgaria. One night, when he was guarding the sheep, he saw a strange, powerful light that illumined the entire flock. Greatly rejoicing, he began to consider where such a light could have arisen: perhaps day had suddenly dawned and the sun had risen while he dozed a little, leaning on his staff. While he was thus pondering, the light began gradually to recede and ascended into the Heavens. And again night and darkness came. Having greatly wondered at this, Clement came to the Holy Mountain and, finding in the skete of Morphinou a simple monk, but one who was pious and virtuous, became his novice, but learned from him only the prayer: "Lord, have mercy." After some time that light began again to appear little by little and filled Clement's soul with Divine grace. Clement was a very simple and artless man and attended only to God. Since the elder commanded him to confess to him all his thoughts, he told him of the vision he had had, asking him to reveal what it might mean. The elder, being incapable of this, went with Clement to the divine Gregory, to whom they told everything, fervently asking him to receive them and enroll them in his brotherhood. Imitating Christ and desiring the salvation of all, the venerable one received them with joy and, separating them from everyone, taught them all that is necessary for the salvation of the soul, commanding them to have patience, humility, constant hope in God—from Whom comes every good thing to men—never to neglect the rule given to them, and to think constantly of death. Having received with great humility what was commanded by the divine father, Clement promised to fulfill everything unceasingly. He began to struggle in the labor according to God with such zeal and diligence that soon his nous was enlightened by the light of Divine grace, and he ascended not only to the contemplation of beings but, ascending from contemplation to contemplation, attained the supra-natural state. If a soul, simple by nature, truly approaches to serve God and zealously dedicates itself to Him, it becomes godlike, receives rest, and enters the supra-natural state. Clement recounted that when the divine Gregory sent him to the Holy Lavra, each time the fathers laboring there reverently began to sing "More honorable than the Cherubim...," a luminous cloud would descend from the Heavens and wondrously cover the Lavra until the hymn was finished, after which the cloud would again ascend into Heaven.

Clement received great spiritual benefit from the teachings of the venerable one, and not only he but also all those who heard his divine words and received them with love and reverence. Almost all the monks would come to him, being completely unable to remain without his teachings, for the venerable one was counted worthy to receive from God great spiritual wisdom and grace, which brought benefit to his listeners, as those who experienced this for themselves related to me. That God-bearing father offered to his disciples spiritual and God-pleasing discourses, which were accompanied by Divine grace. When he began to speak of the purification of the soul and of how a person becomes a god by grace, then wondrous and exceeding Divine love would come into our souls. Just as when the great Peter taught in the house of Cornelius the centurion and the Holy Spirit descended upon them, so also it happened with those whom the divine Gregory taught, according to the testimony of his very disciples. The ever-blessed one made many efforts to incline all the fathers—both hermits and those in the cenobitic life—to practice prayer of the nous and guarding of the nous.

However, the enemy of good, the devil, did not rest but stirred up against the venerable one the more educated monks, who, like ordinary people, succumbed to the passion. They envied the divine Gregory and set as their goal to drive him off the Holy Mountain. In ignorance, others also agreed with them who, confusing stubbornness with pride and arrogance, said to the venerable one: "Do not teach us this way of which we know nothing," meaning prayer of the nous and guarding of the nous. Seeing that instead of peace, envy was being kindled, and that good was giving place to malice, the venerable one, with one of his disciples and a certain ascetic named Isaiah, who was the first of all to build himself a cell in the skete of Magoula, departed from there to the Protaton. Let us say a few words about Isaiah. This blessed one suffered much from the Latin-minded Emperor Michael Palaiologos, because he did not wish to commune with the then Patriarch John Bekkos on account of his innovations in the Orthodox faith. Moved by zeal for God, Isaiah struggled much for Orthodoxy, tirelessly taught, and applied all his striving and diligence to unite all more closely with the Orthodox Church of Christ. Together with this wondrous disciple the venerable one came to the Protaton, but the then protos, although he received them with joy, began to taunt the divine Gregory, as if in a friendly manner. He did this not because Gregory taught about nepsis and prayer of the nous—for how can one oppose the truth and the venerable one, who was a Spirit-bearing man and clearly preached about God for the common benefit—but because Gregory taught without his permission. Having learned, however, of the extraordinary virtue of this holy man and the loftiness of his Divine teaching, the protos abandoned all his mockery and, being reconciled with him, gained great benefit for himself. Conversing with Gregory and Isaiah, the protos said: "Today I am conversing as if with the chief apostles Peter and Paul." Seeing with what care the protos of the Holy Mountain received them, and also learning of his praises, the other fathers also came to know the truth, and from that time all—both hermits and those in the cenobitic life—received the divine Gregory with great spiritual joy as their common teacher. However, because of the multitude of people who came to him, it was not easy for the venerable one to find rest. Therefore, loving hesychia, he changed his place of residence many times. Sometimes he went to the venerable monastery of Saint Simon and remained in its vicinity for hesychia, for the road there was difficult to traverse; and sometimes he practiced hesychia in a deep wooded ravine called Jegreia. In these deserted places too he built cells, far from the road, and in them he often hid from those who came to him, because he greatly loved the solitary life and did not wish even for one hour to interrupt his spiritual contemplation.

But what happened next? Once, a barbarous tribe of Hagarenes suddenly attacked the Holy Mountain and, seizing all the monks who were laboring there, reduced them to slavery. Reflecting, on the one hand, on the great evil that had befallen him when he had been reduced to slavery by these barbarians, as I said at the beginning, and on the other hand, that the commotion produced had scattered his nous and the barbarians had disturbed his hesychia, the venerable one resolved to go again to Sinai in order to practice hesychia there on the peak of the mountain. Together with several disciples we went to Thessaloniki, and then, after two months, secretly from everyone, only with me and another monk, we boarded a ship and sailed to Chios. There we met a monk who was on his way to Jerusalem. I do not know what he said to the venerable one, but it prevented us from going to Sinai. We set off for Mytilene, from where, having spent a short time on Mount Lebanon and being unable to find hesychia, we came to Constantinople. On account of the severe winter we spent six months there, hiding as strangers. Emperor Andronikos Palaiologos, a zealot and champion of Orthodoxy, having learned that Gregory was in Constantinople, graciously invited him to come to him. The emperor had long desired to see the ascetic, for he knew of the great fame of the venerable one. Andronikos even promised to give him rich gifts, but the saint, avoiding the glory of men, would by no means agree to come to the emperor. Leaving Constantinople, we set off by sea for Sozopolis, where we remained but a short time, for a certain monk, Amiralis, who dwelt in the deep wilderness of Paroria, learned of us and invited the venerable Gregory to come to him. Having visited Amiralis, the venerable one thought that this place was quiet and would be conducive to fulfilling his God-pleasing purpose, and resolved to settle there. The venerable one and his disciples built small cells with their own hands, at a distance of one mile both from the place where Amiralis labored, who also had his own disciples, and from one another. Among them was also one monk named Luke, who at the very beginning had been a disciple of the divine Gregory on the Holy Mountain. But now the passion of envy had attacked him, and he was completely unable to restrain himself on account of the malice that had taken root in him. Once, having greatly insulted the holy Gregory, he rushed at him with a knife in great shamelessness. If other disciples of Amiralis had not prevented him, the wretched one would have committed murder. The venerable Gregory, as a true disciple of the meek and peace-loving Christ, became in this case also an example for imitation and not only was not filled with hatred but was not even the least disturbed and did not plot any evil against Luke. He showed him enormous love and even thanked him. For the benefit of Luke's soul, the venerable one wrote one hundred fifty chapters on nepsis, both practical and contemplative.

After some time, Amiralis himself also, under the influence of the primally evil enemy, envied the saint and, being inflamed with anger, shouted at him outrageously and threatened that if he did not leave as quickly as possible, he would hire a multitude of brigands who would come and kill everyone—which he later did. Such was the reward that the one who pretended to be a monk gave to the divine Gregory. But in vain did the madman labor, for God, through the prayers of the venerable one, preserved us all unharmed. Departing from there with all the monks who had gathered for his sake, our divine father Gregory came to a mountain called Katakekrimeni. After several days, that envious Amiralis sent brigands who, attacking us like lions, seized everyone and bound the venerable one (O woe!) with a cloth and began to search for money from one who, since his young years, had not wished to have a single obol. Having found nothing, they released us.

Since envy had completely taken hold of Amiralis's soul and this passion does not pass easily, we departed from there and came again to Sozopolis, from where in December we returned to Constantinople. Having remained there until spring, we came with the venerable one to the Holy Mountain. The monks of the Lavra received him with great joy, considering his arrival a spiritual celebration. Near the Holy Lavra, in various places, the saint built several cells. He asked the Lavra for permission to occupy also some kathismata suitable for hesychia and, laboring there, conversed alone with the One God. By God's permission, the barbarous tribe again burst upon the Holy Mountain. It became impossible to practice hesychia outside the monastery, and the divine father entered the Lavra, but conversations with the monastery's inhabitants distracted him from hesychia. Grieving greatly over this and desiring solitude, ascent, and contemplation, having no rest at all, he told no one, took a disciple, and sailed by ship to Adrianople. Then by land he came to Paroria, where, having gathered a multitude of monks, he settled on Mount Katakekrimeni. Brigands also lived there. Here any prudent person would immediately think that this was from the evil one, who envied the good and feared lest the venerable one should make this wilderness a dwelling of monks for the unceasing glorification of God—which, as we see today, by the grace of Christ, has indeed come to pass. He not only founded the Great Lavra but also contributed to the settlement of the wilderness by monks. Moreover, by the good will of the holy God, Who glorifies the divine man, because of the multitude of monks who had gathered, three other Lavras were built in the cave of Mesomilos and in the place called Pezuva. The man of God, putting his trust in God, was not the least frightened by the trial from the brigands, but devised what was good. Through the monks who had become his disciples, he informed the Bulgarian Tsar Alexander that he had left the Holy Mountain because of the frequent incursions of the barbarous tribe of Hagarenes and, having come to this wilderness for the sake of hesychia, had again encountered a trial in the form of brigands. Knowing that the tsar was a lover of God, pious, merciful, and helpful in all things to those in need, the venerable one asked him, by means of the wisdom and power granted him by God, to hinder the attacks of the brigands.

And that wondrous tsar, greatly honoring virtue and virtuous men, received the words of the venerable one with joy and immediately sent men who built a strong, high tower, a church, cells, and stables for animals. The tsar also provided everything else necessary for the monks, as all those testify who go there for the benefit of their souls and for veneration. Alexander sent much money and provisions for the monks who were there, donated villages to the monastery, a lake with a fish pond, oxen, an innumerable quantity of sheep, and a multitude of mules. Such were the wonderful and generous gifts of the Bulgarian Tsar.

It was always the desired work of the divine Gregory to traverse the world in the apostolic manner and by his teaching to attract all Christians to the ascent to God by means of practical virtue and to raise them to the height of contemplation through the frequent repetition of the prayer of the nous. Of the great Gregory one can say in the words of Scripture: *"Their sound has gone out to all the earth, and their words to the ends of the world"* (Psalm 18:5), because he desired with all his heart to enlighten everyone with the light of the Most Holy Spirit and left almost no place, not only among the Romans and Bulgarians but even among the Serbs, and among others as well, where the good teaching about hesychia and prayer of the nous did not spread through him and his disciples. And as on the Holy Mountain he led the fathers to strict and pure hesychia and prayer of the nous, so also everywhere, wherever he himself or his disciple went, they passed on to all Christians this God-pleasing work of prayer of the nous. Even out of Paroria, the deep wilderness to which the venerable one had come, he made a spiritual workshop, changing those who came to him for the better. Thus, for example, it happened with those wild brigands and murderers, whose malicious character he transformed into a gentle one by his very appearance alone, making them shepherds of sheep. Those who were formerly cruel and bloodthirsty were completely changed through the prayers of the venerable one and, falling at his feet, rolled on the ground in fervent compunction and repentance. What things they said and did, displaying their former life, which testified to the correction of their souls! Most of them, having had their minds enlightened by the teachings of the divine father, truly served God and obtained salvation for their souls.

Such are but a few of the many struggles of Saint Gregory. Such was his life and the struggles according to God of his blessed soul, in which he persevered until his last breath. Having been ill for a short time, he committed his blessed soul into the hands of God and ascended to the Heavens, there to enjoy in perfection the Desired Christ, to Whom be glory, and honor, and worship, with the Father and the Holy Spirit, unto the ages of ages. Amen.

(Written by Kallistos, the most holy Patriarch of Constantinople)

The Life, Glorious Struggles, and Miracles of Our Venerable and God-Bearing Father Maximos Kausokalyvites, Who Struggled on the Holy Mountain of Athos in the Fourteenth Century

This venerable father of ours Maximos came from Lampsacus, from parents who were noble, pious, and virtuous. Being childless, they asked God with tears to grant them a child. God heard their prayer and gave them this blessed Maximos, whom they named Manuel in Holy Baptism. Receiving him as a gift from God, as was indeed the case, his parents raised him with great love and care, teaching him also sacred letters. When the child grew older, they brought him to the church of the Most Holy Theotokos and dedicated him to God. Abiding in the church of the Theotokos, Manuel with love for God chanted hymns and always prayed to the Mother of God with great compunction for his salvation. Growing older and advancing in grace, he was truly like Samuel. Everyone praised and loved him because he did not think as a child, but from the very beginning had an elder's mind and often visited the venerable fathers who practiced hesychia nearby, in order to hear their soul-profitable instructions. Associating with them and serving them when there was opportunity (because he was still under the authority of his parents), Manuel was instructed by them in a God-pleasing way of life. His heart was kindled with divine love, which compelled him to leave the world for hesychia and to be clothed in the holy monastic schema. Therefore the venerable one often removed his worldly garments and put on the clothes of the poor, freezing and shivering from the cold. He secretly gave bread to the hungry with generosity and, in order to conceal his virtue, pretended to be mad before his parents and others. However, his virtue was not hidden from them. Forgetting that they had dedicated him to God, his parents began to prepare him for marriage, so as to bind him with worldly bonds and, while they lived, to have their beloved son with them.

But the good Manuel, maintaining thoughts of God in his mind, at the age of seventeen left his parents, his homeland, and the world, and went to the mountain called Ganos. He put on the monastic garb, received the name Maximos, and entered into obedience to an experienced and active elder named Mark, in order to learn from him the monastic way of life. Since he himself was already accustomed to the monastic life, he proved to be a monk who was proficient and worthy in all things: fasting, vigil, prayer, sleeping on the bare ground, contempt for all that is vain and for his own body. Everyone loved him, and his own elder even reproached him for excessive bodily asceticism.

But a short time passed and his elder, who had shone forth with his virtue throughout all Macedonia, departed to the eternal dwellings. After this, the divine Maximos left that place, traversed Macedonia and the surrounding mountains in search of an equally virtuous elder. God fulfilled his desire. Coming to Mount Papikion, he found holy men like those of old, who dwelt on the mountain, in caves, in desert places, and had nothing except the old garments that they wore. Remaining with them for a long time, he acquired all the superhuman virtues, just as wax receives the form of a seal. Then the venerable one came to Constantinople, visited its beautiful churches and venerated the saints who abide in them as a most precious treasure, and then came to the church of Our Most Holy Lady Theotokos called the Hodegetria. Having venerated the sacred objects of the church, the venerable one began to reflect upon the glory that the Mother of God has in the Heavens. Being in ecstasy, he remained in the church for the night. He had neither footwear nor head covering, but only old garments. And because he was in ecstasy, he seemed mad to everyone. Then he himself began to feign madness, like that great Andrew, Fool-for-Christ. Therefore everyone marveled and considered him a fool for Christ, and not truly mad.

Having learned of Maximos, the great emperor Andronicus Palaeologus invited the venerable one to his palace for a conversation. The divine Maximos answered the emperor with words from the writings of Gregory the Theologian, as was his custom, and from Sacred Scripture, so that all the rhetoricians marveled at how he could know the teaching of Gregory. Maximos sometimes mispronounced words, contrary to the art of grammar, and the great logothete Caniclius once, turning to those present, said: *"The voice is Jacob's voice, but the hands are the hands of Esau"* (Genesis 27:22). Hearing these words, the venerable one immediately departed, calling them vainly wise and foolish, and no longer went to the palace. But to the patriarch of that time, the holy Athanasius, he came often and with joy listened to his sweetest words, calling him a new Chrysostom. Knowing of his virtue, the patriarch tried to keep the venerable one in a coenobitic monastery in Constantinople, but he did not want to leave the Blachernae church of the Mother of God, in the courtyard of which he spent all his nights, struggling in hunger, thirst, vigils, standing, prayer, tears, and constant sighing. During the day he feigned madness, being in truth most wise, so that the wind of people-pleasing would not tear away the fruit of his virtue.

Having spent sufficient time there, he came to Thessalonica to venerate the great Demetrius the Myrrh-streamer, and having fulfilled his desire, he set out for the Holy Mount Athos. Having visited all the monasteries and venerated their sacred objects, he finally came to the Lavra of Saint Athanasius. Reflecting upon the struggles of the saints Athanasius and Peter of Athos, marveling at the asceticism of hesychia of Peter and the coenobitic life of Athanasius, thinking much about the zeal and diligence of both in keeping the commandments of God, Maximos desired to remain on the Holy Mountain and imitate the life of both of them. However, before the God-wise one began his ascetic struggle, he asked the counsel of the holy fathers who were struggling there. They advised him first to enter into obedience to an elder and, as is fitting, to train himself in the struggles of blessed patience. Only after he had laid a good foundation upon the rock of Christ in the form of divine patience, which is the beginning and root of all virtues, would he be able to struggle alone in hesychia.

Having listened to all the counsels, the venerable one became a novice under the abbot and settled together with the other brethren. First he was tested in the simplest obediences, as is customary, then he was appointed to sing in the church to the glory of God, for in his youth he had been taught music. He sang with understanding, comprehending the meaning of the words, and at the same time elevated his mind to God who was being hymned, and from compunction shed abundant tears. He experienced the same thing when reading the verses of Sacred Scripture. Praying in ecstasy, he marveled at the boundless love of God for mankind, who through the Holy Spirit granted us, while still in the body, the grace of understanding Sacred Scripture. The heart of the venerable one shone with divine fire, and his inward parts burned from the Divine grace that dwelt in him, and although he was together with everyone, he was as though alone, in the desert, and nothing hindered him in performing the mental prayer: "Lord Jesus Christ, Son of God, have mercy on me." He uttered it constantly, for it arose with his every thought, which is very rare and difficult to find among ascetics. But this blessed Maximos, for his virtue and reverence toward the Most Holy Theotokos, had been rewarded with the gift of prayer from childhood. Remaining in obedience to the monastic authorities and zealously fulfilling all that was commanded him, he led his life just as before, afflicting his body just as in the Blachernae church. In the Lavra he had neither a cell nor any corner where he might rest bodily, and at meals he took food with restraint, only so as not to die from hunger. Instead of a dwelling, he had the stasidion (a special wooden chair) in the narthex of the church, where he always, according to his custom, struggled in all-night standing and vigil.

But just as Mount Sinai called Moses, Mount Carmel called Elijah, and the desert called John the Baptist, so did the flower of mountains—Athos—call the venerable Maximos, that the righteous one might blossom here and bring forth the fruits of the Holy Spirit. Once, on the feast of All Saints, the Theotokos appeared to him, with the Lord in her arms, and said: "Follow Me, faithful Maximos, and ascend to the summit of Mount Athos, that you may receive the grace of the Holy Spirit, as you yourself desire." This vision was repeated three times, after which he left the Great Lavra and in seven days ascended to the summit of the Mountain on Saturday, the eve of Pentecost. There he spent the night in vigil together with other monks, who departed after the Divine Liturgy. But the divine Maximos remained alone and for three days and nights prayed unceasingly with mental prayer to God and the Mother of God. Who can tell of the temptations with which the enemy assailed him, in order to drive the saint from there? It seemed to him that thunder roared, lightning flashed, the Great Mountain of Athos itself was shaking, that stones were falling upon him. All this happened that night as if in a phantasm, by demonic delusion, in order to frighten the saint. During the day, terrible voices were heard, a great noise as if from a multitude of people nearby; men frightful in appearance came from all sides of the Mountain, ascending to the summit. Rushing at the venerable one with spears and slings, they wanted to cast him down from the summit, because the accursed ones did not want him to live there. But the divine Maximos, having within himself the grace of the Holy Spirit, was not at all frightened and paid no attention to these apparitions, but gave himself to mental prayer and glorified God and the Theotokos, his Protectress and Guardian.

And behold, the Theotokos appeared to him in great glory, surrounded by a multitude of young nobles, in the image of a queen, again holding in her arms the Son, the Creator of all creation. The saint recognized Her by the unbearable Divine light that came forth from the Sovereign Lady and illuminated everything around. The venerable one understood that this was not demonic delusion, but a Divine vision and a genuine apparition of the Theotokos. Maximos joyfully said: "Rejoice, O Full of Grace, the Lord is with Thee." Then he fell down and worshipped the Lord together with the Lady Theotokos, received a blessing from the Lord, and heard from the Theotokos the following words: "Receive grace against demons, O sacred victor, and settle at the foot of Mount Athos. Such is the will of My Son, that you ascend to the height of virtue and become a teacher and guide for many, whom you will save." For the repose of his body, he was given heavenly bread, for he had already been fasting many days. As soon as the ascetic placed the bread in his mouth, Divine light sent from above surrounded him, and he heard the Angelic hymn, after which the Theotokos ascended to Heaven. The Divine light and fragrance still continued to remain on the summit, and the saint, being in ecstasy, did not want to descend to the foot of the Mountain, so as not to be deprived of them.

After three days, Maximos descended from the Mountain, according to the command of the Theotokos, and came to Her church called Panagia. Having stayed there several days, he again ascended to the summit of the Mountain and began to kiss the place where the Theotokos had stood in glory. He asked with tears that the vision be repeated, but he only beheld the light and insatiably breathed in the fragrance, being entirely filled with ineffable joy and gladness. The venerable one ascended to the summit three more times, but no longer saw the Theotokos.

Later he went to the church of the Prophet Elijah and, finding there an elder-hermit, told him about his vision on the summit of the Mountain. However, the elder thought that the divine Maximos had fallen into delusion, and the vision was demonic. Therefore he called him who was a luminary and teacher of those who had gone astray, one who was deluded. From that time, everyone began to call Maximos deluded and, turning away, drove him off. But this luminary who was in fact not deluded accepted the appellation "deluded" rather than "holy" with great joy, and always pretended to be deluded, and if he spoke, he pretended to be mad, so as thereby to destroy people-pleasing and pride, and bring forth the fruit of humility, which preserves the grace of the Holy Spirit in a person. Therefore the venerable one did not remain in one place like the others, but moved from place to place. And wherever he came, he would build a small kaliva out of branches, so that his ascetic body could fit inside, and after some time he would burn the kaliva and go to another place, where he would build another. Such was his superhuman non-acquisitiveness, for he never had either a hoe, or a rake, or a bag, or a bench, or a table, or a pot, or flour, or salt, or wine, or bread, practically nothing of what a person needs for life. He led an almost immaterial life in the deserts and inaccessible places, building small kalivas, which after some time he burned. Therefore the venerable one was called both a "wanderer" and Kausokalyvites (one who burns his kaliva), for people did not know that Divine grace covered him, hope gave him coolness, and constant prayer gave him sweetness. Who can describe the hunger and thirst that the venerable one endured, how he could bear nakedness, cold, winter frost, and summer heat, having neither a roof over his head, nor a second garment, nor footwear? Very rarely did he yield to natural needs and come to some brother to taste a little bread with salt and drink a bit of wine. One may affirm that it was precisely about such as he that Jesus Christ spoke in the Gospel: *"Look at the birds of the air, for they neither sow nor reap nor gather into barns; yet your heavenly Father feeds them"* (Matthew 6:26), for this saint was indeed like a bird of the air, or rather, he dwelt in that desert like one without a body. Truly the ever-memorable Maximos, in the words of the Apostle Paul, crucified *"the flesh with its passions and desires"* (Galatians 5:24).

Who will not marvel at this angelic life, who will not be amazed upon hearing of his supernatural struggles: his great patience, all-night standing, constant tears, unceasing prayer, repentance, beating of his head against the stone, hesychia, meekness, humility? He became a dwelling place of the Holy Spirit, another Peter of Athos, a new Athanasius the Great, whose lives he strove with all his might to imitate. It may be said that he took as examples the founders of monasticism: Paul of Thebes and Anthony the Great, having attained the height of their virtues. Therefore his mind also, like theirs, was caught up in contemplations, and the venerable one saw the revelation of mysteries. When did others learn of all this? When he became acquainted with and began to associate with other holy elders and great ascetics, who had previously marveled at the divine Maximos for his great struggles, but thought that he was deluded, for so they had heard of him. But having associated with him personally, they came to know the Divine grace that dwelt in him, and ceased to call him "deluded," but rather "honored Maximos" and "most radiant luminary."

At this same time, the venerable Gregory of Sinai came to the Holy Mountain and settled in the skete of Magoula. He was loved by all the Athonites, and especially by the hesychasts, for he was a wondrous teacher of hesychia and mental prayer, and he knew well the wiles of the demons, which is very rare. He taught all the hesychasts the mysteries of mental prayer, as well as the ways of discerning true grace and the enemy's delusion. Some of the fathers mentioned the venerable Maximos as well, telling of his supernatural way of life and feigned madness. The divine Gregory was amazed and wished to see Maximos and converse with him. He sent his disciples to the sacred Maximos and invited him to come to him. But the messengers did not find him in his kaliva, and having searched for two days in the surrounding area, they also did not find him. It was winter, and Maximos lived in caves, not in the forest. Having spent much time searching and being exhausted from the cold, the messengers took refuge in the cell of Saint Mamas. And suddenly there came to them, quite unexpectedly, the divine Maximos, whom they had been seeking for so long, greeted everyone by name, and told of the desire of the venerable Gregory to leave the Holy Mountain and go to Paroria. The messengers conveyed to Maximos the invitation of their elder, and the venerable one immediately set out with them on the journey, singing along the way: *"I will lift up my eyes to the mountains; from whence shall my help come?"* (Psalm 120:1). When they approached the cell of Gregory, the divine Maximos said: "The elder is now resting, because he labored much in prayer. You also go and rest a little, and I too will go to rest." But Maximos himself went into the forest and began to pray with tears, chanting: *"O Lord... I will guard my ways... Deliver me from all my transgressions"* (Psalm 38:2, 9). When he finished the psalm, the divine Gregory called him, and he immediately entered his cell. They exchanged a kiss, after which Gregory asked everyone to go outside, leaving the God-bearing Maximos alone, wishing to learn from him personally what he had heard about him from others before.

And Maximos answered:

"Forgive me, father, I am a man who has gone astray."

"Leave that, and tell me, for the Lord's sake, about your virtue, and enlighten me. If not, at least let us instruct each other in virtue and receive mutual benefit. For I am not like others, who ensnare their neighbor with their words, but I love each one as myself."

Then the divine Maximos told him everything about himself, from his youth: about his zeal for God, about his flight from the world, about how he was in obedience, about his feigned madness, about his ascetic labors, about the awesome vision of the Theotokos, about the light that then surrounded him and sometimes surrounds him now, about demonic temptations. Interrupting him, Gregory said:

"I ask you, tell me, honorable father, do you hold the mental prayer?"

And he answered with a smile:

"I do not wish to hide from you, father, that miracle of the Mother of God that happened to me. From my youth I had strong faith in my Lady the Theotokos and asked Her with tears to grant me the grace of mental prayer. One day, coming to Her church as usual, I began to ask Her with extraordinary fervor in my heart. And when I kissed Her holy icon with love, I immediately felt in my chest and heart a certain warmth and fire that entered me from the holy icon. This fire burned me and at the same time refreshed me, gave sweetness and caused great compunction in my soul. From that time, father, my heart of itself utters this prayer, and my mind is sweetened by the remembrance of the vision of my Jesus and the Mother of God, and is always united with this remembrance of Them. From that time, this prayer has not ceased for a second in my heart. Forgive me."

"Tell me, O holy one, did you experience after the prayer: 'Lord Jesus Christ, Son of God, have mercy on me, a sinner,' a divine change, or perhaps you entered into ecstasy, or had some other fruit of the Holy Spirit?"

"Father, for this very reason I went to desert places and always desired hesychia, so as to enjoy even more the fruit of prayer, which is exceedingly great love for God and the rapture of the mind to the Lord."

"I ask you, father, tell me, do you possess the gift of which you speak?"

Smiling again, the divine Maximos answered him:

"Give me something to eat and do not inquire into my delusion."

"Ah, would that I too were such a deluded one. I ask you, tell me, when your mind is caught up in vision, what do you see with the noetic eyes? Can the mind together with the heart perform prayer?"

"No, it cannot, because when through prayer the grace of the Holy Spirit comes to a person, then prayer ceases, for the mind is already entirely filled with grace. It can no longer activate its powers, but remains idle, submitting to the Holy Spirit, who leads it wherever He wills. Either to the immaterial Divine light, or to another ineffable contemplation, and often to conversation with God. In short, as the Holy Spirit wills, so He consoles His servants. Whatever grace each one needs, such He gives to each. What I am speaking of was with the prophets and apostles, who were deemed worthy to behold many visions, although people laughed at them, considering them deluded and drunk. The prophet Isaiah saw the Lord *'sitting on a throne, high and lifted up,'* surrounded by Seraphim (Isaiah 6:1). The Protomartyr Stephen saw *'the heavens opened and the Son of Man standing at the right hand of God'* (Acts 7:56). So also now the servants of Christ are deemed worthy to behold various visions, which some do not believe and completely reject as true, considering them delusion, and the contemplatives themselves as deluded. I am greatly amazed at this and am perplexed at how hardened these people are, blind in soul, not believing what God truly promised through the mouth of the prophet Joel: *'And it shall come to pass afterward that I will pour out My Spirit on all flesh; your sons and your daughters shall prophesy, your old men shall dream dreams, your young men shall see visions'* (Joel 2:28). The Lord gave us this grace, gives it now, and will give it until the end of the age, according to His promise to all His faithful servants. When this grace comes to someone, he sees not ordinary things, not the sensible objects of this world, but what he has never seen and has never even imagined. Then the mind of that person is taught by the Holy Spirit the lofty mysteries, according to the words of the Apostle Paul: *'Eye has not seen, nor ear heard, nor have entered into the heart of man the things which God has prepared for those who love Him'* (1 Corinthians 2:9). And that you may understand how our mind sees this, reflect upon what I shall tell you. When a candle is far from fire, it is solid, and you can take it in your hands, but when you light it, it melts, burns, and becomes entirely light, and it is impossible for it not to melt and become like water. So also the mind of a person, when it abides without God, comprehends only what is within its power. But when it draws near to the fire of the Godhead and the Holy Spirit, then it is entirely seized by the Divine fire and becomes light, burns in the fire of the Holy Spirit and melts from the Divine meanings, and in the fire of the Godhead it cannot think only of its own things and of what it wants."

"There is another thing similar to this, but it is a sign of delusion."

"The signs of delusion are one thing, and those of grace are another. The evil spirit of delusion, when it approaches a person, troubles his mind and embitters it, hardens and darkens the heart, causes cowardice, fear, pride, makes the whole body tremble, before the eyes appears a light that is not radiant and pure, but red. The mind becomes ecstatic and becomes like a demon, the lips utter shameful and blasphemous words, and the one who sees this spirit of delusion is filled with anger, knowing absolutely nothing of humility, true mourning, or tears. Such a person always boasts of his struggles, glorifies himself without restraint and without the fear of God. In the end, he loses his mind and comes to complete perdition, from which may the Lord deliver us by your prayers. The signs of grace are the following. When the grace of the Holy Spirit comes to a person, it concentrates his mind, he becomes attentive, humbles himself, grace brings him the remembrance of death, of sins, of the future Judgment, of eternal torments, and easily leads the soul to compunction, mourning, and sorrow. Day and night the eyes of such a person are filled with tears, and the more grace approaches a person, the more meek he becomes in soul. By the Holy Passions of our Lord Jesus Christ and His boundless love for mankind, grace brings consolation to a person. Grace is the source of lofty true contemplations: about the incomprehensible power of God, about how God by a single word brought all things from non-being into being, about the boundless power that upholds and governs all things and has care for all, about the incomprehensible mystery of the Most Holy Trinity and the unspeakable sea of the Divine Essence, and other things. When the mind of a person is caught up by the Divine light and enlightened by Divine knowledge, then his heart becomes exceedingly calm and meek and pours forth the fruits of the Holy Spirit: joy, peace, longsuffering, kindness, compassion, love, humility. And the soul delights in ineffable gladness."

Having heard this, the holy Gregory was astounded and marveled at all that Maximos told him, and no longer called him a man, but an earthly angel. He asked him for a long time: "Please, from now on cease burning your cell and remain in one place, as the wise Isaac says, so as to bring forth greater fruit and render benefit to many others, as one most experienced in virtue, because you have reached old age, and death often comes unexpectedly. Pass on the talent and gift you have received, and the Divine seed of your teaching to the people of God, before death overtakes you, and then you will receive a greater reward in Heaven for having benefited others. For even the Lord, who gave the apostles the grace of the Holy Spirit, did not command them to spend their lives in the mountains, but sent them to the people, so that they too might partake of their grace and, through their holiness, become holy themselves instead of sinners. Therefore He also said to His apostles: *'Let your light so shine before men'* (Matthew 5:16), and not 'before the mountains.' So also let your light shine before men, *'that they may see your good works and glorify your Father in heaven'* (Matthew 5:16). Cease pretending to be a fool, for it serves as a scandal to those who know of your struggles. Hear my counsel and do as I, your best friend and brother, tell you, since, as Sacred Scripture says, a brother who receives help from a brother is *'like a fortified city'* (Proverbs 18:19)."

The other great elders also learned of these counsels of the divine Gregory, and they too joined in the requests and were able to persuade the venerable Maximos to settle in one place. And so the divine Maximos found a cave which was at a distance of three miles from the cave of Isaiah, made in it a partition one orgyia wide and long out of branches and grass, according to his custom, using absolutely neither stones, nor wood, nor boards, nor nails, so that something like a cell came about. He ceased burning cells from that time on, and lived in this cave almost until the end of his life, in his customary non-acquisitiveness and supernatural asceticism, like the bodiless ones. Then, near the cell, the venerable one dug himself a grave and constantly wept beside it and chanted the exapostilaria (troparia) on the departure of the soul: "Thou who hast adorned the heaven with stars, as God," which he himself had composed.

While he was thus struggling, demons, gathering together, waged daily warfare against the saint, trying to drive him from that place. But the venerable one drove them away with mental prayer, and they, like smoke, dispersed. Moreover, the saint was covered and protected by the invincible and unconquerable power of God, which appeared in the form of fire to those worthy of such a vision, and it also consumed his enemies. As far as we know, the venerable Maximos healed a multitude of the sick, cast out demons from the possessed, and sending the healed home, he commanded them, so that they would always be healthy, to abstain from bearing grudges, injustice, perjury, drunkenness, fornication, from meat, to give alms according to their ability, to purify themselves by repentance from every sin, and on the great feasts to be sure to commune of the Most Pure Mysteries.

Once the venerable one induced a certain monk named Mercurius to cast out a demon from one who was possessed, and the latter, in the presence of the venerable one, rebuked the evil spirit in the name of Jesus Christ and wondrously healed the demoniac.

On another occasion, having met on the road the novice of a certain elder who was being cruelly tormented by a demon, the venerable one commanded him to remain in obedience to his elder, to abstain from cheese, wine, every defilement, and then he, in the name of Jesus Christ, would be healed. Immediately the miracle occurred, and by the word of the venerable one, that novice received healing.

One time, monks from the Lavra came to the venerable one for spiritual conversation, and with them was a certain layman. As soon as the venerable one saw him, while still at a distance, he did not let him approach, saying that this was an unbelieving Akindynist, although none of his companions suspected this. The saint said much about this man, calling him "dangerous," "like a demon," "a partaker of every heresy and a servant of the Antichrist." The venerable Maximos drove away such heretics publicly and anathematized them.

Once certain monks arrived on the Holy Mountain, but when the venerable one saw them, he cried out loudly: "First drive away the Massalian from yourselves" (for so was one of them called), "and then come to me." Hearing this, the monks were frightened and, having driven away that Massalian, came to the saint.

A certain monk wanted to sail by ship on some business to Constantinople from Thessalonica, but the venerable one would not let him go, predicting the destruction of the ship, and indeed, after three days the ship with all its passengers sank.

There was an occasion when a ship docked at the Lavra's harbor and its passengers brought to the venerable one a demoniac possessed by a demon of insatiability. Every day this man ate food sufficient for five men and was not satisfied. Falling at the feet of the venerable one, they together with the possessed man asked the saint to deliver him from the demon. Taking a dried biscuit, the venerable one gave it to the sufferer with the words: "In the name of our Lord Jesus Christ, eat exactly this much, be satisfied, and be at peace." That man was delivered from the demon of insatiability and from that time ate no more than that dried biscuit which the venerable one had given him. Having renounced the world and what is in the world, he became a monk. Guided by the saint, this brother, with the help of Divine grace, progressed in virtue and became a most skilled monk.

Once the venerable one was rebuking a certain monk named Barlaam for his disobedience to his spiritual father, and said that for his sins there would follow a bad end for him, and he would die from cold and frost, which indeed came to pass later, in fulfillment of the prophecy of the venerable Maximos.

To another monk named Athanasius, the venerable one predicted death at the hands of the Ishmaelites, and this too was fulfilled. This blessed one was so rich in the grace of the Holy Spirit that he saw, as if nearby, what was happening at a great distance, and predicted the future as though it were the present.

The venerable one also predicted the coming of the emperors, saying: "Emperors of the Romans will come to me to hear prophecies and learn the future, but not for their own benefit." A short time passed, and John Cantacuzenus came to the saint together with John Palaeologus, who were then reigning, and he predicted what would happen to them and all the calamities that would occur. Then, wishing to instruct them, he said much for the benefit of their souls and what was fitting for emperors. When the emperors were already preparing to depart, the saint said to Cantacuzenus: "Behold, the abbot of a monastery," and to the other John: "Hold on to what cannot be held, and do not be deceived, for your reign will be long but unstable, and will bring you many troubles." After this, the venerable one dismissed them, saying: "Farewell, go in peace." A short time passed, and the saint sent to Constantinople to Cantacuzenus a dried biscuit, an onion, and garlic, predicting that he would become a monk and would eat such food. All this soon came to pass. Being compelled by John Palaeologus, he became a monk against his will, and when he was given a dried biscuit for food, he remembered the prophecy of the venerable one and marveled. John Palaeologus was likewise amazed, remembering the prophecy of the venerable one when everything began to come about according to his prediction.

Setting out together with his clergy for Serbia for the sake of the unity and peace of the Church and passing near the Holy Mountain, the Patriarch Kallistos stopped to visit the venerable Maximos in his kaliva. Coming out to meet him, the venerable one received the patriarchal blessing and after the greeting said jokingly to those present: "This elder has lost his elder." Having conversed for some time, the venerable one stood up and walked before the patriarch and his companions, chanting: *"Blessed are the undefiled in the way, who walk in the law of the Lord"* (Psalm 118:1), thereby foretelling their death and burial. Having arrived in Serbia, the patriarch together with the clergy soon reposed, having been poisoned, as many said; they were buried in Serbia, in a church. Thus were fulfilled the prophecies of the venerable one about the emperors and the patriarch.

A certain ascetic, Methodius, once coming to the venerable one, saw Divine light shining in his kaliva. Methodius did not dare to approach Maximos until the venerable one himself called him.

They also told something extraordinary about the venerable one, for example, that he was fed with heavenly bread. Thus, once in winter, the Lavra's infirmarian Gregory came to visit him, along with another brother. The place where the venerable one lived was covered with snow from heavy snowfalls, and human footprints were nowhere to be seen. Having found the path with difficulty, they brought bread, wine, and other food that serves to comfort nature into the cell of the venerable one. However, entering the kaliva of the ascetic, the brothers saw there hot and pure bread, from which there came forth such wondrous and strong fragrance that it filled the entire dwelling. Looking carefully around and not finding in the kaliva any sign of fire, they fell at the feet of the saint and asked him to give them at least a particle of that bread. Taking pity on them, Maximos cut off half for them and handed it to them with the words: "Take, eat, but do not tell anyone about this while I am alive." The venerable one also gave them water to drink that was pleasant to the taste. All this, calling God to witness, these brothers told us after the repose of the venerable one. And other monks related that the venerable one transformed salty sea water into fresh and drank it himself, and then gave it to them to drink as well.

Once, during the harvest season, two monks came to the venerable one. Having conversed with them, Maximos gave them a dried biscuit and said: "Quickly go to the monastery of Dorotheus, so that you are not exposed to danger from bad weather on the road." It should be said that the weather at this time was clear, and there were no clouds at all. However, before they reached the monastery of Dorotheus, a strong wind arose, lightning flashed, thunder roared, and such heavy rain fell with hail that it destroyed the entire harvest. The ungathered grapes all perished, for the hail "gathered" this harvest. Seeing this, those two monks cried out: "Lord, have mercy!" and told everyone about the prophecy of the venerable one.

Once a certain learned scribe from Constantinople came to him. As soon as the venerable one saw him, he knew of his crafty thoughts and began to admonish him: "Have you seen the struggles and contests of the saints and the grace given them by God, that you blaspheme them, saying that the saints struggled little, and those who write their lives show them kindness and add much that is false, which they did not do; and the grace of wonderworking given to them you consider false? Cease from these satanic thoughts and do not anger God, lest He consume you with fire, for the saints, having dedicated themselves entirely to God, pleased Him through their thoughts and deeds. Tell me, who will be able to describe the life of the saints as it actually was, who knows it in detail? Therefore they write only about a little of the numerous testimonies of their holiness, and you should know that the grace of the Holy Spirit given to the saints is not only that which people learn of, but is much richer and incomprehensible. It surpasses all mind and thought. If you wish to be truly wise, leave off Hellenic foolishness and be still, as David says, in order to know God. With the help of this knowledge and spiritual hesychia, you will become familiar with God, as far as this is possible, and then you will know the grace of the Holy Spirit, the incomprehensible wonders of God, and will accuse yourself, having learned what darkness you were in before. Without light it is impossible to know darkness. Come out into the light of hesychia and prayer, and the former darkness will flee from you, you will see the grace and power of the saints, which you yourself will desire." Hearing this, the scribe became frightened, for the venerable one had uncovered his hidden thoughts, and receiving great benefit from these words, he abandoned his blasphemous thoughts, beginning from that time to correct others as well with the most wise teaching of the saint.

"And I myself," says the writer of this life, "God is my witness, I shall not hide what I saw from the venerable one, for I was acquainted with him and had communion with him. Once I went out from the Vatopedi monastery with a certain monk and went to the venerable one. Not finding him in his kaliva, I grew sad and began to look around. Going around behind the kaliva and climbing a little higher, I looked at the road to Elijah. And suddenly I saw him in the ravine of Agelariou, at a distance of about two miles. The path to that place was difficult and stony, there was no level road at all. But—O miracle!—I suddenly saw how the saint rose high above the ground and, like a swift-winged eagle, flew over the forest and cliffs, approaching me. Seeing him flying in this manner, I was frightened and exclaimed: 'Great art Thou, O Lord!' From fear I moved back a little, and in the twinkling of an eye the saint descended with singing to where I had just been standing. But what he sang, because of the miracle, I do not remember. Falling at his feet, I embraced him. He asked me how much time I had spent in that place, and then, taking me by the hand, led me into the kaliva. After the venerable one had taught and instructed me for a long time, he finally said: 'See that you tell no one of what you have seen as long as I am alive. Know also that you will become an abbot, and then Metropolitan of Ohrid, and will suffer much. However, endure, imitating Christ who was hung upon the Tree, for He will be your Helper in the temptations that will occur as a testimony to your struggle.' All this, according to the prophecy of the saint, was fulfilled in me.

"But I cannot pass over in silence something else that I myself saw. A certain monk from the Lavra named Jacob came to ask the saint to write him a letter with which he could collect alms for the ransom of his brother from slavery. After waiting a little, the venerable one sternly answered him: 'Go, take out the sixty gold pieces that you have hidden in the wall of the tower, and give them for the ransom of your brother. Do not be covetous and deceitful, lest you too fall into slavery.' Hearing this, Jacob told the truth and asked the venerable one for forgiveness for his audacity.

"On another occasion, a certain layman came to the venerable one and said to him with tears: 'Help me, O holy one of God, for a certain priest excommunicated me from Communion, and he has died; now I, wretched man, do not know what to do.' Taking pity on him, the saint answered: 'Go to the Metropolitan of Veria, who was the hierarch of the dead priest, and he will absolve you according to the law.' And at once the venerable one said to a certain monk who was with him: 'You too go to Father John, that he may also absolve you while he is alive, for he has excommunicated you from Communion from the time when you reviled him and struck him.' Marveling that the venerable one told him of a sin of which he himself did not know, the monk and the layman went to Veria and received forgiveness.

"Once the Metropolitan of Trajanopolis and his deacon decided to test the venerable one, to see whether he was truly clairvoyant. On the road, the bishop put on the robe of the deacon, and gave the hierarchical mantle to the deacon. The hierarch, in the guise of a deacon, was the first to approach the saint and said: 'Bless, father,' after which he remained standing before the kaliva, awaiting an invitation to enter. But the saint answered: 'You are a hierarch, you bless me, and do not deceive, because I was at the top of the ravine when you exchanged garments.' With these words, the saint made a prostration, and the hierarch, marveling, blessed him and embraced him.

"The saint spoke about the venerable and God-bearing Niphon of Athos, that above his kaliva there was a small cave. Once Niphon entered this cave and fell asleep. Awakening, he saw before the cave a woman dressed in beautiful garments. Understanding that this was a trick of the evil demon, he crossed himself three times, and she vanished.

"About himself the venerable one said that once on Monday a monk whom he had never seen came to him and sat before his kaliva. 'This monk was dried up from extreme abstinence. On Tuesday morning, he came to me and we conversed. Since neither of us had either bread or anything else to eat, he went out and sat higher up from my kaliva, and on Thursday morning he again came in to me and we conversed. Then he went out again and sat in the same place until Saturday morning. When I went out of the kaliva for a need, I no longer saw him.'"

Having lived in this cave fourteen years, the venerable Maximos came out from it and settled near the sacred Lavra, so as to hear its bells. Here he built a small cell and remained in it until the end of his life.

Much more can be told about the divine Maximos, about his clairvoyance, great wonderworking, God-wise instructions, which he gave both to laypeople and to monks and to people of every rank. However, because of the multitude of these accounts, it is impossible to include them all in this book. And what we have written is all the same as drawing a glass of water from an entire sea. But even this is quite sufficient for Christians to learn that God not only in ancient times glorified His saints, but glorifies now and always those who glorify Him with good deeds. God magnifies them with signs and wonders, which bear witness to that eternal glory which they will enjoy in the Kingdom of Heaven. Passing over much, I shall tell of the sacred repose of the saint.

A certain monk named Nicodemus came to the saint for counsel, and Maximos said to him: "Brother Nicodemus, I shall die soon." He revealed to him the day of his falling asleep and named by name those who would be present at his burial. On the very day predicted, the venerable Maximos reposed, being ninety-five years old. This occurred on the thirteenth of January. They buried him in the grave which he himself had dug near his kaliva, and at the burial were present only those whom he had named, for he did not want a multitude of people to learn of his prediction. The venerable one gave orders that his remains not be transferred to another place, and that no one should take any part from them, but leave them intact. He did this so as not to be glorified by men.

When all the fathers of the Holy Mountain learned of the repose of the venerable one, they were greatly grieved and wept much, for they were orphaned and deprived of a God-wise teacher of the monastic life and a most radiant luminary. Always speaking of his struggles and divine gifts, every year they reverently celebrate with honor the service in memory of the saint. Thus people glorified and glorify the venerable Maximos on earth, and in the Heavens, having received his most pure and holy soul, the Holy Trinity settled him in the tabernacles of the saints and glorified him with the ineffable and incomprehensible light of the Godhead. He now stands before Christ, whom he desired from his youth, and rejoices together with the Angels and the saints, and unceasingly prays for us.

The unceasing miracles at his grave showed that the grace of the Holy Spirit abides inseparably with his divine relics. A certain monk Dionysius, called Kondostephanos, suffered greatly from headaches. He came to the tomb of the venerable one and with faith and tears asked God and the saint to give him health. Dozing off a little, when he awoke he felt that he was well. Glorifying God and the saint, the monk took earth from the grave, which proved to be like wondrous myrrh, filling everything around with ineffable fragrance.

"And I myself," says the author of the life, "who saw the saint soaring in the air, when I became gravely ill and drew near to death, called upon the saint with tears. He appeared to me in a dream, healed me, and I recovered, glorifying and thanking God and the saint for the fact that I was already dead, but rose again."

A certain hieromonk of holy life named Niphon, together with another ascetic, came to the grave of the saint and, digging it up, took part of his holy relics. At this, such fragrance spread forth that they could not bear it. Having wiped with a sponge moistened in water the particle of relics they had taken, they anointed themselves with this sponge in faith, after which they again placed the relics in their place, fulfilling the commandment of the venerable one, who had ordered that his relics be left intact. They again covered the grave with earth, as it had been before, and glorified God, who thus glorifies His saints. In great joy, they visited the grave of Saint Maximos every day and breathed in the fragrance that came forth. Likewise did all those who struggled near the place of his burial, delighting in the fragrance, to the glory of Christ our God, to Whom is due all glory, honor, and worship, with His Beginningless Father and His Most Holy and Life giving Spirit, now and ever, and unto the ages of ages. Amen.

(Written by Theophanes Peripheoriu, former Abbot of the Vatopedi Monastery)

The Life and Ascetic Labors of Our Venerable and God-Bearing Father Niphon of Athos, Who Flourished in the Fourteenth Century

This our venerable father was from Argyrokastro by birth, from the village of Lukovi. His father was a priest, a man most pious and fearing God. When the venerable one was ten years old, his uncle took him with him to the monastery of Saint Nicholas, where he was ecclesiarch. This monastery was built by the ever-memorable Emperor Constantine Monomachos at a place that is still called Mezhdurechye (Between the Rivers).

At first his uncle taught him the sacred letters, and then clothed him in the monastic schema. Since Niphon progressed both in learning and in monastic obedience, he was appointed reader, and when he came of age and had progressed even more spiritually, he was ordained to the priesthood. Being exceedingly gifted and diligent, the venerable one read the Holy Scriptures and the lives of the saints, through which he became very learned. The love of God pierced his very heart, and the desire for hesychia so burned within him that it consumed his mind and thought. Therefore he left the monastery of Saint Nicholas and came to a certain virtuous ascetic on Mount Geromeri, from whom he learned the strict monastic life. Having tasted the honey of hesychia, he could no longer remain in the world, but, despising homeland, kinsmen, friends, and all possessions, he hastened with zeal to the Holy Mountain, and there, by the guidance of God, came to the region of the Great Lavra, to the kathisma (a building near a monastery for one monk) of Saint Peter of Athos. Finding there an ascetic of wondrous life named Theognostos, he gave himself over to him in complete obedience. After three years, having learned that Niphon was a priest and having seen his many and great virtues, the elder no longer wished Niphon to be his disciple, but a brother, equal to him. The venerable one, for his part, objected and said: "It is not possible for a monk to practice hesychia alone if he has not first humbled himself through obedience," and asked to remain as before among the disciples. But on account of his extraordinary humility, Theognostos would not agree, and the divine Niphon, enriched with the gift of tears, was compelled to depart from there. He moved to the kathisma of Basil the Great, which was nearby, where he remained in extreme hesychia for fourteen years, eating all that time only a little dry bread, and that only once a week.

At that time an epidemic of plague occurred in the Great Lavra, from which many of the brethren died. Since few priests remained in the monastery, the abbot called the saint, but he, out of love for hesychia, refused, saying to him: "Forgive me, father, for I am unlearned and ignorant." Then the abbot asked him to serve at least in the kathismata outside the Lavra, and he, out of his humility, submitted, spending three years in this obedience. Since, however, the desire for hesychia continued to burn in the heart of the venerable one, he departed from there and came to Voulevteria, where the skete of Saint Anna is now located. Eating only the grass of the earth, he spent many years there in hesychia, having no shelter over his head, not even a kaliva.

However, there were certain brethren who could not bear to look upon such a lofty life of the venerable one. Moved to envy by the hater of good, the devil, they accused the ascetic of delusion before the abbot of the Lavra, claiming that he ate grass because he disdained bread. The abbot summoned Niphon to the monastery and asked: "My brother and child, why do you labor in such a severe and lofty life, from which arise pride and delusion, instead of following the middle and non-deluded path, which is easier and does not conceal in itself the abysses of delusion? The ancient fathers ate grass in the deserts because they had no bread, but here there is both bread and other food. You must eat all this with temperance, and then you will drive away demonic pride and delusion." Out of his extreme humility, the venerable one obeyed the abbot, and, leaving Voulevteria, came to the kathisma of the Transfiguration, where he lived for many years in succession, celebrating the Divine Liturgy there. Having learned of him, a multitude of brethren gathered at the kathisma who wished to become his disciples and to have the venerable one as their instructor and teacher of the monastic life. But the multitude of people caused the ascetic great disturbance, and he departed from there to the venerable Maximos Kausokalyvites, together with whom he practiced hesychia for many years. And such love did they have for one another that it seemed they had one soul in two bodies. Saint Maximos gave his kaliva to Saint Niphon, and built another for himself, nearby.

Since many came to Saint Maximos on account of the miracles and prophecies he performed, after some time Saint Niphon, being unable to endure this disturbance, departed from there to a cave situated opposite the kathisma of Saint Christopher, where he remained in hesychia. Later, a certain monk named Mark came from his homeland and asked to be taken as his disciple, in order to learn the monastic life. The venerable one received him, but commanded him to build another kaliva near his own, for his brother. Amazed at the words of the saint, Mark replied: "Father, is it possible that my brother would come here? He is a layman and has a family." Then with his characteristic great humility the saint said: "Brother, I have lost my mind, and therefore do not know what I am saying. Do as you wish." On the feast of Saint Athanasius, the venerable one sent Mark to the Lavra on some necessity, saying: "Returning from the feast, bring your brother with you as well, and we shall look upon him." Mark, again amazed, answered him with the very same words. However, upon arriving at the Lavra, he found his brother sitting at the gates. Understanding the clairvoyance of the saint, he joyfully embraced his brother, although he also felt pangs of conscience for not having believed his elder. Calling his brother to follow him, Mark brought him to the saint and, falling at his feet, asked forgiveness for his unbelief. After some time, Mark was struck by severe paralysis; he could neither walk nor move hand or foot. He asked the saint to have compassion on him and heal him, but the saint, wishing Mark to recognize his sin of unbelief and disobedience, said: "Only the holy wonderworkers and unmercenary saints can heal you, child, but God does not hear me, a sinner and unworthy one." The brother of Mark, out of compassion for him, earnestly asked the saint to forgive him. Niphon took oil from the lampada and anointed the body of the sick man, and — O miracle! — Mark was immediately healed and rose from the bed on which he lay. Then the saint said to him: *"See, you have been made well. Sin no more, lest a worse thing come upon you"* (John 5:14). But Mark again fell into disobedience. He asked the blessing of the elder to go fishing, but, not receiving it, he nevertheless went down to the shore, supposedly to wash his clothes, but in reality began to fish. And while he was doing this, suddenly an enormous shark leaped out of the water with open jaws to swallow him. The frightened Mark called upon the elder in his prayers and, drawing back a little, barely managed to escape the monster. He immediately ran to the saint, holding his catch in his hands. The saint, looking at him, said: "Be not unbelieving, you disobedient one, for he who transformed himself into a serpent before the first parents and taught them disobedience, that same one transformed himself into a shark because of your disobedience, which he taught you beforehand, desiring to cast you into the pit of perdition both spiritually and bodily. But Christ, who came into the world that we might have life, helped you today, awaiting, in His boundless goodness, your repentance. I, however, will never eat the fish of disobedience." Hearing this, Mark threw the fish far away and, falling at the feet of the saint, with fervent tears asked forgiveness. Out of his extraordinary compassion, the saint forgave him. From that time, Mark always remained in complete obedience to his instructor, until his earthly life ended and he passed to the other world with good hopes for a thousandfold reward for his obedience. As successor to his obedience, to serve the saint, Mark named his nephew Gabriel, whose father was called Dositheos. This Dositheos once asked the saint to send Gabriel on some errand to the Vatopedi monastery, and the saint sent him, appointing, however, a precise day for his return. The appointed day came, but Gabriel was not there. Dositheos began to weep, thinking that his son had been taken into slavery, for he had heard that those regions were subject to pirate raids by the Hagarenes. The saint, however, perceiving with his spiritual eyes, learned what had happened and said: "Do not weep, Elder Dositheos, for your son, because he is free." And indeed, Gabriel, who had suffered no harm, arrived before sunset.

Knowing that in six months Saint Maximos would fall into his final sleep, the saint said to his fellow-ascetics: "Let us go to Saint Maximos and enjoy his company, for we shall no longer see him in the present life." When they came to him and gave him a final kiss, Saint Maximos said: "Rejoice in Christ, beloved brethren. This is our last greeting, because we shall see each other no more." And this was the true prophecy of the saints.

Many years passed, and on the Holy Mountain an epidemic of plague again began. This illness also struck Gabriel, who was threatened with death. His father wept inconsolably, and the saint comforted him thus: "Do not weep, brother, for your son will not die now, because God so wills, since he has served me." Turning toward the east, the saint began to pray secretly to the All-Merciful God for the sick man, and this prayer lasted rather long, after which a miracle occurred and the sick man rose up healthy, glorifying God. Then, turning to Gabriel, the saint said: "Behold, our brother, with the help of God, has recovered his health, but I shall die during the Apostles' Fast."

The Apostles' Fast arrived. On the first Saturday of the fast, the saint arose, prayed, communed of the Most Pure Mysteries, and then said to the brethren: "My children, beloved in the Lord. Behold, the time has come for me to go to the Lord, whom my soul has desired from my youth." Seeing that all were troubled, he had compassion on them and said: "Children, you must not grieve for me, for henceforth I shall be an intercessor for you before God, entreating Him for your salvation. Only keep His commandments."

On Sunday, he commanded the brethren first to set the table, and then to dig and prepare a grave for him, so that, as he said, he might return *"to the ground from which he was taken"* (Genesis 3:19). After all was done, the saint arose, lifted his eyes to Heaven, and prayed for a long time with upraised hands. Then, having blessed and forgiven the brethren, and having received forgiveness from them, he crossed his hands upon his chest and gave his holy soul into the hands of God. At this, his face shone like the sun, thereby showing his boldness before God. This ever-memorable father reposed on the fourteenth of June, at the age of ninety-six years, having performed many miracles during his lifetime, some of which we shall relate.

A certain spiritual and virtuous elder named Theodulos once wished to go to the saint for the profit of his soul. On the way, near a precipice, he slipped and struck his foot against a large stone. From the severe bleeding and pain he nearly died. Foreseeing that the elder was in such a pitiful state, Niphon cried out from the depths of his soul: "Lord Jesus Christ, Son of God, if Thy servant Niphon has boldness before Thee, then let the bleeding stop and the pains of Theodulos cease, so that, by his prayers, I may come to myself, and not be devoured here by wild beasts." As soon as he uttered this prayer, a miracle occurred: the blood stopped, the pains ceased, and the elder, who until then was half-dead, arose and again walked along the road, glorifying God.

A certain Lavra monk who had great reverence for Saint Niphon sent him a vessel of oil with a friend. But that friend, walking along the road, stumbled and fell. Everything he was carrying broke, except for the vessel of oil, which remained whole, and when the brother gave it to the saint, the saint said with a smile, anticipating him: "Do you see what power the faith of the brother who sent the oil has? It both delivered you from danger and kept the vessel from breaking, unlike everything else." The brother who had brought the oil marveled at the clairvoyance of the saint and glorified God.

Another monk, suffering from headaches for many years, spent large sums on physicians but received no healing. Coming to the saint and falling at his feet, he fervently begged him to heal him, saying: "I know, most holy father, that whatever you ask of God, He will give you, for it is out of love for Him that you have chosen this desert for yourself." The saint, out of his humility, replied: "Father, I am a sinner, and God does not hear sinners." The sick man, however, did not cease falling at his feet with tears and asking for healing. Overcome by his natural kindness and compassion, the blessed Niphon read a prayer over the head of the sick man, after which a noise was heard as of a mighty wind, and — O miracle! — the sick man was healed, thanked the saint, and glorified God.

Another monk, a kelliot, trusted in himself and in his own knowledge, and therefore did not open his thoughts to a more experienced spiritual father. Thus he lived as his thought suggested to him. As a result, the unfortunate one fell into delusion and accepted an angel of darkness as an Angel of light. Having been taught many improprieties by him, the monk fell into pride and thought that by his virtues he surpassed everyone. Once he came to Saint Niphon. To the question of why he had come, he answered:

"To look upon you, who are famous for your virtue."

The saint remarked:

"How is it that you, so great and wondrous, have condescended to come to me, wretched and lowly?"

"God has bestowed His beneficence upon me, and the gift that I have is from God."

"Brother, the gift of God is humility. A thought from God is to think of yourself as the very last of all; a thought from God is to attain great virtues and think that you are worse than everyone. But what you have imagined about yourself is delusion from Satan, who taught you all this."

After such words of the saint, the monk came to himself, as it were, and said:

"Father, if my pride is from the evil one, then drive it away, I beg you, by your prayer, and deliver me from arrogance."

Lifting the eyes of his soul to the heavens, the blessed Niphon said:

"Lord Jesus Christ, who sought and found the lost sheep and numbered it with the rest that had not gone astray, who drove away the noetic wolf that sought to destroy it, and showed us the way of salvation: do Thou, O Master, deliver this Thy servant, who through his simplicity and through the cunning of the devil the deceiver has fallen into delusion, from demonic arrogance — that he may know Thee, the True God, who for our sake endured the Cross and death, and may glorify Thy holy name unto the ages. Amen."

Thus the venerable one prayed, and immediately scales, as it were, fell from the eyes of the brother, and he clearly recognized into what evil he, the unfortunate one, had fallen. From that time, having been delivered from satanic arrogance, he began to lead a God-pleasing life with prudence and humility.

A certain monk was expelled from the holy Lavra for some transgression, and he came to Saint Niphon and complained that he had been driven out unjustly. This brother asked if it might be possible to remain with him as a disciple. However, the saint, foreseeing the future, commanded him to return to the monastery and fall at the feet of the abbot with repentance and humility, so that the abbot might receive him again. "If you do not return," said the saint, "you will not be able to endure all the hardships here either, and you will lose that good which you could receive in the monastery. For if you return, after some time you will become ecclesiarch, and then abbot. However, above all you must have humility." With a smile the saint continued: "When, with God's help, you become abbot, remember us, and allot us means from the portion of the common life." When the monk returned to the monastery, he indeed, after some time, according to the prophecy of the venerable one, became ecclesiarch, and then abbot, and sent the saint all that was necessary for life.

Three monks wished to visit the venerable one, but since one of them was beardless, they left him on the road, far from the kathisma of the venerable one. When these two monks came to the saint, he asked them: "Why did you not bring with you that youth also, who will become an abode of the Holy Spirit?" Amazed at the words of the saint, they went and brought the youth. Having received great benefit from conversation with the venerable one and having received his blessing, all three departed, glorifying God. That youth, having progressed in virtue, according to the word of the saint, shone forth in the monastic life.

Dositheos, the father of Gabriel, of whom we have already spoken, asked the saint to allow Gabriel to go on some business to the Iveron monastery. Foreseeing the danger that was revealed to him by God's Providence and that was to befall him, he objected. However, Dositheos maintained that there was no danger, and that the next day he would go to the Amalfion monastery, now called Morphinou. Niphon objected: "And if Gabriel is taken into slavery at the Amalfion monastery, what then? Let him go; it will not be my fault what happens to him." Dositheos believed the words of the saint and no longer objected. That very evening a certain brother came to them and announced that a ship with pirates had departed from the Morphinou monastery, and they had captured three monks who happened to be on that road.

Once, a certain Lavra monk came to the venerable one and announced that the hieromonk Joannicius had been sent by the abbot together with other brethren to the island of Skyros, but at sea the monastery ship was attacked by pirates, and all were taken captive. The Lavra fathers had collected money for their ransom, and this monk gave one gold coin from himself. At that moment Niphon said to him: "It would have been better, child, if you had given this gold coin to the poor, because Joannicius and the others have already been freed, and they are well. Ah, if only we could participate in that consolation which they have now!" Having heard these words, the monk remembered the day when Saint Niphon said this, and upon the return of Joannicius to the Lavra, told him of the prophecy of the venerable one. It should be noted that on that very day Joannicius and the brethren caught a great quantity of fish, and therefore they received great consolation, to the glory of God who glorifies those who glorify Him. Amen.

The Life and Struggles of Our Father Among the Saints Gregory Palamas, Archbishop of Thessalonica, Wonderworker, Who Shone Forth in the Fourteenth Century

This divine father of ours Gregory was born of parents who were noble and virtuous. His father was so worthy a man that when Andronikos II ascended the imperial throne, he appointed him one of the members of the synkletos (the state council). But not only did the earthly king bestow honors upon him, but also the Heavenly King, Who glorified him with miracles while he was yet alive. Foreseeing his death, he received the monastic schema and from Constantine became Constantios. Having left all earthly things, he at last departed to the heavenly. After the death of his father, Gregory began to study the external wisdom. He was still of a young age, and memorization came with difficulty to him, therefore he resolved that he would not approach his studies until he made three prostrations with prayer before the icon of the Lady Theotokos. And thus, with prayer, learning became easier for him. The Theotokos also helped him by inclining the soul of the emperor toward him, and the latter generously gave Gregory all that was needful for life. A little time passed, and Gregory showed such progress that all marveled at his wisdom, which he displayed in affairs of state. For this reason the emperor was greatly gladdened and intended to give him a significant position. However, the mind of the venerable one was set on things more great and lofty: the Heavenly King and His Kingdom, while for earthly things Gregory cared nothing at all. The venerable one constantly associated with monks of the Holy Mountain who came to Constantinople, and the ascetics advised him to withdraw from the city and go to Athos. They also advised him to exercise himself a little in the virtues before leaving the city, and the venerable one, to the astonishment of all, began to show such indifference to garments, preferring the most wretched of them, and so altered his life and habits that some thought he had gone mad. But the courageous Gregory gave no thought whatsoever to dishonor and shame, and with zeal devoted himself to abstinence and fasting, satisfying his bodily needs for food and drink with only bread and water, never eating his fill. Likewise, beyond measure, he labored in the other virtues. Gregory was twenty years old when he began to live thus, yielding neither to the persuasions of the emperor nor to the promises of great honors. Having persuaded his household, close relatives and certain servants who were well-disposed to receive the angelic schema, he placed them in monasteries, while he himself together with his brothers withdrew from Constantinople. Coming to the Holy Mountain, he settled in the Lavra of Vatopedi and became a disciple of the divine Nikodemos, who was a wondrous hesychast, shining both in the struggles of contemplation and in practical struggles. From him the venerable one received the angelic habit. And now be attentive and you will understand what progress Gregory showed in those very same struggles, both practical and contemplative.

Two years had passed since he dedicated himself to God through fasts, vigils, concentration of thoughts, unceasing prayer, having as his Guide, Protectress and Intercessor the Mother of God, and at every moment in his prayers he turned to Her help. One day, when he was thus keeping hesychia alone and all his thoughts were turned inward and toward God, suddenly there appeared to him a majestic man (this was the holy John the Theologian) and, looking upon him with meekness, said:

"Child, the Most Holy Queen of all has sent me to ask you why you cry out to God all the time with the words: 'Enlighten my darkness, enlighten my darkness?'" To this Gregory answered thus:

"And what else should I, a passionate one full of sins, ask for, if not mercy and enlightenment, that I may know and do His holy will."

"The Lady of all, through me Her servant, promises to be your Helper."

"And where will the Mother of my Lord help me, here or in the future life?"

"Both in the present life and in the future."

Having said this and filled Gregory's heart with ineffable gladness from the promises of the Theotokos, the holy John the Theologian disappeared.

Three years had passed since the divine Gregory became a disciple of the elder. When the elder departed to the Lord, the venerable one left that place and came to the Lavra of Saint Athanasios. The fathers there received him with great honors, because they had heard of his virtues. He spent three years in the Lavra, and all that time the brethren marveled at his manner of life and wisdom. The abbot blessed the venerable one together with other monks to serve at the brotherhood's trapeza and to sing on the kliros with the other chanters. By his zeal for the obediences, Gregory amazed everyone; he strove extraordinarily to acquire all the virtues, and his soul was truly an abode of spiritual blessings. Henceforth all saw in him an example of virtue, for this wondrous Gregory conquered not only the irrational passions and lusts, but also the natural needs. Being in the body, he struggled to become bodiless. Gregory conquered sleep, and for three whole months did not sleep, as one without a body, allowing himself only a brief rest after eating, so as not to injure his mind. However, his love of hesychia did not allow him to remain in the Lavra until the end of his life, and he left there for his beloved wilderness together with like-minded ascetics who possessed the same virtues.

That skete, where many other anchorites dwelt, was called Glossia. Their leader was another Gregory, also from Constantinople, in that time a great and renowned practitioner of hesychia, nepsis and contemplation. From him the venerable one learned the highest mysteries of mental activity and the vision of God. Keeping hesychia alone, the saint was deemed worthy to receive from God many secret gifts, of which it is impossible to tell in words. He always came to such tenderness of heart that tears flowed unceasingly from his eyes. This gift the venerable one possessed all his life. However, it was not possible to enjoy this good hesychia in Glossia all the time, because of the attacks of the Hagarenes upon the monks who struggled outside the walls of the monasteries. Fleeing the danger, Gregory and his brotherhood, twelve in number, were compelled to move to Thessalonica. Having consulted among themselves, they decided to go to Jerusalem to venerate the holy places and remain there in hesychia until the end of their lives. However, the divine Gregory, wishing to know whether this was pleasing to God, began to pray alone. Dozing off a little, he immediately saw the following vision: "It seemed to me that I and the brethren found ourselves before a palace. There upon a throne sat a king in majesty, surrounded by bodyguards, nobles and other officials. From among them a certain archon separated himself, approached us and, embracing me, as it were drew me after him. Turning to my fellow brothers, he said: 'I shall keep this one with me, for so the king has commanded, but you go where you wish, no one will hinder you.'" Enlightened by God, the great Gregory related to the brethren the vision that had come to him, and all thought that this noble who had detained the divine Gregory was the great Demetrios (of Thessalonica, the wonderworker), therefore they decided to remain in Thessalonica, the homeland of the great martyr Demetrios. While in Thessalonica, the brethren asked the divine Gregory to receive the sacred rank. But at first he did not agree, until he came to know that this was the will of God.

After his ordination they came to Beroea, to a certain skete, and built a small monastery, where the divine Gregory, truly filled with every good, together with his fellow ascetics again began to struggle and exercise himself in perfection according to God. Five days a week he did not go out anywhere from the monastery, and received no one in his cell. Only on Saturdays and Sundays did he go out to celebrate the Liturgy and hold spiritual conversations with the brethren for their benefit. He was then thirty years old, his health and bodily strength were in perfect order, therefore he began more severe struggles and manner of life. The venerable one dried out his body with fasts, long vigils, refined and unceasingly purified the mental eyes of his soul through perfect abstinence and collection of thoughts, his habitual fountain of tears, always raised his mind to God in unceasing prayer, striving to completely subject the flesh to the spirit.

From such a godlike manner of life were born also the fruits of the Holy Spirit, as the apostle says. All his fellow ascetics, the monks of that mountain, and even the inhabitants of Beroea, saw in him an example of virtue: not only his angelic life caused wonder and amazement, but also his teachings and his supernatural wisdom according to God. Sometimes he was all attention, cleaving to God alone and being washed by wondrous tears, and sometimes his countenance was supernaturally radiant, enlightened and glorified by the fire of the Most Holy Spirit, especially when he came out of church after the conclusion of a service, or from his cell where he had been keeping hesychia. At this time the mother of Gregory, Kallista, a woman of great virtues, departed to the Lord. Her daughters and fellow ascetics at once sent a letter to the great Gregory with news of their mother's death, asking him to come to them for their spiritual instruction. He came to Constantinople to his sisters and, having sufficiently enlightened them, wished to return to Beroea. The sisters followed after him. Having placed them in a women's monastery, he ordered them to lead the customary ascetic life, after which he returned to his cell on the mountain that was near Beroea. There the venerable one became acquainted with an aged ascetic named Job, of a very simple character. Once, listening to the divine Gregory, who was saying that "not only ascetics, but all simple Christians must pray unceasingly according to the apostle," he did not agree, asserting that this is the duty of monks only, but not of laypeople. The saint was silent, because he hated many words; however, God Himself showed the justice of his words, because when Job returned to his cell and began to pray, he saw a radiant Angel of God, who said to him: "O elder, do not doubt that which the sacred Gregory has just told you. And you too must think thus and confess."

For five years the most wise Gregory kept hesychia on that mountain, but because of the frequent raids of the most vile Albanian race, he was compelled to return again to the Holy Mountain, to the Lavra of Saint Athanasios, where with great joy he was reunited with friends, fathers and brothers. He settled outside the walls of the monastery, in the hesychasterion of Saint Savvas, and went out from it only on Saturdays and Sundays, if he was asked to serve in the Lavra; he did not wish to see anyone, to converse with anyone, nor did he want others to see him. The aim of his life was contemplation according to God.

Once in the evening during Passion Week, according to ancient custom, a majestic All-Night Vigil was being celebrated in the Lavra, at which the saint was also present. Since, however, certain of the chanters were engaged in vain conversations and did not wish to cease them, the man of God was grieved, but considered it unwise to make a remark to them. Therefore the venerable one withdrew his mind from their chatter, as well as from the hymns, and turned inward and toward God, as he had already grown accustomed, and at that time his soul was illumined by the Divine light, by which the eyes of his soul and body were enlightened, and he clearly saw that which was to happen many years hence. And he saw Makarios, the abbot of the Lavra, vested in hierarchical vestments, who ten years later became the metropolitan of the city of Thessalonica, where he ended his life.

On another occasion the saint was praying in his cell to the Theotokos for himself and his brotherhood, asking Her to ease their ascent to God and make their spiritual life unimpeded, so that they might easily and without labor find all that was needful for life, not spending time in searching and thereby being distracted from spiritual matters. And the Lady of all appeared to him in the light of day in the modest form of a Virgin, as we see Her depicted on icons, and addressed those who accompanied Her (and there were many of them, all in bright garments), with the words: "Henceforth you will take care of all that is necessary and give it to Gregory and his brotherhood." Having given this command, the Mother of God became invisible. Saint Gregory said that from that time they always received what was necessary without difficulty, wherever they might be.

In the third year of his stay in the hesychasterion of Saint Savvas, one day, when the saint was ascending in mind to God through sacred prayer, it seemed to him that he was in a light sleep and was seeing the following picture. As though he were holding in his hands a vessel with milk and it suddenly began to overflow. Then suddenly it turned out that the milk had been transformed into excellent wine with a wondrous fragrance, which flowed abundantly over his hands and moistened his garments, filling them with sweet fragrance. And when he was delighting in this fragrance, it seemed to him that a certain man in military dress, filled with light, suddenly appeared to him and said: "Gregory, why do you not give others to drink of this wondrous beverage, which pours forth so abundantly, and it is going to waste? Do you not know that this is a gift of God, and the stream will never cease?" Gregory answered that it was impossible to give others to drink of this beverage, since there were none who truly had need of it. But the one who had appeared declared that although at the present time there were indeed none who passionately sought it, he must nonetheless fulfill his duty and distribute it. And those who wished to drink would be found by the Master Jesus Christ. Then that radiant warrior vanished, and the saint, shaking off sleep, was for a long time surrounded by the Divine light. The transformation of the milk into wine signified that from moral and most simple teaching he must pass to dogmatic and heavenly teaching. Following the divine vision and led by the Holy Spirit dwelling within him, Gregory began not only to give the brethren oral instruction, but also to write with a reed wondrous compositions. Since it was unjust that such a great brother in virtues and words should be hidden, the following occurred. He was appointed abbot of the Esphigmenou Monastery, in which two hundred monks lived. How he governed the monastery and all the sacred brotherhood, there is no need to tell in words, for the deed itself showed everything. In that monastery lived a certain virtuous monk named Eudokimos, whom the devil beguiled with false visions and caused to imagine of himself that he was higher in virtue than Gregory. Foreknowing that Eudokimos had been subjected to a demonic attack, the venerable one sometimes with an instructive word, sometimes with his own secret prayers with tears, and sometimes with the common supplications of all the brotherhood, put a barrier to this demonic activity and by the grace of the Most Holy Spirit made him truly Eudokimos (from the Greek εὐδόκιμος—renowned).

Once the monastery ran out of oil, and since there was great need of it, the saint together with the brethren came to the storehouse and, having prayed to God with faith, blessed the vessel, which immediately filled with oil, and this oil sufficed for that whole year, though it was used abundantly. Learning that there was no oil because the monastery's olive trees bore no fruit, the venerable one came together with the brethren to the trees. When he blessed them in the name of the Father, and of the Son, and of the Holy Spirit, they began to bear fruit. As proof of the miracle that had occurred, any tree that the saint touched immediately became covered with a multitude of fruit.

A little time passed, and the venerable one, having left the abbacy, returned again to the Lavra to his beloved hesychia. Just at that time there came from Calabria the most foul Barlaam, who with all his might was proving that he was in agreement with the Eastern

Church and wished to become a monk. In confirmation of this he composed discourses against his fellow Latins. However, having heard his arguments, the divine Gregory understood that Barlaam's refutations of the Latins were feigned and deceptive, and in reality were directed against the truth. This served as the reason that Barlaam became his enemy. Coming to Constantinople, Barlaam began to associate with certain simple monks, practitioners of mental prayer and nepsis, pretending that he wished to be their disciple and friend. Having learned from them what beginners in mental prayer must guard against, he vilely called them "heretics" and wrote articles directed against sacred prayer and meditation on God. Before these blasphemies of his became known, he was shamed before the Ecumenical Patriarch for other disgraceful and impious deeds of his and departed Constantinople in disgrace, returning to Thessalonica. But there too he continued to repeat his accusations against the monks and, what is worse, was not content merely with slandering the monks of his time, but strove to prove that the cause of the monastic error were the God-bearing fathers and teachers of the Church.

For this reason the monks of Thessalonica wrote a letter to Saint Gregory, fervently asking him to come and defend the truth from Barlaam. The saint immediately set out for Thessalonica and tried by various means to correct Barlaam. Many times he persuaded him in private, wishing to bring him into agreement with the Orthodox Church. Since, however, Barlaam did not cease shamelessly attacking the Church both in conversations and in writings and would not be corrected, the saint was compelled to polemicize with him also in writings, defending the Orthodox faith from Barlaam's lies. As soon as Barlaam learned that his writings had been refuted by the wondrous compositions of the saint on sacred hesychia and on the truth of Orthodoxy, he ceased writing treatises against the monks and attacked the divine Gregory. But he could not dispute with him face to face, and again from Thessalonica he returned to Constantinople.

Saint Gregory remained in Thessalonica for three years and all that time delivered teachings, wrote wondrous compositions on the true glory of God. His free time he spent in his customary weeping, in complete solitude and silent prayers. Since his beloved wilderness was not nearby, he built a small cell in the back part of the house in which he lived, and, when there was opportunity, he kept hesychia there. Once, on the day of the commemoration of Anthony the Great, the disciples and fellow ascetics of the saint together with the wondrous Isidore were serving a vigil to the divine Anthony. And—O miracle!—Anthony the Great appeared on that day to Saint Gregory. When the divine Gregory was praying, suddenly the Divine light surrounded him, as had already happened many times, and together with the light appeared Anthony the Great and said: "Good is prayer in mental hesychia, because it purifies the mental eyes of the soul and vouchsafes a person ineffable revelations of God. However, sometimes a monk needs communion and meeting with like-minded brethren, so that you might pray and chant together. Therefore, you must now go to the brethren who are serving the vigil, for they have great need of your care." After this, Anthony became invisible. The divine Gregory at that very hour went to the brethren, who received him with joy, and all that night they spent in the festal vigil. Having returned to the Holy Mountain, he showed the hesychasts and those chosen from the monasteries his compositions written in defense of Orthodoxy against the errors of Barlaam. The monks marveled, praised them, and unanimously approved them all.

The following also occurred. When Gregory was just preparing to set out for the Holy Mountain, he learned that his sister Theodota was at the point of death. The disciples and friends asked the saint what to do about the burial. The saint, however, foreseeing the future through Divine Providence, answered: "You need not ask me about this now, since, if it be pleasing to God, I shall return by that time and shall be here before her death." As he said, so it happened. When the last hour of Theodota came, she began to call for the divine Gregory, her good brother and spiritual guide. Hearing that he was on the Holy Mountain, she was grieved with all her heart and complained that she had not been deemed worthy to see him one last time and converse with him. Soon she fell silent and became completely calm, as if she had sunk into herself. Those present were already preparing everything for the burial, but a miracle happened! Eight days passed, during which Theodota lay without food, without sleep, not speaking, feeling no pains, and only faint breathing and movement of the eyes indicated that she was still alive and waiting for her brother. On the evening of the eighth day the long-awaited brother came from the Holy Mountain and, approaching his sister, spoke. She heard the sweetest voice of her brother, opened her bodily eyes, and together with them also her spiritual eyes and, since she could not speak, raised her hands a little to God to thank Him, and after a few moments, glorifying God, she gave up her spirit into the hands of God.

After the burial of his sister, the great Gregory again devoted himself to hesychia, nepsis, prayer and unceasing meditation on God. But the enemy of hesychia and contemplation of God, the loathsome Barlaam, came to Constantinople, as we have already said, and held out as bait for those who gaped at such things the external wisdom, bringing almost the whole city to his impiety in a short time, and first of all the Patriarch. He almost convinced everyone to renounce Orthodoxy, while its divine preachers—Saint Gregory and his like-minded brethren—were summoned by a patriarchal letter to the judgment of the Church. Taking Isidore, Mark, Theodore, his friends, the saint arrived in Constantinople. Having become convinced that almost all the eminent men, with the exception of one or two, had believed Barlaam's babble, Gregory by his conversations, with the help of the grace of the Holy Spirit, returned them all, including the Patriarch himself, to the bosom of the Orthodox Church. Having read the wondrous compositions of Gregory written against the teaching of Barlaam and his blasphemies, they proclaimed him a teacher of piety in agreement with the divine fathers of the Church. The Patriarch himself thanked the saint exceedingly.

In order to root out Barlaam's error, they decided to convene a general Council as soon as the emperor returned. By divine command, all the ascetics from various regions who were of one mind with Gregory came to the Council in the capital: the venerable David with his fellow ascetics, Dionysios, who had predicted by means of a divine vision the victory of the wondrous Gregory over the heretics, and others. Last of all arrived the emperor. The Council took place in the church of Hagia Sophia and condemned Barlaam and his blasphemous writings, threatening him with excommunication. And if he had not pretended that he had repented, accepted and truly confessed Orthodoxy and condemned his own false heretical writings, he could not have remained alive due to the anger of the people. Having been thus shamed, Barlaam returned to his beloved Latins. But that same cunning one made successor and heir of Barlaam's error another Gregory, surnamed Akindynos. Again a Church Council was assembled, no less than the previous one (against Barlaam), and again Gregory, the great ascetic and renowned defender of Orthodoxy, destroyed all the errors with proofs from Holy Scripture and the teaching of the Orthodox Church. Hardly two months had passed after the Council when a civil war began, which was provoked by Patriarch John, surnamed Kalekas. Since the divine Gregory was against the war and counseled the making of peace, the Patriarch sought every possible way to punish Gregory. Forgetting all the honors and praises that he himself had formerly shown him, unable to invent any slander against Gregory, the Patriarch turned against Orthodoxy, unleashing terrible warfare upon the Church and its divine dogmas, all in order to punish the venerable one, as if he were defending heretical teaching. The Patriarch brought into the Orthodox Church Akindynos, the guardian of the heresy, ordaining him to the diaconate and preparing to consecrate him a priest and teacher of the Church. Saint Gregory, however, the preacher of the truth, slandered as an instigator of war, he condemned to imprisonment in a dungeon.

The empress Anna of that time, hearing that Akindynos, who had been anathematized at two Holy Councils, had been ordained to the diaconate, expelled him from the Church. The divine Gregory, however, remained in prison for four years, although he was very ill and in need of daily treatment. Gregory, with God's help, steadfastly endured all the hardships of prison. In the end, the Patriarch who had slandered him became hateful to the emperors and was condemned to imprisonment; by a conciliar decision he was deprived of his sacred rank for heresy and excommunicated from the Church. His perdition became perdition for the heresy and a testimony to the truth of Orthodoxy. Immediately the civil war also ceased. The great Gregory was released from prison and solemnly, with the crown of a confessor, returned to his beloved and loving brethren. To omit what is superfluous, I shall say that later he was ordained metropolitan of Thessalonica, and both the emperor and Patriarch Isidore earnestly asked him to accept the rank. Since there was also some civil strife in Thessalonica, Gregory, the hierarch of God, was again expelled from the Church, and he returned again to the Holy Mountain, precisely on the feast of the Nativity of the Theotokos. A certain pious priest who was in charge of the care of orphans persuaded the priests serving the Liturgy to pray to God that He might show them by a sign what boldness Gregory had before God and in what rank he would abide in the Heavens. This pious priest secretly prayed to God that He might manifest a sign through his paralyzed daughter, and that she might be healed (it must be said that the members of her body had been withered and immobile for three years). And God, Who glorifies His servant, for whose sake the supplication was offered, suddenly raised the girl from her bed; she began to walk freely and, forgetting her former illness, ran healthy throughout the whole house.

On the Holy Mountain, where the hierarch had withdrawn, he was visited by the ruler of Bulgaria, Stefan, who long tried to persuade him to go with him to his kingdom, but achieved nothing. Being greatly urged by this Stefan, Saint Gregory was sent as an ambassador to Constantinople to the emperors. After some time Gregory again returned to his diocese, since both the emperor and the Patriarch thought that the dissensions in Christendom had already ended. However, the disagreements intensified, the hierarch could not enter his metropolitanate in Thessalonica, and by a determination of the Great Church he went to Lemnos, where he was an exemplary archpastor and manifested numerous miracles. When Gregory was on Lemnos, a plague occurred in a certain small town. Having made a procession of the cross together with the people and having fervently prayed to God, the hierarch was able to stop the deadly disease.

In the end the Thessalonians decided to bring back their beloved archpastor. At the government's expense they fitted out a ship, and the church hierarchy arrived at Lemnos. After a few days they brought the pastor to his flock. On the day when the saint arrived in Thessalonica, there was great joy everywhere, as on the luminous day of Resurrection. The customary psalmody at the hierarchical entry was abandoned and by inspiration from God all began to sing: "It is the day of Resurrection…Let us purify our senses and we shall behold…Shine, shine." The miracle was that there was no one who advised the chanters to sing these troparia, nor was there anyone who first began to sing them. After three days the hierarch appointed a general assembly and procession of the cross with the holy icons, and after it delivered a teaching on concord and peace. He served the Liturgy and offered the Bloodless Sacrifice to sanctify the people, and it was then that God glorified him with a miracle. That priest, the orphanotrophos, had a son suffering from lunacy, and the disease was becoming more and more progressive. At the Liturgy the father concelebrated with the hierarch and asked him to commune the child. After Communion the disease immediately departed, and the child, glorifying God, was healed. After the Liturgy the hierarch gathered all the clergy and spoke to them at length about the loftiness of the priestly rank, and throughout his life he did not cease to teach both in churches, and in private conversations, and in sermons for all, but especially he taught by his own example, striving to lead all to salvation.

Since the followers of Barlaam and Akindynos did not cease to disturb the Orthodox Church, the emperor together with the Patriarch decided to convene a Council again in the capital in order to carefully examine what they were saying, for they constantly requested this. First of all the most worthy divine Gregory was summoned to Constantinople. After the solemn and great Council had assembled, at the earnest request of the emperor and the Synod, the saint stood up and expounded the Orthodox teaching before the Council. At the conclusion of the Council's work the hierarch wished to return as quickly as possible to his flock, but he was again prevented from returning to Thessalonica, this time not by the inhabitants of his metropolitanate, but by John Palaiologos, who was residing there. Because of this the venerable one returned again to the Holy Mountain, and only three months later, at the request of this John, was he able to return again to his diocese to shepherd his flock and bring them spiritual and bodily benefit. Once, when Gregory came to one of the women's monasteries on the feast of the Nativity of the Theotokos, during the Liturgy there came the nun Eleodora, who several days before had lost sight in one eye, and secretly, like the woman with the issue of blood in the Gospel, grasping the hierarchical vestment, brought it to her sick eye, and at that very moment wondrously received healing.

Having been in his diocese for one year, the hierarch fell gravely ill; his body was tormented by unbearable pains and many temptations, so that all thought he would die. However, God unexpectedly again granted him life, for, as a courageous ascetic, He was preparing him for further struggles. And although the illness had not yet completely departed, he was compelled by the numerous insistent requests of John Palaiologos to go to Constantinople and intercede for him before his father-in-law, the emperor John Kantakouzenos, in order to reconcile them, since it was precisely because of their quarrel that Palaiologos was residing in Thessalonica. However, the Most High God, King of kings, directed the hierarch Gregory to another service, for on his way to Constantinople he was taken captive by the Achaemenids. Under the guise of a slave he was brought to Asia, and as a true evangelist and preacher of the faith he helped the Christians who were in bondage and strengthened them with his teachings. How many and what kinds of discussions he held in Prousa and Nicaea with the Turks about the Orthodox faith, how he stopped their mouths, with what teachings he strengthened the Christians there—whoever is interested can learn about this from the extensive life of the saint. After a year God moved certain upright Bulgarians, who willingly gave the Turks much money and freed the saint.

And again there occurred a wondrous miracle. When the saint was sailing on a ship and approaching the harbors of Constantinople, in the air there was heard chiming and wondrous hymns, as if coming from the ship, but those who heard understood that these were not human but angelic melodies, for angels were invisibly accompanying the saint. Having spent some time in the capital, Gregory went to his diocese, which was suffering from a drought and the absence of the Divine word. Gregory wondrously refreshed his children both spiritually and bodily. The saint had a friend, a pious hieromonk Porphyrios. Once at night, on the feast of the Transfiguration of the Lord, he had such severe pain in his side that even when he lay down, the pain did not let him go. Since the saint was serving the Liturgy, Porphyrios approached him and asked him to heal him. Making the sign of the cross over the ailing side, Gregory with tenderness and contrition of heart pronounced the troparion: "O crucified Master…may Christ heal thee." O miracle! The sufferer was immediately delivered from the unbearable pain and returned healthy to his cell.

On another occasion Porphyrios had such a sore throat that he could not swallow even a small amount of water. He suffered for eight days, and death already threatened him, but the great Gregory made the sign of the cross over the ailing place with his sacred right hand and with tears pronounced, addressing Christ, the troparion: "Without suffering any passion Thou hast remained…" After this the sick man was healed in a wondrous manner.

A certain goldsmith had a five-year-old child who for fifteen months had been suffering from a terrible bleeding, and no one could heal him. The child was doomed. However, the saint made the sign of the cross over him with prayer and handed him back healthy into the arms of his parents.

However, Saint Gregory was nonetheless a man subject to human infirmities. Three years after his last visit to the capital, Gregory fell ill and took to his bed. Even while lying on his deathbed, he continued to instruct his children, foretold his death, naming also its day. He told his friends that his death would occur after the feast of the hierarch John Chrysostom, that is, after the fourteenth day of the month of November. In a dream this hierarch appeared to him and called him to himself as one of the same form and beloved. In all, the wondrous Gregory lived sixty-three years, of which for one and a half years in the hierarchical rank he pastured the Church of God. When his blessed soul was separated from his body, the grace of the Most Holy Spirit wondrously manifested to those present the inner radiance of his soul, since that cell in which his sacred relics lay was filled with a wonderfully bright light. His face, which had withered long before his death, was shining. Witnesses of this supernatural radiance of his face were almost all the inhabitants of the city, who came to the burial of the sacred remains of the hierarch. The grace of the Most Holy Spirit abode inseparably both with the hierarch and with his relics, and henceforth, having shown his holy tomb as an abode of divine light, made it a source of miracles, sacred gifts and a common physician of all. Because of this the hierarch was also called "wonderworker." He is truly a wonderworker, and how I would wish, if time permitted, to tell of his many miracles, but I am compelled to pass over those which occurred after his death. They are described in his extensive life and those who wish may learn of them. I, however, shall briefly tell of only one miracle, which testified that Gregory was truly glorified by God.

The Latins often accuse our holy Eastern Church that after her separation from the Western there have been no saints among us, and there have been no miracles that they performed. The sacred Nektarios, who became Patriarch of Jerusalem in 1660, wishing in his ardent zeal for the truth to stop the foul mouths of the Latins and prove that they are liars and slanderers, enumerated many new saints of the Eastern Church who shone forth after the schism. He testified to many wondrous miracles, including also the miracles of the hierarch Gregory. On the island of Santorini, on the day of the hierarch's commemoration, the second Sunday of Great Lent, certain Latins were relaxing, riding in a boat, or, as Patriarch Dositheos of Jerusalem says, the Franks put children in a boat who were riding on the water, clapping their hands and crying: "Anathema to Palamas! If he is a saint, let him make us drown." Thus they blasphemed the hierarch, but a miracle occurred. At that time, without any storm, in complete calm, the boat together with all its passengers capsized and sank. The bodies of the blasphemers sank into the sea, while their foul souls went into the eternal fire of hell. Thus was the sanctity of the divine Gregory confirmed, and all marveled at God, wondrous in His saints, to Whom be glory and dominion unto the ages of ages. Amen.

(Written by Philotheos, Most Holy Patriarch of Constantinople)

The Life and Struggles of Our Venerable and God-bearing Father Niphon, Archbishop of Constantinople, Who Struggled on the Holy Mountain of Athos in the Monastery of Dionysiou in the Fifteenth Century

This divine father of ours, Niphon, was by birth from the Morea and came from parents of noble and honorable descent, but more renowned for their piety. Their names were Manuel and Maria. The infant was named Nicholas at his Baptism. When the boy had grown a little, he was given to learn the sacred letters. From a young age, possessing an elderly mind, he was not carried away, like other children, by their games. Attending upon most wise and virtuous teachers, he gathered the honey of virtue like a bee, listening to and imitating all that was good—the soul-profiting lessons and examples. He had such a sharp mind that the boy soon surpassed all his peers in learning. Nicholas often read the Lives of the holy fathers, from which his soul rejoiced, and he endeavored, as much as possible, to imitate them in virtues. The venerable one was distinguished by remarkable chastity and was so zealous in abstinence that he satisfied his bodily needs for food and drink with only bread and water. In the same way he also labored in all the other virtues.

In those days a certain hieromonk named Joseph came to the school, an excellent teacher and a most virtuous man. Having communicated and conversed with him sufficiently, this good Nicholas asked the monk to take him with him, but in such a way that no one would know about it, because he feared that he might be hindered. Receiving him with joy, Joseph secretly departed with him and began to teach him philosophy. Coming to Epidaurus, they heard that in that region a certain hermit Anthony was struggling, most virtuous and an imitator in all things of Anthony the Great, and they went to him for a blessing. Having conversed with him for some time and received his divine instructions, they rejoiced in soul. Then Joseph, having asked a blessing from the elder, departed, while Nicholas, casting himself at the feet of Anthony, asked with tears for permission to remain with him. Referring to the labors of the ascetic, the cramped conditions, and especially the young age of Nicholas, Anthony tried to dissuade him, but Nicholas, burning with love for God, insisted and pleaded all the more: "Father, whatever you command me, I will fulfill with joy, only do not deprive me of communion with yourself." Seeing his strong zeal, the elder received him, gave him a cell and an ascetic rule. And the good Nicholas gave himself over to ascetic labors, imitating the elder in all things, and soon asked him to clothe him in the monastic garb. The divine

Anthony answered him: "Since you, child, wish to receive the monastic habit, know that you will have to give yourself over to great struggles and labors, so that the enemy does not find you sleeping and tear you apart, for he is cunning and envious toward us monks. Therefore we must struggle greatly, so that by the narrow and sorrowful path we may come to the enjoyment of eternal life." After this the elder clothed Nicholas in the monastic garb, renaming him Niphon.

From that time the blessed Niphon began to struggle even more in the labors of monastic life. When a thought about wealth would come to him, or about his parents, for the enemy constantly caused him to remember them in order to seduce him, he would immediately run to the elder, fall at his feet and confess with tears, and, strengthened and consoled, would return with prayer and blessing to his cell. Niphon earned his bread by copying books, for he was an excellent copyist. Moreover, he never engaged in idle talk, never laughed in the skete, never read any church book without tears, and never spoke without the elder's blessing. After some time he became perfect in all the ranks of monastic life, but soon the ever-blessed Anthony reposed in the Lord. Niphon wept inconsolably, because he had lost his spiritual father.

Having buried the elder, he spent quite a long time in solitude, but one day he heard that in the city of Narda there was a most wise and very virtuous teacher named Zacharias, who had recently come from the Holy Mountain. Desiring to receive from him the fruit of wisdom and to learn the customs of the Holy Mountain, Niphon came to him and, having confessed, asked to remain with him, and Zacharias began to teach the youth what he so desired.

At that time there was great turmoil in the Churches because of the false Council of Florence, which had been held under John Palaeologus. The Eastern Churches by no means wished to agree with its decisions. Therefore the most wise Zacharias together with the sacred Niphon went to Ascalon, teaching the Christians to stand firmly in Orthodoxy, to follow the teaching of the holy apostles, and to observe the decrees of the Ecumenical Councils. Departing from Ascalon, they came to a certain city whose ruler was George Skanderbeg. He received them with great honors and reverence, because he had heard of them before. Having shown them hospitality, the ruler detained them at the palace, and he made the most wise Zacharias his spiritual father. At that time in Constantinople Emperor John Palaeologus died and in his place his brother Constantine ascended the throne. Having convened a Council, he declared the decisions of the Council of Florence invalid. After some time, evidently by the judgments of God, in the year 1453 the Turks took Constantinople. Everywhere there was great bloodshed, and Christians rushed from place to place seeking refuge. Zacharias and Niphon, until this slaughter subsided, hid for some time on a mountain, and then went to Ohrid, to the monastery of the Most Holy Theotokos. There they remained, and Niphon continued to study diligently from his teacher Zacharias.

At that time the Bishop of Ohrid, Nicholas, reposed in the Lord. To appoint a new bishop, the hierarchy, clergy, and a multitude of people assembled, asking Zacharias to accept the hierarchal rank, for he was known to all for his virtue and wisdom. But he humbled himself, saying that he was unworthy to take upon himself the burden of the salvation of so many souls, since he could barely save his own. But they did not cease asking and entreating him until he agreed.

After several days the sacred Zacharias was ordained bishop, and the blessed Niphon asked his blessing to go and keep stillness on the Holy Mountain. The bishop said to him: "You are very much needed by me now, child, that I may be consoled and the burden which I have taken upon my shoulders against my will might be somewhat lightened. Will you really leave me now? In case of necessity friends and children are needed to help parents who are in danger. My child, Niphon, do not deprive me of the happiness of seeing you." While the bishop was saying all this with tears, tears streamed from the eyes of the divine Niphon like a river, and he could not answer anything. That night they both remained in vigil, and at dawn the hierarch saw a dream. A holy Angel commanded him to release Niphon, because he was a chosen vessel of the holy God. In the morning, having said a prayer, the hierarch released the divine Niphon with the words: "Go, child, where the Lord shall lead you, Whom I, unworthy, ask to allow me to see you again in this life, if it be pleasing to His Divine Providence."

With the hierarch's blessing, the blessed Niphon, like a swift-winged eagle, hastened to the Holy Mountain. Coming to the Vatopedi monastery and venerating the wondrous shrines of the Most Holy Theotokos, he found a multitude of virtuous men, whom he gladly followed in all things. Coming to Karyes, he met the protos of the Holy Mountain named Daniel, a most virtuous and discerning man, who, seeing him, rejoiced and, having embraced him, said: "O most wise Niphon, from many I have heard of you, and I have prayed to God to deem me worthy to see you before my death. Behold, the All-good God has heard my humble prayer. I ask you, give instruction to the brethren who have gathered to hear you." The humble-minded Niphon objected: "Most venerable fathers, I am unworthy to give remedies to healthy and experienced physicians, but I myself am in need of their healing." Then the divine Daniel said: "You should not keep the words of God only for yourself, father, but must transmit them to others, so as to bring benefit to them also."

Then, bowing his head and making the customary prostration, the saint began to speak words of wisdom, and all marveled at their reasonableness. It was so pleasant to listen to him that it was impossible to tear oneself away, and from the sweetness of his words even bodily food was forgotten. Going about the sketes of Karyes, the venerable one found a multitude of virtuous men and his soul rejoiced. Then he came to the sacred Pantokrator monastery. Having spent sufficient time there, he went to the Cave of Crete, in which wondrous ascetics dwelt, leading their life in great hardship. Having marveled at their extraordinary patience, Niphon spent some time with them, teaching and learning, and earned his bread by copying books.

Soon the abbot of the Great Lavra, holy Athanasius, invited him to come to the monastery so that the brethren might receive benefit from his honey-flowing words. In order not to be disobedient, he accepted the invitation with great joy, readily imitating the Master, and taught them for a sufficient time. At that time he also learned of the monastery of the Honorable Forerunner, called the Dionysian, where many virtuous men were struggling, who truly led an equal-to-the-angels life and kept all the ordinances of monastic life, for everything among them was held in common, according to the rules of Basil the Great. The venerable one left the Lavra and came to this monastery. Seeing that the place was difficult of access and austere, the blessed one so rejoiced that it seemed to him as though he saw the divine Forerunner himself, living in mountains and caves and eating locusts and wild honey. All night Niphon spent in vigil, praying to the Honorable Forerunner to deem him worthy to remain in this place. In the morning the abbot clothed him in the divine and angelic schema. When the brethren began to ask him to accept the priestly rank, the venerable one answered with humility that he was unworthy. They asked him again and again, and finally he obeyed and was ordained in order as reader, subdeacon, deacon, and priest. Having received the rank, Niphon began to struggle even more in his spiritual struggles, in vigils, fasts, prayers, and immaculate love toward all. In short, the thrice-blessed one was a great lamp, illumining not only the monastery of Dionysiou but the entire Holy Mountain. As a certain virtuous elder named Petronius testifies, who spent one night together with the divine Niphon outside the monastery, at night he arose to pray and saw that the holy Niphon was standing with his hands raised to Heaven and his eyes lifted up, all filled with Divine light, which reached to Heaven and was poured out everywhere. Unable to bear such light, Petronius fell to the ground as if dead. Amazed, the saint raised him up. When he came to himself, he fell at the feet of Niphon, but the blessed one wished to hide the divine vision from him. However, Petronius secretly told the abbot about the vision, and the abbot said: "This, Father Petronius, reveals the extraordinary purity of the man, for through him many will be enlightened. Beware, tell no one of this, lest he hear and leave us, fleeing praise. Otherwise we shall lose such a man, whom the holy God has granted us as a refuge and strengthening in our days."

At that time two archons from Thessalonica came to venerate the honorable monasteries of the Holy Mountain. Finding themselves in the monastery of Dionysiou on the day when the saint was serving the Liturgy in the katholikon, and hearing his honey-flowing teachings, they marveled, although they themselves were educated men. After the service, having conversed with the saint, they rejoiced at his soul-profiting instructions. Returning home to Thessalonica, the archons told everyone about the divine Niphon.

In those days the Metropolitan of Thessalonica, Parthenius, reposed. The bishops and all the clergy of Thessalonica assembled and unanimously decreed that the most wise Niphon would be their shepherd. They sent two bishops and several clergy for him, who came to the monastery of Dionysiou and, having spoken privately with the senior elders of the monastery, asked them to persuade the saint to accept the metropolia. Sighing heavily, the elders answered: "Holy hierarchs, who gives away his teacher to others? We ourselves hunger and thirst, so how can we give away our food and drink? Have the famous Thessalonians really come to such a point that you have no other worthy person, and you have come to us, the lowly, to deprive us of the light of our eyes? You yourselves see that we are deprived of the most necessary things and dwell in ruinous and impassable places. The Lord has sent us a consoler in our sorrows, so must we, the wretched, be deprived of him? It seems to us that truly a great danger awaits us if we are deprived of such a lamp, and all the brethren will experience immeasurable sorrow." With these words the elders departed.

Having become convinced that they had accomplished nothing, the bishops and clergy began with tears to fervently beseech the holy God and the Honorable Forerunner to help them. When the holy Niphon inquired of the abbot about them, the abbot, from strong sorrow, answered nothing. Enlightened by the grace of the Holy Spirit, the saint understood everything and said: "Father, do not grieve, for I shall be with you again and in this place shall pay our common debt, as I asked of the divine Forerunner when I came to this monastery, and he has heard my prayers." Then the abbot answered him: "May it be to you, beloved, as you yourself have asked of the divine Forerunner. Do you see those about whom you asked me? They are bishops from Thessalonica. They have been sent by the clergy and people to make you their shepherd. But we shall be left orphans, and I shall never see you again." He said this, being enlightened by God, because when the blessed Niphon came to the monastery the second time, the abbot had already passed away and, according to his prediction, did not see him again.

After the abbot's words, the humble-minded Niphon fell to the ground and, pouring out tears, said: "Who am I, a foul-smelling sinner, to take upon my wounded neck such a heavy yoke?" Hearing the weeping of the saint, all the brethren came running to the church to see who was grieving so heavily. When all the brethren had assembled in the church, the abbot announced why the bishops and clergy had come. As soon as the brethren heard this, they surrounded the saint with such weeping and lamentation that the bishops and clergy also entered the church and delivered to the saint the letter from the entire clergy of Thessalonica. The saint said with weeping: "Holy hierarchs, I, wounded by the multitude of my sins, have come to this place to keep stillness and to die here. How can I now depart from the path of repentance and take upon myself the care of so many souls, when I can barely save my own sinful soul?" To this the bishops answered: "Father, do not oppose the Divine decision, because all with one mind and one voice wish you to be their shepherd." Then the abbot, enlightened by the Holy Spirit, said: "Go, honorable father, for such is the will of God, for you have increased your talent, and through you many have been saved. But always remember this sacred monastery, our love and the brethren, and help us by your frequent prayers, and also in our earthly needs. And we shall always remember you as a resident and child of our holy monastery, because the Lord this night commanded me, the unworthy, not to place obstacles in your path." With these words he embraced the blessed Niphon, and the other brethren did the same with tears. Finally the venerable one said: "My fathers and brethren, may the will of the Lord be done, as you desire, yet great danger awaits me, the unworthy, therefore pray for me to the Lord."

When the bishops, clergy, and the holy Niphon came to Thessalonica, they were met by a multitude of people who wished to see the venerable one and receive his blessing, and each one hastened to get ahead of the other. When Sunday came, he was ordained hierarch—to shepherd the people of God. After several days Niphon understood that the Christians were experiencing confusion from the Latin-minded innovations of the false Council of Florence, and he began constantly to teach the people the Divine commandments of the apostles, basing himself on the decrees of the Councils, completely refuting the sophistical proofs of the Latins and commanding them to hold firmly to Orthodoxy. He also consoled his flock during the disorders and temptations caused by the recently established Hagarenes, urging them to bear without murmuring the sorrows and torments of captivity for the sake of hope in the promised blessings.

By his most wise teachings he moved unmerciful and cruel rich men to mercy toward the poor, for he himself was so merciful and loving of the poor that many times he went about alone at night to give all that was necessary to the sick and infirm. By the meekness of his words he attracted all to the Divine will. The most wise one even brought many unbelievers to the Christian faith, having turned them from error. The report of him spread everywhere, so that many came to him. They heard of him even in the Great Church and wished to see him.

After two years the Council of hierarchs of the Church of Constantinople summoned him to the capital on urgent Church matters. This happened by the dispensation of God, since a lamp set on a higher place gives light to all. When the saint arrived in Constantinople, the Patriarch, the hierarchs, all the clergy, and the people received him with all honors for his virtue and most wise guidance of his flock. Zacharias was also there, and they embraced and rejoiced beyond measure. Thus was fulfilled the prophecy of the divine Zacharias that they would meet again in this life. However, after several days the most holy Zacharias, having fallen ill, departed to the Lord, and the divine Niphon reverently committed his honorable remains to burial with all honors.

After a short time the Patriarch of Constantinople also reposed in the Lord, and immediately, without delay, all the hierarchs and clergy by imperial authority elevated the most wise Niphon to the Ecumenical Throne, against his will. Having in his holy soul zeal for God, he began to proclaim loudly, like a new apostle, the Divine teaching, admonishing, forbidding in due measure, striving in every way to drive the wolves away from the flock of Christ and to strengthen Orthodoxy. By his divine and most wise words he saved many unbelievers, who received Divine Baptism from him and, strengthened by his prayers, returned to their homelands. After Baptism they tried to keep apart in order to avoid danger from the impious.

The Church of Christ rejoiced, having such a lamp shining throughout the whole world, and in those times there was no other like him. But the hater of good, the devil, could not bear the renown of the venerable one and stirred up certain scandal-making clergy to separate the saint from his flock. Having conspired against the good shepherd, they expelled him from the Patriarchate by a decree of the sultan.

Not understanding why he was being expelled with such senseless anger, the saint was perplexed and sorrowful, but not because he had been deprived of the throne, but because the Christians were being deprived of salvation. Knowing that all this was the cunning of the evil one, he entreated the Lord to forgive the sins of those scandal-makers, to convert them and give them the opportunity to repent. But he himself rejoiced that he had been freed from cares and could enjoy the desired stillness. He returned to Sozopolis, to the monastery of the Honorable Forerunner, and began to keep stillness. He led a life that was extraordinary in the highest degree, and the report of him spread through many regions, so that Christians came to see the saint and hear his soul-profiting teaching.

After he had lived in the monastery for two years, he was again invited to Constantinople, and Niphon for the second time occupied the Ecumenical Throne. He again began to shine like a lamp on a lampstand, illumining the whole world with his wondrous teachings. But the devil again could not bear the boldness of the saint and therefore devised to expel him by another means. Once, when the venerable one was returning to the Patriarchate from the church where he had served, he suddenly met the sultan on the road. Stepping aside, the Patriarch greeted him as befitting his rank, but the proud sultan, who wished to be honored as God, insulted the saint, declaring that he did not know how to honor emperors as was fitting. Answering nothing, the humble-minded Niphon departed, thinking to himself: "This too is your doing, wicked demon." When the sultan returned to the palace, he ordered the saint to be exiled to Adrianople, accompanied by two soldiers. On the road to Adrianople the soldiers caused him much harm, but God preserved him unharmed. Upon arriving at the place, he was permitted to live in the church of Saint Stephen under strict guard. Thanking God, Who had allowed him to live and serve as a consolation in the church of the Protomartyr, the holy Niphon rejoiced and glorified the Lord, for he was devoted to Him with all his soul and did not hope for help from men.

Since the report of the saint had spread even to Wallachia, the Wallachian voivode Radu wished to visit the saint. Traveling to Constantinople to pay the imperial tax, he was passing through Adrianople. Using every possible means, he received permission from the sultan's men to visit the saint. Coming to Niphon, he bowed his head, venerated him with great reverence, and having lovingly kissed the right hand of the saint, said: "Holy Master, I greatly desired to see your thrice-blessed face, to be deemed worthy of your prayers, and to receive a blessing from you. Blessed be God, Who has deemed me worthy today to enjoy the sight of you. However, I greatly grieve because of the trials to which you are being subjected." The saint answered: "Most illustrious ruler, *We must through many tribulations enter the kingdom of God*' (Acts 14:22), says the Lord. And the divine Paul writes that *'the sufferings of this present time are not worthy to be compared with the glory which shall be revealed in us'* (Romans 8:18). So we also must bear the vicissitudes of this present life with joy, as the divine apostles bore them, who rejoiced when the Jews beat them, for they were dishonored for the name of the Lord, as the divine Luke describes in the Acts of the holy apostles (Acts 5:41). The blessed Paul writes in his epistles: *'I now rejoice in my sufferings'* (Colossians 1:24). The thrice-blessed ones rejoiced in sorrows, bearing them with gratitude, because they awaited the blessed hope, but we are fainthearted, and what can we bear?"

Having heard this, the voivode was moved to compunction and said: "I ask your hierarch's office to come to Wallachia to teach us, because we are deprived of spiritual teaching and a spiritual shepherd. There you will find rest, and all will receive you with joy. Only allow me to ask the impious for permission for you." The saint agreed, and Radu interceded for him with the Turks, after which he returned to Wallachia together with the venerable one, where all received Niphon as an apostle of the Lord. The voivode said to him: "From now on, father, you will be our guide and shepherd, who will lead us on the path of salvation. You will have authority in Church matters, and as you command, so shall everything be."

The divine Niphon answered him: "I praise you for your good character; preserve it to the end. But I ask you to receive with gratitude everything I shall undertake for your correction. Even if you yourself should sin, you will receive spiritual admonition, for when the common people see that their ruler accepts correction through repentance, then they too are easily corrected. And on the contrary, when a ruler tramples on the law and violates the sacred canons, then a great fall occurs, because people easily incline toward evil." The voivode said to the saint in reply: "Everything you do, father, for the benefit of our souls, we shall accept with joy." And then the most wise Niphon commanded that a Local Council be convened. All the priests, abbots of monasteries, and archons together with the voivode assembled, and the blessed one began to preach the Divine teaching, exhorting them to observe good morals, bringing proofs from Holy Scripture and the writings of the holy fathers, persuading them to turn away from evil customs. Having received his honey-flowing teachings and obeying his divine words, they began to strive to correct every disorder and their morals. The holy Niphon also ordained two bishops, commanding them to diligently care for the flock of Christ, for they would give an account for those entrusted to them before the Dread Judge. Then, turning to the voivode, the saint said in a loud voice: "And you, child Radu, who have power in your hands, must admonish your citizens, punish wrongdoers without regard for persons, whether great or small, but render righteous judgment, because, as Holy Scripture says, judgment belongs to the holy God."

Having delivered his teachings with great humility, the saint dismissed the Council, detaining for some time the priests and monks from distant places so that they might be corrected. All glorified God, Who had sent them such a lamp, who had guided them on the true path, and they called him "the new Chrysostom." Niphon served every Sunday and on feast days so that all who came to church could hear his teaching. And the wondrous Niphon strove by any means to turn them away from the bad custom of drunkenness, because almost all were addicted to this passion in the extreme, from which all mortal sins arise, and especially fornication and the abominable sin of sodomy, for many were subject to it. Therefore the most wise one strove to extinguish the flame of drunkenness and by his unceasing teachings turned a great multitude of people to repentance. However, the hater of good, the devil, again devised intrigues against the saint in order to hinder his Divine preaching.

A certain noble archon from Bogdania, wicked in character and doing much evil, left his homeland to escape the power of his ruler. He abandoned his home, wife, children, and arrived in Wallachia. Having become friends with the voivode Radu, he wished to settle in his realm and marry another woman. Knowing that Bogdan had a wife in his homeland, the voivode scorned the ancestral laws and canons and gave him his own sister in marriage. Learning of this, the lawful wife of Bogdan wrote a letter to the holy Niphon in tears, informing him that he was married and had children. Having received the letter, the saint called the archon and with meekness and humility began to admonish him to leave his lawlessness and return to his lawful wife. However, the wicked and unrepentant Bogdan left the saint with threats and, coming to the voivode, inclined him to anger, demanding that the hierarch be expelled from Wallachia. Not in the least fearing the threats, the divine Niphon came to the palace to the voivode in the morning and first gave him the letter sent by the wife of the archon, and then, having opened the book with the laws of God, he besought him not to despise the decisions of God and the canons of our Church. Having cast off the mask of his former piety, Radu grew angry with the saint and said: "Master, you should not be so severe, but you should have shame and fear before the voivode. I wanted to tell you before that as soon as I brought you here, you trampled on and abolished all our customs and orders, changing them according to your own judgment. Henceforth we no longer wish you to teach us; we do not need your customs and your orders, because we are worldly people and cannot follow you."

Not expecting such a rebuff, the saint answered him: "Most illustrious voivode, did I think that you would say such things to me? Did not your illustriousness together with your archons come to me twice and thrice, and did you not ask me to come here for the benefit of your souls? Show me what bad custom and order I have introduced among you, and what custom of yours I have abolished? Alas! Now I clearly see that a great wrath shall come upon you, and therefore I grieve for your souls. About myself I am not at all concerned, because I place all my boldness in Him Whom from my youth I have desired and still desire. For love of Him I shall joyfully pour out, if necessary, even my own blood. Know then, voivode, that all my strength is the law of the Church, for which my Lord poured out His Most Pure Blood in order to cleanse her from every sin and sanctify her. He desires that she be pure and holy in the doing of the commandments of God, which I wish to fulfill to the end of my life."

With these words Niphon left the palace and, having come to the church, commanded the people to be assembled. Having said a long sermon to them, he put on the hierarchal vestments and excommunicated from the Mysteries of Christ the lawless archon and those who helped him in lawlessness together with that adulteress, for violating the law. Then, having instructed the people further, he predicted what would happen in Wallachia: that Radu and the archon would die an evil death and perish together with their lawlessness. After this the hierarch placed the hierarchal vestments on the altar and, having kissed the holy icons, departed.

Learning of this, Radu issued a decree throughout the entire realm: not to call the saint a hierarch any longer, not to show him any honor or care, and if it became known that anyone had given him bread or anything else, or received him in his house, such a one would lose his life, and his property would go to the state. The saint, so as not to arouse even greater anger, went as far as possible from the capital, where he settled in a small house on the outskirts, placing all his hope in God. And He, the All-merciful, sent him all that was necessary, as in ancient times He sent food to the prophet Elijah through a raven, and to Daniel through Habakkuk. A certain noble youth of the Basarab family named Neagoe, a spiritual child of the saint, seeing that the holy Niphon was in such constraint, was greatly grieved and out of reverence himself secretly, fearing the wrath of the ruler, brought him all that was necessary.

After some time Radu, reflecting on the curse of the saint and fearing lest the wrath of God should suddenly come upon him (for although he was set against the saint, he knew that he was righteous in all things and God-fearing), brought Niphon back to the palace with honors, hoping that by flattery he could obtain forgiveness. He said to him: "Divine and most wise father, forgive us who have sinned against you as men, and your all-holiness shall receive forgiveness from us for what you have said and done against us. We ask you, do not be angry with us for our sins, and we shall give you as much money and clothing as you need, and shall send you with honor wherever you wish. And to wherever you shall live, we shall send all that is necessary. And do not be concerned about the cohabitation of the archon, because he has received forgiveness from the entire Hierarchal Synod of the Church of Constantinople; let your All-holiness also give forgiveness, as is fitting." Sighing from the depths of his soul, the divine Niphon answered: "Radu, I do not need your money, nor your clothing, nor your honors; may that not be. Do you remember how you persuaded me to come to Wallachia, so that I would teach you the word of God? If I have dealt lawlessly with you, testify to it. But I have been appointed by my Lord to denounce lawlessness, and in this lawlessness I never wish to be a participant, because it is not permitted by any law. You yourself brought me here, you yourself also drive me away. I go where the Lord shall lead me. But you shall die in lawlessness, in many sorrows and diseases, and many misfortunes shall occur in your land. Then you will seek me, *and shall not find Me'* (John 7:34)."

With these words the saint departed and, finding his spiritual child Neagoe, said to him in private: "I see, my child, that a great wrath is coming upon this land. You together with your family will be in danger, but the All-merciful God will preserve you from every evil. If you fulfill the commandments that I have given you, you will not only be delivered from every danger but will also be held in great honor, and your name will be heard in all corners of the land. Remember me, your spiritual father, and I, if I find boldness before the Man-loving God, shall entreat Him for you." The saint blessed his child and embraced him, and Neagoe wept, lamenting his coming orphanhood. With his disciples Macarius and Joasaph, Niphon set out for Macedonia, and from there to Ptolais, teaching and strengthening the Orthodox Christians. Then he came to the Holy Mountain, to the sacred Vatopedi monastery, where the fathers there received him with all reverence and joy, glorifying God Who had deemed them worthy to see such a lamp of God and teacher. Learning of his arrival, the Holy

Mountain ascetics constantly came to him for a blessing and attended to his soul-profiting teachings.

His disciple Macarius, imitating the virtues of the saint in all things and struggling in many labors, ascended to such a height of Divine love that his heart was kindled with the desire to end his life in martyrdom. Niphon, to whom he had told of his desire, knew that the aim of Macarius was in accordance with the Divine will, and said: "Go, child, on the path of martyrdom, for according to your zeal you will be deemed worthy to receive the martyr's crown and will eternally rejoice with the martyrs and venerable ones." With these words he blessed him and made the sign of the cross over him. Everything happened according to the prophecy of the saint. Coming to Thessalonica, the truly blessed one boldly appeared before the Ottomans and for preaching Christ was subjected to merciless torments. In the end his head was cut off, and thus he received the martyr's crown. This was revealed to the divine Niphon by the Holy Spirit, and he said to his other disciple, Joasaph: "Know, child, today your brother Macarius has passed away and has gone to Heaven in joy."

After some time Niphon together with Joasaph secretly departed from the Vatopedi monastery and, unrecognized by anyone, came to the monastery of Dionysiou, in which, as they say, the following custom was established by the founder. Anyone who wished to become a monk in the monastery had to work as a muleteer, or carry wood, or perform other obediences for as long as the abbot appointed. Only then was he received into the monastery and tonsured. But if the candidate was already a monk, he was immediately enrolled among the brethren. And so, unrecognized by anyone, Niphon came to the monastery in the guise of a poor monk. When the abbot asked if he agreed to perform all the obediences, Niphon made a prostration and agreed. Just at this time, while he still remained unrecognized, messengers came to the monastery from the Great Church of Christ, who were seeking Niphon in order to elevate him again to the Ecumenical Throne by decree of the sultan. Not finding him, they departed.

Once the holy Niphon was assigned to be at the lookout point on the high mountain opposite the monastery, for at that time pirates suddenly attacked the Holy Mountain, enslaved many, and carried off whatever they could. In the middle of the night, when the saint was standing at prayer at this lookout point, certain virtuous monks who were keeping vigil at night saw a pillar of fire ascending from the earth to heaven. And one of the brethren who was doing his obedience together with the saint, having awakened, saw that the saint was all in fire. Frightened, he ran to the monastery and told of his terrifying vision to the senior elders of the monastery. The other monks told the same thing. Then, having assembled in the church, they began to pray to the holy God that He would reveal to them who this man was who was accompanied by such signs. And the Lord heard their prayer, revealing the secret in the following manner. The abbot of the monastery saw in a dream that he was standing in the middle of the church and saw the divine John the Forerunner, who said: "Gather all the brethren and go out to meet the Patriarch Niphon. That humility which he has shown by becoming a muleteer is sufficient, otherwise you will lose a great priest." Waking up, the abbot was frozen in amazement. Coming to himself after some time, he began to strike the semantron and, having called all the brethren together, related to them the dream he had seen. Only then did they learn that the poor monk was the Patriarch Niphon. When the blessed one, driving the mules, was returning to the monastery in the evening, all the brethren came out to meet him with candles and incense and met him with great solemnity. As soon as the wondrous Niphon saw this procession, he threw himself to the ground and began to pour out tears upon it. Having made a prostration, the abbot kissed his holy hands and said: "It is enough, O ecumenical lamp, to test your patience, enough to bear the extreme torments which you bear of your own will. That humility which you have already shown is sufficient, and we, the wretched, did not even suspect it." And all the brethren wept, and especially those who in their ignorance had grieved him; they fell at his sacred feet and asked forgiveness.

Then with many tears the saint said: "My fathers and brethren, for this reason the Lord hid me in this soul-saving place, as I asked Him, so that I might be delivered from worldly cares and receive mercy at the Dread Judgment, for if we do not renounce parents, relatives, and every human glory and attachment of this world, as He Himself commands us, we shall be unworthy to follow Him. If we gain the whole world but harm our soul, what profit is there in that?" And to those who asked forgiveness, he said: "O my children and brethren! Those who struggle in virtue must have meekness and love toward their neighbor, not be angry at them even if they should suffer a thousand evils from them, for we are all men, and none of us is pure." Having instructed them thus, that they should not do evil to others but without anger and murmuring fulfill each one his own obedience, helping one another as much as possible, he blessed them and embraced them.

Then the saint returned to the monastery, and it is impossible to describe what struggles and labors the blessed one bore. Although Niphon was already old and extremely wearied by dangers and exiles, he served the monastery in all its needs like one of the least monks. With his help many buildings were erected in the monastery, he visited the sick, consoled the sorrowing, and many times, when I (the hieromonk Gabriel) came to him for his soul-profiting teachings, I saw him digging in the garden, helping at the mill, going down to the monastery's harbor when ships arrived, and laboring together with the other novices so that they would not murmur and lose the reward of their labors. But the hater of good, the devil, did not cease warring against the saint, for even in the monastery he found certain monks who, at his instigation, rose up against Niphon, condemned and insulted him, calling him a hypocrite and a talker. By the Providence of God the cunning of Satan was revealed to him, and he asked God to strengthen him to bear all temptations, and to forgive and save the offenders by His love of mankind. In such humility, patience, hardship, and voluntary poverty the ever-blessed one struggled, paying no attention whatsoever to his hierarchal rank and to the fact that he had been Ecumenical Patriarch, but counted all this human glory as nothing.

Once, by the action of the Holy Spirit, he foreknew that the brethren who were transporting provisions for the monastery by ship from the dependencies were threatened by danger from a storm that had broken out. The saint went out to the ship, because it was not far from the monastery, and immediately the storm ceased and a complete calm set in. Falling at his sacred feet, the brethren said:

"Most sacred father, we believe that whatever you ask of God, He will give you. Therefore we ask, pray to the Lord, as one having boldness before Him, that we may continue to sail safely and without loss deliver the provisions to the monastery."

"If you will fulfill your prayer rule, will not give yourselves over to idle talk, will not utter shameful and unworthy words, then the Lord will easily hear you and deliver you from all distresses."

Then, bending his knees, he raised his eyes and hands to Heaven and for a long time prayed secretly. Rising, he blessed the boat-hook that was on the ship three times and said:

"Brethren, always be sure to place this boat-hook in a clean place, and when danger arises, lower it into the sea, and then you will sail in safety."

From that time this miracle occurred every time they were threatened by danger at sea. As soon as a storm arose, reverently invoking the name of the Lord and of the saint, the monks lowered the boat-hook into the sea, after which the sea grew calm. The monks so revered that boat-hook that during the censing at divine services they censed that boat-hook also, imagining that they saw the saint. When a storm arose at sea, the brethren cried out:

"Lower, lower 'the Patriarch' into the sea, so that the storm may cease."

Like a most precious treasure, this boat-hook was preserved in the monastery for more than one hundred fifty years.

Having reached a ripe old age (ninety years) and knowing by revelation from the Lord that the time had come for him to pass over to the Desired Christ, the saint called all the brethren together and told them of his departure, commanding them to strictly fulfill the rules of monastic life and to struggle with all their strength so as to be deemed worthy of the Kingdom of Heaven. All the brethren bitterly lamented their orphanhood. And the two brothers who in their ignorance had formerly reviled him wept inconsolably, asking his forgiveness. Having instructed and consoled them, the saint gave his blessing and said to those standing by: "My brethren, if you have any spiritual request, ask before I commit my spirit to the Lord." And all answered: "All-holy father, give us your prayers in writing; we shall read them at the burial of each monk, so that he may receive remission of sins." Obedient to the end, the saint did not scorn their request but, having prayed to God about it, said with warm tears to his disciple Joasaph: "Child, write down on paper what I say, so that my words may remain as a constant consolation to the brethren."

When Joasaph had written down the absolution prayers, the saint said to him: "I go to the Desired God, and you, child, go to Constantinople and do as I have commanded you. There you will receive the crown of martyrdom and will eternally rejoice in Heaven." Then, having received forgiveness from the brethren, the Patriarch received the Most Pure

Mysteries and gave up his blessed soul into the hands of God. This happened on the eleventh of August. All the brethren wept that they had been deprived of a good shepherd, and all the fathers from the monasteries and sketes who learned of the repose of Niphon hastened to the monastery to kiss his sacred relics. A multitude of people gathered for the funeral, they served an All-Night Vigil, and in the morning, with great solemnity, they committed to the earth the radiant lamp of the world, the adamant of patience, the courageous one in dangers and trials, tested like gold in a furnace, who had endured all things for love of the Lord.

This is how the ever-blessed Niphon lived his life, and in such struggles, combats, and virtues he shone forth in the world. Being Patriarch, he regenerated in Divine Baptism a multitude of Armenians, Jews, and Turks, and by his divine and honey-flowing teachings brought to the Lord a countless number of the saved. He also sent his disciples to God in martyrs' crowns. Thus, the blessed Joasaph after the repose of the saint came to Constantinople and, according to the commandment of the saint, boldly preached the Holy Trinity before the Hagarenes, for which he was given over by them to terrible torments, and, according to the prophecy of the saint, he received the crown of martyrdom.

And now the time has come to tell of what happened in Wallachia, as the divine Niphon had predicted. As soon as the saint departed from there, in the Wallachian Church arose a great confusion and great scandals from the clergy themselves and from the archons. From strong winds there began in the country drought and a terrible famine, and only then did all understand that this was punishment from God for having driven away the saint. Then the voivode Radu sent to search for him in all corners of the earth, but did not find him, as Niphon had predicted.

After the repose of the saint, Radu fell ill with some terrible incurable disease: his entire body was pitted with holes and gave off an unbearable stench, so that no one could approach him. Thus in great torments he passed away and was buried in the monastery of Saint Nicholas, called the Distant, which he himself had built. After his burial, to the horror of those present, the grave shook for three days, as also happened with Empress Eudoxia in the time of John Chrysostom. All were in fear, for they remembered that all this had happened according to the prophecy of the holy Niphon. Danger also befell the good Neagoe, the spiritual son of the hierarch, as he had predicted to him. He was threatened by the tyrant voivodes who ruled after the death of Radu: first Mihnea, and then Vlăduț. But, according to the prophecy of the hierarch, Neagoe by his intercession not only was delivered from all dangers but, at the request of the people, became voivode of all Ungro-Wallachia.

Neagoe, who saw that all the prophecies of his spiritual father had been fulfilled, reflecting on his Divine teachings, was inflamed with love for God and wished to transfer to Wallachia the holy relics of Niphon, so that his country, punished by calamities from God, and he himself might receive a blessing from them. Especially he wished that Radu, whom the saint had cursed, might receive blessing. Thus Neagoe became like Theodosius, who for the sake of his mother Eudoxia transferred from Cucusus the relics of the hierarch John Chrysostom, for to Neagoe the divine Niphon was "the new Chrysostom." The voivode sent the abbots of two monasteries and two archons to the Holy Mountain, to the monastery of Dionysiou, with a letter to the sacred authorities and many gifts.

Coming to the monastery, the messengers delivered the letter to the abbot. When it was read aloud, all the brethren were silent for a long time. Then one of the elders addressed the messengers with these words: "All-honorable fathers, abbots, and pious archons, we can neither disregard the command of the voivode nor stretch out our hands to the tomb of the saint. We, the wretched, cannot bear the loss of such a treasure, which serves as consolation to our monastery. Because as during his life the holy Niphon was our savior and guardian, so now, after his repose, his sacred relics give us great consolation in all the sorrows and hardships that we constantly experience from the impious, and in the other misfortunes to which we are subjected. You see in what a difficult and dangerous place we live, having no other consolation except the holy relics of the hierarch Niphon, who struggled in our monastery. And if you now take them and carry them away to another place, this will cause unprecedented sorrow and suffering to all."

The messengers answered thus:

"Venerable fathers, listen to us and do according to the word of our voivode. Bless the translation of the holy relics and choose two of you who will go together with us. We promise that the voivode will send you great help, will bestow many benefactions on your monastery, and after a little while will return the holy relics."

"We do not dare to dig; do it yourselves, as you wish." Then one of the archons, a great logothete by rank, took a spade and, having crossed himself, said: "By the faith and piety of my sovereign I shall do this, and I trust that by the intercession of the saint I shall suffer no harm." He began to dig, and when he reached the holy relics (O Thine ineffable wonders, O Christ!), an indescribable fragrance spread through the air. Taking the holy relics, the monks placed them in a reliquary and brought them into the church, which was filled with a wondrous aroma. All the brethren assembled and served an All-Night Vigil. This event was heard of in the nearby cells, sketes, and monasteries, and therefore many fathers came to kiss the holy relics with faith and reverence.

Wishing even after his repose to glorify the saint for his extraordinary ascetic labors and privations, Almighty God manifested a miracle. A certain deaf-mute monk came to kiss the holy relics, and as soon as he approached them, a miracle occurred. He began to speak freely and, thanking the Lord and the saint, told of this miracle everywhere. Another brother, blind in both eyes, led by a guide, also came to kiss the relics. Having rubbed his eyes near the holy relics, he regained his sight. The holy Niphon also performed many other miracles, which I omit for the sake of brevity. But even the little that I have described shows what boldness the saint had before God.

After three days, taking the holy relics, the messengers together with several monks of the monastery set out for Wallachia. Having crossed the Danube, they notified the voivode, and he immediately sent out hierarchs, priests, deacons, and monks to meet the relics of the saint. When the holy relics reached Bucharest, the pious voivode himself came out to meet them together with a multitude of people, with candles and incense. Embracing the reliquary, he kissed the holy relics with reverence and tears. Having raised on his shoulders the reliquary with the relics, he together with the other archons brought them to the Distant monastery and placed them on the grave of Radu. They began to serve an All-Night Vigil, fervently praying to the saint to forgive the lawlessness of the unfortunate Radu. In the middle of the night, at the height of the vigil, the voivode Neagoe fell asleep and saw in a dream that the tomb of Radu opened, and from it appeared his completely black body, from all the members of which pus was flowing and an unbearable stench was spreading. Unable to endure it, Neagoe began fervently to entreat the Lord and the holy Niphon to have mercy on the unfortunate Radu. And after some time he saw that water flowed from the reliquary of the saint. Niphon washed with this water the foul-smelling body of Radu, and it became radiant. Then the tomb of Radu closed again. The holy Niphon approached Neagoe and said: "Behold, child, I have heard your prayer. Only I command you, always be at peace with your people and do not forget to send back my relics to the monastery for the consolation of the brethren who are struggling there." Then the saint again lay down in the reliquary. Waking up, the God-loving Neagoe remained in amazement for a long time, reflecting on what he had seen. When he finally came to himself, he said aloud: "Glory to Thee, O Heavenly King, Who hast glorified Thy servant, the beloved holy Niphon, with ineffable glory." The hymns had already concluded, and the voivode told everyone of his dream, and all glorified God. In the morning, when the Divine Liturgy was being celebrated, a multitude of people gathered from the lands bordering Wallachia; they brought with them a countless number of sick people who, kissing the relics of the saint with tears and faith, by prayer to God obtained healing. The lame began to walk, the blind received sight, those tormented by seizures were healed, and almost every disease was driven away from those who turned to the saint with faith.

Since miracles were constantly being performed from the relics of the saint, the voivode convened a Local Council, at which they established the commemoration of the saint on the eleventh of August, the day of his repose, and composed a service to the saint. After this the God-fearing Neagoe commanded that a precious golden reliquary be cast, incrusted with precious stones and adorned with enamel, on the lid of which they placed an image of the saint, and next to it, by command of the voivode, Neagoe kneeling, and in the reliquary they placed the relics of the saint. In Wallachia Neagoe left only the holy head and hand of Niphon, and, with the consent of the fathers, gave them in exchange the all-honorable head of the Forerunner and Baptist of the Lord John, in a golden casket adorned with precious stones, which he sent to the monastery of Dionysiou together with the relics of the holy Niphon. The voivode also rendered great material help to the fathers of the monastery, erecting many buildings in the monastery, where he is unceasingly commemorated as a founder. And the holy head and hand of the divine Niphon the ever-blessed Neagoe during his lifetime always kept with him wherever he went, for sanctification and the repelling of every enemy. After his repose the holy objects were donated to the astonishingly beautiful Argeş monastery, which the voivode himself had built, and where they remain to this day, to the glory of the Father and of the Son and of the Holy Spirit. Amen.

A Brief Life and Ascetic Struggles of Our Venerable and God-bearing Father Nectarius, Who Struggled in the Fifteenth Century on the Holy Mountain Athos, in the Skete of Karyes, in the Cell of the Archangels, Called the Igarion Cell

This divine Nectarius was from a locality now called Betolia. His parents were righteous and pious people. Once the mother of the venerable one, being at the threshing floor, fell asleep and saw in a dream the Most Pure Theotokos, Who commanded her to take her husband and children and depart from that country as quickly as possible and hide somewhere, for the Hagarenes wished to attack their locality and enslave the inhabitants. Upon awakening, she immediately ran home, told her husband what she had seen in the dream and, taking the children, they departed, hiding themselves, as it seemed to them, securely. And indeed, soon the barbarians plundered their country and the surrounding regions. After some time the parents of the divine Nectarius came out of hiding, preserved unharmed by the protection and intercession of the Theotokos, Whom they thanked with all their soul, simultaneously grieving and rejoicing. They grieved on account of the barbarian invasion and the captivity of Christians, which had been permitted to the inhabitants for their sins, and they rejoiced on account of the extraordinary deliverance which they had been deemed worthy of through the intercession of the Theotokos.

By agreement with his wife, the father of the venerable Nectarius, being already of advanced age, taking Nectarius and his second son with him, left the world and all that is in the world, and came to the monastery of the Holy Unmercenaries Cosmas and Damian, which was situated at the foot of the mountain. In monasticism he was named Pachomius. He began to keep stillness there, praying to God, attending to himself and raising his sons in the fear and admonition of the Lord, as the divine Paul commands (Ephesians 6:4).

And so Pachomius lived in the monastery, and God worked such a miracle during the days of his sojourn there. The Christians who lived near the monastery had a custom of giving a portion of the fruits gathered from the land, according to the discretion of each, to the monastery for the maintenance of the monks dwelling therein, so that they might each year celebrate the commemoration of the holy unmercenaries Cosmas and Damian. When the day of their commemoration arrived, the monks and Christians from the nearby villages were solemnly celebrating this feast after the service, when suddenly they ran out of wine. The elder Pachomius lit a candle and together with his children went to wash a vessel. But when he wished to take the vessel in his hands, he discovered—O wonder!—that it was full of fragrant wine. With joy and amazement the elder glorified God, Who glorifies the holy unmercenaries, and for their sake had worked such a miracle.

Now Nicholas, the son of the elder Pachomius, who was later named Nectarius, and of whom we shall now speak, from his very childhood being intelligent and enlightened by God, having seen the miracle that occurred and remembering the dream that his mother had seen (concerning their deliverance from the barbarians through the intercession of the Theotokos), was pierced in his heart with love for God and thirsted to delight in the desired Christ. With fervent feeling he wished to dedicate himself to God, and *"he who seeks finds,"* as the Lord says in the Gospel (Matthew 7:8). Forgetting all things carnal, he went to the Holy Mountain, where he became acquainted with a most virtuous elder by the name of Dionysius, whom everyone called Iagaris. Being the son of a senator and first archon of Constantinople, Dionysius loved our Lord Jesus Christ with all his soul. He left behind riches, glory, nobility of lineage, and all that an earthly man considers happiness, clothed himself in the wretched and poor monastic garments, and went into obedience to the elder Philotheus, simple in speech but most skilled in virtue, and the elder led him along the path of virtue.

To this wondrous Dionysius Iagaris Nicholas cleaved, fervently asking permission to remain. What then did the wondrous Dionysius, that most compassionate and man-loving soul, do—did he reject Nicholas for his ignorance or treat him with contempt on account of his poverty? No, but taking pity on him, the elder acceded to his request and, bringing him to his spiritual father, the elder Philotheus, presented Nicholas. Adorned with the gift of clairvoyance and foreknowledge of the future by the Providence of God, having made a prayer, Philotheus cordially greeted the youth, calling him by name:

"Thou, child Nicholas, son of Pachomius, dost wish to live with us?"

"Whence dost thou know me, honorable father?"

"God, our Father, Who sent thee to us, He revealed thee to me."

Hearing this, Nicholas was moved to compunction and with great reverence and readiness went into obedience to the elder.

Soon the elder clothed him in monastic garments and with the tonsuring of his hair Nicholas cut off all worldly thoughts. Removing from himself his worldly garments, he removed together with them the *"garments of skin"* (Genesis 3:21) received by us as a result of disobedience, and became the monk Nectarius. But the venerable one did not stop at this, as most monks do today, who think that monasticism consists only in putting on the schema and black garments and do not concern themselves with the virtues that monks ought to practice. Nor do they consider that, putting on the angelic monastic schema, it is necessary to observe the canons and strictness of the monastic life, imitating the life of the Angels. But the divine Nectarius did not act thus. Having received the angelic schema, he immediately began with all his strength to struggle in the fulfillment of monastic works, imitating the angelic way of life, subjecting the flesh to the spirit through obedience, cutting off of the will, humility, fasting, unceasing prayer, vigil, and all the other virtues befitting monks.

However the envious devil could not endure this; observing how Nectarius was advancing in the virtues, he began to war against him with thoughts. He endeavored to deprive him of communion with such a virtuous elder, so that afterwards, as one young and deprived of the elder's help, he might cast him into the nets of sin. The vile one knew that as long as the youth remained with the elder, he would not be able to ensnare him, because he was relying on the prayers and fatherly instructions of the elder. But the demon was still unable to ensnare Nectarius through this noetic warfare, because God was protecting the youth. And what then did the all-malicious one devise? He kindled the heart of a fellow brother and disciple of the same elder with envy, and set him against Nectarius to such a degree that he openly cried out: "Either drive Nectarius away, or one of the two must be killed." Hearing this, the elder together with Dionysius Iagaris became greatly frightened and began to persuade him with words from Sacred Scripture and the writings of the holy fathers, that he should cease his envy and malice against Nectarius. Sometimes they calmed the passion of anger with peaceful and gentle words, sometimes they frightened the disciple with the unquenchable fire of torment to which the envious and haters of the brethren shall be subjected, but they achieved nothing and asked Nectarius to withdraw from their community for a time, hoping that this would bring the envious brother to his senses. Having blessed Nectarius, the elders sent him to the then prōtos of the Holy Mountain, Daniel, with whom he was to spend some time, until the Lord would arrange all things. Thus the divine Nectarius came to the prōtos and was received with joy, for he was virtuous and had experience of the monastic life. The prōtos came to love him greatly and continued to teach him the rules of the monastic way of life.

At the time when Nectarius was with the prōtos, Philotheus, who was already a very old man, reposed and departed to the Desired Lord. The wondrous Dionysius Iagaris, being unable to endure the hatred of the brethren from that brother, wished to live together with Nectarius. He invited him also because they were both children of one and the same spiritual father and elder. And they struggled together for a long time, as we have already said. Having found a small monastery which had been consecrated in honor of the Heavenly Bodiless Powers, or Kouphō, they received permission from the prōtos of the Holy Mountain, Daniel, to settle there. The ascetics began to live in this monastery, pleasing God, earning their bread by handiwork, and helping all those in need according to their ability. But that hater of the brethren, remaining unrepentant, wandered about the Holy Mountain like a madman, and then went out into the world. There he led a dissolute and intemperate life and ended it by casting forth his soul on the road, having neither house nor roof over his head, and even without the final prayer that is read over all Christians.

Do you see, brethren, what an evil thing is hatred and disobedience? Hatred and envy blind the eye of the soul, that is, the mind of him who is possessed by them. Disobedience separates a man from the servants and friends of God, deprives him of their help and protection, and casts him like a blind man into the depths of perdition. Let us hate disobedience and hatred with all our strength, if any of us does not wish to be separated from the glory of God. Let us love obedience and love for our brethren, that through them we may be able to delight in the Kingdom of God. This is all.

The blessed Dionysius Iagaris, having lived a praiseworthy and venerable life in all the virtues and especially in humble-mindedness, in extreme old age departed to the Desired God. The divine Nectarius buried his remains with reverence and honors. From that time he abode in deep sorrow, for he no longer had communion with the ever-blessed Dionysius, and grieved that he himself had not departed to the Desired Christ together with the wondrous Philotheus and the blessed Dionysius, and being on earth, was deprived of the possibility of delighting in communion with them. Nectarius, according to the Apostle, *"forgetting those things which are behind and reaching forward"* (Philippians 3:13), did not consider his own ascetic struggles and virtues to be perfect, but strove to achieve more. The ascetic constantly ascended from strength to strength, adding desire to desire and ascetic struggles to ascetic struggles. Therefore, seeing his intentions, God did not despise the venerable one, but wishing to give him a greater crown in Heaven, permitted him to fall into many terrible bodily illnesses, which the blessed one endured with extreme magnanimity and thanksgiving. Having lived a life truly venerable and worthy of the saints, he was deemed worthy of a peaceful and God-pleasing end, committing his blessed soul into the hands of God in the year 1500 from the Birth of Christ, on the fifth day of the month of December, and was numbered in Heaven with his beloved venerable fathers Philotheus and Dionysius. His disciples buried him with all reverence, and after four years his holy relics were uncovered, from which there came forth an ineffable fragrance. In the northern part of the church, in a beautiful tomb, with reverence and honors they placed his most honorable relics. The saint's countenance was depicted on an icon, which was placed above the relics. Many who came here with reverence sensed the spiritual fragrance from the holy relics, and received sanctification of soul and body, to the glory of Christ our Lord and as proof of the God-pleasing life of the venerable Nectarius, through whose prayers may we also be deemed worthy of the Heavenly Kingdom. Amen.

The Martyrdom of the Holy
New Martyrs Gabriel and Kirmidolos,
Who Accomplished Their Struggle in Egypt in 1522

These holy new martyrs were born in Egypt; their parents were Christians and gave them a good upbringing. Gabriel and Kirmidolos were martyred in their homeland during the time of Sultan Suleiman, son of Osman. This is how it happened.

In those days the ruler of Egypt was a certain Emir Khaer Mek. The impious came to him and slandered the holy martyrs, reporting: "There are here two Christian youths, and not only are they of a different faith, but they also do us much harm; since their houses are located next to the mosque, they throw garbage into it, pour out dirty water and other filth. None of us can make any remark to them, because they are secretaries of great officials. They act in this manner every day, and we, unable to bear this disgrace, have come to you with a complaint, and you do as you please." These vile and impious ones spoke thus out of envy, because the youths were of noble birth, had succeeded in many endeavors, and were worthy secretaries. They were capable by nature, well educated, and raised by their parents in good manners, and therefore they were envied and slandered before the terrible ruler.

Upon hearing the complaint, the emir immediately sent soldiers, who arrested the youths and brought them to him. Seeing how handsome and young the youths were, the emir began to flatter them with gentle words and question them about their faith. The youths freely and with great boldness told him that they were Christians and believed in our Lord Jesus Christ. Finding that they would not yield to persuasion to change their faith, the emir commanded the soldiers to lead them to the judges. Dragging them like evildoers, cruelly insulting them and beating them inhumanly, the soldiers brought them to the judges. These again questioned them about their faith, and they, without fear, with joyful faces, firmly answered them the same things as they had the emir. The Hagarenes, who had gathered at the trial in great numbers, for they wished to learn the outcome of the matter, upon hearing their words, grew angry, and all as one cried out that the martyrs should renounce their faith in Christ and accept Islam. But the youths answered with great fearlessness: "We received our Christian faith from our ancestors, and we shall not renounce it, but shall remain with it to the end. Your faith we despise and abhor, for it is false and vain." Upon hearing this, the judges grew angry and said: "If you do what you are commanded, then you will escape many torments and save your lives, and you will be honored with great honors and glory. But if you do not accept our faith, you will be put to a painful death." During this tribunal, while the judges were speaking, the mother of Saint Kirmidolos came to see and comfort her son, who was undergoing such danger, but as soon as the Hagarenes saw her, they fell upon her like wild beasts, beat her cruelly, tore her garments, and drove her out of the tribunal.

Seeing this, the blessed Gabriel stood in their midst and declared: "O unrighteous and lawless judges! Nothing shall separate us from the love and faith of Christ—neither riches, nor glory, nor love for parents, nor torments, nor even a terrible and painful death. Here is our neck, and do with us what you will." In like manner Kirmidolos also answered: "I too agree with my companion and am ready to die for my Christ." Then one of the Hagarenes standing by, angered by the martyr for these words, struck him with a sword in the chest and threw him to the ground. Another Moor, rushing upon him with fury, struck him in the chest with his feet with all his might, from which the youth became half-dead. A third, taking up a huge stone, struck the martyr on the head, splitting it in two. But even with this the inhumane ones were not satisfied. One of them ran up and tore out the youth's eyes with his fingers. Thus the ever-memorable Kirmidolos was counted worthy of a blessed end and received the crown of martyrdom from Christ the Bestower of crowns. The blessed Gabriel was thrown to the ground by one of the soldiers who, striking him with a sword, cut off his right shoulder, and then his honorable head as well. Thus the ever-blessed Gabriel also received the crown of martyrdom.

After the martyrs had been so cruelly and inhumanly put to death, ropes were tied to their feet, and the bodies, by order of the judges, were dragged to a place called Khimet Ilguman, that is, to the soldiers' tents. Having built a great fire, they threw the bodies of the martyrs into it. Two days passed, but the bodies did not burn. Then the lawless ones built an even larger fire, added wood, poured on oil, and again placed the relics of the holy martyrs into the fire. After the fire went out and the ashes cooled, the Hagarene slaves collected what remained of the bones of the holy martyrs and sold them to Christians. The holy head of the martyr Gabriel was first secretly taken by one of the soldiers and sold to a certain Christian Elias, a goldsmith, the son of Muphra. Having taken the head, Elias gave it to Joachim, the most blessed Patriarch of Alexandria. Everyone who bought a particle of the holy relics of the martyrs gave them to the Patriarch. Having collected with reverence all the particles of the relics, he anointed them with fragrant spices and placed them in a reliquary, keeping it in his cell. After many days the Patriarch took the reliquary and, with many candles, hymns, and chanting, transferred it and placed it in the temple of our father among the saints, Nicholas. There the relics remain to this day, working wondrous miracles by Divine grace for those who come to them with faith and reverence and kiss them. These saints were about twenty years old when they endured their martyrdom. This good struggle in the name of Christ they accomplished on the eighteenth day of the month of October. Through their prayers, may God have mercy on us and save us, for He is good and the Lover of mankind. Amen.

The Life and Struggles of Our
Venerable and God-Bearing Father Hierotheos

This blessed Hierotheos, who shone forth in ascetic struggle like another Elijah, was born in 1686 from the Nativity of Christ in one of the villages of Kalamata, in the region of the Morea, to pious and wealthy parents, Dimos and Asimina. While he was still in his mother's womb, she asked a certain virtuous ascetic who was then in their village, whom everyone revered as a saint and a prophet: "What will be born to me?" He answered: "Go home; you will bear a good son, pleasing to God."

When the boy had passed beyond infancy and reached seven years of age, his parents sent him to school. In a short time, to the amazement of those around him, he mastered the entire cycle of general ecclesiastical studies, so that he could read and understand any book that came into his hands. Having from the beginning a mature mind and firm will, he did not give himself over to childish games like other children. His heart burned with love for learning; he thought about it alone day and night, believing that with its help he would easily understand Holy Scripture. He had heard that the holy fathers of our Church, especially Basil the Great and Gregory the Theologian, urge young people to study the sciences.

While still in Kalamata, he sufficiently learned ancient Greek and Latin, because Latin is no less useful for all knowledge than Greek. In his studies he was greatly helped, along with zeal and fervor, by sharpness of mind, memory, and the capacity for reasoning, that is, those natural gifts which, combined with diligence, contribute to the greater advancement of one who possesses them.

The venerable one was progressing in his studies, but his parents wanted to marry him off, wishing to see him happy in this life. Many, when they marry off their children, think they will be happy having a wife, children, and other worldly goods, but the vain do not know that it is better to encourage them toward virginity, which is freedom and greater happiness than marriage, which is bondage. As the Apostle says, those who are married *"will have trouble in the flesh,"* that is, sorrows and misfortunes (1 Corinthians 7:28).

Being occupied with these concerns, the parents were arranging a marriage through betrothal. But the blessed Hierotheos grieved and was indignant, because the engagement had taken place against his will. However, he submitted to his parents' command, according to the precept of Scripture: *"Children, obey your parents in all things, for this is well pleasing to the Lord"* (Colossians 3:20), but at the same time he did not cease to ask God from all his heart, and His Providence, to prevent the marriage, so that he might remain a virgin his whole life and have time to freely devote himself to learning.

Seeing the piety that the divine Hierotheos had toward God from his youth, the Lord fulfilled his desire, for *"He will fulfill the desire of those who fear Him"* (Psalm 144:19). Sixteen days after the betrothal, the Lord took both parents to the other life, not because He desired their death, but because such a decision was just for His inscrutable judgments. In precisely this way the saint was able to preserve his virginity and advance in learning. So as not to give reason for suspicion to the parents of the girl betrothed to him that he wished to leave, and so that they would not hinder him, the venerable one left the doors of his house open and set off for the island of Zakynthos, taking nothing of his property with him. He stayed there briefly, devoting all his time to learning, and then wealthy relatives living on that same island offered to send him at their expense to the West to study philosophy. But the ever-blessed Hierotheos, having learned that on the Holy Mountain there were men who, like bees, produced the honey of virtues, preferred to go there to taste this honey, prudently reasoning that if afterward in the West he should encounter some bitterness, either in regard to dogmas or to morals, he would be able to overcome it with the sweetness of virtues.

Coming to the Holy Mountain, Hierotheos settled with a certain hermit in the cell of Saint Artemius, where in stillness he diligently devoted himself to reading Holy Scripture and the lives of the venerable fathers. Having become convinced from them that hermits, even after twenty, forty, and even sixty years spent in desert asceticism, are deceived by the devil, he began to seek another path for the salvation of the soul, shorter and safer, but he could think of nothing except martyrdom for Christ. But martyrdom too must be according to rank and according to law; one cannot simply go thoughtlessly and give up one's life, as if reviling the impious and thus requesting death for oneself. Even the divine Paul opposes such martyrdom, saying: *"And also if anyone competes in athletics, he is not crowned unless he competes according to the rules"* (2 Timothy 2:5). The cause of martyrdom must come from the impious themselves; only then will it be lawful suffering for Christ. After these reflections, the blessed one came to the Iveron Monastery, was clothed there in the riassa, and, accompanying the abbot of the monastery, came with him to the capital. There were other brethren among the companions as well. The venerable one thought that, seeing a Christian monk in the city, the heterodox would find a pretext to beat and revile him, and he would resist reasonably so as to bring his martyrdom to completion. He often prayed about this, desiring to know whether it was the Lord's will that his aim be crowned with a good result. Hierotheos spent a considerable time among the impious. But while his fellow companions were reviled and beaten by the opponents of the faith, he was not touched at all, although he often gave some cause for abuse. Apparently, Divine Providence was preserving him for the benefit of many others. Seeing that his desire was not being fulfilled, Hierotheos once left the city with great sorrow in his heart and headed with his companions toward the northern regions of the country. From there he returned to Wallachia and began to study under Mark of Cyprus, the teacher of the school there, where he was also ordained a deacon by Metropolitan Auxentius of Sophia. Some time later, Hierotheos returned to Constantinople and was taught the philosophical sciences by Iakoumis of Argos, the teacher of the local school. However, the venerable one was not satisfied with these sciences and set off for Venice, having learned that there they taught more than what he had already learned, and with the help of studying new sciences he would be able to bring forth greater fruit. Then Hierotheos returned again to the Holy Mountain, already having mastered many sciences and philosophy, and settled in the Iveron Monastery, in the cell of Chagi, the first stage of his initial struggles. The venerable one leaves the external school and comes to the spiritual one, where one can easily learn the true art of arts and science of sciences: advancement according to God, the all-desired virtue. And immediately, with the help of spiritual discernment, which he constantly studied from the Holy Scriptures, the venerable one began to examine what he had learned, casting aside the useless and gathering the useful into his spiritual storehouses. Thus he began with joy to devote himself to meditations upon God.

Knowing that for the purification of the mind by such meditations and its elevation to Heavenly contemplations, it is necessary to exercise oneself in other virtues as well, both bodily and spiritual, the venerable one began to struggle with great diligence in the strictest fasting, vigil, and prayer, for which he was deemed worthy of the divine gift of the priesthood at the age of thirty from the Metropolitan of Neocaesarea, Jacob, who was then laboring in that same Iveron Monastery. After this, the venerable one continued to add struggles to struggles and sweat to sweat, striving to become *"an example to the believers in word, in conduct, in love, in spirit, in faith, in purity"* (1 Timothy 4:12). Knowing that fasting is the foundation of all virtues, and that the Lord blesses *"those who hunger now, for they shall be filled"* (Luke 6:21), that is, voluntary hunger or involuntary hunger borne with thanksgiving, the saint sometimes ate his barley bread, and that without salt, once in two or three, and sometimes even four days. At other times, instead of bread, he ate beans so rotten that with great difficulty he forced himself to swallow them. Once, when he was reproached by his disciple Meletius, who considered him a suicide, he said: "No, a suicide is one who eats nothing and dies of hunger, but I give it (that is, the belly) food, whether it likes it or not." The venerable one always collected crumbs from the table, moistened them with water or wine, put them in a bag, and kept them until they dried out and began to give off an unpleasant smell. Only then did he eat them. Very often he ate what is usually used to grease baking utensils and then thrown away. With this he consoled himself after a many-day fast. During Great Lent, he ate once a week, trying to surpass the ancient ascetics themselves, and reached the point where for fifteen days he ate absolutely nothing. If he had to eat together with others, he ate everything that a monk is permitted to eat, so that others would not see his virtue, and to humble his pride, according to the Venerable John of the Ladder. But even on these rare occasions, Hierotheos ate very moderately. He slept just as moderately, following the words of Arsenius the Great: "One hour of sleep a day is sufficient for a monk. If he is an ascetic, let him exercise in these two virtues so that he may easily, as if on wings, ascend to other, higher virtues." When sleep overpowered the ascetic very strongly, he walked around the monastery and prayed with tears and sighing: "Lord Jesus Christ, Son of God, have mercy on me." Such was the occupation of the ever-blessed one, and he strove, if it was possible and there was no hindrance from people, not to leave this prayer either with his mind or with his lips.

From his excessive ascetic labors, Hierotheos came into such weakness that he traversed the distance from the shore to the monastery with two or three stops, although the path was short and the road level. Thanks to his labors, the venerable one also attained blessed weeping and joy-creating tears, which elevate one to the height of humility and contempt for oneself. At the end of his life, he also came to know God-imitating love and no longer feared losing it, according to the Apostle: *"love never fails"* (1 Corinthians 13:8). Therefore, if any poor person asked Hierotheos for alms, he, having neither gold nor silver, would take off his clothing and give it away. Sometimes he gave a poor person even his night blanket. When they learned of this in the monastery, they gave him another, but he gave that one away again. Because of this love, he agreed to the persistent requests of the Skopelites, to whose island he had crossed along with many other monks because of an epidemic of terrible plague. Having lived on the island for eight years, he taught various subjects in the schools, preached in the churches, heard confessions, and thus fulfilled in deed the prophetic saying: *"The mouth of the righteous speaks wisdom, and his tongue talks of justice"* (Psalm 36:30).

From bodily and spiritual virtues, he was elevated to Heavenly contemplation, not wishing to know anything about earthly things. Constantly illumined by immaterial visions, the venerable one rejoiced with inexpressible joy and, contemplating divine beauty, became Divine by grace, although he was still in the body. Noetic contemplation of God and the Jesus Prayer alternated in him with the study of Holy Scripture. When the venerable one ceased to occupy himself with this as well, he gave lessons or delivered moral instruction, seasoned with salt. However, after some time, desiring to enjoy profound stillness and to give himself over to Divine contemplations in order to unite more fully with God (or perhaps foreseeing his approaching end) and to escape human glory, the venerable one, together with one of his beloved disciples, the hieromonk Meletius, who was himself very virtuous and as it were reflected the struggles of the blessed one, Saint Hierotheos set off for the completely deserted island of Yura. This island had always served emperors as a convenient place of exile. Having spent a short time here in ascetic struggle together with two other brethren, the venerable one became ill and after several days, on the thirteenth of September 1745, left this temporal life and passed on to the eternal one, having lived on earth fifty-nine years. He departed to that joyful Glory and Light for the sake of which he had undertaken here excessive labors and struggles, and left the brethren who were with him, especially the aforementioned Meletius, in boundless sorrow. After Meletius buried the venerable one, he again returned to the Iveron Monastery and appeared again on the island only for the translation of the relics of the venerable one. The holy relics of Hierotheos poured forth Divine grace. Meletius took the precious head with the jaw and brought them to the Iveron Monastery, where they are kept to this day and venerated. The saint not only during his life was deemed worthy to receive from Christ the power of wonderworking, but even after death from his relics there issues ineffable fragrance and miracles occur, of some of which two hierodeacons and one layman were witnesses. They came to the Iveron Monastery to the most honorable Meletius, the disciple of the venerable one, and asked him to bring out for their veneration the precious head of the ever-blessed elder. When Meletius took the head out of the reliquary, a wondrous miracle occurred: the whole cell was filled with such a fine and pleasant fragrance that it became clear this was a gift of Heaven. Those who had come were amazed, because they had never before perceived such a wondrous aroma, and they told of it everywhere. Further I shall give only a small testimony of the grace that the venerable one received.

In his youth, when the venerable one was struggling the good struggle, a certain censorious monk, envying his chastity, condemned him, and immediately experienced upon himself the Divine wrath. By the judgments of God, both his body and his lips swelled, for thus are punished *"lying lips which speak insolent things proudly against the righteous"* (Psalm 30:18)! Moreover, his lips swelled so greatly that his acquaintances could neither place food in his mouth nor pour in any drink. Having pried open his mouth with the help of a knife, they poured a little juice into his mouth; by this he lived until the guileless venerable one, whom no one had called, appeared to him of his own accord and, having prayed to the Lord, healed him. The same thing happened to another monk who had likewise slandered the saint, and punishment befell him, and he received the same healing through the prayers of the venerable one.

After the death of the saint, a certain Kallinikos, a monk of the Iveron Monastery, was in Constantinople; he had with him a portion of the holy relics of the venerable one. At that time, a certain woman became ill: her eyes filled with bile, her vision deteriorated, and the unfortunate woman experienced terrible pain. The monk healed her in a wondrous manner with the help of these relics, through prayers to the Lord, and she began to glorify God and thank the venerable one, for before this she had spent much money on physicians without any benefit.

Another woman lay bedridden for three years, tormented by pain. That same Kallinikos, with the help of the relics, freed her from these pains and raised her from her bed.

A certain infant cried unceasingly and gnashed his teeth for an entire year. He likewise received healing from the relics, through prayers to the Lord.

And on the Holy Mountain of Athos, with the help of the holy relics, some were healed of bodily illnesses, and others were freed from toothache. Such is the power of the prayer of a righteous man, especially after death, for he prays to the Lord with greater boldness for those who call upon him with faith.

Such, brethren, is the life of our venerable father Hierotheos. Thus he struggled, thus he labored, and thus he conquered, so that he too can say boldly together with the Apostle Paul: *"I have fought the good fight, I have finished the race, I have kept the faith. Finally, there is laid up for me the crown of righteousness, which the Lord, the righteous Judge, will give to me on that Day"* (2 Timothy 4:7–8). For he too, by his own free choice, became a bloodless martyr who gave himself for Christ, and as a venerable one he endured many sufferings and hardships, truly becoming an example for imitation in virtue for all, as the Lord also commands: *"Let your light so shine before men, that they may see your good works and glorify your Father in heaven"* (Matthew 5:16). The Venerable Hierotheos truly honored in his times God Himself, the Orthodox people, his homeland, and his monastery. The negligent lovers of the flesh cannot now say that those times have already passed when there were saints to whom God gave His grace and who piously struggled against sin, even unto blood.

O most divine father, just as throughout your life you cared more for the benefit of the brethren than for your own, so now, standing before the Throne of God, intercede, we beseech, to the Lord for us sinners, who still journey upon this stormy sea of life, who are still troubled by this earthly marketplace, who still contend upon this dangerous noetic arena. Intercede to the Lord that we may reach the peaceful harbor, that this trading may end in success and gain, that we may conquer our invisible enemies and worthily receive the crown of victory from Christ, the Founder of the struggle, and that we may glorify you with an annual celebration on the day of your memory, and to the God Who is One in Trinity may we ceaselessly offer services and thanksgivings, to Whom belongs all glory, dominion, and praise unto the ages. Amen.

A Remarkable Narrative Concerning a Miracle Performed by Saint George, and Concerning the Saracen Who Beheld a Vision in His Church

Once the emir of Syria sent his nephew on business to the city of Diospolis, which the Saracens call Rebli. In this city there is a temple of Saint George, wondrous in beauty. Seeing the temple from afar, the Saracen ordered his servants to carry his belongings into the narthex of the temple, where he decided to stay, and to lead his twelve camels there as well. The priests who served in this temple asked him not to commit this vile act. However, the envoy with threats ordered the animals to be led inside, but as soon as the camels were led into the temple, they immediately fell down and died. Seeing such a sign, the nephew of the emir marveled at the great power of Saint George and ordered the bodies of the camels to be carried out of the temple.

On the next day, when the priest came to the temple to serve, the Saracen from the narthex wanted to observe what he would do. But our God, the Lover of mankind, opened the noetic eyes of the Saracen and showed him a dread vision. At the moment when the priest was performing the Proskomedia, the Saracen saw that he "slew" a small child, poured the blood into the holy Chalice, cut the body into pieces, and placed them on the holy diskos. And then, during Communion, the unbeliever saw how the priest gave the people the flesh and blood of the infant, and he was amazed. Upon the completion of the Divine Liturgy, the priest brought the best prosphoras as a gift to the Saracen. He asked what this was, and the priest answered: "My lord, these are prosphoras, on which we serve in our church." Then the Saracen exclaimed with anger: "Was it on these that you served today? Did I not see how you slew a child, poured his blood into the cup, cut his body into pieces and placed them on the diskos, and then gave them to the people? Did I not see all that you did, foul murderer?"

Hearing these words, the priest trembled and, falling at the feet of the Saracen, said:

"May the Lord be glorified, Who has deemed you worthy, my lord, to see this dread Mystery. I believe in my God that you are a great man, and you are numbered among the saved before Him."

Amazed at the words of the priest, the Saracen answered:

"Was it not all as I saw it?"

"Yes, my lord, it is so, and we believe that the bread and wine which we prepare at the Liturgy are the Body and Blood of our Lord Jesus Christ, the Son of God. But to behold this vision I have never been deemed worthy, because I am a sinner, and I see before me only bread and wine. Since, however, my Lord and God has deemed you worthy, my lord, to see this Mystery, I believe that you are a great man, for only great fathers of our Church, being in the highest degree worthy, have seen this wondrous Mystery."

Hearing this and being greatly amazed, the Saracen pondered for a long time, and then, as if rising from sleep, he came to himself and ordered his servants to go out, saying to the priest:

"As I see and am assured, the Christian faith is true. Woe to me, who have spent my life in the false and vain faith of the Saracens, which is truly impure. But since God desires that I be saved, baptize me, that henceforth I may serve God with a pure conscience."

"My lord, I do not dare to baptize you, because your uncle is a king, and if he learns that I have baptized you, he will kill me and destroy our churches. If you wish, depart from here secretly and go so that no one recognizes you, to the Patriarch of Jerusalem, and he will baptize you."

After these words, the Saracen found a hair shirt, put it on, and secretly departed by night. Coming to the Patriarch of Jerusalem, he fell at his feet and asked him to baptize him. After Baptism, on the eighth day, the former Saracen again came to the Patriarch and said:

"Behold, by the grace of God I have become a Christian. What must I do to be saved?"

"If you wish to be saved, go to Mount Sinai, where pious and virtuous monks dwell, become a monk, and keep the commandments of God."

Coming to Sinai and receiving the tonsure, he lived there for three years, attaining a great measure of virtues, after which he began to ask the abbot to release him to go to Rebli. Having received permission, he came to the city, to the temple of Saint George, and met with that God-fearing priest whom we mentioned earlier. He revealed to him who he was and said:

"Behold, by Divine grace and your favorable prayers I have become a Christian and a monk, but I have a strong desire to see the Lord Jesus Christ, therefore I fervently ask you, fulfill my desire."

Glorifying God, the priest answered:

"Go to your uncle the emir and before him and all the Saracens confess that our Lord Jesus Christ is the Son of God and God, the Creator of all Creation, that He became man and performed wondrous miracles, was crucified, and buried, and rose on the third day, and with glory ascended into Heaven. Having done so, you will be able to behold the Lord with boldness."

After this, that ever-blessed monk, having obeyed the divine words of the pious priest, set out for that land where his uncle lived. By night he ascended the minaret of the mosque and began to cry out in a loud voice: "Run here, Saracens, I want to tell you something." Hearing the call, they came running with candles and, having discovered a monk, asked what he wanted to tell them. The monk answered them: "What will you give me if I tell you where the nephew of the emir, who secretly departed, is to be found?" They promised him as much money as he himself would want. And then the monk said: "Take me to the emir; I myself will tell him." They gladly led him to the emir, explaining: "This monk knows where your nephew is." The emir asked him whether it was true that he knew the place where his nephew was, and the monk answered: "Yes, I know, because I am your nephew, but now I am a Christian, and I believe in the Father and the Son and the Holy Spirit, One Godhead, and I confess that the Son of God was incarnate of the Ever-Virgin Mary and performed great miracles in the world, and was crucified, and on the third day rose, and ascended into Heaven, and sat down at the right hand of God the Father, and shall come again to judge the living and the dead."

Hearing these words, his uncle the emir asked with amazement: "What has happened to you, wretched one, why have you left your home, riches, glory, and wander about in disgrace like a beggar? Why do you not wish to return to your faith and confess Muhammad as a prophet, and come to your former state?" The monk answered this: "All that I had then, when I was a Saracen, all was from the devil. But this hair shirt which I now wear is my boast, and wealth, and the betrothal of glory which I shall enjoy for my true faith in my Christ. But Muhammad, who has deceived you, and his faith, I curse and abhor." Taking pity on him, the emir said to the Saracens who were with him: "He has lost his mind and does not know what he is saying. Lead him out and drive him away." But they objected to him: "Do you want to release one who has cursed our prophet and our faith, and who is worthy of a thousand deaths? What, should we also renounce our faith and become Christians?"

Fearing that they would rebel against him, the emir allowed them to do with his nephew whatever they wished. Gnashing their teeth, they seized this blessed monk, led him outside the city, and stoned him, while he called upon the name of our Lord Jesus Christ. Thus the ever-blessed one died in a good confession and immediately, having gone with boldness to the Lord Whom he had so desired, received the crown of martyrdom. But for a long time still, every night above the pile of those stones there shone a bright star, illuminating the place of martyrdom. Seeing this, the Saracens marveled. After a long time had passed, the emir finally permitted the Christians to remove the holy relics of the martyr from beneath the stones. And, O miracle, his body was found completely whole and incorrupt, and emitted a strong fragrance. Having reverently venerated it, the Christians buried the martyr with hymns and psalmody, glorifying our Lord Jesus Christ, to Whom be glory and dominion unto the ages. Amen.

A Spiritually Beneficial Narrative of Abba Elpidius

A certain monk named Elpidius, while keeping stillness in his cell, was warred against by the sin of negligence and carelessness. And since the warfare of carelessness had overcome him for a long time, he left his cell and set out for the inner desert, called the Elos Desert. Along the way he met a very aged hermit, completely naked, who, seeing Elpidius, ran from him. The monk Elpidius chased after the hermit and asked him to stop. The hermit stood still and, according to custom, offered a prayer, and then asked Elpidius:

"Who are you, brother, and how did you come here?"

"I was warred against by the sin of carelessness and went into the desert so that the sin might depart from me. I wished to find some servant of God who might entreat God on my behalf. And behold, the Lord has looked past my sins and sent me your holiness. I beg you, father, for the Lord's sake, entreat God for me, a sinner, and allow me to live with you."

Embracing me and praying to God on my behalf, the hermit said:

"To live with me in the desert, child, is impossible, for this has not been given to you by God."

"Tell me, father, for the Lord's sake, how you came here to the desert, how many years you have lived here, and what gift God has given you?"

"I came here almost seventy years ago, because I am a sinner and desired to be saved, and since that time, until this day, I have not seen a human face here. Several years ago, through the working of the hater of good, I became exalted, thinking that I had attained a great measure of virtues, having surpassed all the desert fathers. However, by God's Providence, a thought came to me to ask God to reveal to me with whom He would number me in His Kingdom, and whether there is anyone on earth like me in virtue. I prayed to God with my whole soul for seven days in a row, and on the eighth day there came to me a voice that said I would be numbered with Sergius of Alexandria, a keeper of a brothel. Hearing this, I was greatly grieved and thought: 'Woe to you, humble Pyrrhus. Behold, you have labored for God in such hardships for so many years, yet you will be numbered with a keeper of a brothel.' In my exaltation I thought that this voice was not from God, but from the enemy, and therefore I did not believe it. I began to pray to God for another seven days, and on the eighth, in like manner, I heard the voice: 'I shall number you with Sergius.' Then I said to myself: 'Since it pleases God to number me with Sergius, I shall not die until I see who this Sergius is.' At once I set out for Alexandria and began to seek Sergius, whom I found sitting in a tavern. He was playing with harlots and feasting, because he was their master. Then I said to him: 'Brother, I very much wish that you show me love, and that we eat together.' He answered: 'As it pleases you, abba, let us eat. Sit down.' He at once ordered the tavern-keeper to bring their usual food, and I was compelled to eat all this after so many years of abstinence in the desert. After the meal we both went out of the tavern, and I asked him if he had a house. He answered that he did. Then I said: 'Let us go to your house, because I must tell you something.' When we came to his house, I offered a prayer and said: 'Brother, for the Lord's sake, tell me what good you have done in your life?' Marveling at the question, he answered: 'Man of God, you found me in a tavern with harlots, over whom I am master, and still wish, as you say, to know how I live? What good could I possibly do?' Since I pressed and adjured him even more, telling him of the voice that came from Heaven, I compelled him to tell of his virtues. Marveling at God's love for mankind and sighing deeply from his heart, he began his story: 'I remember how, one day, entering the tavern, I saw a woman of wondrous beauty sitting at her work: she was sewing for sale. I greatly desired her and asked the tavern-keeper's wife to go and tell her that I wished to sleep with her. The tavern-keeper's wife answered me: "I cannot tell her this, because she is of very noble birth, and has come to such a condition because the governor of this city put her husband in prison, for he owed him a hundred coins, and took his two children into slavery. So she works day and night like a slave, to free them." I again proposed to the tavern-keeper's wife: "Tell her that if she agrees to sleep with me, I shall give her a hundred coins." The tavern-keeper's wife objected: "I cannot tell her such a thing, because she is very chaste and will not agree to sin." Since I continued to press her greatly, she nonetheless told the noblewoman of my proposal. Groaning from the depths of her heart, the noblewoman answered the tavern-keeper's wife with weeping: "For so many years I have worked day and night to free three beloved ones, but I cannot. I shall have to agree to what you propose to me, and may God the Lover of mankind forgive me this sin, which I commit against my will, for He knows that until now I have known no other man." The tavern-keeper's wife came to me and said that the beauty had agreed. Then I brought a hundred coins and gave them to her. With groaning and weeping she entered the bedchamber with me, saying: "Lord, Thou knowest my sorrow, forgive me." At these words of hers I was wounded in my very heart and said to myself: "If this poor woman so grieves over this sin, then why should I not lie with one of those harlots over whom I have charge, and with a harlot satisfy my lust, and leave this woman untouched, for there will be no difference for me in this lawless deed." So I released her, and she at once went to the governor, gave him the hundred coins, and freed her husband and children.

Hearing this account from Sergius, I glorified God and said:

"Brother, truly it is just that I be numbered with you in the Kingdom of Heaven."

Again sighing deeply, Sergius answered:

"If it truly pleased the good God what I did, as you say, and you, father, have come to me, a sinner, from God to learn how I live, then I have remembered another good deed, perhaps even better than this one.

Once there came to our city a foreign ruler, debauched and sin-loving. Every day he took from me two or three harlots. One day, visiting a women's monastery, he saw beautiful sisters who were nuns. Desiring them, he ordered his soldiers to surround the convent and, entering it, he counted all the sisters, who numbered seventy. Handing them over to me, he said: 'Behold, I give them to you, do with them what you will, but each day you shall send me as many maidens as I ask of you, until I have slept with all seventy.' Sighing from the depths of my heart, I thought: 'Woe to me, a sinner; for so many years these sisters have kept their virginity for God, exhausting their bodies with fasting, vigils, and other ascetic labors, so as to stand before God pure and undefiled, and now, because of me, these unfortunate ones will be defiled by this impious ruler and lose their ascetic struggle. May it not be that I should consent to such impiety and betray so many pure souls to destruction!' I began to ask God to enlighten me and show me a way by which they might be delivered from such defilement. And God the Lover of mankind put a good thought in me: I went to the harlots over whom I had charge, gave them much of my possessions, persuaded them at length to put on monastic garments, and then brought them to that monastery. The sisters at that time hid in another place. And so each day I sent to that pitiful ruler those harlots of mine, until he had slept with seventy. Later that debauched ruler left the city, and I brought the sisters to the monastery and wished to lead the harlots out of it, but they did not wish to leave, saying: 'Since God has deemed us worthy to put on this holy monastic schema, may it not be that we should return again to our former impurity.' Thus those harlots remained in the monastery to lead a life pleasing to God, in true and perfect repentance."

Hearing such an account, I glorified God even more and said to Sergius: "I have now come to know, brother, that you are not only equal to me, but higher than me, and therefore, I ask you, bless me for my journey." Sergius answered: "What are you saying? That I should bless you to leave? Since you said that we shall be together in the Kingdom of Heaven, I shall no longer be parted from you on this earth, but shall go with you, in the name of my Lord Jesus Christ." Asking me to wait for him one day, he distributed his remaining possessions to the poor and followed me. Having lived with me for three years, he severely afflicted himself, laboring for the Lord with great zeal, and four days ago he reposed in the Lord. I think, child Elpidius, that you have come here by God's dispensation, so that I might tell you this. And now go to your cell, and in three days, I ask you, come here again, because I must tell you something." Returning to my cell, I returned after three days and found that Abba Pyrrhus had reposed. As I had been commanded, I buried him next to Abba Sergius and departed, glorifying and blessing God, to Whom be glory and dominion unto the ages of ages. Amen.

A Wondrous Discourse by the Philosopher Theodore Prodromos on How the Honorable Chains of the Holy Chief Apostle Peter Were Translated from Old Rome to Constantinople

Great is the Apostle Peter, and who else could be the supreme head and bulwark of all the disciples of Christ? Truly great is the Apostle Peter, and it is difficult to praise him worthily with a human tongue. And so I, unworthy and impure, would never have been able to dare to compose a discourse of praise to the Apostle Peter and his miracles, if he himself had not encouraged me, appearing in a vision. I was greatly frightened and hesitated, being unable to dare to undertake such a feat. But since from that vision I received, as it were, strength, therefore I now dare to tell you about the chains of the apostle and how they were translated from Old Rome to New Rome, that is, to this reigning city. As Gregory the Theologian says, it is good to show briefly one's refusal to compose a discourse on account of weakness, but then again to readily have recourse to the apostle who called me by the power of Him Who called him.

Who, then, was this great and chief Apostle Peter by birth, fortune, and trade? He was a Jew, a poor fisherman, whom Jesus Christ called to become His disciple. And he immediately left everything and followed Jesus Who called him, becoming, as I believe, an example and model of perfect renunciation of the world for those who pass from the salty and bitter sea of sins and the nets of the devil to the sweetness and simplicity of the Holy Gospel. It is superfluous to tell what zeal and what fervent love for the teaching of Christ the Apostle Peter had, and what gifts he possessed, on account of which he was preferred over the other apostles. Instead of his former name Cephas, he was named Peter, being deemed worthy to hear from the Lord that he is the unshakable rock of the Church, and that to him are entrusted the keys of the Kingdom of Heaven and the spiritual care of the rational sheep of Christ.

Who among Christians who have read the Divine Gospel and the Acts of the Holy Apostles does not know about Peter, about how he once walked on the waves of the sea together with his Teacher, how he loudly confessed Christ as the Son of God, how he paid the didrachma together with Christ, how he ascended with James and John onto Mount Tabor and beheld the light of the Transfiguration of God, how he did not consent to the washing of feet by the most pure hands of his Teacher, how he fought for the betrayed Christ with both hands and sword, how he was called by name on the mountain in Galilee, and how he ran together with the Apostle John to see the Resurrection of the Lord, and how before John he entered the tomb. O how much could be told about the Apostle Peter, but I by my own will pass over these events for the sake of brevity. I shall mention only the ordination which the Apostle Peter performed over Matthias, the twelfth apostle, chosen in place of the traitor Judas, but I cannot fail to recall also the fearful judgment upon Ananias and Sapphira, and Simon Magus, who offered him silver for ordination and whom the apostle drove away and cursed. I cannot fail to speak also of the teachings imparted by Peter, and of his long journeys which the apostle undertook for the sake of preaching, of how he healed various sick people, for which sometimes only the shadow of the apostle was sufficient, of the lame beggar who was healed by one word of Peter and walked on straight legs, of Aeneas the paralytic from Lydda, whom the apostle healed from his disease, and of Tabitha from Joppa, who was raised by one word of Peter. I pass over in silence the other miracles about which the divine Clement, the disciple and successor of Peter, narrates, because if I should wish to enumerate all the exploits of the saint and recount them precisely, not only a day but even an entire age would not suffice for me.

And so, if it seems fitting to you, at present we shall leave all this aside and tell of it in another discourse. We shall also pass over in silence the journeys of the chief apostle to Rome, his teachings and miracles, his dialogues with Simon Magus, and the cross on which he was crucified head downward, and his death, and we shall turn to the subject of the discourse, that is, we shall speak, insofar as this is possible, about the chains of Peter, or better to say, we shall mentally picture the apostle bound in chains and imprisoned in a dungeon, we shall mentally see how he is freed from the chains, led out of the prison by an Angel of God, and walks with unfettered feet. One might say that we shall translate these honorable chains of Peter from Old Rome to the New, the reigning city.

If after the salvific sufferings and death of our Savior Jesus Christ "for our salvation," the honorable Joseph of Arimathea asked Pilate for His dead body, reverently taking Him down from the Cross, and anointed Him with myrrh, wrapped Him in a clean shroud and laid Him in the tomb, then for the body of the chief apostle, after his death on the cross head downward, no one asked the ruler Nero for burial. Several pious Christians, seeing that the body had been left unattended, secretly took it, and having placed it in a woven basket, buried it, out of fear, as I think, of the murderous-minded inhuman idolaters. The Christians feared that they might cast the remains of the apostle either into the fire or into the sea, and the believing Christians would have been deprived of a great treasure. For a time the earth concealed the relics of the apostle hidden in its depths, since he whom the Teacher named Peter was the rock upon which He built His Church. Consequently, according to the rules of construction, the foundation of a building is laid in the earth, and the apostle, as the foundation, had first to be laid in the earth. But once a necessity arose for this honey-flowing spring to flow forth from the earth, and for manna to come forth upon its surface, like that ancient manna which descended from heaven into the wilderness in the times of Moses. Rome was honored by the Apostle Peter far more than Palestine, because this land did not flow with honey like Palestine, but brought forth manna from its hidden depths. And so that which was formerly hidden appeared on the earth again, and by means of an earthquake brought the relics of the apostle forth from the earth, when the war of the idolaters had somewhat subsided. And once again the first preacher of the Gospel shone upon the world, and rose together with Christ, with Whom he was united by death (see Romans 6:4–10).

Since the Teacher likened him to wheat, as is seen from the Holy Gospel, when Christ says, *"Indeed, Satan has asked for you, that he may sift you as wheat"* (Luke 22:31), the apostle also receives the properties of wheat, just as a grain which, having fallen into the earth and being hidden in the earth, dies, and thus brings forth fruit a thousandfold and many thousandfold. Imitating his Teacher, out of fear of Herod and the idolaters, he seeks refuge in the earth as in a certain Egypt, and after the destruction of the persecutors again goes to the mountains of Galilee. As his Teacher out of fear of Herod departed into Egypt, and after his death returned again to Nazareth of Galilee, so also the apostle out of fear of the idolaters was hidden in the subterranean parts of the earth, and after the destruction of the persecutors returned again to the earth. But let us pass to our theme. When the persecutions ceased and Constantine the Great came to reign, the believers removed the relics of the chief apostle from the grave and built in his name a magnificent temple, in the upper part of which they erected a vaulted cathedra, after the manner of a certain sanctuary, into which it was not permitted to enter, and within they placed a throne, upon which they set the holy relics, showing, as I think, by means of the throne and cathedra the following. First, that he who sits upon the throne is alive in Christ, although according to the laws of human nature he has died, and second, that it is he who, at the future universal Judgment, will sit upon the first of the twelve apostolic thrones and judge the twelve tribes of Israel. To the Galileans, who at the time of the Ascension marveled at the fleshly ascent into the Heavens of the Master Christ, the heavenly Angelic powers said: *"Men of Galilee, why do you stand gazing up into heaven?"* (Acts 1:11), as Jesus ascends? Why do you marvel at the new and wondrous ascent, seeing a body weightless, rising upward? With this body, which now ascends, He will come again to judge the whole world." And to the Romans who were standing by and marveling that the relics of the apostle were on the throne, it seems to me that the Roman hierarchs said: "Men of Rome, why do you stand marveling at this apostolic cathedra? In this same manner, sitting upon a throne not built, not made by the hand of man, the apostle will judge the people of Israel."

The cathedra which received the relics of the apostle, and the throne upon which, as if living, the holy relics sat in confirmation of the word of the Lord: *"He who believes in Me, though he may die, he shall live"* (John 11:25), were not surrounded by linen or other curtains, in the manner in which Bezalel enclosed the sanctuary of the ancient tabernacle, but were securely closed by double doors. And if the rest of the temple was open to all, this sanctuary was opened only three times a year for the veneration of the holy relics. All the Romans venerated the relics of the apostle, and love for them increased due to the rare opportunity to behold them, and also because the holy relics were adorned with all manner of precious things. Therefore they decided to keep the holy relics behind double doors, under locks, to protect them from thieves, sacrilegious persons, and grave robbers. For the soles of the saint's footwear were of pure gold, and the upper part of the footwear was adorned with bright pearls and precious stones. The apostle's garment was embroidered with gold and also adorned with pearls. The poor fisherman was clothed after death like a king, and he who did not know where to find a didrachma to pay the tax collector now lay all in gold. The apostle during his life had authority only over the pebbles scattered along the shore of the sea, but now he was clothed in garments embroidered with pearls, and truly beautiful was he who proclaimed to the world peace and good things, according to the word of the Prophet Isaiah: *"How beautiful upon the mountains are the feet of him who brings good news, who proclaims peace"* (Isaiah 52:7).

At the time when the relics of the apostle, adorned in this manner, were kept with every precaution in the sanctuary, the divine chains of the apostle were found outside the temple. They were always in view, and everyone could venerate them at any time, and various miracles occurred through them for those who asked with faith. Such is the wisdom of the Spirit, that it catches the sophist of evil, the devil, in his own nets and casts him into the pit which he himself dug, and he is slain by his own sword, just as David slew Goliath. Satan devised the Cross as a death-dealing weapon against our Lord Jesus Christ, but the wretch erred, because the Cross proved to be the instrument of our salvation, and for him the instrument of destruction. The same thing he experienced also when he forged chains as an instrument of torment for the Apostle Peter. But the miserable one did not know that he had made an instrument of wonder-working, from which would come innumerable healings for believers.

Many miracles did the chief apostle work through these chains, a multitude of wondrous miracles occurred through them. But it is sufficient for us to recount only that miracle which more than others shows their ineffable power. These chains heal not only bodily diseases, but through them sins are also forgiven and loosed, which is altogether incredible.

At that time there came to the Pope of that day, a man wondrous and most wise in Divine matters, a certain Christian, who confessed to him great and mortal sins. With many tears he asked forgiveness of him. The Pope joyfully received his confession and repentance and gave him a rule which he was to perform. But the loosing of sins the Pope left in the power of the chief apostle. Therefore he commanded that the hands, feet, and whole body of the penitent be bound with the chains of the apostle, and thus he was to crawl seven times through the temple, and at the end approach the sanctuary where the holy relics were, and strike his head against the closed doors. If the doors were to open of themselves, then this miracle would be a sign of the forgiveness of his sins. But if they did not open, then the sinner would remain under the penance given to him. The Christian did as the Pope commanded and began to strike his forehead against the doors of the sanctuary, calling upon the apostle for help. O swift to compassion, O chief Apostle of Christ, Peter! In that same hour you broke the seal, opened the locks, opened the doors, and led the bound man inside, freed him from the bonds of the chains, loosed him from his sins, and returned him to his home in joy and gladness. If the keys of the Kingdom of Heaven were entrusted to you by Christ, and you open it when you wish and to whom you wish, what is strange in the fact that the doors of the present sanctuary you justly close to the unworthy and open to those who have cleansed themselves by fitting repentance? And now that which the Pope, moved by God, commanded that Christian to do, became an inviolable law, for the Popes a manner of action, and for those Christians who had confessed, a way to learn whether their sins were forgiven.

And so you must also attend well with your mind to the narrative, because further I shall tell you a most pleasant story. When the report of this miracle spread to all the lands lying around Rome, another Christian, who had once been a wealthy merchant transporting goods by sea, and then became an utter pauper, because the sea had swallowed all his merchandise (for such is the nature of gold—to enrich quickly and just as quickly to make one destitute), so that Christian of whom I spoke, having repeatedly been caught in storms at sea and barely escaped, experienced another storm—that of thoughts, on account of cares for daily bread. Nowhere could he earn bread—neither for himself, nor much less for his family. He devised various means of earning a living, but nothing worked for him. In the end, he remembered the chains of the apostle and that miracle which had occurred. He mentally pictured the relics of the chief apostle, those precious garments that were upon him, the golden soles of the footwear and the pearl trim on the upper part. Mentally addressing the apostle and shedding tears in prayer, he silently conversed with him, asking more by the movement of his heart than by the sound of his lips:

"You, O man of God, when you lived in this world, chose poverty of your own volition and, according to the commandment of your Teacher, had not only no gold or silver, but not even copper. For this reason you rejected the silver of Simon Magus and cursed it together with Simon himself, who brought it to you. And often in your teachings you condemned gold and together with your Teacher blessed the poor, convincing all: *'It is easier for a camel to go through the eye of a needle than for a rich man to enter the Kingdom of God'* (Mark 10:25). And if any of the believers offered you gold or silver, you distributed it to the poor, widows, and orphans, having chosen for yourself forever poverty, destitution, the whip and the rod, and all that you endured for love of Jesus Christ. So it was while you were alive, but now that you are dead, you wear golden footwear and garments that shine with precious stones and pearls. But I, who yesterday and the day before seemed richer than other men, now suffer greatly from poverty and hunger. Going to the rich, I seek consolation in my poverty, but not one has been found who would look upon me with sympathy and hear my request. All turn away from me. I have despaired of receiving help from men, and therefore have come to your sacred feet and, like the divine Moses of old, say to you: *'Take your sandals off your feet and give them to me, that I may be clothed in the garment of salvation'* (Exodus 3:5). You know very well, O divine apostle, the woes of those who suffer shipwrecks. So I too transported goods by sea, and often was caught in storms, and twice was in danger of drowning. Once, when you were together with your Teacher Jesus Christ, Who was sleeping in your boat, you along with the other disciples were frightened of death, and so ran and awakened Jesus, that He might save you. And another time, when you cast yourself into the sea to meet your Teacher, you nearly drowned, had Jesus not come to you first and extended a helping hand, delivering you from death. But I ask of you a sandal not as a gift, but as a loan. If you give it to me, I shall buy goods and now, I am certain, shall sail successfully. And thus I shall be delivered from the

445

storm of poverty, and you shall receive your debt with interest, because, with the help of God, returning from my journey, I shall make for you magnificent footwear far more precious, while your foot, which will be without footwear for a time, will neither freeze, nor will a thorn enter it, nor will it stumble against a stone or be soiled with mud. This place in which you abide has a roof above and a floor below covered with gleaming tiles, especially since you have long since completed your earthly journey and nothing can compel you to set out on the road."

Thus spoke that unfortunate merchant, and since necessity compels such a one to be more inventive than any other, the merchant found a way to enter the sanctuary. "If it please you, O chief of apostles, I shall pretend that I have committed a mortal sin and go to the Pope to make a false confession of a mortal sin. He, as I well know, will prescribe for me, according to custom, to be bound with your chains and to go around the temple seven times, and then to knock with my head against the doors of your sanctuary. And after that everything will depend on your love for mankind and compassion—perhaps you will open the door to me, let me in, and consent to the theft of your sacred sandal." Thus, with tears, telling the apostle of his plans and sorrows, the merchant fell asleep. In sleep the apostle appeared to him and approved his plan. The merchant went to confess a feigned sin, received a penance, bound himself with the chains, went around the temple seven times, and began to knock with his forehead against the doors of the sanctuary. And what happened after this? *"Who can utter the mighty acts"* of the apostle, *"who can declare all His praise?"* (Psalm 105:2). The doors of the sanctuary opened of themselves, and the apostle himself permitted the theft to be committed. For as soon as the doors opened, the thief was, as it were, invited by the divine Peter himself to enter (truly, brethren, my hair stands on end at this fearful narrative). Then, I say, the apostle slightly extended his foot and of his own will gave his sandal to the merchant. The merchant, with the footwear under his arm, came out of the sanctuary filled with joy and gratitude to his benefactor.

I know that you, readers, are amazed at this strange miracle, and I myself would have marveled at the firmness and power of the chains of the apostle, which work such wonders, had I not known beforehand that by the shadow alone of the Apostle Peter the dead were raised. But that through the chains which touched the body of Peter and were sanctified, such miracles are worked, this is not so very strange. That miracles were worked by the shadow that followed Peter, this was more strange. But if that miracle occurred and was believed, then undoubtedly the prudent will believe this miracle also and will always honor it.

And so, as I have already said, rejoicing and thanking the apostle, the merchant came out of the sanctuary together with the sandal, and the power that had formerly opened the doors now again closed them. Neither the Romans nor even the Pope himself learned of the theft until the day came when, according to custom, the sanctuary with the relics of the apostle was opened for the veneration of the people. Entering within, the Pope saw that on one foot of the apostle there was no footwear. He was amazed and greatly grieved at this sacrilege, for he could not understand how it had been committed—the doors were closed, and the seals were found unbroken. Having considered that all had occurred not without the will of God, because without the will of the apostle no one would have dared such a thing, the Pope commanded that another sandal of the same kind be sewn for the foot of the apostle.

And the merchant, having received much money from the sale of the apostle's footwear, bought much merchandise, sold it, and became extraordinarily wealthy, but instead of hastening as quickly as possible to repay the creditor his debt and thank his benefactor according to his promise (I do not know, perhaps his soul was corrupted by great wealth and he begrudged the money, or he heard that the Pope had commanded that another sandal be sewn), the merchant thought that it would be superfluous to sew a third sandal, reasoning that three sandals were not needed for the apostle, who had only two feet. Therefore he did not render gratitude for the benefaction, being negligent, so to speak, in paying his debt. But the Apostle of God Peter did not long permit him to remain in this negligence and sloth. He appeared to him at night and reminded him of the debt, asking for that which was promised. After this the merchant made a magnificent sandal and set out for Rome. After he again confessed to the Pope, he was again bound with chains, and again knocked on the doors, which again opened. The merchant entered, and here a miracle occurred. The apostle again extended his foot, and the merchant, removing the sandal made by the Pope's command, put on him his own, the new one. But the Pope's sandal he fearfully placed between the feet of the apostle, which of themselves, as if alive, one rose slightly above the other, making room for the third sandal. Having fulfilled his promise, the merchant departed in joy and gladness.

The adorned relics of the apostle remained thus for a long time, and then, it is unknown why God so arranged it—*"for who has known the mind of the Lord? Or who has become His counselor?"* (Romans 11:34)—the integrity of the relics was disturbed, and everything separated: the head, the spine, the forearms, the thighs, the shoulder blades, the fingers—perhaps in order to punish the Roman people for their lawlessness, because they removed the throne from the sanctuary, abolished the former precautions, removed the ornaments and sandals of the apostle, and placed his relics in a reliquary and set it in the court of the temple.

Many years passed, and a certain inhabitant of Constantinople of high rank, God-fearing, the best archon of the synkletos, coming to Rome on some necessity, was deemed worthy to venerate the relics of the apostle, and out of love for his homeland and God conceived to perform a deed bold and dangerous. He wished to steal the relics and transport them to Constantinople. Perhaps he would have succeeded in his design if he had acted like that merchant, first informing the apostle of his intention and asking his permission. But this archon set about the matter shamelessly. Having stolen the relics, he placed them in a clean new sack and set out for Constantinople on a mule. What then did the divine Peter do this time? I do not know whether because he did not wish his relics to be in Constantinople, since the theft occurred without his permission, or because he wished to remain forever the guardian and savior of Rome, but at night he appeared in a dream to the Pope of Rome and told him everything: he reported the theft of the relics, named the thief, and said that he was heading for Constantinople. Greatly troubled by this dream, the Pope immediately assembled many horsemen and soldiers and sent them in pursuit of the thief. They soon overtook the thief and returned the relics of the apostle to Rome. The archon was shamefully beaten and brought bound before the Pope. Learning that the archon was of noble birth, held a high position, and had stolen the relics out of love for God and the apostle, the Pope commanded that he be unbound and began to speak with him gently, as a spiritual father, directing his efforts toward peace. The relics of the apostle were securely placed beneath the Holy Altar, and to the archon, instead of the relics, the Pope granted the honorable chains of the Apostle Peter so that, on the one hand, by the gift he might lessen the great sorrow of the archon over the dishonor caused to him, and on the other hand, console him in the love which the archon had for the apostle. And so in this manner the honorable chains were translated to us—an unfailing treasure of souls, an inexhaustible fountain of healings, an ever-flowing river of miracles, and a gift to the pious—better and more precious than any other gift. For the city of Constantinople the chains are fetters that hold and strengthen, which on all sides bind and protect it; for foreigners they are a chain for strangling, which oppresses and subdues them; and for our souls they are a chain ascending to Heaven, which unites us with the divine Peter and with Christ the Savior.

O chief Apostle Peter, you who were revealed by the Unoriginate Father Himself and preached the Only-begotten Son, you who loosed and bound on earth whatsoever you loose and bind in Heaven, you, the foundation of the Church, key-bearer of the Kingdom of Heaven, to whom paradise is entrusted, but not in order to guard its doors like the Cherubim and hinder those who wish to enter, but in order to open and ease entry for those who desire it, you who are the amazement of the Heavenly hosts, the praise of earthly beings, the terror of those in the netherworld, O great Peter, we beseech you, visit us from on high with a gentle gaze and strengthen the Church, shaken by the wiles of the devil, the Church which your Teacher redeemed with His own Blood and built upon you, the unshakable rock. And preserve this city and hold it with the all-embracing chains of peace, be to our pious sovereigns a fellow combatant and helper, becoming for them a firm rock fit to drive away enemies; to foreigners be a rock of offense and stumbling. We entreat you, to that pious Christian who moved me to write this discourse, bountifully recompense for the ardent love which he has for you, and receive me graciously because I, by the weakness of my tongue and not from coldness of thought, have not praised according to their worth your supernatural greatnesses, but have been deficient in what befits you. And here, in the present life, we pray you, correct the sins of the world, heal the infirm of body, and in the other life place the weight of your intercessions on the right pan of the scales, propitiating for us the Judge and our God, to Whom is due glory unto the ages. Amen.

The Martyrdom of the Holy Martyr George, Who Suffered in New Ephesus in 1801

Blessed is God! However much the enemies rise up with fury against Christianity, so much more does the East clearly proclaim and magnify, through its feats, the True God, the Savior of the world and Judge of all, our Lord Jesus Christ. In addition to what you, my brethren Christians, have read in the previously published martyrology, we are adding here, in the New Ecologion, accounts of these new ascetics of Christ, so that your love may not be deprived of the benefit of reading their lives.

And so, we announce to you that in 1801, in New Ephesus, commonly called Kusantasi, the new martyr George suffered for Christ. He suffered in the following manner. George was a native of that city, and his father was named Nicholas Lanchus. George was forty-two years old and had a lawful wife and children. However, he lived in sin, debauchery, and drunkenness. In July of 1798, without any external compulsion or prompting, but from the darkening of drunkenness, he went to Crete and in the presence of many denied (O woe!) the faith in Christ. But before undergoing the rite of circumcision, he sobered up and, becoming deeply grieved, he chose a time and crossed over to the nearby island of Samos. In those days on Crete, by permission of the sultan, a Christian church was being built. The opponents of the Christian faith resolved out of envy to destroy it. They convinced everyone that the Christians had killed George because he had denied the faith, and that they had hidden his body under the foundation of the church. Because of this, a great multitude of foreigners gathered around the church, wishing to destroy the foundation and extract the body. Seeing how agitated the crowd had become, and that the church wardens and other Christians might be killed and the church destroyed, the Christians sent their elders to the judge and in the presence of the local authorities assured everyone that that man was on Samos, and proposed to send people there to verify this themselves. And so they did. Men were sent who found George and cast him, bound in irons, into prison. Finally, after three days, he underwent the rite of circumcision and was assigned as an attendant in a mosque. But if George had changed his faith, he was unable to change his drunkenness, and gave himself over to it to such an extent that he nearly turned the mosque into a tavern.

He served in the mosque for ten months, and then departed from there and lived sometimes on Samos and sometimes on Patmos in repentance and confession of his transgression. On the first of March 1801, he returned to his homeland, but not as a debauchee and drunkard, rather as a man of temperance and sorrow, in profound contrition and with many tears. He frequently asked forgiveness of all his acquaintances and friends and seemed to be preparing himself to accomplish a great feat. Moreover, he prepared for it with great prudence. Before openly declaring his intention, he took care to send his children to a safe place, and three days before the event, he went to the place where the martyr Polydore had been hanged on a mulberry tree and gazed intently at that tree. Before his denial, George had a Christian friend, a fellow countryman, who afterwards began to avoid him. On the day when George resolved to present himself before the foreigners, they met in a coffeehouse, and that Christian, seeing that George's feet were swollen and wounded, asked with a heavy heart what was wrong with his feet. He answered that it was from an illness. "What kind of illness is it if it affects only your feet, while there is nothing on the rest of your body?" asked the Christian. Then George told him the truth: that while on Samos, he had come before the local governor and confessed himself to be a Christian, whereupon the governor ordered him to be stretched out and given a thousand blows to his feet, after which he was cast into prison. Then the community elders of Samos came and with the help of money persuaded the governor to release him from prison and drive him away. So before this courageous man appeared in Ephesus, he already bore sufficient marks of martyrdom on his body. Having somehow dulled the pain from the unbearable beating, he returned to his homeland in order to enter into the perfect feat, and George resolved to accept the desired end for Christ his Savior.

And so, in order to provide a pretext, George attempted to start a fight with the owner of the coffeehouse, thus laying a good beginning. But seeing that his plan was not succeeding, he abandoned such a lengthy method, and on the third of April, a Wednesday, at the third hour of the day, he came and presented himself before the judge. The judge asked him:

"What do you want?"

"I had an excellent thing pledged, but you took it from me and gave me another in exchange. Here, I return it to you, and give me back mine."

With these words, he removed his cap from his head and threw it on the ground.

"Who are you," the judge asked him, "and what is your business?"

"I was a Christian and denied my faith, and now I have come here to confess before you that I was and am, by the grace of God, a Christian."

Then the judge asked how he had denied his faith, and he answered that it was by his own will and without any compulsion.

"Perhaps you are drunk or mad?"

"No, I am not mad. I am in my right mind and sober, but since I have come to know and am convinced that my faith is holy and immaculate, I have returned to this holy faith of mine. I wish to be a Christian, and I say this and declare: I was a Christian and remain one. My name is George."

Angered by such boldness, the judge ordered him immediately to be taken bound to the prison. Then the martyr addressed the one who was about to lead him to prison:

"Man, why do you intend to bind me? Am I a thief or a murderer? I came here of my own will to confess my holy faith and that I am a Christian."

But he was nonetheless taken to prison and had a large chain placed around his neck, and his feet were locked in stocks. What torments they subjected him to that night! On Thursday evening, he was brought out for trial and urged to confess the Muslim faith, with promises that they would then give him much money, after which they began to threaten him. But the martyr only repeated: "I am a Christian and wish to die a Christian." Then these inhuman ones, seeing his steadfastness, in their fury squeezed his testicles and tore them.

On Friday, everyone again gathered for the trial and ordered the martyr to be brought forth. He was led out as one condemned, with his hands bound behind his back. The judge began to speak to him with gentleness, persuading him as a father:

"Come now, child, repent, and then you may go wherever you wish and be whatever you wish. If you want, you may be a Turk, and if you want, you may be a Roman."

But the martyr answered:

"I am a Christian and wish to remain in my faith."

Then one of them said:

"He is not at fault, but their priests are at fault, who teach that wherever they denied their faith, there they must also confess it again."

"Let us not hang him, but rather behead him with a sword."

Then he turned to the martyr:

"Which is greater, ninety or one hundred?"

"What you ask me, even infants know."

The mufti asked him this in order to determine whether he was of sound mind, because if it had turned out that he was mad, they would have driven him away. Finally, understanding his steadfastness, the judge pronounced the sentence: beheading by the sword. The executioners seized the martyr and led him to the place of execution. They made George kneel, and one of the executioners brandished his sword to frighten him. At that moment, a Turk named Osman approached who, showing as if he pitied him, said:

"Men, wait, what are you about to do?"

Then he addressed the martyr:

"Man, spare your life. Just say that you have sinned, and you will be released, you will go from here and live as you wish."

"I am the Christian George and have no need of your explanations."

After this, the executioner asked him:

"Do you repent?"

"I am a Christian."

"Bow your head."

The martyr bowed with a joyful countenance, and the executioner cut off his holy head on Friday, the fifth of April, at the third hour of the day. His blessed soul departed to the Desired Christ and received the unfading crown. The Divine grace illumined his holy relics, for in the night from Friday to Saturday, at dawn, many people, not only Christians but also Hagarenes, saw that the relics of the martyr were shining, emitting a wondrous light, as a mirror shines when the sun is reflected in it. That light proceeded from the blood of the martyr while it was still upon that level and stone-paved place. With the coming of Saturday, the whole people learned of the miracle, and the judge ordered the holy relics to be placed in the tomb of the holy great-martyr Polydore. While the relics were being carried to the tomb, some of the Christians plucked several hairs from the martyr's head, and others took his bloodstained garments. Later they reported that those who suffer intense fever are healed from these garments. One of the foreigners took a piece of the clothing for his brother, who was lying in a fever.

This martyrdom served to the incurable shame of the adversaries, but for the pious it became spiritual joy and ineffable gladness, to the glory of our Lord Jesus Christ with the Father and the Holy Spirit, unto the ages of ages. Amen.

The Life of Our Venerable and God-bearing Father Theona, Archbishop of Thessalonica and Founder of the Monastery of Saint Anastasia the Deliverer from Bonds

"Having walked the narrow path in life, O Father, now you rejoice in Heaven. The spirit of Theona was sent hence to the glorious City."

Neither written documents nor traditions have conveyed to us where this venerable and God-bearing father of ours Theona, the honored founder, instructor, and teacher of Thessalonica and all Thessaly, most holy chief shepherd, glory of ascetics, adornment of hierarchs, and excellent praise of all Christians, had his earthly homeland, from what parents he came, and how he became bishop of Thessalonica. Perhaps this occurred because, out of perfect hatred for all things earthly, the saint revealed to no one either the name of his fatherland or the names of his parents (as many other saints also did), and considered his homeland to be the Heavenly Jerusalem, as his new fatherland predestined for him, his parents to be our Lord Jesus Christ and the Lady Theotokos, and his brethren and kinsmen to be all the saints from the ages, or perhaps because all-consuming time has erased all memories and accounts of the saint's life. We know of him only what is mentioned in the life of the venerable-martyr James the New, who labored on the Holy Mountain of Athos, where the skete of the Honorable John the Forerunner now stands. In that life it is said that the holy father Theona, adorned with the sacred rank, first lived in the monastery of Pantokrator. Loving the hesychastic life more than the coenobitic, he was accustomed to take prosphoras, a little food, and go to the holy James, who was known among the Fathers of the Holy Mountain for the mystical revelations and Heavenly gifts which he had been vouchsafed to receive from God. Theona frequently visited James and was instructed by him in the lofty science of monastic life, and after many requests, he finally became his disciple, joining his brotherhood. He rejoiced that he had been vouchsafed to hear of the divine visions of the elder, and that his teacher and elder was such a Heavenly man. Moved by divine revelation, James went out into the world and settled in Navpaktos, in the monastery of the Honorable Forerunner, near the village of Trevestika. He was accompanied by the holy Theona, who with his own eyes beheld the Divine light which in a wondrous manner appeared above the monastery of the Forerunner for three evenings in a row before the divine James arrived there. For his faithful and close disciple, the holy Theona, James obtained from Bishop Acacius of Arta a written permission to hear the confessions of Christians who came to Arta. Later, when the holy James had already been condemned to torment by the order of the bey, the other disciples lost heart and returned to the monastery of the Forerunner, but the holy Theona feared nothing. Instead, burning with love, he accompanied his beloved teacher, suffering with him and striving to ease the torments to which he was being subjected. Once, together with another disciple of the elder named Marcian, they asked the holy James, who was in prison with Dionysius and the deacon James, his disciple: "Tell us, Father, what will become of our monastery and the brethren after your death?" And the venerable one answered them enigmatically: "When God is pleased to deliver us from the hands of the sultan, then we shall go first to the Patriarch, then to Great Wallachia, and when we arrive there, we shall no longer fear temptations. After this we shall come from the north, and you from the south, and we shall gather near Thessalonica, and by God's help a monastery shall be found for your dwelling, and we shall be inseparable both in this age and in the future."

This riddle, my brethren, was the saint's prophecy about what would happen afterward. And its explanation is as follows: "The Patriarch" is our Lord Jesus Christ; "Great Wallachia" is paradise, where the souls of the righteous dwell. As for their coming from the north and the others from the south, it means that after the martyric death of the holy James with his disciples James and Dionysius, the other disciples of James (who had departed from Trevestika, as we said, and were on Mount Athos at the monastery of Simonopetra), and especially our father Theona, having heard from a certain priest Nicholas from Arta that the relics of the saints were buried near Adrianople, sent men to dig up their graves, extracted the relics, and departed from the Holy Mountain. Not reaching Thessalonica, that is, here, in this place, they found the monastery of the Honorable Anastasia, which was at that time a small, ancient, ruined monastery. They restored it from its foundation, built a sufficient number of cells for the brethren, and by the grace of Christ up to one hundred fifty monks gathered in the monastery, who led a coenobitic life. Over the buildings and all the brethren, the holy Theona was abbot and superior. And the riddle indicated that the disciples of the saint would come from Navpaktos and the Holy Mountain, while the relics of the saints would come from Adrianople. Thus they would gather in this monastery and remain inseparable, both the living and the dead, in this life through their bodies, and in the other through their souls. And so it came to pass.

The divine James left this venerable Theona as his successor and superior over his other disciples, as is evident from the letter which he sent them at the end of his life. In it the venerable one writes: "Submit to Father Theona as to me myself, and confess your thoughts to him."

These words are quite sufficient to show us that in virtue the holy Theona was equal to his teacher, and therefore it was none other but him that James left as head and abbot over the flock, commanding them to honor him as himself. Having Theona as abbot, they were to think that he was James, as it were his image and reflection. In the life of the holy James it is said that a certain hieromonk named Barlaam, while laboring with his disciples in the monastery, once disobeyed the abbot, who was evidently the holy Theona, for which he was subjected to demonic possession. The demon tormented him severely, attacking up to thirty times a day, and the wretched man would roll on the ground, foaming at the mouth. Seeing this, the brethren bound him hand and foot and began to await the arrival of the abbot from Thessalonica. As soon as the holy Theona learned of what had happened, he served a moleben with the blessing of water before the relics of the holy James and, giving the sick man the holy water to drink, he healed him by the grace of God and the intercession of his teacher. The holy Theona lived in the year one thousand five hundred twenty-five from the Nativity of Christ.

When he had well established this coenobitic monastery according to the monastic rule of Basil the Great and ordered the life of the brethren and built a hermitage, he would for some time withdraw from the community and keep hesychia there, praying to God alone, and then he would return again to his disciples, frequently comforting them with his divine teaching and strengthening them in the labors of the monastic life. The holy Theona fulfilled both great commandments: *"You shall love the Lord your God with all your heart, with all your soul, and with all your mind... You shall love your neighbor as yourself"* (Matthew 22:37, 39). And the hermitage which he built, where he conversed with God and was inflamed with love for Him, is proof that he loved God with all his soul, with all his heart, and with all his mind. While this monastery, which he built and through which he saved an innumerable number of souls, is living proof that he loved his neighbor. Having fulfilled these two commandments, upon which the whole law and the prophets depend, he attained the measure of perfection. Who can recount the labors which the blessed one undertook when he became bishop of Thessalonica and all Thessaly? He added fast to fast, vigil to vigil, *"became all things to all men"* (1 Corinthians 9:22), according to the apostle, so that as a true shepherd and truest disciple of the Chief Shepherd Christ, he might save all the Christians entrusted to him and preserve his flock from the attacks of both sensible and noetic wolves. But why should I say more, why do I leave aside what is most important, proving the sanctity of our venerable father with a most active argument? If we, brethren Christians, let us suppose, had no other proof or testimony that Theona is a saint, it would be sufficient that glory which God Himself bestowed upon him, preserving his relics after death completely incorrupt, contrary to the laws of nature, for they are luminous, of a yellowish color, they emit a wondrous fragrance, and they work miracles for those who turn to him with faith. Theona is truly a saint, he pleased God, and he lived an angelic life. There is no other way to obtain holy relics unless you have been cleansed of the passions both of soul and of body, unless you have become a dwelling place of the Holy Spirit, and unless divine grace has united itself to your heart, your marrow, your bones and joints. Just as a tree is known by its fruit, so also by the holiness of Theona's relics we know that he was equal to the ancient saints and lived a holy and superhuman life. This honor and praise which God bestowed upon him surpasses all other praises that the most wondrous rhetoricians in the world might utter.

These sacred and honorable relics remain to this day whole and incorrupt in the monastery of Saint Anastasia, emitting ineffable fragrance, pouring forth miracles, and granting healings to those who approach them with faith. His memory is celebrated by the honorable fathers of this monastery on the fourth Sunday of the Fast, keeping vigil and a festal divine service, to which Christians from the surrounding villages gather, in imitation of the commemoration of Gregory Palamas on the second Sunday of Great Lent, to whom the blessed Theona was an equal successor, not only on the throne, but also in virtue and sanctity.

Let us also imitate him, brethren, emulating his virtuous life. Children should resemble their father, disciples their teacher, and sheep should follow their shepherd. The holy Theona is our father, teacher, and shepherd, and we are his children, disciples, and sheep, and therefore we must follow his way of life and become like him. If we do not resemble him, then it is in vain for us to boast that he is our founder and shepherd. And he himself will not acknowledge us as his children and disciples if we do not preserve the order of the coenobitic monastery and, especially, of the church services inviolate. Let us love non-possessiveness, let us hate love of money and accursed wealth, let us turn away from love of our kinsmen and desire Christ more than them, Who says: *"He who loves father or mother more than Me is not worthy of Me. And he who loves son or daughter more than Me is not worthy of Me"* (Matthew 10:37). Let us preserve virginity and chastity, keeping far from those who tempt us, and let us fulfill all our promises which we gave to God during the tonsure, that by the intercession of the holy Theona, and also of James and his disciples, we may be vouchsafed the Kingdom of Heaven in Christ Jesus, to Whom belongs glory unto the ages of ages. Amen.

IC XC
NIKA
BASED BOOKS
Based-Books.com